D0563190

Tasmania

Devonport &
the Northwest
p199

Launceston
& Around
p170

The
East
Coast
p136

Midlands
& Central
Highlands
p124

Cradle Country
& the West
p231

Hobart & Around
p52

Tasman Peninsula
& Port Arthur
p94

The
Southeast
p107

Charles Rawlings-Way, Virginia Maxwell

Contents

CRADLE MOUNTAIN P250

MARIA ISLAND NATIONAL PARK P141

KUNANYI/MT WELLINGTON P54

HOBART'S WATERFRONT P59

TAYLOR WILSON SMITH / SHUTTERSTOCK ©

CYRUS_2000 / SHUTTERSTOCK ©

KATIE STEVENS PHOTOGRAPHY / SHUTTERSTOCK ©

ARTIE PHOTOGRAPHY (ARTIE NG) / GETTY IMAGES ©

Contents

UNDERSTAND

SURVIVAL GUIDE

SPECIAL FEATURES

Welcome to Tasmania

Revelling in isolation, Tasmania is busting out with fab festivals and sensational food and drink, riding a tourism-fuelled economic boom that's the envy of all Australia.

Festival Frenzy

From wine, beer and food festivals to hot-ticket arts and music events, Tasmania packs a lot of parties into the calendar. Hobart's photogenic docks play host to many, from Taste of Tasmania over New Year to the heritage glories of the Australian Wooden Boat Festival. Art and culture get their game on during Ten Days on the Island, while winter's brooding, edgy Dark MOFO is building to rival the New Year party procession. MONA FOMA and Festivale bring the celebrations to Launceston, and The Unconformity unearths Queenstown's character. Escape for a long weekend.

History Lesson

To understand Australian colonial history you first need to understand Tasmanian colonial history...and before that Tasmanian Aboriginal history. Tragic stories of the island's past play out through its haunting, Gothic landscape: the sublime scenery around Port Arthur only reinforces the site's grim history. It's just as easy to conjure up visions of the raffish past in Hobart's Battery Point and its atmospheric pubs. Elsewhere, architectural treasures include convict-built bridges at Ross, Richmond and Campbell Town.

Into The Wild

From squeaky white sand and lichen-splashed granite to bleak alpine plateaus, Tasmania punches well above its weight when it comes to natural beauty. Hiking opportunities range from short, waterfall-punctuated forest trails to multiday wilderness epics with no one else in sight. You can explore the island's craggy coastlines and wild rivers by kayak, raft, yacht or cruise boat. Tassie's unique native wildlife casts a watchful eye over proceedings.

Tastes of Tasmania

First it was all about apples...but now the Apple Isle's contribution to world food extends to premium seafood, cheese, bread, honey, nuts, truffles, stone fruit, craft beer, whisky, gin and intensely flavoured cool-climate wines. Many smaller producers are owned and operated by passionate foodies: Tasmania is seemingly custom-built for a driving holiday spent shunting between these farm-gate suppliers, boozy cellar doors and niche provedores. After you've sampled the produce, book a table at a top restaurant and see how the local chefs transform it.

Why I love Tasmania

By Charles Rawlings-Way, Writer

I spent my childhood in Hobart, wheeling my bike between the beach and the bush. It was the '70s, man – Tasmania was a magical, laid-back place to be a kid. Like so many other islanders, I was lured away in my 20s by the mainland big smoke – but I return to the small smoke as often as possible, and am thrilled to see MONA firing Tasmania's cultural scene and turning the world's understanding of the island on its head. Not to mention the beer, the wine, the whisky... Who's for a drink?

For more about our writers, see p320

Above: Cape Bruny Lighthouse (p111), Bruny Island

Tasmania

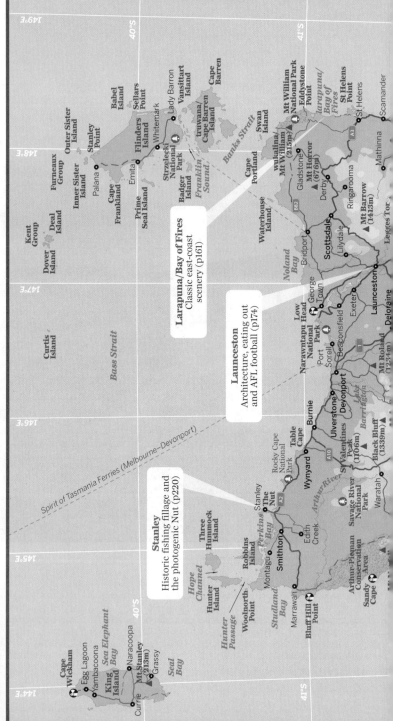

Stanley
Historic fishing fillage and
the photogenic Nut (p220)

Launceston
Architecture, eating out
and AFL football (p174)

Larapuna/Bay of Fires
Classic east-coast
scenery (p161)

Spirit of Tasmania Ferries (Melbourne–Devonport)

0 50 km
0 25 miles

Bass Strait

Cape Wickham
Egg Lagoon
Yambacoona
Naracoopa
King Island
Currie
Grassy
Sea Elephant Bay
Mt Stanley (213m)
Seal Bay

Kent Group
Dover Island
Deal Island

Curtis Island

Outer Sister Island
Inner Sister Island
Cape Frankland
Prime Seal Island
Palana
Emita
Flinders Island
Whitemark
Lady Barron
Stanley Point
Babel Island
Sellars Point

Furneaux Group

Strzelecki National Park
Badger Island
Franklin Sound
truwana/Cape Barren Island
Vansittart Island
Cape Barren
Banks Strait
Swan Island

Cape Portland
larapuna/Bay of Fires
Eddystone Point
wukalina/Mt William (215m)
Mt William National Park
St Helens Point
St Helens
Scamander

Hunter Passage
Hunter Island
Three Hummock Island
Robbins Island
Woolnorth Point
Studland Bay
Montagu
Smithton
Edith Creek
Marrawah
Bluff Hill Point
Hope Channel
Perkins Bay
Stanley
The Nut
Arthur-Pleman Conservation Area
Sandy Cape

Rocky Cape National Park
Table Cape
Wynyard
Burnie
Ulverstone
Valentines Peak (1106m)
St Arthur River
Savage River National Park
Black Bluff (1339m)
Waratah

Low Head
George Town
Narawntapu National Park
Port Sorell
Beaconsfield
Exeter
Devonport
Lake Barrington
Mt Roland (1234m)
Deloraine
Launceston

Noland Bay
Waterhouse Island
Bridport
Gladstone
Mt Horror (676m)
Derby
Scottsdale
Lilydale
Ringarooma
Mt Barrow (1413m)
Legges Tor
Mathinna

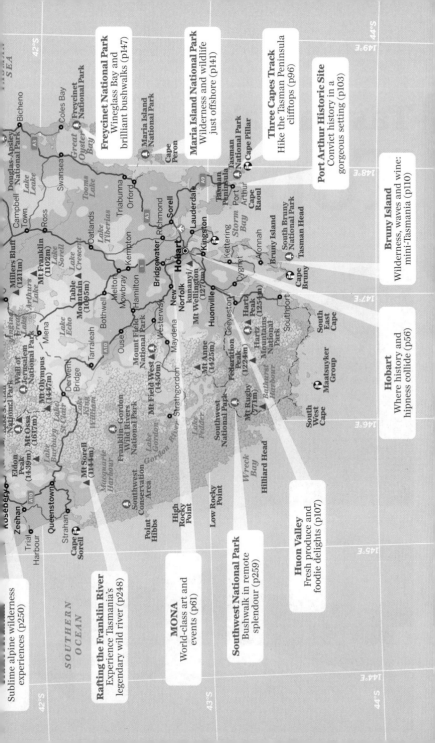

Sublime alpine wilderness experiences (p250)

Rafting the Franklin River
Experience Tasmania's legendary wild river (p248)

MONA
World-class art and events (p61)

Southwest National Park
Bushwalk in remote splendour (p259)

Huon Valley
Fresh produce and foodie delights (p107)

Hobart
Where history and hipness collide (p56)

Bruny Island
Wilderness, waves and wine: mini-Tasmania (p110)

Port Arthur Historic Site
Convict history in a gorgeous setting (p103)

Three Capes Track
Hike the Tasman Peninsula clifftops (p96)

Maria Island National Park
Wilderness and wildlife just offshore (p141)

Freycinet National Park
Wineglass Bay and brilliant bushwalks (p147)

SOUTHERN OCEAN

TASMAN SEA

Tasmania's
Top 15

MONA

1 The brainchild of Hobart philanthropist David Walsh, the Museum of Old & New Art (MONA; p61) has turned the Australian art world on its head. Subversive, confronting, funny and downright weird, this is art for grown-ups. Give yourself half a day to explore the darkened underground galleries. Laugh, be appalled, be turned on, then have a glass of wine…there's nothing quite like it anywhere else in the country. To get here, catch a ferry upriver from the Hobart waterfront and eyeball the museum, carved out of a sandstone headland like a vast rusty bunker, from the water.

Three Capes Track

2 An epic trail on the Tasman Peninsula southeast of Hobart, the Three Capes Track (p96) takes hikers on a four-day, 46km cliff-top tour. From the Port Arthur Historic Site a boat takes walkers to see Cape Raoul, before you hit the trail to Cape Pillar, Cape Hauy and around the coast to Fortescue Bay, with a bus ride back to Port Arthur to end your adventure. Accommodation en route is in architect-designed huts that are almost as good-looking as the eye-popping coastal scenery.
Below: Cape Raoul

Hobart

3 Hobart (p56) – Australia's south-ernmost state capital and home to around 227,000 Tasmanians – has come into its own in the last decade. Affordable airfares, internet exposure and the arrival of the astonishing MONA have really put Hobart on the map, and put a spring in the city's collective step. Don't miss history-rich Battery Point, the Saturday-morning Salamanca Market, a tour of Cascade Brewery, a trip up the leafy (and in winter, snowy) flanks of kunanyi/Mt Wellington and a beer at a harbourside pub.

Top: Salamanca Market (p61)

Freycinet National Park

4 Gin-clear water, blindingly white beaches and pink-granite headlands splashed with flaming-orange lichen – Freycinet National Park (p147) is a painterly natural domain. It's also home to Tasmania's most photographed beach: Wineglass Bay. Sweat it out on the climb to the lookout above the bay, then descend to the sand and dunk yourself under the waves. Escape the camera-clutching crowds on the three-day Freycinet Peninsula Circuit, or explore the peninsula on a cruise, in a kayak or from the air. Luxe accommodation awaits at the end of the day. Bottom: Friendly Beaches (p148)

Port Arthur Historic Site

5 Tasmania's number-one tourist drawcard, the Port Arthur Historic Site (p103) is a compelling mix of gorgeous coastal scenery and the sombre legacy of the past – engrossing, quiet and disquieting. Take a guided tour to understand the site's grand layout before exploring in depth the separate ruined buildings and constructions. While Port Arthur's overall scale impresses, it's the personal histories of the former prisoners that leave the strongest impression. Visit the Isle of the Dead Cemetery and the Point Puer Boys' Prison to uncover the most poignant memories.

Cradle Mountain & the Overland Track

6 A precipitous comb of rock carved out by millenniums of ice and wind, Cradle Mountain (p250) is Tasmania's most recognisable mountain peak. For unbelievable panoramas over Tasmania's alpine heart, take the all-day hike (and boulder scramble) to the summit and back. Or you can stand in awe below and fill your camera with perfect mountain views across Dove Lake. Then, if you're feeling really intrepid, the Overland Track, Tasmania's legendary six-day alpine hike, kicks off from here. Bottom: Dove Lake (p251)

Larapuna/Bay of Fires

7 Licked by azure ocean and embraced by eucalypt forests and granite headlands, the larapuna/Bay of Fires (p161) is arguably Tasmania's most scenic slice of coastline. To the south, Binalong Bay is perfect for surf or a rough-and-tumble swim, and has dive sites full of crayfish and abalone. Mt William National Park in the north is bristling with wildflowers, bounding kangaroos and beachfront camp sites. Visit the bay under your own steam or be guided by the experts on the Bay of Fires Lodge Walk.

Rafting the Franklin River

8 Rafting the Franklin River (p248) in Tasmania's remote southwest may be the ultimate wilderness journey. Deeply (and often literally) immersed in nature, you'll feel as far from the rest of humanity as it's possible to be. River trips involve up to 10 days on the water, navigating as the river dictates: floating in a world of reflections, battling surging white water and chasing rapids through deep, echoing gorges. Nights are spent in rainforest-fringed camp sites where the river hushes you to sleep.

NINA B / SHUTTERSTOCK ©

PETER WALTON PHOTOGRAPHY / GETTY IMAGES ©

Tasting Gourmet Produce

9 Tasmania – aka the Apple Isle – has much more than just Huon Valley (p118) apples in its lunch box these days. The island's fresh air, fertile soil and clean waters sustain truffles, walnuts, blueberries, pears, plums, gooseberries, raspberries, stone fruit, seafood, trout, beef and lamb, while skilled producers are turning out artisan cheeses, honey and premium wine, beer, whisky and gin...the whole island is one big excuse to eat and drink! Festivals and farmers markets present the best of local produce, all on tap for Tassie's restaurateurs.
Top left: Salamanca Market (p61)

Maria Island National Park

10 A short ferry ride off Tasmania's east coast, exquisite Maria Island (p141) is like an island zoo – minus the fences. You don't even need to leave the historic settlement of Darlington to see kangaroos, pademelons, wombats (pictured top right) and Cape Barren geese. On a bushwalk you might spot a prickly echidna, a Tasmanian devil or a forty-spotted pardalote, one of Tasmania's rarest birds. Oh, and did we say historic? There's World Heritage convict history here too, complete with a former penitentiary you can bunk down in for the night.

Stanley

11 Almost completely encircled by the sea, the little fishing village of Stanley (p220) on Tasmania's northwest coast is unbelievably photogenic – a tight clutch of heritage buildings at the foot of an enormous volcanic 'plug' called the Nut (a squat table-topped mountain, in effect). As you'd suspect, Stanley's maritime history, if it was written into a book, would be a storied, sea-salty tale. Bunk down in top-notch boutique accommodation, explore heritage sites, eat at some classy Mod Oz restaurants, or just scale the Nut and soak up the nautical vibes. Bottom right: Highfield Historic Site (p220)

Guided Walks

12 Tasmania's wilderness is just begging to be explored on foot. But if you're new to bushwalking, cringe at the prospect of sleeping in a tent or can afford a little luxury, a catered guided hike could be for you. There are several of these upmarket experiences across the state, including walks along the Overland Track and around Maria Island, the larapuna/Bay of Fires (p161) and Freycinet Peninsula. Accommodation is often in flash bush lodges, and meals reach gourmet heights. A guided walk of the Three Capes Track opened in late 2018. Top: Overland Track (p234)

Launceston

13 Tasmania's northern hub, Launceston (p174) is an affable town that has shed its redneck rep and become the perfec pocket-sized city. Against a backdrop of amazingly well-preserved domestic architecture, lush parks, misty riverscapes and the wilds of Cataract Gorge, 'Lonnie' makes a great weekender. Expect a clutch of good restaurants and cafes, plus some cool bars, patisseries and provedores. In winter, catch an Australian Football League (AFL) game, then explore the Tamar Valley wineries or surrounding heritage towns the next day.

Bruny Island

14 A 15-minute ferry chug from Kettering in the southeast, windswept Bruny Island (p110) is a sparsely populated microcosm of Tasmania. A thriving foodie scene has emerged here, producing handmade cheeses, oysters, smoked seafood, fudge, berry products, craft beer and wines. Plentiful wildlife includes penguins, seals and marine birds: check them out on a boat cruise around Bruny's jagged south coast. Bushwalking and surfing opportunities abound around South Bruny National Park, while accommodation is often absolute beachfront. Top: The Neck (p110)

Southwest National Park

15 Within Southwest National Park in Tasmania's deep south, the hushed, mirror-still waterways of Bathurst Harbour and Port Davey are true natural wonders. Tannin-tinged waters, craggy peaks, white quartzite beaches and underwater kelp forests – there can be few places left on the planet quite so untouristed and untouched. You can sail here on a yacht (p65) from Hobart, or fly in by light plane to the gravel airstrip at Melaleuca – an adventure in itself – then kayak and camp your way around this incredible watery wilderness. Top: Bathurst Harbour (p257)

Need to Know

For more information, see Survival Guide (p293)

Currency
Australian dollar ($)

Language
English

Visas
All visitors to Australia, and thus Tasmania, need a visa. Apply online through the Department of Immigration & Border Protection (www.border. gov.au), unless you are a New Zealander (Kiwis are granted a special visa upon entering Australia).

Money
ATMs widely available. Credit cards accepted in most hotels and restaurants.

Mobile Phones
European phones will work on Australia's network, but most American and Japanese phones will not. Use global roaming or a local SIM card and prepaid account.

Time
Australian Eastern Standard Time (AEST; GMT/UCT plus 10 hours)

When to Go

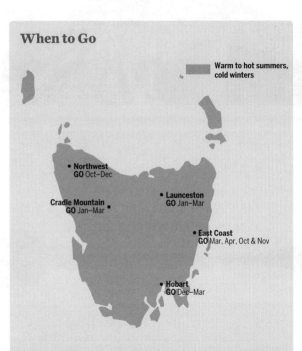

Warm to hot summers, cold winters

Northwest
GO Oct–Dec

Cradle Mountain
GO Jan–Mar

Launceston
GO Jan–Mar

East Coast
GO Mar, Apr, Oct & Nov

Hobart
GO Dec–Mar

High Season
(Dec & Jan)

➜ Accommodation prices scale lofty heights: book ahead.

➜ Festival season hits its straps; beaches (and water temperatures) are at their best.

➜ Expect crowds at big-ticket destinations (and the cricket).

Shoulder
(Feb–Apr, Oct & Nov)

➜ Easter is busy with Aussie families on the loose.

➜ Book ahead for Easter camping grounds, motels and ferries.

➜ April is harvest time, with blazing vine colours and brilliant produce statewide.

Low Season
(May–Sep)

➜ Accommodation prices plunge to manageable levels.

➜ Outside Hobart and Launceston, some eating and sleeping options shut up shop for winter.

➜ Snow closes some bushwalking tracks... but you can ski (just!).

Useful Websites

Discover Tasmania (www.discovertasmania.com) Tasmania's official tourism site.

Lonely Planet (www.lonelyplanet.com/australia/tasmania) Destination information, hotel bookings and traveller forum.

Parks & Wildlife Service (www.parks.tas.gov.au) National-parks information, maps and passes.

Tasmanian Beer Trail (www.tasbeertrail.com) The low-down and the latest on Tasmania's booming craft-beer scene.

Tasmanian Food Guide (www.tasmanianfoodguide.com.au) Restaurant reviews, touring routes and foodie events.

Tasmanian Travel & Information Centre (www.hobarttravelcentre.com.au) Statewide info and bookings.

Important Numbers

Ambulance, fire & police	📞000
Australia's country code	📞61
Directory assistance	📞1223
International access code	📞0011
Tasmania's area code	📞03

Exchange Rates

Canada	C$1	$1.02
Euro zone	€1	$1.52
Japan	¥100	$1.14
New Zealand	NZ$1	$0.90
UK	UK£1	$1.71
US	US$1	$1.31

For current exchange rates, see www.xe.com.

Daily Costs

Budget: Less than $150

➡ Hostel dorm bed: $25–35

➡ Hostel double room: $80–110

➡ Budget pizza or pasta meal: $15–20

➡ Local bus ride: from $3.30

Midrange: $150–300

➡ Motel or B&B double room: $130–250

➡ Breakfast or lunch in a cafe: $20–30

➡ Car hire per day: from $35

➡ Short taxi ride: $25

Top End: More than $300

➡ Boutique-hotel double room: from $250

➡ Three-course meal in a top restaurant: $80

➡ Guided wilderness day tour: from $120

➡ Decent bottle of Tasmanian wine: from $32

Opening Hours

Opening hours are fairly consistent: you'll more likely find venues closing for certain days during winter rather then shortening hours on the days they remain open.

Banks 9.30am to 4pm Monday to Thursday, to 5pm Friday

Cafes 7.30am to 4pm

Post offices 9am to 5pm Monday to Friday; some open Saturday morning in cities

Pubs and bars 11am to 10pm (closing later in cities)

Restaurants Lunch noon to 2pm, dinner 6pm to 8.30pm

Shops 9am to 5pm Monday to Friday, to noon or 5pm Saturday, 'late-night' Hobart shopping to 8pm Friday

Arriving in Tasmania

Hobart Airport Prebooked shuttle buses (adult/child $20/18) run by Hobart Airporter (www.airporterhobart.com.au) meet every flight and take you door-to-door. Book ahead. A taxi into the city (20 minutes) costs around $50.

Launceston Airport Door-to-door Launceston Airporter (www.airporterlaunceston.com.au) shuttle buses to central Launceston meet every flight (one way adult/child $15/14). Book ahead. A taxi into the city (15 minutes) costs about $35.

Spirit of Tasmania (Devonport) Redline and Tassielink buses meet every ferry and offer express services into Launceston (Redline/Tassielink $18.30/24.50), continuing to Hobart ($60/59). Book ahead.

Etiquette

Although largely informal in their everyday dealings, Tasmanians do observe some (unspoken) rules of etiquette.

Greetings Shake hands when meeting someone for the first time and when saying goodbye. Female friends are often greeted with a single kiss on the cheek.

Invitations If you're invited to someone's house for a barbecue or dinner, don't turn up empty-handed: bring a bottle of wine or some beers.

Shouting No, not yelling. 'Shouting' at the bar means buying a round of drinks: if someone buys you one, don't leave without buying them one too.

For much more on **getting around**, see p32

What's New

Three Capes Lodge Walk
In 2018 the Tasman Peninsula's excellent 46km Three Capes Track started offering the upmarket Three Capes Lodge Walk experience, complete with lovely accommodation and fab food and wine. (p97)

Hobart Craft-Beer Scene
Hobart has a slew of new craft-beer brewery bars: start with Hobart Brewing Company, T-Bone Brewing Co and Shambles Brewery. (p80)

Pumphouse Point, Lake St Clair
World-class accommodation is on offer in an extraordinary five-storey, 1930s hydro-electric pumphouse in the middle of Lake St Clair, accessed by a narrow walkway. There are further rooms and a restaurant in the Shore House. (p250)

Clarendon Arms Hotel
The owners of Hadspen's Red Feather Inn have restored the endearing Clarendon Arms Hotel in Evandale, and installed a microbrewery, a restaurant and accommodation. (p197)

Old Kempton Distillery
Old Kempton Distillery (formerly Redlands Distillery) recently uprooted its whisky-soaked self from the Derwent Valley and landed in noble Dysart House in Kempton, in the Tasmanian Midlands. (p128)

Kingston Beach Cafes
Little Kingston Beach south of Hobart, long commercially mired somewhere between 1983 and 1987, finally has a hip new cafe, a wine bar and a fabulously renovated tavern. (p86)

Bangor Wine & Oyster Shed
In unassuming little Dunalley on the Tasman Peninsula is this excellent new oyster bar and wine room, in an equally unassuming shed with fabulous views. (p98)

MACq 01
On Hobart's waterfront, the Macquarie Wharf No 1 shed has morphed into the very flashy MACq 01 luxury hotel, with harbour views aplenty. (p70)

Port Arthur Visitor Centre
The fab new visitor centre at the Port Arthur Historic Site on the Tasman Peninsula includes a restaurant called 1830 (the year Port Arthur was established). (p103)

Bay of Fires Eco Tours
In Binalong Bay's last original timber shack, Bay of Fires Eco Tours runs excellent boat trips to parts of the bay you can't reach by car (that is, most of it). (p161)

Mountain-Biking Hot Spots
Little Derby in the northeast has become a global mountain-biking hot spot, with one leg of the 2017 Enduro World Championships held here. Opened in 2018, the Maydena Bike Park in the southwest hopes to similarly wow the two-wheelers. (p162)

Fat Pig Farm
At Fat Pig Farm near Cygnet in the southeast, former Sydney food critic Matthew Evans cooks and runs cooking classes (and prays that no critics show up). (p117)

For more recommendations and reviews, see lonelyplanet.com/tasmania

If You Like...

Beer, Wine & Whisky

Old Kempton Distillery Nose your way into some fine single malt at this Midlands whisky distillery. (p128)

Seven Sheds Railton's micro-brewery is home to organically brewed boutique beers. (p212)

Puddleduck Vineyard A charming family-run vineyard in the Coal River Valley. Sip some wine and picnic by the lake. (p85)

Bruny Island Premium Wines Wines from Australia's southernmost vineyard buddy up nicely with island oysters and cheeses. (p111)

Cascade Brewery Take a tour of Australia's oldest brewery and sample the super product. (p60)

Weldborough Hotel A one-stop shop for Tasmanian craft beers (of which there are dozens – plan on staying the night). (p162)

Hellyers Road Distillery Hellyers makes vodka too, but golden single malt is why you're here. (p216)

T-Bone Brewing Co The hippest of Hobart's craft-beer breweries is on the fringe of the North Hobart strip. (p81)

Jansz Wine Room The 'Méthode Tasmanoise' sparkling white from Jansz is liquid happiness. (p192)

Bushwalking

Cradle Mountain Give yourself a full day to reach the summit of this iconic mountain. (p250)

Three Capes Track Raoul, Pillar, Hauy – tick them off your list on this four-day Tasman Peninsula hike. (p96)

Wineglass Bay You've seen the photos...now do the walk. It's a three-hour return hike over the saddle to the sand. (p149)

Bay of Fires Lodge Walk Four-day guided walk with all the perks of luxury accommodation and gourmet food. (p161)

Kunanyi/Mt Wellington Check out some challenging tracks a short drive from Hobart. And how about them views! (p54)

Mt Field National Park In spring and summer Mt Field's high-country tracks are awash with wildflowers, chuckling streams, tarns and waterfalls. (p91)

Overland Track Tassie's big-ticket trail is an epic through 65km of majestic highlands and forests. (p234)

South Coast Track Ever been to the edge of the known world? Here's your chance. (p259)

Maria Island Walk Luxury guided (and catered) four-day hike along Maria Island off the east coast. (p143)

Gourmet Food

Farm Gate Market Grab a bagful of top local produce at Hobart's Sunday-morning farmers market. (p83)

Fat Pig Farm Sydney food critic turned TV *Gourmet Farmer* Matthew Evans cooks and eats with you in Cygnet. (p117)

Bruny Island Home to a cheese-maker, an oyster farm, a smoke house, a berry farm, a whisky bar and a fudge maker. (p110)

Freycinet Marine Farm Briny oysters, mussels, octopuses and crayfish, fresh from the sea. (p152)

King Island Dairy Show-stopping dairy on remote King Island with a walk-in tasting room...enjoy! (p228)

Harvest Launceston's excellent foodie market happens every Saturday morning. (p184)

Summer Kitchen Bakery This little bakery hidden in the south-east bakes the best sourdough you'll ever taste. (p119)

Taste of the Huon This annual Huon Valley festival plates up much more than just apples. (p119)

Melshell Oysters Far-flung, forlorn oyster shack in the dunes somewhere near Swansea. Magic! (p147)

Colonial History

Port Arthur Historic Site Beautiful coastal scenery (almost) masks the tragic melancholy infused in every building. (p103)

Callington Mill Organic flour from this meticulously restored 1837 mill in Oatlands is transformed into baked treats around the state. (p129)

Hobart Historic Tours Take a guided walking tour and uncover the history of Australia's second-oldest capital city. (p66)

Midlands towns Piece together Tasmania's rural history in photogenic Oatlands, Ross and Campbell Town. (p124)

The Ship That Never Was Hear a true tale of convict escape in this entertaining production in Strahan. (p242)

Evandale The whole town's listed by the National Trust. Don't miss historic Clarendon mansion! (p196)

Woolmers Estate Longford farming estate dating from 1819; one of the 11 Unesco World Heritage Australian convict sites. (p195)

Stanley Historic northwest fishing village sheltering beneath the Nut. (p220)

Richmond Bridge The oldest road bridge in Australia is in picture-perfect little Richmond, near Hobart. (p88)

Native Wildlife

Maria Island National Park For all things furry and feathered. The wombats are supersized! (p141)

Top: Tasmanian devil (p288)

Bottom: Richmond Bridge (p88)

Mt William National Park Rare Forester kangaroos gambol on the grassland behind the beaches. (p163)

Trowunna Wildlife Park Check out some Tasmanian devils, koalas and wombats in the northwest. (p209)

Tasman Island Cruises Astonishing coastal scenery and the chance to see seals, dolphins and the occasional passing whale. (p65)

Bonorong Wildlife Centre Conservation-savvy wildlife centre near Hobart, starring Tasmanian devils, koalas, wombats, echidnas and quolls. (p88)

Bruny Island Winning bird-watching, including penguins and mutton birds at Bruny Island Neck. (p110)

Cradle Mountain–Lake St Clair National Park Wombats, birds, possums, devils, snakes…any visit here (especially along the Overland Track) is a zoo-like experience. (p250)

King Island Everything seems so healthy and well fed here: the cows, the seagulls, the snakes… (p228)

Festivals

Dark MOFO Cometh the winter solstice, cometh Dark MOFO – an eerie, unnerving and very hip winter festival. (p67)

Falls Festival This touring music fest visits Marion Bay around New Year's Eve. (p69)

Taste of Tasmania Tassie's top food festival is a true gourmet feast. (p67)

Cygnet Folk Festival Folky good times and groovy summer vibes south of Hobart. (p117)

The Unconformity The west coast can be bleak, but this quirky Queenstown festival warms the mood. (p245)

Ten Days on the Island Tasmania's loftiest arts festival. (p67)

Festivale Launceston's showpiece event is a delicious melange of food, wine and good times. (p180)

Festival of Voices Tune up your pipes for a little winter singalong in Hobart. (p67)

Targa Tasmania How does Tasmania look from inside a speeding sports car? Classic cars, classic scenery. (p23)

Beaches & Swimming

Boat Harbour Beach Locals say the water here is the warmest in Tasmania! (p220)

Ocean Beach Long, wild beach walks, giant waves and west-coast sunsets. (p238)

South Cape Bay It's a two-hour walk from Cockle Creek to one of the world's wildest ocean beaches. (p123)

Douglas-Apsley National Park Cool off in the deep, dark waterholes of Douglas River on the east coast. (p154)

Seven Mile Beach Hobart's best beach: safe swimming, undulating dunes and nearby camping. Righto, that's summer sorted. (p87)

Fortescue Bay Gloriously isolated and definitely worth the national-park entrance fee. Camping a must! (p102)

Binalong Bay The southernmost beach in the Bay of Fires is just begging for swimmers. (p161)

Kingston Beach South of Hobart, this little suburban beach has safe swimming and before/after distractions (pub, bar, cafes). (p86)

Luxury Stays

Red Feather Inn Gorgeous accommodation and slow-food cookery classes at Hadspen. (p194)

MACq 01 Hobart's latest waterfront wharf revival has seen MACq 01 take shape – architecturally amazing and superplush. (p70)

Henry Jones Art Hotel A true Hobart highlight: amazingly unpretentious for such a hip hotel. (p70)

Saffire Freycinet Hands down Tasmania's most spectacular accommodation, amid the improbable landscapes of the Freycinet Peninsula. (p152)

Avalon Coastal Retreat A glass-and-steel east-coast haven with endless views ('beach house' just doesn't cut it). (p146)

Pumphouse Point Amazing accommodation actually *on* Lake St Clair (or on the shore, if you like). (p255)

Quamby Estate True class, in a meticulously restored, ultra-elegant historic Hagley homestead. (p194)

Peninsula Experience Amazing 19th-century homestead near Dover, with Asian-chic design and a private beach. (p122)

Islington This historic South Hobart home is awash with lavish trappings. (p72)

Month by Month

January

As New Year's Eve hangovers recede, the summer festival season kicks off with varied events in the north and south. It's school-holiday time across Australia, so expect high demand for family-friendly motels and camp sites.

MONA FOMA

The Museum of Old & New Art (MONA) runs the Festival of Music & Art (FOMA), thus MONA FOMA aka MOFO. It's as edgy, progressive and unexpected as the museum itself. Launceston is looking likely as the festival venue from 2019. (p67)

Cygnet Folk Festival

More woolly sock than arena rock, the Cygnet Folk Festival, a day trip south of Hobart, is a three-day hippie fiesta with good vibes, low-key performances, discussions and workshops. (p117)

Hobart BeerFest

Apart from myriad Tassie brews, you can try hundreds of beers from around the world at the Hobart BeerFest, held in January on the Hobart waterfront. Beer-and-food-matching masterclasses are also held. The Esk BeerFest (www.esk.beerfestivals.com.au) is Launceston's parallel event. (p67)

Hobart International

As a prelude to the Australian Open tennis championship in Melbourne later in January, the weeklong Hobart International women's tournament draws plenty of big-name players. (p67)

February

Hobart's maritime heritage comes to the fore on and off the sea (which is at its warmest – swimming!). Meanwhile, Launceston's biggest party of the year is a chance to sip some Tamar Valley wines.

Festivale

Launceston's City Park hosts three days of eating, drinking, arts and entertainment at Festivale. It's a chill-out-on-the-grass affair, with Tasmanian food, wine and beer, and plenty of live tunes. (p180)

Australian Wooden Boat Festival

In odd-numbered years, the Australian Wooden Boat Festival brings a fleet of beautifully crafted yachts, dinghies and tall ships to Hobart's waterfront, filling the harbour with heritage nautical vibes. (p67)

Evandale Village Fair

The National Penny Farthing Championships happen south of Launceston at the annual Evandale Village Fair. In between wobbly bike races there are markets and musical interludes from pipe bands. (p197)

Royal Hobart Regatta

The three-day Royal Hobart Regatta sees the Derwent River bobbing with aquatic craft of all shapes and sizes. Don't miss Hobart's resident tall ships, the *Lady Nelson* and *Windeward Bound*. (p67)

March

Summer's warmth lingers into dusky evening – perfect for an island-wide arts celebration. March is also harvest time: grapevines blaze with colours and roadside stalls are crammed with fresh produce. Book ahead for Easter accommodation.

✹ Ten Days on the Island

Towing a trad arts line, Ten Days on the Island is the state's premier arts event, running for (you guessed it) 10 days biennially (odd-numbered years) in March. Theatre, music, visual arts, literature and film across the state. (p67)

✗ Taste of the Huon

Ranelagh showgrounds near Huonville hosts the two-day Taste of the Huon, a showcase of the best Huon Valley produce. Apples, cherries, wine, salmon, mushrooms, honey, bread...no one goes home hungry. Bucolic splendour! (p119)

April

Autumn kicks in with cool days and cooler nights. Easter often falls in April: book ferry crossings, motels and camping grounds as far in advance as humanly possible. Oh, and football season gets started!

☆ Football Season

Biceps and tight shorts! Competing in the Australian Football League (AFL; www.afl.com.au), the North Melbourne Kangaroos play some home games at Hobart's Blundstone Arena, while the Hawthorn Hawks play a few at Launceston's Aurora Stadium. Grab a beer and a meat pie and get into it.

May

Cool blue-sky days make May the perfect time for a Tassie sojourn. The low late-autumn light is stellar for photography, and accommodation owners sometimes offer off-peak discounts. Good driving weather too!

☆ Targa Tasmania

Held in late April or early May, Targa Tasmania is a statewide road rally for classic cars of all descriptions (but generally the fast ones). Crowds line the roadsides to ogle the magnificent speeding beasts.

June

Winter is here. Yes, it's colder than elsewhere in Australia, but crisp mornings and Hobart and Launceston's wood-smoky ridge lines are deeply atmospheric. With the coming of the winter solstice, Hobart gets its Gothic going.

✹ Dark MOFO

In the still depths of the Hobart winter, MONA's Dark MOFO arrives. Skirting the frayed edges of Tasmania's guilty conscience, this noir package delivers a taut, seductive and joyful series of happenings, installations and performances that will rattle your rusty cage. (p67)

July

As winter rolls on, hunker down for the indoor pleasures of choirs and chocolate. Outside of Hobart and Launceston, expect some accommodation to be closed, especially in coastal areas.

✹ Festival of Voices

The quirky Festival of Voices turns Hobart into a singing city for three days. Gospel gangs, choirs and a cappella groups showcase the versatility of the human voice. (p67)

August

Winter snow dapples Tasmania's Central Highlands. Unless you're masochistic, it's probably best to leave the bushwalking to experienced hikers. Some tracks become impassable and, besides, hotel accommodation is at its cheapest around the state.

⭐ Ski Season

When winter blows in (roughly from July to September), snow bunnies and powder hounds dust off their skis and head for Ben Lomond National Park. Coverage can be unpredictable: check snow reports before you head for the mountain. (p197)

September

As winter packs itself away, spring heaths bloom in the Central Highlands and muddy tracks start to dry out. Time for a bushwalk? Accommodation is still affordable: treat yourself to a boutique hotel when you wander in from the wilderness.

Junction Arts Festival

Launceston's offbeat Junction Arts Festival is five days of live music, theatre, installations, street art, walking tours and dance. A real shot in the arm for the arts up north. (p180)

October

The spring is sprung, with (usually) more settled weather and two of Tasmania's smallest (but loveliest) festivals. In Hobart and Launceston, the country-comes-to-town royal shows put pressure on accommodation: book ahead.

Bloomin' Tulips Festival

Celebrate spring with food, music, burgeoning blooms and maybe a bit of a dance at Table Cape's annual Bloomin' Tulips Festival. The Wynyard waterfront is where it's at. (p219)

Bruny Island Bird Festival

Twitchers, rejoice! The gloriously isolated landscapes and coastlines of Bruny Island host the annual three-day Bruny Island Bird Festival. Bring your patience and your binoculars. (p113)

Royal Hobart Show

Tasmania's rich agricultural heritage collides with shifty carnies, terrifying rides, fairy floss and junky plastic show bags at the Royal Hobart Show. The Royal Launceston Show also happens in October. 'Dad, I feel sick...'. (p67) (p180)

November

Accommodation around the state is still reasonably priced before the peak tourist season arrives (mid-December to January). After the football and before the cricket, sports fans twiddle their thumbs.

Tasmanian Craft Fair

Running for four days before the first Monday in November, Deloraine's Tasmanian Craft Fair lures 30,000 artsy bods from around Australia. Pottery, textiles, glassware and sculpture all get an airing. (p207)

December

Ring the bell, school's out! Accommodation is at a premium, especially after Christmas and around New Year's Eve, when Hobart really cranks up the festival schedule. Book accommodation well in advance. Happy days – it's summer!

☆ Sydney to Hobart Yacht Race

The world's most arduous open-ocean yacht race is the Sydney to Hobart, departing Sydney Harbour on Boxing Day. The winners sail into Hobart around 29 December...four days at sea is a good excuse for a party! (p77)

Taste of Tasmania

Tassie's big-ticket culinary event, Hobart's Taste of Tasmania is a frenzied waterfront food fest over a week around New Year's Eve. It generates a huge buzz: grab a glass of something cold, a plate of something hot and tune in to some live bands. (p67)

☆ Cricket Season

Cricket fans can catch Tasmania's state team, the Tasmanian Tigers (www.crickettas.com.au/teams/tasmanian-tigers), cracking the willow over summer. In the quick-fire Big Bash League, the Hobart Hurricanes (www.hobarthurricanes.com.au) are good bang for your buck.

☆ Falls Festival

Tasmania's biggest outdoor rock fest, the Falls Festival happens at Marion Bay south of Hobart around New Year's Eve. Expect left-of-centre internationals and a slew of Australian talent (Fleet Foxes, Liam Gallagher, Angus & Julia Stone). BYO tent. (p69)

Itineraries

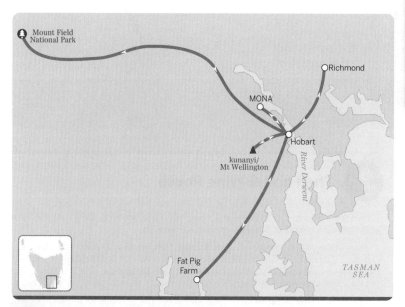

4 DAYS Hobart as a Hub

Fancy a long weekend in Hobart? Take advantage of Tasmania's short driving distances by day-tripping around the hip southern capital.

Spend a day mooching around the **Hobart** waterfront and Battery Point, taking a boat trip up the Derwent River to the dazzling **MONA**, and ending with dinner and drinks in North Hobart. Next day, drive out to history-rich **Richmond**: don't miss the stoic Richmond Bridge, the interesting Bonorong Wildlife Centre and a lazy picnic lunch at Puddleduck Vineyard.

On day three, continue the foodie theme with a prebooked cooking class at **Fat Pig Farm** near Cygnet, where food-critic-turned-farmer Matthew Evans runs entertaining cook-it-then-eat-it classes.

If you have another day up your sleeve, truck out to **Mt Field National Park** for an accessible alpine bushwalk, or book a place on the Mt Wellington Descent – a 22km downhill mountain-bike run from the summit of **kunanyi/Mt Wellington** behind Hobart to the waterfront.

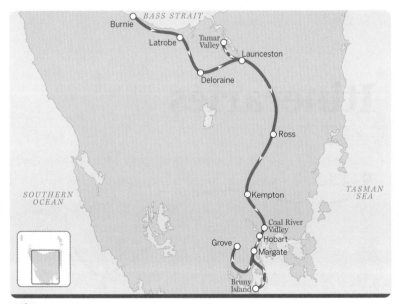

3 WEEKS The Food & Wine Route

With a few weeks at your disposal and a powerful thirst/appetite, you'll find that Tasmania plates up a bounty of delights for your consumption.

Start in the island's northwest. Near **Burnie**, Hellyers Road Distillery leads the charge of Tasmanian whisky makers. At the House of Anvers in **Latrobe** you can fill the chocolate-shaped voids in your life. Further south, in **Deloraine**, visit Truffles of Tasmania for a look at some funky fungi.

Modest little **Launceston** offers some fine urban dining: book for dinner at Geronimo or Pierre's. Coffee culture is firmly entrenched here too: try Sweetbrew or Milkbar for a cup of the good black stuff. Launceston is also a beery sort of town: tour the impressive Boag's Brewery (going since 1881) or enjoy a few craft beers at St John. More into wine? The cool-climate **Tamar Valley Wine Region** is just north of town.

Trucking south through the Midlands, stop at **Ross** for a classic Tasmanian curried-scallop pie at Bakery 31, and at **Kempton** for further single-malt indulgences at Old Kempton Distillery, before assessing the wineries in the **Coal River Valley Wine Region** near Richmond (Puddleduck Vineyard is our pick).

In **Hobart**, fill your hamper with local produce at the Saturday-morning Salamanca Market or Sunday-morning Farm Gate Market. Top restaurant picks here include the endearing Templo and high-end Aloft. Cafes are everywhere: try Pilgrim Coffee and Jackman & McRoss. Thirsty? Sign up for a tour of Australia's oldest brewery, Cascade, or pinball between the pubs and bars in North Hobart or around the waterfront.

Continuing south, stop by Devils Brewery on the old **Margate Train** for a craft-beer tasting. A short ferry ride from Kettering, **Bruny Island** offers plenty for wandering foodies: oysters, cheese, smoked meats, beer, whisky and Australia's most southerly vineyard. Back on the 'mainland', the Huon Valley is Australia's apple basket. Don't miss the Apple Shed cider house in **Grove**. Enjoy!

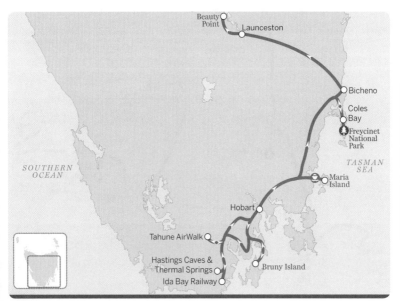

2 WEEKS Tasmania with Kids

Tasmania is a naturally active destination: if you've got kids in tow you'll find plenty of challenges, fun times and exercise opportunities right across the island (sometimes all at once).

In **Hobart**, give the family a musical education with some live Friday-night tunes at the Salamanca Arts Centre Courtyard, followed by a crash course in busking at Saturday's Salamanca Market. Other highlights include harbourside fish and chips (try Flippers), an afternoon at the Tasmanian Museum & Art Gallery, and a drive up kunanyi/Mt Wellington for a walk or some winter snowball hurling. If the weather's looking good, Roaring 40s Kayaking runs kid-friendly paddles around Hobart's docks.

Tracking into the state's sublime southeast, check out the wild beaches of **Bruny Island** or explore the craggy coastline with Bruny Island Cruises. Don't miss the lofty **Tahune AirWalk** near Geeveston, some underground action at **Hastings Caves & Thermal Springs** (even in winter, the pool here is lovely and warm), and a chug along the supercute **Ida Bay Railway**, the most southerly railway in Australia, at Lune River.

Rolling up the east coast, consider a boat trip to **Maria Island**, a beautiful national park overrun with native wildlife. Hire some mountain bikes and explore the trails. An endless sequence of brilliant squeaky-sand beaches unfurls as you continue north. Talk to Freycinet Adventures about some low-key kayaking at **Coles Bay**, or tackle the hike up to Wineglass Bay Lookout in **Freycinet National Park**. Ogle some hungry Tasmanian devils at Natureworld near **Bicheno**, or go on a night-time walk to spot the town's resident penguins.

Tracking northwest, **Launceston** offers plenty of distractions for small humans. Get interactive at the Queen Victoria Museum, then check out the Japanese macaques at home in City Park. Defy gravity on the chairlift over Cataract Gorge (you can swim here too, in summer), or try some cable hang-gliding in nearby Trevallyn. Further north up the Tamar Valley, check out the odd little residents at **Beauty Point** with a visit to Seahorse World and Platypus House.

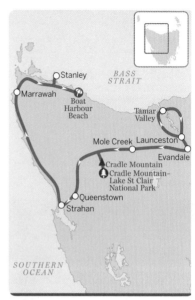

 East Coast Classic
(10 DAYS)

 Cradle Country & the Northwest
(2 WEEKS)

Hobart, Port Arthur, Freycinet and the gorgeous Bay of Fires: check out four of Tasmania's greatest hits on this sunny east-coast cruise.

Hear the heartbeat of **Hobart**: great pubs and cafes, brilliant restaurants and heritage vibes. Don't miss Salamanca Pl, the amazing MONA and the view from atop kunanyi/Mt Wellington.

From Hobart, head southeast to the dramatic coastal crags of the **Tasman Peninsula** and the grim convict stories of **Port Arthur Historic Site**. Near Copping, short-cut to the east coast via the Wielangta Forest Drive. Hop on a ferry out to **Maria Island National Park** for mountain biking, camping, bushwalking and wildlife-spotting.

Stop at some east-coast wineries near **Swansea**, then get your camera primed for **Freycinet National Park** and Wineglass Bay, and follow with sea kayaking and oyster appreciation at Coles Bay. Continue north to the chilled-out fishing town of **Bicheno** for some penguin-spotting, then unwind among the rocky lagoons and headlands of **larapuna/Bay of Fires**.

Launceston, the west coast, Cradle Mountain and the northwest: this is certainly the least visited corner of Tasmania. Enjoy!

Kick off with a couple of days in ebullient **Launceston**: check out Cataract Gorge and the excellent Queen Victoria Museum & Art Gallery (QVMAG), and have dinner at Stillwater and drinks at St John.

From Launceston, explore the eclectic enticements of the **Tamar Valley**: seahorses, gold mines, lighthouses and wineries. Loop south through historic **Evandale** before drifting west through Deloraine to the **Mole Creek** caves. Don't miss a few days exploring the northern end of impressive **Cradle Mountain-Lake St Clair National Park**, the starting point for the famous Overland Track.

From Cradle Mountain, skate southwest to the lunar landscapes of **Queenstown** and ride the West Coast Wilderness Railway to **Strahan**. From Strahan, head north to check the surf at **Marrawah**, then clamber up the Nut in **Stanley** on the north coast. An ocean dip at photogenic **Boat Harbour Beach** awaits.

Above: View of Hobart from the summit of kunanyi/Mt Wellington (p54)

Right: Sea kayaking at Coles Bay (p149)

LKONYA / SHUTTERSTOCK ©

Off The Beaten Track

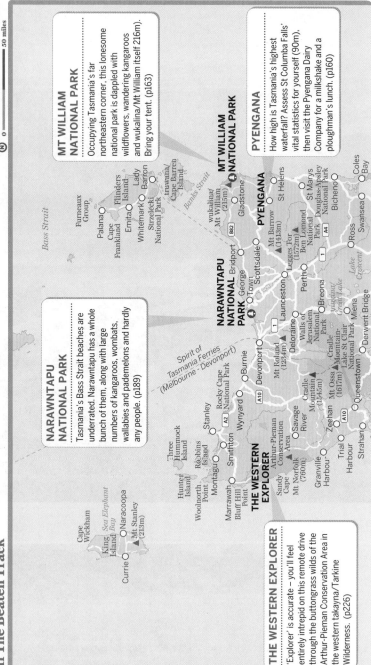

MT WILLIAM NATIONAL PARK

Occupying Tasmania's far northeastern corner, this lonesome national park is dappled with wildflowers, wandering kangaroos and wukalina/Mt William itself (216m). Bring your tent. (p163)

PYENGANA

How high is Tasmania's highest waterfall? Assess St Columba Falls' vital statistics for yourself (90m), then visit the Pyengana Dairy Company for a milkshake and a ploughman's lunch. (p160)

NARAWNTAPU NATIONAL PARK

Tasmania's Bass Strait beaches are underrated. Narawntapu has a whole bunch of them, along with large numbers of kangaroos, wombats, wallabies and pademelons and hardly any people. (p189)

THE WESTERN EXPLORER

'Explorer' is accurate – you'll feel entirely intrepid on this remote drive through the buttongrass wilds of the Arthur-Pieman Conservation Area in the western takayna/Tarkine Wilderness. (p226)

TASMAN SEA

Freycinet National Park

Maria Island National Park

⊘ **COAL MINES HISTORIC SITE**

Oatlands

Bothwell

TARRALEAH ○

A10

A1

Richmond

○ HOBART

Port Arthur

Tasman Peninsula

Mount Field National Park

Bridgewater

kunanyi/ Mt Wellington (1270m) ▲

Huonville

TINDERBOX

Mt Sorell (1144m) ▲

Franklin-Gordon Wild Rivers National Park

Strathgordon

Lake Gordon

Lake Pedder

Southwest National Park

HARTZ ⊘ ▲ **MOUNTAINS NATIONAL PARK**

Hartz Peak (1254m)

Southport

Bruny Island

Southwest Conservation Area

Point Hibbs

Wreck Bay

South West Cape

South East Cape

Low Rocky Point

Hilliard Head

SOUTHERN OCEAN

COAL MINES HISTORIC SITE

Not far from Port Arthur is this less well-known convict site, where prisoners once dug coal to fuel Port Arthur's fires. The tiny solitary confinement cells can only hint at the hardships suffered here. (p99)

TINDERBOX

Bring your snorkel and explore an underwater eco-trail at this hidden little headland. Bruny Island is just across the D'Entrecasteaux Channel: locals skim across to Dennes Point in their boats for a beach BBQ. (p82)

TARRALEAH

This former hydro-electric workers' town in the Central Highlands has been transformed into a tourist village, with a café, whisky-filled bar/restaurant, accommodation and activities aplenty. (p134)

HARTZ MOUNTAINS NATIONAL PARK

Up a long, wiggly dirt road behind Geeveston, this is one of the most accessible corners of the Tasmanian Wilderness World Heritage Area. It's an alpine wonderland of lakes, peaks and trails. (p120)

Getting Around Tasmania

For more information, see Transport (p304)

Little island, big journeys: Tasmania mightn't look too sizeable on the map, but most of the highways here are two-lane wigglers, slowed by the rigours of traversing the island's complex topography. Allow more time than instinct suggests to get from A to B.

Travelling by Car

Getting around in a car or campervan affords maximum efficiency, flexibility and the ability to play loud music. Bringing your vehicle on the *Spirit of Tasmania* ferry can be cheaper than hiring one once you arrive.

Car Hire

Tasmania has the usual slew of international and local car-rental agencies. Campervans are an increasingly popular way to get around: hire one big enough for you to sleep in and you'll save buckets on accommodation.

International company rates are pricey here: expect to pay upwards of $90 per day for a week's hire of a small car in any season. Book in advance for the best prices. Small Tasmanian and Australian firms rent cars for as little as $30 a day, depending on the season and the duration of the hire. The smaller companies don't often have desks at arrival points but can usually arrange for your car to be picked up at airports and the ferry terminal in Devonport.

Campervan rental rates start at around $90 (two berth) or $150 (four berth) per day, usually with a minimum five-day hire period.

For car- and campervan-rental agencies, see p307.

RESOURCES

Automobile Associations

The **Royal Automobile Club of Tasmania** (RACT; ☎03-6232 6300, roadside assistance 13 11 11; www.ract.com.au; cnr Murray & Patrick Sts, Hobart; ⊙8.45am-5pm Mon-Fri) provides an emergency breakdown service to members, with reciprocal arrangements with services in other Australian states and some overseas organisations.

Road Conditions

Road conditions in Tasmania are generally pretty good, but watch out for slippery 'black ice' in alpine areas, wandering native wildlife (particularly at night), log trucks and cyclists.

Insurance

Mandatory third-party personal-injury insurance is included in vehicle registration costs. If you're renting a vehicle, it's prudent to increase your insurance to include third-party property cover (for when you dent that Ferrari in the hostel car park).

No Car?

Bus

There are no passenger-train services in Tasmania, but reliable (if sometimes infrequent) buses run between most major cities and towns. Visiting remote areas can be frustrating due to irregular or nonexistent buses.

The main town-to-town players are Tassielink and Redline, with smaller operators servicing more far-flung areas: the most useful of these are Calow's Coaches on the east coast, two Tamar Valley operators (Lee's and Manion's) and Sainty's North East Bus Service in (you guessed it) the northeast.

Adequate services run within the large cities (Hobart, Launceston, Devonport and Burnie).

Bicycle

Bicycles are great way to get around Tasmania in summer; in winter, not so much... Most roads here are in reasonable condition, and once you're out of the cities, there's not a whole lot of traffic around to cause you grief. Hills and rain (in any season) are more notable deterrents.

Plane

If you're cashed up and time poor, you might consider chartering internal flights point-to-point within Tasmania. But in most instances, catching a bus will be just as quick. Internal flights are, however, the only sane way to visit King and Flinders Islands in the middle of Bass Strait.

Classic Tassie Road Trips

East coast A collusion of pretty seaside settlements, utterly magnificent coastline and some of the best wildlife-watching anywhere in Australia.

Heritage Highway Tasmania's main north–south road connects the state's two biggest cities and rumbles through (or just past) the historic towns of Tasmania's heartland.

Tasman Peninsula Staggering coastal landscapes, sandy beaches and one of Australia's most celebrated historic locations, all within striking distance of Hobart – need we say more?

Tamar Valley Funnelling 64km north from Launceston, the Tamar River Valley is fringed with emerald hills and cool-climate wineries. It's one of Australia's finest wine-touring areas.

West coast From Strahan to Launceston via the takayna/ Tarkine and Cradle Mountain, this journey is one of Australia's premier rainforest and wilderness drives, with historic villages, lonely beaches and amazing wildlife.

PLAN YOUR TRIP GETTING AROUND TASMANIA

DRIVING RULES

→ Drive on the left; the steering wheel is on the right (...in case you can't find it).

→ Give way to the right at intersections.

→ Blood alcohol limit 0.05%.

→ Highway speed limit 100km/h or 110km/h; urban areas 50km/h; near schools 40km/h in the morning and afternoon.

	Hobart	Launceston	Devonport	Strahan
Launceston	200			
Devonport	280	100		
Strahan	300	270	225	
Swansea	135	140	220	370

Plan Your Trip

Walking in Tasmania

Forget the convict history, the food, the architecture... For many, the number-one reason to visit Tasmania is to go bushwalking. Brimming with outdoor opportunities, the island's unique wilderness areas pack a whole lot of diversity into a small space. So break out the thermals and the tent and step to it.

Best Bushwalks for...

Wildlife

Maria Island National Park for Cape Barren geese, wallabies, pademelons, wombats, echidnas and Tasmanian devils.

Mt William National Park for Forester kangaroos.

Families

Easy 20-minute boardwalk track to Cape Tourville on Freycinet Peninsula.

Short walks at Cradle Mountain for a look at the peak, Dove Lake and probably some wildlife.

Scenery

Frenchmans Cap (peer over the cliffs if you dare) and Cradle Mountain for views across Tasmania's alpine heartland.

Tasman Peninsula: the improbably scenic Three Capes Track and Tasman Coastal Trail.

A Challenge

Federation Peak – arguably Australia's toughest bushwalk.

The rugged South Coast Track: fly into Melaleuca, then walk out to Cockle Creek.

When to Go

Summer

Summer (December to February) offers long days and a higher likelihood of warmer, settled weather. But summer is also peak season and popular tracks do get crowded. Try to head off midweek to avoid the crush. In alpine regions, snow still sometimes falls during summer.

Autumn

Mild weather and the gorgeous golden tones of autumn (March to May) are a great time to experience the Tasmanian wilderness. Easter (late March/early April) and Anzac Day (25 April) see higher walker numbers on popular tracks.

Winter

Winter (June to August) can be a mixed bag in Tasmania. Crisp, blue-sky mornings offset the very real possibility of snow, especially in the highlands. Days are short and deep snow can make some tracks impassable. Walking in winter is definitely only for the intrepid and very experienced.

Spring

Rain and wind can be the defining characteristics of spring (September to November) in Tasmania. Tracks can be muddy and slippery – add melting snow to the equation and river levels can be at their highest.

Resources

Books & Brochures

Lonely Planet's *Walking in Australia* has info on some of Tasmania's best (longer) walks. Available free from visitor centres, online and as a mobile-phone app is the Parks & Wildlife Service's (PWS) excellent brochure, *60 Great Short Walks,* listing the state's best quick ambles – anything from 10 minutes to all day (app also available).

Other compilations of walks throughout the state include the following:

➡ *A Visitor's Guide to Tasmania's National Parks* by Greg Buckman

➡ *100 Walks in Tasmania* by Tyrone Thomas and Andrew Close, covering short and multiday walks

➡ *Day Walks Tasmania* by John Chapman and Monica Chapman

➡ *South West Tasmania* by John Chapman

➡ *Cradle Mountain–Lake St Clair & Walls of Jerusalem National Parks* by John Chapman and John Siseman

Jan Hardy and Bert Elson's short-walk books, covering Hobart, Mt Wellington, Launceston, the northeast and the north-west, are also worth hunting down.

Online

Parks & Wildlife Service (www.parks.tas.gov.au) Superb site for essential predeparture information: safety hints, equipment checklists, weather information, bushfire updates, track-closure notifications, podcasts, track notes and fact sheets.

Bushwalk Australia (www.bushwalk.com) Online forum for up-to-date trip reports and feedback from local bushwalkers.

Bushwalk Tasmania (www.bushwalktasmania. com) Information on tracks and transport.

TasTrails (www.tastrails.com) Ninety-three trails around the state, with track info and photos.

Maps & Track Notes

Tasmap (www.tasmap.tas.gov.au) produces excellent maps, which are available from visitor centres, outdoor stores and Parks & Wildlife Service offices around the state. In Hobart you'll find them at Service Tasmania (p299) and the Tasmanian Map Centre (p299). Maps can also be ordered online.

Track notes for the Overland Track, Three Capes Track, Walls of Jerusalem, Freycinet Peninsula Circuit, Frenchmans Cap and South Coast Track are available online from the PWS website: click on 'Recreation', then 'Great Walks' and follow the link under 'Great Bushwalks'.

National-Park Fees & Track Bookings

Visitors' fees apply to all national parks. If you're planning on doing a lot of bushwalking, purchasing a day pass (per person/vehicle $12/24) each time will soon become an expensive exercise. Instead, buying an eight-week holiday pass (per person/vehicle $30/60) or annual pass (per vehicle $96) might be a smart move. You'll definitely need a holiday or annual pass for any of the multiday hikes within national parks.

Because of its popularity, from October to May the Overland Track has a limit on the number of walkers, a compulsory north-to-south walking direction and a booking system in place. You'll also have to pay the Overland Track fee (adult/child $200/160) during this period (not applicable June to September). Book online at www.parks.tas.gov.au.

The Three Capes Track also has capped walking numbers (48 per day), a one-way route and booking costs (adult/child $495/396). Book online at www.threecapes track.com.au.

Prior booking of other tracks and walks in Tasmania is not required.

Guided Walks

Guided hikes are a great way to see remote parts of Tasmania without the risks of getting lost, stranded, hungry or even particularly exhausted. Some of Tasmania's guided hikes are fully catered and include accommodation; others have more of a DIY vibe.

Eight of Tasmania's guided multiday walks have been handily grouped together for marketing purposes as the **Great Walks of Tasmania** (www.greatwalks tasmania.com). Together they cover around 335km, traversing rainforest, alpine areas, islands and beautiful coastal scenery.

Bay of Fires Lodge Walk (p161) Four-day luxury walk along this photogenic, rock-strewn stretch of the northeast coast.

Freycinet Experience Walk (p151) Fully catered, lodge-based, four-day stroll down the famous peninsula.

Maria Island Walk (p143) Another four-day option, this time on Maria Island. Nifty hut accommodation.

Cradle Mountain Huts (p234) Six epic days on the Overland Track with hut accommodation.

Tasmanian Expeditions (p257) Tackle the South Coast Track over nine days (with a rest day in the middle).

Tarkine Trails (p227) Six days in the takayna/ Tarkine wilderness in the remote northwest.

Tasmanian Expeditions (p209) A six-day 'Walls of Jerusalem Experience', returning to base camp at night.

Bruny Island Long Weekend (p113) A three-day, 35km walk through some of Bruny's wildest corners.

The four-day Three Capes Track (p96) on the Tasman Peninsula also has guided options (though not taking in the whole trail), with Park Trek (p96) and Life's An Adventure (p97). The guided **Three Capes Lodge Walk** started operations in late 2018; see www.taswalkingco.com.au for bookings.

On the Trail
Tasmanian Weather

In Tasmania (particularly in the west and southwest), a fine day can quickly become cold and stormy at any time of year. Always carry warm clothing, waterproof gear and a compass. Bring a tent too, rather than relying on finding a bed in a hut – particularly on popular walks such as the Overland Track.

On all extended walks, you must carry extra food in case you have to sit out a few days of bad weather (rather than having to rely on the goodwill of better-prepared hikers). In the worst of circumstances, such lack of preparation puts lives at risk – if the bad weather continues for long enough, everyone suffers.

Tasmanian walks are famous for their mud, so waterproof your boots, wear gaiters and watch where you're putting your feet.

Responsible Bushwalking

To help preserve the ecology and beauty of Tasmania, consider the following when bushwalking.

Code of Ethics

Click on 'Recreation' then 'Leave No Trace' on the PWS website for info on how to best experience Tasmania's wilderness and leave it as you found it. PWS literature is also available at Service Tasmania and national-park visitor centres around the state.

Camping & Walking on Private Property

➜ When camping, always use designated camping grounds where possible. When camping away from established sites, try to find a natural clearing in which to pitch your tent.

➜ Always seek permission to camp from landowners.

Rubbish Disposal

➜ Carry all your rubbish out with you; don't burn or bury it.

➜ Don't overlook easily forgotten items (orange peel, cigarette butts, plastic wrappers).

➜ Make an effort to carry out rubbish left by others.

➜ Never bury your rubbish. Digging disturbs soil and ground cover and encourages erosion. Buried rubbish will likely be dug up by animals anyway, and they may be injured or poisoned by it.

➜ Minimise waste by using minimal packaging.

➜ Sanitary napkins, tampons, condoms and toilet paper should be carried out, despite the inconvenience.

Human Waste Disposal

➜ Use toilets where provided.

➜ In the absence of toilets, dig a small hole 15cm deep and at least 100m from any watercourse. Cover waste with soil and a rock.

➜ Ensure these guidelines are also applied to portable toilet screens/tents if they're being used by a large bushwalking party. Encourage all party members to use a common site.

Washing

➜ Don't use detergents or toothpaste in or near watercourses, even if they are biodegradable.

TASMANIA'S TOP 10 WALKS
....

Walking is absolutely the best way to see Tasmania's wilderness in its full glory (and it's not a bad way to walk off all that great local food and wine, either). Pack comfy walking shoes and thick socks, and make happy trails. Following are our favourite walks, from 20 minutes to six days in length.

Three Capes Track (p96) Tasmania's newest multiday hike is fast becoming thought of as the best.

Overland Track (p234) A stunning six-day alpine endeavour through Cradle Mountain-Lake St Clair National Park.

Wineglass Bay (p149) Climb over the saddle and down to Freycinet's famous beach, a superscenic return walk of around three hours.

Cataract Gorge (p174) Explore Launceston's gorgeous gorge, which cuts into the heart of the city.

Tasman Coastal Trail (p97) Awesome three- to five-day trail along the Tasman Peninsula cliff tops. Keep an eye out for migrating whales.

Truganini Track (p71) Hilly, two-hour return climb through sclerophyll bushland between Mt Nelson, behind Hobart, and the southern suburb of Taroona.

Russell Falls (p91) A short jaunt from the car park at Mt Field National Park.

Dove Lake Circuit (p251) A three-hour lake lap at Cradle Mountain-Lake St Clair National Park.

South Coast Track (p260) An 85km monster along the coast in Southwest National Park.

Waterfall Bay (p100) A 90-minute return hike into Tasman Peninsula National Park to see sea cliffs and a waterfall cascading into the ocean.

➡ For personal washing, use biodegradable soap and a water container at least 50m away from any watercourse. Disperse waste water widely to allow soil to absorb it.

➡ Wash cooking utensils 50m from watercourses using a scourer, sand or snow instead of detergent.

Erosion

Hillsides and mountain slopes, especially at high altitudes, are prone to erosion.

➡ If a well-used track passes through a mud patch, walk through the mud so as not to increase the size of the patch.

➡ Avoid removing the plant life that keeps topsoil in place.

➡ Stick to existing tracks and avoid short cuts.

Fires & Low-Impact Cooking

Don't depend on open fires for cooking, as the collection of firewood in popular bush-walking areas causes rapid deforestation. Bring your own fuel stove instead. Other considerations:

➡ National parks are fuel-stove-only areas.

➡ Cook on a lightweight kerosene, alcohol or Shellite (white gas) stove. Avoid those powered by disposable butane gas canisters.

➡ Boil all water for 10 minutes before drinking, or use water-purifying tablets.

➡ If you're walking with a group, supply stoves for the whole team. In alpine areas, ensure group members wear adequate clothing so that fires aren't necessary for warmth.

➡ Fires may be acceptable below the treeline in winter in areas that get very few visitors. If you do light a fire, use an existing fireplace and only dead, fallen firewood. Leave some wood for the next walker as a courtesy.

➡ Ensure you fully extinguish fires after use. Spread embers and flood them with water.

➡ On days of total fire ban, don't light any fire whatsoever, including fuel stoves.

Wildlife Conservation

➡ Hunting is illegal in Tasmanian national parks.

➡ Don't attempt to exterminate animals in huts. In wilderness areas, they're likely to be protected species.

SHORT BUT SWEET

Here's concise proof that walking in Tasmania is not just suited to gung-ho outdoor types with industrial-strength thermals and a week's worth of powdered milk and instant noodles. If you like what you see here, hunt out the *60 Great Short Walks* brochure. It's freely available at visitor centres, and lists 60 of the state's best short walks, with durations from 10 minutes to all day.

Wineglass Bay (p149) An isthmus circuit at Freycinet.

Cape Tourville Lighthouse (p149) Take the boardwalk out to the lookout.

Liffey Falls (p196) A nice forest wander in the Liffey Valley.

Russell Falls (p91) In Mt Field National Park

Coal Mines Historic Site (p99) On the Tasman Peninsula.

Hartz Peak (p120) In the Hartz Mountains National Park.

Cape Hauy (p103) Close to Fortescue Bay.

Waterfall Bluff (p100) Near Eaglehawk Neck.

Organ Pipes (p54) Walk on Hobart's kunanyi/Mt Wellington.

Labillardiere Peninsula (p111) On Bruny Island.

➡ Leaving food scraps around encourages wildlife to hang around camps. Place gear out of reach and tie packs to rafters or trees.

➡ Feeding wildlife can lead to unbalanced populations, disease and animals becoming dependent on handouts.

➡ Don't bring pets into national parks.

Bushwalking Safety

Bushfires

Bushfires are an annual reality in Tasmania. In hot, dry and windy weather, be extremely careful with any naked flame and don't throw cigarette butts out of car windows. On a total-fire-ban day it's illegal to use even a camping stove in the open.

When a total fire ban is in place (common from November onwards), delay your hike until the weather improves. Stay attuned to updates from the Tasmania Fire Service (www.fire.tas.gov.au). If you're out in the bush and you see smoke, even a long way away, take it seriously – bushfires move very quickly and change direction with the wind. Go to the nearest open space, downhill if possible. A forested ridge, on the other hand, is the most dangerous place to be.

Hypothermia & Blizzards

Hypothermia is a significant risk in Tasmania, especially during winter. Strong winds produce high chill factors that can result in hypothermia even in moderate temperatures. Early signs include the inability to perform fine movements (such as doing up buttons), shivering and a bad case of the 'umbles' (fumbles, mumbles, grumbles and stumbles). Key elements of treatment include moving out of the cold, changing out of wet gear into dry, windproof, waterproof clothes, adding insulation and providing fuel (water and carbohydrates). Shivering is a good thing – it builds internal temperature. In severe hypothermia, shivering actually stops: this is a medical emergency requiring rapid evacuation in addition to the above measures.

Blizzards can occur in Tasmania's mountains at any time of year. Bushwalkers should be prepared for such freezing eventualities, particularly in remote areas. Take thermals and jackets, plus windproof and waterproof garments. Carry a high-quality tent suitable for snow camping, and enough food for two extra days, in case you get snowed in.

Creepy-Crawlies

This is Australia, so there are also things that can bite, suck and sting you and generally ruin your hike: ticks, jack jumper and bull ants, leeches and snakes (p300) are the most common.

Plan Your Trip
Activities

If Tasmania were a person, it would very much be the 'outdoors type'. The bushwalks (p34) here are among Australia's best, while white-water rafting on the Franklin River is charged with environmental grandeur. Abseiling and rock climbing are thrill-a-minute adventures, and cycling and sea kayaking are magical ways to explore the state.

On the Land
Mountain Biking

There are plenty of fire trails and off-the-beaten-track routes around Tasmania to explore. Dedicated trails include the Glenorchy MTB Park (p64) north of Hobart and the new mountain-bike park at Hollybank Treetops Adventure (p193) north of Launceston. There's also the new 'gravity-focussed' Maydena Bike Park (www.maydenabikepark.com) in the southwest, which opened in 2018.

On the competition front, the multisport Freycinet Challenge (p151) is held every October. Little Derby (p162) in the northeast has become a biking hot spot of late, with the 2015 and 2016 Australian Cross Country Marathon Mountain Bike Championships held there, and one of the six events in the 2017 Enduro World Series.

Resources

Parks & Wildlife Service (www.parks.tas.gov.au) Mountain-biking code of conduct for low-impact biking. Click on 'Recreation', 'Other Activities', then 'Mountain Biking'.

Tassie Trails (www.tassietrails.org) Online guide to all things mountain biking in Tasmania.

Ride Tassie (www.ridetassie.com) Comprehensive guide to Tassie's mountain-bike trails.

Tasmanian Trail Guide to this blockbuster 480km multi-use trail from Devonport to Dover.

Best Activities for...

Families
Swimming at Seven Mile Beach or Boat Harbour Beach.

Winter snow action at Ben Lomond National Park.

Daredevils
Abseiling down the 140m-high wall of the Gordon Dam.

Careering down the slopes of kunanyi/Mt Wellington on a mountain bike.

Taking it Easy
Cruising the Gordon River on a yacht or boat.

Casting a fly across the Central Highland's trout-filled lakes.

Getting Wet
Rafting the Franklin River, a classic 10-day river run.

Diving through underwater kelp forests off the Tasman Peninsula.

THE TASMANIAN TRAIL

The Tasmanian Trail (www.tasmanian trail.com.au) is a 480km multi-use route from Devonport to Dover that's geared towards walkers, horse riders and mountain bikers. Most of the trail is on forestry or fire trails and country roads: it passes farms, forests and towns en route, with camping spots every 30km or so (and lots of opportunities to sleep in a real bed!). All the information you need to tackle some or all of the trail is in the *Tasmanian Trail Guide Book*, available online as a digital file ($24). As a rough guide, mountain bikers should allow around eight days complete the trail, walkers around 25 days. Have fun!

Tasmanian Mountain Bike Guide Book (Travis and Jane Deane; www.mtbguidebook.com) Details rides through 40 locations, complete with difficulty and 'skull' ratings (danger factor).

Tours

An essential part of any visit to Hobart should be a knobbly, two-wheeled Mt Wellington Descent (p54). Beyond the capital, try Mountain Bike & Rock Climbing Tasmania (p177).

Cycling

Cycling is a terrific way to tour Tasmania and engage with the island landscapes, especially on the dry east coast. To cycle between Hobart and Launceston along either coast, allow between 10 and 14 days. For a two-wheeled 'lap of the map', give yourself 18 to 28 days.

Short- and long-term bike rental is available in Hobart and Launceston. Cycling-tour operators include Green Island Tours (p159) and Tasmanian Expeditions (p309).

Resources

Bicycle Network Tasmania (www.biketas.org.au) Cycling blog and links to route descriptions, online maps and publications: click on 'The Knowledge', then 'Maps and Routes' under 'Rides & Riding'.

Discover Tasmania (www.discovertasmania. com) Download the *Self Guided Cycle Touring in Tasmania* PDF, or ask for it at the Hobart Visitor Information Centre.

Where to Ride: Tasmania (Andrew Bain) Details 45 rides with maps, altitude profiles and difficulty ratings. Look for it in bike shops.

Trout Fishing

Brown trout were introduced into Tasmania's Plenty River in 1866, and into Lake Sorell in 1867. Innumerable lakes and rivers have subsequently been stocked and trout have thrived. Let's go fishing!

Where to Fish

The Central Highlands are home to the state's best-known spots for brown and rainbow trout: Arthurs Lake, Great Lake, Little Pine Lagoon, Western Lakes (including Lake St Clair), Lake Sorell and the Lake Pedder impoundment. On some parts of Great Lake you're only allowed to use artificial lures, and you're not allowed to fish any of the streams flowing into Great Lake.

Information & Gear

Bone up on Tassie trout with a copy of *Tasmanian Trout Waters* by Greg French. Also worth a look is the two-monthly *Tasmanian Fishing & Boating News*, current and back issues of which are available online at Tasfish (www.tasfish.com). Trout Guides & Lodges Tasmania (www.troutguides tasmania.com.au) lists trout-fishing guides and Central Highlands accommodation options. In Hobart, buy equipment and licences at Spot On Fishing Tackle (p132).

Learning to Fish

Tasmanian trout can be difficult to catch. They're fickle about what they eat, and the right lures are needed for the right river, lake, season, weather... Check out Rod & Fly Tasmania (p132) or Trout Guides & Lodges Tasmania (www.troutguidestasma nia.com.au) for info on guides and lessons.

Licences & Costs

A licence is required to fish Tasmania's inland waters, and there are bag, season and size limits on most fish.

An annual licence runs for 12 months from 1 August to 31 July ($75.50). Short-term licences are also available: $23 for 48 hours, $38.50 for a week. Licences are available from the **Inland Fisheries Service** (☑03-6165 3808; www.ifs.tas.gov.au), Service Tasmania (p299), fishing stores and some visitor centres.

In general, inland waters open for fishing on the Saturday closest to 1 August and

Above: Rock climbing on the Totem Pole, Cape Hauy (p102)

Right: Mountain biking at Derby (p163)

ANDREW BAIN / GETTY IMAGES ©

ALTERNATIVE ACTIVITIES

Yes, yes, we know – everyone is here to hike the Overland Track, go mountain biking in Derby, fly-fish in the Central Highlands and go rafting on the Franklin River. These avid pursuits are all fantastic and have deservedly put Tasmania on the map. But what of you're after something a little more niche?

Caving Tasmania's limestone karst caves are among the most impressive in Australia. The Mole Creek and Gunns Plains caves in the north and Hastings Caves in the southeast are open to the public daily, with troglodytic cave tours.

Canoeing For a sedate paddle sans-rapids, try the Arthur and Pieman Rivers in the northwest, and Ansons River and Coles Bay on the east coast. You can rent canoes and/or kayaks at Arthur River, Corinna and Coles Bay. The Huon, Weld, Leven and North Esk Rivers also attract their fair share of canoes. Canoe Tasmania (www.tas. canoe.org.au) has canoe- and kayak-club info around the state.

Sailing The D'Entrecasteaux Channel and Huon River south of Hobart are deep, wide and handsome places to set sail, with more inlets and harbours than you could swing a boom at. Fleets of white sails often dot Hobart's Derwent River in summer – many locals own yachts and consider an afternoon sailing on the estuary to be Hobart's greatest perk. Of course, when the annual Sydney to Hobart Yacht Race (p77) winds up in Hobart just before New Year's Eve, the whole state goes yacht crazy. Check out the big ocean-going maxi-yachts as they bump and sway at their moorings around Sullivans Cove. Contact the Royal Yacht Club of Tasmania (www.ryct. org.au) for sailing advice for around the island.

Ocean fishing Saltwater rod fishing is allowed year-round without a permit, but size restrictions and bag limits apply. Eaglehawk Neck on the Tasman Peninsula and St Helens on the east coast are good spots for fishing-boat charters. Online, Tasfish (www.tasfish.com) is a wealth of fishy info.

close on the Sunday nearest to 30 April. The best fishing is between October and April.

Rock Climbing & Abseiling

Rock climbing and abseiling are alive and well in Tasmania. There are some awesome cliffs for climbing, particularly along the sunny east coast. The Organ Pipes on kunanyi/Mt Wellington above Hobart, the Mt Killiecrankie cliffs on Flinders Island and Launceston's Cataract Gorge also offer brilliant climbing on solid rock. The soaring coastal cliffs on the Tasman Peninsula are rock-climbing nirvana – especially the legendary Totem Pole and Candlestick dolerite stacks – but they're impossible to access if there's any kind of ocean swell.

See the Discover Tasmania website (www.discovertasmania.com) for a general introduction: click on 'What to Do', then 'Outdoors and Adventure'. Operators around the state include Tasmanian Expeditions (p309), Rock Climbing Adventures Tasmania (p65) and Mountain Bike & Rock Climbing Tasmania (p177).

Abseiling around the state doesn't get much better than dangling your way down

the 140m-high face of the Gordon Dam near Strathgordon: contact Aardvark Adventures (p259).

Skiing

There are two petite ski resorts in Tasmania: Ben Lomond (p197), 55km southeast of Launceston, and Mt Mawson (p92) in Mt Field National Park, 80km northwest of Hobart. Both offer cheaper (though much less developed) ski facilities than mainland resorts. The ski season usually runs from July to mid-September, but snowfalls tend to be patchy and unreliable.

See www.ski.com.au/reports/australia/ tas for snow conditions. The only place you can hire gear is at Ben Lomond itself, through Ben Lomond Snow Sports (p198)

On the Water
Sea Kayaking

Sea-kayaking hot spots include Hobart, where you can explore the suburban waterline and docks with an on-the-water fish-and-chip feast; the D'Entrecasteaux Channel south of Hobart; the Tasman Peninsula; Coles Bay on the east coast; and the remote waterways of Bathurst Harbour and Port Davey on the south coast.

Key operators include **Roaring 40s Kayaking** (☎0455 949 777; www.roaring40skayak ing.com.au), Freycinet Adventures (p149) and Tassie Bound (p90).

Online, the Parks & Wildlife Service website (www.parks.tas.gov.au) has tips on minimal-impact sea kayaking: click on 'Recreation', then 'Other Activities'.

Rafting

Tasmania is famed for white-knuckle white-water rafting on the Franklin River. Other rivers offering rapid thrills include the Derwent (upstream from Hobart), the Picton (southwest of Hobart) and the Mersey in the north.

Check out the Parks & Wildlife Service website (www.parks.tas.gov.au) for rafting-operator listings and lots of solid advice: click on 'Recreation', then 'Other Activities'.

Surfing

Tasmania has dozens of buckin' surf breaks, but the water is damn cold – pack an iron will and a thick steamer wetsuit.

Where to Surf

Close to Hobart, the most reliable spots are Clifton Beach and Goats Beach (unsigned) en route to South Arm, and Park Beach near Sorell. Eaglehawk Neck on the Tasman Peninsula is also worth checking out. The southern beaches on Bruny Island – particularly Cloudy Bay – offer consistent swells.

The east coast from Bicheno north to St Helens has solid beach breaks when conditions are working. Binalong Bay, at the southern end of the Bay of Fires, is an accessible option; Ironhouse Point is more hard core; and Spring and Shelly Beaches near Orford have consistent breaks.

Further north, King Island cops some big Bass Strait swells, while Marrawah on the west coast is famous for its towering waves. Australia's heaviest wave, the utterly gnarly Shipstern Bluff off the Tasman Peninsula, isn't recommended for anyone other than serious pros.

Island Surf School (p98) offers lessons at Park Beach.

Resources

Check out the following for surf reports.

Magic Seaweed (www.magicseaweed.com)

Surfing Tasmania (www.surfingaustralia.com/tas)

Tassie Surf (www.tassiesurf.com)

Scuba Diving & Snorkelling

National Geographic once claimed that Tasmania offered the 'most accessible underwater wilderness in the world'. You may well find yourself in agreement. Visibility ranges from 12m in summer to 40m in winter, with temperate waters offering unique biodiversity.

Where to Dive

There are excellent underwater opportunities around Rocky Cape in the north, on the east coast and around the shipwrecks off King and Flinders Islands. At Tinderbox near Hobart and off Maria Island there are marked underwater snorkelling trails. There's also an artificial dive site created by the scuttling of the *Troy D* off the west coast of Maria Island; contact the Tasmanian Scuba Diving Club (www.tsdc.org.au) for info.

TOP TASSIE BEACHES

Pack your swimsuit, brace yourself for a cold-water collision, and jump right in!

Binalong Bay (p161) Binalong time since you had a dip? Head for this crescent of sand north of St Helens.

Boat Harbour Beach (p220) The drive down the steep access road offers postcard-perfect beach views.

Seven Mile Beach (p87) Safe swimming, rolling dunes and an occasional point break near Hobart.

Fortescue Bay (p102) A little slice of heaven, complete with low-key camping ground.

Trousers Point (p167) Take your trousers off at this magnificent Flinders Island beach.

Resources

Discover Tasmania (www.discovertasma
nia.com) has info on diving in Tasmania,
including lists of diving businesses and
equipment-hire operators around the
state.

Learning to Dive

Contact the following operators if you
want to learn to breathe underwater:

Bicheno Dive Centre (p154) On the east coast.

Eaglehawk Dive Centre (p100) On the Tasman
Peninsula.

Flinders Island Dive (p168) On Flinders Island.

Leven Scuba Club (www.levenscubaclub.com.au)
In Devonport.

Beach Swimming

The east coast has plenty of sheltered,
white-sand beaches offering excellent
swimming, although the water is (to
understate it) rather cold. There are also
sheltered suburban beaches in Hobart,
including Bellerive and Sandy Bay, but the
water here can often be a little soupy –
things get clearer further south at Taroona, Kingston and Blackmans Bay, or east
at Seven Mile Beach.

In the north, Bass Strait beaches such as
Sisters Beach and Boat Harbour Beach are
great spots for a quick ocean dip. On the
west coast, the surf can be ferocious and
the beaches aren't patrolled – play it safe.

Indoor Activities

When the rain comes down – which,
despite Tasmania's chilly rep, isn't as common as you might think – there's plenty
going on indoors.

Swimming Pools

Cold out? Indoor swim centres are a great
way to beat a retreat from the bleak. In
Launceston, head for the Launceston Leisure & Aquatic Centre (p177); in Hobart,
try the Hobart Aquatic Centre (p63). The
usual waterslides, gyms, yoga rooms and
cafes are in attendance.

Climbing Gyms

When there's snow on kunanyi/Mt Wellington and scaling the rock formations
at the summit doesn't seem wise, head to
the indoor Rockit Climbing (p65) gym in
central Hobart.

Cooking Schools

Tasmania is rapidly becoming renowned
globally as a destination for passionate
foodie travellers. The state's fruit and
vegetables, seafood, meat, cheese, whisky,
wine and beer are held in high regard
by star mainland chefs such as Tetsuya
Wakuda, and local chefs are also forging
an international reputation. It's the kind of
superior produce that any self-respecting
home cook would love to get into. Here's
your chance.

Agrarian Kitchen (☑03-6261 1099; www.
theagrariankitchen.com; 650 Lachlan Rd, Lachlan;
classes per person from $385) – located in a
19th-century schoolhouse in the Derwent
Valley village of Lachlan, about 45 minutes' drive from Hobart – is Tasmania's
first hands-on, farm-based cookery school.
The surrounding 5 acres provide sustainable, organically grown vegetables, fruit,
berries and herbs. Other ingredients are
sourced from local farmers, fishers and
artisan producers.

One of the most popular classes is the
Agrarian Experience (per person $385), a
daylong celebration of the seasons, com-
mencing with choosing the freshest of fruit
and vegies in the garden and then cooking
up a storm before settling in for lunch with
Tasmanian wines and beers from the nearby Two Metre Tall (p90) craft-beer brewery. Other classes specialise in charcuterie
and gourmet sausage making, pastries and
pasta, bread-making and desserts.

In Hobart itself, Corinda (p73) B&B in
Glebe has a Spanish chef who runs regular
Iberian cooking classes for guests ($249).
South of Hobart in Cygnet in the Huon
Valley, Matthew Evans, star of the SBS TV
series *Gourmet Farmer,* has opened a res-
taurant and cooking school on his Fat Pig
Farm (p117). See the website for info on his
cook-and-eat classes, starting at $300.

If you're travelling in Tasmania's north,
Hadspen's Red Feather Inn (p194) also
offers cooking classes, inspired by the Slow
Food movement.

Plan Your Trip
Travel with Children

As any parent will tell you, getting from A to B is the hardest part of travelling with children. Fortunately, in Tasmania, A is never very far from B. This will leave your family feeling unhurried, stress-free and ready to enjoy the state's beaches, rivers, forests and wildlife parks.

Tasmania for Kids

Tasmania is a naturally active destination, with plenty of challenges, fun times and exercise opportunities for children (sometimes all at once). Cruise past coastal scenery to spy on seals and dolphins, or paddle a kayak around Hobart's docks. Explore the forest canopy, or ride a mountain bike down Mt Wellington.

On the gentler side are riverbank bike paths and feeding times at Tassie's excellent wildlife parks. And when the kids have hiked, biked and kayaked all day, treat them to superfresh local fruit from a roadside stall, or some alfresco fish and chips.

Accommodation

Many motels and better-equipped caravan parks can supply cots. Caravan parks also often have playgrounds, games rooms and hectares of grass on which to burn off some cooped-up-in-the-car kilojoules.

Top-end, and some midrange, hotels are well versed in the needs of guests with children. Some may also have in-house children's movies and child-minding services. B&Bs, on the other hand, often market themselves as blissfully child-free.

Best Regions for Kids

Hobart & Around

A musical education: live Friday-night tunes at Salamanca Arts Centre followed by Saturday's Salamanca Market buskers. Other highlights include harbourside fish and chips, the Tasmanian Museum & Art Gallery and kunanyi/Mt Wellington for mountain biking and winter snowball throwing.

The Southeast

Check out Bruny Island's wild coastline by boat. Don't miss the Tahune AirWalk, Hastings Caves & Thermal Springs and the Ida Bay Railway.

The East Coast

Brilliant beaches, Coles Bay kayaking, hungry Tasmanian devils at Natureworld and Bicheno's cute penguins.

Launceston & Around

Curious critters: City Park's Japanese macaques and the odd little residents at Beauty Point's Seahorse World and Platypus House. Defy gravity with the Cataract Gorge chairlift or some Cable Hang Gliding.

Eating Out with Children

Dining with kids in Tasmania rarely causes any hassles. If you sidestep the flashier restaurants, children are generally welcomed. Cafes are kid friendly and you'll see families getting in early for dinner in pub dining rooms. Most places can supply high chairs.

Dedicated kids menus are common, but selections are usually uninspiring (ham-and-pineapple pizza, fish fingers, chicken nuggets etc). If a restaurant doesn't have a kids menu, find something on the regular menu and ask the kitchen to adapt it. It's usually fine to bring toddler food in with you.

If the sun is shining, there are plenty of picnic spots around the state, many with free barbecues. During summer, Tassie is also a great place to buy fresh fruit at roadside stalls.

Breastfeeding & Nappy Changing

Most Tasmanians are relaxed about public breastfeeding and nappy changing: a parent using the open boot of a car as a nappy-changing area is a common sight! Hobart and most major towns also have public rooms where parents can go to feed their baby or change a nappy; ask at the local visitor centre or city councils. Items such as infant formula and disposable nappies are widely available.

Babysitting

In Hobart contact the Mobile Nanny Service (p74), or check out the statewide listings on www.babysittersrus.com.au.

Admission Fees & Discounts

Child concessions (and family rates) generally apply to tours, museum admission and bus transport, with discounts as high as 50% of the adult rate. Nearly all tourist attractions offer kids' prices, with kids aged under four or five often admitted free. However, the definition of 'child' can vary from under 12 to under 18 years. Accommodation concessions often apply to children under 12 years sharing the same room as adults. On the major airlines, infants up to three years of age travel free (provided they don't occupy a seat).

Children's Highlights

Beaches & Swimming

Seven Mile Beach (p87) The best safe-swimming beach near Hobart.

Sisters Beach (p221)

Douglas-Apsley National Park (p154) Take a dip in a deep, dark river waterhole ('Was that an eel?').

Fortescue Bay (p102) If you've made the effort to drive in here, you might as well camp for the night. And have a swim.

Cataract Gorge (p174) Cool off in the free outdoor swimming pool at First Basin.

We're Hungry!

Flippers (p75) Fish and chips on Hobart's Constitution Dock. Launceston's equivalent is Fish 'n' Chips (p182) by the river.

Sorell Fruit Farm (p98) Bag your own fruit (cherries, strawberries, apricots, apples etc) on the doorstep of the Tasman Peninsula.

Doo-Lishus Food Caravan (p100) Scallop pies for lunch! Then a short walk to Eaglehawk Neck's blowhole.

Hillwood Farmgate (p190) Berry picking/scoffing near George Town.

House of Anvers (p206) For a quick-fire choc fix near Devonport.

Getting Active

Tarkine Forest Adventures (p227) Slip down a 110m-long slide into a deep-forest sinkhole.

Tahune AirWalk (p120) Make like a possum in the treetops along walkways 20m above the ground; near Geeveston.

Tasmazia (p211) Totally ridiculous maze and theme park near Lake Barrington.

Hollybank Treetops Adventure (p193) Swing through the trees with the greatest of ease at this adventure park near Lilydale.

Killiecrankie Enterprises (p168) Fossick for 'diamonds' (well, semiprecious topaz) on Flinders Island.

A History Lesson

Historic Ghost Tour (p105) The Port Arthur Historic Site by day is creepy enough, but come back at dusk for extra atmos-fear.

Ida Bay Railway (p310) Historic WWII-era rattler, running 14km through bushland to the beach near Southport.

Callington Mill (p129) Oatlands' old-time mill is cranking out flour again.

Beaconsfield Mine & Heritage Centre (p188) Hands-on gold-mining displays and plenty of heritage.

Mawson's Huts Replica Museum (p59) Antarctic heritage in Hobart.

Meeting the Locals

Maria Island National Park (p142) Close-up encounters with wallabies, echidnas, honking Cape Barren geese and maybe even a Tasmanian devil.

Bonorong Wildlife Centre (p88) A whole bunch of beasts, not far from Hobart. The emphasis is on conservation and education.

Bicheno Penguin Tours (p154) Watch the waddling locals come home to roost.

Seahorse World (p189) On the waterfront at Beauty Point.

Natureworld (p153) Daily Tasmanian-devil feeding sessions at this wildlife centre near Bicheno. Show the progeny a tiger snake without the accompanying fear and peril.

Messing About in Boats

Bruny Island Cruises (p113) Boat tours of the island's southern coastline, cliffs and caves (...and the ferry ride to the island itself is fun!).

Lady Nelson (p67) Tall-ship sailing on Hobart's Derwent River.

Freycinet Adventures (p149) Easygoing sea-kayak paddles around sheltered Coles Bay. Sunset tours a bonus.

Huon Jet (p118) Jet-boat rides on the otherwise-tranquil Huon River in the southeast.

Arthur River Canoe & Boat Hire (p225) Paddle around on the Arthur River in a Canadian canoe.

Planning

Lonely Planet's *Travel with Children* contains buckets of useful information for travel with little 'uns. To aid your planning once you get to Tassie, pick up the free *LetsGoKids* magazine (www.letsgokids.com.au) at visitor centres for activity ideas, kid-friendly-accommodation listings and event discount vouchers.

What to Pack

Tasmania's weather is truly fickle, even in summer, so a diverse wardrobe with lots of layers is recommended. Definitely pack beach gear for your summer holiday, but also throw in a few thermal long-sleeve tops, beanies and jackets. A compact beach tent will also be handy, given Tasmania's capricious winds. Don't forget hats and sunglasses – essential for Tasmania's sharp southern rays.

When to Go

When it comes to family holidays, Tasmania is a winner during summer. Having said that, summer is peak season and school-holiday time: expect pricey accommodation and a lot of booking ahead for transport and beds (especially interstate flights, rental cars, the *Spirit of Tasmania* ferry, camping grounds and motels).

If your own kids don't need to be at school, a better bet may be the shoulder months of March and April (sidestepping Easter) and November, when the weather's still good and there's less pressure on the tourism sector. Winter is even better (if you don't mind the cold and aren't into swimming and camping) – you'll have the whole place to yourselves!

PLAN YOUR TRIP TRAVEL WITH CHILDREN

Regions at a Glance

Hobart & Around

Arts Scene
Gourmet Travel
History

Festival Frenzy

On the quiet rim of the world, Hobart hosts some dizzyingly good arts festivals. Ten Days on the Island hits the cultural high-water mark; Dark MOFO is disquieting and brilliant. In between times, the Salamanca Pl galleries keep the arts brew bubbling.

Fine Food & Wine

Get a food-and-wine infusion from Hobart's fab festivals, hip cafes and restaurants, atmospheric pubs and craft-beer bars. Day-trip to the nearby Coal River Valley wine region, then finish up with fish and chips at Constitution Dock.

Old Hobart Town

Salamanca Pl and tight-knit Battery Point are awash with memories of a challenging past. Huddled under kunanyi/Mt Wellington, Cascade Brewery and the Female Factory Historic Site illuminate two very different aspects of early Van Diemen's Land life.

p52

Tasman Peninsula & Port Arthur

Activities
History
Wildlife

Coastal Exploring

Experience the Tasman Peninsula's rugged coast in a sea kayak, on a surfboard, on a boat cruise, or on foot along the superscenic Three Capes Track. Camping at remote Fortescue Bay is a must.

Port Arthur & Beyond

Both melancholy and photogenic, Port Arthur is only the starting point for history buffs. Don't miss the underrated Coal Mines Historic Site and the history of the Dogline at Eaglehawk Neck.

Devils & Dolphins

Get a good look at a Tasmanian devil at the Tasmanian Devil Unzoo, then eyeball some seals, dolphins and whales on a sea-salty cruise around Tasman Island.

p94

The Southeast

Gourmet Travel
Wildlife
Natural Landscapes

Gourmet Delays

Throw your schedule out the window and stop off at the southeast's vineyards, cider houses and roadside fruit stalls. Across on Bruny Island, smoked seafood, fresh oysters, berry pies, beer and handmade cheeses create further delays.

Bruny Island Birdlife

Penguins and muttonbirds are the immediate stars on Bruny Island, but an in-depth birdwatching excursion will reveal a veritable gaggle of pelagic species. Visit in October for the annual Bruny Island Bird Festival.

Caves & Peaks

Explore the subterranean caverns and geothermal springs of the Hastings Caves & Thermal Springs area, then venture into a wilderness of glacial peaks and tarns in Hartz Mountains National Park.

p107

Midlands & Central Highlands

History
Fishing
Whisky

Heritage Highway

Imagine stage coaches and bushrangers as you rattle into historic towns along the Midland Hwy. Ross' bridge is a sturdy entry point to the town, and Callington Mill stands out amid Oatlands' fine sandstone buildings.

Trout-Fishing Nirvana

On a misty morning the Central Highlands' elevated waterways feel otherworldly...and the trout fishing is out of this world too! Reminisce about the one that didn't get away at a snug lakeside pub.

Singleminded About Single Malt

Time for a dram? Historic Dysart House in Kempton, home to Redlands Distillery, is well worth a trip. See if Nant Distillery in Bothwell is taking tours, or detour to Tarraleah and choose from the lodge's cache of 200 single malt whiskies.

p124

The East Coast

Beaches
Gourmet Travel
Wildlife

Sandy Shores

Wineglass Bay and the Bay of Fires get all the press, but equally deserving are Redbill Beach, Spring Beach and Honeymoon Bay. Cool off after a bushwalk, camp behind the dunes or kayak the coast.

Picnic Supplies

The fertile east coast offers up seasonal berries, oysters, chocolate, fresh seafood and wonderfully whiffy cheeses. Craft beer and excellent wines will also make it onto your beach-picnic menu.

Maria Island Locals

Maria Island National Park offers a miniselection from Dr Dolittle's contact list: wallabies, pademelons, kangaroos, wombats, echidnas, tiger snakes, Cape Barren geese and a healthy population of Tasmanian devils. Offshore are seals, dolphins and wandering whales.

p136

Launceston & Around

Festivals
Architecture
Wine

Arty Events

Festivale is Launceston's annual summer arts festival. The city also hosts events during the Tasmania-wide Ten Days on the Island festival. The Junction Arts Festival is edgy, while MONA FOMA looks like becoming a Launceston mainstay from 2019.

Historic Properties

Tasmania's second city has a compelling architectural heritage, with grand public buildings and well-preserved domestic architecture. Around the city are heritage estates: Franklin House, Woolmers Estate, Clarendon, Entally Estate...

Tamar Valley Wine Region

Tamar Valley vineyards produce world-class cool-climate wines. Our favourites include Holm Oak Vineyards in Rowella, Bay of Fires Wines at Pipers River, Leaning Church Vineyard in Lalla and Tamar Ridge in Rosevears. Who's driving?

p170

Devonport & the Northwest

Gourmet Travel
National Parks
Coast

Beer, Chocolate & Whisky

You've got the three major food groups all covered here! In between sampling chocolate, single malt whisky and craft beer, make some room for local smoked salmon, cheeses and fresh berries.

Camping & Caving

Head to the Walls of Jerusalem National Park for superb bushwalking – rug up for snowy winter camping. Not far away, turn off your torch and check out the glow-worms at Mole Creek Karst National Park.

Life by the Sea

Life in the northwest is inextricably linked with the sea. Take a dip at Boat Harbour Beach, delve into maritime heritage at Stanley, and enjoy seaside cafe culture in Penguin and lighthouse tours at Table Cape.

p199

Cradle Country & the West

Bushwalking
Kayaking
History

Alpine Heartland

Tasmania's untamed southwest proffers endless bushwalking opportunities – up peaks, traversing tarn shelves and across moorlands. The return hike up Cradle Mountain is a robust eight hours; the Overland Track is a six- to eight-day spectacular.

Remote Waterways

Paddle onto mirror-flat Bathurst Harbour in a kayak, or set sail along the isolated Gordon and Pieman Rivers. For an adrenalin hit, a multiday white-water-rafting trip on the Franklin River will redefine your concept of wilderness.

Riding the Rails

Ride the historic West Coast Wilderness Railway through rainforest between Queenstown and Strahan. The towns' differences couldn't be more stark: Queenstown's rugged, unabashed mining ambience versus Strahan's cutesy (but undeniably lovely) harbourside vibes.

p231

On the Road

Hobart & Around

Best Places to Eat

➡ Templo (p74)

➡ Jackman & McRoss (p76)

➡ Aløft (p76)

➡ Flippers (p75)

➡ Picnic Basket (p85)

Best Places to Stay

➡ Henry Jones Art Hotel (p70)

➡ Alabama Hotel (p69)

➡ Montacute (p71)

➡ MACq 01 (p70)

Why Go?

Australia's second-oldest city and southernmost capital, Hobart dapples the foothills of Mt Wellington, angling down to the slate-grey Derwent River. The town's rich cache of colonial architecture and natural charms are complemented by innovative festivals, eclectic markets and world-class food and drink experiences.

It's a gorgeous place, but until quite recently Hobart was far from cosmopolitan or self-assured – it's taken a while for Hobartians to feel comfortable in their own skins. Paralleling this shift (or perhaps driving it), the mainland Australian attitude to Hobart has changed from derision to delight: investors now recognise that Tasmania's abundant water, stress-free pace and cool climate are precious commodities.

Not far past the outskirts of town are some great beaches, alpine areas and historic villages. And don't miss MONA, Hobart's dizzyingly good Museum of Old and New Art, which has vehemently stamped Tasmania onto the global cultural map.

When to Go

➡ For a week either side of New Year's Eve, Hobart heaves with sailors, travellers, food festivals and concerts. This is prime-time Hobart, when the old town treads the boards of the world stage.

➡ During the long days of summer – January into March – the time is right for eating, drinking, afternoons at the cricket and maybe even a swim (the sea around Hobart is warm... almost).

➡ When the southern winter blows in (June to August), catch some AFL football, throw snowballs on kunanyi/ Mt Wellington or Mt Field and cosy-up by an open fire in a pub. Crowds are down – take your pick of the waterfront accommodation. Dark MOFO broods in the half-light.

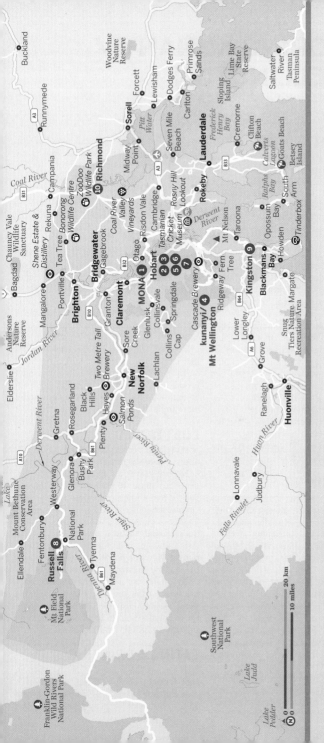

Hobart & Around Highlights

1 MONA (p61) Being inspired, turned on, appalled, educated and amused.

2 Salamanca Market (p61) Losing yourself in the Saturday morning crowds.

3 Battery Point (p60) Whiling away an afternoon exploring this historic enclave.

4 kunanyi/Mt Wellington (p54) Careering down from the summit on a mountain bike.

5 Roaring 40s Kayaking (p64) Paddling around the Hobart waterfront.

6 Constitution Dock fish punts (p75) Devouring fresh fish and chips.

7 North Hobart (p61) Seeing what's cooking along this evolving restaurant strip.

8 Russell Falls (p91) Bracing yourself for a spray at Mt Field National Park.

9 Kingston Beach (p86) Splashing in the chilly sea south of Hobart.

10 Richmond (p87) Getting a dose of heritage in this photogenic town.

EXPLORING KUNANYI/ MT WELLINGTON

THE SUMMIT

The sealed 12km Pinnacle Rd from Fern Tree to the **kunanyi/Mt Wellington** (Mount Wellington; ☑ 03-6238 4222; www.wellingtonpark. org.au; Pinnacle Rd, via Fern Tree) summit was the brainchild of Albert Ogilvie, premier of Tasmania in the 1930s. When the Great Depression hit hard in Hobart, Ogilvie deemed that all those unemployed hands would be best engaged in doing something constructive for the community. After several years of backbreaking labour, Pinnacle Rd opened in 1937. Initially very visible from the city and not entirely popular, the road became know as 'Ogilvie's Scar'.

These days the road has mostly been obscured by trees; much morew visible are the two huge transmission towers at the peak. There's a nifty little curvy-roofed viewing room here, too, in which you can shelter from the wind and check out the eye-popping views. A drive to the summit to assess the city below is now a near-mandatory Hobart experience. Don't be deterred if the sky is overcast – often the peak rises above cloud level and looks out over a magic carpet of cotton-topped clouds.

HIKING & BIKING

The mountain is criss-crossed by numerous hiking paths, bike tracks, horse-riding trails and fire roads, some well-trodden and wide, some overgrown and intriguing. Popular tracks include the Radfords Track, Pinnacle Track, Fern Glade Track, the steep Zig Zag Track and the Organ Pipes Track below the trademark cliffs of *kunanyi*. Check out www.greaterhobarttrails.com.au for detailed track and planning info. Download maps at www.wellingtonpark.org.au/maps, or pick up the free *Wellington Park* walk map or detailed *Wellington Park Recreation Map* ($12) from the Hobart Visitor Information Centre (p84) or Service Tasmania (p84).

On two wheels, sign up for the exhilarating **Mt Wellington Descent** (Map p62; ☑ 1800 444 442; www.underdownunder.com.au/tour/ mount-wellington-descent; adult/child $85/65;

⊙ 10am & 1pm daily year-round, plus 4pm Nov-Feb): take a van ride to the summit then cruise 22km downhill on a mountain bike. It's terrific fun, with minimal energy output and maximum views. Tours start and end at 4 Elizabeth St on the Hobart waterfront, and last 2½ hours.

WINTER SNOW

Sure, Canberra has subzero nights and Melbourne requires one to don a woolly hat occasionally, but do any Australian cities other than Hobart have direct access to ACTUAL SNOW!? 'No', is the resounding response. kunanyi/Mt Wellington wears a white cloak for most of the winter (June to August), with snowfalls often reaching down into the suburbs. Local kids grow up knowing what it's like to build a snowman, hurl a snowball and pile a snow mound on the car bonnet for the ride back to sea level, watching in anticipation for the moment it melts and slides off onto the road.

LOST WORLD

A real local secret, **Lost World** (☑ 03-6238 4222; www.wellingtonpark.org.au; off Pinnacle Rd, via Fern Tree) is an amazing boulder field near the summit of kunanyi/Mt Wellington, backed by a miniature version of the famous Organ Pipes dolerite cliffs below the summit, further to the south. Rock climbers, boulder hoppers and bushwalkers venture here to lose a few hours in surreal solitude, check out the views or play hide-and-seek among the massive fractured hunks of stone.

To get to Lost World, take the little track heading north from the car park at 'Big Bend', 9km up Pinnacle Rd from Fern Tree – the last major hairpin bend before the summit. It's a 45-minute walk one-way.

EATING & DRINKING

Halfway up the mountain at the Springs, **Lost Freight** (☑ 0417 719 856; www.facebook. com/lostfreight; Pinnacle Rd, via Fern Tree; items $3-6; ⊙ 9am-4pm Tue-Fri, to 4.30pm Sat & Sun,

Cloaked in winter snow, kunanyi/Mt Wellington (1271m) towers over Hobart like a benevolent overlord. The citizens find reassurance in its solid presence, while outdoorsy types find the space to hike and bike on its leafy flanks.

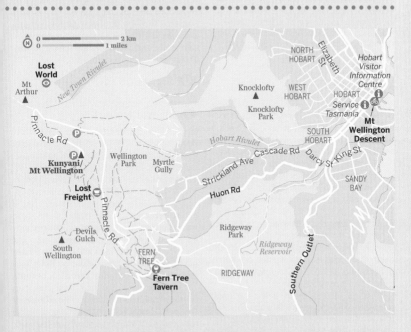

shorter hours in winter) is a hip little coffee caravan providing a welcome warm-up.

At forested Fern Tree a bit further down the slope, the rudimentary **Fern Tree Tavern** (☑03-6239 1171; www.facebook.com/ferntree tavern; 680 Huon Rd, Fern Tree; ◷noon-8pm Tue-Thu, to 9pm Fri, 10.30am-9pm Sat & Sun) has cold beer and warm fires.

INFORMATION & ACCESS

The Wellington Park (www.wellingtonpark. org.au) website is a fabulous resource, with maps, history and bushwalking and mountain-biking info.

At any time on the mountain, expect rapid and extreme weather shifts: this ain't no walk in the park (well, it is, but you know what we mean – be prepared). Pinnacle Rd is often closed by winter snow; for updates call the **Pinnacle Road Information Line** (☑03-6278 0200), or check www.hobartcity.com.au (click on 'Community' then 'kunanyi/Mount Wellington').

If you don't have wheels, local buses 448 (direct) and 449 (indirect) stop at Fern Tree halfway up the hill, from where it's a five- to six-hour return walk to the top. Alternatively, the **Hobart Shuttle Bus Company** (☑0408 341 804; www.hobartshuttlebus.com; transfers & tours per adult/child from $30/20) runs daily two-hour tours to the summit.

ⓘ Getting There & Away

If you're flying into Tasmania, more often than not you'll be landing at Hobart Airport (p84), 19km east of the city centre. **Tassielink** (☏03-6235 7300, 1300 300 520; www.tassielink.com.au) and Redline Coaches (p84) buses also use Hobart as a base for their statewide operations. Behind the wheel, Hobart makes a handy hub from which to explore the surrounding area, extending to the Southeast, the Tasman Peninsula, Midlands and Central Highlands without too much drama.

HOBART

☏03 / POP 226,750

No doubt about it, Hobart's future is looking rosy. Tourism is booming and the town is humming with low vacancy rates, high real-estate prices and new-found self-confidence.

Hobart is a harbour town – a port city, where the world rushes in on the tide and ebbs away again, bringing with it influences from afar and leaving the locals buzzing with global zeitgeist. Or so the theory goes. And these days, Hobart's waterfront precinct is certainly a buzz, with old pubs alongside new craft-beer bars, myriad restaurants and cafes, museums, festivals, ferries, accommodation...and all of it washed with sea-salty charm and a sense of history.

North of the city centre is the dazzlingly successful MONA; west is kunanyi/Mt Wellington, the brooding silent mountain that shelters the city below.

History

Hobart's original inhabitants were the semi-nomadic Mouheneenner and Muwinina bands of the Southeast Aboriginal tribe, who called the area Nibberloonne. Mt Wellington, towering behind Hobart, was a place of refuge and reward for the Muwinina, who called it *kunanyi* – a name only recently reassigned to the mountain by the city council.

In 1803 the first European settlers in Van Diemen's Land pitched their tents at Risdon Cove on the Derwent's eastern shore, which promptly became the site of the first massacre of the Mouheneenner (Risdon Cove was returned to the Aboriginal community by the state government in 1995). The colony relocated a year later to the site of present-day Hobart, where water running off Mt Wellington was plentiful.

When Britain's jails overflowed with sinners in the 1820s, Hobart's isolation loomed as a major selling point. Tens of thousands of convicts were chained into rotting hulks and shipped down to Hobart Town to serve their sentences in vile conditions.

With the abolition of convict transportation to Tasmania in 1853, Hobart became marginally more moral and the town came to rely on the apple and wool industries for its fiscal fortitude. In the 20th century Hobart stuttered through the Great Depression and both world wars, relying on the production of paper, zinc and chocolate, and the deep-water Derwent River harbour, to sustain it.

◉ Sights

◉ Central Hobart

Hobart Convict Penitentiary HISTORIC SITE
(Map p58; ☏03-6231 0911; www.national trust.org.au/places/penitentiary; cnr Brisbane & Campbell Sts; tours adult/child/family $20/12/40; ⊙tours 10am, 11.30am, 1pm & 2.30pm Mon-Fri, 1pm & 2.30pm Sat & Sun) The courtrooms, cells and gallows here at 'the Tench' had a hellish reputation in the 1800s: a stint here was to be avoided at all costs. This perhaps goes some way towards explaining how these amazing old convict-built structures have survived in the middle of Hobart in original condition into the 21st century. Take the excellent National Trust–run tour, or the bookings-mandatory **Penitentiary Chapel Ghost Tour** (https://nationaltrusttas. rezdy.com/43790/the-tench-ghost-tour; tours $25; ⊙8pm Mon & Fri Jun-Aug, 9pm Mon & Fri Sep-May).

Theatre Royal HISTORIC BUILDING
(Map p62; ☏03-6233 2299; www.theatreroyal.com. au; 29 Campbell St; 1hr tour adult/child $15/10; ⊙tours 11am Mon, Wed & Fri) Take a backstage tour of Hobart's prestigious (and very precious) Theatre Royal. Host to bombastic thespians since 1837, and despite a major fire in 1984, it remains Australia's oldest continuously operating theatre.

Hobart Real Tennis Club HISTORIC BUILDING
(Royal Tennis Club; Map p62; ☏03-6231 1781; www. hobarttennis.com.au; 45 Davey St; ⊙9am-6pm Mon-Fri) Dating from 1875, this is one of only three such tennis courts in the southern hemisphere (the others are in Melbourne and Ballarat). Real (or 'Royal') tennis is an archaic form of the highly strung game, played in a jaunty four-walled indoor court. Visitors can watch, take a lesson ($50) or hire the court ($40 per hour per two players).

**Allport Library
& Museum of Fine Arts** MUSEUM
(Map p62; ☑03-6165 5584; www.linc.tas.gov.au/all
port; 91 Murray St; ☺9.30am-5pm Mon-Fri, to 2pm
Sat) FREE The State Library is home to this
excellent collection of rare books on the Aus-
tralia-Pacific region, as well as colonial paintings, antiques, photographs, manuscripts,
decorative arts and furniture. Special exhibits
get dusted off for display several times a year,
and there are monthly talks and seminars.
Marvellously nerdy and interesting.

Franklin Square SQUARE
(Map p62; www.hobartcity.com.au; cnr Macquarie
& Elizabeth Sts; ☺24hr) Encircling a statue of
Sir John Franklin, Lieutenant-Governor of
Van Diemen's Land (aka Tasmania) from
1837–43, Franklin Sq is one of central Ho-
bart's main public spaces (along with the
Elizabeth St Mall). Sit on the grass, munch
some lunch, wait for a bus, push some giant
chess pieces around, or turn up on Friday
night during summer for the Street Eats @
Franko (p74) food market.

Gasworks Cellar Door WINERY
(Map p62; ☑03-6231 5946; www.gasworks
cellardoor.com.au; 2 Macquarie St; tastings from
$2.50; ☺noon-4pm Sun-Wed, 11am-5pm Thu-Sat)
If you don't have the time (or inclination)
to visit Tasmania's wine regions to sip a few
cool-climate drops, duck into the Gasworks
Cellar Door at the bottom end of Macquarie
St instead. Creatively crafted displays take
you on a virtual tour, highlighting the best regional bottles (which you can buy here, too).

◉ Salamanca Place & the Waterfront

★**Salamanca Place** HISTORIC SITE
(Map p62; ☑03-6238 2843; www.salamanca.com.au;
Salamanca Pl) This picturesque row of three-
and four-storey sandstone warehouses is a
classic example of Australian colonial architecture. Dating back to the whaling days of
the 1830s, Salamanca was the hub of Hobart's
trade and commerce. By the mid-20th century
many of the warehouses had fallen into ruin,
before restorations began in the 1970s. These
days Salamanca hosts myriad restaurants,
cafes, bars and shops, and the unmissable Saturday morning Salamanca Market (p61).

The development of the quarry behind
the warehouses into **Salamanca Square**
has bolstered the atmosphere, while at the

HOBART IN...
....

Two Days
Get your head into history mode with an amble around Battery Point (p60) – coffee
and cake at Jackman & McRoss (p76) is mandatory. Afterwards, wander down Kelly's
Steps to Salamanca Place where you can check out the craft shops and galleries at
the Salamanca Arts Centre (p59). Bone up on Hobart's Antarctic heritage at the
Mawson's Huts Replica Museum (p59) before a promenade along the Sullivans Cove
waterfront with fish-and-chips for dinner from the floating Flippers (p75) fish punt. Leave
the seagulls to finish off your chips and head for a classy drink at the Glass House (p79)
or earthy Jack Greene (p79) back on Salamanca Place.

On day two, recuperate over a big breakfast at Retro Café (p75) on Salamanca (if
it's a Saturday, Salamanca Market (p61) will be pumping), then catch the ferry out to
MONA (p61) for an afternoon of saucy, subversive, mindful distraction. Come down to
earth with dinner and drinks in North Hobart (p61) then some live music at Republic
Bar & Café (p81).

Four Days
If you've got a bit more time on your hands, grab breakfast at Ginger Brown (p76) then
blow out the cobwebs with a mountain-bike ride down kunanyi/Mt Wellington (p54) – on
a clear day it'll be hard to keep your eyes on the road. Tucked into the foothills of the mountain in South Hobart is the legendary Cascade Brewery (p60): take a tour and sip a few.
Snooze the afternoon away on the sunny lawns of the Royal Tasmanian Botanical Gardens (p61), then boot it back into the city for dinner at Templo (p74).

Still here? On day four take a photo-worthy day trip to nearby Richmond (p87) or the
waterfalls and alpine peaks of Mt Field National Park (p91). Wine buffs will find plenty
to quaff en route to Richmond in the Coal River Valley (p85) wine region.

Hobart

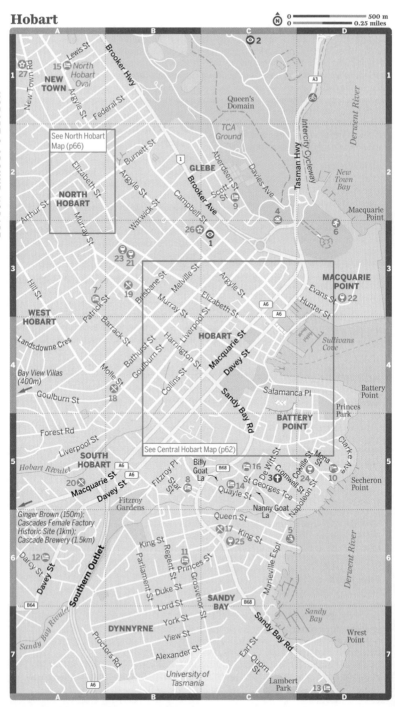

N
0 ——————— 500 m
0 ——————— 0.25 miles

Hobart

eastern end of Salamanca, the conversion of four old wheat silos into plush apartments has also been a hit.

Operating behind the scenes is a vibrant and creative arts community. The non-profit **Salamanca Arts Centre** (SAC; Map p62; ☑ 03-6234 8414; www.salarts.org.au; 65-77 Salamanca Pl; ⊙ shops & galleries 9am-5pm) occupies seven Salamanca warehouses, home to 70-plus arts organisations and individuals, including shops, galleries, studios, performing-arts venues and versatile public spaces. Check the website for happenings.

To reach Salamanca from Battery Point, descend the well-weathered 1839 Kelly's Steps (p60), wedged between warehouses at the eastern end of the main block of buildings.

★**Tasmanian Museum
& Art Gallery**   MUSEUM
(TMAG; Map p62; ☑ 03-6165 7000; www.tmag.tas.gov.au; Dunn Pl; ⊙ 10am-4pm daily Jan-Mar, 10am-4pm Tue-Sun Apr-Dec) **FREE** Incorporating Hobart's oldest building, the Commissariat Store (1808), this revamped museum features Aboriginal and colonial relics and excellent wildlife displays. The gallery curates a collection of Tasmanian colonial art. There are free guided tours at 1pm and 2pm from Wednesday to Sunday (hordes of school kids might be a little less interested in proceedings than you are), plus special themed tours

at 11am; check the website or call to see what's on. There's a cool cafe and shop, too.

Mawson's Huts Replica Museum   MUSEUM
(Map p62; ☑ 03-6231 1518, 1300 551 422; www.mawsons-huts-replica.org.au; cnr Morrison & Argyle Sts; adult/child/family $12/4/28; ⊙ 9am-6pm Oct-Apr, 10am-5pm May-Sep) This excellent waterfront installation is an exact model of one of the huts in which Sir Douglas Mawson hunkered down on his 1911–14 Australasian Antarctic Expedition, which set sail from Hobart. Inside it is 100% authentic, right down to the matches, the stove and the bunks. A knowledgable guide sits at a rustic table, ready to answer your Antarctic enquiries. Entry fees go towards the upkeep of the original huts at Cape Denison in Antarctica.

Waterfront   AREA
(Map p62; off Davey St) Hobartians flock to the city's waterfront like seagulls to chips. Centred on **Victoria Dock** (a working fishing harbour) and **Constitution Dock** (chock-full of floating takeaway-seafood punts and the odd wayward seal), it's a brilliant place to explore. The obligatory Hobart experience is to sit in the sun, munch some fish and chips and watch the harbour hubbub. If you'd prefer something with a knife and fork, there are some superb restaurants here, too – head for **Elizabeth Street Pier**.

Parliament House
HISTORIC BUILDING

(Map p62; ☑03-6212 2200; www.parliament.tas.gov.au/parliament/tours.htm; Parliament Sq; ☺tours 10am & 2pm Mon-Fri on nonsitting days) **FREE** Presiding over an oak-studded park adjacent to Salamanca Place, Tasmania's sandstone Parliament House (1840) was originally a customs house. There's a tunnel under Murray St from Parliament House to the Customs House pub opposite: the official line is that no one knows what it was used for, but we'd hazard a guess... Free 90-minute tours run when parliament isn't sitting (call for availability).

Maritime Museum of Tasmania
MUSEUM

(Map p62; ☑03-6234 1427; www.maritimetas.org; 16 Argyle St; adult/child/family $10/8/20; ☺9am-5pm) Highlighting shipwrecks, boat building, whaling and Hobart's unbreakable bond with the sea, the Maritime Museum of Tasmania (out the back of the Town Hall) has an interesting (if a little static) collection of photos, paintings, models and relics (try to resist ringing the huge brass bell from the *Rhexenor*). Kids under 13 get in free.

⊙ Battery Point, Sandy Bay & South Hobart

★Battery Point
HISTORIC SITE

(Map p62) An empty rum bottle's throw from the waterfront, the old maritime village of Battery Point is a tight nest of lanes and 19th-century cottages, packed together like shanghaied landlubbers in a ship's belly. Spend an afternoon exploring: stumble up **Kelly's Steps** (Map p62; Kelly St) from Salamanca Place and dogleg into South St, where the red lights once burned night and day. Spin around picturesque Arthur Circus, refuel in the cafes on Hampden Rd, then ogle **St George's Anglican Church** (Map p58; ☑03-6223 2146; www.stgeorgesbatterypoint.org; 30 Cromwell St; ☺9.15am-2.15pm Tue-Fri, services 8am & 10am Sun).

★Cascade Brewery
BREWERY

(☑03-6212 7800; www.cascadebrewery.com.au; 140 Cascade Rd, South Hobart; brewery tour adult/child 16-18yr $30/15, Cascade Story tour adult/child $15/5; ☺tours daily) Standing in startling, Gothic isolation next to the clean-running Hobart Rivulet, Cascade is Australia's oldest brewery (1824) and is still pumping out superb beers. Ninety-minute tours involve plenty of history, with tastings at the end. Note that under-16s aren't permitted on the main brewery tour (take the family-friendly Cascade Story tour instead), and that brewery machinery might not be running if you're here on a weekend (brewers have weekends, too). Bookings essential. To get here, take bus 446, 447 or 449.

★Cascades Female Factory Historic Site
HISTORIC SITE

(☑1800 139 478, 03-6233 6656; www.femalefactory.org.au; 16 Degraves St; adult/child/family $5/5/15, tour $15/10/40, 'Her Story' dramatisation $20/12.50/60; ☺9.30am-4pm, tours hourly 10am-3pm, except noon) Enshrined by Unesco as a World Heritage Historic Site, this was where Hobart's female convicts were incarcerated and put to work. Rather amazingly, one in four convicts transported to Van Diemen's Land was a woman. You can explore the site under your own steam – it's a hauntingly spare sequence of courtyards and interpretive installations. Or to better understand the site (which looked very different back in the early 1800s), take a guided tour or the excellent 'Her Story' dramatisation. To get here by public transport, take bus 446, 447 or 449.

Combined guided and 'Her Story' tour tickets are also available (adult/child/family $30/20/85), starting with an 11am guided tour followed by 'Her Story' at noon.

Narryna Heritage Museum
MUSEUM

(Map p62; ☑03-6234 2791; www.tmag.tas.gov.au/narryna; 103 Hampden Rd, Battery Point; adult/child $10/4; ☺10am-5pm Tue-Sat) Fronted by a babbling fountain, this stately Greek-Revival sandstone mansion (pronounced 'Narinna') was built in 1837 by trader Captain Andrew Haig. Set in established grounds, it's a treasure trove of domestic colonial artefacts, and is Australia's oldest folk museum.

Not far away is the adjunct **Markree House Museum** (Map p62; ☑03-6165 7001; www.tmag.tas.gov.au/markree; 145 Hampden Rd; adult/child $10/4; ☺10.30am-4.30pm Sat Oct-Apr, tours 3pm Tue-Sun year-round), putting a 1920s spin on Hobart domestic life. The combined ticket price for the two museums is adult/child $16/10.

Lower Sandy Bay Beach
BEACH

(Long Beach; Beach Rd, Lower Sandy Bay) This sweet little beach is a decent spot for a stroll or a dip on a hot afternoon: swim out to the pontoon and warm up in the sun before re-entering the chilly brine. The Hobart Twilight Market (p83) happens nearby.

☉ MONA & Northern Hobart

★ **MONA** MUSEUM, GALLERY

(Museum of Old & New Art; ☑03-6277 9900; www.
mona.net.au; 655 Main Rd, Berriedale; adult/child
$28/free, Tasmanian residents free; ⊙10am-6pm
daily Jan, 10am-6pm Wed-Mon Feb-Apr & Dec, 10am-
5pm Wed-Mon May-Nov) Twelve kilometres
north of Hobart's city centre, MONA occupies
a saucepan-shaped peninsula jutting into the
Derwent River. Arrayed across three underground levels, abutting a sheer rock face,
the $75-million museum has been described
by philanthropist owner David Walsh as 'a
subversive adult Disneycascadland'. Ancient
antiquities are showcased next to contemporary works: sexy, provocative, disturbing and
deeply engaging. Don't miss it.

To get here catch the MR-1 ferry or MONA
Roma shuttle bus from Hobart's Brooke St
Pier. Book everything online.

Also at MONA is the cellar door for **Moorilla** (☑03-6277 9960; www.moorilla.com.au;
tastings/tours $10/20; ⊙tastings 9.30am-5pm
Mon-Wed, tours 3.30pm Wed-Mon), a winery
established here in the 1950s. Duck in for
a wine or Moo Brew beer tasting, or have
lunch upstairs at the outstanding restaurant, **The Source** (☑03-6277 9904; www.
mona.net.au/eat-drink/the-source-restaurant;
mains $22-38; ⊙ 7.30-10am & noon-2pm Mon, Wed,
Thu & Sun, 7.30-10am, noon-2pm & 6pm-late Fri &
Sat). You can also catch a summer concert
on the lawns, check out the **MONA Market**
(⊙11am-4pm Sun Feb-Apr), or maybe splash
out for a night in the uber-swish **Pavilions**
(www.mona.net.au/stay/mona-pavilions; d from
$700; P ❋ ☎ ⛱).

MONA is also the driving force behind
Hobart's annual MONA FOMA (p67) arts
and music festival, and the disquieting Dark
MOFO (p67) winter festival.

At the time of writing a new hotel was
being built at MONA (they're always doing
something new); watch this space.

★ **North Hobart** NEIGHBOURHOOD

(Map p66) Hobart at its most bohemian and
multicultural, the Elizabeth St strip in North
Hobart (or 'NoHo' to those with a sense of
humour) is lined with dozens of cafes, restaurants, bars and pubs – enough to keep
you coming back meal after meal after meal.
Also here is the excellent art-house State
Cinema (p82), and Hobart's best live music
room, the Republic Bar & Café (p81). Must-
do Hobart!

DON'T MISS

SALAMANCA MARKET

Every Saturday morning since 1972, the
open-air **Salamanca Market** (Map p62;
☑03-6238 2843; www.salamanca.com.au;
Salamanca Pl; ⊙8am-3pm Sat) has lured
hippies and craft merchants from the
foothills to fill the tree-lined expanses of
Salamanca Place with their stalls. Fresh
organic produce, secondhand clothes
and books, tacky tourist souvenirs, ceramics and woodwork, cheap sunglasses,
antiques, exuberant buskers, quality food
and drink. It's all here, but people-watch-
ing is the real name of the game. Rain or
shine – don't miss it!

To get here, it's about a 3km walk from
the city centre up gently sloping Elizabeth
St, or jump on bus 551, 552, 553 or 550 from
the city centre.

**Royal Tasmanian
Botanical Gardens** GARDENS

(Map p58; ☑03-6166 0451; www.rtbg.tas.gov.au;
Lower Domain Rd, Queen's Domain; ⊙8am-6.30pm
Oct-Mar, to 5.30pm Apr & Sep, to 5pm May-Aug)
FREE On the eastern side of the Queen's
Domain, these small but beguiling gardens
hark back to 1818 and feature more than
6000 exotic and native plant species. Picnic
on the lawns, check out the Subantarctic
Plant House or grab a bite at the restaurant
or cafe. Across from the main entrance is the
site of the former Beaumaris Zoo, where the
last captive Tasmanian tiger died in 1936.
Call to ask about guided tours.

Lady Franklin Gallery GALLERY

(☑03-6228 0076; www.artstas.com.au/our-history/
lady-franklin-gallery; Ancanthe Park, 268 Lenah Valley Rd, Lenah Valley; ⊙11am-4pm Sat & Sun) **FREE**
In an exquisitely proportioned colonnaded
1842 sandstone building called Ancanthe
(Greek for 'vale of flowers' – enough of a reason to visit alone), the gorgeous Lady Franklin Gallery displays contemporary work by
Tasmanian artists. To get here without your
own wheels, take bus 551, 552 or 553.

Tasmanian Transport Museum MUSEUM

(☑0428 386 843, 03-6272 7721; www.railtasmania.
com/ttms; Anfield St, Glenorchy; adult/child $8/4;
⊙1-4pm Sat & Sun) Trainspotter? Tram fan?
Train rides happen at this transport mecca
on the first and third Sundays of each month
(admission increases to $10/5 per adult/

Central Hobart

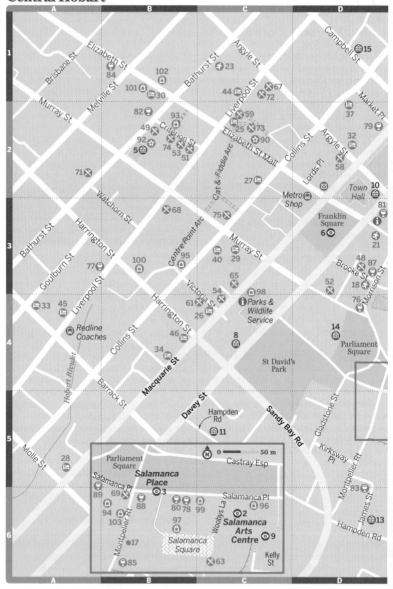

child on these days). At other times, you can mourn the loss of Tasmania's passenger-train network, which called it quits in the mid-1970s. To get here, catch any of the many buses headed for the Glenorchy interchange. The museum is a short walk from here.

◉ Eastern Shore

Tasmanian Cricket Museum MUSEUM
(☑03-6282 0433; www.blundstonearena.com.au/museum; 15 Derwent St, Bellerive; adult/child $2/1; ◷10am-3pm Tue-Thu) Cricket fans should

tonian) Ricky 'Punter' Ponting. There's still no commemoration of David Boon's 52 cans of beer quaffed on a Sydney-to-London flight in 1989, though. Buses 624 and 625 from the city run close to the oval.

Rosny Hill Lookout   VIEWPOINT

(off Riawena Rd, Rosny) For a classic view of Hobart, the Derwent River and the hulking mass of kunanyi/Mt Wellington in the background, drive up to this seldom-visited hilltop lookout. Council thoughtfully lops the tops off any trees that dare impede the view. To get here, cross the Tasman Bridge, head for Rosny, turn right at the lights onto Riawena Rd and follow the signs.

🏃 Activities

Swimming & Surfing

Hobart's city beaches look inviting, especially at Bellerive and Sandy Bay, but the water here tends to get a bit soupy. For a safe, clean swim, you'll be better off heading further south to the beaches at Kingston (p86) and Blackmans Bay (p86).

The most reliable local surfing spots near Hobart are Clifton Beach (off South Arm Rd, Clifton Beach) and Goats Beach (off South Arm Rd, South Arm), en route to South Arm – about 30km and 35km from Hobart, respectively.

Hobart Aquatic Centre   SWIMMING

(Map p58; ☎ 03-6222 6999; www.hobartcity.com. au/community/doone-kennedy-hobart-aquatic-centre; 1 Davies Ave, Glebe; adult/child/family $8/5/20; ⏱ 6am-9pm Mon-Fri, 8am-6pm Sat & Sun) The excellent Hobart Aquatic Centre at the foot of the Queen's Domain (officially the 'Doone Kennedy Hobart Aquatic Centre', named after a former mayor) offers recreational moisture, even when it's raining. Inside are leisure pools, lap-swimming pools, a spa, a sauna, a steam room, gym, aqua aerobics, and regular aerobics for landlubbers.

Cycling & Mountain Biking

Hobart isn't big on bike lanes, but there's a terrific cycling path here running from Macquarie Point on the waterfront all the way north to MONA, following an old railway line. It's called the Intercity Cycleway (www. greaterhobarttrails.com.au/track/intercity cycleway), and is about 20km one-way. Bike hire is available from the MONA ferry terminal or several other spots around the waterfront; try Hobart Bike Hire (Map p62; ☎ 0447 556 189; www.hobartbikehire.com.au; 1a

steer a well-directed cover drive towards Blundstone Arena (p82), aka Bellerive Oval. There's a beaut cricket museum and library here, plus oval tours. Don't miss the corner of the museum dedicated to the achievements of former Australian captain (and Launces-

Central Hobart

Brooke St; bike hire per day/overnight from $25/35; ⊕9am-5pm).

On the mountain-biking front, there's one seriously big mountain here. Tackle the Mt Wellington Descent (p54), or go off-road on some challenging trails; see www.wellingtonpark.org.au/bikes. A more managed environment is the excellent **Glenorchy MTB Park** (☑03-6216 6315; www.gcc.tas.gov.au/content/glenorchy_mountain_bike_park.gcc; off Tolosa St; ⊕daylight hours) FREE in the northern suburbs.

Spoke Bike Hire　　　　　　　　CYCLING
(Map p58; ☑03-6232 4848; www.spokebikehire.com.au; 20 McVilly Dr, Cenotaph; bike hire per hr/day/2 days from $15/25/45; ⊕9am-5pm Sep-May, shorter hours Jun-Aug) Mountain bikes, hybrids and kids' bikes for hire, plus loads of advice on riding around the city and beyond. You can hop on the bike track here and roll all the way to MONA (about 20km).

On the Water

★**Roaring 40s Kayaking**　　　　KAYAKING
(Map p58; ☑0455 949 777; www.roaring40s kayaking.com.au; Marieville Esplanade, Sandy Bay; adult/child $90/60; ⊕10am daily Oct-Apr, plus 4pm Nov-Mar) Hobart is perhaps at its prettiest when viewed from the water. Take a safe, steady, 2½-hour guided paddle with Roaring 40s, named after the prevailing winds at these latitudes. You'll cruise from Sandy Bay past Battery Point and into the Hobart docks for some fish and chips while you float, before returning to Sandy Bay.

Ask about other paddling trips around the Tasman Peninsula and Storm Bay's cliffs, caves and beaches, at the mouth of the Derwent River.

Hobart Yachts　　　　　　　　SAILING
(☑0438 399 477; www.hobartyachts.com.au; 3hr sail adult/child $140/100) Set sail on a skippered yacht jaunt on the Derwent River, aboard a 62ft luxury ocean racer. Minimum

three people. Longer trips also available, to the East Coast and Port Davey.

Windeward Bound BOATING
(Map p62; 0418 120 243, 0498 120 092; www.windewardbound.com.au; Elizabeth St Pier, Hobart; 3hr sail incl lunch adult/child/family $90/45/225; ⊙ sailings 1pm Oct-Mar, 12.30pm Apr-Sep) An elegant replica square-rigged tall ship with lots of opportunities to get involved with the actual sailing. Three-hour harbour sails happen year-round. Also runs occasional eight-day voyages around Port Davey and Recherche Bay ($3650 per person).

Rock Climbing
Rock Climbing
Adventures Tasmania CLIMBING
(0438 087 477; www.rcat.com.au) Customised lessons and rock-climbing and abseiling trips for beginners and experienced climbers. A half-/full-day climbing trip to kunanyi/Mt Wellington costs $250/390 per person (cheaper per person for groups).

Rockit Climbing CLIMBING
(Map p62; 03-6234 1090; www.rockitclimbing.com.au; 54 Bathurst St; adult/child/family incl gear $25/12/60; ⊙ noon-9pm Mon-Fri, to 6pm Sat & Sun) Rockit offers world-class climbing walls inside a converted warehouse. Don your nifty rubber shoes and harness (included in the admission price), chalk up your paws, and up you go.

🧭 Tours

★**Pennicott Wilderness Journeys** BOATING
(Map p62; 03-6234 4270; www.pennicottjourneys.com.au; Dock Head Bldg, Franklin Wharf; tours adult/child from $125/100; ⊙ 7am-6.30pm) Pennicott offers half-a-dozen outstanding boat trips around key southern Tasmanian sights, including trips to Bruny Island, Tasman Island, the Tasman Peninsula, D'Entrecasteaux Channel and the Iron Pot Lighthouse south of Hobart. The Tasmanian Seafood Seduction (full-day trip $685) trip is a winner for fans of all things fishy. Highly recommended.

North Hobart

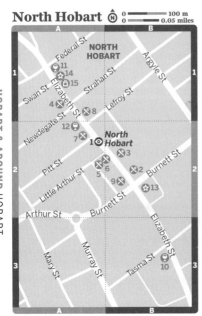

0 — 100 m
0 — 0.05 miles

North Hobart

◎ **Top Sights**
1 North Hobart A2

⊗ **Eating**
2 Annapurna B2
3 Berta B2
4 Born in Brunswick A1
5 Burger Haus A2
6 Capital B2
7 Pancho Villa A2
8 Vanidol's A1
9 Veg Bar B2

◎ **Drinking & Nightlife**
10 T-Bone Brewing Co B3
11 The Winston A1
12 Willing Bros A2

⊛ **Entertainment**
13 Republic Bar & Café B2
14 State Cinema A1

◉ **Shopping**
15 State Cinema Bookstore A1

Hobart Historic Tours WALKING
(☑03-6234 5550; www.hobarthistorictours.com.
au; tours from $30) Informative, entertaining
90-minute walking tours of Hobart and historic Battery Point. There's also an Old Hobart
Pub Tour, which sluices through some water-

front watering holes, and a three-hour Grand
Hobart Walk. Call or see the website for times
and bookings. Reduced winter schedule.

Drink Tasmania DISTILLERY
(☑0475 000 120; www.drinktasmania.com.au;
tours per person $300; ⊙Fri & Sat) Tasmanian
whisky has been getting plenty of press since
Sullivans Cove Whisky won the coveted 'Best
Single Malt' gong at the World Whisky Masters in 2014. Take a day tour with this passionate outfit, visiting three distilleries with
tastings of top Tassie single malts. Minimum
four passengers. Wine tours also available.

Gourmania WALKING, FOOD
(☑0419 180 113; www.gourmaniafoodtours.com.au;
tours from $90) Fabulous, flavour-filled walking
tours run by passionate local foodies, taking
in Salamanca Place and central Hobart. Expect plenty of tasting opportunities and chats
with restaurant, cafe and shop owners.

Long Lunch Wine Tour Co FOOD & DRINK
(☑0409 225 841; www.longlunchtourco.com.au;
per person $180) Time for a wine? Sign up for
a full-day minibus tour around some fine
southern wineries, mostly in the Coal River
Valley region. Lots of tastings and tasty food.
Longer tours up the east coast also available.

Par Avion SCENIC FLIGHTS
(☑03-6248 5390; www.paravion.com.au) Scenic
helicopter flights above Hobart (20 minutes
per person $175) and fixed-wing flights into
the southwest from Cambridge Aerodrome
near Hobart Airport. A four-hour Southwest World Heritage Tour, including a boat
ride on Bathurst Harbour, costs $395/345
per adult/child. An eight-hour Day in the
Wilderness tour costs $495/445, including
lunch and a visit to Port Davey.

Red Decker BUS
(☑03-6236 9116; www.reddecker.com.au; 20-stop
pass adult/child/family 24hr $35/20/90, 48hr
$40/25/110) Commentated sightseeing on
an old London double-decker bus. Buy a
20-stop, hop-on-hop-off pass (valid for one
or two days), or do the tour as a 90-minute
loop. Pay a bit more and add a Cascade
Brewery (adult/child $65/55) or kunanyi/Mt
Wellington ($65/40) tour to the deal.

Tours Tasmania TOURS
(☑1800 777 103; www.tourstas.com.au) Small-
group full-day trips from Hobart, including
trips to Port Arthur, Hastings Caves and
a 'Mt Field, Wildlife & Mt Wellington' tour
with lots of walks and waterfalls (adult/con-

cession $130/120). Park fees included; BYO lunch.

Lady Nelson
BOATING

(Map p62; ☑03-6234 3348; www.ladynelson.org. au; Elizabeth St Pier; adult/child $30/15; ⊙11am & 1pm Sat & Sun) Sail around the harbour for 90 minutes on a replica of the surprisingly compact brig *Lady Nelson,* one of the first colonial ships to sail to Tasmania. Longer trips are occasionally on offer; check the website. There's an extra 3pm sailing on Saturday and Sunday from mid-December to April.

Ghost Tours of Hobart
& Battery Point
WALKING

(Map p62; ☑0467 687 004; www.ghosttours ofhobart.com.au; adult/child $25/15) Walking tours of Battery Point oozing ectoplasmic tall tales, departing the 7D Cinema on Montpelier Retreat at dusk most nights. Bookings essential, and no kids under eight. At the time of writing its city-centre tour was being reinvented.

Hobart Historic Cruises
CRUISE

(Map p62; ☑03-6200 9074; www.hobarthistoric cruises.com.au; Murray St Pier; 1hr cruises adult/ child/family $25/22.50/70; ⊙cruises 11am-4pm) Chug up or down the Derwent River from Hobart's waterfront on cute old ferries. Also runs longer lunch (adult/child/family $35/35/120) and dinner ($58/55/180) cruises travelling both up and down the river. Call for times and bookings.

Gray Line
BUS

(☑1300 858 687; www.grayline.com.au; city coach tour per adult/child from $49/24.50) Mainstream city coach tours, plus longer tours to destinations including kunanyi/Mt Wellington ($49), Mt Field National Park ($135), Bruny Island ($225), the Huon Valley ($160) and Port Arthur ($125). Three Capes Track bus transfers also available (one-way $45). Children go half price.

★ Festivals & Events

The 2018 MONA FOMA (MOFO; www.mofo. net.au; ⊙Jan) festival might have been the last time it features in Hobart; Launceston is looking likely as the venue from 2019 on. Check the website.

Hobart International
SPORTS

(www.hobartinternational.com.au; ⊙Jan) As a prelude to the Australian Open tennis championship in Melbourne later in January, the Hobart International draws plenty of big-name players (just the ladies) for a week-

long tournament. Games are played at the Domain Tennis Centre in Glebe.

Australian Wooden Boat Festival
CULTURAL

(www.australianwoodenboatfestival.com.au; ⊙Feb) Biennial event (odd-numbered years) in mid-February to coincide with the Royal Hobart Regatta. The festival showcases Tasmania's boat-building heritage and maritime traditions. You can almost smell the Huon pine. The next event is in 2019.

Hobart BeerFest
BEER

(www.hobart.beerfestivals.com.au; ⊙Feb) More than 200 brews from around Australia and the world, with brewing classes and lots of opportunities for waterfront snacking, foot tapping and imbibing.

Royal Hobart Regatta
SPORTS

(www.royalhobartregatta.com; ⊙Feb) Three days of yacht watching and mayhem on the Derwent River. Held annually in mid-February, coinciding with the Australian Wooden Boat Festival every second year.

Ten Days on the Island
CULTURAL, ART

(www.tendays.org.au; ⊙Mar) Tasmania's premier cultural festival is a biennial event (odd-numbered years) celebrating Tasmanian arts, music and culture at state-wide venues. Expect concerts, exhibitions, dance, film, theatre and workshops.

★ Dark MOFO
ART, MUSIC

(www.darkmofo.net.au; ⊙Jun) The sinister sister of MONA FOMA, Dark MOFO broods in the half-light of June's winter solstice. Expect live music, installations, readings, film noir, bonfires, red wine and midnight feasts, all mainlining Tasmania's Gothic blood flow.

Festival of Voices
MUSIC

(www.festivalofvoices.com; ⊙Jul) Sing to keep the winter chills at bay during this quirky vocal festival, featuring myriad performances, workshops, cabaret and choirs at venues around town.

Royal Hobart Show
FAIR

(www.hobartshowground.com.au/show; ⊙Oct) Enduring rural-meets-urban festival showcasing Tassie's primary industries. Overpriced show bags, hold-on-to-your-lunch rides, carnies and the fecund aromas of nature – you get the picture.

★ Taste of Tasmania
FOOD & DRINK

(www.thetasteoftasmania.com.au; ⊙Dec-Jan) On either side of New Year's Eve, this weeklong

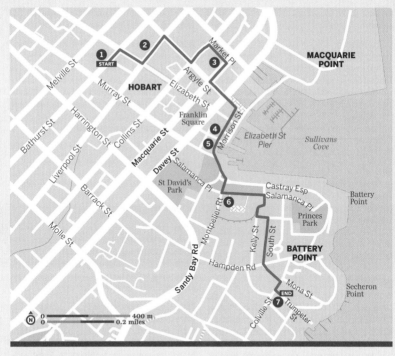

City Walk
Hobart Pub Crawl

START NEW SYDNEY HOTEL
FINISH SHIPWRIGHT'S ARMS HOTEL
LENGTH 2.5KM; FIVE HOURS

Hobart has always been a hard-drinking town, and many of the city's most atmospheric old pubs are still here. Kick off your booze cruise at the ❶ **New Sydney Hotel** (p79), a welcoming Bathurst St pub with open fires, excellent beers and plenty of quiet corners in which to pursue the lost art of conversation. On a low-lying stretch of Liverpool St nearby, the ❷ **Brunswick Hotel** (p79) dates back to 1827 – allegedly Australia's second-oldest pub! A savvy architectural makeover exposes key bones in its old skeleton.

If the Brunswick is Australia's second-oldest pub, the ❸ **Hope & Anchor** (p79) is the oldest. Licensed since 1807, if the walls here could talk it'd be a helluva loud conversation. Closer to the waterfront, act like a thirsty deckhand and mosey into the old art-deco

❹ **Telegraph Hotel** (p80). Despite being afflicted by an infectious rash of 1990s turquoise tiles and corrugated iron, 'the Telly' still has boat-loads of charm.

Across the road from Parliament House the sandstone ❺ **Customs House Hotel** (p80) is in a prime waterfront position. Resisting the urge to gentrify, it's a resolutely old-school spot for a beer.

Over on Salamanca Place, the ❻ **Whaler** (p80) is an uncomplicated, open-to-all-comers kind of pub – something of an anomaly on this slick promenade.

When the Sydney to Hobart Yacht Race fleet sweeps into Hobart just prior to New Year's Eve, most of the yachties end up at the ❼ **Shipwright's Arms Hotel** (p81), a backstreet Battery Point boozer that's been here since 1846. And indeed, a shipwright or two has passed through here over the years – Hobart's original shipyards are right at the bottom of Trumpeter St. Wander down to the little park at the bottom of the street for a look-see before calling it a night.

harbourside event is a celebration of Tassie's gastronomic prowess. The seafood, wines and cheeses are predictably fab, or branch out into mushrooms, truffles, raspberries and much more. Stalls are a who's who of the Hobart restaurant scene. Live music, too. Just brilliant.

Falls Festival MUSIC
(www.fallsfestival.com.au; ⊘ 29 Dec-1 Jan) The Tasmanian version of the Victorian rock festival is a winner. Three nights and four days of live Oz and international tunes (Fleet Foxes, Liam Gallagher, Angus & Julia Stone) at Marion Bay, an hour east of Hobart.

🛏 Sleeping

Hobart has plenty of budget hostels and pubs offering accommodation, some salubrious, some not so much. Like the rest of Tasmania, midrange accommodation here isn't exactly a bargain (B&Bs and motels, mostly), but top-end accommodation can be quite reasonable. If your budget stretches beyond $250 per night, you can afford something quite special: designer hotels, historic guesthouses and mod waterside apartments. Booking ahead is always a good idea, regardless of season.

🛏 Central Hobart

★ **Alabama Hotel** HOTEL $
(Map p62; ☑ 0499 987 698; www.alabamahobart. com.au; L1, 72 Liverpool St; d/tw from $80/90; 🛜) 🖉 Sweet home Alabama! This old art-deco boozer – once a grim, sticky-carpet lush magnet – has been reborn as a boutique budget hotel. None of the 17 rooms has a bathroom, but the shared facilities are immaculate and plentiful. Decor is funky and colourful with retro-deco flourishes, and there's an all-day bar with a sunny balcony over the street.

The Nook HOSTEL $
(Map p62; ☑ 03-6135 4044; www.thenookback packers.com; 251 Liverpool St, Hobart; dm/d from $28/110; P 🛜) It's less of a nook, more of a reconfigured old pub, but the Nook is doing things right hostel-wise. Fourteen tidy rooms extend above a sociable open-plan kitchen space, with a neat BBQ deck out the back. A busy cleaning crew works hard in the shared bathrooms.

Tassie Backpackers HOSTEL $
(Brunswick Hotel; Map p62; ☑ 03-6234 4981; www. brunswickhotelhobart.com.au; 67 Liverpool St; dm from $28, d with/without bathroom from $110/90; ❄ 🛜) Upstairs at the venerable old Brunswick Hotel (p79) is one of Hobart's better backpackers, with plenty of shared spaces, good security, a kitchen and a laundry. Energetic management also runs the pub downstairs – head for the beery courtyard out the back.

Hobart Central YHA HOSTEL $
(Map p62; ☑ 03-6231 2660; www.yha.com.au; 9 Argyle St; dm from $31, d & tw with/without bathroom from $130/103, f from $160; 🛜) Attached to a historic pub, this simple but clean YHA offers bright, secure accommodation right in the middle of town. Spread over three maze-like levels are dorms of all sizes, including nifty en-suite rooms and family-sized rooms. No parking, but you're within walking distance of everything here.

Hobart's Accommodation & Hostel HOSTEL $
(Map p62; ☑ 03-6234 6122; www.hobarthostel. com; cnr Goulburn & Barrack Sts; dm from $30, s/d without bathroom $80/95, d & tw with bathroom from $110; @ 🛜) In a former pub (the ever-rockin' Doghouse), Hobart Hostel offers clean redecorated dorms, with good-value en-suite twins and doubles upstairs. Downstairs there are huge red sofas, and well-behaved backpackers going about their business (party somewhere else).

★ **Old Woolstore Apartment Hotel** HOTEL $$
(Map p62; ☑ 03-6235 5355; www.oldwoolstore. com.au; 1 Macquarie St; d from $170, 1-/2-bed-room apt from $200/265; P ❄ 🛜) Oodles of parking and superfriendly staff are the first things you'll notice at this large, lavish hotel-apartment complex in a once-seedy area of Hobart known as Wapping in colonial times. You won't notice much wool lying around – it hasn't been a woolstore for 100 years. Roomy apartments have kitchens and laundry facilities. A consistently good performer.

★ **Astor Private Hotel** HOTEL $$
(Map p62; ☑ 03-6234 6611; www.astorprivate hotel.com.au; 157 Macquarie St; s/tw/d/tr with shared bathroom from $77/93/93/140, d with bathroom from $150, all incl breakfast; 🛜) A rambling downtown 1920s charmer, the Astor retains much of its character: stained-glass windows, old furniture, lofty ceilings (with ceiling roses) and the irrepressible Tildy at the helm. Older-style rooms have shared bathrooms, which are plentiful, while the more recently refurbished rooms have en suites.

ibis Styles Hobart Hotel   BUSINESS HOTEL **$$**

(Map p62; ☑03-6289 8500; www.ibis.com; 173 Macquarie St; r from $160; P❋@�⊜) A major new hotel being built in Hobart has been a rare event in recent decades, but this is the first of several the city council has approved. The vibe is very upmarket-corporate, but the location is central and everything (as you'd expect) is shiny, new and professional. Love the living green walls in the lobby. The excellent Mr Goodguy (p74) restaurant is here, too.

Travelodge Hobart   HOTEL **$$**

(Map p62; ☑1300 886 886; www.travelodge.com.au/hotel/hobart; cnr Harrington & Macquarie Sts; d/tr from $190/210; P❋�) The safe-bet Travelodge rises 10 red-brick floors above the Macquarie St fray. Rooms are compact but stylish, and great value this close to the action. One of the old breed of Hobart hotels that's still making a good fist of it.

Hadley's Orient Hotel   HISTORIC HOTEL **$$**

(Map p62; ☑03-6237 2999; www.hadleyshotel.com.au; 34 Murray St; d/f from $190/275, 2-bedroom apt from $370; P❋@�) This sumptuous place has clocked up more than 170 years of hospitality in the heart of the CBD. It's acquired plenty of modern embellishments since its colonial beginnings – some good, some not so good – but the current management has poured millions into restoring its heritage charms. Some rooms are a tad poky, but wasn't everything in 1834?

Edinburgh Gallery B&B   B&B **$$**

(Map p62; ☑03-6224 9229; www.artaccom.com.au; 211 Macquarie St; r incl breakfast $110-230; P�) This funky, art-filled hotel puts an eclectic stamp on a 1909 Federation house, just west of the CBD. Six of the 10 rooms have private bathrooms; the rest share. All have DVD players and quirky, artsy decor (try for a verandah suite). Continental breakfast (breads, honey and jam, yoghurt, cereals and chocolate-chip cookies!) is served in the bright communal kitchen.

Central Hotel   PUB **$$**

(Map p62; ☑03-6234 4419; www.centralhotel hobart.com.au; 73 Collins St; d/tw incl breakfast from $180/190; P❋�) Downstairs is a mainstream Aussie pub with gaming machines, cheap meals and big-screen sports; upstairs are 11 surprisingly decent en-suite rooms with TVs and hip furniture. Pricey for pub rooms, but you'll struggle to find anywhere more central (we can't take issue with the name). Off-site parking $15 per day.

★**Hayloft**   APARTMENT **$$$**

(Map p62; ☑03-6298 1441; www.hayloft.com.au; 100 Elizabeth St; apt from $285; �) Out the back of Ettie's (p75) restaurant and up a set of stairs in this excellent little urban bolt-hole for two – formerly a hayloft above some old red-brick stables. It's an open-plan arrangement with a feature stone bathtub in which to sit, soak and sip. It cops a bit of restaurant noise occasionally (but perhaps you'll be eating there too). Super-central.

RACT Hobart Apartment Hotel   HOTEL **$$$**

(Map p62; ☑03-6270 8600; www.racv.com.au/resorts; 154-6 Collins St; d from $220, 1-/2-bedroom apt from $250/475; P❋�) One of Hobart's new high-rise hotels (they're popping up all over the place), this eight-level, 125-room effort won't win too many architectural awards, but it's super-central and has stylish interiors, good views and excellent staff. Good off-season rates and big discounts for auto-club members.

Mantra Collins Hotel   HOTEL **$$$**

(Map p62; ☑03-6226 1111; www.mantra.com.au; 58 Collins St; d from $250, 1-/2-bedroom apt from $290/460; ❋@�) One of Hobart's newer hotels effortlessly shows up other places around town as a little old and weary. A youthful energy at reception flows through all 10 floors of spacious rooms and apartments, some with super views of kunanyi/Mt Wellington's gargantuan bulk. There's also a relaxed cafe-bar downstairs. No parking is the only drawback. Cheaper winter rates.

🏛 Salamanca Place & the Waterfront

★**Henry Jones Art Hotel**   BOUTIQUE HOTEL **$$$**

(Map p62; ☑03-6210 7700; www.thehenry jones.com; 25 Hunter St; d from $290; P❋@�) Super-swish HJs is a beacon of sophistication. In the restored waterfront Henry Jones IXL jam factory, with remnant bits of jam-making machinery and huge timber beams, it oozes class but is far from snooty (this is Hobart, not Sydney, after all). Modern art enlivens the walls, while facilities and distractions (bar, restaurant, cafe) are world class.

MACq 01   HOTEL **$$$**

(Map p62; ☑03-6210 7600; www.macq01.com.au; 18 Hunter St; r from $260; P@�) Old Macquarie Wharf No 1 is now MACq 01, a very sassy new waterfront hotel with 144 rooms over four levels. All wood panelling, concrete and jaunty angles, it's as lovely externally as it is comfortable and stylish inside and all rooms have balconies. Just try to tear yourself away from the view in the bar.

Somerset on the Pier APARTMENT $$$
(Map p62; ☑ 03-6220 6600, 1800 766 377; www.somerset.com; Elizabeth St Pier; 1-/2-bedroom apt from $275/325; P❄@☎) In a definitively Hobart location, on the upper level of the Elizabeth St Pier, this cool complex offers luxe apartments with beaut harbour views and breezy, contemporary design. You'll pay more for a balcony, but with these views you won't need to do any other sightseeing. Right in the thick of things, but still very private. Limited parking.

Sullivans Cove Apartments APARTMENT $$$
(Map p62; ☑ 03-6234 5063; www.sullivans coveapartments.com.au; 5/19a Hunter St; 1-/2-/3-bedroom apt from $295/350/640; P❄☎) Exclusive, boutique, luxury, private: all apply to these classy apartments, dotted around the Hobart waterfront in five locations (check-in for all is at 5/19a Hunter St). Our faves are the hip architect-designed units inside the charismatic old Gibson's City Flour Mill on Morrison St, where the mill's original timber and steel structures are highlighted in the interior design.

🛏 Battery Point, Sandy Bay & South Hobart

★**Montacute** HOSTEL $
(Map p62; ☑ 03-6212 0474; www.montacute.com.au; 1 Stowell Ave, Battery Point; dm/tw/d from $35/100/110; P@☎) Many Hobart hostels are cheap remodellings of old pubs, but Montacute – a renovated house in Battery Point – sets the bar a mile higher, with immaculate rooms and shared bathrooms, nice art, quality linen and mattresses, a lovely lounge with open fire, bikes for guests, proximity to cafes, and young internationalists swanning about the kitchen. Nice one!

★**Quayle Terrace** RENTAL HOUSE $$
(Map p58; ☑ 0418 395 543; 51 Quayle St, Battery Point; d $190-250, extra person $20; P❄☎) Tracing the boundary between Battery Point and Sandy Bay, Quayle St features a long run of photogenic terrace houses (ignore the power lines and this could be 1900). Quayle Terrace is one such edifice – a two-storey, two-bedroom, tastefully renovated house with a cosy gas fire and mountain views

MT NELSON

The Old Signal Station atop **Mt Nelson** (352m; Nelson Rd) (352m) provides immaculate views over Hobart and the Derwent River estuary. The Mt Nelson semaphore station (established 1811) was once the major link between Hobart and the Port Arthur penal colony further south. To get here, drive up Davey St then take the Southern Outlet towards Kingston and turn left at the top of the hill. Local buses 457, 458 and X58 also come here.

There's a sassy **restaurant** (☑ 03-6223 3407; www.signalstation.com.au; 700 Nelson Rd, Mt Nelson; breakfast mains $13-23, lunch $24-32; ☺10am-4pm Mon-Fri, 9am-4pm Sat & Sun) beside the signal station, plus barbecues and picnic tables. You can also walk to the top via the 90-minute return **Truganini Track**, which starts at Cartwright Reserve beside the Channel Hwy in Taroona.

from the shower. Free street parking; minimum three-night stay.

Lenna HERITAGE HOTEL $$
(Map p62; ☑ 1800 030 633, 03-6232 3900; www.lenna.com.au; cnr Salamanca Pl & Runnymede St, Battery Point; d/f/penthouse from $205/310/1000; P❄☎) Is Lenna old, or does it just look old? Not a question anyone would want to face personally, but for this iconic hotel the answer is 'both'. There's an old bit (1870s) and a new bit (1970s), but all rooms are thoroughly contemporary. Free parking and wi-fi; great location. Fab penthouses, too, plus mod apartments (Salamanca Terraces) across the street.

St Ives Motel MOTEL $$
(Map p58; ☑ 03-6221 5555; www.stivesmotel.com.au; 67 St Georges Tce, Battery Point; d from $140, 2-bedroom units from $240; P❄☎) Within walking distance of Battery Point, Salamanca and the city is this excellent option, a curvalicious '80s building with dozens of rooms, all with kitchens. A recent flash makeover has introduced the property to the 21st century – pleased to meet you. Good last-minute deals online; free parking and wi-fi.

Grosvenor Court Apartment Hotel APARTMENT $$
(Map p58; ☑ 03-6223 3422; www.grosvenor courtapartments.com.au; 42 Grosvenor St, Sandy Bay; 1-/2-bedroom apt from $160/260;

COMPACT COFFEE

Need caffeine, pronto? Roll into one of these great little downtown coffee nooks.

Mulberry Street Espresso (Map p62; 📱0404 214 082; www.facebook.com/mulberry streetespresso; 137 Macquarie St; items $4-9; ⏱6.30am-4pm Mon-Fri, 7am-2pm Sat) It's actually on Macquarie St, but we're not concerned. This little black coffee nook knows exactly what it's all about: top-notch coffee to go or to sip at the window seats, plus excellent tarts, sandwiches, muffins and panini. Good one.

Ecru (Map p62; 📱0448 738 014; www.ecrucoffee.com.au; 18 Criterion St; items from $3; ⏱7am-3pm Mon-Fri, 8.30am-12.30pm Sun) If you're spending any time at all in central Hobart, you might accrue a few visits to Ecru, a hole-in-the-wall coffee joint with an enthusiastic, chatty barista. The coffee here, made with beans from **Villino** (Map p62; 📱03-6231 0890; www.villino.com.au; 30 Criterion St; items $5-12; ⏱8am-4.30pm Mon-Fri, 9am-3pm Sat) just up the street, is borderline divine.

Two Folk Espresso (Map p62; 📱0439 302 678; www.facebook.com/twofolkespresso; Bank Arcade, 64-68 Liverpool St; items $3-5; ⏱7am-4pm Mon-Fri, 9am-2pm Sat) You can fit more than two folk in here (well, one or two more – it's little). But size means nothing when the coffee, interior design and morsels are this good. Two Folk is a snappy outfit at the end of the increasingly interesting Bank Arcade, serving buttery croissants, muffins, biscuits and Danish pastries along with good black stuff.

Yellow Bernard (Map p62; 📱03-6231 5207; www.yellowbernard.com; 109 Collins St; items from $3; ⏱7am-4pm Mon-Fri) With a global selection of interesting blends, Yellow Bernard (great name!) takes its coffee *very* seriously. If you're in a hippie mood, its chai – made with local honey and the cafe's own spice blend – is a perfect way to tune in while wandering Hobart's CBD. Biscuits and corners of cake to go.

P ❄ 🛜) On a demure Sandy Bay backstreet, Grosvenor Court is a tidy enclave of 20 apartments over three levels, built in the 1970s but recently rejuvenated. All have kitchens, the odd curious antique and spiffy bathrooms. Ask about its three- and four-bedroom houses available nearby if you're travelling with a group/big family.

Motel 429　　　　　　　　MOTEL $$
(Map p58; 📱03-6225 2511; www.motel429.com.au; 429 Sandy Bay Rd, Sandy Bay; d/3-bedroom unit from $150/265; P ❄ 🛜) This motel's ongoing facelift has given the rooms a sleek designer sheen. The staff are friendly, everything is clean and shipshape, and the restaurants of Sandy Bay are a short drive away. The deluxe rooms are super-comfortable, and Wrest Point Casino is across the road if you're feeling lucky. There's also a good-value three-bedroom unit available.

★**Islington**　　　　　BOUTIQUE HOTEL $$$
(Map p58; 📱03-6220 2123; www.islington hotel.com; 321 Davey St, South Hobart; d from $345; P ❄ 🛜) At the top of Hobart's accommodation tree, classy Islington effortlessly merges heritage architecture with antique furniture, contemporary art and a glorious garden. Service is attentive but understated,

with breakfast served in an expansive conservatory. In the evening, wind down with a wine in the guest library, music room or drawing room. Exquisite private dinners also available. No children under 15 years.

★**Grande Vue Private Hotel**　　B&B $$$
(Map p58; 📱03-6223 8216; www.grandevue hotel.com.au; 8 Mona St, Battery Point; 1-/2-bedroom units from $235/325; P 🛜) 'Vues' from the best rooms at this tastefully restored 1906 mansion take in a broad sweep of Sandy Bay and the Derwent River, or Mt Wellington in the other direction. Sleek new bathrooms, kitchenettes and super-friendly service lift Grande Vue to the top of the Battery Point B&B pile. Breakfast (including fresh muffins!) costs a very reasonable $15.

Salamanca Wharf Hotel　　APARTMENT $$$
(Map p62; 📱03-6224 7007; www.salamancawharf hotel.com; 17a Castray Esplanade, Battery Point; d/ apt from $215/265; P ❄ 🛜) Filling a slender gap between historic sandstone ordnance stores just east of Salamanca Place, these 22 slick studios and one-bedroom apartments offer nifty kitchens, cool art, affable staff and an unbeatable location. Units at the front have balconies, those at the back have baths (take your pick). Penthouse suites also

available (from $375). There's a cool cafe downstairs.

Apartments on Star   APARTMENT $$$
(Map p58; ☑03-6225 4799, 0400 414 656; www.apartmentsonstar.com.au; 22 Star St, Sandy Bay; 1-/2-/3-bedroom apt from $210/250/380; P ☎) This old brick house at the bottom of Star St comprises two hip apartments, bolstered by an adjacent building housing a further two slick units. Cool kitchens, big TVs, quality furnishings and Sandy Bay's buzzing restaurant scene are just metres away.

🛏 MONA & Northern Hobart

Hobart Cabins & Cottages   CARAVAN PARK $
(☑03-6272 7115; www.hobartcabinscottages.com.au; 19 Goodwood Rd, Goodwood; powered sites $35, cabins d & f from $125, 3-bedroom house $230; P ☎ 🐾) An unflattering 8km north of the city across the road from Hobart's racetrack in Goodwood, the modest Hobart Cabins & Cottages offers a few powered sites, a range of tidy cottages and cabins and a three-bedroom house sleeping up to 10. Not a bad alternative to a motel.

Altamont House   APARTMENT $$
(Map p58; ☑0427 842 140; www.facebook.com/altamonthouse; 109 Patrick St, West Hobart; d $200, extra adult/child $50/30; P ☀☎) Are there rules about how steep a street can be? The town planners weren't paying attention when they laid out Patrick St...but the views are great! Occupying the ground floor of a gorgeous old stone-and-slate house (1854), Altamont offers a plush double suite with an extra room that can be opened up as required.

Bay View Villas   APARTMENT $$
(☑1800 061 505, 03-6234 7611; www.bayviewvillas.com; 34 Poets Rd, West Hobart; 1-/2-/3-bedroom apt from $200/215/330; P ☀☎🏊) A few kilometres up the steep West Hobart slopes from the city, this family-focused option offers a games room and an indoor pool (follow the scent of chlorine from reception). There's a rank of tarted-up motel-style units out the front, and 12 stylish apartments behind with magical river views.

Graham Apartments   APARTMENTS $$
(☑03-6278 1333; www.grahamapartments.com.au; 15 Pirie St, New Town; d/q from $160/220; P ☎) One of Hobart's best-value family options, this trim complex of a couple of dozen self-contained apartments sits in established gardens in subdued New Town. Units range from one to three bedrooms, updated in contemporary style. A playground, cots, toy boxes and high chairs make it a solid family choice. Aim for the red-brick section out the front.

Rydges Hobart   HOTEL $$
(Map p58; ☑03-6231 1588; www.rydges.com; 393 Argyle St, New Town; d/ste from $130/160; P ☀☎) In a prime hillside position overlooking North Hobart Oval (any football this weekend?), great-value Rydges comprises 64 hotel rooms centred on a former school for blind and deaf kids, built in 1889. Most rooms have views, and range from interesting heritage units in the gabled roof space of the old school, to modern apartment-style suites.

Corinda   B&B, COTTAGE $$$
(Map p58; ☑03-6234 1590; www.corindacollection.com.au; 3c Aberdeen St, Glebe; r & cottages incl breakfast from $250; P ☎) Gorgeous Corinda, a renovated Victorian mansion with meticulously maintained parterre gardens, sits high on the sunny Glebe hillside a short (steep!) walk from town. There are multiple B&B rooms, two contemporary garden pavilions or three self-contained cottages to choose from, each providing mod comforts and no twee, old-world guff. Breakfast is DIY gourmet (eggs, muffins, fresh coffee etc).

🍴 Eating

Hobart's city centre proffers some excellent cafes and rapid-fire lunch venues, but when the sun sinks behind the mountain, there's not a whole lot going on here (with some notable exceptions). Instead, head for the waterfront, the epicentre of the city's culinary scene, where there's quality seafood everywhere you look. Here, Salamanca Place is an almost unbroken string of excellent cafes, bars and restaurants, especially busy during Saturday morning market festivities.

Battery Point's Hampden Rd cafes and restaurants are always worth a look, while Elizabeth St in North Hobart (aka 'NoHo') has evolved into a diverse collection of cosmopolitan eateries: Indian, Asian, Mexican, cafes, patisseries and pubs. The Sandy Bay food scene is also bubbling along nicely with some quality options at all price levels.

🍴 Central Hobart

★Bury Me Standing   CAFE $
(Map p62; ☑0424 365 027; www.facebook.com/burymestandinghobarttown; 104 Bathurst St; bagels $5-10; ☺6am-2.30pm Mon-Fri, 8am-1pm Sat

HOBART FOR CHILDREN

Parents won't break the bank keeping the troops entertained in Hobart. The free Friday-night Rektango (p81) music event in the courtyard at the Salamanca Arts Centre is a family-friendly affair. Street performers, buskers and visual smorgasbord of Saturday's Salamanca Market (p61) captivate kids of all ages. There's always something going on around the waterfront (p59) – fishing boats chugging in and out of Victoria Dock, yachts tacking in Sullivans Cove...and you can feed the tribe on a budget at the floating fish punts on Constitution Dock.

Rainy-day attractions to satisfy your child (or inner child) include the excellent Tasmanian Museum & Art Gallery (p59), Maritime Museum of Tasmania (p60) and the Antarctic-chilly Mawson's Huts Replica Museum (p59).

Just beyond the outskirts of Hobart there are some great animal parks, beaches and walks to explore. Check the view from atop Mt Nelson (p71), then hike down Truganini Tack to Taroona. Seven Mile Beach (p87) is beaut for a swim, or pack the teens into the Kombi and go surfing (p63). Alternatively, truck out to nearby Richmond and see some wild things (p88).

If you're in need of a romantic dinner for two, contact the **Mobile Nanny Service** (☑ 0437 504 064, 03-6273 3773; www.mobilenannyservice.com.au). Pick up the free *Lets-GoKids* (www.letsgokids.com.au) magazine at the Hobart Visitor Information Centre (p84) for activity ideas.

& Sun) Run by a chipper Minnesotan who ended up in Hobart accidentally, this brilliant little coffee-and-bagel joint is literally a hole in the wall of a car park. Bagels are pot-boiled (a traditional method ensuring a sticky outer and chewy inner) – don't go past the Reuben version. A couple of milk crates and dinky tables, and Dylan piped through little speakers.

Street Eats @ Franko MARKET $
(Map p62; ☑ 0408 543 179; www.facebook.com/streeteatsfranko; Franklin Sq, 70 Macquarie St; ☺ 4.30-9pm Fri Nov-Apr) Launched in 2016, Street Eats @ Franko is a buzzy night market showcasing fabulous southern Tasmanian food, with live music and plenty to drink, too. It's run by the same folks who organise the Sunday morning Farm Gate Market (p83).

Criterion Street Cafe CAFE $
(Map p62; ☑ 03-6234 5858; 10 Criterion St; mains $8-18; ☺ 7am-4pm Mon-Fri, 8am-3pm Sat & Sun) It's a short menu on a short street, but Criterion Street Cafe effortlessly meets the criteria for keeping both breakfast and lunch fans sated, and caffeine fiends buzzing through the day. Try the Spanish omelette, or Aunt Mabel's porridge with blackberry compote and apple crumble. Beers and wines, too.

R Takagi Sushi SUSHI $
(Map p62; ☑ 03-6234 8524; 132 Liverpool St; sushi from $4; ☺ 10.30am-5.30pm Mon-Fri, to 4pm Sat,

11.30am-3pm Sun) Central Hobart's best sushi spot – a favourite with downtown desk jockeys – makes the most of Tasmania's great seafood. Udon noodles and miso also make an appearance.

★**Templo** ITALIAN $$
(Map p58; ☑ 03-6234 7659; www.templo.com.au; 98 Patrick St; mains $24-32; ☺ noon-2.30pm & 6pm-late Thu-Mon) Unpretentious little Templo, on a nondescript reach of Patrick St, has assumed the mantle of Hobart's 'must-do' restaurant. With only about 20 seats (bookings essential), and only three or four Italian-inspired mains to choose from, Templo is an exercise in selectivity and sharing (your personal space, and your food). Survey the pricey-but-memorable wine list at the cute bar.

★**Mr Goodguy** ASIAN $$
(Map p62; ☑ 03-6289 8516; www.mrgoodguy.com.au; 173 Macquarie St; small plates $12-14, mains $20-28; ☺ 6.30am-10pm) Aiming for a future-Asian *Bladerunner* look, this good-looking good guy is a hawker-style restaurant revolving around a central bar, on the ground floor of the new ibis Styles Hobart Hotel. Order the wallaby shank massaman curry, a plate of crispy-skin pork belly and a cold longneck of Tsingtao and work on your Ryan Gosling scowl.

★**Pilgrim Coffee** CAFE $$
(Map p62; ☑ 03-6234 1999; www.pilgrimcoffee.com; 48 Argyle St; mains $15-20; ☺ 6.30am-

4.30pm Mon-Fri, 8am-2pm Sat & Sun) With exposed bricks, timber beams and distressed walls, L-shaped Pilgrim is Hobart's hippest cafe. Expect wraps, panini and interesting mains (try the house black beans with pulled pork) and expertly prepared coffee. Fall into conversation with the locals at big shared tables. Down a laneway around the back is the Standard (Map p62; ☑ 0458 050 612; www.standard-burgers.com; Hudsons Lane; burgers $8-14; ⊙ 11am-10pm), a burger nook run by the same tattooed crew.

Small Fry CAFE **$$**
(Map p62; ☑ 03-6231 1338; www.small-fry hobart.com.au; 129 Bathurst St; mains $18-28; ⊙ 7.30am-3pm Mon-Fri, 8.30am-1pm Sat & Sun) 🥐
Hip Small Fry sure is small, but what it lacks in size it makes up for in character. Conversation comes naturally at the shared steel counter: sip some soup, a coffee or a glass of wine; talk, listen, laugh, chew some brisket or power into an omelette. It's a flexible vibe designed to 'avoid labels'.

Ettie's MODERN AUSTRALIAN **$$**
(Map p62; ☑ 03-6231 1165; www.etties.com.au; 100 Elizabeth St; plates $12-36, fixed-price lunch $25; ⊙ 10.30am-11pm Mon-Sat) Ettie's shows three faces to the city: a bistro, wine bar and bottle shop (move through all three in sequence). Meals are in the share-plate mode, including the likes of country terrine with sherry prunes and roast duck ravioli in broth. The baby-grand in the wine bar downstairs (open until 2am on Friday and Saturday) gets a good workout.

Fico ITALIAN **$$**
(Map p62; ☑ 03-6245 3391; www.ficofico.net; 151a Macquarie St; mains $28-30, set menus $50-75; ⊙ noon-3pm Fri-Sun, 6-10pm Tue-Sat) This stylish Italian restaurant on the business flanks of Macquarie St somehow manages to feel intimate despite the traffic thundering past (jazz, bentwood chairs and moody lighting all help). Risottos and handmade pastas are the standouts – order the fresh spaghetti with sea urchin and a bottle of peppy Sicilian red. Sunday lunch is a set-menu affair ($75 per person).

Astor Grill STEAK **$$$**
(Map p62; ☑ 03-6234 3122; www.astorgrill.com.au; 157 Macquarie St; mains $29-69; ⊙ noon-4pm & 5.30-11.45pm Mon-Fri, 5.30-11.45pm Sat) Indulge in old-school meaty treats at this sumptuous stalwart, in a blood-coloured 1920s art-deco brick building on the CBD fringe. Start with

some oysters, then choose your prime cut, or perhaps the wallaby fillets with onion mash, beetroot and pepper-berry sauce. Classy.

Franklin MODERN AUSTRALIAN **$$$**
(Map p62; ☑ 03-6234 3375; www.franklin hobart.com.au; 30 Argyle St; mains $20-40; ⊙ 4.30am-late Tue-Thu, 11.30am-late Fri & Sat) In a lofty industrial space (the former *Hobart Mercury* newspaper printing room – the papers would roll straight out the front window), Franklin is all concrete, steel beams, cowhide and curtains. Have a drink at the bar, or settle in for a creative Mod Oz meal cooked in the central kitchen.

🍴 Salamanca Place & the Waterfront

★ **Retro Cafe** CAFE **$**
(Map p62; ☑ 03-6223 3073; 31 Salamanca Pl; mains $11-20; ⊙ 7.30am-5pm Mon-Fri, 8am-5pm Sat & Sun) So popular it hurts, funky Retro is ground zero for Saturday brunch among the market stalls (or any day, really). Masterful breakfasts, bagels, salads and burgers interweave with laughing staff, chilled-out jazz and the whirr and bang of the coffee machine. A classic Hobart cafe.

★ **Flippers** FISH & CHIPS **$**
(Map p62; ☑ 03-6234 3101; www.flippersfishand chips.com.au; Constitution Dock; meals $10-31; ⊙ 9.30am-8.30pm; 🐾) There are quite a few floating fish punts moored in Constitution Dock, selling fresh-caught seafood either uncooked or cooked. Our pick is Flippers, an enduring favourite with a voluptuous fish-shaped profile. Fillets of flathead and curls of calamari – straight from the deep blue sea and into the deep fryer.

Daci & Daci BAKERY, CAFE **$**
(Map p62; ☑ 03-6224 9237; www.dacianddaci bakers.com.au; 11 Murray St; mains $8-20; ⊙ 7am-6pm) Full of public servants and parliamentarians on the loose, Daci & Daci is an excellent bakery-cafe serving quiches, pasties, salads, sandwiches, pies (try the lamb, red wine and rosemary version) and cloud-like meringues the size of softballs. The daily soup with house bread is great value at $12.50. Sit inside if it's wet, or on the split-level street-side deck if it's not.

Machine Laundry Café CAFE **$**
(Map p62; ☑ 03-6224 9922; 12 Salamanca Sq; mains $8-18; ⊙ 7.30am-5pm Mon-Sat, 8.30am-5pm Sun) Hypnotise yourself watching the

tumble dryers spin at this bright retro cafe, where you can wash your dirty clothes ($5) while discreetly adding fresh juice, soup or coffee stains to your clean ones. Don't miss the chilli-infused roti wrap for breakfast.

Black Footed Pig
TAPAS $$

(Map p62; ☑ 03-6224 2222; www.theblackfootedpig.com.au; 8 Brooke St; tapas $8-21, mains $25-30, set menu per person $70; ☺ 6-10pm Tue-Sat) Exposed brick, white marble tables, black leather seats – the colours and textures here are appropriately dramatic for an upbeat waterfront diner, serving tapas (seared scallops with cauliflower cream, grilled chorizo with honey glaze) and larger *raciones* (spiced lamb cutlets, ravioli with marscapone and spinach). The wine list splits itself neatly between Tasmania and Spain, and they love their gin here.

Fish Frenzy
SEAFOOD $$

(Map p62; ☑ 03-6231 2134; www.fishfrenzy.com.au; Elizabeth St Pier; mains $13-35; ☺ 11am-9pm; ☎ ⓘ) A casual, waterside fish nook, overflowing with fish fiends and brimming with fish and chips, fishy salads (warm octopus with yoghurt dressing) and fish burgers. The eponymous 'Fish Frenzy' ($21) delivers a little bit of everything. Quality can be inconsistent, but good staff and buzzy harbourside vibes compensate. No bookings.

★ Aløft
MODERN AUSTRALIAN $$$

(Map p62; ☑ 03-6223 1619; www.aloftrestaurant.com; Brooke St Pier; mains $34-36, banquets from $70; ☺ 6pm-late Tue-Sat; ☑) Staking a bold claim as Hobart's top restaurant, Aløft occupies a lofty eyrie in the floating Brooke Street Pier. Menu hits include yellow fish curry with beetroot and fennel, and chargrilled quail with lime and white pepper. If you can drag your gaze away from the view, service and presentation are both excellent, in an unpretentious Hobart kinda way.

Peacock & Jones
MODERN AUSTRALIAN $$$

(Map p62; ☑ 1800 375 692; www.peacockandjones.com.au; 33 Hunter St; snacks $13-20, mains $32-36; ☺ 4-10pm) Almost difficult to find in the courtyard behind the Henry Jones Art Hotel, Peacock & Jones is a marvellously atmospheric space with huge timber beams and a ceiling hung with old jam-making machinations. Drinks and snacks roll out from 4pm (ocean trout pastrami, chicken liver parfait); dinner starts at 6pm (try the braised pig's tail and mushrooms). Casual but classy.

Frank
SOUTH AMERICAN $$$

(Map p62; ☑ 03-6231 5005; www.frankrestaurant.com.au; 1 Franklin Wharf; mains $39-49; ☺ 11am-10.30pm) At the base of the much-maligned Marine Board Building, Frank brings fabulous South American–inspired flavours to the Hobart waterfront. Everything is designed for sharing, from empanadas to small plates (crispy squid, confit lamb ribs), vegetable dishes (charred sweet potato and goat's-milk curd), and sensational steaks (big ones cost up to $89). Frank is one well-dressed hombre, with a super-hip design.

✘ Battery Point, Sandy Bay & South Hobart

★ Jackman & McRoss
BAKERY $

(Map p62; ☑ 03-6223 3186; 57-59 Hampden Rd, Battery Point; items $4-14; ☺ 7am-5pm) Make sure you stop by this neighbourhood bakery-cafe, even if it's just to gawk at the display cabinet full of delectable pies, tarts, baguettes and pastries. Early-morning cake and coffee may evolve into a quiche for lunch, or perhaps a duck, cranberry and walnut sausage roll. Staff stay cheery despite being run off their feet. There's also a city branch (Map p62; ☑ 03-6231 0601; 4 Victoria St, Hobart; items $4-14; ☺ 7am-4.30pm Mon-Fri).

★ Ginger Brown
CAFE $

(☑ 03-6223 3531; 464 Macquarie St, South Hobart; mains $10-20; ☺ 7.30am-4pm; ☑ ⓘ) When a food business is this well run, the mood infects the entire room: happy staff, happy customers and happy vibes. Try the slow-cooked lamb panini with cornichons and hummus, or the signature kimchi pancake. Very kid- and cyclist-friendly, and the coffee is the best in South Hobart. Last orders 3pm.

Liv-eat
CAFE $

(Map p58; ☑ 03-6224 1999; www.liveat.com.au; 15 Magnet Ct, Sandy Bay; mains $7-14; ☺ 6am-8.30pm; ☑ ⓘ) Soups, grilled salads, rolls, sandwiches, wraps, juices and smoothies – all of it fresh and/or made on the spot, and none of it deep-fried. It's a healthy formula not necessarily in accord with the lifestyles of the beer-soaked students who seem to flock here. It might be the good coffee they're after...

Don Camillo
ITALIAN $$

(Map p58; ☑ 03-6234 1006; www.facebook.com/doncamillohobart; 5 Magnet Ct, Sandy Bay; mains $18-32; ☺ 5.30-9.30pm Tue-Sat) Quite possibly the oldest restaurant in Hobart (since 1965!), little Don Camillo is still turning out a tight menu of classic Italian pastas, risottos and meat dishes.

Ristorante Da Angelo
ITALIAN $$

(Map p62; ☑ 03-6223 7011; www.daangelo.com; 47 Hampden Rd, Battery Point; mains $17-38; ☺ 5pm-late) An enduring (and endearing) Italian *ristorante,* Da Angelo presents an impressively long menu of homemade pastas, veal and chicken dishes, calzones, and pizzas with 20 different toppings. Colosseum images and Carlton Football Club team photos add a unique authenticity. Takeaway, BYO and open late.

Magic Curries
INDIAN $$

(Map p62; ☑ 03-6223 4500; www.magiccurries.com.au; 41 Hampden Rd, Battery Point; mains $14-22; ☺ 5-9.30pm Sun-Thu, to 10pm Fri & Sat; ☑) There's a photo on the wall here of the Indian cricket team's visit in 2004 – a while ago, we know, but if it's good enough for Anil Kumble, it's good enough for us. Sip a Kingfisher beer in the magically coloured interior and await your face-meltingly hot beef vindaloo. Excellent vegetarian options.

Kosaten Japanese Restaurant
JAPANESE $$

(Map p62; ☑ 03-6135 4018; www.kosaten.com.au; 17 Castray Esplanade, Battery Point; small plates $5-15; ☺ 11am-3pm & 5pm-late Mon-Sat; ☑) We could say this darkened Japanese bunker in an old stone ordnance store near Salamanca Place is a sushi-train joint, but that would be underselling it. Plates of gorgeously prepared Wagyu, pork belly, soft-shell crab tempura and grilled scallops travel the train tracks along with more predictable sushi and sashimi, best consumed with a cold Asahi. Good vegetarian options, too.

Chippies
FISH & CHIPS $$

(Map p62; ☑ 03-6286 8137; www.chippiesfishandchips.com.au; 45 Hampden Rd, Battery Point; mains $18-35; ☺ 5-9pm) Fancy fish and chips comes to Battery Point, giving the right-royal treatment to good local seafood (the carpets here are the same as those in Buckingham Palace!). Polish off your grilled flathead, mushy peas and chip butty, then head to the secret speakeasy out the back for a quick gin (can you find the door?).

Me Wah
CHINESE $$$

(Map p58; ☑ 03-6223 3688; www.mewah.com.au; 16 Magnet Ct, Sandy Bay; mains $19-42, banquets per person from $65; ☺ noon-2.30pm & 6-9.30pm

> ### SYDNEY TO HOBART YACHT RACE
>
> Arguably the world's greatest and most treacherous open-ocean yacht race, the **Sydney to Hobart Yacht Race** (www.rolexsydneyhobart.com; ☺Dec) winds up at Hobart's Constitution Dock some time around New Year's Eve. As the storm-battered maxis limp across the finish line, champagne corks pop and weary sailors turn the town upside down. On New Year's Day, find a sunny spot by the harbour, munch some lunch from the Taste of Tasmania food festival and count spinnakers on the river. New Year's resolutions? What New Year's resolutions?

Tue-Sun; ☑) From the outside, Me Wah looks just like any suburban shopping-mall joint. But inside it's an elegant confection of chinoiserie, almost bordering on over-the-top. The food is equally stellar, including terrific ways with seafood and world-famous-in-Hobart yum cha sessions from 11am on weekends. Plenty of vegetarian choices.

Prosser's on the Beach
SEAFOOD $$$

(☑03-6225 2276; www.prossersonthebeach.com; 19 Beach Rd, Lower Sandy Bay; mains $35-48; ☺ noon-2pm Thu-Sun, 6pm-late Wed-Sat) A glass-fronted, elevated pavilion by the water in Lower Sandy Bay, classy Prosser's is big on seafood: try the Bass Strait scallops with mushroom and lemon, or the signature Cajun-spiced fish of the day with mash and citrus butter. It's a taxi ride from town, but worth the trip. Bookings recommended.

✕ MONA & Northern Hobart

★Burger Haus
BURGERS $

(Map p66; ☑ 03-6234 9507; www.theburgerhaus.com.au; 364a Elizabeth St, North Hobart; burgers $11-16; ☺ 11.30am-10pm) Blaring 1980s rock and boasting big beefy burgers and a little terrace on which to sit, chew and contemplate the moody hues of kunanyi/ Mt Wellington – this place has got it all! The Haus Burger (with bacon, onion rings, caramelised pineapple and mustard mayo) reigns supreme. Secret alleyway location.

★Pigeon Hole
CAFE $$

(Map p58; ☑ 03-6236 9306; www.pigeonholecafe.com.au; 93 Goulburn St, West Hobart; mains $14-20; ☺ 7.30am-4.30pm Mon-Fri, 8am-3.30pm

WHALES IN THE DERWENT

In the 1830s Hobartians joked about walking across the Derwent River on the backs of whales, and complained about being kept awake at night by the noise of the ocean giants cavorting in the river. In typical Tasmanian style, the ensuing whaling boom was catastrophic, driving local populations of southern right and humpback whales to near extinction. Though still endangered, the occasional forgiving whale returns to the Derwent during the June–July northbound and October–November southbound migration. If you spy one, call the Parks & Wildlife Service Whale Hotline (✆0427 942 537).

Sat & Sun) This compact, friendly bakery-cafe is the kind of place every inner-city neighbourhood should have. A serious coffee attitude comes together with paddock-to-plate cafe food that's definitely a cut above. The freshly baked panini are the best you'll have, while the eggs *en cocotte* (baked eggs) with serrano ham is an absolute knockout.

Veg Bar VEGETARIAN $$
(Map p66; ✆03-6231 1593; www.vegbar.com. au; 346 Elizabeth St, North Hobart; mains $14-23; ⊙11.30am-9pm; ⊛) 'Plant-based eatery' may be a coded way of saying 'vegetarian joint', but there's really no need for disguises. Veg Bar is a quality outfit, from the snappy design (swing seats, polished concrete, faux-turf wall) to the menu of veg classics (kimchi fried rice, massaman curry) and wholesome burgers, wraps and bowls – all organic and local. Beer, wine and cocktails, too.

Born in Brunswick CAFE $$
(Map p66; www.borninbrunswick.com.au; 410 Elizabeth St, North Hobart; mains $14-24; ⊙8am-3pm Tue-Sun) Born in Brunswick is a stylistically elevated Hobart cafe (blond timbers, huge colourful bird murals and white everywhere else) with a creative menu of all-day offerings (coffee-and-cake takes on a new meaning when the 'cake' is blood lime and macadamia cheesecake with honeycomb). Try the house-smoked Huon salmon with crispy egg, black sesame and Tasmanian wasabi. It's all quite impressive.

Capital ITALIAN $$
(Map p66; ✆03-6231 1101; www.capitalrestaurant.com.au; 364 Elizabeth St, North Hobart; mains $24-38; ⊙5-10pm Mon-Wed, 11.30am-10pm Thu-Sun) Authentic Italian pizza, pasta and *dolci* (dessert) in the thick of the Elizabeth St action – an experience made even better by one of Hobart's best interiors (think pressed tin, rusted steel, polished concrete and wreathes of dried chillis; the owners did it themselves – talented!). Try the porcini mushroom gnocchi with three-cheese sauce, or the Calabrese salami pizza. Always busy – a good sign.

Berta CAFE $$
(Map p66; ✆03-6234 4844; www.bertahobart. com.au; 323a Elizabeth St, North Hobart; mains $13-26; ⊙8am-3.30pm Mon-Fri, to 4pm Sat, to 2.30pm Sun) Atmospheric NoHo cafe with perfect people-watching window seats, pressed-tin ceilings, classy cafe fare and a wine list travelling from Tasmania to Tuscany. Kick-start your day with some slippery sardines with tomato, garlic, chilli, pickled Spanish onion and basil; or maybe the pulled pork and sweet potato hash with crispy onion rings, spinach, poached eggs and Cajun hollandaise. And maybe a wine.

Vanidol's ASIAN $$
(Map p66; ✆03-6234 9307; www.vanidolsnorth-hobart.com; 353 Elizabeth St; mains $18-27; ⊙5.30pm-late, closed Mon Jun-Aug; ⊛) A pioneering North Hobart restaurant, Vanidol's has a diverse menu that travels effortlessly around Asia with dishes including spicy Thai beef salad, Nepalese lamb curry and Balinese chicken. Expect a well-thumbed passport full of vegetarian dishes, too. Also in South Hobart (Map p58; ✆03-6224 5986; www.vanidolsouth.com; 361a Macquarie St,; lunch mains $15-22, dinner $22-31; ⊙11am-2pm & 5.30-9pm Tue-Sat).

Annapurna INDIAN $$
(Map p66; ✆03-6236 9500; www.annapurnaindiancuisine.com; 305 Elizabeth St, North Hobart; mains $16-26, banquets $25-34; ⊙5-10pm; ⊛) It seems like half of Hobart lists modest Annapurna as their favourite eatery (you'd better book). Northern and southern Indian options are served with absolute proficiency: the *masala dosa* (south Indian crepe filled with curried potato) is a crowd favourite. Takeaway and good-value group banquets available. Hard to top.

Pancho Villa MEXICAN $$
(Map p66; ✆03-6234 4161; www.panchovilla.com. au; cnr Elizabeth & Pitt Sts, North Hobart; small

plates $14-23, large plates $26-37; ⊙ 5.30pm-late) A dour red-brick bank turned super-moody tequila bar and restaurant (Day of the Dead skulls, pressed metal lanterns), where you order selections from the menu – creative tacos, enchiladas, quesadillas and corn and bean dishes – and knock them back with the aforementioned white spirit (tasting flights from $20). Head for the courtyard on Saturday and Sunday nights.

Cornelian Bay
Boat House   MODERN AUSTRALIAN $$$
(⊉ 03-6228 9289; www.theboathouse.com.au; Queen's Walk, Cornelian Bay; mains $29-38; ⊙ noon-2pm daily, 6-8.30pm Wed-Sat) About 3km north of the city, this stylish, light-filled restaurant-bar occupies a converted beach pavilion on shallow Cornelian Bay – the swimming destination of choice for sweaty Hobartians circa 1900. The menu is highly evolved, starring quality local produce and delivered with super service. Try the Boat House chowder or the Scottsdale pork loin with smoked pineapple and cider-and-sage jelly.

🍷 Drinking & Nightlife

Hobart's younger drinkers are 10,000 leagues removed from the rum-addled whalers of the past, but the general intentions remain true – drink a bit, relax a lot, and maybe get lucky and take someone home. Salamanca Place, the waterfront and North Hobart are the main drinking and nocturnal hubs.

🍷 Central Hobart
⭐ New Sydney Hotel   PUB
(Map p62; ⊉ 03-6234 4516; www.newsydney hotel.com.au; 87 Bathurst St; ⊙ noon-10pm Mon, to midnight Tue-Sat, 4-9pm Sun) This low-key city pub is the best boozer in the CBD, with open fires, creative pub food (think duck tortillas; mains $15 to $39) and a terrific 15-tap beer selection, including an ever-changing array of island craft beers (try the Bruny Island Beer Co IPA). No poker machines or TVs!

Rude Boy   BAR
(Map p62; ⊉ 03-6236 9816; www.rudeboy hobart.com.au; 130 Elizabeth St; ⊙ 4pm-late Tue & Wed, 3pm-late Fri & Sat) Old-time Havana mural, pastel-coloured stools, palm fronds painted on the windows, gallons of rum behind the bar – Rude Boy channels a little bit of the Caribbean into downtown Hobart. The cocktails here are killer: make your way through a 'Death in the Afternoon' (ab-sinthe, lemon, passionfruit and sparkling wine) and you'll be inclined to stay for another. Reggae rules.

Brunswick Hotel   PUB
(Map p62; ⊉ 03-6234 4981; www.brunswickhotel hobart.com.au; 67 Liverpool St; ⊙ 11.30am-midnight Mon-Sat, 3pm-midnight Sun) Purportedly Australia's second-oldest pub (some of the sandstone walls here date back to 1816), the Brunswick has received a schmick makeover, dragging it into the current century. There's a backpacker joint (p69) upstairs and the 'Yard' – an excellent inner-city beer garden (movies, live music, trivia, street food etc) – out the back.

Hope & Anchor   PUB
(Map p62; ⊉ 03-6236 9982; www.hopeand anchor.com.au; 65 Macquarie St; ⊙ 11.30am-late) Depending on who you believe (don't listen to the barman at the Fortune of War in Sydney), this is the oldest continually licensed pub in Australia (1807). The woody interior is festooned with nautical knick-knacks (duck up the stairs to see the museum-like dining room). Not a bad spot for a cold Cascade or three.

Flamingos Dance Bar   GAY & LESBIAN
(Map p62; ⊉ 03-6294 6173; www.facebook.com/ flamingosdancebar; 201 Liverpool St, Hobart; ⊙ 10pm-5am Fri & Sat) Hobart's only dedicated gay bar is Flamingos, with pumping dance/ disco and a bedazzling schedule of theme parties and drag events.

🍷 Salamanca Place & the Waterfront
⭐ Jack Greene   BAR
(Map p62; ⊉ 03-6224 9655; www.jackgreene.com. au; 49 Salamanca Pl; ⊙ 11.30am-late) The gourmet burgers here nudge $20, but atmospheric Jack Greene (a European hunting lodge on the run?) is worthwhile if you're a wandering beer fan. Glowing racks of bottled brews fill the fridges, and there are at least 16 beers on tap from around Australia and New Zealand. Occasional acoustic troubadours perch next to the stairs.

Glass House   COCKTAIL BAR
(Map p62; ⊉ 03-6223 1032; www.theglass.house; Brooke St Pier; ⊙ noon-late) The very fancy Glass House sits in the prow of the floating Brooke St Pier, a huge window-wall affording uninterrupted views down the Derwent River estuary. Put on your best duds, order

a Hobartian Sidecar and soak it all in. Fab bar food, too (small plates $15 to $36). Is Charlie, the quintessential Hobart barman, working tonight?

Society Salamanca
COCKTAIL BAR

(Map p62; ☑03-6223 1497; http://society salamanca.com; 22 Montpellier Retreat; ☻4pm-late Tue-Sat) Society Salamanca is an atmospheric gin-and-whisky bar occupying the ground floor of a brutal-looking concrete building just up the hill from Salamanca Place. Try some Brocken Spectre gin, distilled a few hundred metres away in Battery Point. Tapas on Tuesday from 6pm.

Waterman's Beer Market
CRAFT BEER

(WBM; Map p62; ☑0424 176 745; www.watermans beermarket.com.au; 27 Salamanca Pl; ☻11am-2am Tue-Sat, to midnight Sun) 'Since 1840' is the tagline here... Well, the building maybe. But 'WBM' is one of a new brigade of Salamanca Place booze rooms, focused on excellent craft and small-batch beers and live music Thursday to Saturday. Order a pint of Iron Pot Rye Porter from Hobart Brewing Company and head for the moody row of booths. 'Lawn' courtyard out the back.

IXL Long Bar
BAR

(Map p62; ☑03-6210 7700; www.thehenryjones. com; Henry Jones Art Hotel, 25 Hunter St; ☻5-10.30pm Mon-Thu, 3-10.30pm Fri & Sat, 5-9pm Sun) Prop yourself at the glowing bar at the Henry Jones Art Hotel (p70) and check out Hobart's fashionistas over a honey porter. If there are no spare stools at the bar, flop on to the leather couches in the hotel lobby. Moo Brew on tap, killer whiskies and live jazz Thursday to Saturday.

Hobart Brewing Company
CRAFT BEER

(Map p58; ☑03-6231 9779; www.hobartbrewing co.com.au; 16 Evans St; ☻3-10pm Thu, 3-11pm Fri, 2-11pm Sat, 2-5.30pm Sun) In a big shed on Macquarie Point, fronted by the Red Square community space, Hobart Brewing Company is doing good things with craft beer. There are plenty of creative brews on tap (try the Harbour Master ale, or hook into a tasting paddle), plus there's live music most weekends and often-laughing staff.

Grape
WINE BAR

(Map p62; ☑03-6224 0611; www.grapebar.com. au; 55 Salamanca Pl; ☻11am-11.30pm Sun-Thu, to 2am Fri & Sat; ☻) In search of civility amid the nocturnal Salamanca fray? Grape is possibly your best bet, a woody wine bar with a superb list of Tasmanian drops, wandering occasionally across Bass Strait (like most Tasmanians) into Victoria and South Australia. Beers are mainstream; cocktails are more interesting. Love the cork-filled bar frontage.

T-42°
BAR

(Map p62; ☑03-6224 7742; www.tav42.com.au; Elizabeth St Pier; ☻10am-10pm Mon-Thu, 10am-1.30am Fri, 8.30am-1.30am Sat, 8.30am-10pm Sun) Stylish waterfront T-42° makes a big splash with its food (mains $18 to $32), but also draws well-dressed, late-week barflies with its minimalist interior, spinnaker-shaped bar and ambient tunes. If you stay out late enough on Friday or Saturday night, breakfast offers redemption from your nocturnal misdemeanours.

The Whaler
PUB

(Map p62; ☑03-6200 1854; www.thewhaler.com. au; 39 Salamanca Pl; ☻11am-late) Until several years ago this pub was called 'Knopwoods Retreat', an endearing old boozer and a perennial Friday-night favourite. The Whaler is doing its best to live up to the tradition, its unpretentious service and interiors making it something of an incongruity on the otherwise highly polished Salamanca Place.

Telegraph Hotel
PUB

(Map p62; ☑03-6234 6254; www.facebook.com/ telegraphhotel; 19 Morrison St; ☻11am-late) The slinky, low-slung, art-deco 'Telly' has long been the boozer of choice for local dock workers and visiting nautical types. They're still here (despite the naff '90s interior design), along with live-music fans here to see bands on Friday and Saturday night.

Customs House Hotel
PUB

(Map p62; ☑03-6234 6645; www.customs househotel.com; 1 Murray St; ☻7am-11pm Sun-Thu, to 12.30am Fri & Sat) The old sandstone Customs House (1846) dabbles in a lot of areas: accommodation, food, live music, and often successfully so. But what most folks are here for is an uncomplicated, unpretentious cold beer, more often than not from Cascade Brewery just down the road in South Hobart. Nothing too new-century here, other than the fab new beer terrace out the front.

🍺 Battery Point, Sandy Bay & South Hobart

World's End Brewpub
CRAFT BEER

(Map p58; ☑03-6135 5903; www.facebook.com/ worldsendbrewpub; 236 Sandy Bay Rd, Sandy Bay;

4pm-midnight Wed-Sat) The bad old Mayfair Tavern is long gone: in its place is the arty World's End, with an emphasis placed squarely on craft beers and cool tunes ('70s funk is a mainstay). Retro couches and Persian rugs forgive any spillage.

Preachers   BAR
(Map p62; ☑ 03-6223 3621; www.facebook.com/ preachershobart; 5 Knopwood St, Battery Point; ⊙ noon-late) Grab a retro sofa seat inside this 1849 sailmaker's cottage, or adjourn to the ramshackle garden bar, in which an old Hobart bus is now full of beer booths. Lots of Tasmanian craft beers on tap, plus cool staff and a resident ghost! A steady flow of burgers and tapas keeps the beer in check.

Shipwright's Arms Hotel   PUB
(Map p58; ☑ 03-6223 5551; www.shipwrights arms.com.au; 29 Trumpeter St, Battery Point; ⊙ noon-10pm Mon-Wed, 11.30am-11pm Thu-Sun; 🛜) Backstreet 'Shippies' is one of the best old pubs in town. Soak yourself in maritime heritage (and other liquids) at the bar, then retire to your clean, above-board berth upstairs or in the newer wing (doubles with/without bathroom $150/90). Other bonuses include hefty pub meals and the delight in saying you're having a drink on Trumpeter St.

🍷 MONA & Northern Hobart

⭐ **Shambles Brewery**   CRAFT BEER
(Map p58; ☑ 03-6289 5639; www.shamblesbrewery. com.au; 222 Elizabeth St, North Hobart; ⊙ 4pm-late Wed & Thu, noon-late Fri-Sun) Excellent brew-stuff just south of the NoHo strip, with minimalist interiors, concrete block bar and chunky Tasmanian oak tables. Tasting paddles are $12, or refill your 'growler' (1.9L bottle) to take home and savour. Terrific beery bar food, too: burgers, ribs, steak sandwiches and the like.

⭐ **The Winston**   PUB
(Map p66; ☑ 03-6231 2299; www.thewinstonbar. com; 381 Elizabeth St, North Hobart; ⊙ 4pm-late) The grim old art-deco Eaglehawk pub has been transformed into the Winston, a craftbeery, US-style alehouse. Grab a pint of the house stout from one of the beardy guys behind the bar and check out the wall of US registration plates near the pool table. Calorific bar food and live music, too.

Bar Wa Izakaya   COCKTAIL BAR
(Map p58; ☑ 03-6288 7876; www.facebook. com/barwaizakaya; 216-218 Elizabeth St, Hobart;

> ### FRIDAY-NIGHT FANDANGO
>
> Some of Hobart's best live tunes get an airing every Friday night at the **Salamanca Arts Centre Courtyard** (Map p62; ☑ 03-6234 8414; www.salarts. org.au/rektango; Salamanca Arts Centre, 65-77 Salamanca Pl, Hobart; ⊙ 5.30-7.30pm Fri), just off Woobys Lane. It's a free community event that started in about 2000, with the adopted name 'Rektango', borrowed from a band that sometimes graces the stage. Acts vary from month to month – expect anything from African beats to rockabilly, folk and gypsy-Latino. Drinks essential (sangria in summer, mulled wine in winter); dancing near-essential.

⊙ noon-midnight) Backed by glowing shelves of whisky tumblers, Bar Wa Izakaya is a darkened, atmospheric Japanese bar with more sake, Sapporo and Japanese whisky on offer than seems plausible. Order a plate of tempura mushrooms or kingfish sashimi (bar food $6 to $16) to temper your whisky tasting flight ($27).

Willing Bros   WINE BAR
(Map p66; ☑ 03-6234 3053; www.facebook. com/willingbros; 390 Elizabeth St, North Hobart; ⊙ 3pm-midnight Tue & Sun, to 1am Wed-Sat) Hey – a classy wine bar! Just what NoHo ordered. Pull up a window seat at the front of the skinny room and sip something hip from the tightly edited menu of reds, whites and bubbles. Food drifts from Moroccan fish cakes to spicy lamb empanadas – perfect fodder for a post-movie debrief.

T-Bone Brewing Co   CRAFT BEER
(Map p66; ☑ 0407 502 521; www.tbonebrewing. com.au; 308 Elizabeth St, North Hobart; ⊙ 4pm-late Wed & Thu, 2pm-late Fri-Sun) Obsessively brewed real ales steal the show at this new North Hobart brew-bar, a stylish black beer-bunker reviving an old corner shop, just a short wobble from the main Elizabeth St action. Sit by the fold-back windows, or play peek-a-boo with the beer vats, bubbling beyond a hole in the wall. Tasting flights $16.

⭐ Entertainment

⭐ **Republic Bar & Café**   LIVE MUSIC
(Map p66; ☑ 03-6234 6954; www.republicbar. com; 299 Elizabeth St, North Hobart; ⊙ 11am-late; 🛜) The Republic is a raucous art-deco pub

OFF THE BEATEN TRACK

TINDERBOX

From Kingston, drive through Black-mans Bay and continue 10km to the delightfully named Tinderbox: the views en route are eye-popping, and at Tinderbox itself there is a small beach bordering **Tinderbox Marine Reserve** (☑03-6121 7026; www.parks.tas.gov.au; Tinderbox Rd; ☉ 24hr) FREE. Here you can snorkel along an underwater trail running alongside a sandstone reef, marked with submerged information plates explaining the rich local ecosystem.

Roaring 40s Kayaking (www.roaring 40skayaking.com.au) runs day tours around this coast (adult/child $180/150) on Sundays between November and April.

From Tinderbox, continue around the peninsula to Howden and then back to Kingston via the Channel Hwy.

hosting live music every night (often with free entry). It's the number-one live-music pub around town, with an always-interesting line-up, including international acts. Loads of different beers and excellent food (mains $21 to $33; try the Jack Daniels–marinated rump steak). Just the kind of place you'd love to call your local.

★**State Cinema**   CINEMA
(Map p66; ☑03-6234 6318; www.statecinema.com. au; 375 Elizabeth St, North Hobart; ☉10am-late Mon-Fri, 9.30am-late Sat & Sun) Saved from the wrecking ball in the 1990s, the multiscreen State (built in 1913) shows independent and art-house flicks from local and international film-makers. There's a great cafe and bar on-site, plus a rooftop screen (with another bar!), a browse-worthy **bookshop** (☑03-6234 6318; www.statecinemabookstore.com.au; 373 Elizabeth St, North Hobart; ☉10am-6.30pm Sun-Thu, to 9pm Fri & Sat) and the foodie temptations of North Hobart's restaurants right outside. Magic.

Theatre Royal   THEATRE
(Map p62; ☑1800 650 277, 03-6233 2299; www. theatreroyal.com.au; 29 Campbell St; ☉box office 9am-5pm Mon-Fri) This venerable old stager is Australia's oldest continuously operating theatre, with actors first treading the boards here back in 1837 (the foundation stone says 1834, but it took them a few years to finish

it). Despite a bad fire in 1984, theatre-goers can still expect an eclectic range of music plus ballet, theatre, opera and university revues. Guided tours (p56) are available.

Blundstone Arena   SPECTATOR SPORT
(Bellerive Oval; ☑tickets 13 28 49, tours 03-6282 0400; www.blundstonearena.com.au; 15 Derwent St, Bellerive; tours adult/chld $15/5; ☉tours 10am Tue & Wed, 1pm Thu) Hobart's home of cricket and football is across the Derwent River from the city in Bellerive. The AFL's North Melbourne Football Club plays three home games here a year, while international test, one-day and T20 cricket matches also pull good crowds. Guided arena tours run if there's not a game happening, and take in the Tasmanian Cricket Museum (p62).

Playhouse Theatre   THEATRE
(Map p62; ☑03-6234 1536; www.playhouse.org. au; 106 Bathurst St; ☉box office opens 1hr prior to performances) This vintage city theatre (1864 – a former church) is home to the Hobart Repertory Theatre Society (musicals, Shakespeare, kids' plays). Book online.

Brisbane Hotel   LIVE MUSIC
(Map p58; ☑03-6234 4920; www.facebook. com/thebrisbanehotelhobart; 3 Brisbane St; ☉5-8.30pm Tue, noon-1am Wed & Thu, noon-4am Fri, 4pm-4am Sat, 4-10pm Sun) The bad old Brisbane has dragged itself up from the pit of old-man, sticky-carpet alcoholism to be reinvented as a progressive, student-filled live-music venue. This is where anyone doing anything original, offbeat or uncommercial gets a gig: punk, metal, hip-hop and singer-songwriters.

Jokers Comedy Club   COMEDY
(Map p58; ☑0427 726 123; www.jokerscomedy.com. au; Polish Corner, cnr New Town & Augusta Rds, New Town; ☉shows at 8pm Wed, bar from 6pm) Live weekly stand-up comedy at Hobart's Polish Club, just north of the main North Hobart strip. Cheap drinks and big laughs from Australian and overseas comics. Book through **Centretainment** (Map p62; ☑03-6234 5998; www.centertainment.com.au; 53 Elizabeth St Mall; ☉9am-5.30pm Mon-Fri, 10am-2pm Sat).

Federation Concert Hall   CLASSICAL MUSIC
(Map p62; ☑03-6232 4450, 1800 001 190; www. tso.com.au; 1 Davey St; ☉box office 10am-4pm Mon-Fri) Welded to the Hotel Grand Chancellor, this concert hall resembles a huge aluminium can leaking insulation from gaps

in the panelling. Inside, the Tasmanian Symphony Orchestra does what it does best.

🛍 Shopping

⭐ Farm Gate Market
MARKET
(Map p62; ☑03-6234 5625; www.farmgate market.com.au; Bathurst St, btwn Elizabeth & Murray Sts; ⊙8.30am-1pm Sun) 🍴 The waterfront Salamanca Market has dominated for decades, but this hyperactive foodie street-mart is giving it a run for its money. Trading commences with the ding of a big brass bell: elbow your way in for the best local fruit, veg, honey, wine, baked goods, beer, smoked meats, coffee, cheese, nuts, oils, cut flowers and jams.

⭐ Fullers Bookshop
BOOKS
(Map p62; ☑03-6234 3800; www.fullersbook shop.com.au; 131 Collins St; ⊙8.30am-6pm Mon-Fri, 9am-5pm Sat, 10am-4pm Sun) Hobart's best bookshop has a great range of literature and travel guides, plus regular book launches, signings and readings, and the writerly Afterword Café in the corner. Fullers has been a true hub of the Hobart literary scene for around 70 years.

⭐ Handmark Gallery
ART
(Map p62; ☑03-6223 7895; www.handmark.com. au; 77 Salamanca Pl; ⊙10am-5pm Mon-Fri, to 4pm Sat & Sun) A key tenant at the Salamanca Arts Centre (p59), Handmark has been here for 30 years, displaying unique ceramics, glass, woodwork and jewellery, plus paintings and sculpture – 100% Tasmanian, 100% exquisite.

Poet
BOOKS
(Map p62; ☑03-6245 3870; www.facebook.com/ poetstore; 130 Macquarie St; ⊙9.30am-5pm Mon & Sat, to 5.30pm Tue-Fri) In a lovely old city sandstone shopfront, Poet specialises in nonfiction and philosophy, plus its own line of stationery (including hats, leather goods and cards) and fair-trade Sri Lankan tea (see www.poettea.com).

Tommy Gun Records
MUSIC, CLOTHING
(Map p62; ☑03-6234 2039; www.facebook.com/ tommygunhobart; 127 Elizabeth St; ⊙10am-5.30pm Mon-Fri, 11am-3pm Sat, 10am-2pm Sun) For all your vinyl, secondhand CD, studded-leather wristband and black heavy-metal T-shirt requirements.

Cool Wine
WINE
(Map p62; ☑03-6231 4000; www.coolwine.com. au; Shop 8, MidCity Arcade, Criterion St; ⊙9.30am-6.30pm Mon-Sat) Excellent selection of Tasmanian wine, spirits and craft beers (plus a few global interlopers). Open Sunday by appointment. Freight available.

Wursthaus Kitchen
FOOD
(Map p62; ☑03-6224 0644; www.wursthauskitchen. com.au; 1 Montpelier Retreat; ⊙8.30am-6pm Fri, 8am-5pm Sat, 10am-5pm Sun) Follow your nose into this brilliant fine-food showcase just off Salamanca Place, selling cheeses, cakes, breads, olives, wines and pre-prepared meals. Oh, and amazing sausages!

Hobart Twilight Market
MARKET
(HTM; ☑0448 997 748; www.facebook.com/ hobarttwilightmarket; 17 Beach Rd, Lower Sandy Bay; ⊙4.30-9pm Fri Oct-Mar) Filling the lawns behind Lower Sandy Bay Beach (aka Long Beach; about 5km south of central Hobart), the HTM is a relatively new and hugely popular phenomenon. The official line goes, 'eats, drinks, artisans, music' – add to that valet bike parking and heaps of dogs, and you get the picture.

Hobart Book Shop
BOOKS
(Map p62; ☑03-6223 1803; www.hobartbook shop.com.au; 22 Salamanca Sq; ⊙9am-6pm Mon-Fri, to 5pm Sat, 10am-5pm Sun) Step into the hushed Hobart Book Shop, with its excellent array of reads and dedicated wall full of Tasmanian authorly efforts.

Drink Co
WINE & SPIRITS
(Map p62; ☑0414 896 930; www.drinkco.club; Galleria Arcade, 33 Salamanca Pl; ⊙10am-8pm Mon-Thu, to 10pm Fri & Sat) Excellent little bottle shop down an otherwise unremarkable arcade of Salamanca Place. Top-shelf Tassie wines and spirits are the names of the games – and you can sit on a stool and sip a few before you decide which ones to brown-bag and take home. Free interstate shipping for orders over $200.

ℹ️ Information

EMERGENCY

Hobart Police Station (☑03-6230 2111, non-emergency assistance 13 14 44; www.police.tas. gov.au; 43 Liverpool St; ⊙24hr) Hobart's main cop shop.

MEDICAL SERVICES

City Doctors & Travel Clinic (☑03-6231 3003; www.citydoctors.com.au; 188 Collins St; ⊙9am-5pm Mon-Fri) General medical appointments and travel immunisations.

My Chemist Salamanca (☑03-6224 9994; www.mychemist.com.au; 6 Montpelier Retreat;

☺8.30am-6pm Mon-Fri, to 5pm Sat, 10am-4pm Sun) Handy chemist just off Salamanca Place.
Royal Hobart Hospital (☑03-6166 8308; www.dhhs.tas.gov.au; 48 Liverpool St; ☺24hr) Accident and emergency, running round the clock.

POST

General Post Office (GPO; Map p62; ☑03-6236 3575; www.auspost.com.au; cnr Elizabeth & Macquarie Sts; ☺8.30am-5.30pm Mon-Fri, 9am-12.30pm Sat) Forget about the mail and check out the heritage architecture! It was built in 1905 in lavish Edwardian baroque style.

TOURIST INFORMATION

Hobart Visitor Information Centre (Map p62; ☑03-6238 4222; www.hobarttravelcentre.com.au; cnr Davey & Elizabeth Sts; ☺9am-5pm) Poised perfectly between the CBD and the waterfront. Information, maps and state-wide tour, transport and accommodation bookings. A few Tasmanian books and gifts, too.

Parks & Wildlife Service (Map p62; ☑1300 135 513; www.parks.tas.gov.au; 134 Macquarie St; ☺9am-5pm Mon-Fri) Information, maps, passes and fact sheets for bushwalking in national parks (including the Overland and Three Capes tracks). Located inside the Service Tasmania (☑1300 135 513; www.service.tas.gov.au; ☺9am-5pm Mon-Fri) office.

❶ Getting There & Away

AIR

In an irony that doesn't elude the locals, Hobart's 'international' **airport** (☑03-6216 1600; www.hobartairport.com.au; 6 Hinkler Rd, Cambridge) has only domestic flights, with services operated by Qantas, Virgin Australia, Jetstar and Tiger Air. Direct flights arrive from Melbourne, Sydney, Brisbane and (less regularly) Adelaide and Canberra. The airport is in Cambridge, 19km east of the city.

BUS

There are two main intrastate bus companies operating here, **Redline Coaches** (Map p62; ☑1300 360 000; www.redlinecoaches.com.au; 230 Liverpool St; ☺8am-6pm) and Tassielink (p306), and both run state-wide routes. Tassielink buses leave Hobart from 64 Brisbane St and a temporary stop on Elizabeth St, across the road from the Hobart Visitor Information Centre (a permanent bus depot is being planned – call or check the website for updates).

❶ Getting Around

TO/FROM THE AIRPORT

There's no public transport to Hobart airport.
A taxi into the city will cost around $50 and take about 20 minutes.

Prebooked **Hobart Airporter** (☑1300 385 511; www.airporterhobart.com.au; adult/child $20/18 one way, return $35/31) shuttle buses meet every flight and can deliver you door-to-door.

BUS

The local bus network is operated by **Metro Tasmania** (☑13 22 01; www.metrotas.com.au), which is reliable but infrequent outside of business hours. The **Metro Shop** (Map p62; ☑13 22 01; www.metrotas.com.au; 22 Elizabeth St; ☺8am-6pm Mon-Fri, plus Sat morning Dec-Mar) handles ticketing and enquiries: most buses depart from this section of Elizabeth St, or from nearby Franklin Sq.

CAR & MOTORCYCLE

Timed, metered parking predominates in the CBD and tourist areas such as Salamanca Place and the waterfront. For longer-term parking, large CBD car parks (clearly signposted) offer reasonable rates.

The big-boy rental firms have airport desks and city offices. Cheaper local firms offer daily rental rates from as low as $30. Car-rental companies include the following:

AAA Car Rentals (☑03-6231 3313; www.aaacarrentals.com.au; 73 Warwick St; ☺8.30am-5pm Mon-Sat)

AutoRent-Hertz (☑1300 030 222, 03-6234 1955; www.autorent.com.au; cnr Bathurst & Harrington Sts; ☺8am-5pm)

Avis (☑03-6214 1711; www.avis.com.au; 2/4 Market Pl; ☺8am-5.30pm Mon-Fri, to 4pm Sat & Sun)

Bargain Car Rentals (☑1300 729 230, 03-6234 6959; www.bargaincarrentals.com.au; 173 Harrington St; ☺8am-5pm Mon-Fri, 9am-3pm Sat & Sun)

Budget (☑03-6234 5222, 1300 362 848; www.budget.com.au; 96 Harrington St; ☺7.30am-5.30pm Mon-Fri, to 4.30pm Sat, 9am-2pm Sun)

Europcar (☑03-6231 1077, 1300 131 390; www.europcar.com.au; 112 Harrington St; ☺8am-5.30pm Mon-Fri, to 1pm Sat & Sun)

Rent For Less (☑1300 883 728, 03-6231 6844; www.rentforless.com.au; 92 Harrington St; ☺8am-5pm Mon-Fri, 8.30am-5pm Sat, 9am-1pm Sun)

TAXI

Hobart's taxi services pick up the slack from the bus network, with ranks in key areas such as Salamanca Place, North Hobart and the CBD. Ride-share operator Uber also operates in Hobart.

131008 Hobart (☑13 10 08; www.131008hobart.com) Standard taxis.

Hobart Maxis (☑13 32 22; www.hobartmaxi taxi.com.au) Wheelchair-accessible vehicles, and taxis for groups.

Yellow Cab Co (☑13 19 24; http://hobart. yellowcab.com.au) Standard cabs (not all of which are yellow).

AROUND HOBART

Taroona

☑03 / POP 2000

Ten kilometres south of Hobart lies the laid-back residential beach suburb Taroona, its name derived from an Aboriginal word meaning 'chiton' (a type of marine mollusc). In the 1970s there was a real sense of community here, since eroded by the closure of the shopping centre, the petrol station, the newsagent, the doctors' surgery and (especially) the pub. But maybe things are looking up: there's now an excellent cafe occupying the old petrol station.

◉ Sights & Activities

On the suburb's northern fringe is **Truganini Reserve** and the bottom end of the 2km Truganini Track, which leads up a wooded valley to the old signal station at Mt Nelson (p71). At the southern end of the 'hood, the excellent 3.5km Alum Cliffs Track heads off towards Kingston from just below the Shot Tower.

Shot Tower HISTORIC BUILDING
(☑03-6227 8885; www.taroona.tas.au/history/ shot-tower; Channel Hwy; adult/child/family $8/4/20, tearoom items $6-12; ⊘9am-5pm Sep-Apr, to 4pm May-Aug, tearoom 10am-4pm) On Taroona's southern fringe stands the Shot Tower, a 48m-high, circular sandstone turret (1870) built to make lead shot for firearms. Molten lead was once dribbled from the top, forming perfect spheres on its way down to a cooling vat of water at the bottom. The river views from atop the 318 steps are wondrous. You can also devour a Devonshire tea on the stone rampart outside.

✖ Eating

★**Picnic Basket** CAFE $
(☑0459 466 057; www.facebook.com/thepicnic basket.com.au; 176 Channel Hwy; mains $6-17; ⊘7.30am-3.30pm Mon-Fri, 8am-3.30pm Sat & Sun; ☑) This old petrol-station building has been reworked as an earthy cafe, with a quirky retro interior, staff dancing in the kitchen and herbs growing in planter boxes – a far remove from its petrochemical past. Order some Dr Seussian green eggs and ham, a breakfast burrito, some sweet-potato waffles, a salad or some homemade muesli with local yoghurt. Wake-you-up coffee, too.

❶ Getting There & Away

To get to Taroona from Hobart, drive south along Sandy Bay Rd (10km) or take **Metro Tasmania** (p84) buses 426–429 from Franklin Sq ($4.60).

COAL RIVER VALLEY WINE REGION

Richmond and nearby Cambridge are at the centre of Tasmania's fastest-growing wine region, the Coal River Valley. Some operations here are sophisticated affairs with gourmet restaurants; others are small, family-owned vineyards with cellar doors open by appointment. See www.winesouth.com.au for more info.

Puddleduck Vineyard (☑03-6260 2301; www.puddleduck.com.au; 992 Richmond Rd, Richmond; ⊘10am-5pm) Puddleduck is a small, family-run vineyard producing just 1500 cases per year: shoot for the riesling, pinot noir or 'Bubbleduck' sparkling white. Snaffle a cheese or vineyard platter ($25 to $48), or fire up the BBQs (BYO meat) for lunch by the lake with Lucky the duck and Polly the wine dog. Tastings start at $5.

Frogmore Creek (☑03-6274 5844; www.frogmorecreek.com.au; 699 Richmond Rd, Cambridge; ⊘10am-5pm, restaurant 11.30am-3pm) Overlooking the Mt Pleasant Observatory, 9km southwest of Richmond, flashy Frogmore Creek has a smart restaurant (mains $17 to $25) serving lunch, along with excellent chardonnay, pinot noir and sticky botrytis riesling. Don't miss *Flawed History,* an in-floor jigsaw by local artist Tom Samek. Bookings recommended.

Pooley Wines (☑03-6260 2895; www.pooleywines.com.au; 1431 Richmond Rd, Richmond; ⊘10am-5pm) In a lovely old two-storey Georgian sandstone house on the edge of town, Pooley has been doing good things with wine since 1985 (and on more recent Sunday afternoons, wood-fired pizza). The pinot noir is why you're here.

HOBART & AROUND TAROONA

Kingston

03 / POP 14,830

Sprawling Kingston, 12km south of Hobart, is a booming outer suburb. Once a sleepy beach enclave, Kingston changed in the 1980s when the Southern Outlet roadway established a rocket-shot route into town. The beach here is great for a chilly swim on a sunny afternoon, and there are some lovely places to eat and drink along the beachfront.

Sights

Blackmans Bay Beach BEACH
(Ocean Esplanade, Blackmans Bay) About 3km from Kingston, Blackmans Bay has a safe-swimming beach and a blowhole. The water is usually quite cold, and there's rarely any surf...but it sure is pretty! If you wander around the cliff base near the blowhole, you'll find a local-secret swimming gulch, with waves surging in and out of a deep channel (not so secret now, eh?).

Kingston Beach BEACH
(Osborne Esplanade) This relaxed swimming and sailing spot has steep wooded cliffs at each end of a long arc of sand. There's a picnic area at the northern end, accessed by a pedestrian bridge over the pollution-prone (and therefore aptly named) Browns River. The 3.5km **Alum Cliffs Track** from near the Shot Tower (p85) in Taroona finishes here. Behind the sailing clubhouse at the beach's southern end is a track leading to a secret little swimming cove called **Boronia Beach**.

Australian Antarctic Division SCIENCE CENTRE
(03-6232 3209; www.antarctica.gov.au; 203 Channel Hwy; ⊗8.30am-5pm Mon-Fri) **FREE** Just south of Kingston is the government HQ responsible for administering Australia's 42%

wedge of the frozen continent. Australia has a long history of exploration and scientific study of Antarctica: it's one of the original 12 nations that ratified the Antarctic Treaty in 1961. Visitors can check out the displays here, which feature Antarctic equipment, clothing and scientific vehicles, plus ecological info and some brilliant photographs. There's an on-site cafe.

Eating & Drinking

★**Beach** CAFE $$
(03-6229 7600; www.thebeachrestaurant.com.au; 14 Ocean Esplanade, Blackmans Bay; breakfast mains $9-23, lunch & dinner $13-34; ⊗10am-late Mon-Fri, 9am-late Sat & Sun) It's worth driving a few kilometres over the headland from Kingston to the sunny terrace of this angular cafe-bar on Blackmans Bay beach. Wood-fired pizzas, steaks, lamb shanks, big salads and pasta are all done with flair. There's a great range of Tasmanian wines and beers, if you feel like settling in for the afternoon.

Beachfront 32 CAFE $$
(03-6229 4891; www.facebook.com/beachfront32; 32 Osbourne Esplanade; mains $10-23; ⊗8am-10pm Mon-Sat, to 9pm Sun) What are all those people doing over there? Oh, they're eating and drinking at Beachfront 32, a cafe-bar right on Kingston Beach. Scan the menu (pinned to a vintage placemat) and order a Greek lamb burger, some sweet-potato and zucchini fritters with poached eggs, or a lemon-pepper calamari salad. Good beers and wines and attentive staff round things out.

★**Salty Dog Hotel** PUB
(03-6229 6185; www.thesaltydog.net.au; 2 Beach Rd; ⊗10am-late) A superb reworking of a weary old 1970s tavern (the term given to low-roofed, architecturally lazy, suburban

---

CROWN PRINCESS MARY OF DENMARK (AKA MARY DONALDSON OF TAROONA)

A few Tasmanians have found themselves in the spotlight over the years, but no one has garnered more international attention than Mary Donaldson, the girl from Taroona, now living a modern-day fairy tale in Europe. Mary was born in Hobart in 1972, the youngest of four children. She attended Taroona High School before graduating from the University of Tasmania (in commerce and law) in 1993.

Mary met Denmark's Crown Prince Frederik at the Slip Inn pub in Sydney during the 2000 Olympic Games: the prince was in Oz with the Danish sailing team. The pair sailed into a relationship that sent the paparazzi into a frenzy, until Mary and Fred announced their engagement in 2003. They married in a lavish ceremony in Copenhagen in 2004 with a sea of well-wishers lining the streets, waving Danish and Australian flags.

Tasmanian pubs), the Salty Dog is bright, contemporary and interesting, with terrific Tasmanian food (Huon Valley mushrooms, Spring Bay mussels), excellent beers and wines, a grassy beer garden and the beach right across the road.

Robbie Brown's WINE BAR
(☑03-6229 4891; www.robbiebrowns.com.au; 32 Osbourne Esplanade; ☺4pm-midnight Mon-Thu, noon-midnight Fri-Sun) Sweet relief on a hot evening, this wine bar is a moody little spot, with tall bentwood stools, craft beers on tap, local-spirits cocktails and an eccentric array of potted succulent plant species hanging on the wall. Sit in the window and watch the waves.

❶ Getting There & Away

To get to Kingston Beach from Hobart by bus ($4.60), take Metro Tasmania (p84) bus 427 via Taroona, or 407, 409 or 411 via the Southern Outlet. The 407, 409 and 427 also run to Blackmans Bay beach.

By car, as you branch off from the Southern Outlet and approach Kingston, continue straight ahead at the first set of lights – this road takes you down to the beach. If you're trundling down the Channel Hwy from Taroona, turn left at these lights.

Seven Mile Beach & Around

☑03 / POP 450

Out near the Hobart Airport, 15km east of Hobart, is this brilliant, safe swimming beach backed by shacks, a corner store and pine-punctured dunes, plus an oyster farm nearby.

Seven Mile Beach does get some decent surf a handful of times a year – when the swell is working the point break here is magic – but usually there's just gentle knee-high ripples rolling in. For waves you can more reliably ride on, head 18km south of Seven Mile Beach through nearby Lauderdale to Clifton Beach, or Goats Beach about 5km further along towards South Arm.

◎ Sights

Barilla Bay Oysters FARM
(☑03-6248 5458; www.barillabay.com.au; 1388 Tasman Hwy, Cambridge; tours adult/child $39/29; ☺9am-6pm, tours 11am Mon & Wed-Sun) From Seven Mile Beach, follow Surf Rd out past the Hobart Airport runway and around to the left for 2km and you'll come to Barilla Bay Oyster Farm. One-hour tours explore the oyster production process (farming, processing, grading) and include six shucked shells to taste. Call for bookings (kids under 10 free). Afterwards hit the slick restaurant for lunch (mains $18 to $45; also open for dinner on Friday and Saturday), or grab a dozen shucked oysters (from $13) and some Oyster Stout to go.

⌂ Sleeping

BIG4 Hobart Airport Tourist Park CARAVAN PARK $
(☑03-6248 4551; www.hobartairporttouristpark. com.au; 2 Flight St, Cambridge; powered sites from $40, cabins from $135; ☒☜) Filling a long-vacant void in the Hobart tourism sector is this caravan park near Hobart Airport – big, clean and grassy with excellent cabins, and perfectly located if you've got an early flight.

Travelodge Hobart Airport HOTEL $$
(☑03-6248 3555; www.travelodge.com.au/hotel/ hobart-airport; 1 Holyman Ave, Cambridge; d/f from $150/180; ☒☜) Out near the airport, this slick chain hotel caters mostly to business bods with an early flight. Rooms are predictably corporate but immaculate, and there's a cafe-restaurant.

❶ Getting There & Away

To get to Seven Mile Beach, drive towards Hobart Airport and follow the signs. Metro Tasmania (p84) buses 635, 664, X64, 665 and X65 also run here ($4.60).

Richmond & Around

☑03 / POP 1610

Straddling the Coal River 27km northeast of Hobart, historic Richmond was once a strategic military post and convict station on the road to Port Arthur. Riddled with 19th-century buildings, it's arguably Tasmania's premier historic town, but businesses here do tend to err on the 'kitsch colonial' side of tourism.

That said, Richmond is certainly a picturesque little town and the kids will love chasing the ducks around the riverbanks. It's also quite close to the airport – a happy overnight option if you're on an early flight.

◎ Sights

★**Sullivans Cove Whisky** DISTILLERY
(☑03-6248 5399; www.sullivanscove.com; 1/10 Lamb Pl, Cambridge; tour/tasting per adult $30/30, combined $40; ☺10am-4pm Mon-Fri) It doesn't

look much from the outside, but this tin shed near the turn-off to Richmond managed to produce the best single malt whisky in the world, as adjudged at the 2014 World Whiskies Awards. And now there are a dozen distillers around Tasmania. Tours run on the hour; bookings essential (don't even think about not doing a tasting!).

Richmond Bridge
BRIDGE

(Wellington St) This chunky (but not inelegant) bridge still funnels traffic across the Coal River and is the town's proud centrepiece. Built by convicts in 1823 (making it the oldest road bridge in Australia), it's purportedly haunted by the 'Flagellator of Richmond', George Grover, who died here in 1832.

Bonorong Wildlife Centre
WILDLIFE RESERVE

(☑03-6268 1184; www.bonorong.com.au; 593 Briggs Rd, Brighton; adult/child/family $29/15/80; ☺9am-5pm) ✔ The name 'Bonorong' derives from an Aboriginal word meaning 'native companion' – look forward to seeing Tasmanian devils, koalas, wombats, echidnas and quolls at this impressive operation. The emphasis here is on conservation, education and the rehabilitation of injured animals. Nocturnal tours also available (adult/child from $160/85). The centre is about 17km west of Richmond: take Middle Tea Tree Rd, turn left into Tea Tree Rd after 11km, then left again onto Briggs Rd once you get to Brighton. Bonorong is on the left.

Richmond ZooDoo Zoo
ZOO

(☑03-6260 2444; www.zoodoo.com.au; 620 Middle Tea Tree Rd; adult/child $25/13; ☺9am-5pm) Six kilometres west of Richmond on the road to Brighton (Middle Tea Tree Rd), ZooDoo has 'safari bus' rides, playgrounds, picnic areas and half of Dr Dolittle's appointment book, including tigers, llamas, Tasmanian devils, wallabies and a particularly imperious peacock. Hungry white lions chow down at regularly scheduled intervals.

Richmond Gaol
Historic Site
HISTORIC BUILDING

(☑03-6260 2127; www.richmondgaol.com.au; 37 Bathurst St; adult/child/family $10/5/25; ☺9am-5pm) The northern wing of the remarkably well-preserved jail was built in 1825, five years before the penitentiary at Port Arthur, making it Australia's oldest jail (or, rather, gaol). Built to house 60, the jail soon had 100 inmates crammed in here, including at one stage the notorious bushranger Martin Cash.

Like Port Arthur, fascinating historic insights abound, but the mood is pretty sombre.

Old Hobart Town
Historical Model Village
MUSEUM

(☑03-6260 2502; www.oldhobarttown.com; 21a Bridge St; adult/child $15/5, f from $32; ☺9am-5pm) The kids will love this painstaking recreation of Hobart Town in the 1820s, built from the city's original plans. Admission is a bit steep, but it's actually pretty amazing, with some solid historical insights. Doubles as an informal visitor information centre.

🛏 Sleeping

★ Daisy Bank Cottages
B&B $$

(☑03-6260 2390; www.daisybankcottages.com.au; 78 Middle Tea Tree Rd; d from $170, extra person $30; 🖲) A rural delight: two spotless, stylish self-contained units (one with spa) in a converted 1840s sandstone barn on a working sheep farm. There are loft bedrooms, views of the Richmond rooftops and plenty of bucolic distractions for kids. The surrounding farmland has interpretative walks and soaring birds of prey. Breakfast stuff provided on your first morning. Hard to beat.

Richmond Coachmans Rest
MOTEL $$

(☑03-6260 2609; www.richmondcoachmansrest.com.au; 28 Bridge St; d from $130, 2-bedroom unit from $180) A no-fuss, tidy row of three motel-style units on the main street. Unit 1 is a two-storey, two-bedroom affair; the other two are studio-style doubles. Simple, clean and totally sans colonial frills – what a relief!

🍴 Eating & Drinking

★ Richmond Bakery
BAKERY $

(☑03-6260 2628; 50 Bridge St, off Edward St; items $4-8; ☺7.30am-5pm) Come for takeaway pies, pastries, sandwiches, croissants, muffins and cakes, or munch on them in the courtyard. Its version of the Tasmanian classic curried scallop pie more than passes muster. If the main street is empty, chances are everyone is in here.

Coal River Farm
BISTRO $$

(☑03-6248 4960; www.coalriverfarm.com.au; 634 Richmond Rd, Cambridge; breakfast mains $12-17, lunch $24-29; ☺9am-4pm) A snappy piece of hillside architecture, Coal River Farm is a family-friendly spot to try some artisan cheese, chocolate or grab some breakfast or lunch in the bistro – perhaps some smoked wallaby with white bean mash and spicy tomato and capsicum sauce. You can also pick

Richmond

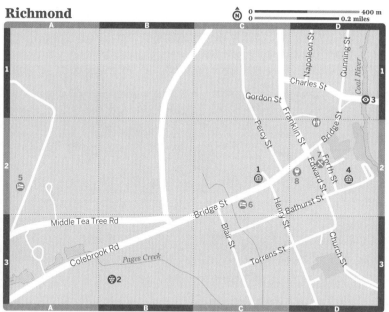

strawberries, feed the goats and collect eggs from the chooks.

Richmond Arms Hotel PUB
(📞 03-6260 2109; www.richmondarmshotel.com.au; 42 Bridge St; ⏱ 11am-10pm) This laid-back sandstone pub (built in 1888), popular with day-tripping, moustachioed bikers, has old-school pub grub (mains $18 to $38; try the pork chops with cider sauce) and boundless cold beer. The streetside tables are where you want to be.

There's also motel-style accommodation (doubles from $120) in the renovated stables out the back.

ℹ Information

See www.richmondvillage.com.au to catch the village vibe.

ℹ Getting There & Away

Richmond is a 20-minute drive east of Hobart: head for the airport and follow the signs.

Tassielink (p306) runs buses from Hobart to Richmond ($7.60, 45 minutes) multiple times daily from Monday to Saturday.

Richmond Tourist Bus (Hobart Shuttle Bus; 📞 0408 341 804; www.hobartshuttlebus.com/richmond-village.html; adult/child return $30/20; ⏱ 12.15pm Sun-Fri) runs services from

Richmond

◎ Sights
1	Old Hobart Town Historical Model Village	C2
2	Pooley Wines	B3
3	Richmond Bridge	D1
4	Richmond Gaol Historic Site	D2

⊜ Sleeping
5	Daisy Bank Cottages	A2
6	Richmond Coachmans Rest	C2

⊗ Eating
7	Richmond Bakery	D2

⊜ Drinking & Nightlife
8	Richmond Arms Hotel	D2

Hobart, with three hours to explore Richmond (unguided) before returning. Call for bookings and pick-up locations. Extensions to Richmond ZooDoo Zoo also available.

New Norfolk & Around

📞 03 / POP 9000

Cropping up unexpectedly amid the lush, rolling countryside (and heavy industry) of the Derwent Valley is New Norfolk, settled by colonists in 1808. Here, 38km north of Hobart, the Derwent River narrows, and black swans rubberneck across the water.

New Norfolk

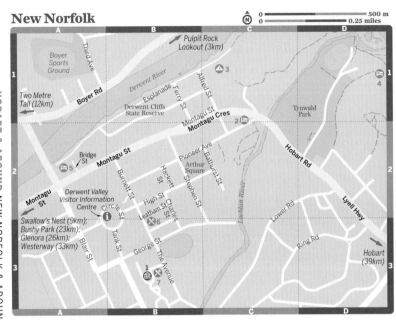

New Norfolk

By the 1860s the valley had become a hops-growing hub (hops are used to give beer its bitterness). Through the 20th century, New Norfolk was sculpted (and stigmatised) by two forces – the insane asylum Willow Court and the Boyer newspaper print mill. These days the asylum is gone, and New Norfolk maintains a small-town, riverside sensibility along with eight antiques shops (eight!).

Near New Norfolk, en route to Mt Field National Park, are the historic towns of Plenty, Bushy Park, Glenora and Westerway. The countryside here is utterly photogenic, with long runs of roadside poplar trees, rambling hop fields and old shingle-roof oast houses (used for drying hops). Bushy Park remains the largest hops-producing town in the southern hemisphere.

◉ Sights

★ **Two Metre Tall**   BREWERY
(☏ 0400 969 677; www.2mt.com.au; 2862 Lyell Hwy, Hayes; ⊙ cellar door 11am-3pm Tue-Thu, bar noon-6pm Fri & Sun) One of Tassie's best craft-beer breweries (where the brewer ain't short) is open for tastings, plus 'Farm Bar' sessions every Friday and Sunday afternoon, featuring hand-pumped ales and ciders, with BBQs available (BYO meat). Hops and barley are sourced from Two Metre Tall's own farm in the Derwent Valley. You'll find the brewery 12km northwest of New Norfolk, en route to Hamilton.

Stefano Lubiana Wines   WINERY
(☏ 03-6263 7430; www.slw.com.au; 60 Rowbottoms Rd, Granton; ⊙ tastings 11am-4pm Wed-Sun) Is this Tuscany? Sonoma Valley, maybe? No, it's Granton, about 20km north of Hobart and 16km southeast of New Norfolk, but the vibe is very international. The wines produced here – notably chardonnay, pinot gris and pinot noir – are first rate, but the rustic, river-view Italian *osteria* (restaurant) is what many come here for (mains $26 to $32, open noon to 2.30pm Thursday to Sunday).

Salmon Ponds FARM
(📋03-6261 5663; www.salmonponds.com.au; 70 Salmon Ponds Rd, Plenty; adult/child/family $8/6/22; ⊙9am-5pm, restaurant 9am-4pm Nov-Apr, 10am-3pm May-Oct) In 1864 rainbow and brown trout were bred for the first time in the southern hemisphere at this hatchery, 9km west of New Norfolk at Plenty. You can feed the fish in the display ponds, visit the hatchery and check out the angling museum. The **restaurant** (mains $11 to $21) here specialises in sweet and savoury crepes (try the smoked salmon and camembert) plus Tasmanian wines, and serves decent coffee.

Willow Court Historic Site HISTORIC BUILDING
(www.newnorfolk.org/~willow_court; 15 George St; ⊙daylight hours) FREE Infamous Willow Court dates from the 1820s and once housed invalid convicts before it became a mental institution. In 1968 it had 1000 patients, but by the 1980s asylums began to be phased out in favour of community-based treatment. In 2000 the asylum finally closed. The stately old buildings are grim but are slowly being repurposed, and now include a motel, the **Patchwork Cafe** (📋0417 916 479; www.patchworkcafe.com; mains $8-12; ⊙10am-2pm Mon, 9am-4pm Tue-Sat, 10am-4pm Sun; 🐾) and an eccentric antiques shop, fronted by rusty American cars.

🏃 Activities

See Agrarian Kitchen (p44) for info on this excellent local cooking school.

⭐**Tassie Bound** CANOEING
(📋0417 008 422; www.tassiebound.com.au; per adult/family incl lunch $135/400) Take a small-group two-hour downstream canoe paddle on a scenic, serene section of the Derwent River, with lunch on the riverbank. Pick-ups from New Norfolk. Five-hour paddles through sections of river rapids ($150/550) also available, plus three-hour evening platypus-spotting trips ($150/300).

🛏 Sleeping

Junction Motel MOTEL $
(📋03-6261 4029; www.junctionmotel.com.au; 50 Pioneer Ave; d/f from $100/160; 🅿🐾) This refurbished 1960s motel has 30 spotless, quirky rooms – including a few Asian-themed luxury options – and energetic ex-Sydney and New Zealand owners forging a new life in Tasmania. There's also an on-site restaurant (mains from $22 to $25, serving 6pm to 8pm Monday to Friday) for guests (good pizzas). Basic breakfast included.

New Norfolk Caravan Park CARAVAN PARK $
(📋03-6261 1268; www.newnorfolkcp.com; 1 The Esplanade; unpowered/powered sites $25/32, cabins d $110, extra adult/child $10/5) This caravan park has shady, poplar-studded grounds on the Derwent River's south bank, with ducks waddling around on the lawns. There are a handful of cabins, all of which have en suites – everyone else uses the amenities blocks.

Tynwald B&B $$
(📋03-6261 2667; www.tynwaldtasmania.com.au; 1 Tynwald St; d incl breakfast $170-255, cottage from $205, extra person $45; 🐾🏊) Run by a couple of chefs, Tynwald is a beautiful, turreted 1830s mansion overlooking the river, with six antique-stuffed guest rooms, a heated pool, rambling gardens and cooked breakfasts. There's also a lovely self-contained stone cottage, sleeping three. Outside guests are welcome at the excellent restaurant (mains $38 to $40; call for dinner bookings).

Woodbridge on the Derwent BOUTIQUE HOTEL $$$
(📋0417 996 305; www.woodbridgenn.com.au; 6 Bridge St; d from $385; 🐾) 'Small luxury hotel' is the billing at Woodbridge, which is indeed next to the bridge across the Derwent River on New Norfolk's northern fringes. It's an elegant, cream-painted brick homestead (1825) with wisteria-hung trellises and lush riverside lawns. The classiest place to stay in a country mile (actually, many country miles). No kids, but 'young adults' tolerated.

🍴 Eating

⭐**Cheeky Little Place** CAFE $
(📋0427 461 889; 38 Burnett St; mains $5-15; ⊙7am-2pm Mon-Fri, 5-8pm Thu & Fri) The best spot for a coffee in New Norfolk is this cheeky little cafe occupying a minuscule shopfront in the middle of town. On the menu are soups, curries, French toast and an excellent smoked salmon, cream cheese, tomato and onion tart. 'It's bit groovy for Norfick!', says one chuffed customer. Sometimes opens on weekends in summer; pasta nights Thursday and Friday.

ℹ Information

Derwent Valley Visitor Information Centre
(📋03-6261 3700; www.newnorfolk.org; Circle St; ⊙10am-4pm) The local info hub handles accommodation bookings and dishes the local

low-down. The free photocopied brochure *New Norfolk* will guide you around the old-time sights.

ℹ️ Getting There & Away

Tassielink (p306) runs between Hobart and New Norfolk ($8.30, 50 minutes), with buses once daily on Tuesday, Thursday, Friday and Sunday. **Derwent Valley Link** (🖉 03-6261 4653; www.derwentvalleylink.com.au) buses ply the same route, with at least three buses daily ($8.30, 45 minutes).

Mt Field National Park

🖉 03 / POP 170 (NATIONAL PARK TOWNSHIP)

Mt Field, 80km northwest of Hobart and 7km beyond Westerway, was declared a national park in 1916. It is famed for its alpine moorlands, lakes, rainforest, impressive waterfalls, walks, skiing and rampant wildlife. It's an accessible day trip from Hobart, or you can bunk down overnight. Either way, things can get mighty chilly here – bring a woolly hat!

🏃 Activities

The visitor information centre has maps and advice on the various walks around the park. Sign the intentions book here if you're heading off on a longer hike.

Short Walks

The park's most touted attraction is the cascading, 45m-high **Russell Falls** (www.parks.tas.gov.au; off Lake Dobson Rd; ☉daylight hours), which is in the valley close to the park entrance. It's an easy 20-minute circuit walk from the car park along a wheelchair-suitable path. From Russell Falls, you can continue past **Horseshoe Falls** and the **Tall Trees Circuit** to **Lady Barron Falls**, a two-hour return walk past mountain ash (the world's tallest flowering plants).

For kids (and adults!) who don't mind a longer walk, there's the **Pandani Grove Nature Walk**. This 30-minute walk traces the edge of Lake Dobson (any platypuses today?) through magical stands of endemic pandanis – comedic-looking palms that grow up to 12m high before toppling over. Park at Lake Dobson car park, 15km from the park entrance.

High-Country Walks

There are some awesome walks at the top of the range, where glaciation has sculpted steep cliffs and bruised deep valleys into what was once a continuous plateau. Shimmering lakes perforate the valley floors, and smaller tarns adorn the ridge tops.

If you're setting out on a walk to the high country, take waterproof gear and warm clothing – the weather is changeable year-round, so check weather and track conditions with the visitor centre before you set out. Walks here include those to **Seagers Lookout** (two hours return), **Mt Field East via Lake Nicholls** (four to five hours return) and **Lakes Belton and Belcher** (five to six hours return).

Tarn Shelf Track

The **Tarn Shelf Track** is a brilliant walk year-round in clear weather. In summer the temperature is mild, and in autumn deciduous beech trees along the way turn golden. In winter you may need skis or snowshoes. In spring the sound of melting snow trickling beneath the boardwalk enhances the silence.

Most people walk from the Lake Dobson car park, taking the Urquhart Track to the ski fields, at the top of which is the start of the Tarn Shelf Track. The track is fairly level, with a boardwalk protecting delicate vegetation and keeping walkers out of the mud. Either continue as far as you like along the track and then backtrack, or circle east past Twisted Tarn, Twilight Tarn and Lake Webster, which all up takes five or six hours return from the car park.

Skiing

Mt Mawson   SKIING

(🖉03-6288 1149; www.mtmawson.info; off Lake Dobson Rd; skiing adult/child full day $30/15, half-day $20/10, ski tow deposit $10; ☉10am-4pm Sat & Sun mid-Jul–mid-Sep) Skiing was first attempted here on Mt Mawson in 1922. A low-key resort with clubby huts and rope tows has evolved, and when nature sees fit to offload some snow (infrequently in recent years) it makes a relaxed change from the commercial ski fields on mainland Australia. Check the website for snow reports and cams.

🛏️ Sleeping

Mt Field National Park Campground   CAMPGROUND $

(🖉03-6288 1149; www.parks.tas.gov.au; off Lake Dobson Rd; unpowered/powered sites per 2 adults $16/20, family $22/30) Run by the park administration, this self-registration campground is a few hundred metres past the visitor information centre and has decent facilities (toilets, showers, laundry and free

BBQs). No bookings. Site prices are additional to national park entry fees.

Government Huts
CABIN $

(☑ 03-6491 2271; www.parks.tas.gov.au; Lake Dobson Rd; cabins up to 6 people $45) Get back to your rootsy mountaintop essence at these three simple, six-bed cabins 15km inside Mt Field National Park. Built in the 1940s, the cabins are equipped with mattresses, cold water, wood stove and firewood (there's no power), with a communal outdoor toilet block. BYO gas lamps, cookers, utensils and bedding. Book online.

★Duffy's Country Accommodation
COTTAGE $$

(☑ 03-6288 1373; www.duffyscountry.com; 49 Clark's Rd, Westerway; d $135-165, extra adult/ child $25/20; ☞) Overlooking a field of raspberry canes at Westerway (8km east of Mt Field National Park) are these great-value, immaculate self-contained cottages: one studio-style cabin for couples, and one two-bedroom relocated rangers' hut from Mt Field National Park for families. There are also a couple of cute two-bed bunkhouses where you can file the teenagers. Breakfast provisions available. Wallabies are a distinct possibility.

★Platypus Riverside Cottage
COTTAGE $$

(☑ 0413 833 700; www.riverside-cottage.com; 1658 Gordon River Rd, Westerway; d from $150, extra person $30; Ⓟ) ✐ You can't miss this little red shiplap cottage by the Tyenna River in Westerway, 8km from Mt Field National Park. Winning features include a little outdoor deck overlooking the river (spot a platypus, hook a trout) and a little BBQ. Everything's little! The owners try to minimise guests' environmental impact (ecofriendly toiletries and detergents all the way). Sleeps four.

✗ Eating

Possum Shed
CAFE $$

(☑ 03-6288 1364; www.thepossumshed.com.au; 1654 Gordon River Rd, Westerway; mains $15-20; ☺10am-4pm Mon-Fri, to 9am-5pm Sat & Sun; ☎) At Westerway, en route to Mt Field about 30km from New Norfolk, you'll find this vivacious riverside haunt, with outdoor seating, a resident platypus (sightings are not guaranteed – you have to be really quiet) and lunches and snacks (salads, burgers, pan-

---

ⓘ ROAD WARNING

If you're staying in the Government Huts, skiing at Mt Mawson or tramping the high-country walks, you'll have to drive the 15km unsealed Lake Dobson Rd. In winter you'll need chains and antifreeze for your car; contact the **visitor centre** (p93) for advice.

---

cakes, muffins, BLTs) with locally sourced ingredients. The coffee is good to go.

National Park Hotel
PUB FOOD $$

(☑ 03-6288 1103; www.nationalparkhotel.com.au; 2366 Gordon River Rd, National Park; mains $9-28; ☺1-8pm Mon-Wed, noon-10pm Thu, noon-midnight Fri, noon-11pm Sat, noon-8pm Sun) A few hundred metres past the park turn-off is this old country pub (1920), cooking up mixed grills, chicken dishes and steaks. The bartender shakes her head and says, 'They love their meat round here...' The bar scenes from the 2011 Willem Dafoe movie *The Hunter* were filmed here. Expect open fires, retro furniture and occasional live music.

ⓘ Information

Mt Field National Park Visitor Information Centre (☑ 03-6288 1149; www.parks.tas.gov. au; 66 Lake Dobson Rd; park day pass per person/vehicle $12/24; ☺8.30am-5pm Nov-Apr, 9am-4pm May-Oct) The Mt Field National Park Visitor Information Centre houses the Waterfalls Cafe and displays on the park's origins. It sells park day passes, and has reams of information on walks and ranger-led activities, held from late December until early February. There are excellent day-use facilities around the centre, including BBQs, shelters, lawns and a children's playground.

ⓘ Getting There & Away

The 80km drive from Hobart to Mt Field through the Derwent River Valley and Bushy Park is an absolute stunner, with river rapids, hop fields, old oast houses, rows of poplars and hawthorn hedgerows. There's no public transport to the park, but some Hobart-based tour operators offer Mt Field day trips; try Tours Tasmania (p66).

Derwent Valley Link (p91) runs buses from Hobart to New Norfolk ($8.30) three to 13 times daily, with one service daily continuing to Westerway ($13.30) and Ellendale ($17.80).

HOBART & AROUND MT FIELD NATIONAL PARK

Tasman Peninsula & Port Arthur

Best Places to Eat

➡ Doo-Lishus Food Caravan (p100)

➡ Bangor Wine & Oyster Shed (p98)

➡ Dunalley Waterfront Café & Gallery (p98)

➡ Cubed (p100)

Best Places to Stay

➡ Larus Waterfront Cottage (p102)

➡ Brick Point Cottage (p105)

➡ Sea Change Safety Cove (p105)

Why Go?

Just an hour from Hobart lie the staggering coastal landscapes, sandy beaches and historic sites of the Tasman Peninsula. Bushwalking, surfing, sea-kayaking, diving and rock-climbing opportunities abound – all good reasons to extend your visit beyond a hurried day trip from Hobart.

Don't miss visiting the peninsula's legendary 300m-high sea cliffs – the tallest in the southern hemisphere – which will dose you up on natural awe. Most of the cliffs are protected by Tasman National Park, a coastal enclave embracing chunky offshore islands and underwater kelp forests. Within the national park, the fabulous Three Capes Track is enticing hikers from across the planet to experience this amazing landscape.

Waiting portentously at the end of Arthur Hwy is Port Arthur, the infamous and allegedly escape-proof penal colony dating from the early 19th century. Today kids kick footballs and families cook sausages on the BBQs here, but it's impossible to totally blank out the tragedy of this place, both historically and more recently.

When to Go

➡ Tasman Peninsula weather is at its most reliable from November to March, but from December to February be prepared for crowds at the Port Arthur Historic Site (especially on weekends). Alternatively, visiting Port Arthur during winter (June to August) makes the experience even more confronting and atmospheric.

➡ Tackling the Tasman Peninsula's surf breaks and bushwalking tracks – including the epic Three Capes Track – is definitely best done during the warmer months: aim for January to April.

➡ Fresh-fruit fans should visit from December to January, when boughs at the Sorell Fruit Farm hang heavy with ripe varieties.

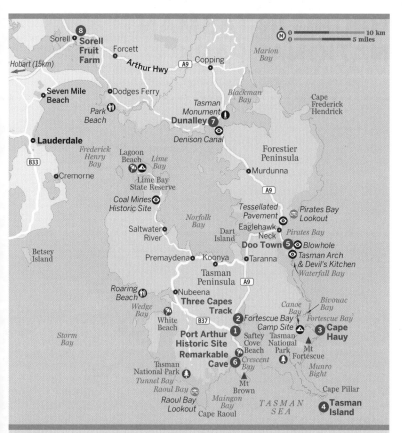

Tasman Peninsula & Port Arthur Highlights

❶ Port Arthur Historic Site (p103) Paying your respects to the past, both distant and recent.

❷ Three Capes Track (p96) Ticking this epic walking trail off your 'to do' list.

❸ Roaring 40s Kayaking (p103) Exploring the wild, broken coastline around Cape Hauy.

❹ Tasman Island Cruises (p105) Spotting seals and dolphins (and maybe even a whale) on a cruise around Tasman Island from Port Arthur.

❺ Doo Town (p99) Reading 'doo' name plaques en route to the Blowhole, Tasman Arch and Devil's Kitchen.

❻ Remarkable Cave (p102) Watching the waves surge in and out of this remarkable gulch.

❼ Bangor Wine & Oyster Shed (p98) Slurping down some briny bivalves and excellent local wine in Dunalley.

❽ Sorell Fruit Farm (p98) Picking some fresh raspberries, apricots, silvanberries, strawberries, cherries, apricots, peaches...

❶ Getting There & Away

Tassielink (p306) is the main bus-service provider on the Tasman Peninsula, stopping at all the major towns en route from Hobart down to Port Arthur, Monday to Saturday (Monday, Wednesday, Friday and Saturday only during school holidays). If you're driving, the same route is an easy 1½-hour drive if you don't dawdle.

HIKING IN TASMAN NATIONAL PARK

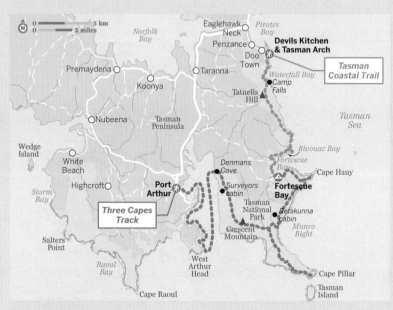

THREE CAPES TRACK

START PORT ARTHUR HISTORIC SITE
END FORTESCUE BAY
DURATION/DISTANCE 4 DAYS/46KM
DIFFICULTY MODERATE

The **Three Capes Track** (☎ 1300 827 727; www.threecapestrack.com.au; adult/child $495/396) is a four-day, three-night hike, with a boat trip from Port Arthur Historic Site to the trailhead, a bus ride back to Port Arthur at the end, and excellent hut accommodation en route. Walkers don't actually set foot (boot) on Cape Raoul: the boat from Port Arthur skirts around the coastline (caves, bays, sea cliffs), then drops you at Denmans Cove, from where it's a two-hour, 4km hike to the Surveyors cabin. Cape Raoul shows itself spectacularly from the deck here. Day two involves a longer hike (11km, up to five hours) via eucalypt forests, Mt Arthur and Crescent Mountain, before bunking down in Munro cabin with view of Munro Bight and Cape Hauy. Day three (17km, up to six hours) winds up at Retakunna cabin, after trekking out to the vertiginous Cape Pillar. Day four (14km, up to seven hours) sees hikers tackling Cape Hauy, before finishing up on the sandy shores of Fortescue Bay. There might even be time for a swim before the bus ride back to Port Arthur.

The three fabulous eco-cabins en route are set up like youth hostels, with four- and eight-bed dorms and comfortable mattresses, plus communal areas with heating, gas cooktops, tables, seating and panoramic decks (even board games, phone chargers and yoga mats!). A resident ranger is on hand.

Since opening in late 2015 the track has proved to be hugely popular – so much so that numbers are capped at 48 walkers per day, walking in one direction, so there will always be a bunk available. Book online, waaay ahead. Kids can walk the trail too.

If you don't want to walk the trail independently, there are a couple of commercial guided-walk companies operating here, including **Park Trek** (☎ 03-5639 2615; www.park

The ambitious Three Capes Track traverses the majestic cliff tops of Cape Raoul, Cape Pillar and Cape Hauy within Tasman National Park. Also here is the Tasman Coastal Trail: shorter, easier and (almost) as scenic.

- -

trek.com.au) and **Life's An Adventure** (☑0457 002 482, 02-9975 4553; www.lifesanadventure. com.au; per person from $1499). The upmarket guided, fully-catered Three Capes Lodge Walk (same walk, fancier accommodation) opened in late 2018; see www.taswalkingco. com.au for the latest.

TASMAN COASTAL TRAIL

START DEVIL'S KITCHEN, EAGLEHAWK NECK
END FORTESCUE BAY
DURATION/DISTANCE 2 DAYS/19KM
DIFFICULTY EASY

Within Tasman National Park, the 19km **Tasman Coastal Trail** (☑03-6250 3980; www. parks.tas.gov.au; Tasmans Arch Rd, Doo Town; park day pass per person/vehicle $12/24; ☺24hr) between Fortescue Bay and Devil's Kitchen has been somewhat outshined recently by the big-ticket Three Capes Track, which everybody clamours to do. But this excellent track still packs a superscenic punch, and won't burn nearly as big a hole into your wallet (only standard national park entry fees apply).

You can walk the trail in either direction – north–south from Devil's Kitchen near Eaglehawk Neck to Fortescue Bay, or the other way around – and knock it off in a brisk nine hours if you put your head down. But if your head is down, you'll miss all the views! We recommend making it an overnighter: bring a tent and a fuel stove, and camp at either Bivouac Bay (if you're walking from the north) or Camp Falls (if you're walking from the south). You can also camp at photogenic Fortescue Bay itself, before or after your hike.

From the north, park your car (or arrange to be dropped off) at the Devil's Kitchen car park. Devil's Kitchen is a spectacularly collapsed archway in the sea cliffs, with waves surging in and out below. Tasman Arch nearby is the 'before' model, with the massive stone arch still intact. From here it's around a 2km hike to Waterfall Bay, via coastal heathlands and cliff-top viewing platforms. At Waterfall Bay itself, a feathery white plume falls 200m from the cliff tops into the sea (the amount of water falling depends on recent rains).

Passing Camp Falls and the adjunct camp site, the trail departs the cliff tops and ascends Tatnells Hill, before returning to the coast near becalmed Bivouac Bay, where you can camp (basic toilets). The trail then hugs the coast for 10km to Fortescue Bay, via Canoe Bay where you can snorkel out to see a rusty wreck of the *William Pitt* protruding from the brine. Cool off with another dip in Fortescue Bay itself and camp another night (toilets, cold showers, fireplaces and gas BBQs; bookings advised in summer). From here it's a 12km dirt-road drive back out to the Arthur Hwy. There's no public transport into Fortescue Bay, so arrange to have someone pick you up.

Sorell

☑ 03 / POP 2480

Sorell is one of Tasmania's oldest towns, settled in 1808 primarily to supply locally processed wheat and flour to the rest of the colony, but its historic aura has tarnished over time. These days it's a T-junction service town with more petrol stations and fast-food joints than anything else, but it remains the gateway to the Tasman Peninsula. Most people just breeze through, but there are a couple of decent places to eat and stay around here.

◉ Sights & Activities

Sorell Fruit Farm   FARM
(☑03-6265 3100; www.sorellfruitfarm.com; 174 Pawleena Rd; per container from $8; ☺10am-4pm Oct & Mar-May, 9am-5pm Nov-Feb) Pick your own fruit (15 different kinds including strawberries, raspberries, cherries, apricots, peaches, apples and loganberries) at this intensively planted 5-hectare farm, or grab a bite and a coffee at the cafe (items $8 to $16). December and January are the best months for variety, but different fruits are in season at different times – check the website for a nifty chart. Head east through Sorell towards Port Arthur; you'll see Pawleena signposted on your left.

Island Surf School   SURFING
(☑ 0400 830 237, 03-6265 9776; www.islandsurf school.com.au; Park Beach, Dodges Ferry; 2hr group lesson per person $40) Hit the surf with a lesson or two at Park Beach at Dodges Ferry, not far south of Sorell. All gear, including wetsuits, is provided. Bookings essential.

🛏 Sleeping & Eating

Steele's Island Retreat   RENTAL HOUSE $$
(☑0438 733 215, 03-6265 8077; www.steeles island.com; via River St, Carlton Beach; d/houses from $125/540, extra adult/child $20/10) Wanna play castaway? This private headland (accessed over a sandy causeway via a little bridge) is at the mouth of the Carlton River, 16km south of Sorell. On offer is a large beach house sleeping 12, and two two-bedroom cottages for couples or small families. It's a terrific spot, with gentle surf and sunset views across the water.

Velvet   CAFE $
(☑03-6265 2444; 21 Gordon St; mains $8-17; ☺5am-4pm Mon-Fri, 6am-4pm Sat & Sun) Open early to snare the passing trucker trade, Velvet is a modest-looking, brown weatherboard cafe on Sorell's main street, decked out with retro furniture. On your plate are trucker-sized burgers, schnitzels and seafood fry-ups, plus cakes, muffins and sandwiches. Kick-starting coffee too, if you're not too long out of bed. Great value.

ℹ Information

Sorell Visitor Information Centre (☑03-6269 2924; www.tasmanregion.com.au; 16 Gordon St; ☺10am-4pm May-Sep, 9am-5pm Oct-Apr; ☎) For maps and peninsula info. Pick up the *Tasman – The Essence of Tasmania* booklet, which covers the peninsula's key sites.

ℹ Getting There & Away

The Tassielink (p306) service down the Tasman Peninsula from Hobart stops at Sorell ($7.60, 40 minutes).

Dunalley

☑ 03 / POP 310

The thickly timbered Forestier Peninsula – the precursor peninsula you'll cross en route to the Tasman Peninsula – is connected to mainland Tasmanian soil by the isthmus town of Dunalley. Much of the area was ravaged by bushfires in 2013, but is greening up again nicely. At Dunalley itself, the Denison Canal (1905) bisects the isthmus, providing a short cut for small boats. There's not a whole lot to do here, nor anywhere outstanding to stay, but there are a couple of good foodie haunts if you're hungry.

🍴 Eating

★**Bangor Wine & Oyster Shed**   SEAFOOD $$
(☑03-6253 5558; www.bangorshed.com.au; 20 Blackman Bay Rd; 12 oysters from $28.50, mains $18-49; ☺10am-5pm; ☎) Turn left 1km beyond the Denison Canal to discover this excellent foodie haunt. It's a black-stained timber shed, hosting a winery cellar door (the cool-climate pinot noir rocks) and restaurant, where you can sample the local oysters (try the Mignonette dressing: red wine vinegar, shallots and pepper), a tasting platter, or more substantial mains (sautéd abalone, calamari salad).

★**Dunalley Waterfront Café & Gallery**   CAFE $$
(☑03-6253 5122; www.dunalleywaterfrontcafe. com; 4 Imlay St; mains $16-43; ☺9am-4pm Wed-Mon) With its broad outdoor deck and views across the water, this bright, airy cafe

COAL MINES HISTORIC SITE

At Premaydena, take the signposted turn-off (the C431) 13km northwest to Saltwater River and the restored ruins at the Coal Mines Historic Site (☑ 03-6251 2310, 1800 659 101; www.coalmines.org.au; Coal Mine Rd, via Saltwater River; ☺ daylight hours) FREE , a powerful reminder of the colonial past. Excavated in 1833, the coal mines were used to punish the worst of the convicts, who worked here in abominable conditions. The poorly managed mining operation wasn't economically viable, and in 1848 it was sold to a private enterprise. Within 10 years it was abandoned. Some buildings were demolished; fire and weather put paid to the rest.

These days the site is managed by the Port Arthur Historic Site Management Authority and is one of the Unesco Australian Convict Sites World Heritage properties. A low-key contrast to Port Arthur, the old mines are interesting to wander around, following a trail of interpretative panels. You can snoop around the well-preserved solitary-confinement cells, which are torturously small and dark. If you want to stay nearby, Tigerbay Retreat (☑ 0414 851 962; www.tigerbayretreat.com.au; 719 & 724 Saltwater River Rd, Saltwater River; houses $210-285) comprises two self-contained historic homes – the Surgeon's Cottage (sleeping six) and Semaphore House (sleeping eight) – both dating back to the convict era, now lovingly restored and with plenty of beds.

is a Dunalley culinary hot spot. The menu ranges from seafood pie with potato gratin to a pulled-pork sandwich with fennel slaw and chilli aioli. Homemade cakes, pizzas, brilliant coffee and Tasmanian wines are further excuses to linger. The funky gallery showcases local artists.

❶ Getting There & Away

The Tassielink (p306) Tasman Peninsula service will take you to Dunalley from Hobart ($14, one hour).

Eaglehawk Neck

☑ 03 / POP 340

Eaglehawk Neck is the second isthmus you'll cross heading south to Port Arthur, this one connecting the Forestier Peninsula to the Tasman Peninsula. In convict days, the 100m-wide Neck had a row of ornery dogs chained across it to prevent convicts from escaping – the infamous Dogline. Timber platforms were also built in narrow Eaglehawk Bay to the west, and stocked with yet more ferocious dogs to prevent convicts from wading around the Dogline. To discourage swimming, rumours were circulated that the waters were shark infested – the occasional white pointer does indeed shimmy through these waters, but 'infested' is an overstatement. Remarkably, despite these measures, several convicts made successful bids for freedom.

Eaglehawk Neck is the northern access point to Tasman National Park. The natural landscape around here is astonishing, with huge stone arches, blowholes, cliffs, craggy shoreline terraces and a superb surf beach.

◉ Sights

Pirates Bay Lookout   VIEWPOINT
(www.eaglehawkneck.org/attractions/pirates-bay-lookout; Pirates Bay Dr) FREE As you approach Eaglehawk Neck from the north, turn east onto Pirates Bay Dr for eye-popping views across Pirates Bay, the Neck and the jagged coastline to the south. Is the Cubed (p100) coffee van in attendance?

Blowhole, Tasman Arch
& Devil's Kitchen   LANDMARK
(www.eaglehawkneck.org/attractions; off Blowhole Rd, Doo Town) FREE For a close-up look at the spectacular coastline just south of Eaglehawk Neck, follow the signs to the Blowhole, Tasman Arch (a cavern-like natural bridge) and Devil's Kitchen (a rugged 60m-deep cleft). Watch out for sporadic bursts at the Blowhole, and keep behind the fences at the other sites – the cliff edges tend to decay. On the road to the Blowhole, look for the signposted 4km gravel road leading to Waterfall Bay, which has further photo-worthy views.

Doo Town   VILLAGE
(www.eaglehawkneck.org/attractions/doo-town; Blowhole Rd, Doo Town) No one is really sure how it all started, but the raggedy collection of fishing shacks at Doo Town (3km south of Eaglehawk Neck on the way to the Blowhole) all contain the word 'Doo' in their names.

There's the sexy 'Doo Me', the approving 'We Doo', the Beatles-esque 'Love Me Doo', and (our favourite) the melancholic 'Doo Write'. We doo hope the new breed of architecturally adventurous beach houses here maintain the tradition. Definitely worth a dootour.

Eaglehawk Neck
Historic Site   HISTORIC SITE, MUSEUM
(☑03-6214 8100, 1300 135 513; www.parks.tas.gov.au; Arthur Hwy; ⊙24hr, museum 9am-3.30pm) **FREE** Down on the Eaglehawk Neck isthmus – where once the barking Dogline dissuaded convicts escaping from Port Arthur and the Tasman Peninsula to the south – the only remaining structure from the convict days is the **Officers Quarters Museum** (1832; as it happens, the oldest wooden military building in Australia). Inside is a series of rooms loaded with historical info, covering the Dogline, escapee prisoners and the erudite bushranger Martin Cash.

Tessellated Pavement   LANDMARK
(www.eaglehawkneck.org/attractions/tesselated-pavement; off Pirates Bay Dr) **FREE** At the northern end of Pirates Bay, a short trail leads to a rocky coastal terrace that has curiously eroded into what looks like tiled paving (bring your camera). At low tide you can walk along the foreshore to **Clydes Island**, where there are several graves and wicked coastline panoramas down to Cape Hauy.

🏃 Activities

The excellent 19km Tasman Coastal Trail (p97) kicks off at the Devil's Kitchen car park near Doo Town (the Waterfall Bay Walk forms the first part of this longer hike).

Waterfall Bay Walk   WALKING
(☑03-6250 3980; www.parks.tas.gov.au; Tasmans Arch Rd, Doo Town; park day pass per person/vehicle $12/24) From the car park at Devil's Kitchen, take the 1½-hour return hike to Waterfall Bay inside Tasman National Park. Much of the walk is through a forest that somewhat obscures the view, but the track stays close to the water and there are plenty of places to stop and gawp. The namesake waterfall plunges into the sea after rains.

Eaglehawk Dive Centre   DIVING
(☑03-6250 3566; www.eaglehawkdive.com.au; 178 Pirates Bay Dr) Runs underwater explorations (sea caves, giant kelp forests, a sea-lion colony and shipwrecks) and a range of Professional Association of Diving Instructors (PADI) courses. A one-day introduction to diving costs $325 (no experience necessary); a two-day learn-to-dive PADI course is $655. Two boat dives per person with/without gear is $215/115. Basic accommodation for divers also available (powered sites/dorm/double $30/30/80).

🛏 Sleeping & Eating

Lufra Hotel & Apartments   HOTEL, APARTMENT $$
(☑03-6250 3262; www.lufrahotel.com; 380 Pirates Bay Dr; hotel tw/d/f from $145/145/185, 1-/2-bedroom units from $210/300; ☎) This chowder-coloured old naughty-weekender (1949) is an icon in this neck of the woods (neck of the Neck?), with million-dollar views over Pirates Bay. The owners are progressively renovating the modest rooms in the original building, or there are newer self-contained one- and two-bedroom units off to one side. The downstairs cafe-bistro plates up pub classics (mains $20 to $35).

★ Doo-Lishus Food Caravan   FAST FOOD $
(☑0437 469 412; www.tasmanregion.com.au/doo-lishus; Blowhole Rd, Doo Town; meals $5-17; ⊙8.45am-6pm late Sep-Apr) At the Blowhole car park in Doo Town, this unexpected caravan serves up fresh berry smoothies, beaut fish and chips and the best curried-scallop pies in Tasmania (we should know – we conducted an extensive survey). Excellent rabbit and venison pies too.

★ Cubed   CAFE $
(☑0439 001 588; www.facebook.com/cubed espresso; Pirates Bay Lookout, Pirates Bay Dr; snacks from $3.50; ⊙9am-3pm Thu-Mon, closed Jun-Aug) 🌿 This restored 1957 caravan parks at the Pirates Bay Lookout and doles out fastidiously prepared coffee and snacks to passers-by. It's a low-impact, sustainable operation – solar powered, and using milk, coffee and ingredients traceable back to local farm level. If it's sunny, the cheery NZ-German owners provide a telescope to amuse and Persian rugs and cushions to perch on.

ℹ Getting There & Away

Tassielink (p306) can bus you from Hobart to Eaglehawk Neck (1½ hours, $21).

Taranna
☑03 / POP 280

Taranna is a small town strung out along the shores of Norfolk Bay about 10km north of Port Arthur, its name coming from an

Aboriginal word meaning 'hunting ground'. Historically important, it was once the terminus for Australia's first railway, which rattled its way here from Long Bay near Port Arthur. This public transport was powered by convicts, who pushed the carriages uphill, then jumped aboard for the downhill run. Not far offshore, Dart Island was used as a semaphore station to relay messages from Port Arthur to Hobart. Today, the waters near the island are used for oyster farming. Back on dry land, you'll find some passable accommodation, plus a couple of diverting pit stops.

◉ Sights

Tasmanian Devil Unzoo WILDLIFE RESERVE
(☑ 1800 641 641; www.tasmaniandevilunzoo. com.au; 5990 Arthur Hwy; adult/child/family $35/19.50/85, tour incl admission $99/55/249; ☺ 9am-5pm, to 6pm Dec-Feb) Taranna's main attraction is this 'unzoo', an unfenced enclave of native bushland where wildlife comes and goes of its own accord. Species you might encounter include native hens, wallabies, quolls, eagles, wattlebirds, pademelons and, of course, Tasmanian devils, which you can see being fed every hour. Walking trails extend to 2.5km, or take a Devil Tracker 4WD tour to learn about the fight against Devil Facial Tumour Disease (DFTD), which afflicts a huge percentage of the wild population.

⌂ Sleeping

Taranna Cottages CABIN $
(☑ 03-6250 3436; www.tarannacottages.com.au; 19 Nubeena Rd; unpowered/powered sites from $10/20, d $112-138, extra adult/child $24/12) This value-for-money enterprise at the southern end of Taranna features self-contained accommodation in two neat-as-a-pin apple-pickers' cottages relocated from the Huon Valley, and a railway building from the Midlands. It's a quiet bush setting, with open fires and breakfast provisions (free-range eggs, homemade jams) for a few dollars extra. Camp sites also available.

The lovingly curated **Tasman Historical Museum** (adult/child/family $10/5/25; www. tasmanhistoricalmuseum.com.au) is here too, looking at local Aboriginal, convict and social history, with a little adjunct cafe if you're feeling peckish.

Mussel Boys CABIN $$
(☑ 03-6290 0073; www.themusselboys.com.au; 5927 Arthur Hwy; d from $195; ❋) These four nattily designed studio cabins are all grey and navy blue, with compact kitchens, king-size beds, spa baths, polished floorboards and leather couches. They're cleverly spaced around a grassy embankment above the main road, affording a degree of privacy and views across the road to the bay. Sit on your dinky deck and see what you can see.

❶ Getting There & Away

The Tassielink (p306) Tasman Peninsula service calls in at Taranna ($21, 1¾ hours) en route from Hobart to Port Arthur.

Koonya, Nubeena & White Beach

Just past Taranna is the Nubeena Rd turn-off, depositing you 6km later in diminutive Koonya (population 100). It was originally called 'Cascades', and 400 convicts once toiled on the farms here, but there's not a whole lot of shakin' going on these days.

About 12km further along is Nubeena (population 490), the largest town on the peninsula, fanned out along the shore of Wedge Bay. It's much more low-key than Port Arthur – it's really just an easygoing holiday destination for locals – but if all the other accommodation on the peninsula is booked out (trust us, it happens, you might be able to find a bed here. There's also a supermarket, a tavern and a good cafe.

White Beach (population 290) is yet another snoozy holiday enclave about 6km southwest of Nubeena. There are no shops or services here, but the beach is lovely for a swim (yes, it's white).

⚘ Activities

The main things to do around Nubeena are swimming and chilling out on nearby White Beach, or fishing from the jetty or foreshore. Down a side road 3km south of Nubeena is some energetic walking to **Tunnel Bay** (five hours return), **Raoul Bay Lookout** (two hours return) and the exquisitely named **Cape Raoul** (five hours return). Just off this part of the coast is **Shipsterns Bluff**, known by surfers as the gnarliest, meanest, heaviest, biggest wave in Australia (not for beginners). To the north is **Roaring Beach**, which also gets wicked surf, but isn't safe for swimming.

DON'T MISS

REMARKABLE CAVE

About 7.5km south of Port Arthur is Remarkable Cave (www.eaglehawkneck.org/gateway-to/remarkable-cave; Safety Cove Rd) FREE, a long tunnel eroded from the base of a collapsed gully, under a cliff and out to sea. The waves surge through the tunnel and fill the gully with sea spray (and sometimes water – watch out!). A boardwalk and 115 steps provide access to a metal viewing platform. Believe it or not, hard-core surfers often brave the cave, paddling out through the opening to surf the offshore reefs beyond.

From the car park here follow the coast east to Maingon Blowhole (one hour return) or further on to Mt Brown (four hours return), from which there are magical views. Isolated Crescent Bay is also a four-hour return walk – a magical arc of white sand, seemingly on the edge of the known universe.

🛏 Sleeping & Eating

White Beach Tourist Park CARAVAN PARK **$**
(☑03-6250 2142; www.whitebeachtouristpark.com.au; 128 White Beach Rd, White Beach; unpowered sites $20-33, powered sites $25-40, cabins from $100, extra adult/child $20/10) This beachfront park rests in quiet splendour south of Nubeena. Facilities include laundry, shop, playground, prim cabins with awnings and barbecue areas with impossibly well-manicured lawns. Ask about local walks (though you'll probably only get as far as the beach).

★**Larus Waterfront Cottage** RENTAL HOUSE **$$**
(☑0457 758 711; www.larus.com.au; 576 White Beach Rd, White Beach; d $205-240) Contemporary design, a marine colour scheme, audacious views and all mod cons (big-screen TV, gas cooking, flash barbecue) equate to a great Tasman Peninsula bolthole. It's in a quiet spot with just a narrow strip of scrub between you and the sea. You'll be spending a lot of time sitting, sipping and admiring the sunset from the wraparound deck. Sleeps four.

★**Lucky Ducks** CAFE **$$**
(☑03-6250 2777; 1665 Main Rd, Nubeena; breakfast $10-20, lunch & dinner $23-38; ☺5-8pm Sun-Wed, 9.30am-8pm Sat) With huge picture windows, this bright, all-day waterfront food room is perfect for coffee and cake, a beer, a glass of wine, or all of them in sequence.

Other options include excellent gourmet pies, tarts, filo rolls and a spicy lamb *tagine*. The huge bacon-and-egg breakfast with 24-hour-marinated mushrooms is famous (in Nubeena, at any rate). Winter hours are much reduced.

ℹ Getting There & Away

Tassielink (p306) will take you from Hobart to Koonya (1¾ hours, $24.20). The bus continues to Nubeena (also $24.20, two hours), before looping around to Port Arthur.

Fortescue Bay & Tasman National Park

Sequestered 12km down a gravel road from the highway (the turn-off is halfway between Taranna and Port Arthur) is becalmed Fortescue Bay, with a sweeping sandy arc backed by thickly forested slopes. The sheltered bay was one of the semaphore-station sites used during the convict period to relay messages to and from Eaglehawk Neck. Early last century a timber mill was in operation, and the boilers and jetty ruins are still visible near Mill Creek, plus the remains of tramways used to collect the timber. The mill closed in 1952.

Fortescue Bay is one of the main access points for Tasman National Park (☑03-6250 3980; www.parks.tas.gov.au; via Fortescue Bay or Eaglehawk Neck, Tasman Peninsula; park day pass per person/vehicle $12/24), encompassing the territory around Cape Raoul, Cape Hauy, Cape Pillar (home to the Three Capes Track), plus Tasman Island and up the rugged coast north to Eaglehawk Neck. Here you'll find the tallest sea cliffs in the southern hemisphere (300m!), while offshore, dolphins, seals, penguins and whales are regular passers-by.

🚶 Activities

Several walking tracks kick off at Fortescue Bay, including the excellent Tasman Coastal Trail (p97), tracing the shoreline to the Devil's Kitchen car park at Doo Town near Eaglehawk Neck (nine hours one way).

Fortescue Bay is also the finishing point for the Three Capes Track (p96), winding its way here via Cape Raoul, Cape Pillar and Cape Hauy. You can walk some of the way in the other direction (east) from Fortescue to Cape Hauy (four to five hours return) – a well-used path leading out to sea cliffs with sensational views of the famous Candlestick and Totem Pole sea stacks. To get into some rainforest, follow the same track towards Cape Hauy, then take the steep side track to Mt Fortescue (six to seven hours return).

★Roaring 40s Kayaking   KAYAKING
(☎0455 949 777; www.roaring40skayaking.com.au; per person $220; ⊗8am Mon & Fri Nov-Apr) Roaring 40s conducts epic sea-kayaking day tours around the Tasman Peninsula, paddling past the monumental coastline of Cape Hauy in Tasman National Park. Prices include equipment, lunch and transfers from Hobart. Minimum age 16.

🛌 Sleeping

Fortescue Bay Camp Site   CAMPGROUND $
(☎03-6250 2433; www.parks.tas.gov.au; Fortescue Rd; unpowered sites per 2 people/family $13/16, extra adult/child $5/2.50) Dream the night away to the sound of gentle surf within Tasman National Park. There are no powered sites and showers are cold, but fireplaces and gas BBQs compensate. National-park fees apply (park day pass per person/vehicle $12/24) in addition to camping fees. Book ahead during summer and BYO supplies. There's a basic shop.

ℹ️ Getting There & Away

No public transport runs to Fortescue Bay. Unless you're bussing out of here after completing the Three Capes Track, you'll need your own vehicle. The turn-off is midway between Taranna and Port Arthur; it's a 12km gravel road down to the bay.

Port Arthur

🎵 03 / POP 250

In 1830 Governor Arthur chose beautiful Port Arthur on the Tasman Peninsula as the ideal place to confine prisoners who had committed further crimes in the colony. It was a 'natural penitentiary' – the peninsula is connected to the mainland by Eaglehawk Neck, a strip of land less than 100m wide, where ferocious guard dogs and tales of shark-infested waters deterred escape.

Despite its redemption as a major tourist site (the ruins here are undeniably amazing), Port Arthur remains a sombre place. Don't expect to remain unaffected by what you see: there's a sadness here that's palpable, and a Gothic pall of woe that can cloud your senses on even the sunniest of days. Compounding this, in April 1996 a young gunman fired bullets indiscriminately at the community, murdering 35 people and injuring 37 more. After burning down a guesthouse, he was finally captured and remains imprisoned north of Hobart.

After a major upgrade and redevelopment, the main visitor centre and restaurant at the site reopened in late 2017.

History

Between 1830 and 1877, 12,500 convicts did hard, brutal prison time at Port Arthur. For most it was hell on earth, but those who behaved often enjoyed better conditions than they'd endured in England and Ireland. Port Arthur became the hub of a network of penal stations on the peninsula, its fine buildings sustaining thriving convict-labour industries, including timber milling, ship-building, coal mining, shoemaking, and brick and nail production.

Australia's first railway literally 'ran' the 7km between Norfolk Bay at Taranna and Long Bay near Port Arthur: convicts pushed the carriages along the tracks. A semaphore telegraph system allowed speedy communication between Port Arthur, other peninsula outstations and Hobart. Convict farms provided fresh vegetables, a boys' prison was built at Point Puer to reform and educate juvenile convicts, and a church was erected.

◉ Sights

★Port Arthur Historic Site   HISTORIC SITE
(☎1800 659 101, 03-6251 2310; www.portarthur.org.au; 6973 Arthur Hwy; adult/child/family $39/17/99; ⊗tours & buildings 9am-5pm, grounds to dusk) This amazing Unesco World Heritage–listed convict site is one of Tasmania's big-ticket attractions. The dozens of structures here are best interpreted via guided tour (included with admission). The feared Separate Prison was built to punish prisoners through isolation and sensory deprivation (bad vibes? What bad vibes?). The 1836 church burned down in 1884; the penitentiary was originally a granary. The shell of the Broad Arrow Café, scene of many of the 1996 shootings, has been preserved as a memorial garden. Buggy transport around the site can be arranged for people with restricted mobility. The ferry plying the harbour is also wheelchair accessible.

Port Arthur

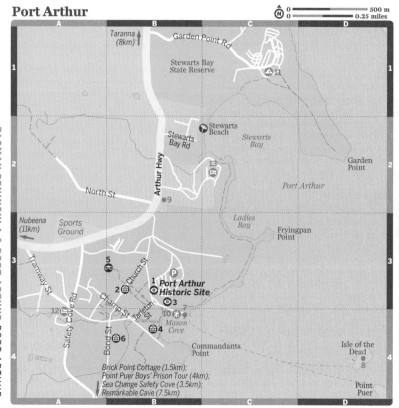

Port Arthur

Tours

The 40-minute Port Arthur Historic Site **guided tour** is included in the admission price and departs regularly from the visitor centre. It's an excellent introduction to the site, visiting all the old buildings. Also included in the ticket price is a 25-minute **harbour cruise**, with commentary, past Point Puer Boys' Prison and the Isle of the Dead cemetery. When you buy your ticket you'll be told the times of the next tour and cruise. You can also download an **audio tour** ($3) app for the site, or pick up an audio tour iPod ($6) at the main entrance.

★**Tasman Island Cruises** BOATING
(Pennicott Wilderness Journeys; ☎03-6250 2200; www.tasmancruises.com.au; 6961 Arthur Hwy; adult/child/family $135/85/430; ⓧ9.15am year-round, plus 1.15pm mid-Dec–mid-Apr) Boat trips departing the Pennicott Wilderness

Journeys office near Port Arthur incorporate a three-hour adventure cruise past the Tasman Peninsula's most spectacular coastal scenery, plus Port Arthur admission. You can also start the tour at Hobart, taking the tour bus down to Port Arthur, then back again after the boat ride (adult/child $225/165 not including Port Arthur admission, $260/180 including Port Arthur).

Ghost Tour TOURS
(✆1800 659 101; www.portarthur.org.au/activities/port-arthur-ghost-tour; Port Arthur Historic Site, 6973 Arthur Hwy; adult/child/family $26.50/15/75; ☉dusk) This 90-minute, lantern-lit tour of the Port Arthur Historic Site leaves from the main entrance nightly at dusk (rain or shine), visiting a number of historic buildings, with guides relating ghoulish occurrences. Bookings essential; leave the little kids at home.

Isle of the Dead Cemetery Tour TOURS
(✆1800 659 101; www.portarthur.org.au/activities/isle-of-the-dead; Port Arthur Historic Site, 6973 Arthur Hwy; combined site entry & tour adult/child/family $59/27/144; ☉site 9am-5pm) A detailed guided tour through Port Arthur's old burial ground on a spooky island in the harbour, with more than 1000 long-slumbering residents. Usually departs at 11am and 1pm daily, with additional tours during peak seasons (summer, school holidays, Easter).

Point Puer Boys' Prison Tour TOURS
(✆1800 659 101; www.portarthur.org.au/tickets/site-entry-point-puer-boys-prison-tour; Port Arthur Historic Site, 6973 Arthur Hwy; combined site entry & tour adult/child/family $59/27/144; ☉site 9am-5pm) This tour visits the first reformatory in the British Empire built for juvenile male convicts (aged nine to 18). Two-hour tours usually depart at 1.40pm daily.

Tours from Hobart

Under Down Under TOURS
(✆1800 444 442; www.underdownunder.com.au; per person $115) Guided backpacker-style day trips to Port Arthur, including accommodation pick-up, admission fees, a guided walk and a harbour cruise. There's also a quick look at Richmond en route.

Tours Tasmania TOURS
(✆1800 777 103; www.tourstas.com.au; per person $125) Good-value, small-group day tours to Port Arthur (including admission fees, walking tour and harbour cruise) via Richmond,

ℹ️ PORT ARTHUR ADMISSION

The basic Port Arthur historic site (p103) entry pass includes admission to the site, a 40-minute guided tour and a 25-minute harbour cruise, and is valid for daytime entry for two consecutive days. Optional tours to Isle of the Dead and Point Puer Boys' Prison (or both) can be added to the pass. Tickets to the Ghost Tour are independent of site admission (you don't have to buy a site entry pass to go on the Ghost Tour).

It's possible to prebook passes and tours online or by phone – recommended during summer and school holidays.

Devil's Kitchen and Tasman Arch. Backpacker focused.

🛏️ Sleeping

Port Arthur Holiday Park CARAVAN PARK $
(✆1800 607 057; www.portarthurhp.com.au; Garden Point Rd, Port Arthur; unpowered/powered/en suite sites from $31/38/49, cabins from $120; ❄️ 🛜) Spacious and with plenty of greenery and singsong bird life, this park is 2km before Port Arthur within Stewarts Bay State Reserve, not far from a sheltered beach. Facilities are abundant, including a camp kitchen, wood BBQs, petrol pump and shop. The best (and only) budget option around these latitudes.

⭐ Brick Point Cottage RENTAL HOUSE $$
(✆0438 070 498; www.brickpointcottage.com.au; 241 Safety Cove Rd; up to 4 people from $170) Fronted by a dinky little white garage and some mysterious crumbling ruins (convict bricks?), Brick Point Cottage is an old-school Tassie shack with two bedrooms, compact kitchen, wood heater, sunny deck and daisy-dotted lawn arcing down to a sheltered reach of Carnarvon Bay. There are few more unpretentious, untouristy and affordable places to stay on the whole Tasman Peninsula.

Sea Change Safety Cove B&B $$
(✆03-6250 2719; www.safetycove.com; 425 Safety Cove Rd; d $200, 2-bedroom apt d $250, extra person $40; 🛜) Whichever way you look from this guesthouse, 4km south of Port Arthur, there are fantastic views: misty cliffs, sea-wracked Safety Cove Beach or scrub-by bushland. There are a couple of B&B rooms inside the house plus a self-contained

unit downstairs that sleeps five. Outside, camellia-filled gardens roll down to a beaut deck overlooking the beach (G&T anyone?).

Stewarts Bay Lodge
RESORT **$$**

(☑ 03-6250 2888; www.stewartsbaylodge.com.au; 6955 Arthur Hwy; 1-/2-/3-bedroom units from $165/260/340; ❄ 🛜) Arrayed around a gorgeous hidden cove (seemingly made for swimming and kayaking), Stewarts Bay Lodge combines older, rustic log cabins with newer deluxe units, some with private spa baths. You can cook something good in your contemporary kitchen, but you'll probably spend more time in the sleek Gabriel's on the Bay restaurant.

Port Arthur Villas
MOTEL **$$**

(☑ 03-6250 2239; www.portarthurvillas.com.au; 52 Safety Cove Rd; d/2-bedroom units from $210/235, extra adult/child $25/15; ❄ 🛜) This place has tidy self-contained units sleeping up to five, horseshoeing around the garden and outdoor barbecue area. Externally it's all faux-Victorian lace and brickwork, but inside things are a little more stylish, with mod bathrooms and kitchenettes. Walking distance to the historic site. Cheaper for multinight stays.

Eating

The newly refurbished restaurant at the historic site is called 1830 (serving dinner from 6pm). During the day, there's a cafe in the main visitor centre; drinks and snacks available at the restored Visiting Magistrate's House; and light meals at the Museum Coffee Shop in the old asylum.

Gabriel's on the Bay
MODERN AUSTRALIAN **$$**

(☑ 03-6250 2888; www.stewartsbaylodge.com.au; Stewarts Bay Lodge, 6955 Arthur Hwy; mains lunch $20-24, dinner $30-46; ⊙ 8-10am & noon-2pm daily, 5.30-8.30pm Thu-Mon) Oddly clad in orange-stained timber like a giant packing crate, upmarket Gabe's showcases local produce with Eaglehawk Neck oysters, pan-fried Tasmanian scallops with chilli, pancetta and garlic, and Tasmanian eye fillet with brandy pepper sauce. Definitely worth a detour if you're overnighting anywhere nearby. Bookings recommended.

Port Arthur Lavender
CAFE **$$**

(☑ 03-6250 3058; www.portarthurlavender.com.au; 6555 Arthur Hwy; mains $13-26; ⊙ 9am-8pm Jan & Feb, 9am-4pm Mar & Dec, 10am-4pm Apr-Nov) This contemporary shed just north of Port Arthur is part lavender farm, part lavender distillery, part lavender shop, but is mostly worth a stop for its all-day cafe. Expect the likes of seafood chowder, chilli-soy marinated squid, and deep-fried Tasmanian camembert with cucumber, beetroot and mint salad. Buy some lavender-infused hand cream afterwards if you must.

ⓘ Getting There & Away

Regional public-transport connections are surprisingly poor. Tassielink (p306) runs a weekday bus from Hobart to Port Arthur ($24.20, 2¼ hours) during school terms (reducing to Monday, Wednesday and Friday during school holidays), plus a morning and afternoon bus on Saturday. No bus on Sunday. Buses stop at the main towns en route.

The Southeast

Best Places to Eat

➡ Get Shucked Oyster Farm (p114)

➡ Lotus Eaters Cafe (p117)

➡ Summer Kitchen Bakery (p119)

➡ Pepperberries Garden Cafe (p116)

Best Places to Stay

➡ Red Gate Cottage (p113)

➡ 43 Degrees (p113)

➡ Jetty House (p122)

➡ The Shackeau (p123)

Why Go?

Still harbours, country villages and misty valleys – Tasmania's southeast has much to entice. The apple-producing heartland of the Apple Isle, this fertile area now also produces cherries, apricots, Atlantic salmon, wines, mushrooms, cheeses...and apple cider! The wide, tea-coloured Huon River remains the region's lifeblood. Courtesy of these southern latitudes and myriad waterways, the southeast is also known for its rainbows.

As you head south the fruity hillsides of the Huon Valley give way to the sparkling inlets of the D'Entrecasteaux Channel, with Bruny Island awaiting offshore. Hartz Mountains National Park is not far inland and, further south, the epic South Coast Track kicks off at magnificent Recherche Bay.

All sounding a bit French? French explorers Bruni d'Entrecasteaux and Nicolas Baudin charted much of the region's coastline in the 1790s and early 1800s, a good decade before the Brits hoisted the Union Jack at Risdon Cove near Hobart in 1803.

When to Go

➡ Peckish? Summer – from December to February – is definitely the time to visit the Southeast. The Huon Valley harvest is in, and roadside stalls are jam-packed with fresh produce, including juicy cherries and crisp apples

➡ The cool southern waters around Bruny Island are much more inviting in the summer sunshine. Alternatively, birdwatching fans should wing it here in October for the annual Bruny Island Bird Festival.

➡ January is the time to be in funky-hippie Cygnet for the annual Cygnet Folk Festival.

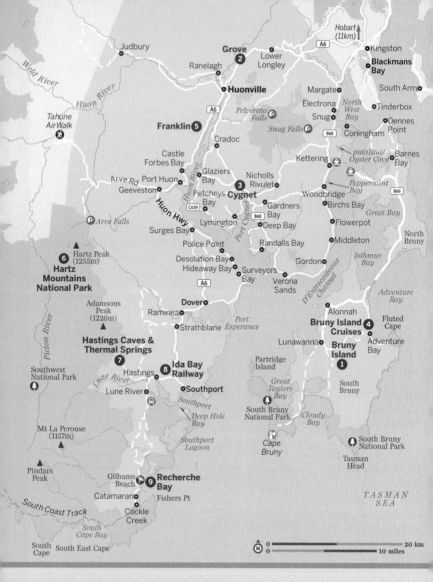

The Southeast Highlights

1 Bruny Island (p110)
Dropping in and out of mobile-phone reception for a couple of days.

2 Apple Shed (p118)
Sipping fine Huon Valley cider in Grove.

3 Cygnet Folk Festival (p117) Tuning in at this folksy January jamboree.

4 Bruny Island Cruises (p113) Exploring Bruny's ragged southern coastline.

5 Wooden Boat Centre (p118) Seeing a Huon-pine hull built in Franklin.

6 Hartz Mountains National Park (p120) Smiling at your reflection in an alpine tarn.

7 Hastings Caves & Thermal Springs (p122) Spelunking and swimming in warm pools.

8 Ida Bay Railway (p122) Riding this cute railway.

9 Recherche Bay (p123) Imagining French explorers anchored in this remote harbour.

ℹ️ Getting There & Away

There are bus services from Hobart through the main towns in the southeast, but having your own vehicle will give you much more flexibility and freedom to explore.

The ferry (p115) from Kettering to Bruny Island runs many times each way daily – it's a fun 20-minute ride across the D'Entrecasteaux Channel.

Margate

📞 03 / POP 3630

About 23km south of Hobart is small-town Margate, which sometimes feels more like a suburb of Hobart than a town in its own right. There are a few engaging pit stops here, including cafes, an excellent regional museum and an ancient train, stopped in its tracks and full of curious shops.

◉ Sights

★ **Channel Heritage Centre** MUSEUM
(📞03-6267 2333; www.channelheritagecentre.org; 1755 Channel Hwy; admission by donation; ⊙10am-4pm) This fabulous community-owned museum on the roadside just south of central Margate is well worth a stop. A series of intimate, passionately curated display spaces shines a light on local history, covering (among other things) Aboriginal culture, forestry, boating, fishing, whaling, schooling, toys, bushfires and military and migrant history. And check out the amazing collection of 700-plus cameras! An outstanding little museum.

Margate Train LANDMARK
(📞03-6267 1667; www.facebook.com/margatetrain; 1567 Channel Hwy; ⊙9am-5pm Sat-Thu, to 8pm Fri) FREE Margate Train is a chance for train geeks to gawk at Tasmania's last passenger train, the good ol' *Tasman Ltd,* which stopped chugging in 1978. It stands idly on a redundant section of track by the highway just north of town, and houses craft shops, a bookshop, antique dealers, a craft brewer, a pancake cafe and a provedore for picnic supplies.

Inverawe Native Gardens GARDENS
(📞03-6267 2020; www.inverawe.com.au; 1565 Channel Hwy; adult/child $12/4; ⊙9am-6pm Sep-May) Behind the Margate Train is Inverawe Native Gardens, a private, 9.5-hectare property with landscaped native gardens, trails, water views and 80 species of blow-through birds, including the 12 species endemic to Tasmania.

🍴 Eating & Drinking

Pancake Train Restaurant CAFE $$
(📞03-6267 1120; www.pancaketrain.com.au; Margate Train, 1567 Channel Hwy; snacks $5-10, mains $10-29; ⊙9am-5pm; 🚋) This upbeat flapjack shack occupies a carriage of the going-nowhere Margate Train. Order the Tasmanian-salmon version with creamy caper sauce.

Devils Brewery CRAFT BEER
(📞0412 163 772; www.devilsbrewery.com.au; Margate Train, 1567 Channel Hwy; ⊙10am-5pm Sat-Thu, to at least 6pm Fri, reduced winter hours) One of Tasmania's creative new breed of small craft-beer brewers (there were 21 of them last time we counted), Devils Brewery occupies a restored carriage in the stationary Margate Train (love the fire-extinguisher beer taps and the Tasmanian-oak bar). Tasting paddles are $10, or go straight for a pint of rye porter or wide-awake coffee stout.

ℹ️ Getting There & Away

Margate is connected to Hobart by Metro Tasmania (p84) buses, with routes 412, 413 and 415 to 418 trundling through town ($6.40, 40 minutes). Otherwise, it's a 25-minute drive south of Hobart.

Kettering

📞 03 / POP 990

Photogenic Kettering's sedate harbour shelters fishing boats and yachts in Oyster Cove Marina, next to the Bruny Island ferry terminal. Most folks just blow through en route to Bruny, but it's a pretty spot to pause for half a day if you've been running yourself ragged on your Tour de Tassie. For a little previsit inspiration, check out the Australian TV miniseries *The Kettering Incident* (2016), a small-town Gothic murder-mystery filmed hereabouts.

🧭 Tours

Sail Bruny BOATING
(📞0428 674 747; www.sailbruny.com; Oyster Cove Marina; per person $225, self-catered $195) Sail over to Bruny Island from pretty Kettering aboard the *Ubique of Hobart* yacht – technically a 32ft Bristol Channel Cutter. Day sails last 7½ hours, and include lots of local insights and lunch. Maximum four sailors.

🛏️ Sleeping & Eating

Herons Rise Vineyard COTTAGE $$
(📞03-6267 4339; www.heronsrise.com.au; 100 Saddle Rd; cottages from $175) Just north of town, Herons Rise has two upmarket self-contained

cottages set among pinot noir vines. Both have log fires and lots of Tasmanian timbers (no, not to burn). We especially like the roomy apartment above the barn (good for families). Dinners by arrangement; breakfast optional ($15 per person for provisions).

Oyster Cove Inn PUB FOOD **$$**
(✆03-6267 4446; www.oystercoveinn.com.au; 1 Ferry Rd; mains $24-30; ⊘bar 11am-late, meals noon-1.45pm & 5.30-7.45pm Mon-Sat, noon-1.45pm Sun) This tarted-up monolith lords over Kettering's boat-bobbing harbour, with a couple of broad deck areas and a span of sunny grass rolling down towards the water. The short-but-sweet menu of pub favourites (also tarted up) might lure you into the bistro from the busy bar. Try the wallaby sausages.

ⓘ Information

Bruny D'Entrecasteaux Visitor Information Centre (✆03-6267 4494; www.brunyislandaccommodationandtours.com; 81 Ferry Rd, Kettering; ⊘9am-5pm) The main Bruny Island visitor centre is actually at the ferry terminal in Kettering (ie not on the island). It's a one-stop shop for info on island accommodation and services, including driving advice, bushwalking maps and South Bruny National Park passes (per vehicle/person per day $24/12). There's also a cafe here.

ⓘ Getting There & Away

Kettering is connected to Hobart by Metro Tasmania (p84) bus routes 415 to 417 ($8.30, 50 minutes). By car, it's a 35-minute drive south of Hobart. The ferry (p115) to Bruny Island leaves from Kettering.

Bruny Island

✆ 03 / POP 620

Bruny Island is almost two islands, joined by a narrow, 5km-long sandy isthmus called the Neck. Renowned for wildlife (little penguins, echidnas, muttonbirds), it's a windswept, sparsely populated isle, blown by ocean rains in the south, and dry and beachy in the north. Access is via a short car-ferry chug from Kettering.

Bruny's coastal scenery is magical. There are countless swimming and surf beaches, plus good ocean and freshwater fishing. South Bruny offers the steep, forested South Bruny National Park, with beautiful walking tracks, especially around Labillardiere Peninsula and Fluted Cape.

Tourism is increasingly important to the island's economy but remains low-key. There

are (as yet) no homogenised resorts, just plenty of beachy cottages and houses. Too many visitors cram their Bruny experience into one day: if you can handle the peace and quiet, stay a few days. Bruny Island takes hold slowly, then tends not to let go.

History

The island was spied by Abel Tasman's beady eyes in 1642, and between 1770 and 1790 was visited by Furneaux, Cook, Bligh and Cox. It was named after Rear Admiral Bruni d'Entrecasteaux, who explored the area in 1792. Strangely, confusion reigned about the spelling – in 1918 it was changed from Bruni to Bruny.

Nuenonne Aboriginals called the island Lunawanna-Alonnah, a name given contemporary recognition (albeit broken in two) as the titles of two island settlements. Among their numbers was Truganini, daughter of Mangana, chief of the Nuenonne. Truganini left Bruny in the 1830s to accompany George Robinson on his infamous statewide journey to win the trust of all the Tasmanian Aboriginals. Many of Bruny's landmarks, including Mt Mangana, are named after the isle's original inhabitants.

The island has endured several commercial ventures. Sandstone was mined here and used for the post office and Houses of Parliament in Melbourne, and coal was also mined. Both industries gradually declined due to lofty transport costs. Only farming, aquaculture and forestry have had long-term viability.

◉ Sights

The Neck NATURE RESERVE, VIEWPOINT
(www.brunyisland.org.au/about-bruny-island/the-neck; Bruny Island Main Rd) FREE Park halfway across the isthmus – aka the Neck – between North and South Bruny and climb the 279 steps (count them!) to the **Truganini Memorial** for broad views of both ends of the island. Another timber walkway crosses the Neck to the beach on the other side. Keep to the boardwalk in this area: muttonbirds and little (fairy) penguins nest here. Your best chance of seeing the penguins is at dusk in the warmer months.

Bruny Island Premium Wines WINERY
(✆0409 973 033; www.brunyislandwine.com; 4391 Bruny Island Main Rd, Lunawanna; ⊘11am-5pm) If you're working up a thirst, swing into the

cellar door at Australia's most southerly vineyard. Pinot noir and chardonnay rule the roost; burgers, platters and meaty mains also available (mains $17 to $34). Also open for dinner on Saturday night from November to March.

South Bruny National Park
NATIONAL PARK

(☏03-6293 1419; www.parks.tas.gov.au; South Bruny; park day pass per person/vehicle $12/24) South Bruny National Park comprises extensive coastal and wooded hinterland areas. At Fluted Cape near Adventure Bay, an easy trail leads to the old whaling station at Grass Point (1½ hours return). From here, Penguin Island is accessible at low tide, or tackle the challenging Cape Circuit (2½ hours return).

The park's southwestern portion comprises the Labillardiere Peninsula, featuring jagged coastal scenery and Cape Bruny Lighthouse (☉reserve access vehicles 9.30am-4.30pm, pedestrians 24hr). Walks here range from leisurely beach meanderings to a seven-hour peninsula circuit.

Bligh Museum of Pacific Exploration
MUSEUM

(☏03-6293 1117; www.southcom.com.au/~jontan/index.html; 876 Adventure Bay Rd, Adventure Bay; adult/child/family $4/2/10; ☉10am-4pm) This curio-crammed, windowless, brick museum details the local exploits of explorers Bligh, Cook, Furneaux, Baudin and, of course, Bruni d'Entrecasteaux. The engaging collection includes maps, charts and manuscripts, many of them originals or 1st editions.

Inala Nature Museum & Jurassic Garden
NATURE RESERVE

(☏03-6293 1217; www.inalanaturetours.com.au; 320 Cloudy Bay Rd, South Bruny; adult/child $10/5; ☉10am-4pm Mon-Fri) 🌱 A 600-hectare spread of wonderful island wilderness on South Bruny, with hundreds of plant species and almost as many birds to quietly observe (including the 12 endemic Tasmanian species). The Nature Museum houses an amazing collection of shells, fossils and minerals, while the Jurassic Garden is a thoughtfully laid-out botanic park, showing how some species hark back to the days of the ancient Gondwana continent. Tours and accommodation also available (cottages $340); see the website for details.

Bruny Island Quarantine Station
HISTORIC SITE

(☏0435 069 312; www.facebook.com/brunyquarantinestation; 816 Killora Rd, Barnes Bay; ☉10am-4pm

Thu-Mon Nov-Mar, Sat & Sun only Apr-Oct) FREE On an isolated peninsula, this historic maritime quarantine station operated from 1884 until 1919, treating immigrants with typhoid and smallpox, and health-checking 9000 WWI troops on their return to Tasmania. There aren't many buildings left, but there's copious historical information, enthusiastic volunteer staff, lots of wildlife to see and some lovely walking trails over 322 acres.

Court House History Room
MUSEUM

(☏03-6260 6287; www.brunyisland.net.au/history.php; 3893 Bruny Island Main Rd, Alonnah; ☉10am-4pm) FREE At the council offices in Alonnah is this megamodest, volunteer-run museum (in an old courthouse – no prizes for guessing that) displaying newspaper clippings, photos and records of the island community's social and whaling past, plus info on walks and attractions around Bruny Island.

🏃 Activities

Cloudy Bay
SURFING

(Cloudy Bay Rd, Cloudy Bay) Beautiful Cloudy Bay at the bottom of South Bruny has the most reliable waves on the island, working best with an offshore northerly breeze...and the best view from a public toilet in Australia!

Bruny Island Cycle Tours & Hire
CYCLING

(☏0477 495 339; www.brunyislandcycletoursandhire.com.au; 66 Ferry Rd, Kettering; hire per day mountain/e-bike $40/65, 2 days $75/120; ☉office 8am-8pm) Take a self-guided tour of Bruny on a nifty 'e-bike', which can give you a boost of up to 25km/h courtesy of a little rechargeable electric motor. Pick-up in Kettering across the road from the ferry. See the website for suggested touring routes. Regular mountain and road bikes also available.

THE SOUTHEAST BRUNY ISLAND

Bruny Island

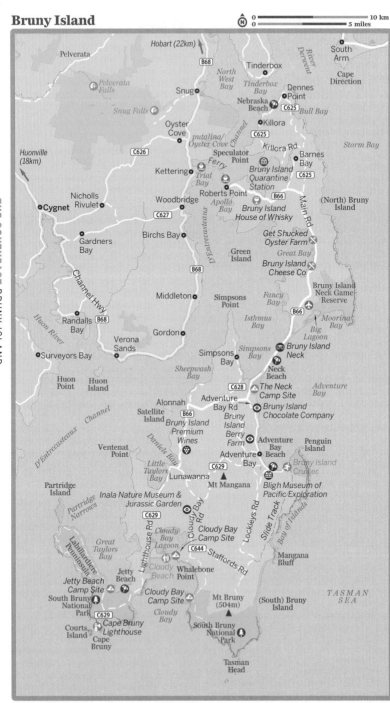

0 ———— 10 km
0 ———— 5 miles

Pelverata

Hobart (22km)

B68

Tinderbox

South Arm

Cape Direction

Pelverata Falls

North West Bay

Tinderbox Bay

Dennes Point

Snug

Nebraska Beach

C625

Bull Bay

Snug Falls

Killora

Oyster Cove

putalina/ Oyster Cove

C625

Killora Rd

Barnes Bay

Storm Bay

Huonville (18km)

C626

Speculator Point

Kettering

Trial Bay

Bruny Island Quarantine Station

C625

(North) Bruny Island

Nicholls Rivulet

Cygnet

Woodbridge

Roberts Point

Apollo Bay

C627

Bruny Island House of Whisky

B66

Main Rd

Gardners Bay

Birchs Bay

Get Shucked Oyster Farm

Green Island

Great Bay

Bruny Island Cheese Co

B68

Middleton

Simpsons Point

Fancy Bay

Bruny Island Neck Game Reserve

Channel Hwy

B66

Moorina Bay

Isthmus Bay

Big Lagoon

Huon River

Randalls Bay

B68

Gordon

Verona Sands

Simpsons Bay

Simpsons Bay

Bruny Island Neck

Surveyors Bay

Sheepwash Bay

Neck Beach

Adventure Bay

Huon Point

Huon Island

C628

The Neck Camp Site

Alonnah

Adventure Bay Rd

Bruny Island Chocolate Company

Satellite Island

B66

Bruny Island

Ventenat Point

Bruny Island Premium Wines

Daniels Bay

Bruny Island Berry Farm

Adventure Bay Beach

Penguin Island

Little Taylors Bay

Adventure Bay

C629

Bruny Island Cruises

Partridge Island

Lunawanna

Mt Mangana

Bligh Museum of Pacific Exploration

Inala Nature Museum & Jurassic Garden

Partridge Narrows

C629

Lockleys Rd

Slide Track

Cloudy Bay Lagoon

Cloudy Bay Camp Site

Bay of Islands

Great Taylors Bay

C644

Staffords Rd

Mangana Bluff

Labillardiere Peninsula

Jetty Beach

Cloudy Beach

Whalebone Point

Jetty Beach Camp Site

Cloudy Bay Camp Site

Mt Bruny (504m)

TASMAN SEA

South Bruny National Park

C629

Cloudy Bay

South Bruny National Park

(South) Bruny Island

Courts Island

Cape Bruny Lighthouse

Cape Bruny

Tasman Head

D'Entrecasteaux Channel

D'Entrecasteaux

Bruny Island

Channel

Speculator Point

Ferry

👉 Tours

⭐ **Bruny Island Cruises** BOATING
(Pennicott Wilderness Journeys; ☎03-6234 4270; www.brunycruises.com.au; 915 Adventure Bay Rd, Adventure Bay; adult/child/family $135/85/430) Run by Pennicott Wilderness Journeys, this excellent three-hour tour of the island's awesome southeast coastline takes in rookeries, seal colonies, bays, caves and towering sea cliffs. Trips depart Adventure Bay jetty at 11am daily, with an extra 2pm cruise in summer; make your own way there.

You can also take the tour as a full-day trip from Hobart, or leave your car at Kettering and take the tour bus, which goes onto the ferry and down to Adventure Bay (additional charges apply).

Bruny Island Traveller TOURS
(Pennicott Wilderness Journeys; ☎03-6234 4270; www.brunyislandtraveller.com.au; per person $155) Operated by Pennicott Wilderness Journeys (the same folks who run Bruny Island Cruises; p113), this is a full-day tour ex-Hobart for landlubbers who don't fancy the idea of too much time in a boat. The itinerary includes beaches, wildlife, Bruny Island Cheese Co (p114), the isthmus and lunch at Bruny Island Premium Wines (p111). Prices include transfers, ferry crossings and lunch.

Bruny Island Safaris TOURS
(☎0437 499 795; www.brunyislandsafaris.com.au; per person $149, lighthouse tour only adult/child/family $10/5/35) Full-day tours departing Hobart, focusing on Bruny's history and landscapes. Look forward to opportunities to sample the island's culinary bounty, including oysters, salmon, cheese, wine and berries, and a visit to the old Cape Bruny Lighthouse. If you're already on the island, you can meet the tour at the lighthouse for a look inside (see www.brunyislandlighthousetours.com.au).

Bruny Island Long Weekend WALKING
(☎0437 256 270; www.brunyislandlongweekend.com.au; per person $1795) Indulgent (but still active) three-day tours around Bruny's best bits, with expert guides. Food, drinks, accommodation, national-parks passes and transfers included.

🎉 Festivals & Events

Bruny Island Bird Festival WILDLIFE
(www.brunybirdfestival.org.au; ⊙late Oct) A three-day celebration of all things avian. There are about 150 bird species present on the island, including all 12 of Tasmania's endemic species. Bring your binoculars and your patience.

🛏 Sleeping

Self-contained cottages have economical weekly rates (though they are generally pricey for shorter stays; few have wi-fi). Adventure Bay has the lion's share of accommodation, but there are places at Alonnah, and at Barnes Bay and Dennes Point on North Bruny.

Bruny's cheapest lodgings are the bush camp sites within South Bruny National Park. There's also a camp site at Neck Reserve near the isthmus.

Captain Cook Holiday Park CARAVAN PARK $
(☎03-6293 1128; www.captaincookpark.com; 786 Adventure Bay Rd, Adventure Bay; unpowered/powered sites $25/30, on-site vans/cabins from $70/150; ❄) Across the road from the beach in Adventure Bay, this park could do with a few trees but has decent facilities, including some swish one-bedroom cabins with little decks out the front. And is this the only caravan park in Tasmania that actually has caravans you can stay in? Kayaks for hire; wi-fi still on the horizon...

⭐ **Red Gate Cottage** RENTAL HOUSE $$
(☎0411 030 445; www.redgatecottage.weebly.com; 178 Nebraska Rd, Dennes Point; houses from $185) A charismatic old shiplap-board beach shack on Dennes Point dunes, with a red gate (two of them, in fact) leading down to the west-facing beach (great sunsets). 'Retro-shack-classic' would best describe the architecture, but inside it's all thoroughly comfortable, with a kitchen that's entirely new-century. Sleeps four in two bedrooms, plus a couple of spare mattresses for extra bods. Two-night minimum stay.

⭐ **43 Degrees** APARTMENT $$
(☎03-6293 1018; www.43degrees.com.au; 1 Lumeah Rd & 948 Adventure Bay Rd, Adventure Bay; d/apt from $195/250) At 43°S latitude, the accommodation here neatly bookends Adventure Bay beach: there are three tidy, roll-roofed studios (sleeping two) at the western end; and two similarly styled apartments (sleeping four) at the eastern end near the jetty. Double glazing keeps the heat out/in, depending on the season.

Bruny Beach House RENTAL HOUSE $$
(☎0419 315 626; www.brunybeachhouse.com; 91 Nebraska Rd, Dennes Point; house from $165) High above the sandy sliver of Nebraska Beach

THE SOUTHEAST BRUNY ISLAND

on North Bruny is this lovely, good-value, woody beach house sleeping four. It's got all the requisite facilities, a wood heater and a north-facing deck on which to sip and scan. BYO supplies; two-night minimum stay.

Lumeah
RENTAL HOUSE $$

(📞0419 870 341, 03-6293 1265; www.lumeah-island. com.au; 3a Lumeah Rd, Adventure Bay; house from $165; 🛜🐕) Lumeah, an Adventure Bay saw-miller's cottage knocked up 120-something years ago, offers accommodation perfect for groups or families. It has three bedrooms and two bathrooms (sleeping 11) and is fully self-contained, 50m from the beach. It also has a BBQ area, spa and casual craft gallery out the front. Two-night minimum stay.

Bruny Boathouse
RENTAL HOUSE $$$

(📞0400 130 354; www.facebook.com/brunyboat houseaccommodation; 13a Ritchie St, Alonnah; house from $210; 🐕) Overlooking Satellite Island and the Alonnah town jetty (made from part of Hobart's old floating bridge), this bright, stylish option, built in 2015, features Tasmanian-oak floorboards and a sunny deck on which to sit and consume your novel. Sleeps four in two bedrooms. The pub and a beaut coastal trail are both within walking distance (choose your destiny).

Captain's Cabin
RENTAL HOUSE $$$

(📞03-6293 1078, 1800 144 633; www.brunyisland holidayrentals.com.au; 258 Nebraska Rd, Dennes Point; house from $280; 🐕) Someone here ask for a private north-facing beach? There's 1.6km of private sunny sand at Captain's Cabin, a stylish, two-bedroom, woody cottage standing on stilts on a cleared slope of terrain near Bligh Point. There are two bed rooms inside (pardon the naff four-poster bed), with skilfully designed windows maximising both privacy and views.

All Angels Church House
RENTAL HOUSE $$$

(📞03-6293 1271, 0427 931 271; www.brunyisland. org.au/accommodation/all-angels-church-house; 4561 Bruny Island Main Rd, Lunawanna; house from $235) Your prayers have been answered with this restored 1912 church near Daniels Bay, now rental accommodation with three bedrooms and a soaring-ceiling open-plan lounge. Fire up the BBQ in the sheltered garden, eat alfresco on the picnic table or dine inside at the huge shared table. Sleeps five.

✕ Eating

For self-caterers, options are limited to the general stores at Adventure Bay and Alon-

nah. There are no stores on North Bruny. Your best bet is to bring everything you need from the mainland.

★ Bruny Island Cheese Co
CHEESE $

(📞03-6260 6353; www.brunyislandcheese.com. au; 1807 Bruny Island Main Rd, Great Bay; tastings free, meals from $12; ⊙9.30am-5pm) Hankering for a quivering sliver of cheese? Head to the Bruny Island Cheese Co, where Kiwi cheese-maker Nick Haddow draws inspiration from time spent working and travelling in France, Spain, Italy and the UK. Bruny Island Beer Co operates under the same auspices: try the Oxymoron dark pale ale, or some arti-san wood-fired sourdough bread with your cheese platter.

★ Get Shucked Oyster Farm
SEAFOOD $$

(📞0439 303 597; www.getshucked.com.au; 1735 Bruny Island Main Rd, Great Bay; 12 oysters un-shucked/shucked from $10/16; ⊙9.30am-4.30pm) Get Shucked cultivates the 'fuel for love' in chilly Great Bay. Visit the tasting room and wolf down a briny dozen with lemon juice and Tabasco and a cold flute of Jansz bubbles. Shucking brilliant.

Jetty Cafe
CAFE $$

(📞03-6260 6245; www.facebook.com/jettycafe brunyisland; 18 Main Rd, Dennes Point; mains $15-35; ⊙10am-4pm Fri-Mon, extended summer hours) Part cafe-restaurant, part provedore, part local art gallery – the stylish Jetty Cafe (designed by ace architect John Wardle) is a North Bruny highlight. Duck in for a coffee or some line-caught fish and chips – seasonal menus showcase local produce. Phone ahead (opening hours sway in the sea breeze). Open seven days in summer, including some nights.

Hotel Bruny
PUB FOOD $$

(📞03-6293 1148; www.hotelbruny.com; 3959 Bruny Island Main Rd, Alonnah; mains $22-34; ⊙11am-late; 🛜) A simple but progressively marketed affair in Alonnah, Bruny Island's only pub is the architectural cousin of an Idaho roadhouse, with a few outdoor water-view seats and an all-day menu heavy on local seafood and grills (great oysters!). Live bands monthly, and island cider on tap. (Captain Bligh planted Tasmania's first ap-ples on Bruny in 1788.)

🍷 Drinking & Nightlife

Bruny Island House of Whisky
BAR

(📞03-6260 6344; www.tasmanianhouseofwhisky. com.au; 360 Lennon Rd, North Bruny; ⊙9.30am-5.30pm, reduced winter hours) Stand in awe before this lustrous, dazzling bar, full of bottles containing Tasmania's best single malt whiskies (there are a lot of them these days, including the house Trappers Hut whisky). Gourmet platters also available. Don't blame us if you miss the last ferry back to Kettering…

ℹ Information

The Bruny D'Entrecasteaux Visitor Information Centre (p110) is actually back in Kettering on the mainland, at the ferry terminal. You can buy South Bruny National Park passes here (per vehicle/person per day \$24/12).

Note that mobile-phone coverage on Bruny can be patchy.

ℹ Getting There & Away

Buy your return ticket (cash only, no bookings) for the **Bruny Island Ferry** (☑03-6273 6725; www.brunyislandferry.com.au; Ferry Rd, Kettering; car return \$33-38, motorcycle/bike/foot passenger return \$6/6/free) from the drive-up ticket booth at Kettering. There are no such formalities on the way back – just queue up and drive on.

The ferry shuttles cars and passengers from Kettering across to Roberts Point on North Bruny, with at least 10 services daily each way (20 minutes) on two boats. The first ferry leaves Kettering at 6.30am (7.30am Sunday); the last one at 7pm. The first ferry from Bruny sails at 7am (8.30am Sunday); the last one at 7.15pm.

On summer weekends and over Christmas and Easter there are often long queues waiting to board the ferry, despite extra sailings. You'll likely spend a significant chunk of the day queuing for the ferry at either end. Our advice: make it an overnighter rather than a day trip.

Note that the ferry timetable does vary occasionally – double-check departure times.

ℹ Getting Around

You'll need your own wheels to get around on Bruny – there are no buses. A bicycle is a great option, but be prepared for long rides between outposts of civilisation. Bicycle and e-bikes can be rented from Bruny Island Cycle Tours & Hire (p111) . Bruny has some narrow, winding gravel roads, the slippery, log-truck-infested road over Mt Mangana being the prime case in point. Not all car-rental companies are cool with this concept. Petrol is available at Adventure Bay.

Woodbridge

☑03 / POP 450

Established in 1874 as Peppermint Bay (after the area's peppermint gums), Woodbridge was eventually renamed by a landowner nostalgic for his old home in England. It's a quiet village sitting squarely on the tourist trail, thanks to the sexy Peppermint Bay Hotel development, which has consumed the old Woodbridge pub.

◉ Sights

Hartzview Vineyard WINERY
(☑03-6295 1623; www.hartzview.com.au; 70 Dillons Rd, Gardners Bay; tastings from \$2; ⊙10am-5pm) Hartzview is a scenic 8km drive up the hill from Woodbridge (or 11km from Cygnet), off the road to Gardners Bay. For your palate's pleasure there are fruit liqueurs, ports, peppery pinot noir and smooth mead. Lunch is also a goer (local produce and cheese platters; \$19 to \$25). There's also **accommodation** (house from \$180; ☎) here if you need a little lie-down.

Grandvewe Cheeses FARM
(☑03-6267 4099; www.grandvewe.com.au; 59 Devlyns Rd, Birchs Bay; tastings free; ⊙10am-5pm Sep-May, to 4pm Jun-Aug) About 3km south of Peppermint Bay is this top stop for foodies. Grandvewe Cheeses churns out organic cheese from sheep's milk – Tasmania's only sheep cheesery. Snack on a cheese platter (the pecorino and blue are perfection; \$10 to \$15) and nose into some pinot noir from local wineries or some rather amazing sheep-whey vodka!

🛏 Sleeping

★**Peppermint Ridge Retreat** RENTAL HOUSE **\$\$**
(☑03-6267 4192; www.peppermintridge.com.au; 290 Woodbridge Hill Rd; houses from \$185) ✎ Two amazing handmade straw-bale-and-stone studios, complete with composting toilets, recycled timbers, spa baths, lofty ceilings and brilliant D'Entrecasteaux Channel and Bruny Island views. Each sleeps five, with breakfast supplies included. 'Hippie-savvy' best describes proceedings.

Fox Hole COTTAGE **\$\$**
(☑0408 732 215; www.facebook.com/thefoxhole woodbridge; 25 Granquist Rd; cottage from \$189; ☎) Encircled by wandering chickens, this compact grey-painted weatherboard cottage is just a few streets from the Woodbridge water, with a couple of comfy chairs on the porch in which to sit and watch the weather. Inside you'll find one bedroom (plus fold-out couch), and a mod kitchen with

THE SOUTHEAST CYGNET

CYGNET COAST ROAD

If you're not in a rush, don't miss the scenic coast road (C639) between Cradoc and Cygnet. The more direct route along the Channel Hwy (B68) is about 7km (this is the route for roadside apple stalls), but the coastal route is a lazy, meandering 27km past Petcheys Bay and Glaziers Bay.

One kilometre from the Cradoc junction, on a north-facing bank of the Huon River, is the pioneering Panorama Vineyard (☑03-6266 3409; www.facebook.com/panoramavineyard; 1848 Cygnet Coast Rd, Cradoc; tastings free; ☺11am-5pm Wed-Mon). Stick your nose into some pinot noir, chardonnay, merlot, riesling and an unusual white port.

An impressive place to stay at Glaziers Bay is Riverside (☑03-6295 1952; www.huon-riverside.com.au; 35 Graces Rd, Glaziers Bay; d $250), a luxe contemporary abode (good for two couples) with Huon views from wide verandahs. Fresh flowers, quality linen and homemade breakfast provisions seal the deal. Minimum three-night stay: look forward to slowing the holiday tempo right down.

Tasmanian-timber benchtops. Dinner by arrangement. Sleeps four.

Satellite Island RENTAL HOUSE $$$
(☑nonbooking info 0417 141 635; www.satelliteisland.com.au; Satellite Island, via Alonnah or Middleton; house from $1800) An island, off an island, off an island... Adrift in the D'Entrecasteaux Channel, this amazing private-island lodge (boatshed-chic) offers self-contained accommodation for up to eight castaways. Kayaks and fishing rods for distraction; walking trails and oyster-clad rocks for exploring. Private-boat access from Alonnah on Bruny Island or Middleton on the Tasmanian 'mainland'. Two-night minimum (though you'll want to stay longer). Breakfast is included.

✕ Eating

★ **Pepperberries Garden Cafe** CAFE $$
(☑03-6267 4078; www.fleurtys.com.au/cafe.html; 3866 Channel Hwy, Birchs Bay; mains $6-17; ☺10am-4pm Thu-Sun; ☑) ✿ Just south of Woodbridge at Birchs Bay, hidden up a winding dirt track, Pepperberries is a sophisticated little glass-fronted cafe in the trees. Utilising the biggest kitchen garden you'll ever see, the cafe turns out beaut breakfasts and lunches – the likes of warm roasted apple and granola; or olive, feta and caramelised- onion tart. Lots of vegetarian and gluten-free offerings.

Peppermint Bay Hotel MODERN AUSTRALIAN $$
(☑03-6267 4088; www.peppermintbay.com.au; 3435 Channel Hwy; mains $10-35; ☺9am-5pm Mon-Wed & Sun, to 9pm Thu-Sat) On a mesmeric D'Entrecasteaux Channel inlet, jaunty Peppermint Bay is a cool, contemporary bar/bistro, open all day for coffee (or a drink),

for lunch daily and dinner Thursday to Saturday. The emphasis is squarely on local produce, with seafood, fruits, meats, cheeses and other ingredients from just down the road. Bookings advised. Excuse the postfunk Stevie Wonder soundtrack...

ℹ Getting There & Away

Woodbridge is connected to Hobart by Metro Tasmania (p84) bus routes 415 to 417 ($10.80, one hour). Otherwise, it's a 40-minute drive south of Hobart.

Cygnet

☑03 / POP 1460

Groovy Cygnet was originally named Port de Cygne Noir (Port of the Black Swan) by Bruni d'Entrecasteaux, after the big *noir* birds that cruise around the bay. Youthfully reincarnated as Cygnet (a baby swan), the town has evolved into a dreadlocked, artsy enclave, while still functioning as a major fruit-producing centre. Weathered farmers and banjo-carrying hippies chat amiably in the main street and prop up the bars of the town's pubs. To the south, the Randalls Bay and Verona Sands beaches aren't far away.

Cygnet has been getting some nationwide screen-time of late, courtesy of *Gourmet Farmer* (www.sbs.com.au/food/programs/gourmet-farmer), the SBS TV series about Sydney food critic Matthew Evans, who moved to Cygnet to try his hand on the land.

◉ Sights

Pagan Cider BREWERY
(☑0448 688 809; www.pagancider.com.au; 7891 Channel Hwy, Cradoc; tastings free; ☺11am-4pm

Mon-Fri, to 5pm Sat & Sun) One of Cygnet's claims to fame is Pagan Cider, the 'champagne of ciders' that's made its way into the taps of pubs around the state. At Pagan, cider ain't just about apples: it also does pear, cherry, strawberry and blueberry cider, plus mead and scrumpy (punchy apple wine). Surprising stuff.

Cygnet Living History Museum MUSEUM

(☑03-6295 1394; 37 Mary St; admission by donation; ☉10am-3pm Mon-Fri, 12.30-3pm Sat & Sun) For a window into Cygnet's soul, the little Cygnet Living History Museum is a quaint history room next to the church on the main street, stuffed full of old photos, documents and curios. Check out the fantastic old apple-crate labels from the 1930s.

Sketchy hours; call in advance.

Courses

Fat Pig Farm COOKING

(☑0415 168 285; www.fatpig.farm; off Dillons Hill Rd, Glaziers Bay; lunch per person $165, cooking classes $300) 🗐 Book yourself in for a cooking class or a fab Friday feast at Fat Pig Farm, the restaurant/cooking school (and actual farm) owned by runaway Sydney food critic Matthew Evans and his partner Sadie Chrestman. Matthew, Sadie and their foodie mates feature in the enduring/endearing SBS TV series *Gourmet Farmer*.

Festivals & Events

Cygnet Folk Festival MUSIC

(www.cygnetfolkfestival.org; ☉2nd weekend of Jan) January's hippie-happy Cygnet Folk Festival is three days of words, music and dance, attracting rootsy left-field local and mainland talent like Jeff Lang, James Kenyon and Monique Brumby. Book early for accommodation and camping.

Sleeping

Cygnet's Secret Garden B&B $$

(☑03-6295 0223; www.cygnets-secret-garden.com.au; 7 Mary St; s/d from $130/140; 🗐) Surrounded by a flower-filled garden, this lovely Federation-style weatherboard house (1913) sits at the bottom of the main street (across from the pub – handy) and has three B&B rooms with plenty of heritage charm. Breakfast is big and cooked, with homemade jams and fruit from the owners' orchard.

Cherryview COTTAGE $$

(☑03-6295 0569; www.cherryview.com.au; 90 Supplice Rd; house $135-160) Backed by a tall stand of eucalypts on 10 quiet hectares, this self-contained studio is a beauty. It's a simple, stylish affair, overlooking a valley with the Hartz Mountains beyond. Love the antique-door bedhead! It's 4km north of Cygnet's bright lights.

Eating

★Lotus Eaters Cafe CAFE $$

(☑03-6295 1996; www.facebook.com/thelotuseaterscafe; 10 Mary St; mains $12-24; ☉9am-4pm Fri-Mon; 🗐) This mighty-fine hippie cafe has rustic decor that belies real culinary savvy: expect terrific eggy breakfasts, curries and soups, with a rigorous focus on the seasonal, the organic, the free-range and the local. Superlative homemade cakes, almond croissants and coffee. Head for the chunky timber tables outside in the sun.

Red Velvet Lounge CAFE $$

(☑03-6295 0730; www.redvelvetlounge.com.au; 24 Mary St; mains $12-24; ☉9am-4pm Wed, Sat & Sun, to 9pm Thu & Fri; 🗐) It's hard to believe, but this place burned down a few years ago. But Red Velvet is back! It's 100% vegetarian these days (this is Cygnet, after all), serving the likes of beetroot burgers, vegan bowls (smoky beans, organic quinoa, dill salsa) and mushrooms with buckwheat noodles. Curry night Thursday; live music and pizzas on Friday nights. Fully Tasmanian booze list.

Shopping

Cygnet Market MARKET

(☑0488 006 873; www.cygnetmarket.com.au; Town Hall, 14 Mary St; ☉10am-2pm 1st & 3rd Sun of month) Food, music and people – three of our favourite things about Cygnet, all on display at this twice-monthly market on the main street. Stalls usually number upwards of 30.

❶ Getting There & Away

Tassielink (p306) buses service Cygnet two or three times daily via Huonville ($12.40, 1¼ hours). Cygnet is also connected to Hobart by Metro Tasmania bus 418 ($10.80, 1¼ hours), running just once in each direction every weekday.

By car, Cygnet is a one-hour drive south of Hobart.

Huonville & Around

☑03 / POP 2540

The biggest town in the southeast, agrarian Huonville flanks the Huon River 35km south of Hobart, not far from some lovely vineyards and small villages. Having made its name as Tasmania's apple-growing powerhouse, it remains a functional, working town – low on charm but with all the services you need.

The Huon Hwy traces the Huon River south, passing the settlements of Franklin, Castle Forbes Bay and Port Huon. These were once important shipping ports for apples, but nowadays the old wharves and packing sheds are decaying like old fruit. Nearby Ranelagh is an agricultural hub, while strung-out Franklin is the oldest town in the Huon Valley. The wide, reedy riverscape here is one of Australia's best rowing courses.

History

The Huon and Kermandie Rivers were named after Huon de Kermadec, second in command to explorer Bruni d'Entrecasteaux. Prior to that, the area was known by the local Aboriginal people as Tahune-Linah. The region was originally steeped in tall forests, and timber milling quickly became a major industry, focusing on the coveted softwood Huon pine. The initial plundering of Huon pine groves nearly wiped the tree out, as it's extremely slow growing. Today, only immature trees survive along the river. Once the forest was levelled, apple trees were planted and the orchard industry blossomed – it's still the region's primary money-spinner.

◉ Sights

★ **Apple Shed**   MUSEUM
(☑03-6266 4345; www.williesmiths.com.au; 2064 Huon Hwy, Grove; admission by donation; ⊙10am-5pm Mon-Thu, to 9pm Fri, to 6pm Sat & Sun) At Grove, 6km north of Huonville, this revamped cafe-provedore-museum is home to Willie Smith's Organic Apple Cider, riding the cider wave that's been sweeping Australia's pubs and bars of late. Swing by for a coffee, a cheese plate, meals (from $14 to $30), a cider tasting paddle ($12), or a more purposeful 1.89L 'growler' of Willie Smith's Bone Dry. The museum zooms in on Huonville's appley heritage, with old cider presses and an amazing wall of different apple varieties.

Live music and extended opening hours on Friday nights...and the apple-brandy distillery is up and bubbling!

Wooden Boat Centre   MUSEUM
(☑03-6266 3586; www.woodenboatcentre.com; 3333 Huon Hwy, Franklin; adult/child/family $15/5/30; ⊙9.30am-4.30pm Mon-Fri, 10.30am-

4pm Sun) This engaging, sea-centric spot incorporates the School of Wooden Boatbuilding, a unique institution running accredited courses (from one to seven weeks) in traditional boat building, using Tasmanian timbers. Stick your head in the door to learn all about it, watch boats being cobbled together and catch a glorious whiff of Huon pine.

Home Hill Wines   WINERY
(☑03-6264 1200; www.homehillwines.com.au; 38 Nairn St, Ranelagh; tastings free; ⊙10am-5pm) In Ranelagh, 3km west of Huonville, is this superstylish winery – all rammed earth and corrugated iron (somehow very Australian) – which has been collecting trophies for its pinot noir, chardonnay and dessert wines. There's also a sassy **restaurant** (mains $25-45; ⊙11.30am-3pm) here.

🏃 Activities

Huon Bikes   CYCLING
(☑0447 270 669; www.huonbikes.com; 105 Wilmot Rd, Huonville; bike hire per half-/full day $25/35; ⊙10am-5pm Mon-Wed, 9am-3pm Thu-Sat) Saddle up on a vintage, retro or mountain bike and go exploring around Huonville. See the website for some ideas on local routes to follow, from 12km to 32km.

Huon Jet   BOATING
(☑03-6264 1838; www.huonjet.com; Esplanade, Huonville; adult/child $80/58; ⊙9am-5pm Sep-Apr, 10am-4pm May-Aug) Jet boating? That's so '80s... Still, these frenetic, 35-minute rides are a great way to see the river up close. Bookings recommended.

Yukon Tours   BOATING
(☑0498 578 535, 0447 972 342; www.yukon-tours.com.au; Franklin Marina, 3333 Huon Hwy, Franklin; tours adult/child/family $50/28/134) Take a 90-minute sailing cruise on the flat, deep Huon River aboard the 1930 *Yukon*. The ship was dredged from the bottom of a harbour near Copenhagen in 2004, restored and then sailed to Tasmania. An amazing old dame! Tours depart at 10.30am year-round, plus 3pm September to April.

🎊 Festivals & Events

Taste of the Huon   FOOD & DRINK
(www.tasteofthehuon.com; ⊙Mar) Visit the Ranelagh showgrounds in mid-March for the annual Taste of the Huon – a showcase of Huon Valley produce (cherries, mushrooms, salmon, wine, berries, truffles...and apples).

🛏 Sleeping

Huon Valley Caravan Park
CARAVAN PARK $

(☑ 0438 304 383; www.huonvalleycaravanpark.
com.au; 177 Wilmot Rd, Ranelagh; unpowered/pow-
ered sites from $35/39, en suite sites $65) At the
junction of the Huon and Mountain Rivers
is this lush, grassy patch, filling a budget-
shaped gap in the local accommodation
market. There are no cabins here (yet), but
there's a fabulous camp kitchen with a pizza
oven, tidy amenities and nifty powered sites
with elevated, brightly painted en suites.
And you can cast a fly into Mountain River.

House on the Hill B&B
B&B $$

(☑ 03-6264 1665; www.houseonthehillbedand
breakfast.com.au; 186 Scenic Hill Rd, Huonville;
d/f from $136/280; 🐾) There are two double
suites and one larger suite sleeping four,
all with bathroom, at this attractive timber
house, high on the hillside just across the
bridge from downtown Huonville. Needless
to say, the views are ace, especially from
the wraparound balcony where you can eat
breakfast when the fickle southeast weather
decides to behave.

Huon Bush Retreats
CABIN $$

(☑ 03-6264 2233; www.huonbushretreats.com;
300 Browns Rd, Ranelagh; unpowered sites $30, te-
pees $125-145, cabins from $245) 🌿 This private,
wildlife-friendly retreat dapples the flanks of
not-so-miserable Mt Misery. On site are five
modern, self-contained, one- and two-bedroom cabins, luxury tepees, tent and campervan sites, plus 5km of walking tracks and
a fantastic BBQ camp kitchen. Superb blue
wrens flit through the branches. Check the
website for directions; it's 12km from Huonville – beware of the steep dirt road!

🍴 Eating

⭐ Ranelagh General Store
CAFE $

(☑ 03-6264 2316; www.facebook.com/ranelagh
generalstore; 31 Marguerite St, Ranelagh; mains
$12-15; ⏱ 9am-4pm Mon & Thu, 8am-8pm Fri &
Sat) The dodgy old Ranelagh General Store
has been reborn as a cafe. Burgers are the
main deal, plus coffee, smoothies, sundaes
and racks full of Huon Valley produce to go.
The 'Dennis' burger (Bruny Island wallaby,
beetroot jam, Tabasco sauce, parsley and
aioli) is an absolute winner.

⭐ Summer Kitchen Bakery
BAKERY, CAFE $

(☑ 03-6264 3388; 1 Marguerite St, Ranelagh; items
$4-8; ⏱ 7.30am-4pm Tue-Fri, 8am-4pm Sat & Sun)
Locals come from kilometres around just

for a loaf of bread from this excellent little
bakery, on a street corner in Ranelagh a few
kilometres out of Huonville. Organic wood-
fired sourdough, sprouted-rye sourdough,
organic beef-and-wallaby pies, pastries,
fiendishly good chocolate croissants and the
best coffee in the Huon. Just terrific.

The Local
CAFE $

(☑ 0484 326 907; www.facebook.com/thelocal
huonville; 17 Wilmot Rd, Huonville; mains $5-15;
⏱ 8am-4pm Mon-Fri, 8.30am-12.30pm Sat) 'Local' is correct at this streetside cafe, which
sources all ingredients from Tasmania and as
many of these as possible from the Huon Valley. The contemporary city fit-out – all ply-
wood, lemon-yellow and grey – is something
of a refreshing anomaly in Huonville. Scan
the menu for soups, pies, pasties, muffins,
toasted sandwiches, wood-smoked bacon-
and-egg rolls and dandelion soy lattes.

DS Coffee
House Cafe
CAFE $

(☑ 03-6264 1226; www.facebook.com/dscoffee
housecafe; 12 Main Rd, Huonville; mains $8-13;
⏱ 7.30am-5pm Mon & Tue, to 6pm Wed-Sun; 🐾)
Despite the mealy-mouthed name, this is
Huonville's funkiest cafe, with quirky retro furniture and uni-student vibes. All-day
breakfasts, sourdough sandwiches, lasagne,
burgers, pies, daily soup specials, myriad
Mona Lisa portraits and Huonville's best
coffee all feature.

🍷 Drinking & Nightlife

Frank's Cider Bar
BAR

(☑ 0438 663 525; www.frankscider.com.au; 3328
Huon Hwy, Franklin; ⏱ 10am-5pm) Inside a little
old 1870s weatherboard church in little old
Franklin, Frank's is a cellar-door bar where
you can sip your way through a few glasses
of apple, pear or cherry-pear cider. Frank
Clark himself was one of many generations of
Clarks who still grow fruit in this part of the
Huon Valley. Check out the old photos inside.

☆ Entertainment

Franklin Palais
ARTS CENTRE

(☑ 0455 568 965; www.franklinpalais.com; 3388
Huon Hwy, Franklin; ⏱ hours vary) This curious
old hall harks back to 1911, when Franklin
was a much less soporific kind of place.
Stick your head in the door (or call ahead)
and see what's happening – perhaps a market, a craft collective, a guided tour or a free
classic-movie screening (6.30pm on the first
Sunday of the month).

OFF THE BEATEN TRACK

HARTZ MOUNTAINS NATIONAL PARK
···
The 65-sq-km Hartz Mountains National Park (☑03-6121 7026; www.parks.tas.gov. au; via Arve Rd; park day pass per person/vehicle $12/24), an alpine wilderness that's part of the Tasmanian Wilderness World Heritage Area, is only 84km from Hobart – easy striking distance for day trippers and weekend walkers. The park is renowned for its jagged peaks, glacial tarns, gorges and alpine moorlands, where fragile cushion-plant communities hunker down in the cold, misty airs. Rapid weather changes bluster through – even day walkers should bring waterproofs and warm clothing.

A century ago, the Hartz plateau was a logging hot spot, and stocks of small varnished gums were harvested for eucalyptus oil, which was distilled in Hobart for medicinal applications. Eventually the area was declared a national park, and in 1989 became part of the Tasmanian Wilderness World Heritage Area.

There are some great hikes and isolated, sit-and-ponder-your-existence viewpoints in the park. Waratah Lookout, 24km from Geeveston, is an easy five-minute shuffle from the road. Other well-surfaced short walks include Arve Falls (20 minutes return) and Lake Osborne (40 minutes return). The steeper Lake Esperance walk (1½ hours return) takes you through beautiful high country. You'll need to be fairly fit and experienced to tackle the steep, rougher track that leads to Hartz Peak (1254m; four hours return), which is poorly marked beyond Hartz Pass (two hours return).

There's no camping within the park – just basic day facilities, including toilets, shelters, picnic tables and barbecues. Access is via the Arve Road from Geeveston: the last 10.5km is unsealed (fine in a regular car) and is sometimes snowed under.

❶ Information

Huon Valley Visitor Information Centre
(☑03-6264 0326; www.huonvalleyvisitorcentre.com.au; 23-25 Main Rd, Huonville; ☺9am-5pm) Southeast tourist information on the way into town from Hobart. Check out the live beehive out the back.

Parks & Wildlife Service (☑03-6121 7026; www.parks.tas.gov.au; 22 Main Rd, Huonville; ☺10am-4pm Mon-Fri) Sells national-parks passes.

❶ Getting There & Away

Tassielink (p306) runs regular daily buses from Hobart to Huonville ($10.40, one hour) via Ranelagh ($10.40, 55 minutes) and continuing to Franklin ($10.40, 1¼ hours) and beyond.

Geeveston & Around

☑03 / POP 1430

A rugged but photogenic town 31km south of Huonville, Geeveston was built by bushmen who came to extract timber from the surrounding forests. It's a utilitarian sort of place, but offers accommodation close to Hartz Mountains National Park and Tahune AirWalk along the Arve Rd.

Geeveston was founded in the mid-19th century by the Geeves family, whose descendants still have fingers in lots of local pies. In the 1980s the town was the epicentre of an intense battle over logging the Farmhouse Creek forests. At the height of the controversy, conservationists spent weeks living in the tops of 80m-tall eucalypts to prevent them being felled. The conservation movement ultimately won: Farmhouse Creek is now protected from logging.

More recently, Geeveston has been the filming location for the fictional town of 'Rosehaven' for the ABC TV comedy series of the same name – a quirky and surprisingly tender insight into small-town Tasmania.

🏃 Activities

Tahune AirWalk WALKING
(☑1300 720 507, 03-6251 3903; www.tahuneairwalk.com.au; Arve Rd, Geeveston; adult/child/family $29/14.50/58; ☺9am-5pm Oct-Mar, 10am-4pm Apr-Sep) About 29km west of Geeveston, Tahune Forest has 600m of wheelchair-accessible steel walkways suspended 20m above the forest floor. One 24m cantilevered section is designed to sway disconcertingly with approaching footsteps. Vertigo? Ground-level walks include a 20-minute riverside stroll through stands of young Huon pine. There's also a cafe (mains $12 to $30) here and lodge accommodation (dorms/doubles/families/cabins $60/121/152/180).

Cable Eagle Hang Glider   ADVENTURE SPORTS
(☑03-6251 3903, 1300 720 507; www.tahuneair walk.com.au/activities/cable-eagle-hang-glider; Tahune AirWalk, Arve Rd, Geeveston; adult/child/family $18/16/59; ⊙9.30am-4.30pm Oct-Mar, 10.30am-3.30pm Apr-Sep) Near the Tahune Air-Walk, wannabe birds of prey are strapped into a hang-glider, which in turn is latched to a 250m-long cable 50m above the Huon River and forest. Fly my pretties! Minimum/maximum weight 25/100kg.

Arve Road Walks   WALKING
(Arve Rd, Geeveston) Walks along the Arve Rd from Geeveston, heading for the Tahune Forest AirWalk, include a ferny forest walk (10 minutes return) at the **Arve River picnic area**. A sub-five-minute walk leads to **Big Tree Lookout**, at an 87m-high swamp gum. **Keogh's Creek Walk** is a 15-minute streamside circuit. **West Creek Lookout** offers views from atop an old tree stump.

🛏️ Sleeping & Eating

Cambridge House   B&B $$
(☑03-6297 1561; www.cambridgehouse.com.au; 2 School Rd, Geeveston; d $140-165) This photogenic 1870s B&B – cottagey but not kitsch – offers three bedrooms upstairs with shared facilities (good for families), and two downstairs en suite rooms. The timber staircase and Baltic-pine ceilings are wonders. If you're quiet, you might spy a platypus in the creek at the bottom of the garden. Cooked breakfast.

Kermandie Hotel   PUB $$
(☑03-6297 1052; www.kermandie.com.au; 4518 Huon Hwy, Port Huon; s/d/tw/f from $110/140/150/210; 🐾) Having a real crack at keeping it contemporary, the highway-side Kermandie Hotel (1932) at Port Huon, just 3km north of Geeveston, has 11 tastefully refurbished bedrooms upstairs, all with bathroom. The best ones have views across the road to the river and marina. Downstairs you can grab a meal in the **bar** (mains $15 to $28) or **restaurant** (mains $28 to $40).

★Masaaki's Sushi   JAPANESE $
(☑0408 712 340; 20b Church St, Geeveston; sushi $9-20; ⊙11.30am-3pm Fri-Sun) What a surprise! Tasmania's best sushi – including fresh Tasmanian wasabi – is in sleepy Geeveston. Opening hours are disappointingly limited (and he usually sells out by 2pm), but you'll also find Masaaki (from Osaka) and his outstanding sushi at Hobart's Sunday morning Farm Gate Market (p83).

Old Bank Of Geeveston   CAFE $$
(☑03-6297 9922; www.facebook.com/theold bankofgeeveston; 13 Church St, Geeveston; mains $10-21; ⊙10am-3pm Thu & Fri, 9.30am-3pm Sat) Local produce, local produce, sustainable local produce...doesn't anyone import anything nasty anymore? But seriously, this cafe (yes, it's an old bank) serves excellent coffee, cakes, pastries and artful breakfasts and lunches, best consumed on the deck beneath huge old cherry-blossom trees. Possum-pelt seat backs and mounted stags' heads conjure a hunting-lodge vibe inside.

ℹ️ Information

Geeveston Visitor Information Centre
(☑03-6297 1120; www.facebook.com/geevestonvisitorcentre; 15 Church St, Geeveston; ⊙9am-5pm, reduced winter hours) In Geeveston's old red-brick town hall, this unofficial visitor centre sells tickets to the Tahune AirWalk and Hastings Caves & Thermal Springs (p122) further south.

ℹ️ Getting There & Away

Tassielink (p306) runs regular daily buses from Hobart to Geeveston ($13.70, 1½ hours) via Huonville ($10.40, one hour). If you're driving it's a one-hour, 60km trip south.

Dover
☑03 / POP 960
A Port Esperance fishing town with a beach and a pier (but sadly no pub – it burned down in 2013), Dover is a chilled-out spot to while away a few deep-south days. The town was originally called Port Esperance after a ship in Bruni d'Entrecasteaux's fleet, but that moniker now only applies to the bay. The bay's three small islands are optimistically called Faith, Hope and Charity.

In the 19th century this was timber territory. Huon pine and local hardwoods were milled and shipped from here (and also from nearby Strathblane and Raminea), heading to China, India and Germany for use as railway sleepers. Today the major industries are fruit growing and aquaculture, with Atlantic salmon reared here then exported throughout Asia.

◉ Sights

St Imre Vineyard   WINERY
(☑0428 373 237; www.facebook.com/st.imrevineyard; 6902 Huon Hwy; tastings free; ⊙10am-5pm) Bottling pinot noir, chardonnay, pinot gris

and the robust 'Tiger Blood', this compact hillside vineyard has a fabulous timber tasting room, built by the Hungarian owner.

🛏 Sleeping

Dover Beachside Tourist Park CARAVAN PARK $
(☑ 03-6298 1301; www.dovercaravanpark.com.au; 27 Kent Beach Rd; unpowered/powered sites from $25/35, cabins from $100; 🐾) Opposite a stretch of shallow, sandy shore and a kids' playground, this decent southern set-up features grassy expanses, trim cream-coloured cabins and a chatty cockatoo in reception.

Fisherman's Wife COTTAGE $$
(☑ 0428 981 574; www.chapellanehall.com/fishermans-wife; 7059 Huon Hwy; cottages from $190) Any closer to the water and this little old roadside cottage would be a boat. Encircled by lush lawns, it's a classic deep-south holiday shack with a wood heater, sunny deck and cute country kitchen – call it retro, with a contemporary twist. A little private jetty juts into Port Esperance. Minimum two-night stay; sleeps four.

★Peninsula Experience RENTAL HOUSE $$$
(☑ 03-6298 1441; www.peninsulatas.com; Blubber Head Rd; houses from $475; 🐾) Poised on a private peninsula beyond some steely gates and a long wiggly driveway, this stately 19th-century farmhouse now exudes 21st-century luxury. Asian-chic design infuses the three bedrooms (it sleeps six) and the elegant kitchen. At dusk, pademelons, wallabies and echidnas patrol the grounds. The Boat House is here too – a slick little waterside cottage for two.

🍴 Eating

★Post>Office 6985 PIZZA $$
(☑ 03-6298 1905; 6985 Huon Hwy; mains $15-30; ⊙4-8pm Thu-Sat) Leonard Cohen and alt-country on the stereo, cool decor, foodie magazines... And that's before you get to the menu, which features excellent wood-fired pizzas (try the scallop, caramelised onion and pancetta version). An evening here will probably have you asking if you can stay an extra night.

ℹ Getting There & Away

Tassielink (p306) runs two buses each weekday, in each direction, between Hobart and Dover ($21, two hours) via Huonville ($10.40, one hour) and Geeveston ($13.70, 1½ hours). If you're driving south from Hobart, it's a wiggly 1¼-hour trip with no pit stops.

Southport & Around
🗐 03 / POP 140

Southport was once called Baie des Moules (Bay of Mussels), one of several names it's had over the years. Many travellers don't take the 2km detour off the main road to visit the town, but it's a worthy diversion if only to stay in its B&Bs, which make good use of the waterside locale. Nearby, the Hastings Caves & Thermal Springs reserve and quirky Ida Bay Railway at Lune River are worthwhile detours.

◉ Sights & Activities

Hastings Caves & Thermal Springs CAVE
(☑ 03-6298 3209; www.parks.tas.gov.au/reserves/hastings; 754 Hastings Caves Rd, Hastings; caves & pool adult/child/family $24/12/60, pool adult/child/family $5/2.50/12; ⊙9am-5pm Jan, 10am-4pm Feb-mid-Apr & Oct-Dec, 10.30am-4pm mid-Apr–Sep) A 7.5km drive inland from the Southport turn-off on the Huon Hwy are the amazing Hastings Caves and their adjunct thermal springs. Admission is via guided tour, leaving roughly hourly (call or check the website). Tours (45 minutes) take you into the impressive dolomite Newdegate Cave, followed by a dip in the thermal pool behind the visitor centre, filled with 28°C spring water. The cafe (mains $10 to $20) at the visitor centre also sells BBQ packs and picnic hampers. The wheelchair-friendly Hot Springs Trail does a big loop from the pool area, taking 20 minutes to navigate.

Ida Bay Railway RAIL
(☑ 03-6298 3110, 0428 383 262; www.idabayrailway.com.au; 328 Lune River Rd, Lune River; adult/child/family $32/17/75; ⊙10am, noon, 2pm & 4pm Jan, 10am, noon & 2pm Feb-Apr, 10am & 12.30pm Thu-Sun May-Dec) Australia's southernmost railway tracks a scenic 14km, 1½-hour narrow-gauge course through native bush from Lune River to Deep Hole Bay: take a picnic, explore the beach then rattle back to Lune River. There's a cafe (light meals $5 to $10) here too serving up simple food.

🛏 Sleeping

★Jetty House B&B $$
(☑ 03-6298 3139; www.endoftheroadtasmania.com; 8848 Huon Hwy, Southport; d/f from $170/220, entire house $440-500; 🐾🐾) This family-run guesthouse near the wharf is a rustic, verandah-encircled homestead built in 1876 for the local sawmill boss. Rates in-

FRENCH CONNECTIONS

Back in the early 2000s, it seemed that Tasmania's pristine deep south was about to change for the worse. In 2004 the Tasmanian government gave private landowners permission to log the forests of the northeast peninsula of Recherche Bay – a decision that stirred up controversy in Tasmania and as far away as France.

In 1792 two French ships under the command of explorer Bruni d'Entrecasteaux, *La Recherche* and *L'Espérance,* anchored in a harbour near Tasmania's southernmost point and called it Recherche Bay (www.tasland.org.au/reserves/recherche-bay-reserve; off Cockle Creek Rd, Cockle Creek). More than a decade before British settlers arrived in Tasmania, the French met the Lyluquonny Aboriginals here and were carrying out the first significant scientific studies on the continent. There are two heritage sites at Recherche Bay with protected status (relics of the French observatory and garden, not accessible to the public), but the explorers' journals record them venturing far into the bush. With the government's announcement, historians, scientists and conservationists became concerned that the area earmarked for clear-felling was home to yet more sites of historical interest to both Australia and France. Needless to say, tensions between the anti- and prologging groups escalated – the prospect of the kinds of protests that took place in Tasmania when the Franklin River was under threat in the mid-1980s loomed large.

Fortunately, in 2006 the landowners agreed to sell the northeast peninsula to the Tasmanian Land Conservancy and it's now protected as a significant site.

clude full cooked breakfast and afternoon tea. Open fires, interesting art and the total absence of doilies complete the package. Dinner by arrangement; cheaper long-stay rates. Kids and pets welcome. Lovely!

★ **The Shackeau** RENTAL HOUSE $$$
(☑ 03-6298 1441; www.shackeau.com; 223 Kingfish Beach Rd, Southport; houses from $295; ❄) The name sounds goofy (a nod to local French history?), but this lovely, absolute-waterfront cottage is anything but. The last in a long row of quirky little beach shacks right above the waterline, it's a cream-coloured weatherboard affair, with mod, beachy interiors, a fabulous deck and an infinity-edge spa pool with unbeatable views. Sleeps four.

ⓘ Getting There & Away

There's no public transport this far south. Behind the wheel, with no pit stops, Southport is a 1½-hour drive south of Hobart.

Cockle Creek

Australia's most southerly drive is the 19km gravel stretch from Ida Bay past the soft-lulling waves of Recherche Bay to Cockle Creek. A grand grid of streets was once planned for Cockle Creek, but dwindling coal seams and whale numbers scotched that idea.

This is epic country, studded with craggy, clouded mountains, sigh-inducing beaches and (best of all) hardly any people – perfect for camping and bushwalking.

🏃 Activities

The challenging South Coast Track starts (or ends) at Cockle Creek, tracking between here and Melaleuca in the Southwest National Park (☑ 03-6288 1149; www.parks.tas. gov.au; via Strathgordon or Melaleuca; vehicle/ person per day $24/12). Combined with the Port Davey Track you can walk all the way to Lake Pedder. Shorter walks from Cockle Creek include ambles along the shoreline to the lighthouse at Fishers Point (two hours return), and a section of the South Coast Track to South Cape Bay (four hours return). National-park entry fees apply.

🛏 Sleeping

There are some brilliant free camping grounds along Recherche Bay, including at Gilhams Beach, just before Catamaran. You can also camp for free at Cockle Creek itself, but national-park fees apply as soon as you cross the bridge. Bring all your own provisions, including fuel or gas stoves. There are pit toilets (no showers) and some tank water.

ⓘ Getting There & Away

There's no public transport this far south. From Hobart, it's a two-hour drive if you don't stop anywhere en route. Tassie Road Trips (p310) provides bushwalker pick-ups from Cockle Creek for bedraggled South Coast Track hikers.

Midlands & Central Highlands

Best Places to Eat

➡ Ross Village Bakery (p130)

➡ Zeps (p131)

➡ Jackson's Emporium (p135)

➡ Feisty Hen Pantry Cafe (p129)

➡ Highlander Restaurant (p134)

Best Places to Stay

➡ Ratho Farm (p133)

➡ Curringa Farm (p135)

➡ Stables (p130)

➡ Tarraleah Lodge (p134)

➡ Blossom's Cottage (p129)

Why Go?

Baked, straw-coloured plains, hawthorn hedgerows, rows of poplars, roadside mansions... Tasmania's Midlands have a distinct English-countryside feel. This is old-school Tasmania, tracing the route between Hobart and Launceston hammered out by convict gangs in the early 1800s. As the road rolled itself out, sandstone garrison towns and pastoral properties appeared: the Midlands soon became the food factory of Van Diemen's Land.

The current course of the Midland Hwy has strayed from its original path – a few meandering detours are required to explore the old towns here, with their Georgian main streets, antique shops and country pubs.

Not far to the west, the undertouristed Central Highlands feature subalpine moorlands and trout-filled lakes. Bounded to the south by the Derwent Valley with its sleepy farming towns, this landscape is quintessentially Tasmanian: wild, underpopulated and hauntingly Gothic.

When to Go

➡ The Midlands and the Central Highlands are definitely at their best from December to March, with warm, settled weather and extended opening hours.

➡ Through the winter months (June to August), snow is quite common around the Central Highlands: atmospheric! A wee dram of local single malt whisky will keep the chills at bay on a cold highland night.

➡ If you're keen on checking out the heritage architecture around Ross and Oatlands, shoot for the shoulder months – October, November, April and May – when accommodation owners crank up the discounts.

Midlands & Central Highlands Highlights

1 **Trout fishing** (p132) Arcing a fly across a stream in the Central Highlands.

2 **Callington Mill** (p129) Ascending the steps inside Oatlands' heritage flour mill.

3 **Ross Bridge** (p129) Looking for the carving of Jorgen Jorgensen, former king of Iceland.

4 **Ratho Farm** (p133) Making par on Australia's oldest golf course in Bothwell.

5 **Campbell Town** (p131) Reading the heinous convict histories in the red bricks along the main street.

6 **Four Corners of Ross** (p130) Questioning your moral direction at the town crossroads.

7 **Old Kempton Distillery** (p128) Nosing your way into a whisky tasting in Kempton.

8 **Tarraleah** (p134) Exploring this curious old hydroelectric town in the middle of nowhere.

ROAD TRIP > HERITAGE HIGHWAY

• •

This journey from south to north connects Tasmania's two premier cities, via a quirky and engaging series of historic towns. The town names, building facades and landscapes here call to mind the rolling farmlands of southern England. All but one of these towns sit just off the main highway and receive far fewer visitors than you might expect.

❶ Kempton

Heading north from Hobart on the Midland Hwy (aka the 'Heritage Hwy, or plain old Rte 1), the first historic town of note is Kempton, 48km away. Named after provocateur settler Anthony Fenn Kemp, it's an agricultural hub that's slipped into sleepy obscurity. The excellent **Old Kempton Distillery** (p128) will warm your spirits.

The Drive > Just 7km kilometres north of Kempton at Melton Mowbray, turn left to Bothwell, a further 21km northwest on the Lakes Hwy (A5).

❷ Bothwell

Echoes of Scotland resonate through quiet little Bothwell, encircling a village green near the trout-filled Clyde River. The excellent **Nant Distillery** (p133) is here, along with Australia's oldest golf course, **Ratho Farm** (p133). Bothwell's street signs are spangled with a winning tartan motif.

The Drive > Retrace your steps to Melton Mowbray (21km), rejoin the Midland Hwy and roll 38km northeast to Oatlands.

❸ Oatlands

With Australia's largest single collection of Georgian architecture, Oatlands feels like a picture-perfect film set. Originally planned as the Midlands' capital, its heyday was the 1830s, when settlers began erecting solid buildings. Today the architecture sets the scene for B&Bs and low-key country pubs. Don't miss the restored **Callington Mill** (p129).

The Drive > Return to the Midland Hwy and trundle 37km further north to the turn-off for Ross.

❹ Ross

A garrison town founded in 1812 to protect Hobart–Launceston travellers from bushrangers, little Ross is utterly photogenic. Dotted with elm trees, heritage stone buildings (including Australia's second-oldest **bridge**; p129), country cafes and a decent pub, it's the perfect place to spend the night.

The Drive > Back on the main highway, Campbell Town is just 12km north of Ross.

2 days / 153 miles / 246km

Great for... History & Culture

Best Time to Go; November to March to dodge winter

⑤ Campbell Town

With far more through traffic than the other Heritage Hwy towns, Campbell Town wears its history a little more lightly. Today, Campbell Town is ground zero for Tasmania's cattle- and sheep-farming industries. The annual **Campbell Town Show** (p131) is the oldest country show in Australia (since 1839).

The Drive > The drive to Evandale (50km) is mostly along the Midland Hwy, with undulating farmland all the way to the Evandale turn-off (B41).

⑥ Evandale

Walk down Evandale's main street and you'll feel like you've time-warped back a century (precisely why the entire town is National Trust–listed). Highlights include February's **National Penny Farthing Championships** (p22) and south of town, the neoclassical **Clarendon** (1838; p196) – straight out of *Gone with the Wind*. The **Australian Fly Fishing Museum** (p197) is also at Clarendon.

The Drive > Continuing north, all roads lead to Launceston. Follow the signs to the city centre.

MIDLANDS

Tracking north–south between Launceston and Hobart, the convict-built Midland Hwy has been Tasmania's main thoroughfare since it opened to horse-and-carriage traffic in 1821. The towns along this route – now also nostalgically known as the 'Heritage Hwy' – were established as garrisons for prisoners and guards, protecting travellers from the menace of bushrangers. These days there are plenty of places to stop and eat, drink and absorb the history here, with some amazing old bridges, homesteads and convict-built remnants to see.

Find out more on www.heritagehighway.com.au.

Getting There & Away

Redline Coaches (📞1300 360 000; www.tasredline.com.au) buses power between Hobart and Launceston ($41.50, 2½ hours) two to four times daily, via Kempton, Oatlands, Ross and Campbell Town. An express Tassielink (p306) service ($35, 2½ hours) plies the same route, not stopping at the Midlands towns.

Kempton

📞 03 / POP 360

Strung-out Kempton, about 50km north of Hobart and bypassed by the main highway, was founded in 1838, making it one of the state's earliest settlements. Originally known as Green Ponds, it was later renamed after one-time resident and notorious rabble-rouser Anthony Fenn Kemp. There's not a

ANTHONY FENN KEMP

Kempton was named after one-time resident Anthony Fenn Kemp. He was a charismatic dude: one-half egotistical bankrupt with scant moral fibre, one-half progressive patriot who was critical in Tasmania's evolution from convict dump to independent colony. Fleeing debts in England, he became a dedicated pastoralist, merchant and political sabre-rattler. Never far from controversy, he made as many friends as enemies, and left behind more than a dozen children – a fact that has seen him dubbed the 'Father of Tasmania'. For a critical (and comical) look at Kemp's exploits, read Nicholas Shakespeare's excellent book *In Tasmania*.

whole lot to see or do here these days, except for a visit to Old Kempton whisky distillery in the stately old Dysart House.

Sights

Old Kempton Distillery DISTILLERY
(📞03-6259 3058; www.oldkemptondistillery.com.au; 26 Main St; tours with/without tastings $35/20; ⊙10am-4pm) Old Kempton (until recently called Redlands Distillery) set up shop in 2012 at historic Redlands Estate near New Norfolk but has relocated to the equally gorgeous Dysart House (1842) in Kempton. Pull off the highway for a whisky tasting ($22), a bite to eat in the cafe, or a guided tour of the distillery and lovely old homestead (1.30pm, bookings advised).

Shene Estate & Distillery DISTILLERY
(📞0432 480 250; www.shene.com.au; 76 Shene Rd, Pontville; ⊙10am-4pm Sun) Dating back to 1819, Shene is a noble sandstone estate on the outskirts of Pontville, 19km south of Kempton. Sure, the old architecture (and occasional polo matches) are amazing, but these days it's gin that's the main lure here. Buy some from its roadside stall on a Sunday, or book a weekend distillery ($35) or estate ($25) tour to get a good look at the place.

Getting There & Away

Kempton is about 41km north of Hobart, just off the Midland Hwy. Hobart–Launceston Redline Coaches stop here on request ($11, 40 minutes from Hobart; $36, 1¾ hours from Launceston), running in each direction three or four times a day.

Oatlands

📞 03 / POP 860

Oatlands contains Australia's largest single collection of Georgian architecture. On the stately main street alone (which feels like a film set) there are 87 historic buildings.

The site for the town was chosen in 1821 as one of four military posts on the Hobart–George Town road, but it was slow to develop. In 1832 an optimistic surveyor marked out 80km of streets on the assumption that Oatlands would become the Midlands' capital. Many folks made the town home in the 1830s, erecting solid buildings with the help of former convicts and soldiers who were skilled carpenters and stonemasons.

These days the town has a few decent places to stay and eat, and makes for a history-soaked stopover.

Sights

Callington Mill   HISTORIC BUILDING

(☑03-6254 5000; www.callingtonmill.com.au; 1 Mill Lane; ⊙grounds 9am-5pm) 🏷 Spinning above the Oatlands rooftops, the Callington Mill was built in 1837 and ground flour until 1891. After decades of neglect, with the innards collecting pigeon poo and the stonework crumbling, it's been fully restored and is once again producing high-grade organic flour. It's an amazing piece of engineering – the only working Lincolnshire-style windmill in Australia. Visitors are free to wander around the grounds.

History Room   MUSEUM

(☑03-6254 1111; www.southernmidlands.tas. gov.au/museums; 107 High St; by donation; ⊙10.30am-4pm Mon, Wed, Sat & Sun, 10am-4pm Fri) At the northern end of town, fronted by bright-orange daisy blooms, this old garage is full of photos, relics, bootmaking and sewing equipment, and sundry historical knick-knacks. It's run by volunteers, so hours may vary.

Sleeping & Eating

Blossom's Cottage   B&B $$

(☑03-6254 1516; www.blossomscottageoatlands. com.au; 116 High St; d from $110; 🛜) In a self-contained garden studio, Blossom's is bright and cheerful, with a cast-iron bed, blackwood-timber floors, leadlight windows, a small kitchenette and a couple of easy chairs under a silver birch. Great value. Generous breakfast basket provided.

Jenny Wren   COTTAGE $$

(☑03-6254 0099, 03-6254 1212; www.southern midlands.tas.gov.au/the-jenny-wren; 103 High St; d $110, extra person $20) Plastic flowers aside, Jenny Wren is a supercute, supertidy 1830s stone cottage on the main street, with a 1940s extension out the back. Sleeps four in two bedrooms, with a trundle (pull-out) bed for guest number five. You can spy the spinning blades of Callington Mill beyond the chunky stone garden wall in the backyard. Breakfast is included.

Feisty Hen Pantry Cafe   CAFE $

(☑0411 232 776; www.feistyhenpantry.com.au; 94 High St; mains $6-15; ⊙9am-3.30pm Tue-Sun) How sweet! This diminutive stone cottage out the back of Oatlands Lodge B&B (☑03-6254 1444; www.oatlandslodge.com; 92 High St; s/d incl breakfast from $100/130, extra person $25) houses a European-style deli-cafe, serving all-day breakfasts, afternoon Devonshire teas, toasted sandwiches, slabs of quiche and slices of carrot cake – using all-local, all-seasonal ingredients. Good coffee too. There's a scattering of sunny tables out the front if the Midlands wind isn't howling.

❶ Information

Southern Midlands Council (☑03-6254 5000; www.southernmidlands.tas.gov.au; 71 High St; ⊙9am-4.30pm Mon-Fri) The local council offices stock tourist brochures, including a self-guided town tour and leaflets on the old town jail, supreme court and military precinct; and the *Lake Dulverton & Dulverton Walkway Information Guide*, for explorations around the lake.

❶ Getting There & Away

Oatlands is 84km north of Hobart, a short detour off the Midland Hwy. Hobart–Launceston Redline Coaches stop here ($21.50, one hour from Hobart; $21.50, 1½ hours from Launceston).

Ross

☑03 / POP 430

Another tidy (nay, immaculate) Midlands town, Ross was established in 1812 to protect Hobart–Launceston travellers from bushrangers. The town became an important coach staging post at the centre of Tasmania's burgeoning wool industry and, before the famous Ross Bridge was built in 1836, a fording point across the Macquarie River. These days the town's elm-lined streets are awash with colonial charm. Plenty of tourist accommodation keeps the town buzzing along.

Sights

Ross Bridge   BRIDGE

(Bridge St) FREE The oft-photographed 1836 Ross Bridge is the third-oldest bridge in Australia. Designed by colonial architect John Lee Archer, it was built by two convict stonemasons, Messrs Colbeck and Herbert, who were granted pardons for their efforts. Herbert chiselled the 186 intricate carvings decorating the arches, including Celtic symbols, animals and notable people (including Governor Arthur and Anglo-Danish convict Jorgen Jorgenson, the farcical ex-king of Iceland). At night the bridge is lit up – the carvings shimmer with spooky shadows.

Four Corners of Ross LANDMARK
(cnr Church & Bridge Sts) **FREE** The crossroads
in the middle of town is known as the Four
Corners of Ross, potentially leading your
soul in one of four directions: temptation
(the Ross Hotel), salvation (the Catholic
Church), re-creation (the town hall) or dam-
nation (the old jail). We know which one we
would choose...

Ross Female Factory HISTORIC SITE
(☑ 03-6381 5466; www.parks.tas.gov.au; cnr Bond
& Portugal Sts; ⊙ 9am-5pm) **FREE** This barren site was once one of Tasmania's five
female-convict prisons (the others were in
Hobart, Launceston, George Town and Cascades on the Tasman Peninsula). Only one
cottage remains, full of interesting historical
info, but archaeological excavations below
the sunburnt grass have revealed much.
Descriptive panels provide insight into the
hard lives these women led. Pick up the *Ross
Female Factory* brochure from the visitor
centre, then traverse the track from the top
of Church St to get here.

Tasmanian Wool Centre MUSEUM
(☑ 03-6381 5466; www.taswoolcentre.com.au; 48
Church St; entry by donation; ⊙ 9.30am-4.30pm
Mon-Fri, 10am-4pm Sat & Sun) This place houses a sheep-centric museum, the town visitor
centre and a craft shop. The museum focuses on convict times and the Australian wool
industry, with samples of wool to feel (so
thick and greasy!) and woolly audiovisual
displays.

🛏 Sleeping

Ross Hotel HOTEL $
(☑ 03-6381 5445; www.rosshotel.com.au; 35
Church St; r without bathroom $75-95, extra person
$15; 🛰) This gracious 1835 hotel is a fasci-
nating old building: a tunnel (now blocked)
runs beneath the street to the old jail; it was
purportedly used to securely transport the
convicts who were constructing the pub
from their cells to the building site. Bathrooms are shared, but the heritage-style upstairs rooms are better than those in your
average boozer.

⭐ **Stables** COTTAGE $$
(☑ 0438 250 161, 03-6381 5481; www.visitross.
com.au/stay/the-stables-cottage; 21 Church St; d
from $140; 🛰) Tucked in behind a larger ac-
commodation business on the main street
is this cosy little gem – stylishly renovated,
two-room former stables sleeping just two.

Contemporary art, a mod little kitchen, a
bedroom nook and exposed-stone walls give
the place oodles more charisma than a mo-
tel room. Nice one.

Ross Motel MOTEL $$
(☑ 03-6381 5224; www.rossmotel.com.au; 2 High
St; d/tw/f from $135/145/215; 🛰) The inde-
pendently owned Ross Motel offers spick-
and-span Georgian-style cottage units (reasonably inoffensive reproductions – albeit
with a retirement-village vibe), each with
microwave, fridge and TV. Family units sleep
four. Quiet and central, with breakfast provisions available ($15 per couple).

Check-in for the **caravan park** (☑ 03-6381
5224; www.rossmotel.com.au/ross-caravan-park; 2
High St; unpowered/powered sites $25/34, cabin d
$70; 🛰) is here too.

🍴 Eating

⭐ **Ross Village Bakery** BAKERY $
(☑ 03-6381 5246; www.rossbakery.com.au; 15
Church St; pies $5-9, mains $10-24; ⊙ 9am-4pm
Wed-Mon; 🛰) Overdose on savoury carbs,
pies and astonishingly tall vanilla slices, plus
virtuous soups and salads of all kinds. The
owners get up before dawn every day to set
the 1860 wood oven blazing. Wood-fired pizzas on Saturday nights in summer.

Bakery 31 CAFE $
(☑ 03-6381 5422; www.bakery31.com.au; 31
Church St; pies $5-8, mains $8-18; ⊙ 7am-5pm)
Home to the Tasmanian Scallop Pie Company, this chipper Ross bakery is a fair way
from the coast...but reserve your cynicism
and wolf down an excellent curried-scallop
pie for lunch. All-day breakfasts and agricultural mains – the likes of lamb's fry (offal),
vegetable soup and rissoles with peas and
mash – are also available.

ℹ Information

Ross Visitor Information Centre (☑ 03-6381
5466; www.visitross.com.au; 48 Church St;
⊙ 9am-4.30pm Mon-Fri, 10am-4pm Sat & Sun)
Inside the Tasmanian Wool Centre.

ℹ Getting There & Away

A short detour off the Midland Hwy, Ross is
120km north of Hobart and 79km south of
Launceston. Hobart–Launceston Redline
Coaches (p128) stop here ($31, 1¾ hours from
Hobart; $14, one hour from Launceston) three or
four times daily.

LAKE LEAKE

The secondary B34 road from Campbell Town heads 33km east to the excellent fishing and bushwalking area around Lake Leake (population 180), continuing for 36km through to Swansea on the east coast. Shimmering Lake Leake itself – an artificial reservoir first dammed in 1884 – is punctuated by ghostly tree stumps and encircled by holiday shacks. East of the little Lake Leake township are Meetus Falls and Lost Falls forest reserves. Meetus Falls is the pick of the two: it's 10km from the signposted turn-off and has a sheltered barbecue area.

If you want to stay the night, the shingle-covered Lake Leake Inn (☑03-6381 1329; www.lakeleakeinn.com.au; 320 Lake Rd; s/d from $40/110) offers decent (albeit basic) pub accommodation with shared bathrooms, and hefty postfishing bar meals (mains $16 to $30; noon to 2pm and 6pm to 8pm daily). There's occasional live country music, or you can rustle some up on the jukebox.

For more fishing opps, Currawong Lakes (☑03-6381 1148; www.currawonglakes. com.au; 1204 Long Marsh Rd; d from $225, extra person $50) is a private trout fishery about 14km south of the Lake Leake turn-off. The property offers trout-filled lakes, a handful of good-quality self-contained cabins, a lodge sleeping up to six (from $600), equipment hire and fly-fishing (no licence required).

Campbell Town

☑03 / POP 1000

A former garrison and convict settlement, Campbell Town makes a handy pit stop: the Midland Hwy still trucks right on through it, which isn't the case in nearby Oatlands and Ross. Along High St, rows of red bricks set into the footpath detail the crimes, sentences and arrival dates of convicts such as Ephram Brain and English Corney, sent here for crimes as various as stealing potatoes, bigamy and murder.

After convict transportation ended, Campbell Town's first white settlers were Irish timber workers who spoke Gaelic and had a particularly debauched reputation. Today, Campbell Town is ground zero for Tasmania's cattle- and sheep-farming industries.

◉ Sights

Red Bridge   BRIDGE
(High St) FREE The convict-built bridge across the slow-moving Elizabeth River at Campbell Town was completed in 1838, making it almost as venerable as the Ross Bridge (p129). Locals call it the Red Bridge because it was built from more than 1.5 million red bricks, baked on-site.

★ Festivals & Events

Campbell Town Show   FAIR
(www.campbelltownshow.com.au; Campbell Town Showgrounds, 21 Church St; ☉early Jun) The annual 'paddock to people' Campbell Town Show is the oldest country show in Australia, running since 1839. The closing cocktail party is a blast.

🛏 Sleeping & Eating

Ivy on Glenelg   B&B $$
(☑03-6381 1228; www.ivyonglenelg.com.au; 9 Glenelg St; r from $160) There are three self-contained arrangements at this backstreet B&B (with kitchen and bathroom), the biggest of which sleeps six; there's also a smaller suite sans kitchen. Shame about the 'no kids' policy – the oval across the street is ripe for football kicking! The vibe is heritage but sidesteps any kitsch overtones...and yes, there's a bit of ivy on the fence. Continental breakfast.

★Zeps   CAFE $$
(☑03-6381 1344; www.zeps.com.au; 92 High St; mains breakfast $8-22, lunch & dinner $10-27; ☉7am-8pm Mon-Fri, 8am-8pm Sat & Sun) A top refuelling spot is the hyperactive Zeps, serving brekky, panini, pasta, fat pies and good coffee throughout the day, plus impressive pizzas and more substantial mains in the evening. This ain't no blow-through truck stop...try the sticky soy pork belly with spicy roast pumpkin and Asian greens.

🛍 Shopping

★Book Cellar   BOOKS
(☑03-6381 1545; www.bookcellar.com.au; 132 High St; ☉10am-4pm) In the vaulted 1833

ABOUT TROUT

Catching brown and rainbow trout in the Central Highlands (aka the Lake Country) should be as easy as getting your feet wet – but you still need to be in the right place at the right time, and fly-fishing takes skill! There are also restrictions on fish size, daily catch allocations and the types of tackle permitted in various areas in different seasons: the **Inland Fisheries Service** (☑03-6165 3808; www.ifs.tas.gov.au) offers priceless advice.

Live bait (impaling a grasshopper, grub or worm on a hook) is tried and true, but bait-fishing is banned in most inland Tasmanian waters – it's too effective to give the fish a sporting chance! Artificial lures and flies are more acceptable, coming in myriad shapes, sizes, weights and colours: 'Cobra' wobbler might work for you in lakes, or a 'Celta' in streams.

In the Lake Country, always bring warm, waterproof clothing, even in summer (snow happens). Engaging a professional guide for lessons, or taking a guided trip, is a stellar idea: try **Rod & Fly Tasmania** (☑03-6266 4480; www.rodandfly.com.au) or **Trout Guides & Lodges Tasmania** (www.troutguidestasmania.com.au). And don't forget your fishing licence; pick one up from **Spot On Fishing Tackle** (Map p62; ☑03-6234 4880; www.spotonfishing.com.au; 87-89 Harrington St, Hobart; ◷9am-5.30pm Mon-Fri, to 3.45pm Sat) in Hobart.

convict-built cellar of what was once a coaching inn, then a B&B, is the unexpected Book Cellar, specialising in Tasmanian tomes. Grab a coffee and have a browse.

ℹ️ Information

Campbell Town Visitor Information Centre (☑ 03-6381 1353; www.campbelltowntasmania.com; Town Hall, 75 High St; ◷10am-3pm Mon-Sat) Local info, plus the **Campbell Town Museum** (www.northerntasmania.com.au; ◷10am-3pm Mon-Sat). The centre is run by volunteers, so hours may vary. Pick up the *Campbell Town – Historic Heart of Tasmania* brochure, which plots sundry historic edifices on a map.

ℹ️ Getting There & Away

Right on the Midland Hwy, Campbell Town is 131km north of Hobart and 68km south of Launceston. Hobart–Launceston **Redline Coaches** (p128) stop here ($30.60, 1½ hours from Hobart; $14, 40 minutes from Launceston).

CENTRAL HIGHLANDS

Tasmania's people-free Central Highlands area is spiked with steep mountains and perforated with glacial lakes, waterfalls, abundant wildlife and unusual flora, including the ancient pencil pine. The plateau's northwestern sector is part of the Tasmanian Wilderness World Heritage Area. The region is also known for its world-class trout fishing and for its socially divisive hydro-

electric schemes, which have seen the damming of rivers, the creation of artificial lakes, the building of power stations and the construction of massive pipelines arcing over rough terrain like giant metal worms.

On the western edge of the Central Plateau is the Walls of Jerusalem National Park (p209), a perennial favourite with bushwalkers and cross-country skiers. Experienced bushwalkers can hike across the Central Plateau into 'the Walls' and also into Cradle Mountain-Lake St Clair National Park (p250). Meanwhile, quirky highland-fringe towns like Bothwell and Hamilton prove to be unexpectedly interesting.

ℹ️ Getting There & Away

The Central Highlands occupy Tasmania's vast heartland. Getting here usually involves having your own transport, though Tassielink (p306) buses heading between Hobart and the west coast skirt past Hamilton and Tarraleah, while Bothwell is serviced by occasional **Derwent Valley Link** (☑ 03-6261 4653; www.derwentvalleylink.com.au) public buses.

Bothwell

☑03 / POP 390

Encircling a village green, Bothwell is a becalmed historic town 74km north of Hobart in the Clyde River valley. Its Scottish heritage runs deep: the town has adopted tartan street signs. Bothwell is best known for its proximity to trout heaven, but the town also lays claim to Australia's oldest golf course,

Ratho Farm, where you can now also rest your golf-fatigued head.

⊙ Sights & Activities

Nant Distillery
DISTILLERY

(☎03-6111 6110; www.nant.com.au; 254 Nant Lane; tours with/without tasting $35/25; ⊙10am-4pm) A key component of Bothwell's mini-Scotland ambience is this distillery, where superb single malt whisky is crafted in an 1820s flour mill. Tours (11am, 1.30pm & 3pm) and tastings were running when we visited, but the restaurant – a cutting-edge piece of architecture that contrasts beautifully with older structures, including the estate's original convict-built homestead – was only open for private functions. Call for tour bookings.

Australasian Golf Museum
MUSEUM

(☎03-6259 4033; www.ausgolfmuseum.com; Market Pl; adult/child/family $5/1/10; ⊙10am-4pm Sep-May, 11am-3pm Jun-Aug) In the same building as the visitor centre, this museum celebrates golfing achievements Down Under. Exhibits have a particular bias towards Ratho Farm, Australia's oldest golf course, which is just up the road. There's a miniature putting green where you can try out old-style clubs, and a stupendous selection of collectable, golf-themed Jim Beam bourbon decanters (sadly, empty).

Ratho Farm
GOLF

(☎03-6259 5553, 0497 644 916; www.rathofarm.com; 2122 Highland Lakes Rd; 9/18 holes $25/40, club/trolley hire $10/5; ⊙8am-dusk) Australia's oldest golf course was rolled out of the dust in 1822 by the Scottish settlers who built Bothwell. It's an eccentric course: watch out for sheep, hedges and hay bales.

There's also in convict-built accommodation (1/2-bedroom units from $185/235; ❉ 🅟) here now, if you feel like a snooze after tackling the course.

ⓘ Information

Central Highlands Visitor Information Centre (☎03-6259 5503; www.centralhighlands.tas.gov.au; Market Pl; ⊙10am-4pm) Pick up the free Browse Bothwell! leaflet from this fancy new visitor centre (revamped in 2016) and check out the wee map, marked with the locations of historic buildings. The Australasian Golf Museum is here too.

ⓘ Getting There & Away

The only transport to/from Bothwell is the **Derwent Valley Link** bus to/from Hobart ($13.30, 1½ hours, one daily Monday to Friday). Otherwise, BYO wheels.

The Lakes

Levelling out at 1050m above sea level in the Central Highlands (technically a large plateau), **yingina/Great Lake** is the largest natural freshwater lake in Australia. In 1870 brown trout were released here and it soon became a fishing fantasia. Rainbow trout were added in 1910 and thrived. Trout have now penetrated most of the streams across the plateau.

In the seminal days of hydroelectric ambition, a small Great Lake dam was constructed to raise water levels near Miena. Yingina/Great Lake is linked to nearby Arthurs Lake by canals, and a pumping station supplies water to the Poatina power station on its northeastern shore.

This part of Tasmania is still wild – expect dirt tracks, lots of mud (and snow!), and very few places to stay and eat.

🛏 Sleeping & Eating

If you don't fancy staying at a fishing lodge or a pub, you can try the basic camping ground at **Dago Point** (☎03-6263 5133; www.centralhighlands.tas.gov.au/tourism/caravan-and-camping-sites; Lake Sorrell; unpowered sites adult/child/family $4/2/10) beside Lake Sorell. A better bet for families is the camping ground on Arthurs Lake at **Pumphouse Bay** (☎0439 503 211; www.centralhighlands.tas.gov.au/tourism/caravan-and-camping-sites; Arthurs Lake; unpowered sites adult/child/family $4/2/10), which has hot showers. Campers self-register at both sites. BYO supplies; boil your tap water.

Great Lake Hotel
PUB $

(☎03-6259 8163; www.greatlakehotel.com.au; 3096 Marlborough Hwy, Miena; cabin s/d/tr/q $50/65/80/95, d $105, unit d/f $120/150) From Miena, take the turn-off to Bronte Park and you'll soon come across this small-town pub, offering accommodation ranging from basic anglers' cabins (sleeping four) with shared facilities to self-contained motel-style units.

The meaty meals in the bar (mains $16 to $30, serving noon to 2pm and 6pm to 8pm) may reduce vegetarians to tears. 'Go bush or go home!' is its motto: who are we to argue?

TARRALEAH

Midway between Hobart and Queenstown, Tarraleah (☑03-6289 0111; www.tarraleah.com; ⊙24hr) FREE (pronounced 'Tarra-*lee*-uh'; population 10) is a surreal place. Built in the 1920s and '30s as a residential village for hydroelectric workers, at its peak it had a population of hundreds, complete with police station, town hall, shops, church, golf course and 100 houses. Once the hydro work dried up, Tarraleah declined and the population plummeted.

Hydro sold off most houses for removal in the 1990s, then put the remainder of the village up for sale. In 2002 Tarraleah was purchased by a family from Queensland ('The Family that Bought a Town', as the tabloids tagged them). They poured in buckets of cash, then sold the whole shebang to private interests who've spent further millions.

Tarraleah still feels like a ghost town if you visit outside peak season. But history is palpable, and even in the mists of July it's curiously engaging.

Activities include mountain biking, bushwalking, golf, birdwatching, fishing (ask about fishing-and-accommodation packages), kayaking and squash. Less outdoorsy types can submit to the pleasures of the lodge's cliff-top spa, or cooking lessons focusing on local produce.

Accommodation here traverses the budgetary terrain, from seasonal caravan-park sites (☑03-6289 0111; www.tarraleah.com/tarraleah/tarraleah-highland-caravan-park; unpowered/powered sites $20/40, cabin $120; ⊙Oct-Apr) to hotel-style rooms (☑03-6289 0111; www.tarraleah.com/tarraleah/scholars-house; Trawala Cres; d from $135), self-contained cottages (☑03-6289 0111; www.tarraleah.com/tarraleah/cottages; Oldina Dr; 2-4 people from $230, extra person $30) and ritzy lodge (☑03-6289 0111; www.tarraleahlodge.com.au; Oldina Dr; d from $285) rooms. Note that none of the accommodation here has wi-fi.

On the food front there's good coffee and big brunches at Teez Café (☑03-6289 0105; www.tarraleah.com/tarraleah/teez-cafe; Pugara St; mains $6-15; ⊙8am-3pm mid-Sep–Apr), and evening bistro meals, Guinness and whisky at the Highlander Restaurant & Bar (☑03-6289 0111; www.tarraleah.com/tarraleah/the-highlander-restaurant-and-bar; Pugara St; mains $25-38; ⊙5-8pm Mon-Sat Nov-Apr).

Tassielink (p306) buses stop here on request on Tuesday, Thursday, Friday and Sunday (and every weekday during school terms), trucking in from Hobart ($28, two hours) and Strahan ($49.30, five hours).

Central Highlands Lodge　　LODGE $$
(☑03-6259 8179; www.centralhighlandslodge.com.au; 7795 Highland Lakes Rd, Miena; d/f from $125/165; ☎) On the southern outskirts of Miena, this jaunty, rough-sawn timber lodge offers clean, comfortable cabins.

The lodge restaurant (mains $20 to $32, open noon to 2pm and 6pm to 8pm) is a snug spot to rejuvenate with a cold beer and a hot meal – venison hot pot, trout, salmon and quail have the authentic tinge of the encircling wilderness.

ℹ Information

For lake and bushwalking info, phone the Parks & Wildlife Service's **Great Western Tiers Field Office** (☑03-6701 2104; www.parks.tas.gov.au) in Deloraine or the Central Highlands Visitor Information Centre (p133) in Bothwell.

Inland Fisheries Service (p132) has advice and fishing licences.

ℹ Getting There & Away

Public-transport services to this area are nonexistent. Bring a 4WD if you can, to really get into the thick of it. Access is via the Lake Hwy, which turns off the Midland Hwy at Melton Mowbray and trucks through Bothwell.

Hamilton

☑03 / POP 300

National Trust–classified Hamilton, on the fringe of the Central Highlands in the Derwent Valley, was planned with great expectations. Settled in 1808 (the same year nearby New Norfolk was established), it was a mid-19th-century boom town. By 1835 it had 800 residents, who were well watered by 11 hotels and two breweries. Grids of streets were surveyed, but the dry local soils defeated many farmers. The town stagnated and several buildings were eventually removed.

These days, historic sandstone buildings adorn the main street, with photo-worthy views of mountain ranges and peaks to the west.

◉ Sights & Activities

If you're driving into Hamilton from Hobart, pick up the *Historic Hamilton* brochure at the New Norfolk visitor centre (p91). It details a walking tour past many of Hamilton's old buildings.

Hamilton Heritage Centre MUSEUM
(☑03-6286 3381; www.aumuseums.com/tas/hobart/hamilton-heritage-museum; Tarleton St; adult/child $1/0.50; ☺noon-3pm Tue) Hamilton's history gets an overview in the little Hamilton Heritage Centre, set up in an 1835 cottage that was once part of a larger jail. Ridiculously limited opening hours might stop you from getting in the door (call to see if the situation has improved).

Curringa Farm TOURS
(☑0418 863 337, 03-6286 3333; www.curringafarm.com.au; 5831 Lyell Hwy; tours per person from $60; ☺by arrangement 10am & 2.30pm Sep-Apr) Take a tour of the locally owned, 300-hectare, working Curringa Farm, 3km west of Hamilton. The owners strike a balance between business and sustainability, an approach applied to the 3000 sheep plus poppies, oats and cabbage seed farmed here. Minimum four people; bookings essential.

There's also accommodation (doubles from $230, extra person $45) in secluded spa cottages.

🛌 Sleeping & Eating

Hamilton Camping Facilities CAMPGROUND $
(☑03-6286 3202; www.centralhighlands.tas.gov.au/tourism/caravan-and-camping-sites; River St; unpowered sites per vehicle $5) No-frills camping on a grassy river flat near Hamilton's old pub, with a barbecue hut, toilets, showers, and a laundry across the street. Muddy if the Clyde River has been running high.

Cherry Villa B&B $$
(☑03-6286 3418; www.discovertasmania.com.au/accommodation/cherryvillabnb; 12 Arthur St; d $140, extra adult/child $45/30) The 1835 Cherry Villa offers three attractive heritage rooms amid buzzy-bee rose gardens. Straight out of an architectural textbook, it's a classically symmetrical Georgian house, with twin dormer windows and chimneys. Breakfast included, dinners by arrangement. Steep stairs!

28 Gates LODGE $$$
(☑03-6286 1319, 0428 371 701; www.28gates.com.au; 662 Marked Tree Rd, Gretna; up to 6 people $500) Fancy wetting a line in some highland lakes? The trout are biting at 28 Gates, a luxury fishing lodge (formerly shearers' quarters) near Gretna, with three bedrooms sleeping up to six. Ask about accommodation and guided fishing packages. Breakfast provisions supplied, lunch and dinner by arrangement. Two-night minimum.

★ Jackson's Emporium CAFE $$
(☑03-6286 3232; www.jacksonsemporium.com.au; 13 Franklin Pl; mains $12-18; ☺9am-9pm, to 8pm Jun-Aug) Enterprising Jackson's (an emporium since the 1850s) offers up locally sourced cafe fare (quiches, burgers, chilli con carne, soups), plus desserts, wine and beer, in its rustic shopfront. Lots of vegetarian options too, plus takeaway jars of local honey, chutney, preserves and pickles.

Heritage accommodation is also available in a self-contained cottage ($305 for up to six people).

ⓘ Getting There & Away

Tassielink (p306) runs between Hobart and Hamilton, with daily buses on Tuesday, Thursday, Friday and Sunday (every weekday during school terms). One-way tickets are $15 (1½ hours).

The East Coast

Best Places to Eat

➜ Pasinis (p156)

➜ Freycinet Marine Farm (p152)

➜ Melshell Oysters (p147)

Best Places to Stay

➜ Beach Path House (p155)

➜ Piermont (p146)

➜ The French House (p159)

Why Go?

White-blond sand, gin-clear water, high blue skies...now strip off and plunge in! But don't stay in for too long – even in summer the water temperatures here can leave you breathless.

Tasmania's east coast is sea-salted and rejuvenating – a land of quiet bays and sandy shores, punctuated by granite headlands splashed with flaming orange lichen. The whole coast is fringed with forests, national parks and farmland.

Tasmania's west coast cops all the rain – by the time the clouds make it out here they're virtually empty! No surprise, then, that this is prime holiday terrain for Tasmanians, with plenty of opportunities to hike, bike, kayak, surf, dive and fish – set up your beachside camp and get into it. At the end of the day, fish and chips on the beacwineh is a sure-fire winner. Or, if luxury is more your thing, you'll find hip lodges and top-flight eateries aplenty.

When to Go

➜ Picture-postcard east-coast images conjure up visions of high summer, but in truth those clear photographers' dream days are often in winter: be open-minded about when you visit.

➜ The whole coast comes alive in summer. A relaxed, vacation vibe prevails, but popular spots get busy and accommodation prices surge. Conversely, in the dead of winter (June to August) many east-coast beach towns are half-asleep and empty.

➜ In autumn (March to April) the sea is at its warmest, and you might have a beach all to yourself.

East Coast Highlights

❶ Wineglass Bay
(p149) Sweating it out on the track to this fabled bay, then cooling off in the sea once you get there.

❷ Maria Island National Park
(p142) Bumping into wombats and wallabies on a bushwalk.

❸ St Helens (p158) Reeling in a deep-sea monster – or at least catching your dinner.

❹ Weldborough Hotel (p162) Drinking your way around the full suite of Tasmanian craft brews.

❺ Mt William National Park (p163) Camping under whispering she-oaks.

❻ Bay of Fires Lodge Walk (p161) Hiking the shore and paddling a kayak on mirror-calm Ansons River.

❼ Binalong Bay
(p161) Dunking your head under the waves at this gorgeous beach.

❽ Devil's Corner
(p146) Quaffing the afternoon away at the slickest of the east-coast wineries.

❾ Flinders Island
(p167) Beachcombing for Killiecrankie diamonds.

CYCLING THE EAST COAST

THE RIDE

START ORFORD
END BICHENO
LENGTH 140KM; ONE WEEK

The east coast proper kicks off at **Orford** (p140), a soporific holiday hub 79km northeast of Hobart, where the glassy Prosser River meets the sea. Fuel up on baked treats (head for the Gateway Cafe) or cool off with a swim at nearby Spring Beach. Darlington Vineyard is here, too, if you have room for a bottle or two in your panniers.

From Orford it's just a 7km pedal to little **Triabunna** (p140), a raffish port town with a fishing fleet, an old pub and a former wood-chipping mill in the throes of (rather controversial) redevelopment. The ferry to **Maria Island National Park** (p142) leaves from the waterfront: if you have a few days up your sleeve, take your bike over, camp and pedal around some brilliant island trails (native animals ahoy!). Otherwise, stay the night in Triabunna (the town caravan park is very decent) and don't miss some fresh fish and chips from the Fish Van on the harbour.

From Triabunna it's a 50km run north to **Swansea** (p144), the next big town. If that seems too far, shoot for **Little Swanport**, 22km away, where there's a lovely (and free) camp site just north of the river. There's another free camp site at beautiful Mayfield Bay, about 15km south of Swansea. Note that just beyond Mayfield Bay the road makes a steep climb – you'll need to put some power into your pedals! Don't miss Spiky Bridge, 7km south of Swansea, a convict-built marvel just off the main road. The golden-sand beaches near here – Kelvedon, Spiky and Cressy – are divine for a dip.

Swansea itself is a busy tourist hub, with lots of cafes, a buzzing tavern and plenty of places to stay for all budgets. Check out the little East Coast Heritage Museum for an overview of local history. Next to the town backpackers, the Bark Mill Tavern & Bakery is the pick of places to eat at any tick of

the clock (doors open at 6am). Load up on goodies, then take a local cycling tour with Swansea Cycle Tours along some gorgeous privately owned coastline (...these guys are also helpful if you're having any mechanical issues).

The east coast is the sunniest, driest part of the state, and the riding along the main coast road is mostly easygoing (with a few steady climbs). There are also plenty of towns en route in which to stop – perfect road-cycling country!

North of Swansea there's a string of brilliant wineries in which to sip and swill (just one or two, of course...). **Gala Estate Vineyard** (p146) is right on the roadside in Cranbrook and makes a handy stop. The architecturally devilish Devil's Corner is brilliant, too, with a crop of eating options on-site and killer views across the coast. But don't linger too long – it's a lengthy 52km haul from Swansea to Coles Bay, your next stop.

Turn off the main road 34km north of Swansea and head 18km south towards **Coles Bay** (p147), an endearing holiday hamlet on the doorstep of the famous Freycinet National Park. Coles Bay, too, has plenty of places to rest your bones, from camp sites to plush villas. There are some great foodie haunts around here, too: don't bypass the oysters at Freycinet Marine Farm on the way into Coles Bay, nor Tombolo Freycinet for a pizza in the township itself. But what most folks are here for is a look at Wineglass Bay, the amazing beach beyond the craggy Hazards granite peaks that form the backdrop to Coles Bay. You can take a ritzy boat cruise to Wineglass Bay from Coles Bay, or cycle into the national park and then hike up over 'The Saddle' to get there; your efforts will be rewarded with a cooling dunk in the impossibly clear ocean.

Backtrack to the highway and continue north to **Bicheno** (p153), 35km from Coles Bay and an unpretentious town in which to end your east-coast tour. Native-wildlife experiences are the name of the game here: check out some Tasmanian devils and snakes at Natureworld, some penguins with Bicheno Penguin Tours, or the undersea realm with Bicheno's Glass Bottom Boat. The Bicheno Motorcycle Museum is an amazing place to visit, too, with more than 60 shiny chrome machines (perhaps next time you tackle this trip your two wheels might be accompanied by an engine?). Celebrate your adventures with dinner and a few more east-coast wines at Pasinis, a local Italian restaurant that leaves the competition floundering in its wake.

❶ Getting There & Away

The road traversing Tasmania's east coast is a long, sinewy route running north–south, with a few detours here and there. Having your own transport will serve you best, but there are bus services here: **Tassielink** (p306) runs up the coast from Hobart as far as Bicheno, stopping at all the towns along the way. North of Bicheno, **Calow's Coaches** (📞 0400 570 036, 03-6376 2161; www.calowscoaches.com.au) takes over, running as far north as St Helens, and also running from Bicheno to Launceston via St Marys. Calow's also connects Bicheno with Coles Bay and the Freycinet Peninsula.

In the northeast, **Sainty's North East Bus Service** (Map p178; 📞 0437 469 186, 0400 791 076; www.saintysnortheastbusservice.com.au) runs from Bridport to Launceston via Scottsdale, and connects Derby and Launceston.

Access to Flinders Island is usually via a flight from Launceston or Melbourne with Sharp Airlines (p169). There's also a freight boat you can catch, running occasionally from Bridport.

Orford

📞 03 / POP 520

First stop on the east coast if you're heading north from Hobart, seaside Orford was once a port for the east-coast whaling fleet and the convict and military settlement on Maria Island, just across Mercury Passage. These days, Orford is a holiday hamlet where Hobartians have their seaside 'shacks' and spend summer holidays on the sand.

The Prosser River flows through Paradise Gorge as it heads towards the town, and is often mirror-calm with perfect reflections. On the north side of the river is a convict-built road that once ran all the way to Hobart; it's now a riverside walking track. Another coastal track (5km) leads from Raspins Beach, along Shelly Beach, around the Luther Point cliffs and onto photogenic Spring Beach, which has improbably clear water and, if the surf gods are smiling, decent waves. The track passes a convict-era quarry that coughed out sandstone for buildings in Hobart and Melbourne.

◉ Sights & Activities

The fish are biting in the Prosser – ideal for messing about in boats. There's also good diving offshore, particularly around the scuppered ship *Troy D*, which has attracted plenty of underwater residents. Contact the Tasmanian Scuba Diving Club (www.tsdc.org.au) for details.

Darlington Vineyard   WINERY
(📞 03-6257 1630; www.darlingtonvineyard.com.au; 63 Holkham Ct; ⊙ 10am-5pm) In the Orford back-blocks up the hill opposite the service station, Darlington Vineyard is the most southerly of the east-coast wineries, producing quaffable riesling. The simple cellar door is open for tastings and sales. Visitors to Maria Island may recognise the logo on the bottles.

🛏 Sleeping & Eating

Sanda House   B&B $$
(📞 03-6257 1527; www.orfordsandahouse.com.au; 33 Walpole St; d $180-195; 🛜) A colonial B&B in Orford's oldest house, a photogenic 1840s stone cottage (actually, some sections date back to 1825!) surrounded by lovingly tended gardens on the south side of the river. Continental breakfasts are served fireside in the dining room (love those stewed fruits). Inside are four rooms, all with bathroom; outside are 20 fruit trees in the garden.

Nosh   RENTAL HOUSE $$$
(📞 0419 117 613; www.noshholiday.com.au; 2 Happy Valley Rd, Spring Beach; house $320) *Star Wars'* Tatooine meets ecofriendly at this holiday home that looks like it was sculpted from white clay and filled with designer furniture. Just up the hill from gorgeous Spring Beach, it sleeps up to six comfortably. Pour a glass of wine, kick back and contemplate another beach day ahead.

Scorchers by the River   PIZZA $$
(📞 03-6257 1033; 1 Esplanade; mains $17-27; ⊙ 4-8pm Mon-Thu, noon-8pm Fri-Sun) Scorchers gets big ticks for superior eat-in or takeaway wood-fired pizzas, of which the Spring Bay seafood disc tops the list (local smoked mussels, scallops, bacon, cheddar, baby spinach and tomato relish). There's also lasagne, salads and a long list of Tasmanian wines by the glass or bottle (go on, upsize – you're on holiday).

❶ Getting There & Away

Daily Tassielink (p306) buses roll into Orford from Hobart ($16.90, 1½ hours).

Triabunna

📞 03 / POP 900

Nondescript Triabunna, 8km north of Orford, was founded as a military outpost in 1830. The town squats on an inlet of Spring Bay and shelters a small cray- and scallop-

THE SAGA OF THE TRIABUNNA MILL

Millionaire Tasmanian conservationists Jan Cameron (co-founder of Kathmandu) and Graeme Wood (founder of Wotif.com) purchased the old Triabunna woodchip mill in 2011, handing over $10 million to controversial (and now defunct) timber company Gunns Ltd. Cameron and Wood shut the mill down, effectively choking the state's wood-chip industry by denying access to the only deep-water port on the east coast.

Furore and confusion ensued. How could these millionaires jeopardise the state's economy like this? Should the state government compulsorily acquire the mill to free up the port? What would become of Triabunna without the mill?

After a wrecking crew put paid to the mill's machinations, most locals resigned themselves to its closure and now seem to want to move on. In 2017 Wood had plans approved to develop Spring Bay Mill (www.springbaymill.com), a multimillion-dollar reimagining of the site as a tourist destination to rival MONA in Hobart. His latest battle, however, is with Tassal salmon farms, which wants to set up a fish farm in neighbouring Okehampton Bay. Wood claims the farm will jeopardise the local marine ecosystem and threaten the viability of his development. Watch this space...

fishing fleet. There's a shambling old waterside pub here and the Triabunna Visitor Information Centre, but not much else of interest to tourists...other than the fact that this is the jumping-off point for magical Maria Island National Park. The old woodchip mill by the harbour has been making headlines in recent years; a major tourism redevelopment here is under way.

Word nerds may be interested to learn that the name Triabunna is a local Aboriginal word for native hen.

Tours

East Coast Cruises   CRUISE
(☑03-6257 1300; www.eastcoastcruises.com.au; tours adult/child from $220/85) ✐ East Coast Cruises runs full-day ecotours from Triabunna to Maria Island, visiting the Ile des Phoques seal colony, the island's Painted Cliffs and the old convict settlement at Darlington.

Sleeping & Eating

Triabunna Cabin & Caravan Park   CARAVAN PARK $
(☑03-6257 3575; www.mariagateway.com; 4 Vicary St; unpowered/powered sites from $30/33, on-site vans/cabins/d from $95/130/140; ⊛) This small-but-progressive compound, surrounded by well-maintained gardens, has all the usual caravan-park facilities, as well as a couple of en suite double rooms in the front of a lovely old house. DVDs for when it's raining; BBQ out the front for when it's not.

★ **The Fish Van**   SEAFOOD $
(☑0407 552 847; www.facebook.com/thefishvan; 19 Esplanade W; meals $8-18; ⊗11am-7pm)

Gobble some east-coast fish and chips from this super-friendly, marina-side caravan. It cooks up flathead, trevalla, barracouta and flake – whatever is fresh from the local fishing boats – along with mountains of chips. Burgers and steak sangers, too. Brilliant.

ℹ Information

Triabunna Visitor Information Centre (☑03-6257 4772; www.tasmaniaseastcoast.com.au; cnr Charles St & Esplanade W; ⊗9am-5pm Oct-Apr, 10am-4pm May-Sep) Cheerily delivered information on the whole east-coast region, plus Maria Island ferry tickets and accommodation bookings. Pick up the handy *Great Eastern Drive* booklet, covering the whole coast.

ℹ Getting There & Away

Tassielink (p306) buses from Hobart ($20.70, 1¾ hours) stop at the visitor information centre every day.

Triabunna is also the departure point for ferries to Maria Island National Park.

Maria Island National Park

Captivating Maria Island (pronounced 'Muh-*rye*-uh'), with its jagged peaks, rises up like a fairy-tale castle across Mercury Passage, which separates it from the mainland. It's a carefree, car-free haven – a top spot for walking, wildlife watching, mountain biking, camping and reading a book on the beach.

Maria is laced with impressive scenery: curious cliffs, fern-draped forests, squeaky-sand beaches and azure seas. Forester

Northern Maria Island

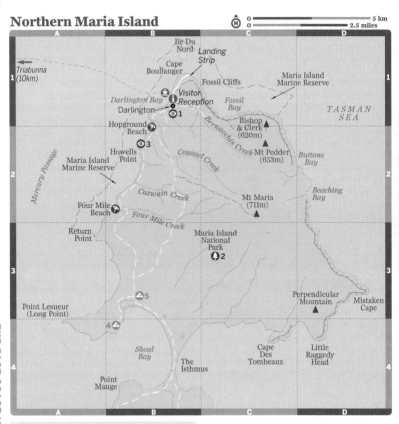

(eastern grey) kangaroos, wombats and wallabies wander around; grey-plumed Cape Barren geese honk about on the grasslands; and an insurance population of Tasmanian devils (they're beset with disease on the mainland), has been released here and is thriving. Below the water there's also lots to see, with good snorkelling and diving in the clear, shallow marine reserve.

In 1972 Maria became a national park (☏03-6257 1420; www.parks.tas.gov.au; park day pass per person $12), as much for its history as for its natural assets, and Darlington is now also a Unesco World Heritage–listed site.

The island doesn't have any shops: BYO food and gear.

History

Maria Island has seen various incarnations as a penal settlement, an industrial site and a farming community. The island was originally home to the Oyster Bay community of Tasmanian Aboriginals, who called it Toarra Marra Monah. They lived primarily on shellfish, and made the crossing to the mainland in bark canoes.

Dutch explorer Abel Tasman landed here in 1642, and named the island in honour of Anthony van Diemen's wife. The island became Tasmania's second penal settlement in 1821 and, for the next 10 years, the convicts were set to work developing it. Many of the surviving buildings, such as the commissariat store (1825) and the penitentiary (1830), are from this era. By the early 1830s Maria Island was becoming too expensive to be viable, so the convicts were shipped back to settlements on the Tasmanian mainland. For the next 10 years, the island was the domain of whalers, farmers and smugglers.

In 1842 Darlington reopened as a probation station and a road was built to a second settlement at Long Point (Point Lesueur). At one stage there were about 600 convicts on Maria, but when convict transportation to Tasmania slowed, numbers dwindled and Darlington was again closed in 1850.

With the arrival of enterprising Italian businessman Diego Bernacchi in 1884, Maria Island began a new era. Darlington's buildings were renovated and structures such as the Coffee Palace (1888) were added. The town of 260 people was renamed San Diego. Over the next 40 years a cement factory and wine and silk-growing industries were developed. This industrial era ended with the advent of the Great Depression, and by the 1940s the island reverted to farming.

In the 1960s the government bought the properties on the island and reintroduced animals such as forester kangaroos, Bennett's wallabies and Cape Barren geese, which had been wiped out since European occupation.

◉ Sights

Darlington   HISTORIC SITE
(☑ 03-6257 1420; www.parks.tas.gov.au; park day pass per person $12) The township of Darlington – officially the Unesco World Heritage-listed Darlington Probation Station – is where you'll start your time on the island. Close to the ferry jetty are some amazing old silos (good for some midnight monastic chanting inside) and the historic commissariat store, now the national park visitor centre. Through an avenue of gnarled macrocarpa trees lies the penitentiary, which once housed convicts (now bunkhouse-style accommodation), as well as the restored Coffee Palace and mess hall.

Painted Cliffs   LANDMARK
(☑ 03-6257 1420; www.parks.tas.gov.au; via Ashley Rd, Darlington; park day pass per person $12) From Darlington it's a one-hour return walk to the Painted Cliffs, at the southern end of Hopground Beach. From the beach you can clamber along the sculpted sandstone cliffs, stained with iron oxide in a kaleidoscope of colours. We suggest a visit in the late afternoon when the sun paints the cliffs a fiery orange.

🏃 Activities

Wildlife Watching   WILDLIFE RESERVE
(☑ 03-6257 1420; www.parks.tas.gov.au; Darlington; park day pass per person $12) Lucky twitchers might spot the endangered forty-spotted pardalote on Maria, or perhaps the aptly named swift parrot. You'll certainly see Cape Barren geese waddling around (and depositing their dietary byproducts on) the lawns at Darlington. Meandering wombats and grazing wallabies are also a common sight. Keep an eye out for echidnas and nocturnal Tasmanian devils on forest tracks.

Darlington Day Walks   HIKING
(☑ 03-6257 1420; www.parks.tas.gov.au; via Darlington; park day pass per person $12) From Darlington, there's a two-hour loop walk to the Fossil Cliffs and the old brickworks. If you have more time (four hours return from Darlington), climb Bishop and Clerk (620m) for a bird's-eye view while you eat your packed lunch on the exposed, rocky summit. Mt Maria (711m) is the island's highest point; it's a seven-hour return hike through the eucalypt forests from Darlington, with brilliant views over the island's isthmus from the top.

Mountain Biking   MOUNTAIN BIKING
(☑ 03-6256 4772; www.encountermaria.com.au; Encounter Maria Island, Charles St, Triabunna) With well-maintained tracks, dirt roads and no cars, Maria is a fantastic place for mountain biking. You can bring your own wheels on the ferry ($10 return), or hire bikes from the ferry company (per day adult/child $33/20). Ask about the best trails at visitor reception on the island.

☞ Tours

Maria Island Walk   HIKING
(☑ 03-6234 2999; www.mariaislandwalk.com.au; per person $2500) Blisters, soggy tents and two-minute noodles? Redefine your concept of bushwalking on this luxury guided four-day hike through Maria's best bits. The first two nights are spent at secluded bush camps, with the third at the historic former home of entrepreneur Diego Bernacchi in Darlington. The price includes amazing

THE EAST COAST MARIA ISLANDNATIONAL PARK

food, fine Tasmanian wines, accommodation, park fees and transport from Hobart.

🛏 Sleeping

There are two ways to sleep on the island: in a tent and in the old convict penitentiary, now a humble lodge. There are no bookings for camp sites – just pay your fees when you arrive on the island.

Darlington Camp Site CAMPGROUND **$**
(📞 03-6257 1420; www.parks.tas.gov.au; Darlington; unpowered sites s/d/f $7/13/16) Grassy unpowered sites at Darlington (fees payable at the island visitor centre; no bookings), plus free sites at **French's Farm** and **Encampment Cove** three to four hours' walk from the ferry pier. Barbecues, toilets and showers ($1) at Darlington. Fires allowed in designated fireplaces (often banned in summer). French's Farm and Encampment Cove have limited tank water – bring your own. National park fees apply.

Penitentiary LODGE **$**
(📞 03-6256 4772; www.parks.tas.gov.au; Darlington; dm/d/f $15/44/50) Darlington's brick penitentiary once housed the island's convicts. These days it's simple, sensible accommodation, with six-bunk rooms, shared bathrooms and coin-operated showers ($1). BYO linen, lighting (there's no electricity), food, cooking gear and ability to dismiss the possibility of ghosts. It's often full of school groups, so plan ahead. Book via the Triabunna Visitor Information Centre (p141).

❶ Information

Buy your national parks passes at the Triabunna Visitor Information Centre (p141) before you get on the ferry, or at **visitor reception** (📞 03-6257 1420; www.parks.tas.gov.au; Commissariat Store, Darlington; ⊘ 9am-5pm) once you get to Maria.

❶ Getting There & Away

Encounter Maria Island (p306) runs three ferries daily in each direction between Triabunna and Darlington, extending to five sailings from September to April. Bike hire per day is adult/child $33/20.

You can land on the grass airstrip near Darlington in a light plane (or just fly overhead): talk with **Par Avion** (📞 03-6248 5390; www.paravion.com.au; 4hr east-coast tour adult/child $395/345).

You can also get a good look at the island with East Coast Cruises (p141), departing Triabunna.

Swansea
📞 03 / POP 780

Unhurried Swansea graces the western shore of sheltered Great Oyster Bay, with sweeping views across the water to the peaks of the Freycinet Peninsula. Founded in 1820 as 'Great Swanport', Swansea also delivers some interesting historic buildings and a museum.

The town's revival since the doldrums of the 1980s has paralleled the boom in tourism across the state, though it manages to retain a laid-back holiday vibe. There are plenty of enticements for visitors in and around town, including myriad accommodation options, beaches, restaurants, cafes and some impressive wineries to the north. Swansea gets busy as a beaver (or perhaps a platypus?) in summer, so book ahead.

◉ Sights

★ **Spiky Bridge** BRIDGE
(off Tasman Hwy) About 7km south of Swansea is the rather amazing Spiky Bridge, built by convicts in the early 1840s using thousands of local fieldstones (yes, they're spiky). The main east-coast road used to truck right across it, but these days it's set beside the highway. Nearby Kelvedon Beach, Spiky Beach and Cressy Beach have deep golden sand and rarely a footprint.

Bark Mill Museum MUSEUM
(📞 03-6257 8094; www.barkmilltavern.com.au/museum; 96 Tasman Hwy; adult/child/family $10/6/23; ⊘ 10am-4pm) Out the back of the Bark Mill Tavern & Bakery, this museum explains the processing of black wattle bark to obtain tannin for tanning leathers. The mill was one of the few industries that operated in Swansea through the Great Depression and helped keep the town afloat. There's also a display on early French exploration along Tasmania's east coast.

East Coast Heritage Museum MUSEUM
(📞 03-6256 5066; www.eastcoastheritage.org.au; 22 Franklin St; entry by donation; ⊘ 10am-4pm) **FREE** Inside Swansea's original schoolhouse – now also home to the Swansea Visitor Information Centre – this engaging little museum covers Aboriginal artefacts, colonial history, schooling in the early days and the plight of the thylacine.

Swansea

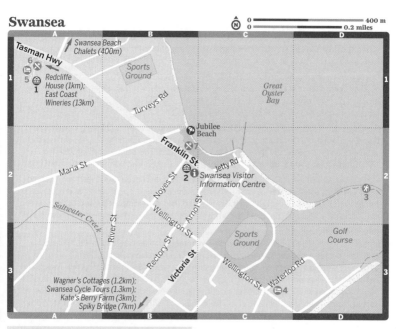

Swansea

⊙ Sights
1 Bark Mill Museum A1
2 East Coast Heritage Museum B2

⊙ Activities, Courses & Tours
3 Loon.tite.ter.mair.re.le.hoin.er
  Walk D2

⊝ Sleeping
4 Schouten House C3
5 Swansea Backpackers A1

⊗ Eating
6 Bark Mill Tavern & Bakery A1
7 Saltshaker B2

✦ Activities

Loon.tite.ter.mair.re.le.hoin.er Walk WALKING
(☑03-6256 7000; www.parks.tas.gov.au; Foreshore) This 2.3km trail skirts the headland
between Waterloo Beach and the Esplanade,
passing a mutton bird (short-tailed shearwater) rookery. During breeding season
(September to April) the adult birds return
at dusk after feeding at sea. Allow 30 to 50
minutes to loop around the trail (you'll need
at least that long to figure out how to pro-
nounce it – it's named after the Aboriginal
community that lived in the area).

Swansea Cycle Tours CYCLING
(☑0400 899 956; www.swanseacycletours.com.
au; 17 Old Spring Bay Rd; tours per person guid-
ed/unguided from $115/60; ☺office 9am-5pm)
Saddle up for one of seven customised bike
tours around super-scenic, private east-coast
farmland, visiting vineyards, oyster beds,
lagoons and rivers. Bike hire also available
(per half-/full day $15/25).

🛏 Sleeping

Swansea Backpackers HOSTEL $
(☑03-6257 8650; www.swanseabackpackers.
com.au; 98 Tasman Hwy; unpowered & powered
sites $25-35, dm/d/tr/q from $39/85/85/90; ☂)
This hip backpackers, next door to the Bark
Mill, was purpose-built a few years ago, and
is still looking sharp. Inside are smart, spacious public areas and a shiny stainless-steel
kitchen. Rooms surround a shady deck and
are clean and shipshape. More than a little
fortuitously, the bar and bottle shop are
right next door.

★Schouten House B&B $$
(☑03-6257 8564; www.schoutenhouse.com.
au; 1 Waterloo Rd; d incl breakfast from $185; ☂)
This brick-and-sandstone 1844 mansion
was built by convicts, and was the centre of
'Great Swanport' before the action shifted

EAST-COAST WINERIES

Along the Tasman Hwy north of Swansea is a string of terrific wineries, the producers here making the most of sunny east-coast days and cool nights. From south to north:

Milton Vineyard (☑03-6257 8298; www.miltonvineyard.com.au; 14635 Tasman Hwy; ⊙10am-5pm) Milton is 13km north of Swansea, with tastings in an elegant, white weatherboard pavilion presiding over the vines. Sip some sparkling rosé and enjoy a cheese platter or some tapas by the lake (mains $14 to $26).

Spring Vale Wines (☑03-6257 8208; www.springvalewines.com; 130 Spring Vale Rd, Cranbrook; ⊙11am-4pm) Down a *looong* driveway in Cranbrook, 15km north of Swansea, this winery is on land owned by the same family since 1875. The cellar door is housed in an 1842 stable, cobbled together by hard-working convict hands. Don't miss the pinot gris.

Gala Estate Vineyard (☑03-6257 8641; www.galaestate.com.au; 14891 Tasman Hwy, Cranbrook; ⊙10am-4pm Sep-May) A funky little cellar door – once a post office, and home to a family with 10 kids (10!) – right on the main road through Cranbrook. Stop by for some pinot gris ('It walks out the door!', says the lady behind the bar), some late-harvest riesling and a picnic hamper.

Devil's Corner (☑03-6257 8881; www.brownbrothers.com.au; Sherbourne Rd, Apslawn; ⊙10am-5pm) Below a devilishly tight turn on the Tasman Hwy, Devil's Corner is one of Tasmania's largest vineyards, run by the estimable Brown Brothers company. The mod cellar door here overlooks Moulting Lagoon, beyond which is Freycinet Peninsula. Even if you're not into wine, stop by to check out the jaunty lookout tower, or to grab a coffee, a sorbet, some oysters or fish and chips from the **food outlets** here, housed in styled-up shipping containers (mains $12 to $25).

Freycinet Vineyard (☑03-6257 8574; www.freycinetvineyard.com.au; 15919 Tasman Hwy, Apslawn; ⊙10am-5pm Oct-Apr, 10am-4pm May-Sep) The Bull family has been growing grapes 'neath the east-coast sun since 1980 – it was the first vineyard on the coast. The vibe at the cellar door is agricultural, not flashy – we like it! Super sauvignon blanc.

a little further north. Decorated in simple, masculine Georgian style (no frills), its huge rooms now house antique beds and bathrooms. The history-buff owners do a mean pancake breakfast, and have perfected the art of making shortbread.

Swansea Beach Chalets　CABIN $$
(☑03-6257 8177; www.swanseachalets.com.au; 27 Shaw St; cabin from $170; ▣⬚⬚) These 20 chic, self-contained, grey-and-blue chalets are just steps from Jubilee Beach. The best ones have amazing 180-degree water vistas – high, wide and handsome. There's also a BBQ pavilion, a games room and an outdoor pool if the beach doesn't do it for you.

Redcliffe House　B&B $$
(☑03-6257 8557; www.redcliffehouse.com.au; 13569 Tasman Hwy; d incl breakfast $140-185; ⬚) This restored, two-storey convict-built farmhouse (1835) is just north of Swansea, backing onto the Meredith River. The five guest rooms have various bedding and bathroom configurations (no kids) and are decked out in rustic style. If you're feeling sociable,

there's a snug guest lounge with decanters of port and sherry awaiting. The iron roof could use a paint!

★**Piermont**　COTTAGE $$$
(☑03-6257 8131; www.piermont.com.au; 12990 Tasman Hwy; cottage from $415; ⬚⬚) Down a hawthorn-hedged driveway, 5km south of Swansea, these 21 stylish stone cabins fan out from an old farmhouse close to the sea. Each unit has a fireplace and a spa. There's also a pool, tennis court, free bikes and kayaks, and a **restaurant** (1/2/3 courses $45/65/75, degustation without/with wine $110/150; ⊙6-8pm) that's been getting positive press. Big on weddings (so book ahead).

★**Avalon Coastal Retreat**　RENTAL HOUSE $$$
(☑1300 361 136, 0428 250 399; www.avalon retreats.com.au/coastal; 11922 Tasman Hwy, Rocky Hills; house incl breakfast $900-1000; ⬚) What a beauty! Like something out of a James Bond movie – all glass and steel and endless ocean views – this is possibly the most luxurious beach house in Tasmania. The kitchen and cellar are well stocked and the beach is near-

by – though you'll hardly want to leave the house. It's 14km south of Swansea. Sleeps six.

Wagner's Cottages
COTTAGE $$$

(☑03-6257 8494, 0419 882 726; www.wagner
scottages.com; 13182 Tasman Hwy; cottage from
$195; ❀ 🐾) Wagner's Cottages entails four
stone cottages in cottage gardens a couple of
kilometres south of town. Cottagey, yes, but
they're characterful and eccentric, variously
with open fires, loft bedrooms and freestone
walling. Breakfast is a DIY affair, featuring
fresh eggs from resident chooks and just-
out-of-the-oven bread.

🍴 Eating

★ Melshell Oysters
SEAFOOD $$

(☑03-6257 0269, 0428 570 334; www.melshell
oysters.com.au; 1 Yellow Sandbanks Rd, Dolphin
Sands; 12 oysters unshucked/shucked from $12/20;
⊙10am-4pm) In the soupy back reaches of
Moulting Lagoon, about 16km northeast
of Swansea off Dolphin Sands Rd (itself off
Swan River Rd – follow the signs), Melshell
is a quirky caravan behind the dunes selling
local Pacific oysters (and sometimes mussels). We like 'em natural, or with a little
splash of Tabasco sauce.

Bark Mill Tavern & Bakery
CAFE $$

(☑03-6257 8094; www.barkmilltavern.com.au;
96 Tasman Hwy; mains bakery $5-15, tavern $17-
43; ⊙bakery 6am-4pm, tavern noon-2pm & 5.30-
8pm) The Bark Mill has two foodie faces: a
busy bakery-cafe and a pubby tavern, both
doing a roaring trade (to the exclusion of
many other businesses in town, it seems).
The bakery serves cooked breakfasts, stuffed
rolls, sweet temptations, neat quiches and
good coffee; the tavern does pizzas and volu-
minous mains (try the kangaroo and cheese
sausage).

Saltshaker
MODERN AUSTRALIAN $$

(☑03-6257 8488; www.saltshakerrestaurant.com.
au; 11a Franklin St; breakfast $9-20, lunch $20-33,
dinner $27-39; ⊙9am-late) Ebullient, all-day
Saltshaker gets the urban vote in Swansea.
This bright, chic, waterfront dining room
serves fresh lunches and classy dinners that
are big on local seafood (try the prawn and
scallop linguine with lemon garlic butter).
There's a wine list as long as your afternoon,
and a takeaway outlet (mains $7 to $25) doing decent pizzas, burgers and pasta.

Kate's Berry Farm
CAFE $$

(☑03-6257 8428; www.katesberryfarm.com; 12
Addison St; meals $13-18; ⊙9.30am-4.30pm)

Sit under the wisteria-draped pergola at
Kate's (3km south of Swansea) and decide
which handmade berry incarnation suits
your mood: berry ice creams, jams, sauces,
chocolates, waffles, pancakes or pies (go for
anything with raspberries involved). Great
coffee and 'potted' pies, too (try the beef and
burgundy). Look for the signs off the Tas-
man Hwy.

ℹ Information

Swansea Visitor Information Centre (☑03-
6256 5072; www.tasmaniaseastcoast.com.
au; 22 Franklin St; ⊙9am-5pm; 🐾) In the
old school building on the corner of Noyes St
(sharing space with the East Coast Heritage
Museum).

ℹ Getting There & Away

Tassielink (p306) buses to/from Hobart ($30,
2¼ hours) stop at Swansea Corner Store (cor-
ner Franklin and Victoria Sts) every day.

Coles Bay & Freycinet National Park

☑03 / POP 310

Coles Bay township sits on a sweep of sand
at the foot of the dramatic pink-granite
peaks of the Hazards on the Freycinet Pen-
insula. It's a laid-back holiday town with
plenty of accommodation (though book well
ahead in summer) and some active tour op-
tions. The sublime Freycinet National Park
(☑03-6256 7000; www.parks.tas.gov.au; via Coles
Bay; parks day pass per person/vehicle $12/24) is
the reason everyone is here: a wild domain
of sugar-white beaches and utterly transpar-
ent water. In the coastal heath and forests,
wildflowers and native critters hold sway.

The park encompasses the whole of the
peninsula south of Coles Bay, including
Schouten Island to the south, and a stretch
of coastal scrub around the Friendly Beaches
further north. The park's big-ticket sight is
the gorgeous goblet of Wineglass Bay. Take
the steep hike up to the saddle and grab
your photo opportunity, or continue down
to the sand on the other side for a (decidedly
nippy) dip in the sea.

History

The first folks to live around Coles Bay and
the Freycinet Peninsula were the Oyster Bay
Aboriginal community. Their diet was rich
in the abundant shellfish of the bay, and

Coles Bay

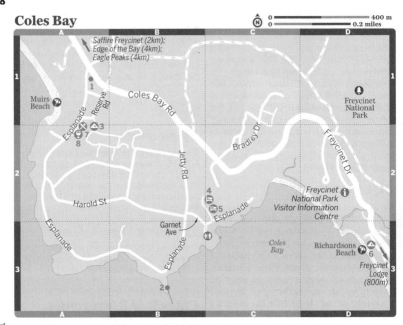

there are shell middens as evidence of this all over the peninsula.

Abel Tasman visited in 1642 and named Schouten Island. In 1802 Baudin's French expedition explored and named Freycinet Peninsula. When subsequent expeditions spied seals lounging around on the rocks, sealers arrived from Sydney to plunder them.

A whale 'fishery' was established at Parsons Cove at the foot of the Hazards in 1824 – the area is still known as the Fisheries. Here southern right whales that were hunted on their migration down the penin-sula were processed; the sparkling waters and blond sands soon became polluted with rotting whale remains. The station was closed by the 1840s – the whales had wised-up and moved elsewhere.

Coles Bay was named after Silas Cole, who arrived in the 1830s and burnt shells from Aboriginal middens to produce lime for the mortar to build Swansea. Since the early field naturalists' expeditions here in the late 1800s, the bay has been a popular holiday spot. In the 1920s the first holiday homes were built, and the area has been a much-loved holiday town ever since.

In the early days of the colony, both Freycinet Peninsula and Schouten Island were farmed, but in 1906 both became game reserves. In 1916 Freycinet shared the honour with Mt Field in becoming Tasmania's first national park; Schouten Island was added in 1977. The Friendly Beaches were added to the park in 1992.

⊙ Sights

★ Friendly Beaches   BEACH
(☑ 03-6256 7000; www.parks.tas.gov.au; Friendly Beaches Rd, Freycinet National Park; parks day pass per person/vehicle $12/24) This wind-swept ocean beach is signposted from the

WINGLASS BAY

You've no doubt seen the photos of Wineglass Bay – its perfect arc of talc-white sand fringed with clear waters. It's a regular on lists of 'World's Top 10 Beaches'. But visiting Wineglass is no lazy day at the beach. Getting here involves a steep, sweaty hike (✐03-6256 7000; www.parks.tas.gov.au; Freycinet National Park; park day pass per person/vehicle $12/24), and to get away from the crowds, you'll need to hike even further.

To reach the bay on foot is at least a half-day expedition, with 800 steep steps each way. If you only climb to the viewpoint over the bay, your Wineglass Bay wineglass will likely be overflowing with a horde of other camera clickers (some of the 250,000 that come here annually).

To beat the crowds, visit early and trudge right down to the bay on the other side of the viewpoint. On the way back, take the shady Isthmus Track from the beach then follow the coastal track along the west side of the peninsula back to the car park (about four hours). Take water, food and sun protection – and have a swim!

If this sort of physical exertion fills you with fear and loathing, you can swoop over the bay on a scenic flight (✐03-6375 1694; www.freycinetair.com.au; off Coles Bay Rd, Friendly Beaches; flights from $130), or cruise in by boat (p151).

main road about 26km north of Coles Bay. A five-minute walk leads from the car park to a vantage point: tumbling surf, an abandoned stretch of sand and views seemingly (if you squint, actually?) all the way to New Zealand.

Cape Tourville
LANDMARK

(✐03-6256 7000; www.parks.tas.gov.au; via Cape Tourville Rd, Freycinet National Park; parks day pass per person/vehicle $12/24) There's an easy 20-minute circuit here for eye-popping panoramas of Freycinet Peninsula's eastern coastline. You can even get a wheelchair or a pram along here. Also here is Cape Tourville Lighthouse, which is totally spectacular when the sun cracks a smile over the horizon at dawn.

Activities

For all national park walks, remember to pick up a parks pass from the Freycinet National Park Visitor Information Centre (p153). For longer walks, sign in (and out) at the car-park registration booth.

Sail Freycinet
BOATING

(✐0419 889 458; www.sailfreycinet.com.au; 3/6hr sail per 2 people $320/550, extra person from $115) Get some wind in your sails on these three- or six-hour sailing trips around sheltered Great Oyster Bay, with excellent views of Freycinet from the water. An overnight option sailing around the peninsula to sleep becalmed in Wineglass Bay is also available (two people $1800). Ex-Coles Bay.

Freycinet Peninsula Circuit
HIKING

(✐03-6256 7000; www.parks.tas.gov.au; Freycinet National Park; park day pass per person/vehicle $12/24, holiday pass $30) This is a three-day, 30km trek around the peninsula, from Hazards Beach south to Cooks Beach (with optional extension to Bryans Beach) then across the peninsula over a heathland plateau before descending to Wineglass Bay. Consult the Freycinet National Park Visitor Information Centre (p153) for advice and maps, and check out Lonely Planet's *Walking in Australia*.

Mt Amos Walk
HIKING

(✐03-6256 7000; www.parks.tas.gov.au; Freycinet National Park; park day pass per person/vehicle $12/24) If your thighs are up to the challenge, make the trek to see the killer views from this summit (454m; three hours return), one of the Hazards peaks. Dangerously slippery in wet weather.

Tours

★ Freycinet Adventures
KAYAKING

(✐03-6257 0500; www.freycinetadventures.com.au; 2 Freycinet Dr, Coles Bay; tour per adult/child $98/88; ⊘tours 8.30am Oct-Apr, 9am May-Sep; ⊞) Get an eyeful of the peninsula from the sheltered waters around Coles Bay on these terrific three-hour paddles. There are also daily twilight tours available, setting off three hours before sunset. No experience necessary. Kayak hire is also available (from $55 per person per day, including safety gear). Ask about overnight and multiday trips, too.

Freycinet National Park

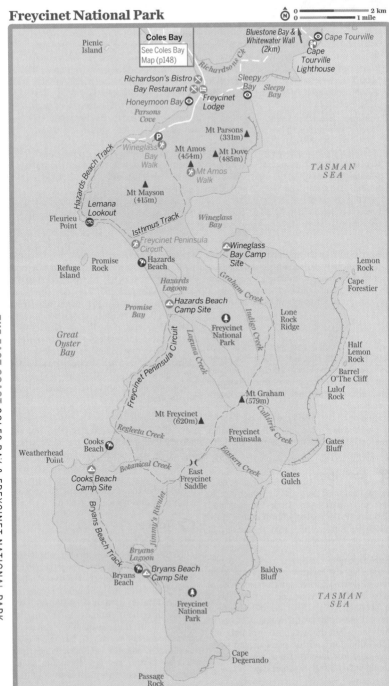

Freycinet Experience Walk
WALKING

(☑ 1800 506 003, 03-6223 7565; www.freycinet.com.au; adult/child $2550/2400; ☺ Nov–Apr) For those who like their wilderness more mild, less wild, Freycinet Experience Walk offers a four-day, fully catered exploration of the peninsula. Walkers return each evening to the secluded, environmentally attuned Friendly Beaches Lodge for superb meals, local wine, hot showers and comfortable beds. The walk covers around 37km.

Wineglass Bay Day Tour
BUS

(☑ 03-6110 9994, 0416 178 469; www.wineglassbaytours.com.au; adult/child $115/80; ☺ daily Nov–Apr, Mon, Tue, Fri & Sun May–Oct) Full-day minibus tours to the gorgeous goblet, departing Hobart at 7.30am and getting back around 7pm. You'll walk into Wineglass Bay, and also see Spiky Bridge, Cape Tourville and Honeymoon Bay.

Long Lunch Wine Tour Co
FOOD & DRINK

(☑ 0409 225 841; www.longlunchtourco.com.au; tour $160) Now this is a great idea! A full-day east-coast gastronomic adventure departing Coles Bay and ducking into four east-coast wineries, with stops for oysters, seafood, pizza and dessert along the way.

Wineglass Bay Cruises
BOATING

(☑ 03-6257 0355; www.wineglassbaycruises.com; Jetty Rd, Coles Bay; adult/child $140/90; ☺ 10am Sep–May, 10am Tue, Thu & Sat Jun & Jul, 10am Tue & Thu Aug) Sedate, four-hour cruises from Coles Bay to Wineglass Bay, including a gourmet chef-cooked lunch. The boat chugs around the southern end of the peninsula, passing Hazards Beach and Schouten Island en route. You're likely to see dolphins, sea eagles, seals, penguins and perhaps even migrating whales in the right season. Book ahead.

✦ Festivals & Events

Freycinet Challenge
SPORTS

(www.freycinetchallenge.com.au; ☺ Oct) Two days of paddling, running, cycling and mountain-biking competition on the Freycinet Peninsula in October. Book your beds in advance!

🛏 Sleeping

Richardsons Beach
CAMPGROUND $

(☑ 03-6256 7000; www.parks.tas.gov.au; unpowered/powered sites from $13/16) Tucked behind Richardsons Beach, near the entrance to Freycinet, these camp sites are seriously pop-

---

> ### ❶ FREE CAMPING AT FREYCINET
>
> Inside Freycinet National Park, beyond the main Richardsons Beach camp sites near Coles Bay, there are free walk-in camp sites at Wineglass Bay (☑ 03-6256 7000; www.parks.tas.gov.au), Hazards Beach (both two to three hours' walk from the car park), Cooks Beach (4½ hours) and Bryans Beach (5½ hours). Further north, there are two basic camp sites with pit toilets at Friendly Beaches. All of these camp sites are free, but national park entry fees apply. The park is a fuel-stove-only area – campfires are not permitted. Limited water may be available, but it's a better bet to bring your own (and wine).

ular. From late December to mid-February and at Easter, site allocation is via a ballot system: download the application form and submit it by 31 July. Outside the ballot period, book via the Freycinet National Park Visitor Information Centre (p153). National park entry fees apply.

BIG4 Iluka on Freycinet Holiday Park
CARAVAN PARK, HOSTEL $

(☑ 03-6257 0115; www.big4.com.au; end of Reserve Rd, Coles Bay; unpowered/powered sites $30/40, hostel dm/tw $30/80, cabins & units $120-195; 🛜 ♨) Iluka is a big, rambling park that's been here forever and is an unfaltering favourite with local holidaymakers – book well ahead. The backpackers section is managed by YHA; there's room for only 32 (refreshingly small) in dorms, twins and doubles, and a predictably decent kitchen. The local shop, bakery and tavern are a short stroll down the hill.

Freycinet Sanctuary
RENTAL HOUSE $$

(☑ 03-6257 0320; www.freycinetsanctuary.com.au; 9 East Esplanade, Coles Bay; house from $180) These two hillside holiday houses – one with two bedrooms, the other with one – are just how Australian beach shacks should be: simple, unpretentious, bright and breezy. Throw in decks with water views and you've got a winning combo. The pine-lined one-bedroom unit is further up the slope and has a loftier outlook.

Freycinet Rentals
ACCOMMODATION SERVICES $$

(☑ 03-6257 0320; www.freycinetrentals.com; 5 East Esplanade, Coles Bay; house from $160) This is your hub for renting (mostly older-style) holiday houses and beach 'shacks' in and around Coles Bay. Prices swing wildly between summer and winter, and minimum stays apply for long weekends and Christmas holidays. One option, 81 On Freycinet, has heaps of charm – the stone-and-timber house has three bedrooms, a spiral staircase and Hazards views (doubles $190).

★ Saffire Freycinet   RESORT $$$

(☎03-6256 7888, 1800 723 347; www.saffire-freycinet.com.au; 2352 Coles Bay Rd, Coles Bay; d incl meals from $2100; ❄@🖥) Saffire is an architectural, gastronomic and wallet-slimming marvel that sets the bar for top-notch Tasmanian hospitality. There are 20 luxe suites here, the curvilicious main building housing a swanky restaurant, self-serve bar, library, art gallery and spa. There's also a menu of activity options, many included in the price. A two-night minimum stay often applies.

Freycinet Retreat   APARTMENT $$$

(☎03-6257 0300, 0408 504 414; www.freycinet. com; d/apt incl breakfast from $350/490; ❄🖥) 🏄 Beat a retreat up Mt Paul, north of Coles Bay, where two carefully crafted ecolodges offer super peninsula vistas, and resident wildlife are your only neighbours. This is a magic spot – you'll want to stay for days. There are also eight studio doubles with views to Saltwater Lagoon, the Friendly Beaches and beyond. Gay friendly, wheelchair accessible, eco-certified...but no kids!

Eagle Peaks   APARTMENT $$$

(☎0419 101 847, 03-6257 0444; www.eaglepeaks. com.au; 11-13 Oyster Bay Ct, Coles Bay; studio/house from $295/315; ❄🖥) These two beautiful Tasmanian-oak and rammed-earth studios are 4km north of Coles Bay. Each unit has its own kitchenette, timber deck and comfortable king-size bed. The immaculate Beach House is here, too, sleeping four. All guests have access to BBQs; eat outside as wattlebirds dart in and out of the foliage. Five-minute walk to Sandpiper Beach. No kids.

Freycinet Lodge   RESORT $$$

(☎03-6256 7222, 1800 236 420; www.freycinet lodge.com.au; Coles Bay Rd, Freycinet National Park; cabin from $329; 🖥) Pioneering Freycinet Lodge is in an amazing location, completely surrounded by the national park at the end of Richardsons Beach. (We doubt the planners would let anyone build here these days!) Classy cabin accommodation is scattered through bushland and linked to the

main lodge building by boardwalks. Staff happily direct you between guided activities, bikes, the tennis court, bar and restaurants.

Richardson's Bistro (mains $20-36; ☺10am-8.30pm; 🚲) and Bay Restaurant (breakfast $10-20, dinner $38-44; ☺7-10am & 6-9pm, reduced winter hours) are here too, both open to nonguests. Note that wi-fi is only available in the main restaurant/reception building.

Edge of the Bay   RESORT $$$

(☎03-6257 0102; www.edgeofthebay.com.au; 2308 Main Rd, Coles Bay; cottage from $295; ❄🖥) Away from the main holiday hubbub, right on the beach about 4km north of Coles Bay, this small resort dances to the beat of its own drum. It has keenly decorated waterside suites, great staff and cottages sleeping five. Once you've woken up, there are mountain bikes, dinghies and tennis courts for guests to serve-and-volley on. There's also an excellent restaurant (mains $30-36; ☺5.30-8pm).

✕ Eating & Drinking

Freycinet Cafe & Bakery   BAKERY, CAFE $

(☎03-6257 0272; www.eastcoasttasmania.com/ business/freycinet-cafe-bakery; 2 Esplanade, Coles Bay; items $6-15; ☺8am-4pm; 🖥) This bakery has fuelled many a Freycinet walking epic. Pick up pies, cakes and sandwiches, or lurch into an all-day breakfast after a night at the tavern next door. Unexpected interlopers such as Greek salad and freshly squeezed juices also make an appearance.

★ Freycinet Marine Farm   SEAFOOD $$

(☎03-6257 0140; www.freycinetmarinefarm. com; 1784 Coles Bay Rd, Coles Bay; plates $20-25; ☺9am-5pm Sep-May, 10am-4pm Jun, 11am-4pm Jul-Aug) Super-popular Freycinet Marine Farm grows huge, succulent oysters (a dozen shucked/unshucked $22/11) in the tidal waters of Moulting Lagoon. Also for your consideration are mussels, rock lobsters, scallops and abalone. Sit on the deck among the cray pots, sip some chardonnay and dig into your seafood picnic, as fresh as Freycinet.

Iluka Tavern   PUB

(☎03-6257 0429; www.facebook.com/ilukatavern. colesbay; 31 Esplanade, Coles Bay; ☺11am-9pm; 🖥) This amiable boozer gets packed to the gills with tourists and locals most nights, elbowing around the pool table and downing a few cold ales. The pub nosh is top shelf: in between the reef 'n' beef and the chicken parmigiana you'll find dishes such as pork loin with mustard sauce and prawn pasta with brandy and chilli (mains $18 to $32).

❶ Information

Freycinet National Park Visitor Information Centre (☑ 03-6256 7000; www.parks.tas. gov.au; Freycinet Dr, Freycinet National Park; ☺ 8am-5pm Nov-Apr, 9am-4pm May-Oct) At the park entrance; get your parks passes here (day passes are popular, or there's a two-month holiday pass for not much more). Ask about free ranger-led activities December to February.

Lonely Planet (www.lonelyplanet.com/ australia/tasmania/coles-bay-and-freycinet-national-park) Destination information, hotel bookings, traveller forum and more.

Wineglass Bay (www.wineglassbay.com) Pretrip planning around the Freycinet Peninsula and Coles Bay: accommodation, eating, activities and maps.

❶ Getting There & Away

Coles Bay is 31km from the Tasman Hwy turn-off. Traverse this stretch slowly between dusk and dawn to avoid hitting any wildlife on the road.

Calow's Coaches (p140) runs buses from Bicheno into Coles Bay ($12, 45 minutes). These buses also pick up passengers from Tassielink (p306) east-coast buses at the Coles Bay turn-off (from Hobart $35.60, three hours).

❶ Getting Around

It's a 7km drive from Coles Bay to the car park where most of the national park walks begin. No car? Did you bring your bike?

Freycinet Adventures (p149) runs aqua-taxis from Coles Bay to Hazards Beach and Cooks Beach within the national park; call for info.

Bicheno

☑ 03 / POP 860

Unlike upmarket Swansea and Coles Bay, Bicheno (*bish*-uh-no) is still a functioning fishing port. With brilliant ocean views and lovely beaches, it's also madly popular with holidaymakers, but the town has never sold its soul to the Tourism Devil and remains rough-edged and unwashed. A busy fishing fleet still comes home to harbour in the Gulch with pots of lobsters and scaly loot. Food and accommodation prices here will seem realistic if you're heading north from Freycinet.

European settlement began here when whalers and sealers came to the Gulch in 1803. The town became known as Waubs

Bay Harbour, to honour an Aboriginal woman, Waubedebar, rescued two drowning men when their boat was wrecked offshore. After her death in 1832, the settlement bore her name until the 1840s when it was renamed after James Ebenezer Bicheno, once colonial secretary of Van Diemen's Land.

◎ Sights

★**Bicheno Motorcycle Museum** MUSEUM (☑ 03-6375 1485; 35 Burgess St; adult/child $9/ free; ☺ 9am-5pm Mon-Fri, 9am-4pm Sat, 9am-2pm Sun, closed Sun Jun-Aug) Andrew Quin got his first Honda at age four, and has been hooked on motorbikes ever since. You don't have to be an aficionado, though, to visit his wonderful museum out the back of his bike-repair shop. It's all shiny chrome and enamel under bright lights, with 60-plus immaculately restored bikes on display, including the rare Noriel 4 Café Racer – the only one of its kind in the world. East-coast bikers wheel in for an oil top-up.

Diamond Island ISLAND (Redbill Beach, off Gordon St) Off the northern end of Redbill Beach is this photogenic granite outcrop, connected to the mainland via a short, semi-submerged, sandy isthmus, which you can wade across. Time your expedition with low tide – otherwise you might end up chest-deep in the waves trying to get back!

Redbill Beach BEACH (off Gordon St) Backed by dunes, Bicheno's fabulous surf beach is long, wide and handsome. There's usually a surf carnival held in the beach breaks here in January.

Waubedebar's Grave LANDMARK (off Old Tram Rd) The final resting place of Waubedebar, the local Aboriginal woman who fished a couple of hapless sailors from the surf in the early 1800s.

Natureworld ZOO (☑ 03-6375 1311; www.natureworld.com.au; 18356 Tasman Hwy; adult/child/family $25/12/65; ☺ 9am-5pm) About 7km north of Bicheno, this wildlife park is overrun with native and non-native wildlife, including Tasmanian devils, wallabies, quolls, snakes, wombats and enormous roos. There are devil feedings daily at 10am, 12.30pm and 3.30pm, and a devil house where you can see these little demons up close. There's a cafe here, too.

Douglas-Apsley National Park　　NATIONAL PARK
(☑ 03-6256 7070; www.parks.tas.gov.au; off Tasman Hwy; per person/vehicle $12/24) Four kilometres north of Bicheno is the turn-off to Douglas-Apsley, an impressive park, with rocky peaks, eucalypt forest, waterfalls, abundant bird and animal life and a river gorge with deep swimming holes – and best of all, none of the midsummer hordes that swarm over Freycinet. Walk to the swimming hole at **Apsley Gorge** (two to three hours return) or to the **Apsley River Waterhole** (15 minutes return). There's basic, walk-in bush camping here, too (free, but national park fees apply).

🏃 Activities

⭐ **Foreshore Footway**　　WALKING
(via Gordon St) This lovely 3km seaside stroll extends from Redbill Beach (p153) to the Blowhole via Waubedebar's Grave (p153) and the **Gulch** (off Esplanade). When the sea is angry (or just a bit annoyed), huge columns of foamy seawater spurt spectacularly into the air at the Blowhole. Don't get too close: even on calm days you can be unexpectedly drenched. Return along the path up **Whalers Hill** (off Foster St), which offers broad views over the town. In whaling days, passing sea giants were spotted from here.

Bicheno Dive Centre　　DIVING
(☑ 03-6375 1138; www.bichenodive.com.au; 2 Scuba Ct; ☺ 9am-5pm) The clear waters off Bicheno offer brilliant temperate-water diving. This crew visits dive sites mainly in the nearby **Governor Island Marine Reserve** (☑ 03-6256 7000; www.parks.tas.gov.au; Governor Island, via Esplanade). One-day charters, including equipment and one/two boat dives, cost $160/200. A guided shore dive with equipment is $150. There's also budget accommodation here for divers.

👉 Tours

Bicheno Penguin Tours　　BIRDWATCHING
(☑ 03-6375 1333; www.bichenopenguintours.com.au; 70 Burgess St; adult/child $35/15; ☺ booking office 9am-5.30pm Mon-Fri, 10am-5pm Sat & Sun) Bicheno is one of the top spots in Tasmania to see penguins: spy them on these one-hour dusk tours as they waddle back to their burrows. Expect a sincere nature experience: no cafes or souvenirs (and no photography allowed). Departure times vary year-round, depending on when dusk falls. Penguin numbers peak from November to January. Bookings essential.

Devils in the Dark　　WILDLIFE WATCHING
(☑ 0401 246 777; www.devilsinthedark.com.au; per person $65; ☺ dusk) Book a nocturnal bus tour to see Tasmanian devils in a secret location near Bicheno. Proceeds go towards battling the Devil Facial Tumour Disease (DFTD), which has decimated devil populations around the state. Pick-ups from various locations around town (ask when you book). No kids under seven.

Bicheno's Glass Bottom Boat　　BOATING
(☑ 03-6375 1294; www.facebook.com/bichenoglassbottomboat; The Gulch, Esplanade; adult/child $25/10; ☺ 10am, noon & 2pm late-Sep–early May) This 40-minute trip will give you a watery perspective on Bicheno's submarine wonders. Tours run late-September to May from the Gulch, weather permitting (bookings advised in January).

🎉 Festivals & Events

Bicheno Food & Wine Festival　　FOOD & DRINK
(www.bichenofestivals.com.au; ☺ Nov) On one frenzied Saturday in November, Bicheno bursts forth with food and wine stalls, cooking classes, live music, home-brew beer competitions and vintage surf exhibits. Great fun!

🛏️ Sleeping

For house rental listings, see www.bichenoholiday.com.au.

Bicheno Backpackers　　HOSTEL $
(☑ 03-6375 1651; www.bichenobackpackers.com; 11 Morrison St; dm/tw/house from $31/75/140; 🌐) This congenial backpackers has dorms spread across two mural-painted buildings, plus a 12-berth self-contained house nearby, set up as six doubles. The communal kitchen is the place to be. There's also free luggage storage, and a walking track to a lookout at the top of the street. Is the new wine centre next door open yet?

Bicheno East Coast Holiday Park　　CARAVAN PARK $
(☑ 1800 904 199, 03-6375 1999; www.bichenoholidaypark.com.au; 4 Champ St; unpowered/powered sites from $30/35, units & cabins from $140; ❄️🌐) This trim, decent park with plenty of grass (not many trees) is right in the middle of town, and has BBQs, laundry facilities and a kids' playground. The neat cedar-coloured cabins sleep up to seven. There's also a new camp kitchen and a couple of bunk rooms on the drawing board.

Bicheno

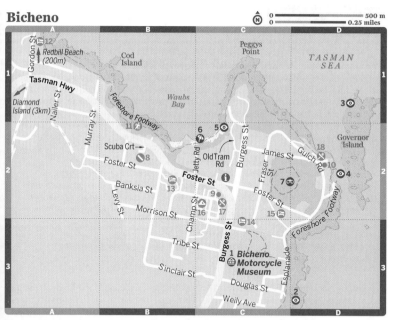

Bicheno

◎ Top Sights
1 Bicheno Motorcycle Museum	C3

◎ Sights
2 Blowhole	D3
3 Governor Island Marine Reserve	D1
4 The Gulch	D2
5 Waubedebar's Grave	C2
6 Waubs Beach	C2
7 Whalers Hill	C2

✪ Activities, Courses & Tours
8 Bicheno Dive Centre	B2
9 Bicheno Penguin Tours	C2

10 Bicheno's Glass Bottom Boat	D2
11 Foreshore Footway	B2

🛏 Sleeping
12 Beach Path House	A1
13 Beachfront Bicheno	B2
14 Bicheno Backpackers	C3
15 Bicheno by the Bay	C2
16 Bicheno East Coast Holiday Park	C2

🍴 Eating
17 Pasinis	C2
18 The Gulch Fish & Chips	D2

★ **Beach Path House** RENTAL HOUSE **$$**
(☏ 03-6375 1400; www.beachpathhouse.com.au; 2 Gordon St; house from $200; ❄) Painted cream and navy, this mid-century beach shack has been reborn as a contemporary holiday house, with three bedrooms, flower-filled gardens, an open fire and a little deck from where you can hear the surf. A couple of old cray pots are strewn about for good nautical measure. Sleeps up to eight. Prices swing wildly with the seasons.

Bicheno by the Bay CABIN **$$**
(☏ 03-6375 1171; www.bichenobythebay.com.au; cnr Foster & Fraser Sts; cabins from $165, motel d from $125; ❄🏊) There are 20 cabins and five motel rooms in a bushy setting here, the biggest sleeping 10. The A-frame sea-view cabins are the pick of the bunch. Facilities include an outdoor heated pool, a tennis court, a communal fire pit, a kids' pirate-boat playground and a canoe lake (being revamped when we visited, ducks waiting patiently).

Beachfront Bicheno MOTEL **$$**
(☏ 03-6375 1111; www.beachfrontbicheno.com.au; cnr Sinclair St & Tasman Hwy; d $145-170; ❄📶🏊) There are renovated ocean-facing rooms with balconies and snazzy bathrooms here, and ranks of view-free rooms out-the-back (the

FINGAL

To escape the east-coast tourist tirade, detour west from St Marys on the A4 and drive through the beautiful, rolling countryside of the Fingal Valley.

Soporific Fingal itself, 21km west of St Marys, was one of the larger agricultural settlements from the early days of the colony and has some sturdy 19th-century buildings on the main street. These days it's a town in steady (approaching rapid) decline, with more historic churches and cemeteries than anything else.

If you're here in March, the kooky **Fingal Valley Festival** (www.fingalvalleyfestival.com.au; ⊙Mar) features the World Roof Bolting and World Coal Shovelling Championships. After all that you'll need a snack: try the **Hayshed Café** (☑03-6374 2171; 31-33 Talbot St; mains $5-12; ⊙8am-3pm Mon-Fri) for a sausage roll or an impressive-looking cake entombed in icing.

For some amazing tree-scapes, check out the **Evercreech Forest Reserve**, 34km north of Fingal near Mathinna. A 20-minute circuit walk through blackwood and myrtle delivers you to the **White Knights**, a group of the world's tallest white gums (*Eucalyptus viminalis*); the loftiest boughs here reach 91m. You can also visit **Mathinna Falls** (follow signs from the Mathinna junction on the B43), an impressive 80m-high, four-tier waterfall. There's a 30-minute return stroll to the base of the falls.

Calow's Coaches runs from St Helens to Fingal ($16, one hour), en route to Launceston.

ones by the pool are nicely dolled-up). The **tavern** here is Bicheno's take on a pub, with footy on the TV and big meals (mains $23 to $38, serving noon to 2pm and 6pm to 8pm).

Aurora Beach Cottage RENTAL HOUSE **$$$** (☑03-6375 1774; www.aurorabeachcottage.com.au; 207 Champ St, Seymour; house from $230) For total seclusion, marvellous Aurora Beach Cottage is a great option. It's a timber-and-stone house 18km north of Bicheno at Seymour, set in the dunes behind a wide span of empty sand. Sit out on the deck and watch the waves, or look for messages in bottles along the shore. Breakfast provisions on request; no kids under eight. Two-night minimum. Accommodates up to four people.

✖ Eating

The Gulch Fish & Chips FISH & CHIPS **$** (☑03-6375 2000; www.tascoastalseafoods.com; 48 Waubs Esplanade; meals $10-18; ⊙11am-7.30pm Oct-Apr, 11am-6pm Mon-Sat May-Sep) Home to Tasmanian Coastal Seafoods, this little shack on the Gulch foreshore cooks brilliant fish and chips, straight off the boat. What's cooking depends on the catch of the day: flathead, trevalla, ling, stripy trumpeter... Crayfish in season, too. Hours can vary – call ahead.

★ Pasinis ITALIAN, CAFE **$$** (☑03-6375 1076; www.facebook.com/pasinis; 70 Burgess St; breakfast $8-20, lunch & dinner $13-33; ⊙8am-8pm Tue-Sat, 8am-3pm Sun) This expertly managed outfit does Italian staples such

as antipasto plates, wood-fired pizzas and lasagne – but oh, so much better than most. The breakfasts border on artisanal, the pastas and gnocchi are homemade and the coffees ('Oomph' brand, roasted in Hobart) are richly delicious. Takeaways, east-coast beers and wines, oysters and sumptuous sandwiches also make the cut. Winner!

❶ Information

Bicheno Visitor Information Centre (☑03-6256 5072; www.eastcoasttasmania.com; 41b Foster St; ⊙9am-5pm Oct-Apr, 10am-4pm May-Sep) Local information and accommodation bookings.

❶ Getting There & Away

Tassielink buses (p306) run from Hobart to Bicheno ($37.80, 3¼ hours) on Monday, Wednesday, Friday and Sunday. North of here, Calow's Coaches (p140) runs to St Helens ($14, 1¼ hours) daily except Saturday, and to Launceston ($34, three hours). Calow's also does the trip into Coles Bay from Bicheno ($12, 45 minutes).

St Marys

☑ / POP

St Marys is an unhurried, pretty little inland village in the Mt Nicholas range, encircled by forests and cattle farms. Visit for the small-town vibe and the craggy heights around town, which you can climb for wicked views over the area.

The top of South Sister (832m), towering over German Town Rd 6km north of town, is a 10-minute walk from the car park. To get to St Patricks Head (683m) turn down Irishtown Rd, just east of town. This long, steep, 90-minute (one-way) climb, with some cables and a ladder, is a real challenge, but at the top there's a stellar vista along the coast.

🛏 Sleeping & Eating

St Marys Recreation Ground   CAMPGROUND
(📋 03-6376 7900; Harefield Rd, off Gray Rd) FREE There are free grassy unpowered sites, toilets and showers next to the town oval. It's a right turn after the rivulet off Gray Rd (A4), heading out of town towards Elephant Pass.

St Marys Hotel   PUB $
(📋 03-6372 2181; www.stmaryshoteltasmania.com. au; 48 Main St; s/d/tw/f $60/80/80/150; 📶) There's accommodation upstairs at this 1910 pub in the middle of town; ask for one of the handsome, newly renovated rooms. It also does huge pub meals (noon to 2pm and 6pm to 8pm, mains $18 to $32) downstairs. 'You don't see too much plate', says one well-fed local.

Addlestone House   B&B $$
(📋03-6372 2783; www.addlestonehouse.com. au; 19 Gray Rd; s & d incl breakfast $150-175; 🅿️📶) This immaculate, 100-year-old B&B (transported here a while ago from nearby Mathinna) is an excellent option. Two guest rooms are beautifully decorated (a tad lacy), there's a snug guest lounge, and the host is a charming gent (a photographer, who'll snap your portrait then email it to you). Easily the nicest place to stay in this neck of the woods.

⭐**Purple Possum Wholefoods**   CAFE $
(📋03-6372 2655; www.purplepossum.com.au; 5 Story St; mains $7-15; ⊙9am-5pm Mon-Fri, 9am-3pm Sat; 📶🖊) 🍽 An unexpected find in a little country town, this chipper wholefoods cafe serves excellent homemade soups, burgers, pasties, vegetarian wraps, fabulous coffee, cakes and slices. There are also vats of nuts, chocolates and spices, and a DIY peanut butter grinder. You'll regret it forever if you don't try the rhubarb cake.

❶ Getting There & Away

Calow's Coaches (p140) stops at St Marys on its way between St Helens and Launceston ($7, 40 minutes from St Helens). If you're driving it's a 40km drive northeast from Bicheno

via wiggly Elephant Pass, or about the same distance heading south from St Helens.

Scamander & Beaumaris

Unfazed by life, the neighbouring towns of Scamander and Beaumaris probably aren't much of an attraction in themselves...but they do have beautiful, long, white-sand beaches where the surf rolls in and you feel like you can wander forever. There are reliable waves around Four Mile Creek, while fisherfolk can toss in a line for bream from the old bridge over the Scamander River, or catch trout further upstream. Shelley Point, just north of town, has rock pools to explore and shells to collect. There's also a craft-beer brewery nearby.

◎ Sights

Iron House Brewery   BREWERY
(📋0409 308 824, 03-6372 2228; www.ironhouse. com.au; White Sands Estate, 21554 Tasman Hwy, Ironhouse Point; tastings $5; ⊙9am-5pm) Get thirsty on the beach? Quench yourself 16km south of Scamander at Iron House, a craft brewery producing flavoursome pale ale, lager, wheat beer, stout, pilsner and porter. The brewery is part of the corporate White Sands Estate accommodation, but beer is why you're here. Sample the good stuff and grab some lunch at the restaurant (mains $22 to $38).

🛏 Sleeping & Eating

Scamander Sanctuary Holiday Park   CARAVAN PARK $
(📋0457 725 311, 03-6372 5311; www.scamander sanctuary.com.au; 1 Winifred Dr, Scamander; unpowered/powered sites $30/35, safari tents from $95) Just south of Scamander township behind the beach is this affable caravan park, with 20 hectares of wild dune and bush landscape. Sleeping options include powered and unpowered camp sites and quirky canvas safari tents (sleeping up to seven) on stilts above the ground, each with a kitchen,

❶ ROAD WARNING

Cyclists riding over **Elephant Pass** to/from St Marys beware: the road is steep, narrow and winding, and drivers tend to get *really* impatient trying to negotiate their way around two-wheelers.

bathroom and little deck. It's a short walk to the beach or into town.

Beaumaris Beach Pad   RENTAL HOUSE $$

(☑ 0400 038 136; www.beaumarisbeachpad.com.au; 191 Tasman Hwy, Beaumaris; house from $185) This new, two-bedroom beach house is architecturally excellent, with dapper grey vertical weatherboards, lots of glass, a broad deck and a stylish internal fit-out. There are surfboards to use on the beach across the road, and a hot outdoor shower for rinsing off afterwards. If only it wasn't right on the highway… Sleeps up to four; two-night minimum stay.

Pelican Sands   APARTMENT $$

(☑ 03-6372 5231; www.pelicansandsscamander.com.au; 157 Scamander Ave, Scamander; d $140-190, f $200-220; ☎) If you want to stay on the waterfront, you can't get much closer than this. The six compact, motel-style, self-contained units here have been tastefully renovated. Lush lawns out the front roll down to the river mouth, beyond which is the beach, then the wild ocean. Grazers (☑ 0455 415 551; www.facebook.com/grazerstas; 157 Scamander Ave, Scamander; mains $25-29; ☉ 5pm-late Tue-Sat, reduced winter hours) is right next door when dinner time rolls around.

Eureka Farm   CAFE $

(☑ 03-6372 5500; www.eurekafarm.com.au; 89 Upper Scamander Rd, Scamander; mains $8-15; ☉ 8am-5pm Oct-Apr, 9am-4pm May-Sep; ☎ ⚹ 🚼) A couple of kilometres south of Scamander is a sign pointing towards this fruitarian's paradise. Try a smoked-salmon omelette for breakfast, or get stuck into the all-day fruit wonders: berry crepes, fruit pies, ice creams, smoothies, summer puddings and an amazing choc-raspberry pavlova.

ⓘ Getting There & Away

Scamander is 53km north of Bicheno; Beaumaris is a further 7km. Calow's Coaches (p140) stops at both towns en route between St Helens and Bicheno.

St Helens

☑ 03 / POP 2180

On the broad, protected sweep of Georges Bay, St Helens began life as a whaling and sealing settlement in the 1830s. Soon the 'swanners' came to plunder, harvesting the bay's black swans for their downy underfeathers. By the 1850s the town was a permanent farming settlement, which swelled in 1874 when tin was discovered nearby. Today, St Helens is a pragmatic sort of town, harbouring the state's largest fishing fleet. This equates to plenty for anglers to get excited about; charter boats will take you out to where the big game fish play. For landlubbers there are some good places to eat, sleep and unwind, with beaches nearby.

◉ Sights

St Helens History Room   MUSEUM

(☑ 03-6376 1479; www.sthelenshistoryroom.com; 61 Cecilia St; adult/family $3/5; ☉ 9am-5pm) Out the back of the town visitor centre is this unexpected little museum, cataloguing the town's social and natural history. Farming, exploring, schooling, whaling, fishing, mining, shells and east-coast wildlife all get a once-over (is that thylacine's head life-sized?), all to the tick-tick-tick of an antique clock. Don't miss the amazing old funeral buggy, and the cheesy-but-interesting film introducing the Trail of the Tin Dragon (p164), focusing on Chinese tin mining in the northeast.

Humbug Point Nature Recreation Area   NATURE RESERVE

(☑ 03-6387 5510; www.parks.tas.gov.au; via Binalong Bay Rd, St Helens) FREE Nature reserve en route to Binalong Bay, loaded-up with native blooms and birdlife (yellow-tailed black cockatoos, gannets, petrels, wattlebirds, honeyeaters, white-breasted sea eagles…). There are surf beaches, walking tracks and free camp sites here too, at Dora Point (☑ 03-6387 5510; www.parks.tas.gov.au; off Binalong Bay Rd) FREE.

⚹ Activities

Fishing

If you are at all into fishing, then St Helens – Tasmania's ocean-fishing capital – is the place to catch the big one that didn't get away (or a small one closer to land). Call charter operators for prices and bookings.

Gone Fishing Charters   FISHING

(☑ 03-6376 1553; www.breamfishing.com.au) Hook a bream or two on a close-to-shore fishing trip with an expert local guide. Call to talk times and prices. No fish, no pay (you have to admire the confidence).

Zulu Fishing Charterz   FISHING

(☑ 0487 351 408; www.zulucharterz.com; up to 6 people half-/full-day charter $650/1200) Chase

St Helens

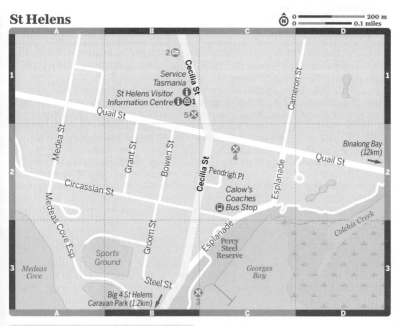

St Helens

◎ **Sights**
1 St Helens History Room B1

🛏 **Sleeping**
2 Artnor Lodge B1

🍴 **Eating**
3 Captain's Catch................................... B3
4 Lifebuoy Cafe C2
5 Mohr & Smith B1

the big fish out in the deep blue sea on a big black boat. Call to discuss requirements.

Walking

Both sides of the entrance to Georges Bay are state reserves and are laced with easy walking tracks. A good track circles around St Helens Point (one hour return) – take St Helens Point Rd to access it. Also on St Helens Point are the impressive Peron Dunes.

On the north side of Georges Bay, off Binalong Bay Rd, is the Humbug Point Nature Recreation Area. Within this park, Skeleton Bay and Dora Point are prime destinations on well-marked tracks. Ask at the St Helens Visitor Information Centre (p160) for a walking map and track notes.

👉 Tours

Green Island Tours CYCLING
(☑ 03-6376 3080; www.cycling-tasmania.com; 7-day tour $1090-2210, 11-day tour $1790-3680) 🍃 Mosey along the east coast by bike – with all the tricky logistics taken care of – on seven-day St Helens to Hobart and 11-day Launceston to Hobart (via the east coast) trips, including transfers, national park fees, breakfasts, lunches and accommodation in varying levels of luxury. Bike hire sans tour and self-guided tours also available.

🛏 Sleeping

BIG4 St Helens Holiday Park CARAVAN PARK **$**
(☑ 1300 559 745; www.sthelenscp.com.au; 2 Penelope St; powered/unpowered sites from $46/35, cabin & villa from $160; ❄ 🛜 🏊) This efficiently run park rolls itself across a green hillside 1.5km south of town and has plenty of family-centric amenities (games room, jumping pillow, playground, swimming pool). Shoot for one of the smart row of blue-and-cream villas running up the hill. Decent camp kitchen. Venture to the top of the slope to find a flat patch for your tent.

★ **The French House** B&B **$$**
(☑ 03-6376 2602, 0414 264 258; www.thefrench housesthelens.com.au; 197 Ansons Bay Rd; d $140-

PYENGANA

About 26km west of St Helens, the turn-off to tiny Pyengana ('Pie-en-*gah*-na' – an Aboriginal word describing the meeting of two rivers) leads to an impossibly emerald-green valley with some interesting diversions.

In the 1890s European pioneers noted the area's high rainfall and brought in dairy cattle, which thrived on the lush grass. Exporting milk from this isolated valley was impractical, but once converted into cheese and butter the produce could last the long journey to market.

These days there's still cheese made here at the **Pyengana Dairy Company** (☑03-6373 6157; www.pyenganadairy.com.au; St Columba Falls Rd; tastings free, cafe mains $14-30; ◷9am-5pm Sep-May, 10am-4pm Jun-Aug). The nearby **Pub in the Paddock** (St Columba Falls Hotel; ☑03-6373 6121; www.pubinthepaddocktas.com.au; 250 St Columba Falls Rd; s/tw/d from $65/95/95) attracts just as many visitors, infamously for its beer-drinking pig. There are also some beautiful waterfalls in the valley, including **St Columba Falls** (St Columba Falls Rd), Tasmania's highest (90m).

To get to Pyengana, head west from St Helens on the Tasman Hwy for 24km to the Pyengana turn-off: from here it's a couple of kilometres in to the dairy and the pub. There's no public transport along this route.

170; ✳☏) About 4km from St Helens, this B&B, built over 20 years ago by a Frenchman homesick for his country home, exudes Gallic charm. Upstairs are four compact en-suite rooms with TV and fridge; downstairs is a country kitchen and guest lounge with herringbone timber floor. Not frilly or kitsch, just simple and stylish. Breakfasts are generous cooked affairs. *Oui, oui!*

Artnor Lodge MOTEL $$
(☑03-6376 1234; www.artnorlodge.com.au; 71 Cecilia St; d without/with bathroom from $90/110) Just off St Helens' leafy main street, this neat, understated, peaceful little motel complex extends from the back of a 1940s house. Clean budget rooms share bathrooms and a tidy little kitchen, plus two renovated en-suite rooms and an en-suite studio at the back of the garden.

Bed in the Treetops B&B B&B $$$
(☑03-6376 1318; www.bedinthetreetops.com.au; 701 Binalong Bay Rd; s/d/tr/q incl breakfast from $250/300/380/460; ☏) Some 7km out of St Helens en route to Binalong Bay, take the (steep) drive up and up through the trees to reach this secluded, stylish timber home. There are two plush apartments, tastefully furnished and with private decks, spas and verdant views. Rates include afternoon tea or predinner drinks, and a cooked breakfast.

✖ Eating

Lifebuoy Cafe CAFE $
(☑0439 761 371; www.facebook.com/thelifebuoy cafe; 29 Quail St; mains $8-16; ◷7.30am-4pm Mon-Fri, to 1pm Sat) This secretive, bookish little coffee joint is tucked in behind an eccentric antiques shop off the main drag. Reliable coffee and homemade soups are what you're here for, plus salmon burgers, waffles, eggs Benedict and good ol' country scones.

Mohr & Smith CAFE $$
(☑03-6376 2039; www.mohrandsmith.com.au; 55-59 Cecilia St; breakfast & lunch $16-22, dinner $24-32; ◷10am-8pm Tue-Sat) Oh look! A slick urban nook! With a sunny front terrace, snug open-fire lounge area, chilled tunes and sexy staff, M&S would feel right at home on Salamanca Place in Hobart. Order a pulled-pork quesadilla or a Japanese pancake with chilli jam and coriander for lunch and see what the afternoon brings. Good for an evening drink, too.

Captain's Catch SEAFOOD $$
(☑03-6376 1170; www.facebook.com/captains catchsthelens; 1 Marina Pde; mains $16-27; ◷10am-8pm) This harbourside fish-and-chipper does wonders with seafood, all of it hook-caught on its boat, the *Insta-gator*. The 'Captain's Basket' is hard to beat: blue eye, scallops, prawns and squid; or try the house chowder. Eat in or take away.

❶ Information

St Helens Visitor Information Centre (☑03-6376 1744; www.visitsthelenstasmania.com. au; 61 Cecilia St; ◷9am-5pm) Just off the main street behind the library. Sells national parks passes. The St Helens History Room (p158) is here too.

Service Tasmania (📞1300 135 513; www.service.tas.gov.au; 65 Cecilia St; ⊘10am-4.30pm Mon-Fri) Sells national parks passes.

ⓘ Getting There & Away

Calow's Coaches (p140) runs from St Helens to Launceston ($33, three hours) via Scamander and St Marys, connecting with Tassielink (p306) buses at Conara, on the Midlands Hwy, for the run to Hobart ($56, four hours). Calow's also runs from St Helens to Bicheno ($12, two hours).

Bay of Fires

Larapuna/Bay of Fires is a 29km-long sweep of powder-white sand and crystal-clear seas that has featured on plenty of 'Most Beautiful Beaches in the World' lists recently. To refer to the Bay of Fires as a single beach, though, is a mistake: it's actually a string of superb beaches, punctuated by lagoons and rocky headlands, backed by coastal heath and bush.

There's no road that runs the length of the bay: the C850 heads out of St Helens to the gorgeous beachside holiday settlement of Binalong Bay, which marks the southern end of the bay. In the bay's northern end are Ansons Bay, a quiet holiday hamlet, and the southern sections of Mt William National Park.

Eddystone Point, just north of Ansons Bay, within Mt William National Park, marks the larapuna/Bay of Fires' northern extremity, the tall Eddystone Point Lighthouse standing as a symbolic exclamation mark.

🏃 Activities

Bay of Fires Lodge Walk WALKING
(📞03-6392 2211; www.bayoffires.com.au; per person $2560; ⊘Oct-May) A four-day, three-night guided adventure through this glorious wave-washed domain. A maximum of 10 guests beachcomb the coastline, led by knowledgeable guides. The first night is spent at a secluded tented beach camp, with the next two at the sublime Bay of Fires Lodge. Fine food and wine included. Magic!

Binalong Bay

📞03 / POP 210

Curling around a sheltered sandy inlet 11km north of St Helens, Binalong Bay is the only permanent settlement in larapuna/Bay of Fires. It was first used by fishermen and farmers around 1900, but no one (no one European, that is) actually lived here until

the 1940s. Now, this quiet spot is a beachy holiday town. There's not much here – the beach, a restaurant and a hillside dotted with pricey holiday houses – but this is precisely why everyone loves it.

There's good surf in and around the bay, and great swimming on calm days. Snorkellers head to Binalong Gulch, where they can pick up abalone (with a licence). This is also one of the best spots in Tasmania for diving: the elusive weedy sea dragon often hangs out here.

🏃 Activities

Bay of Fires Eco Tours BOATING
(📞0499 209 756; www.bayoffiresecotours.au; Titley's Shack, Main Rd; tour per adult/child/family $135/85/380) 🌿 Even with a 4WD it's impossible to access about 60% of larapuna/Bay of Fires coastline...so take a boat trip instead! Based in a little 1935 shack on the Binalong Bay waterfront, this outfit will get you out on the water for three hours to see dunes, dolphins, Aboriginal sites and the lichen-covered coast between Binalong Bay and Eddystone Point.

Tours run at 9.30am daily; shorter tours to the Gardens or St Helens Island run at 2pm.

🛏 Sleeping

Kingfisher Cottage RENTAL HOUSE $$
(📞0467 808 738; www.kingfishercottage.com.au; 74 Main Rd; house from $195; ❄🐾) We like this one: not gregarious, not making a statement, not flashy or pretentious – just the perfect little beach house in a primo location, right in the sandy heart of Binalong Bay, next to the restaurant and a pebble's toss from the beach (the best bit for swimming). Sleeps up to six in two bedrooms.

Bay of Fires Bush Retreat TENTED CAMP $$
(📞0439 343 066; www.bayoffiresbushretreat.com.au; 795 Reids Rd; safari tent d & tw from $155; 🐾) Heading north from Binalong Bay into larapuna/Bay of Fires, this rustic, hippie-goes-boutique bush camping set-up involves interesting 'bell tents' with shared bathrooms and cooking facilities. Gourmet platters and breakfast hampers are available if you don't feel like cooking for yourself (order when you book). The vibe is chilled-out and wholesome.

Arthouse Bay of Fires RENTAL HOUSE $$$
(📞0457 750 035; www.arthousebayoffires.com.au; 61 Lyall Rd; house from $550; 🐾) Lasso some

like-minded amigos and book this architect-designed beach house, with polished floorboards, granite bench tops and a wide curvy deck backed by a phalanx of sliding doors. About 50m away is a classic larapuna/Bay of Fires scene: white sand, rocks studded with orange lichen, and gently rolling waves. Sleeps four; no kids under 12. Two-night minimum stay.

ⓘ Getting There & Away

Binalong Bay is a 13km drive north of St Helens, along Binalong Bay Rd. There's no public transport heading out this way.

Weldborough

🗘 03 / POP 50

As the Tasman Hwy approaches Weldborough Pass – an arabesque cutting famously popular with motorcyclists – it traces a high ridge with vistas of surrounding forests and mountains. Near the top, the Weldborough Pass Rainforest Walk is a 15-minute interpretative circuit through moss-covered myrtle rainforest.

Tiny Weldborough itself is almost a ghost town these days, compared with the busy settlement it must have been in the thick of the late-1800s northeast tin rush. In mining days Weldborough had 800 inhabitants, many of whom were Chinese. There's not much here these days, but the Weldborough Hotel is an essential pit stop.

🏃 Activities

You could base yourself in Weldborough for a day or two to do some hiking or mountain biking around the gorgeous Blue Tier Forest Reserve, where rainforest walks wander past overgrown mining ruins. The mountain bike trails here are developing an enviable reputation among off-road riders, including an epic trail from the Blue Tier to Derby: see www.ridetassie.com/blue-tier.html for details. The St Helens or Scottsdale visitor information centres can also help with maps and advice.

🛏 Sleeping

★ **Weldborough Hotel**   PUB $
(🗘 03-6354 2223; www.weldborough.com.au; 12 Main Rd; unpowered sites $20, d/f without bathroom from $100/150; ⊙ 11.30am-late) The hub of town life, the 1876 Weldborough Hotel is a characterful lunch stop or overnighter. Beer boffins rejoice: product from every Tasmani-

an craft brewery is on hand! The kitchen delivers excellent food (mains $13 to $32) and there's pub accommodation if you've had too many ales to drive. There are also verdant camp sites and hot showers out the back.

ⓘ Getting There & Away

Little blink-and-you'll-miss-it Weldborough is a 22km drive from Derby and 43km from St Helens via winding, hilly roads – so winding and hilly, in fact, that no public transport traverses this route.

Derby

🗘 03 / POP 210

For much of the year, Derby (dur-bee) seems a rather forlorn little town nooked into the Ringarooma River valley, clinging grimly to its tin-mining history, dating back to the 1870s. The tin mines closed in the 1940s, causing an exodus that has never really stopped.

But there's an interesting transformation under way, courtesy of a network of brilliant mountain-biking trails in the surrounding hills. The Australian Cross Country Marathon Mountain Bike Championships (www.mtba.asn.au) was held here in 2015 and 2016, followed by an Enduro World Championships (www.enduroworldseries.com) event in 2017. When the mountain bikers are in town the place goes berserk, and accommodation is booked out from here to St Helens. About 8km west of Derby is Branxholm (population 210) with further sleeping and eating options.

If you're driving into Derby from Weldborough, check out the gigantic trout mural splashed across the cliffs near the bridge into town.

History

One hundred years ago Derby was a thriving mining centre, springing up when tin was discovered here in 1874. The northeast's tin rush attracted thousands, and several mines operated in and around Derby. At its boomtime height, the town numbered 3000 souls. In 1929, after five days of heavy rain, a mining dam burst in Derby and 14 people died in the resulting flood. The mines closed for five years after this tragedy. They reopened in 1935, but closed again after WWII.

⊙ Sights

Derby Schoolhouse Museum   MUSEUM
(🗘 0457 281 257; www.nationaltrust.org.au; 53 Main St; entry by donation; ⊙ 11am-3pm Mar-

OFF THE BEATEN TRACK

MT WILLIAM NATIONAL PARK

Little-known, isolated **Mt William National Park** (☎03-6387 5510; www.parks.tas.gov. au; via St Helens or Gladstone; per person/vehicle $12/24, camping from $13) features long sandy beaches, low ridges and coastal heathlands; visit during spring or early summer when the wildflowers are bloomin' marvellous. The highest point, wukalina/Mt William (1½-hour return walk), stands only 216m tall, yet projects your gaze over land and sea. The area was declared a national park in 1973, primarily to protect Tasmania's remaining forester (eastern grey) kangaroos, which faced extinction in the 1950s and '60s (they've been breeding themselves silly ever since).

Activities on offer in the park include birdwatching and wildlife-spotting, fishing, swimming, surfing and diving. Aboriginal habitation of the area is illustrated by the large shell midden at Musselroe Point, and many others across the region. To the south, the **Eddystone Point Lighthouse** (www.lighthouses.org.au; via Eddystone Point Rd, Mt William National-al Park) **FREE** is clearly visible, its night-time beam a beacon to ships entering dangerous Banks Strait, between the Furneaux Group and mainland Tasmania.

There's beachside camping under the she-oaks at **Stumpys Bay**, at **Top Camp** near Musselroe Bay and beside tannin-stained **Deep Creek** in the park's south. All sites have pit toilets, but no drinking water. Fires are allowed in designated fire spots; BYO firewood and heed fire restrictions. Pay camping fees on-site; pay park fees at the kiosk on the northern access road or, if approaching from the south, buy a pass from Service Tasmania (p161) in St Helens or the St Helens Visitor Information Centre (p160).

The northern end of Mt William National Park is 17km from Gladstone on gravel roads; the southern end is 60km from St Helens (also gravel) – these two towns are the closest petrol stops. From Bridport, take the road towards Tomahawk and continue to Gladstone. Be careful driving at night – these roads are rife with wildlife.

THE EAST COAST DERBY

Nov, 10am-4pm Dec-Feb) In the 1897 school building adjacent to the Tin Centre, there's a display on the social history of Derby as opposed to its mining past, including some amazing old photos. Opening hours can be patchy (volunteer staffing).

Tin Centre　　　　　　　　　　　MUSEUM
(☎03-63541062; www.trailofthetindragon.com.au/derby; 55 Main St; ⊙8.30am-5pm, reduced hours in winter) **FREE** Derby's tin-mining heritage is on display in this architecturally impressive space, part of the Trail of the Tin Dragon tourist route (www.trailofthetindragon.com.au). The **Crank It Cafe** (www.crankitcafederby.com; mains $6-14; ⊙8.30am-5pm) is here too.

🏃 Activities

**Blue Derby Mountain
Bike Trails**　　　　　　　MOUNTAIN BIKING
(☎03-6352 6500; www.rideblueberry.com.au; off Tasman Hwy) **FREE** Derby has become Tasmania's mountain-biking mecca, with the Blue Derby network of 26 trails at the fore. Trails range from easy to extremely difficult, and from 1km to 40km (the latter being the track between the Blue Tier and Derby). Check out the signboards at the southern end of

town for info, or download maps from the website.

For bike hire and shuttle services head to **Vertigo MTB** (☎0488 463 333; www.vertigomtb.com.au; 66 Main St; bike hire per day incl equipment from $99; ⊙8am-5.30pm).

🎉 Festivals & Events

Derby River Derby　　　　　　　SPORTS
(www.neriversfestival.com.au; ⊙Oct) Derby gets up to 10,000 visitors in late October for the annual Derby River Derby, part of the North East Rivers Festival. Around 500 competitors in all sorts of homemade inflatable craft race down a 5km river course. The primary goal is not so much to win, but to sabotage your neighbours' vessels and be the last one afloat. Ha!

🛏 Sleeping

Derby has a few cottages and rental houses to stay in. When the town is full (it happens when the mountain bikers are here), try Branxholm, 7km to the west. At a pinch there's free short-term camping in Derby Park by the Ringarooma River, with unpowered sites, a toilet block, a BBQ hut and the option of an *au naturel* dunk in the river.

Branxholm Lodge
LODGE **$**

(☑ 0447 041 418; www.branxholmlodge.com.au; 32 Albert St, Branxholm; d $100) Breathing new life into what was once the Branxholm Primary School, this budget lodge is set-up well for mountain bikers, with dorm bunks for up to 12 people, bike storage, maintenance and wash-down areas, a kitchen, a laundry, multiple toilet areas and plenty of heaters for chilly northeastern nights.

Tin Dragon Trail Cottages
COTTAGE **$$**

(☑ 0407 501 137; www.tindragontrailcottages.com. au; 3 Cox's Lane, Branxholm; cottage from $170, single-night surcharge $50) 🌢 These five neat, sustainably built cottages sit near the Ringarooma River on a property that has an interesting story to tell from the Chinese mining past. Two interpretative walks here follow some of the original (now dry) mining races built by Chinese miners. More contemporary is the amazing 'micro-hydro' station the owners have built, powering the whole property. Two-night minimum preferred.

There's also a simple six-bed timber **bunkhouse** here, popular with mountain bikers ($40 per person).

Brothers Town Cottage
COTTAGE **$$**

(☑ 0400 030 221; www.brotherstowncottage.com. au; 25 Main St; cottage from $145) Kitted-out well for visiting mountain bikers, this modest two-bedroom weatherboard cottage sits behind a big camellia bush at the northern end of town and sleeps up to eight. Top features include a big outdoor deck with BBQ, a full kitchen and a fab workshop with all the benches, racks and stands you might need to repair or tune-up your trusty steed.

Postmasters Lodge
COTTAGE **$$**

(☑ 0427 496 281, 03-6354 2334; www.postmasters lodge.com.au; 59 Main St; cottage from $195) Wrapping itself underneath and behind Derby's post office, Postmasters Lodge is stylishly renovated cottage accommodation (three bedrooms, sleeping up to seven) with a full kitchen, cosy lounge and dedicated bike storage room for slumbering mountain bikers. Out the back there's lots of lawn to laze around on and a BBQ by the azaleas.

🍴 Eating

Painted Door Art Cafe
CAFE **$**

(☑ 0429 952 276; 62 Main St; mains $6-16; ⊙ 8am-4pm Mon, Tue & Thu-Sat) All-day cooked breakfasts, pizzas, toasties, burgers, baked potatoes, homemade scones and coffee are the order of the day at this art-spangled, main-street cafe, one of Derby's finite eating options.

Imperial Hotel
PUB FOOD **$$**

(☑ 03-6354 6121; www.facebook.com/branxholm imperialhotel; 5-7 Stoke St, Branxholm; mains $16-26; ⊙ bar 11am-late, meals noon-1.30pm & 6-7.30pm Mon-Sat, noon-1.30pm Sun) Locals in the know say Branxholm's monolithic, 114-year-old country pub is the best place for a feed within miles. Expect country-sized plates of steak, seafood, pork chops, surf 'n' turf, schnitzels and roast-of-the-day, plus endless cold beer. There's basic pub-style

---

TRAIL OF THE TIN DRAGON

Tin was discovered in Tasmania's northeast in the late 1800s, attracting thousands of miners. Many came from the goldfields of Victoria, and many were Chinese. At its peak, the Chinese community in and around Derby, Weldborough and Moorina numbered 1000. Documenting this Chinese mining heritage is the tourist route called the Trail of the Tin Dragon.

The trail runs between Launceston and St Helens. Key sites with interpretation panels crop up along the route, including those at Moorina, Branxholm and the Tin Centre (p163) in Derby. Chinese miners also congregated for recreation at Weldborough, where there was once a Daoist temple (or 'joss house'), now in the Queen Victoria Art Gallery (p174) in Launceston. There are also Chinese mining artefacts on display and the Trail of the Tin Dragon film to watch at the St Helens Visitor Information Centre (p160).

Locals are cynical about the trail's success. The flashy, expensive Tin Centre in Derby is seen as something of a white elephant (and no longer screens the *Trail of the Tin Dragon* film); there are usually more mountain bikers in the cafe here than tin travellers. 'Where are all the tourists?' is a common salvo at the bar in pubs around here. Make up your own mind: pick up a trail brochure at the Scottsdale or St Helens Visitor Information Centres, or check out www.trailofthetindragon.com.au.

accommodation upstairs, too, from $35 per person.

ℹ Getting There & Away

Sainty's North East Bus Service (p140) runs the Launceston to Derby service ($22, 2½ hours), once daily Monday to Friday in each direction.

Scottsdale & Around

📞 03 / POP 2470

Scottsdale planted itself on the rich agricultural soils of Tasmania's northeast in the 1850s. It's an industrious, pocket-sized town that looks out to the rolling hills that surround it. Poppies, forestry and potatoes are the town's raison d'être – all of which adds up to an agricultural, utilitarian approach to life and natural resources. It's a veritable metropolis compared with some of the little towns you may have passed through back towards the east coast, but Scottsdale's charms are more subtle than obvious.

If you're passing through the Scottsdale area in summer, don't miss the amazing purple haze of lavender at nearby Nabowla. For mountain bikers, the North East Tasmania Rail Trail (www.railtrails.org.au) kicks off in Scottsdale, tracking 62km southwest to Launceston.

⊙ Sights

Bridestowe Lavender Estate   FARM

(📞 03-6352 8182; www.bridestowelavender.com. au; 296 Gillespies Rd, Nabowla; free Feb-Nov, $10 Dec & Jan; ⊙10am-4pm May-Aug, 9am-5pm Sep-Apr) Near Nabowla, 22km west of Scottsdale, is the turn-off to the largest lavender farm in the southern hemisphere, producing lavender oil for the perfume industry. The purple fields in flowering season (mid-December to late January) are unforgettable. There's also a cafe and gift shop that sells all things lavender: drawer scenters, fudge, ice cream and 'Bobbie Bears' – lavender-stuffed toys that (inexplicably) sell by the thousands.

Between 1 December and late January, the entry fee includes a guided tour of the blooms; tours leave hourly between 9.30am and 3.30pm.

Sideling   VIEWPOINT

(Tasman Hwy, Scottsdale) The road from Scottsdale to Launceston crosses a pass called the Sideling (about 15km south of Scottsdale). Outfitted with toilets, picnic tables and killer

WORTH A TRIP

LEGERWOOD CHAINSAW SCULPTURES

When the small town of Legerwood was forced to lop the gigantic trees along its main street – planted to commemorate its WWI soldiers – it came up with a novel idea. It commissioned chainsaw sculptor Eddie Freeman to carve dramatically posed figures of the soldiers (and other significant local personages) from the tree stumps that remained. For a quick look, detour off the A3 to/from St Helens, 24km south of Scottsdale, onto the C423, signed to Legerwood and Ringarooma.

views as far as Flinders Island on a clear day, it makes a great break from the wiggly road.

🛏 Sleeping

Lords Hotel   PUB $

(📞 03-6352 2319; www.lordshotel.com.au; 2 King St, Scottsdale; s/d $60/80, motel $130/150; 🛜) Lords has been lording it over Scottsdale since 1911 and still pulls in the punters for hefty pub meals (mains $14 to $33). Upstairs are 15 basic pub rooms with shared facilities; out the back are newer motel rooms. The old photos in the dining room of heartbreakingly big trees being felled say much about the town's tenor.

Willow Lodge   B&B $$

(📞 03-6352 2552; www.willowlodge.net.au; 119 King St, Scottsdale; d incl breakfast from $155; 🛜) This endearing Federation-era (1881) B&B is presented with absolute attention to detail. Two bright, colourful rooms overlook garden blooms, and the owners intoxicate guests with after-dinner liqueurs (best consumed in the hot tub); dinners by arrangement). Beaut views of potato fields, cows and horses. Two attic rooms and a pool are on the drawing board.

Beulah   B&B $$

(📞 03-6352 3723; www.beulaheritage.com; 9 King St, Scottsdale; s/d incl breakfast from $120/150; 🛜) This appealing 1878 home has three rooms decked out in tolerable heritage style. Ease into a chair by the fire in the guest lounge, sip a complimentary port or sherry and chew the fat with the affable owners, who also run Cafe Rhubaba (p166) up the street (expect lashings of rhubarb compote on the breakfast menu).

🍴 Eating & Drinking

Cottage Bakery   BAKERY $
(☑ 03-6352 2273; www.facebook.com/cottage bakery; 9 Victoria St, Scottsdale; items $5-8; ⊙ 6am-5pm Mon-Fri, 7am-2.30pm Sat) Duck into this famously good bakery to pick up picnic fodder, biscuits, cakes and real cream pies. It also does a mighty fine curried scallop pie (be here early before they sell out).

Cafe Rhubaba   CAFE $$
(☑ 03-6366 6028; 15 King St, Scottsdale; mains $12-18; ⊙ 8.30am-5.30pm Mon-Fri, 9am-5pm Sat & Sun) Into rhubarb, much? The good folks at Cafe Rhubaba make rhubarb sponge, rhubarb shortcake, rhubarb-and-apple tart, rhubarb syrup, rhubarb cordial, rhubarb jam... Buy some to eat-in or take away, or if you're not a fan of the 'barb, there's meatloaf, salmon-and-asparagus tart, chicken curry, chilli con carne and good old-fashioned curried sausages to fill any lunchtime voids.

Little Rivers Brewing Co   BREWERY
(☑ 03-6352 4886; www.littlerivers.com.au; 22 Victoria St, Scottsdale; tasting paddles $10; ⊙ 11am-5pm Wed, Thu, Sat & Sun, to 8pm Fri) Something new in Scottsdale (believe us, it's unusual), Little Rivers is a backstreet brewhouse turning out five flavoursome beers, including a crisp Dorset lager and a glorious golden ale. There's a fun vibe here, summer Friday nights kicking on with occasional live music and passing food truck.

ℹ Information

Scottsdale Visitor Information Centre
(☑ 03-6352 6520; www.northeasttasmania. com.au; 4 Alfred St, Scottsdale; ⊙ 9am-5pm; 🛜) Info on local accommodation, attractions and transport inside an 1881 courthouse (...the judge looks like he needs a holiday). Free wi-fi.

ℹ Getting There & Away

Sainty's North East Bus Service (p140) runs from Launceston to Scottsdale ($13, one hour).

Bridport

☑ 03 / POP 1250
This well-entrenched, snoozy holiday town squats on the shores of Anderson Bay. Just 85km from Launceston, it's popular with sea-seeking weekenders, with safe swimming beaches and good fishing. There's also trout fishing in nearby lakes and dams. Meanwhile, golfers come from across the globe to play on the two (two!) world-class courses here. Bridport is also the launching point for the slow boat to Flinders Island.

🏃 Activities

Barnbougle   GOLF
(☑ 03-6356 0094; www.barnbougle.com.au; 425 Waterhouse Rd; 18 or 20 holes from $104, club hire from $35; ⊙ 7am-dusk) Who would have thought two of Australia's top-10 public golf courses would be in this remote location, 5km east of Bridport? The Dunes is a challenging par-71 links in rolling sand dunes right on the edge of Bass Strait; Lost Farm is an adjacent 20-hole links 4km down the road. There's **accommodation** (☑ 03-6356 1124; cottage from $165, villa $900; 🌊) and a restaurant here too.

Bridport Walking Track   WALKING
(☑ 03-6356 1881; www.bridportwalkingtrack.com; foreshore) Feel like stretching your legs? Hoof it along this scenic 11km circuit around town, passing beaches, forests, riverbanks and the **Bridport Wildflower Reserve** (☑ 1300 827 727; www.parks.tas.gov.au; off Richard St) – all part of the traditional lands of the Leenerrerter Aboriginal clan. If you really push it, you can do the loop in a couple of hours. Download a map online.

🛏 Sleeping & Eating

Bridport YHA   HOSTEL $
(☑ 03-6356 1585; www.yha.com.au; 47 Main St; dm $28, d with/without bathroom from $82/55; ⊙ closed mid-Jun–mid-Aug; 🛜) There are great water views from this bright, clean, chocolate-brown weatherboard hostel, that feels more like a relaxed beach house than a backpackers. You can hire bikes and canoes, or ogle the shifting sands across the road from the deck.

Platypus Park Country Retreat   APARTMENT $$
(☑ 03-6356 1873; www.platypuspark.com.au; 20 Ada St; d from $110, apt from $140; 🛜) In a quiet spot beside the Brid River, a short drive out of town, Platypus Park has a range of cottagey apartments and doubles, overseen by the friendly owners – fifth-generation Tasmanians who can tell you all about the 'hood. There's trout fishing in dams nearby, and you might spy a platypus in the river.

Bridport Beach Cottages   APARTMENT $$
(☑ 03-6356 1122; www.bridportbeachcottages. com; 103 Main St; apt from $115; 🌊) A snappy-

looking group of seven tidy corrugated-iron-clad one- and two-bedroom units on the main street, each with a deck, bathroom, a small kitchen in the corner and bee-buzzy native garden surrounds. Wobbling distance to the pub and the cafe. Terrific bang for your buck.

★ **Bridport Café**   CAFE $$
(☑03-6356 0057; 97 Main St; mains $15-26; ⊙9am-4pm daily, 6-8pm Fri) With a broad deck, an eclectic scatter of tables and chairs, and a crochet-clad tree out the front, this cafe on the main drag is a real gem. Sidle in for local scallops and chips, pork sliders with apple slaw, some chicken curry or Friday-night tapas. Live weekend music in summer, and Tasmanian beers and wines aplenty. Good one!

❶ Getting There & Away

Sainty's North East Bus Service (p140) runs from Bridport to Launceston ($20, two hours) via Scottsdale once daily in each direction, Monday to Friday.

Furneaux Freight (p169) operates a boat to Flinders Island from Bridport.

Flinders Island

☑03 / POP 840

There's more than one island here, adrift in Bass Strait off the northeastern corner of mainland Tasmania: Flinders is just one of 51 islands in the Furneaux Group archipelago. These rocky, mountainous isles are all that remains of the land bridge that connected Tasmania with mainland Australia 10,000 years ago.

Sparsely populated and naturally gorgeous, Flinders is a rural community that lives mostly from fishing and agriculture. For visitors there's great bushwalking, wildlife spotting, fishing, kayaking, snorkelling, diving and safe swimming in its curvaceous bays. Or you can spend a few leisurely hours combing the beaches for elusive Killiecrankie diamonds (topaz, technically) and nautilus shells.

For online inspiration, see www.visit flindersisland.com.au.

History

Flinders had a lawless early history as the domain of sealers. These pirates slaughtered thousands of seals, lured ships onto the island's rocks with lanterns and kidnapped local Aboriginal women to claim as 'wives',

taking many to Kangaroo Island in South Australia where Tasmanian Indigenous lineage can still be traced. Mainland Tasmanian Aboriginals also suffered here: between 1829 and 1834, 135 Indigenous people were transported to Wybalenna to be 'civilised and educated'. After 14 years, only 47 survived.

⊙ Sights

Furneaux Museum   MUSEUM
(☑03-6359 8434; www.flinders.tas.gov.au/ furneaux-museum; 8 Fowlers Rd, Emita; adult/child $5/free; ⊙1-5pm Jan-Mar, 1-4pm Sat & Sun Apr-Dec) The grounds around the volunteer-run Furneaux Museum are strewn with whalebones, blubber pots and rusty wrecks. Inside are Aboriginal artefacts (including beautiful shell necklaces), plus sealing, sailing and mutton-bird industry relics.

Wybalenna Historic Site   HISTORIC SITE
(☑03-6359 5002; www.visitflindersisland.com. au/explore/culture-heritage; Port Davies Rd, Emita; ⊙dawn-dusk) FREE A few piles of bricks, the chapel and cemetery are all that remain of this misguided settlement built to 'care for' relocated mainland Tasmanian Aboriginal people, operating between 1829 and 1834. Eighty-seven people died here from poor food, disease and despair – among them was Manalargena, chief of the Ben Lomond tribe, whose headstone can be seen here. The site is on Aboriginal land: be respectful.

Unavale Vineyard   VINEYARD
(☑03-6359 3632, 0427 593 631; www.unavale. com.au; 10 Badger Corner Rd, Lady Barron; ⊙10am-4pm) The island's only vineyard produces decent pinot noir, oaked chardonnay and sauvignon blanc. Everything is done onsite, right down to the labels. Roll up for a tasting at the cellar door – call first to make sure someone is around.

⚡ Activities

There's great bushwalking on Flinders. The highlight is a well-signposted track to the peak of Mt Strzelecki (756m; five hours return) for poetry-inspiring views. At the disarmingly named Trousers Point there's a terrific 1.9km coastal circuit walk. Keen for more? Source a copy of *A Walking Guide to Flinders Island and Cape Barren Island,* by Doreen Lovegrove and Steve Summers, or *Walks of Flinders Island,* by Ken Martin. Multiday guided hiking packages are available.

THE EAST COAST FLINDERS ISLAND

It's easy to find your own private beach for **swimming**. A local secret is the **Docks** below Mt Killiecrankie, where granite boulders protect white-sand coves. **Trousers Point Beach** is the classic Flinders swimming spot (with or without trousers). There are picnic tables, BBQs, toilets and unpowered camp sites under the she-oaks here; national park entry fees ($12/24 per person/vehicle per day) apply. **Fishing**, **snorkelling** and **diving** possibilities also abound.

The granite faces of Mt Killiecrankie (319m) offer challenging **rock climbing**. There's also a climbable 200m granite wall on Mt Strzelecki.

Flinders Island Adventures   FISHING, WALKING
(☑03-6359 4507; www.flindersisland.com.au) Book a fishing charter with this local outfit, which also runs land-based guided walking tours (five-day all-inclusive guided walks per person from $2415). A two-night fishing package (with breakfast, lunch, accommodation at Lady Barron and airport transfers) costs $695 per person.

Killiecrankie Enterprises   OUTDOORS
(☑03-6359 2130; www.killiecrankieenterprises. com.au; 7 Lagoon Rd, Whitemark; ⊘9.30am-4.30pm Mon-Fri, to 12.30pm Sat) The elusive Killiecrankie 'diamond' is actually semi-precious topaz. Killiecrankie Enterprises in Whitemark hires shovels ($2) and sieves ($2), and can advise where to fossick (most likely Diamond Creek at Killiecrankie Beach on the island's north shore).

Flinders Island Dive   DIVING
(☑0428 598 529, 03-6359 8429; www.flinders islanddive.com.au; 22 Wireless Station Rd, Emita) There's great diving and snorkelling in the clear waters around the island, among sea caves, shoals and reefs: talk to Flinders Island Dive.

Flinders Island Aviation   SCENIC FLIGHTS
(☑03-6359 3641; www.flindersislandaviation.com; 4 Gunter St, Lady Barron) Scenic flights over the craggy peaks of Flinders and the surrounding isles. Call to discuss pricing/timing.

🛏 Sleeping

See www.visitflindersisland.com.au/plan/stay for accommodation listings.

Department of Parks, Wildlife & Heritage   CAMPGROUND
(☑03-6359 2217; www.parks.tas.gov.au) FREE
Operates a handful of free camp sites around

the island, mostly with toilets and BBQs. North East River, Lillies Beach and Trousers Point are the best of the bunch (though national park entry fees – day pass per person/vehicle $12/24 – apply at Trousers Point).

Island Quarters   APARTMENT $$
(IQ; ☑0427 611 413, 03-6359 2168; www.island quarters.com.au; 12 Patrick St, Whitemark; apt from $180; ❋♠) On a former concrete-mixing yard, this stylish new one-bedroom apartment is right in the middle of Whitemark, and – if you like your regional Tasmania served with a touch of the city – provides a very slick accommodation experience (the lounge is leather, the bench tops are granite and the TV is large).

The Studio   COTTAGE $$
(☑03-6359 4553, 0487 034 844; www.mountain seas.com.au/studio; 811 Trousers Point Rd, Trousers Point; cottage from $130) This lovely little self-contained, steep-roofed bushland cottage is behind an arts retreat where people come to paint, think and pursue their muse. It's a super-private one-bedroom arrangement, with predictably interesting art on the walls.

Lady Barron Holiday Home   RENTAL HOUSE $$
(☑03-6359 3555; www.ladybarron.com; 31 Franklin Pde, Lady Barron; house from $140; ❋) A homely, renovated 1940s place with three bedrooms (sleeping up to six), walking distance to the Lady Barron shops and pub, and with views across Franklin Sound to barren Cape Barron Island. Good for families. Have a look in the veggie garden and see what's sprouting.

Furneaux Tavern   MOTEL $$
(☑03-6359 3521; www.furneauxtavern.com.au; 11 Franklin Pde, Lady Barron; s/d/f from $90/120/150; ♠) An array of nicely updated motel-style cabins with wraparound decks, set amid native gardens. The fish-focused **Kipli Restaurant** (mains $16-33; ⊘noon-1.30pm & 6-7.30pm) is here, too, and you can bend an elbow over the pool table in the bar.

Flinders Island Cabin Park   CABIN $$
(☑03-6359 2188; www.flindersislandcp.com.au; 1 Bluff Rd, Whitemark; cabins & cottages from $110) Near the airport are these busily managed and recently renovated cabins, plus car and campervan hire. Mountain bikes, kayaks and fishing gear also available. Ask about car-and-cabin package deals.

West End Beach House RENTAL HOUSE **$$$**
(☑0488 089 955; www.westendbeachhouse.com.
au; 801 West End Rd, Leeka; house $260-345) 🏄
Architect-designed to have a minimal en-
vironmental footprint, this fabulous, roll-
roofed holiday house en route to Mt Tanner
has a very Australian vibe: corrugated iron,
lots of fold-back glass, sunny decks, outdoor
post-beach shower and a short stroll to the
sand. And the sunken bath is something to
cherish! Two-night minimum stay.

✖ Eating

A Taste of Flinders DELI **$**
(☑0474 889 236; www.tasteofflinders.com.au; 3
Walker St, Whitemark; items from $4; ⊙7am-4pm
Mon & Tue, to 5pm Wed-Fri, 8am-1pm Sat, 11am-4pm
Sun) This savvy cafe-deli does the best coffee
on the island, and has shelves full of fresh
island produce: bread, vegetables, jams, bot-
tled water, wine, honey. Food on your plate
includes the likes of quiches, cakes and vir-
tuous salads.

Flinders Island Bakery BAKERY **$**
(☑03-6359 2105; www.fiaai.org.au/portfolio-item/
bakery; 4 Lagoon Rd, Whitemark; items from $4;
⊙7am-4pm Mon-Fri) Divine wallaby-and-red-
wine pie (or chicken and corn, if you're not
into eating the natives). Passable coffee,
sandwiches, rolls, hamburgers and sausage
rolls also. Open every second Saturday, too.

Interstate Hotel PUB FOOD **$$**
(☑03-6359 2114; www.interstatehotel.com.au;
6 Patrick St, Whitemark; mains $15-30; ⊙noon-
1.30pm & 6-7.30pm Mon-Sat) Chew on some
pub grub while you assess the health and
temper of the locals at the bar. Takeaway
barbecue packs and picnic lunches available. There's pub-style accommodation here,
too (doubles with/without bathroom from
$120/90). If you feel like belting out a ren-
dition of the Stone Temple Pilots' 'Interstate
Love Song' at the bar, we're sure no one will
take offence.

ⓘ Information

Flinders Island Visitor Information Centre
(☑03-6359 5002; www.visitflindersisland.com.
au; 4 Davies St, Whitemark; ⊙9am-5pm Mon-
Fri) is the main hub for island advice.

Service Tasmania (☑1300 135 513; www.
servicetasmania.tas.gov.au; 2 Lagoon Rd,
Whitemark; ⊙11am-3pm Mon-Wed, noon-4pm
Thu & Fri) has walking track advice and national
park passes.

There are no ATMs on the island, but there's
a Westpac bank agency in Whitemark and most
businesses have Eftpos facilities for cash withdrawals.

ⓘ Getting There & Away

Flinders Island Travel (☑0400 111 641; www.
flindersislandtravel.com.au) Has package deals
(flights, accommodation and car rental).

Furneaux Freight (☑03-6356 1753; www.fur
neauxfreight.com.au; Main St, Bridport; adult/
child/car return $115/60/505) Operates a
Bridport–Lady Barron car ferry. The trip takes
eight hours; bookings essential.

Sharp Airlines (☑1300 556 694; www.sharp
airlines.com; Flinders Island Airport, Palana
Rd, Whitemark) Flies between Melbourne
(Essendon Airport) and Flinders Island Airport
at Whitemark (one-way $252), and between
Launceston and Flinders Island (one-way $185).
Fly-drive packages start at $447.

ⓘ Getting Around

Many island roads are unsealed – take care
when driving. Don't drive after dusk unless you
really have to: the native wildlife has suicidal
tendencies.

Flinders Island Cabin Park rents out budget
cars and vans from $75 per day. Both operators
can meet you at the airport.

Flinders Island Car Rentals (☑0415 505
655, 03-6359 2168; www.ficr.com.au; 21 Mem-
ana Rd, Whitemark) has vehicles from $80 for
up to three days, and operates an electricity-
powered (!) airport shuttle between the airport
and your accommodation (one-way from $10).

Launceston & Around

Best Places to Eat

➡ Geronimo (p183)

➡ Stillwater (p183)

➡ Bryher (p181)

Best Places to Stay

➡ Quamby Estate (p194)

➡ The Trig/The Container (p193)

➡ Two Four Two (p180)

Why Go?

It's hard to imagine a pocket-sized city more appealing than Launceston. 'Lonnie', as the locals call it, is certainly large enough for some urban buzz, but small enough for country congeniality to be the rule rather than the exception. The city effortlessly melds the historic with the contemporary, bolstered by vibrant arts and food scenes. Cloaked in bushland, the amazing Cataract Gorge brings the wilds into the heart of town. Those who want to travel a little further out have plenty of choices: the Tamar Valley Wine Route delivers world-class pinot noirs; historic pastoral estates such as Woolmers and Clarendon hit all the heritage high notes; and national parks at Narawntapu and Ben Lomond offer plenty of opportunities to get up close to unspoiled nature.

When to Go

➡ Launceston becomes giddy over summer (December to February) with some excellent festivals and long, still evenings by the river.

➡ In March and April the Tamar Valley vineyards hum with pickers and pruners working among the autumnal vine colours.

➡ In winter (June to August) the region is still, sunny and crisp: nearby peaks are primed for snowman construction (maybe even some skiing). Rug up at night in Launceston, with temperatures frequently dipping down to 0°C.

Launceston & Around Highlights

1 Tamar Valley Wine Route (p192) Sipping sparkling wine at ridiculously picturesque vineyards.

2 Cataract Gorge (p174) Walking, swimming, climbing or cycling at Launceston's outdoor playground.

3 Woolmers Estate (p195) Exploring this amazing World

Heritage–listed pastoral property, along with nearby Brickendon.

4 Seahorse World (p189) Befriending the cute critters at this fascinating enterprise in Beauty Point.

5 Queen Victoria Art Gallery (p174) Admiring colonial and contemporary art.

6 Low Head Penguin Tours (p191) Watching the penguins coming home at dusk.

7 Launceston cafe culture (p182) Digging the city's caffeine scene.

8 Hollybank Treetops Adventure (p193) Making like Tarzan at this family-focused forest activity park.

ROAD TRIP >
TAMAR VALLEY TRAIL

• •

Funnelling 64km north from Launceston, the Tamar River Valley is fringed with emerald hills and cool-climate wineries: it's one of Australia's finest wine-touring areas. You could make this up-and-back journey in a single day, but that would be to miss the point. Meander along the riverbank, go off on a tangent to a winery or two – take your time and really unwind.

❶ Launceston

Laid-back Launceston is a fine starting point for a foodie's exploration of Tasmania's north, with Cataract Gorge providing a dramatic natural counterpoint within walking distance of the city centre. If you're here on a Saturday morning, fill your picnic hamper at the weekly Harvest (p184) market.

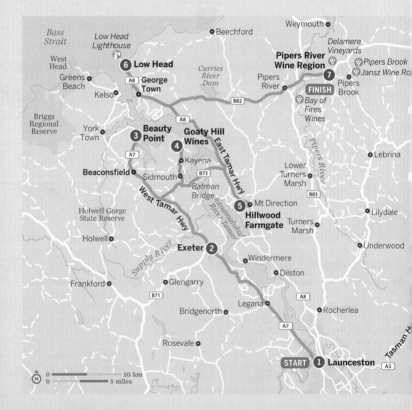

4 days / 144 miles / 232km

Great for... Food & Drink, Outdoors

Best Time to Go; October to May for fine, mild weather

The Drive > From downtown Launceston, take the West Tamar Hwy (A7) 22km northwest to Exeter. The road stays close to the Tamar's west riverbank, and en route you'll catch glimpses of the river, with the best views from well-signposted Brady's Lookout around 5km southeast of Exeter.

② Exeter

The premium cool-climate wines of the Tamar Valley have been swilled at the tables of royalty and to make sure you don't miss the best the region has to offer, check out the Tamar Valley Wine Route (www.tamarvalleywineroute.com.au); pick up a self-drive guide from the Tamar Visitor Information Centre (p187) in sleepy little Exeter. Don't miss a pie from the Exeter Bakery (p187) for lunch!

The Drive > The road northwest from Exeter to Beauty Point (23km) crosses the pancake-flat river flats, which are a deep shade of green for most of the year.

③ Beauty Point

Beauty Point has two winning attractions: Platypus House (p189) is a fine chance to see everyone's favourite monotreme, while Seahorse World (p189) has to be one of the world's more unusual aquariums, with a pot-bellied seahorse the main drawcard.

The Drive > Heading back south, take the turn-off west towards Batman Bridge, then follow the signs to Kayena just before crossing the bridge.

④ Goaty Hill Wines

In the tiny hamlet of Kayena, the family-friendly Goaty Hill Wines (p188) has cellar-door sales and tastings (ring ahead in the depths of winter). It's best known for its top-notch riesling and pinots gris and noir. Acoustic troubadors strum on the deck in summer; impromptu cricket matches happen on the lawns. Bliss.

The Drive > From Kayena, head south to the B73 and Batman Bridge, cross over to the Tamar's east bank, then turn south along the East Tamar Hwy (A8). Almost immediately, watch for signs to Hillwood, which overlooks the river just down off the main road.

⑤ Hillwood Farmgate

At the bounteous Hillwood Farmgate (p190) you can pick your own strawberries, raspberries, loganberries, blackcurrants, redcurrants and blueberries. Afterwards, make a beeline for the cafe (mains $8 to $16) for a berry sundae, a slice of berry-swirl cheesecake or a coffee.

The Drive > Return to the A8, then follow it for 22km north amid the fruit-growing hills above the Tamar's eastern riverbank. Eventually you'll hit George Town, with Low Head 5km further on.

⑥ Low Head

The main attraction here is Low Head Lighthouse (p191); built in 1888, it's a terrific spot to watch the torrent of the Tamar spilling into Bass Strait. Low Head Penguin Tours (p191) leave nightly at dusk from a signposted spot beside Low Head Rd, just south of the lighthouse.

The Drive > Some 7km south of George Town (or 12km from Low Head), the B82 veers east out over the low and verdant Tippogoree Hills and passes through the Den Ranges Forest Reserve before emerging amid the vineyards of Pipers River, just 27km after leaving George Town.

⑦ Pipers River Wine Region

In the eastern Tamar Valley hinterland, the Pipers River Wine Region (www.tamarvalleywineroute.com.au) is a lovely adjunct to the Tamar's charms. Pipers Brook (p192) is the region's most famous vineyard. Next door, savvy Jansz Wine Room (p192) makes fine sparkling wine, aka 'Méthode Tasmanoise'... Bay of Fires Wines (p192) is the home of prestigious Arras sparkling and easy-drinking whites and pinots. On a much smaller scale is affable, family-run Delamere Vineyards (p192).

The Drive > Drive south from Pipers River along the B83 to Lower Turners Marsh (14km), turn right (west) along the C812 to Mt Direction (13km), then rejoin the main Tamar Valley route (A8) all the way into Launceston.

ℹ️ Getting There & Away

Launceston has bus services to Hobart, Devonport and beyond, primarily provided by **Tassielink** (p306) and **Redline Coaches** (p185). **Launceston Airport** (p185) offers flights to the mainland.

LAUNCESTON

📞 03 / POP 86,640

Tasmania's second city has forever been locked in rivalry with big-smoke Hobart to the south. Launcestonians argue that their architecture is more elegant, their parks more beautiful, their surrounding hills more verdant and their food scene zestier. And on many of these points it's hard to argue. This is a city where art and design are highly valued, the locals embrace the outdoors and food and coffee culture thrives. There are a couple of big new hotels being built, the University of Tasmania is doing good things here, and it's an easy and endearing base for those exploring the Tamar Valley or other parts of the north. Nice one, 'Lonnie'.

History

George Bass and Matthew Flinders were the first Europeans to spy Launceston's Kanamaluka/Tamar River when they sailed in here on their 1798 voyage of discovery. The area's first white settlement was established in 1804, when the British, intent on beating the French in claiming the island, built a military post at George Town. Not long after, an expedition scouted south and found the present-day site of Launceston, naming it for the English town in Cornwall – although the Tasmanian version came to be pronounced 'Lon-sess-ton', rather than the traditional 'Lawnston'.

Early Launceston was both a port and a military headquarters. By 1827 it already had a population of 2000, and was shipping wool and wheat from the surrounding districts. By the 1850s the town was Tasmania's second major centre and was proclaimed a municipality. In 1871 tin was discovered at Mt Bischoff, which further cemented Launceston's fortunes as a trading hub. A decade later it opened its own stock exchange. In the 20th century the city was an important service town for the rich agricultural region that surrounds it, and more recently a university town.

◉ Sights

★ Cataract Gorge   PARK

(Map p175; 📞03-6331 5915; www.launceston cataractgorge.com.au; via Cataract Walk, Trevallyn; ⏰24hr) At magnificent Cataract Gorge, the bushland, cliffs and ice-cold South Esk River feel a million miles from town. At First Basin there's a free (chilly) outdoor swimming pool (November to March), the world's longest single-span chairlift (adult/child $15/10; 9am to 5.30pm, to 4.30pm in winter) and Victorian-era gardens where peacocks wander aimlessly. Elsewhere, there are walking and cycling tracks as well as lookouts. Eating options include two cafes and a BBQ area. The whole shebang is floodlit at night.

Two walking tracks straddle the gorgeous gorge (Cataract Walk is level; the Zig Zag Track is steep), leading from Kings Bridge up to First Basin. You can also drive to the First Basin car park – follow the signs from York St to Hillside Cres, Brougham St and Basin Rd.

Just upstream from First Basin is the Alexandra Suspension Bridge. Another walking track (45 minutes one way) leads further up the gorge to Second Basin and further still to Duck Reach, the earliest municipal hydroelectric power station in Australia (1895).

★ Queen Victoria Museum   MUSEUM

(QVMAG; Map p178; 📞03-6323 3777; www.qvmag. tas.gov.au; 2 Invermay Rd, Inveresk; ⏰10am-4pm, planetarium shows 1pm & 3pm Tue-Fri, 2pm & 3pm Sat) FREE The natural, social and technology-focused collections of the QVMAG are exhibited in this annexe housed in historic workshops in the restored and reinvented Inveresk Railyards precinct. The building itself is half the attraction. Inside, the zoology, botany and geology collections are extensive and the planetarium (adult/child/family $6/4/16) is perennially popular. There's also a cafe and a museum shop on-site. Get here on the free Tiger Bus (p185).

Free museum tours run on Sundays at 1pm.

★ Queen Victoria Art Gallery   MUSEUM, GALLERY

(QVMAG; Map p178; 📞03-6323 3777; www.qvmag. tas.gov.au; 2 Wellington St; ⏰10am-4pm) FREE Colonial paintings, including works by John Glover, are the pride of the collection at this art gallery in a meticulously restored 19th-century building on the edge of Royal Park. Other works cover the gamut of Australian painting from Tom Roberts to Fred Williams and Bea Maddock. There's also an

Launceston

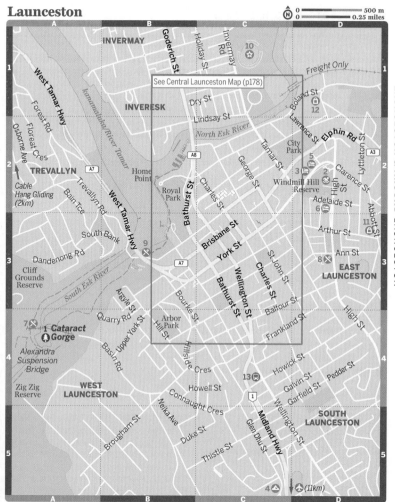

See Central Launceston Map (p178)

Launceston

LAUNCESTON ARCHITECTURE

Launceston has an amazingly well-preserved collation of heritage architecture, across all eras and styles. It probably has something to do with Tasmania's notoriously slow economy – there's just never been enough cash around to knock things down and build something worse! Take a wander around suburban Trevallyn and East Launceston to stickybeak at some beautifully crafted private homes, and keep your eyes open in the city for these notable public edifices.

Albert Hall (Map p178; ✆03-6331 4616; www.alberthalllaunceston-public.sharepoint.com; 47 Tamar St) Now operating as a convention and function venue, this Launceston landmark was built in 1891 in classical Victorian style. Inside the Great Hall is the Brindley Air Organ, Australia's largest pre-1860 organ.

Town Hall (Map p178; ✆03-6323 3000; www.launceston.tas.gov.au; 18-28 St John St; ⊙8.30am-5pm Mon-Fri) Erected in 1864 with soaring neoclassical columns. 'Progress with Prudence' says the coat of arms – duck inside to the council offices on weekdays to see how they're going with that.

State Customs Office (Map p178; 89 Esplanade) This building's magnificent 1888 neoclassical colonnade reflects Launceston's 19th-century prosperity. It now houses offices; not open to the public.

Holyman House (Map p178; cnr Brisbane & George Sts) Built in 1936, this building is a fine example of interwar architecture. Four levels of art-deco detailing surround sundry offices. The future-thinking Holyman transport empire has long since left the building.

Henty House (Map p178; 1 Civic Sq; ⊙8.30am-4.30pm Mon-Fri) Built in 1983, this ziggurat-shaped brutalist building was the subject of a heated conservation battle in 2012. Should it be heritage listed or demolished? The community was divided, but those supporting the heritage listing won the day. It now houses various civic offices.

Launceston City Council has produced a handy walking-tour map called *Launceston Heritage Walks*, which takes in these landmarks and more. It can be downloaded from www.destinationlaunceston.com.au.

---

impressive collection of decorative arts, a popular cafe and a gallery shop.

Boag's Brewery BREWERY
(Map p178; ✆03-6332 6300; www.jamesboag.com.au; 39 William St; adult/child $33/15; ⊙tours 11am, 1pm & 3pm) James Boag's beer has been brewed on William St since 1881. See the amber alchemy in action on 90-minute guided tours; these include a beer and cheese tasting. Alternatively, order a beer paddle ($10) and afterwards take a wander through the free on-site museum, which sheds further light on brewing history (old TV ads, beer labels and photographs aplenty).

National Automobile Museum of Tasmania MUSEUM
(Map p178; ✆03-6334 8888; www.namt.com.au; 86 Cimitiere St; adult/child/family $14/8/36; ⊙9am-5pm Sep-May, 10am-4pm Jun-Aug) Rev-heads get pretty excited over the displays here – it's one of Australia's slickest presentations of classic and historic cars and motorbikes. The 1969 Fiat Spider takes the cake.

City Park PARK
(Map p178; ✆03-6323 3000; www.launceston.tas.gov.au/parks-and-gardens/city-park; cnr Tamar & Cimitiere Sts; ⊙daylight hours) There's loads going on at this shady park. It's home to enormous oak and plane trees, an over-the-top Victorian fountain, a conservatory, a Victorian bandstand and a playground for kids. Everyone loves the glass-walled **Japanese macaque enclosure** (8am to 4pm), a gift from Japanese sister-city Ikeda. There's even free wi-fi.

Launceston Tramway Museum MUSEUM
(Map p178; ✆03-6334 8334; www.facebook.com/launcestontramwaymuseum; 2 Invermay Rd, Inveresk; adult/child $5/2; ⊙10am-4pm Wed-Sun) Launceston had trams until 1952, when the rails were ripped up and the carriages sold off. Now you can visit this volunteer-staffed museum to take a ride on the lustrously restored No 29, on a little track that runs out past Aurora Stadium. The stories of what happened to all the old carriages are nerdishly fascinating.

Design Centre Tasmania
GALLERY

(Map p178; ☎03-6331 5506; www.designtasmania. com.au; cnr Brisbane & Tamar Sts; adult/child $6/ free; ☺9.30am-5.30pm Mon-Fri, 10am-4pm Sat & Sun Oct-Apr, shorter hours rest of year) A two-wing building on the fringe of City Park, this impressive design centre incorporates an old church hall that now houses a shop specialising in handmade Tasmanian crafts, as well as a new purpose-built wing where exhibitions of Tasmanian design are staged.

Prince's Square
PARK

(Map p178; ☎03-6323 3000; www.launceston.tas. gov.au; btwn Charles & St John Sts) Prince's Sq once hosted military drills, public hangings and rowdy political meetings. These days, it's a lovely place to relax. There's a bronze fountain that was purchased at the 1855 Paris Exhibition and a statue of top-hatted Dr William Russ Pugh, the first surgeon in the southern hemisphere to use general anaesthetic.

Franklin House
HISTORIC BUILDING

(☎03-6344 7824; www.nationaltrust.org.au/places/ franklin-house; 413 Hobart Rd, Youngtown; adult/ child $10/5; ☺9am-4pm Mon-Sat, noon-4pm Sun) A relatively short drive south of the city, Franklin House is one of Launceston's most fetching Georgian-era homes. Built in 1838 by former convict and savvy businessman Britton Jones, it was extended in 1848 by schoolteacher William Keeler Hawkes, who ran it as a boys' school until 1866. Later, it became a private residence. Though the furnishings in the house are sparse and modest, the building's history makes it well worth a visit.

Tasmania Zoo
ZOO

(☎03-6396 6100; www.tasmaniazoo.com.au; 1166 Ecclestone Rd, Riverside; adult/child $28/15; ☺9am-4.30pm) There are more than 80 species of feathered, furred and finned critters – native and non-native – at this laid-back wildlife park. This is your chance to see some Tasmanian devils, which you can watch snarling over meaty meals at 10.30am, 1pm and 3.30pm. To get here, take the West Tamar Hwy (A7) out of Launceston to Riverside, turn left into Ecclestone Rd (C734) and continue 12km west.

 Activities

Mountain biking and rock climbing are terrific fun around Launceston. Mountain Bike & Rock Climbing Tasmania (☎0447 712 638; www.mountainbiketasmania.com.au) runs guided rides along the North Esk River

($100), through the Trevallyn Nature Recreation Area ($150) and down the slopes of Ben Lomond ($250) – a downhill rush shedding 1050m in altitude. Derby ($250) and Hollybank ($195) trail tours are also available, as are various trail rides around Hobart. Rock-climbing adventures include full-day climbs and abseils in Cataract Gorge ($225). Introductory sessions are also available for novice spidermen/women ($175). There's a minimum of two people required for both courses. Climbing trips to the Freycinet Peninsula on the east coast are also available.

Tasmanian Expeditions
CLIMBING

(☎03-6331 9000, 1300 666 856; www.tasmanian expeditions.com.au) These guys specialise in guided hikes around the state, but also run rock-climbing adventures on the dolerite cliffs of Cataract Gorge: half-day tour for one person ($250) as well as a full-day tour ($400 one person, $250 per person for two or more).

Launceston Leisure & Aquatic Centre
SWIMMING

(Map p175; ☎03-6323 3636; www.launceston aquatic.com.au; 18a High St; adult/child/family $7.50/5.50/19.50; ☺6am-8pm Mon-Fri, 8am-6pm Sat & Sun) Follow the sniff of chlorine up steep Windmill Hill, with its lush lawns and rooftop views, to Launceston's aquatic centre. There are several pools inside and out, a water slide, fitness centre, a watery playground for kids and a rather salubrious cafe.

Cable Hang Gliding
ADVENTURE SPORTS

(☎0419 311 198; www.cablehanggliding.com.au; Trevallyn Nature Recreation Area, Reatta Rd, Trevallyn; adult/child/tandems/family $20/15/30/60; ☺10am-5pm daily Dec-Apr, Sat & Sun only May-Nov; ▥) Make like a condor with a spot of cable hang gliding in the Trevallyn Nature Recreation Area. You'll hurtle over the edge of a cliff and glide down a 200m-long cable, suspended under wide wings. Stomach-in-your-mouth stuff. Head west along Paterson St and from King's Bridge follow the signs.

 Tours

Tamar River Cruises
BOATING

(Map p178; ☎03-6334 9900; www.tamarriver cruises.com.au; Home Point Pde) Hop aboard the 1890s-style *Lady Launceston* for a 50-minute Cataract Gorge cruise (adult/child/family $33/15/80), or opt for a longer morning or afternoon exploration of the gorge and the riverfront on the modern *Tamar Odyssey* (adult/ child/family $89/40/195). Four-hour cruises

Central Launceston

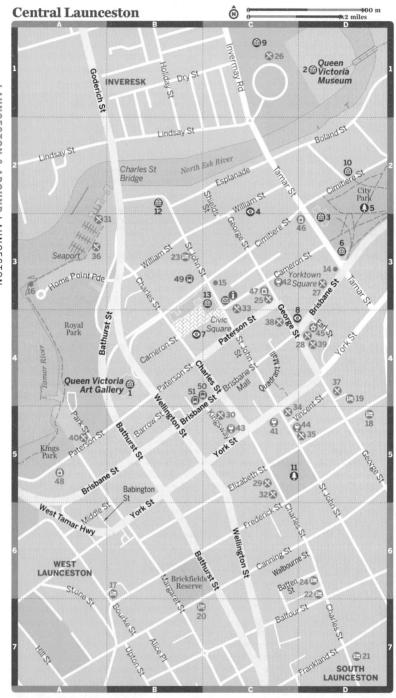

Central Launceston

on the same boat take you downstream to Batman Bridge and back and include a light lunch (adult/child/family $135/70/325). Check the website for sailing times.

Launceston Historic Walks WALKING
(Map p178; ☑03-6331 2213; www.1842.com.au/launceston-historic-walks; cnr St John & Cimitiere Sts; per person $15; ◎4pm Mon, 10am Tue-Sat) Get your historical bearings with a 1½-hour walking journey through the Georgian, Victorian and modern architecture of the city. Walks depart from the '1842' building, on the corner of St John and Cimitiere Sts. Discounted family tickets can be arranged.

Launceston City Ghost Tours WALKING
(Map p178; ☑0421 819 373; www.launcestoncityghosttours.com; 14 Brisbane St; adult/child/family $25/15/55; ◎dusk) Just after sunset, get

spooked on a 90-minute wander around the city's back alleys. Tours depart at dusk from the Royal Oak Hotel (p184) – where Cyril is the resident ghost. Bookings essential; departure time varies throughout the year. Not for children under 10.

Tasmanian Safaris ADVENTURE
(☑1300 882 415; www.tasmaniansafaris.com; 2-/3-day tours from $300/650) One-/two-night tours to Cradle Mountain or the Bay of Fires/Freycinet region (from $350/750; cheaper if you have your own tent). Also offers short (1½ hours) pedal-canoe tours on the Tamar, departing from the pontoon at Seaport ($45). Advance bookings essential.

McDermott's Coaches BUS
(☑03-6330 3717; www.mcdermotts.com.au; tours adult/child $168/84; ◎Sun, Mon, Wed & Fri)

Full-day tours to Cradle Mountain. Price includes hotel pick-up/drop-off and national park fees.

⭐ Festivals & Events

★ MONA FOMA
PERFORMING ARTS

(Museum of Old & New Art Festival of Music & Art; www.mofo.net.au; ☉ Jan) Hobart's fabulous MONA (p61) is sharing the love: its annual summer music fest (aka MOFO) was split between Hobart and Launceston in 2018. Under the stewardship of Brian Ritchie, the bass-man from the Violent Femmes, the good times kicked-off with three days of artful tunes in Launceston, before the carnival relocated down south.

From 2019 (assuming a few funding issues are ironed out), the entire festival will be held in Launceston.

Esk BeerFest
BEER

(www.esk.beerfestivals.com.au; ☉ Jan) A two-day celebration of craft beer, cider, spirits and local produce, held on the Esplanade. An entry ticket must be purchased. Pray that Van Dieman Brewery's summer IPA is on tap.

Festivale
FOOD, ART

(www.festivale.com.au; ☉ Feb) Launceston's foodie-cultural highlight – three festive days in City Park, with eating, drinking, arts and live music (everything from country to cool jazz). Tasmanian food and wine get an appropriate airing. An entry ticket must be purchased.

Launceston Cup
SPORTS

(www.goracingtasmania.com.au; ☉ Feb) The pinnacle event of the Tasmanian Summer Racing Carnival. Champagne, hats and well-presented fillies and colts. An entry ticket must be purchased.

Junction Arts Festival
PERFORMING ARTS

(www.junctionartsfestival.com.au; ☉ Sep) Five excellent days of offbeat and interesting arts performances, installations and gigs in or around Launceston's Prince's Sq.

Launceston Marathon
SPORTS

(www.launcestonmarathon.com.au; ☉ Sep) Gained a kilo or two on your travels? Sweat it out in the annual Launceston Marathon, 42.2km of sweat, pain and suffering (…then you can go and have another burger).

Royal Launceston Show
FAIR

(www.launcestonshowground.com.au; ☉ Oct) Fairy floss, bumper cars, pedigree bulls and all the questionable commerce of the fair over three days in October. An entry ticket must be purchased.

🛏 Sleeping

Sporties Hotel
PUB $

(Sporties; Map p178; ☎ 03-6331 3968; www.sportieshotel.com.au; cnr Charles & Balfour Sts; s $60-70, d with/without bathroom from $90/80; P 🛜) Sporties (Sportsmans Hall Hotel) is a bit of a local institution. The nine upstairs rooms have decent beds and a TV: some have en suites and others have their own private bathrooms down the hallway. The Monday night $15 'pint and parmi' special downstairs lures the hungry masses. Live music on weekends (light sleepers beware).

Launceston Backpackers
HOSTEL $

(Map p178; ☎ 03-6334 2327; www.launcestonbackpackers.com.au; 103 Canning St; dm $27, s/tw/tr $65/69/90, d with/without bathroom $75/65; P 🛜) 🌿 Overlooking Brickfields Reserve, this cavernous Federation-era house is the pick of Launceston's scant budget offerings. Dorms have a mix of bunks and single beds; en-suite doubles have comfy beds. There's a lounge with TV and DVD player, a clean and well-equipped communal kitchen and lovely dining room. Management is eco-attuned, proudly backing local environmental activities.

BIG4 Holiday Park Launceston
CARAVAN PARK $

(Map p175; ☎ 03-6344 2600; www.big4launceston.com.au; 86-94 Glen Dhu St, South Launceston; unpowered/powered sites from $40/45, cabin $125, villa $160-195; P 🛜) BIG4 is the closest camping to the city centre – about 2.5km to the south – but it's right on the highway and is pretty noisy. The new self-contained villas are good-lookin' and comfortable (albeit a bit pricey for the location – the budget cabins are better value). There's an enormous jumping pillow for kids to gambol on.

★ Two Four Two
APARTMENT $$

(Map p178; ☎ 03-6331 9242; www.twofourtwo.com.au; 242 Charles St; studio/apt from $230/270; P ❄ 🛜) Launceston's best self-catering accommodation, super-stylish Two Four Two is on the hip Charles St cafe strip. Two double studios and an apartment sleeping up to four feature fully equipped kitchens with coffee machines, spacious bathrooms and comfortable beds sheathed in quality linen. Each space is fully kitted out with books, DVDs and art…and there are free bicycles!

Auldington
BOUTIQUE HOTEL **$$**

(Map p178; ✆03-6331 2050; www.auldington.com. au; 110 Frederick St; r $130-195, f $170-255; P✴🐾🖥) Built in the late 19th century, this former convent perched high on Frederick St offers 18 frills-free rooms with comfortable beds, kettles, TVs and DVD players. A consistent and enthusiastically managed choice, with awesome city views from some rooms.

Eleanor
APARTMENT **$$**

(Map p178; ✆03-6333 8817; www.herocollec tion.com.au; 23 Elizabeth St; d from $180; P🖥) Secreted away beyond a courtyard off a hilly reach of Elizabeth St, Eleanor is a fab two-storey apartment for two, occupying a renovated 1890s stables building. Prices ascend over weekends; parking is $10 per night. Minimum two-night stay November to mid-May. If Eleanor is busy, the 'Hero Collection' includes two other heroic apartments in the city – check the website.

Hideaway on George
APARTMENT **$$**

(Map p178; ✆0409 806 151; www.facebook.com/ hideawayongeorge; 141a George St; d/ste/apt from $120/130/180; P✴🖥) Positioned somewhere between an upmarket motel and an apartment complex, mustard-coloured Hideaway on George has been recently refurbished, with new paint, carpets, leather couches, kitchens and art. There's plenty of parking and flowery gardens, including a lemon tree for your evening G&Ts. A light breakfast is included, served in a cosy communal dining room.

Hi George
B&B **$$**

(Map p175; ✆03-6331 2144; www.higeorge.com.au; 64 York St; r from $140; P✴🖥) The owners of this quaint 1880 brick B&B on the York St hill have been in the business for decades and know what guests want – a clean, comfortable and well-located base. No frills, but no aesthetic fuss either (when it comes to B&Bs, that can be a blessing). Communal breakfast room; super-plush carpets. Nice one.

Kurrajong House
B&B **$$**

(Map p175; ✆03-6331 6655; www.kurrajong house.com.au; cnr High & Adelaide Sts; r $175-200, cottage $195-225; P🖥) This fastidiously run B&B in a handsome 1887 house near Windmill Hill offers three rooms in the main house and a self-contained cottage in the lovely garden. The pitch is squarely towards 'mature' guests (no kids...and no under-25s either), but attention to detail is exceptional: fresh flowers, fresh milk for in-room tea, homemade jam with breakfast etc.

★ Apartment Sixty Six
APARTMENT **$$$**

(Map p175; ✆0428 430 330; www.stayz.com.au; 66a York St; apt from $220; P✴🖥) The entire ground floor of this 1870s former doctor's surgery is given over to lovely Apartment Sixty Six, sleeping up to six in three bedrooms. Interiors are decked-out in tasteful 'antique' style (not too frilly), and the grandfather clock is a beauty. A super-central location (with parking) and full contemporary kitchen seal the deal.

★ Mantra Charles Hotel
HOTEL **$$$**

(Map p178; ✆1300 987 604, 03-6337 4100; www. hotelcharles.com.au; 287 Charles St; d/apt from $210/413; P✴@🖥) Once a hospital, the Mantra Charles has been given a funky facelift and now rightfully claims the title of Launceston's savviest business hotel. There are a number of room types, including king rooms, two-bedroom apartments and studios with kitchenette. All are spacious, stylish and utterly comfortable. The ground-floor bar/restaurant sees plenty of corporate travellers bending an elbow.

The Sebel Launceston
HOTEL **$$$**

(Map p178; ✆03-6333 7555; www.thesebel launceston.com.au; 12 St John St; d/ste/apt from $230/248/428; P✴🖥) As far as Launceston hotels go, the reliable Sebel is a big 'un (five storeys and half a city block) – plenty of space for suites and two-bedroom apartments with king-sized beds, work desks and small kitchenettes (some also have a laundry). There's an on-site restaurant/bar (being vamped-up when we visited), a gym and parking.

✕ Eating

★ Bryher
CAFE **$**

(Map p178; ✆03-6380 9893; www.bryherfood. com; 91 George St; mains $11-22; ⏱7am-4pm Mon & Wed-Fri, 8am-3pm Sat & Sun) Bryher's super-appealing 1920s stained-glass shopfront and well-loved floorboards set the scene for a rootsy, meaty menu. The baked giant beans, black pudding, bratwurst and poached egg will resolve any hangover issues, or order the venison sausage with red sauerkraut and rocket pesto. There are vintage *Phantom* comics to read, and footpath tables with rugs (or warm up with a whisky hot toddy).

Milkbar
CAFE **$**

(Map p178; ✆0418 258 506; 139 St John St; mains $8-12; ⏱8am-3.30pm Mon-Fri; 🖥) 🍴 Sixties retro cool and 21st-century chic collide at Milkbar, which serves excellent coffee, organic tea, huge milkshakes, delicious sandwiches and home-style cakes (love the jaffa slice). All of the produce is as local and sustainable as possible. There's also a little shop section selling vintage-inspired crafts and knitting gear. Shame it's not open weekends.

Tio Rico
LATIN AMERICAN $

(Map p178; ☑03-6334 8871; www.tiorico.com.au; 80 Paterson St; mains $8-12; ◷8am-4pm Mon-Fri) It's all things Latin (Mexican, Venezuelan, Brazilian, Spanish...) at this brightly coloured corner cantina near Royal Park, plating up great-value burritos, quesadillas, empanadas and other south-of-the-border delights. The *pao de quijo* (Brazilian cheese bread) goes well with almost everything, as does a cold Peruvian cola. Regular $2 taco Tuesdays.

Le Café on St George
CAFE $

(Map p175; ☑03-6334 8887; www.lecafeonstgeorge.com; 39 Ann St, East Launceston; mains $8-16; ◷7am-5pm Mon-Fri, 8am-4pm Sat, 8am-3pm Sun) Crowded with conversations, this local favourite faces onto St Georges Sq on top of the hill in East Launceston. Beyond the beautiful old shopfront (stained glass, art-deco tiles) you'll find fresh juices, cakes, tarts, happy staff and decent coffee. *Très bon.*

Fish 'n' Chips
FISH & CHIPS $

(Map p178; ☑03-6331 1999; 30 Seaport Blvd; mains $18-27; ◷11am-9pm; 🛜🖐) The late-afternoon sun on the riverfront deck here makes for a memorable meal. Seafood is cooked fresh to order, and there are salads, antipasto platters and wines by the glass. Kid friendly, too.

★ Sweetbrew
CAFE $$

(Map p178; ☑03-6333 0443; www.facebook.com/sweetbrewespresso; 93a George St; mains $14-19; ◷7am-5pm Mon-Fri, 8am-4pm Sat & Sun; 🛜🖐) Sweetbrew is the best cafe in the city centre, serving Melbourne's Five Senses coffee and cooking up an interesting brunch menu: baguettes, quiches, classy tarts and pastries, with lots of vegetarian stuff. Love the sneaky booth room out the back! Sweet.

Blue Café Bar
CAFE $$

(Map p178; ☑03-6334 3133; www.bluecafebar.com.au; Inveresk Railyards, Inveresk; breakfast $14-25, lunch $18-34; ◷8am-4pm) 🍃 In a converted chunky-concrete power station next to the Queen Victoria Museum, this cool cafe

serves creative local, organic dishes to architecture students on the run from the books. The wood-fired pizzas are deservedly popular (try the mushroom, olive, blue cheese and smoked chilli edition).

Metz
PUB FOOD $$

(Map p178; ☑03-6331 7277; www.metzcafebar.com.au; 119 St John St; mains $18-38; ◷11am-late; 🖐) Locals recommend family-friendly, unpretentious Metz, a good-time bar/eatery in the former St George Hotel building (the old pub signage and resident ghost malinger upstairs). Menu highlights include seafood chowder, a sticky pork-belly burger and a decent Malaysian chicken curry. There are plenty of gluten-free options, plus a dedicated kids menu to boot. Or just stop by for a beer.

Pickled Evenings
INDIAN $$

(Map p178; ☑03-6331 0110; www.pickledevenings.com.au; 135 George St; mains $17-22; ◷5.30-9.30pm Tue-Sun; 🍴) Pickled evenings and holidays go hand in hand, but a visit to this excellent Indian restaurant will not (necessarily) involve excessive drinking. What you're here for are the traditional curries, which are generous, spicy and well priced. Plenty of vegetarian options and takeaways available.

Pierre's
FRENCH $$

(Map p178; ☑03-6331 6835; www.pierres.net.au; 88 George St; brunch $15-25, dinner $29-39; ◷8.30am-3pm Tue-Sat, 5.30pm-late Thu-Sat) Pierre's has been here since 1956. That's gotta be some sort of record! (French restaurants weren't exactly common in Tasmania in the 1950s.) The brunch menu is borderline Mod Oz (corn fritters, and waffles with mushroom, spinach and miso mayonnaise), while dinner offerings tread more Francophile terrain (roast spatchcock, lamb rack, eye fillet). Impressive wines, good coffee, professional service...and Tasmanian whiskies!

Buddha Thai Restaurant
THAI $$

(Map p178; ☑03-6334 1122; www.headsuplaunceston.com/buddha-thai-menu; 168 Charles St; mains $16-23; ◷10am-3pm Mon, 8am & Sun, 8.30am-3pm Tue-Fri, 5-9.30pm daily; 🍴) A boho vibe, BYO policy and reasonable prices mean this small eatery on the Charles St strip is almost always full – book ahead or get here early to snaffle a table. The dinner menu is the usual barrage of curries, stir-fries, salads and noodles; lunch dishes are lighter and change daily. Leave room for the sticky coconut rice.

Gorge Restaurant
MODERN AUSTRALIAN $$

(Map p175; ☏03-6331 3330; www.launceston cataractgorge.com.au/gorgerestaurant.html; Cataract Gorge; lunch $22-45, dinner $33-45; ☺noon-2.30pm & 6.30-9pm Tue-Sat, noon-2.30pm Sun) It's worth eating here for the photogenic setting alone, especially when sitting outside in summer and watching the peacocks strut their stuff. Walk off your baked brie and your twice-cooked duck on the stroll back to town through Cataract Gorge. Super-romantic at night.

★Geronimo
MODERN AUSTRALIAN $$$

(Map p178; ☏03-6331 3652; www.geronimo restaurant.com.au; 186 Charles St; brunch $9-23, dinner $19-40; ☺5-10pm Mon-Thu, 10.30am-late Fri & Sat, 10.30am-6pm Sun; ☈) Launceston's most savvy eatery, with an up-to-the-moment menu of shared plates, wood-fired pizzas, a formidable wine list and bright interiors. The food is beautiful to behold and even better to taste – Middle Eastern, Asian and Mediterranean flavours with faultless execution. There's also a snack menu ($9 to $17) during the aperitivo hour. Go for the chorizo and braised fennel pizza.

★Stillwater
MODERN AUSTRALIAN $$$

(Map p175; ☏03-6331 4153; www.stillwater.net.au; Ritchie's Mill, 2 Bridge Rd; breakfast $9-25, mains $31-40; ☺8.30am-3pm Sun & Mon, 8.30am-late Tue-Sat; ☈) Still waters run deep at this historic flour mill on the Tamar (parts of which date back to 1832), where Stillwater serves laid-back breakfasts and lunches...then puts on the Ritz for dinner. The menu changes with the seasons and both it and the wine list zero-in on local produce.

Henry's
MODERN AUSTRALIAN $$$

(Map p178; ☏03-6334 7757; www.henryslaun ceston.com.au; 61 Cameron St; 3 plates $45, extra plate $15; ☺4pm-late Tue-Thu & Sat, from noon Fri) Atop the terrazzo steps of the gentlemanly old Northern Club, this handsome red-brick building is now home to a fine-dining restaurant and a sassy lounge bar specialising in craft beer, whisky, gin and vodka. Food in the restaurant is of the share-plate variety – try the sticky honey-and-garlic quail. Bar snacks are three for $18. Don't dress down (caps, hoodies, sneakers and beanies are verboten).

Brisbane Street Bistro
FRENCH $$$

(Map p178; ☏03-6333 0888; www.brisbane streetbistro.com; 24 Brisbane St; mains $42, 6-course menu with/without wine $165/110; ☺6-9pm Tue-Sat) Contemporary French dishes, romantic vibes, knowledgeable staff... what's not to like? Claim a candlelit table in the intimate dining room and order from the daily-changing menu of dishes created with quality, predominantly local, produce. French fare prevails, with the occasional Asian accent (hoisin sauce, chilli jam). Fab wine list, too.

Black Cow Bistro
STEAK $$$

(Map p178; ☏03-6331 9333; www.blackcow bistro.com.au; 70 George St; mains $43-57; ☺5.30pm-late) This classy bistro in an old art-deco butcher shop specialises in Tasmanian free-range, grass-fed, artificial-hormone-free, dry-aged beef. It claims to be the best steakhouse in Tassie, which, judging by the restaurant's runaway success, can't be too far off the mark. Choose from Wagyu ($110 for 450g), porterhouse, scotch fillet and eye fillet with your choice of six butters and sauces.

Mudbar
MODERN AUSTRALIAN $$$

(Map p178; ☏03-6334 5066; www.mudbar.com. au; 28 Seaport Blvd; lunch $29-30, dinner $38-46; ☺11am-late) This is the pick of the eateries in the Seaport enclave. Chill with a beer at the bar, then migrate to your table for superior Asian-inspired fare and wine from the girthsome list. You'll enjoy good service and views of the crews from the North Esk Rowing Club gliding past. The wasabi oysters will lift your lid.

Drinking & Nightlife

★Saint John
BAR

(Map p178; ☏03-6333 0340; www.saintjohncraft beer.com.au; 133 St John St; ☺noon-late Mon-Sat, 2pm-late Sun) The 14 taps here get busy, pouring a vast range of craft beers for regulars of every age and social category. Out the back is an unexpected little food van plating up crispy chicken wings and lamb burgers you can eat in the bar after 5pm. The perfect symbiosis!

Kingsway
BAR

(Map p178; ☏0488 030 307; www.facebook.com/ thekingsway; 33 Kingsway; ☺5pm-midnight Wed-Sat) Cool! A Tasmania-centric bar serving libations of all kinds from around the island: whites, reds, beers and spirits. Slide into a leather lounge or prop yourself on a bar stool for a schooling in all things Tas-oholic. Regular live music. The Charles Bukowski mural is a winner.

Royal Oak Hotel PUB

(Map p178; ☑ 03-6331 5346; www.royaloaktas.com.au; 14 Brisbane St; ⊙noon-late) The 'Leap In, Limp Out' motto is dodgy, but the Royal Oak is still Launceston's best pub. We really don't need to expand on this fact, but it's hard not to – brilliant beers, regular open-mic nights, live music Wednesday to Sunday and ballsy '70s rock on the stereo. If you're too old to be a hipster but still feel culturally valid, this is the place for you.

Bakers Lane BAR

(Map p178; ☑ 03-6334 2414; www.bakerslanebar.com; 81 York St; ⊙11.30am-late Wed-Sat, 3-8.30pm Sun) Next to an alleyway hung with faux ivy, this place delivers dude food (tacos, ribs, burgers), cocktails and craft beer, plus live acoustic acts on Thursday and DJs on Friday and Saturday. It also stays open later than most venues in town. Be there.

Club 54 CLUB

(Map p178; ☑ 03-6331 9951; www.facebook.com/club54launceston; 39 Cameron St; ⊙9pm-2am Wed, Fri & Sat) Launceston is fat with students but thin on clubs – an odd scenario. Club 54 is a far remove from the fabled Studio 54 in NYC, but it's the only passable club option in town. Touring bands of varying merit also grace the stage.

☆ Entertainment

York Park SPECTATOR SPORT

(University of Tasmania Stadium; Map p175; www.facebook.com/universityoftasmaniastadium; Invermay Rd, Invermay) If you're in town during the Australian Rules football season (April to August), come here to see the big men fly. Melbourne-based AFL team Hawthorn (www.hawthornfc.com.au) plays a handful of home games here each season.

Princess Theatre THEATRE

(Map p178; ☑ 03-6323 3666; www.theatrenorth.com.au/princess-theatre; 57 Brisbane St; ⊙box office 9am-5pm Mon-Fri, 10am-1pm Sat) Built in 1911 and incorporating the smaller Earl Arts Centre out the back, the old Princess stages an eclectic schedule of drama, dance and comedy, drawing acts from across Tasmania and the mainland.

🛍 Shopping

★ Design Tasmania Shop ARTS & CRAFTS

(Map p178; ☑ 03-6331 5506; www.designtasmania.com.au/shop; cnr Brisbane & Tamar Sts; ⊙9.30am-5.30pm Mon-Fri, 10am-2pm Sat & Sun) Want to snaffle a souvenir to take home? The beaut shop at the Design Centre Tasmania (p177) stocks a huge array of artisan-made objects, with a particular emphasis on furniture and homewares made from local wood – a veritable hymn to Huon pine. Also stocks jewellery and clothing.

★ Harvest MARKET

(Map p178; ☑ 0417 352 780; www.harvestmarket.org.au; 71 Cimitiere St; ⊙8.30am-12.30pm Sat) 🖉 Excellent weekly gathering of organic producers and sustainable suppliers from around northern and western Tasmania. Craft beer and cider, artisan baked goods, cheese, Mt Direction olives, salmon from 41° Degrees South, honey and veggies are all on offer, plus food trucks and stalls sell treats including *okonomiyaki* (Japanese pancakes; $10).

Old Umbrella Shop GIFTS & SOUVENIRS

(Map p178; ☑ 03-6331 9248; www.nationaltrust.org.au/places/old-umbrella-shop; 60 George St; ⊙9am-5pm Mon-Fri, to noon Sat) Launcestonians once sheltered beneath the umbrellas made here by R Shott & Sons. A rare example of an intact early-20th-century store, complete with its original till and blackwood display cases, it still sells brollies, as well as a range of National Trust and Tasmanian products.

Alps & Amici FOOD

(Map p175; ☑ 03-6331 1777; www.alpsandamici.com.au; 52 Abbott St, East Launceston; ⊙7.30am-6.30pm Mon-Fri, 8am-2pm Sat) Super-chef Daniel Alps has set up this smart providore where you can buy his restaurant-quality meals to take home and adore. Classy cakes, cheeses, meats and seafood, the freshest fruit and veg, and Tasmanian beer and wine also available. Good coffee, too.

Pinot Shop WINE

(Map p178; ☑ 03-6331 3977; www.pinotshop.com; 135 Paterson St; ⊙10am-6pm Mon-Sat) The future of Tasmanian wine may be sparkling whites, but pinot noir is where it's at today. This boutique bottle shop specialises in the latter, plus premium international and 'big-island' (ie Australian mainland) vintages. Australia-wide freight available.

ℹ Information

Launceston General Hospital (☑ 03-6777 6777; www.dhhs.tas.gov.au; 287-289 Charles St; ⊙24hr) Accident and emergency.

Launceston Post Office (GPO; Map p178; ☑13 13 18; www.auspost.com.au; 68-72 Cameron St; ⊙8.30am-5.30pm Mon-Fri, 9am-12.30pm Sat) Next to the visitor information centre.

Launceston Visitor Information Centre (Map p178; ☑1800 651 827, 03-6323 3082; www.destinationlaunceston.com.au; 68-72 Cameron St; ⊙9am-5pm Mon-Fri, to 1pm Sat & Sun) Helpful tourist office that can book accommodation and tours, supply a city map and proffer other information about the city and region. Extended weekend hours from December to March.

Online Access Centre (☑03-6777 2446; www.linc.tas.gov.au; 71 Civic Sq; ⊙9.30am-6pm Mon-Thu, to 7pm Fri, to 2pm Sat) Free computer terminals and wi-fi access.

ⓘ Getting There & Away

AIR

There are regular domestic flights from Melbourne and Sydney to **Launceston Airport** (☑03-6391 6222; www.launcestonairport.com.au; 201 Evandale Rd, Western Junction), and a lesser number of services from Brisbane, with Qantas (www.qantas.com.au), Jetstar (www.jetstar.com) and Virgin Australia (www.virginaustralia.com).

BUS

The depot for most services is the **Cornwall Square Transit Centre** (Map p178; 200 Cimitiere St).

Tassielink (p306) Heads to/from the west coast via Devonport and Cradle Mountain, and from the Devonport ferry terminal to Hobart via Launceston. There's also a service between Launceston, Evandale and Longford.

Redline Coaches (Map p178; ☑1300 360 000; www.tasredline.com.au) Tassielink's main competitor, running from Launceston west to Westbury, Deloraine, Mole Creek, Devonport, Ulverstone, Penguin, Burnie, Wynyard, Stanley and Smithton. Redline also runs south to Hobart via Campbell Town, Ross, Oatlands and Kempton.

Calow's Coaches (p306) Services the east coast (St Marys, St Helens, Bicheno) from Launceston.

Lee's Coaches (Map p178; ☑0400 937 440; www.leescoaches.com) Services the East Tamar Valley region between Launceston and George Town.

Manions' Coaches (Map p178; ☑03-6383 1221; www.manionscoaches.com.au) Local operator that services the West Tamar Valley region (Exeter, Beaconsfield, Beauty Point etc) from Launceston. Both Lee's and Manions' buses stop on Brisbane St.

Sainty's North East Bus Service (p306) Runs buses between Launceston and Lilydale, Scottsdale, Derby and Bridport in the northeast.

ⓘ Getting Around

TO/FROM THE AIRPORT

Launceston Airport is on the road to Evandale, 15km south of the city. The **Launceston Airporter** (☑1300 360 000; www.airporterlaunceston.com.au; adult/child one way $15/14) shuttle bus runs door-to-door services. A taxi into the city costs about $35.

BUS

Metro Tasmania (Map p175; ☑13 22 01; www.metrotas.com.au; 186 Wellington St; ⊙8.30am-5pm Mon-Fri) operates services within the city and has a ticketing/info shopfront.

Tiger Bus (☑03-6323 3000; www.metrotas.com.au) is a free Metro Tasmania bus service, running in a loop from the Inveresk QVMAG on two routes every 30 minutes.

The City Explorer goes to Civic Sq, Prince's Sq, Launceston General Hospital, Windmill Hill Reserve and City Park between 10am and 3pm weekdays. The River Explorer goes to Civic Sq, the QVMAG in Paterson St and Home Point between 10.30am and 3.30pm.

TAXI

Taxi Combined (☑13 10 08; www.taxicombined.com.au)

TAMAR VALLEY

A terrain of undulating emerald hills covered with vineyards, orchards and stands of native forest, this valley is intersected by the wide Tamar River, a tidal waterway running 64km north from Launceston towards Bass Strait. On the river's eastern bank is Launceston's ocean port, Bell Bay, near George Town. The western bank is home to a string of laid-back country hamlets that are popular weekend and summer escapes for Launcestonians. The Batman Bridge unites the two shores near Deviot.

☞ Tours

Valleybrook Wine on Wheels   WINE
(☑0451 965 841; www.valleybrook.com.au; full-/half-day tours $160/130) These small-group tours pick up/drop off in Launceston and visit six cellar doors (full day) or four (half-day). Both tours include lunch.

Prestige Leisure Tours   WINE
(☑0429 030 588; www.prestigeleisuretours.com.au; full-day tours per person from $130) Small-group tours that pick up/drop off in

Launceston and include lunch. Also offers a five-hour boutique beer/wine/cider/honey/spirits tour (from $195 per person).

Tamar Valley Winery Tours   WINE
(☑ 0447 472 177; www.tamarvalleywinerytours.com.au; tours per person $125) Highly regarded small-group tours that pick up/drop off in Launceston and visit four cellar doors on a half-day tour. Includes lunch.

Legana & Rosevears

These two hubs offer the first pit stops heading north out of Launceston along the West Tamar Hwy (A7) – they're almost suburbs of Launceston, they're so darn proximal. Legana is right on the highway; Rosevears adheres to narrow Rosevears Dr, running along the water past moored yachts and swaying reed beds. This is vineyard territory, so bring your downloaded map of the *Tamar Valley Wine Route* (www.tamarvalleywineroute.com.au).

◉ Sights

Tamar Ridge   WINERY
(☑ 03-6330 0300; www.tamarridge.com.au; 1a Waldhorn Dr, Rosevears; ⊙ 10am-5pm; 🚻) Tamar Ridge is best known for its quaffable Pirie sparkling wine. Begin with a free tasting at the counter, choose a bottle to buy then hit the scenic terrace, which overlooks the Tamar, to enjoy a platter (terrine, salmon or cheese; $20 to $25). The kids can spin hula hoops on the lawn, or scrawl on the blackboard wall.

Brady's Lookout State Reserve   VIEWPOINT
(www.parks.tas.gov.au; Brady's Lookout Rd, Rosevears) `FREE` Offering views over the Tamar River and surrounding areas, this reserve was named after nefarious bushranger Matthew Brady, who used the rocky outcrop here to spy prospective victims on the road below. Brady was known as the 'Gentleman Bushranger' for his impeccable mid-theft manners. There are toilet and picnic facil-

ities here, including sheltered BBQs. It's signed off the West Tamar Hwy, between Legana and Exeter.

Tamar Island Wetlands   NATURE RESERVE
(☑ 03-6327 3964; www.parks.tas.gov.au; West Tamar Hwy, Legana; by donation; ⊙ daylight hours) Part of the Tamar River Conservation Area, this wetland reserve has a 2km wheelchair- and pram-friendly boardwalk running through it, strategically positioned so you can ogle the resident birds, and an interpretation centre. The island itself has toilets, BBQs and an elevated bird hide. Scan the reedy swamp alongside the boardwalk for frogs, skinks and the occasional copperhead snake. It's a 10-minute drive north of Launceston.

🛏 Sleeping & Eating

Rosevears Hotel   HOTEL **$$**
(☑ 03-6394 4074; www.rosevearshotel.com.au; 215 Rosevears Dr, Rosevears; d without/with spa $195/255, ste $245; 🅿❄🅿) Recently constructed, these stylish units behind the Rosevears Hotel come in various permutations: choose from a standard room, premium room with outdoor spa, or two-bedroom suite. The suite, premium room and some standard rooms have river-facing balconies. **Meals** (mains $20-36; ⊙ 11.30am-3pm & 5.30pm-late) are available at the hotel.

Timbre Kitchen   MODERN AUSTRALIAN **$$**
(☑ 03-6330 3677; www.timbrekitchen.com; Vélo Wines, 755 West Tamar Hwy, Legana; small plates $10-18, large plates $32-35, banquets per person $40-65; ⊙ 11am-4pm Mon, Thu & Sun, 11am-late Fri & Sat; 🅿) Timbre's chefs draw inspiration from around the globe when constructing their menus of shared-plate dishes – you can move from Japan to the Middle East, France to Italy in the space of a meal. Vegan and gluten-free options are available. Decor is Scandinavian-chic, there's a large wine list and you can sit inside or on the large deck overlooking the vineyard.

ℹ Getting There & Away

Manions' Coaches (p185) operates Monday to Saturday services from Launceston to Rosevears ($7, 30 minutes). Some of these stop at the Legana roundabout ($7, 15 minutes) en route. Manions' also runs a Monday-to-Saturday 'Legana Loop' service, looping back to Launceston rather than continuing north ($4.50, 15 minutes).

ℹ TAMAR TRIPLE PASS

The three-attraction **Tamar Triple Pass** (adult/family $49/135) gives access to both Platypus House and Seahorse World at Beauty Point, as well as the nearby Beaconsfield Mine & Heritage Centre It represents a saving of adult/family $13/18.

Tamar Valley

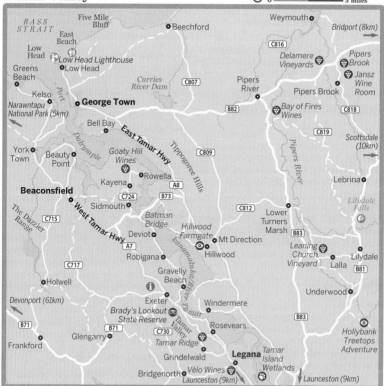

Exeter

📞 03 / POP 390

The land around Exeter is predominantly orchard and farming country, and there are no big-name tourist attractions to claim your attention. The main excuses to pause here are to visit the Tamar Visitor Information Centre and the honey shop. South of the town, Gravelly Beach Rd will take you to Robigana (derived from the Aboriginal word for 'swans'), where the road crosses the Supply River. From here there's a marked walking track (one hour return) beside the Tamar River to Paper Beach.

✕ Eating & Shopping

Exeter Bakery   BAKERY $
(📞 03-6394 4069; 104 Main Rd; items $2-5; ⏰ 7am-5pm Mon-Fri, 8am-3pm Sat, 9am-3pm Sun) The century-old wood-fired oven here produces all manner of pies – from egg-and-bacon to

Thai massaman and glistening custard. Also on offer are old-fashioned cakes and slices – think snowballs, jelly slice and Swiss rolls.

The Beehive   FOOD
(📞 03-6331 9300; www.honeytasmania.com; 124 Main Rd; ⏰ 10am-4.30 Mon-Fri, 10am-2pm Sat) Decorated with an etched mural featuring a rainforest scene, a woven skep hive, a traditional square hive and a natural tree hive, this shop celebrates and sells all things honey-related (including a yummy honey ice cream). There are also display beehives for viewing, a bee-friendly garden to stroll in and tours of a honey-extracting factory.

❶ Information

Tamar Visitor Information Centre (📞 03-6394 4454, 1800 637 989; www.wtc.tas.gov.au/tourism/tamar-visitor-centre; 81 Main Rd; ⏰ 9am-4pm Apr-Sep, to 5pm Oct-Mar; 📞) This helpful information centre sells the Tamar

Triple Pass and national parks passes, stocks a huge array of brochures and offers free wi-fi.

Getting There & Away

Manions' Coaches (p185) operates services between Launceston and Beauty Point from Monday to Saturday, stopping in Exeter ($9, 35 minutes) en route.

Beaconsfield & Around

☑ 03 / POP 1010

This small town set in apple-growing country has had two big moments in the spotlight. The first was when gold was discovered here in 1877; the second was in 2006 when a mine collapse killed one miner and trapped two others in a cage 1km underground for two weeks before they were rescued. Their story is told in the town's one and only tourist draw, the Beaconsfield Mine & Heritage Centre. To the east of town are rolling hills where a number of picturesque vineyards are located.

Sights

Holm Oak   VINEYARD
(☑ 03-6394 7577; www.holmoakvineyards.com.au; 11 West Bay Rd, Rowella; ⊙ 11am-5pm) Winemaker Rebecca Duffy is making a splash in the local scene, producing fantastic pinot noir from grapes grown at this vineyard 4km east of Beaconsfield (try the rich and bold 'The Wizard' or the elegant 'Hot Shot'). Come for a free tasting, or indulge in a flight of pinot noir ($15).

Goaty Hill Wines   VINEYARD
(☑ 1300 819 997; www.goatyhill.com; 530 Auburn Rd, Kayena; tastings per person $3; ⊙ 11am-5pm) The view from the cellar door at this small but scenic vineyard 8km east of Beaconsfield is hard to beat. Come for a tasting (the

chardonnay, pinot noir and riesling are well regarded), but stay to enjoy a full glass or two with a gourmet vineyard platter ($60) or Tasmanian cheese plate ($25). There's live music on weekends in January.

**Beaconsfield Mine
& Heritage Centre**   MUSEUM
(☑ 03-6383 1473; www.beaconsfieldheritage. com.au; West St, Beaconsfield; adult/child/family $15/5/38; ⊙ 9.30am-4.30pm) This centre offers plenty of opportunities to learn about Beaconsfield's fascinating mining heritage. An interactive experience, it includes plenty of buttons to push, levers to pull and tunnels to crawl through. There are special exhibitions about the 2006 mine rescue, and it's possible to wander through the historic Grubb Shaft Engine and Boiler Houses.

Eating

Jubilee Bakery   BAKERY $
(☑ 03-6383 1124; 125-127 Weld St (West Tamar Hwy); items $1.20-6; ⊙ 6.30am-5pm Mon-Fri, 7am-3pm Sat) The baker here puts the wood oven to good use, cooking excellent homemade pies, pasties and sausage rolls. The rich vanilla slices and light-as-air lamingtons are pretty good, too. Grab one to go, or enjoy it with a cup of tea and coffee on the streetside terrace.

Getting There & Away

Manions' Coaches (p185) operates services between Launceston and Beaconsfield ($11, 80 minutes) from Monday to Saturday.

Beauty Point

☑ 03 / POP 1210

While the surrounding hillsides and riverscapes are certainly beautiful, the name of this town actually derives from pulchritude of the bovine variety: a now-immortalised

---

THE BEACONSFIELD MINE COLLAPSE

On 25 April 2006 a small earthquake triggered an underground rock fall at Beaconsfield's historic gold mine. There were 17 miners underground at the time: 14 of them managed to scramble to safety but three were trapped underground. It soon became apparent that one had died in the collapse but the other two were trapped in a cage 1km below the ground. After an exhaustive two-week rescue operation that made global headlines (further sensationalised by the heart-attack death of a TV reporter on the surface), the two miners emerged to a media feeding frenzy. Even Oprah expressed interest in making a movie about their ordeal. Weathering the storm, the miners signed lucrative deals for their story, but to everyone's great disappointment they turned out to be regular blokes – short on charisma and eloquent summations of their ordeal. The Foo Fighters wrote a song...but Oprah never called. The mine reopened in November 2006 but was closed permanently in 2012.

NARAWNTAPU NATIONAL PARK

Formerly called Asbestos Range National Park, park management astutely decided that the name was deterring people from visiting. **Narawntapu** (☑03-6428 6277; www.parks.tas. gov.au; via Bakers Beach Rd, Bakers Beach; vehicle/person per day $24/12; ☺ranger station 9am-4pm Dec-Apr, to 3pm May-Nov) is a magical meld of coastal heath, dunes and bushland that's astoundingly abundant in wildlife (so abundant that it's been called 'Tasmania's Serengeti'). As well as wildlife spotting, there are plenty of opportunities to bushwalk and beachcomb.

Walking trails in the park include a hike round **Badger Head** (six to eight hours) and a trail to **Archers Knob** (114m; two hours return). The one-hour **Springlawn Nature Walk** includes a boardwalk over wetlands to a bird hide.

The beach from Griffiths Point to Bakers Point is good for beachcombing and sunset watching. **Bakers Beach** and **Badger Beach** are the safest swimming spots.

Horse riding is allowed and the park has corrals and a 26km trail; ask at the ranger station.

There are a number of **camp sites** (unpowered/powered sites from $13/16) in the park; all have toilets. The best equipped is at Springlawn, with septic toilets, water tanks, an electric BBQ, a shower block and powered sites. All sites have fireplaces with firewood, but campers are encouraged to use a portable cooking stove.

The main body of the park is accessible via the main entrance at Springlawn, off the B71 near Port Sorell. Take the B71 east of Devonport or B72 north of Westbury. Watch for the marked turn-off to the park (C740).

bullock called Beauty. These days, visitors head here to visit Platypus House and Seahorse World on Inspection Head Wharf. It's also a good base for those following the Tamar Valley Wine Route.

⊙ Sights

★ **Seahorse World** AQUARIUM
(☑03-6383 4111; www.seahorseworld.com.au; Inspection Head Wharf, 200 Flinders St; adult/child/family $22/9.50/55; ☺9.30am-4pm Dec-Apr, 10am-3pm May-Nov) At coo-inducing Seahorse World, eight species of seahorses are hatched and raised to supply aquariums worldwide. Access is via 45-minute guided tours, which run on the hour and take you through the aquarium, which is populated with many bizarre sea creatures from the Southern Ocean and includes a touch pool, as well as the seahorse farm and a display showcasing the wonderful diversity of the species.

Platypus House ZOO
(☑03-6383 4884; www.platypushouse.com.au; Inspection Head Wharf, 200 Flinders St; adult/child/family $25/11/59; ☺9.30am-4.30pm Nov-Apr, 10am-3.30pm May-Oct) Housed in a huge wharf shed, Platypus House puts the world's only two monotremes – the platypus and the echidna – on display for your viewing pleasure. Platypuses gambol in glass-sided tanks and transparent 'burrows', while in the echidna room you can walk among the

trundling creatures as guides dish out scientific facts. Guided tours depart on the hour.

⌘ Sleeping

Beauty Point Tourist Park CARAVAN PARK $
(☑03-6383 4536; www.beautypointtouristpark. com.au; 36 West Arm Rd; powered sites $39, cabins $99-229; ☎❄) There's easygoing camping in a pleasantly landscaped area by the water here (we love the fact that each camp site is hedged), plus tidy cabins (try to score one of the four next to the water, which have air-conditioning, good kitchens, laundries and water-facing verandahs). Easy river access is an added enticement. No camp kitchen, but there is a BBQ area.

★ **Jensens Bed & Breakfast** B&B $$
(☑0410 615 678; www.jensensbedandbreakfast. com.au; 77 Flinders St; r from $175; 🅿❄) If only all B&Bs could be like this. Occupying a handsome Federation-style house surrounded by apple trees and a manicured garden, Jensens has a gracious communal lounge with open fire, two stylishly presented ensuite rooms and a large verandah with distinctive rotunda and spectacular river views. Helpful host Carol cooks her guests a full breakfast in the morning.

Beauty Point Cottages B&B $$
(☑03-6383 4556; www.beautypointcottages. com.au; 14 Flinders St; d $175, cottage $185-195;

❶ HISTORICAL ATTRACTIONS PASS

History fans can save some coin in George Town and Low Head if they purchase a **Historical Attractions Pass**. These cost adult/family $13/50 and permit entrance to the Bass and Flinders Centre, the George Town Watch House and the Low Head Maritime Museum at the Pilot Station. Passes are available at all three attractions.

🛜) Settle into the guest room in this 1880s house (with en suite and private entrance), or opt for one of two self-contained cottages set in the gorgeous garden, which has trees, a tinkling fountain and views over the river. Breakfast provisions are provided, and hosts Colin and Barbara are friendly and helpful. Wi-fi in reception only.

✘ Eating & Drinking

★ River Cafe
CAFE $$

(☑ 03-6383 4099; www.therivercafe.com.au; 225 Flinders St; pizzas $10-24, mains $21-38; ⊙ 9am-4pm; 🛜 ⊞) On sunny days at the River Cafe the windows fold right back and the water feels so close you could touch it. The menu tempts with all-day breakfasts ($10 to $22), gourmet panini, pastas and a delectable array of local seafood – try the signature seafood platter ($38) with a glass of Tamar Valley wine. Takeaway pizzas, too.

Riviera Hotel
PUB

(☑ 03-6383 4153; www.beautypointrivierahotel.com.au; 12 Lenborough St; ⊙ bar 11am-late, bistro noon-2pm & 6-8pm) A majestic art-deco building right on the water's edge, the Riviera has a popular bar with outdoor seating. There's also a bistro on-site (mains $22 to $40).

❶ Getting There & Away

From Monday to Saturday, Manions' Coaches (p185) operates services to/from Launceston ($11, one hour).

George Town
☑ 03 / POP 4310

George Town stands sentinel on the Tamar River's eastern shore, close to where it empties into Bass Strait. Originally the territory of the Leterremairrener or Port Douglas people, it was occupied by Europeans in 1804 as part of the British attempt to stave off settlement by the French, who had been reconnoitering the area. It was the third British town established in the new colony after Sydney and Hobart. A number of buildings in the town centre date from the 1830s and 1840s, when George Town prospered as the port linking Tasmania with Victoria. Today it's in the economic doldrums as a result of employment losses at the nearby Bell Bay Smelter and TEMCO steel plant. It's a rewarding stop for history buffs, though, and also has some pleasant beaches.

◎ Sights & Activities

The information centre and George Town Watch House stock the excellent free *George Town Heritage Trail* brochure, which outlines a self-guided tour of the heritage attractions in George Town and Low Head.

★ Bass & Flinders Centre
MUSEUM

(☑ 03-6382 3792; www.bassandflinders.org.au; 8 Elizabeth St; adult/child/family $10/4/24; ⊙ 10am-4pm, closed Sat & Sun Jun-Oct) Undoubtedly the highlight of a visit to George Town, this small museum in a former cinema houses a red-sailed replica of the *Norfolk,* the sloop used by Bass and Flinders for their 1798 circumnavigation of Van Diemen's Land. There are other old wooden boats here, too, including a replica of *Tom Thumb,* the cramped whale-boat that carried Bass, Flinders and an assistant up the Georges River in New South Wales – it's altogether a rather fabulous collection. There's also a **cafe** (www.facebook.com/gunndeck; mains $6-15; ⊙ 10am-4pm Mon-Fri).

Hillwood Farmgate
FARM

(☑ 03-6394 8180; www.hillwoodfarmgate.com.au; 105 Hillwood Rd, Hillwood; ⊙ 9am-5pm Nov-May) This working farm burgeons with berries in summer. The main crop is strawberries, but there are also raspberries, loganberries and redcurrants. You can pick your own ($10 per kilo) then make a beeline to the **cafe and providore**, which serves coffee, milkshakes and cakes, and sells wine, berries, cheese, chocolates and jams produced in the region. You'll find it just off the East Tamar Hwy, 22km south of George Town.

George Town Watch House
MUSEUM

(☑ 03-6382 4466; www.discovertasmania.com.au/attraction/thewatchhouse; 84-86 Macquarie St; adult/child/family $3/1/8; ⊙ 10am-3pm Mon-Fri, 1-3pm Sat & Sun) Occupying an 1843 lock-up, this endearingly old-fashioned museum also doubles as an ad hoc tourist information office. The centrepiece is a huge, dusty model of the town as it would have appeared in 1850, and there's also a room with exhibits about the George Town Female Factory. This includes Christina Henri's installation *Arrivals & Departures*, which features baby bonnets arranged in the shape of a cross. It's a moving memorial to the many children of female convicts who died in infancy.

Festivals & Events

SteamPunk Tasmania CULTURAL
(www.steampunktasmania.com.au; ⊙ Jun) For one day in June, George Town celebrates the steampunk genre, staging music, exhibitions and displays on maritime and other history and technology.

Sleeping & Eating

The Pier Hotel MOTEL $$
(✆ 03-6382 1300; www.pierhotel.com.au; 5 Elizabeth St; r/unit from $140/220; ❄ 🛜) There's a wing of quiet and modern motel units out the back of this busy pub next to the water, as well as two cheaper rooms upstairs in the main building. The units are your best bet, being well-sized and equipped with kettle and TV. Air-con is in the hotel rooms only.

⭐ **Peppers Tamar Cove** HOTEL, APARTMENT $$$
(✆ 03-6382 9900; www.peppers.com.au/york-cove; 2 Ferry Blvd; r $249, apt from $289; 🛜🍴) This corporate waterfront resort is making waves on the Tamar. It offers generously sized hotel rooms with kitchenettes at the rear of the main building (some with spa, but none with views), but the headline acts are river-facing apartments, which are huge and facility-rich (laundry, full kitchen, lounge and balcony). Wi-fi is only available in the main building.

Cove Restaurant & Bar CAFE $$
(✆ 03-6382 9900; www.peppers.com.au/york-cove/dining; Peppers Tamar Cove, 2 Ferry Bvd; mains $17-30; ⊙ 7-10am & noon-2pm Mon-Wed, noon-2pm Thu & Fri, 8-11am, noon-3pm & 5-8pm Sat & Sun; 🛜🍴) The views over the Tamar River and Stone Quarry Bay from this light-saturated cafe/bistro at Peppers Tamar Cove are wonderful, and can be appreciated over a coffee (the best in George Town), breakfast, light lunch or weekend dinner. The best seating is on the expansive deck.

Information

George Town Visitor Information Centre
(✆ 03-6382 1700; www.georgetown.tas.

gov.au/visitor-information; 92-96 Main Rd; ⊙ 9am-4pm Oct-Mar, 9am-3pm Apr-Sep) This volunteer-staffed centre is located on the main road as you enter from the south. It supplies brochures and maps, makes accommodation bookings and has public toilets.

Getting There & Away

Lee's Coaches (p185) services George Town from Launceston ($13.80, 55 minutes). Buses travel at least four times daily in each direction Monday to Friday, and twice on Saturday. Buses stop in front of the Caltex service station on the main road, and in Elizabeth St in the town centre.

Low Head
📍 03 / POP 440

Low Head and George Town are barely divided – you won't notice leaving one before arriving in the other. Historic Low Head is in a spectacular setting though, looking out over the swirling – and treacherous – waters of the Tamar as it empties into the sea. There's good surf at East Beach on Bass Strait, and safe swimming at Lagoon Beach on the Tamar.

Sights

Low Head Maritime Museum MUSEUM
(Low Head Pilot Station Museum; ✆ 03-6382 1143; www.lowheadpilotstation.com; 399 Low Head Rd; adult/child/family $5/3/15; ⊙ 10am-4pm) In the Low Head Historic Precinct, this museum occupies the whitewashed pilot station, which is Australia's oldest (1805). A series of rooms contains a weird and wonderful array of exhibits about the maritime history of this part of Tasmania. Though dusty, they're quite fascinating. There's a **cafe** (✆ 03-6382 2826; sandwiches $6.50, mains $12-20; ⊙ 10am-5pm Jun-Nov, 9am-5pm Dec-May; 🛜) next door, and accommodation (p192) in a number of cottages in the precinct.

Low Head Lighthouse LIGHTHOUSE
(✆ 03-6382 2826; www.lowheadpilotstation.com; Low Head Rd; ⊙ grounds 9am-5pm) **FREE** Designed by colonial architect John Lee Archer and built in 1888, this red-and-white lighthouse on the end of Low Head itself is a great spot to watch the Tamar River spilling into Bass Strait. On Sunday at noon the foghorn sounds with three ear-splitting bellows.

Tours

Low Head Penguin Tours BIRDWATCHING
(✆ 0418 361 860; www.penguintourstasmania.com.au; 485 Low Head Rd; adult/child $22/10;

DON'T MISS

PIPERS RIVER REGION

Don't miss a long afternoon putting your palate/liver to work at the cellar doors in this wine region, which is an easy day trip north of Launceston. There's no public transport out this way, so see who draws the short straw and has to drive, or book yourself onto a winery day tour out of Launceston: try Prestige Leisure Tours (p185), Tamar Valley Winery Tours (p186) or Valleybrook Wine on Wheels (p185). Online see www.tamar valleywineroute.com.au.

Jansz Wine Room (☑ 03-6382 7066; www.jansz.com.au; 1216b Pipers Brook Rd, Pipers Brook; ⊙10am-4.30pm) Located next door to Pipers Brook, Jansz (named after explorer Abel Jansz Tasman) was originally in partnership with Louise Roederer, so it's not surprising that its *Méthode Tasmanoise* is a more-than-quaffable drop. Ask for a picnic blanket and head outside to enjoy a cheese platter plus two flutes of the sparkling stuff ($40). There are free tastings, too.

Bay of Fires Wines (☑ 03-6382 7622; www.bayoffireswines.com.au; 40 Baxters Rd, Pipers River; ⊙11am-4pm Mon-Fri, 10am-4pm Sat & Sun) The home of prestigious Arras sparkling and workaday Eddystone Point and Bay of Fires wines, this is the most visitor-friendly – and perhaps the most attractive – vineyard in the Tamar. There's a cafe and a tasting area that includes displays about winemaking. After a tasting or light lunch, consider indulging in a game of croquet on the lawn.

Delamere Vineyards (☑ 03-6382 7190; www.delamerevineyards.com.au; 4238 Bridport Rd, Pipers Brook; ⊙10am-5pm) Affable, family-run Delamere is the antithesis of the big-ticket wineries around here. A small set-up, it grows, produces and bottles everything on-site. It produces cider, rosé, chardonnay-dominated sparkling wines (try the Vintage Cuvée or Blanc de Blanc) and pinot noir. Tastings cost $5 per person, redeemable with purchase. It sells some picnic provisions and supplies blankets.

Pipers Brook Vineyard (☑ 03-6382 7527; www.pipersbrook.com.au; 1216 Pipers Brook Rd, Pipers Brook; cafe mains $16-28; ⊙10am-5pm Oct-May, 11am-4pm Thu-Mon Jun-Sep, cafe 11am-3pm) This is the Tamar's best-known vineyard, home to Pipers Brook, Ninth Island and Kreglinger wines (the Kreglinger sparkling is particularly impressive). There's a tasting room (three Ninth Island/Pipers Brook/Kreglinger wines $5/7/10) and a cafe serving simple foods such as chicken baguettes ($18.50) and cheese boards ($28). The tasting fee is waived if you buy a bottle.

⊙sunset) Check out the little penguins that live around the Low Head Lighthouse. Wheelchair-friendly guided tours leave nightly at sunset from a signposted spot beside Low Head Rd just south of the lighthouse. Bookings advised.

🛌 Sleeping

Low Head Tourist Park　　CARAVAN PARK $
(☑ 03-6382 1573; www.lowheadtouristpark.com.au; 136 Low Head Rd; unpowered/powered sites from $22/28, cabins & cottages from $105; ☎🐾) The bad news: this site is cramped, treeless and unattractive. The good news: it's well-maintained and has friendly management and clean amenities blocks. The cabins have a basic kitchenette, cottages have an equipped kitchen and sites have use of a small camp kitchen with BBQ.

★**Low Head Pilot Station Accommodation**　　COTTAGE $$
(☑ 03-6382 2826; www.lowheadpilotstation.com; 399 Low Head Rd; cottage from $150) Low Head's historic pilot station precinct offers nine very smartly refurbished, self-contained cottages sleeping between two and nine; the Pilot's Cottage, Coxswain's Cottage, Lighthouse Cottage and Queenslander have ocean views. All are great for families, as there's plenty of grass and space where little ones can play. Wi-fi is available in the nearby cafe (also the reception).

ℹ Getting There & Away

Lee's Coaches (p185) services George Town from Launceston ($13.80, 55 minutes). Buses travel at least four times daily in each direction Monday to Friday, and twice on Saturday. From Launceston tell the driver if you wish to continue to Low

Head; this is usually possible. Returning from Low Head, you'll need to book in advance.

Lilydale

📍 03 / POP 660

Quiet Lilydale is little more than a main street with a few stores and services. It's a popular pit stop on the Tamar Valley Wine Route (there's a petrol station on Main Rd) and a good place to source picnic provisions if you're planning to visit Lilydale Falls, 3km north of town. Energetic types also propel themselves up Mt Arthur (1188m; five to seven hours return), which looms – high, cold and austere – above the town.

◉ Sights & Activities

★ Hollybank Treetops Adventure
ADVENTURE SPORTS

(📞03-6395 1390; www.treetopsadventure. au; 66 Hollybank Rd, Underwood; ⊙9am-5pm; 🅿) Various adventure experiences are offered at Hollybank, 7km south of Lilydale. Scramble and balance through pine trees at height on a supervised two-hour Ropes Course (various levels of difficulty, adult/child $48/38), or take a guided three-hour Treetops Canopy Tour (adult/child $125/90) where you'll fly through native wet forest on zip lines.

You can also take a 1.5km guided exploration of a forest reserve on a Segway ($100) or hire a hard-tail bike (adult standard/superior bike $30/60 for two hours, child $30) to use in the on-site mountain bike park.

Leaning Church Vineyard
VINEYARD

(📞03-6395 4447; www.leaningchurch.com.au; 76 Brooks Rd, Lalla; ⊙10am-5pm) Producing a quaffable sparkling wine (tastings free), this pretty vineyard is built around an old – and yes, leaning – timber church. Visitors can enjoy a glass of wine and a grazing platter ($52 for two people) or cheese plate ($30) at terrace tables or on picnic blankets. Children can enjoy a lunch box ($12) and a play in the sandpit.

🛏 Sleeping

Cherry Top Accommodation
FARMSTAY $$

(📞03-6395 1167; www.cherrytopfarmstay.weebly. com; 81 Lalla Rd; cottage/villa from $130/220) 🅿 Experience life on the farm at this friendly, sustainably minded property that farms hazelnuts, blueberries and cherries. There are two self-contained options – Eagle Park Villa is much better than Cherry Top Cottage.

Guests can harvest produce from the garden (there's loads) and children love the treehouse and swings. To get here, take the C822 and follow the signs.

★ The Trig/The Container
COTTAGE $$$

(📞0498 189 488; www.thetrig.com.au; 345 Mountain Rd, Mt Arthur; cottage $250-290) 🅿 Self-contained accommodation doesn't get any better than this. Perched on a working farm on the picturesque slopes of broody Mt Arthur, these two well-spaced eco-cabins (one a cleverly converted shipping container) are the perfect romantic retreat. Decorated in retro-chic style, they have excellent kitchens stocked with organic breakfast provisions (included) and gourmet frozen meals from Alps & Amici (p184).

Lilydale Larder
CAFE $$

(📞03-6395 1230; www.lilydalelarder.com.au; 1983 Main Rd; mains $15-30; ⊙9.30am-7pm Sun-Thu, to 9pm Fri & Sat) This providore, cafe and bar is the best in the region in all three categories. Owned by a group of locals who share a love of fine food and beverages, its kitchen uses local produce wherever possible, and its bar concentrates on local tipples. Book ahead for weekend dinners.

❶ Getting There & Away

Sainty North East Bus Service (📞0437 469 186; www.saintysnortheastbusservice.com. au) operates at least one service daily in each direction, Monday to Friday, between Launceston and Lilydale ($8, 30 minutes), continuing either to Bridport or Derby.

SOUTH OF LAUNCESTON

Hadspen & Carrick

Just 15km and 19km southwest of Launceston respectively, historic Hadspen and Carrick are endearing wee hamlets with a few interesting diversions and accommodation options. Slow down, look around and tune in to the historic vibes.

◉ Sights

Entally Estate
HISTORIC BUILDING

(📞03-6393 3200; www.entally.com.au; 28 Rutherglen Rd, Hadspen; adult/concession/family $15/12/35; ⊙10am-4pm Thu-Mon) Built in 1819 by shipping entrepreneur Thomas Haydock Reibey, Entally is one of Tasmania's oldest –

and loveliest – country homesteads, painting a vivid picture of the affluent rural life back in the day. Wander around the sparsely furnished house then roll out a picnic rug in the meticulously tended garden. Interesting fact for the day: Mary Reibey, Thomas' mum, is on the Australian $20 note.

🛏 Sleeping

Entally Lodge
HOTEL $$

(☑ 03-6393 3200; www.entally.com.au; 28 Rutherglen Rd, Hadspen; d from $140; 🛜) Sometimes enthusiastic management can make all the difference. This large hotel and reception centre opposite historic Entally Estate won't win any design awards, but its enthusiastic manager is ensuring that guests enjoy their stay by providing good food in its bistro, a convivial vibe in its bar, stylish refurbished rooms and special events aplenty.

Hawthorn Villa Stables
B&B $$

(☑ 03-6393 6150; www.hawthornvilla.com.au; 1 Church St, Carrick; s/d from $150/160; ❄🛜) Set in the manicured gardens of an historic house, these four two-storey cottages have cosy kitchen/lounge spaces with log fire downstairs and a bedroom upstairs. A breakfast hamper can be supplied for $10 to $15 per person.

★ Red Feather Inn
BOUTIQUE HOTEL $$$

(☑ 03-6393 6506; www.redfeatherinn.com.au; 42 Main St, Hadspen; d/q incl breakfast from $250/450; ❄🛜) The unreservedly gorgeous 1852 Red Feather Inn offers French Provincial–style boutique accommodation, gourmet in-house dining and a well-regarded cooking school. Rooms range from attic doubles to a cottage sleeping eight – the Library Suite and Garden Suite are particularly attractive. Full-day cooking classes (from $195) are held in the country kitchen, which also services the in-house restaurant (three courses $85). No kids under 16.

ℹ Getting There & Away

Metro (☑ 13 22 01; www.metrotas.com.au) bus 78 travels between Launceston and Hadspen ($4.60, 35 minutes) from Monday to Saturday, at least five times daily. There's no Carrick service.

Westbury
☑ 03 / POP 2110

This languid country town has a feast of historic buildings and a decidedly English vibe; it even has a pretty village green. Its tourist attractions are modest, but the Liffey Falls State Reserve (p196) is nearby, as is the craft centre of Deloraine.

◎ Sights

Westbury Maze
MAZE

(☑ 0408 315 611; 10 Meander Valley Rd; $7; ⊙10am-3pm) Lose the kids among the 3000-plant privet hedges of Westbury Maze, then recover in the tearoom. It's great family entertainment.

Pearn's Steam World
MUSEUM

(☑ 03-6393 1414; www.pearnssteamworld.org.au; 65 Meander Valley Rd; adult/child $10/5; ⊙9am-4pm Sep-Jun, 10am-3pm Jul & Aug) Two huge vaulted sheds are filled with (allegedly) the world's largest collection of antique steam engines and relics. If your timing's good, you will see a little petrol engine will be doing laps of the complex.

🛏 Sleeping & Eating

Fitzpatrick's Inn
B&B $$

(☑ 03-6393 1153; www.fitzpatricksinn.com.au; 56 Meander Valley Rd; d incl breakfast $130-150; 🅿🛜❄) Travellers have been overnighting in this inn for nearly two centuries (it was built in 1833). Back in the day, the upstairs rooms provided the only accommodation, but now there are rooms in a modern extension at the rear – those in the original building are the nicest, but families and/or pet owners may prefer the garden rooms.

★ Quamby Estate
BOUTIQUE HOTEL $$$

(☑ 03-6392 2135; www.quambyestate.com.au; 1145 Westwood Rd, Hagley; d $169-349, breakfast $25; ❄❄🛜) Few hotels can match the setting and surrounds on offer at this classy country-house hotel. In a pastoral homestead dating from 1828, it offers 10 stylish en-suite rooms (opt for a downstairs deluxe king suite). Relax in the gorgeous garden or sitting rooms, dine in the ballroom (two/three courses from $60/75), play a round of golf and pretend you're 'to the manor born'.

You'll find it off Meander Valley Rd, between Carrick and Westbury.

Andy's Bakery
BAKERY $

(☑ 03-6393 1846; www.andystasmania.com; 45 Meander Valley Rd; pies/gelato from $6.50/5; ⊙9am-4pm Mon & Tue, 9am-6pm Wed-Sun; 🛜) This roadhouse is a bit of an icon around these parts, with a big reputation for its house-made pies, cakes and gelato. The peppery 'Tassie Devil' pie isn't for the faint-hearted, but the Devonshire teas, which are served with locally made jam and Ashgrove cream, are universally appealing. It closes earlier during winter.

❶ Getting There & Away

Twice-daily Redline (p185) buses from Launceston to the north coast stop in Westbury ($11.20, 35 minutes) and go on to Deloraine ($14.30, 45 minutes).

Longford

📒 03 / POP 3760

Longford was founded in 1807 when free landholding farmers were moved to Van Diemen's Land from Norfolk Island. It's one of the few Tasmanian towns not established by convicts. Two farming estates on the far edge of town, Woolmers Estate and Brickendon, are included on the list of the 11 Unesco World Heritage Australian Convict Sites and should be on your must-see list when visiting this neck o' the woods. Longford is also the birthplace of Man Booker Prize–winning Tasmanian author Richard Flanagan, who won the award in 2014 for his novel *The Narrow Road to the Deep North*.

◉ Sights

Longford spreads itself out around Memorial Park, and is known for heritage buildings such as **Christ Church** (📒03-6391 2982; www.christchurchlongford.com.au; 2 William St; ☺service 9am Sun), the **Town Hall** (📒03-6397 7303; www.northernmidlands. tas.gov.au; 67 Wellington St) and **Queen's Arms Hotel** (📒03-6391 1130; www.facebook. com/qalongford; 69 Wellington St; ☺9am-10pm Mon-Thu, to midnight Fri & Sat, 10am-8pm Sun). The town's other claim to fame is its role as host to the Australian Grand Prix from 1953 to 1968. The **Country Club Hotel** (📒03-6391 2769; www.facebook.com/longford pub; 19 Wellington St; ☺10.30am-10pm Mon-Sat, to 9pm Sun) is a shrine to this racy past, with photos and paraphernalia aplenty.

★ **Woolmers Estate** HISTORIC SITE
(📒03-6391 2230; www.woolmers.com.au; 658 Woolmers Lane; tours adult/child/family $20/7/45; ☺9.30am-4pm) Joining nearby Brickendon on the list of the 11 Unesco World Heritage Australian Convict Sites, this pastoral estate on the Macquarie River was built by

Thomas Archer in 1817 and remained in the ownership of the Archer family until 1994. Admission is via guided tours at 11.15am, 12.30pm and 2pm daily. Wandering through the rooms, which are still furnished with the family's possessions, is a fascinating experience. There are also **farm outbuildings** and a noted **rose garden**.

It's possible to overnight in self-contained **cottages** (cottage from $150) on the site. Be sure to visit the shearing shed (the oldest in Australia still in use) and take the picturesque 2.8km **Convict Trail Walk** to Brickendon across the river.

Brickendon HISTORIC SITE
(📒03-6391 1383; www.brickendon.com.au; 236 Wellington St; adult/child/family $12.50/5/38; ☺9.30am-5pm Tue-Sun Oct-May, to 4pm Jun-Sep) World Heritage–listed Brickendon, one of the 11 Unesco World Heritage Australian Convict Sites, was established in 1824. The homestead is still occupied by the Archer family, so you can't see inside, but you can explore the gorgeous old gardens and the farm village, and take the 2.8km Convict Trail Walk to Woolmers. There's animal feeding for the kids at 10.15am and on-site **accommodation** (cottage from $190; 🐾🐕).

LIFFEY VALLEY

The lush landscape around the Liffey River comprises cool temperate forests on hillsides and rich agricultural land closer to the river. Stretching from the Great Western Tiers (Kooperona Niara or 'Mountains of the Spirits') to the Meander River near Carrick, the river is a popular spot for fisherfolk (feisty brown and rainbow trout). The valley is home to the Liffey Falls State Reserve, and the towns of Deloraine, Hadspen, Westbury, Longford and Evandale are relatively close by.

Around 42km southeast of Longford on the slopes of the Great Western Tiers, the Liffey Falls State Reserve (☑03-6701 2104; www.parks.tas.gov.au; via Bass Hwy, Deloraine) FREE protects one of the most beautiful waterfalls on the island (and part of the Tasmanian Wilderness World Heritage Area). The reserve also sustains a temperate rainforest of myrtle, sassafras and leatherwood. A nature walk (45-minute return) leads from a picnic area near the car park down through forests of towering eucalypts and tree ferns to the falls. A number of smaller falls are passed along the way.

There are two approaches to the falls, which are actually four separate cascades. From the upstream car park (reached by a steep, winding road) it's a 45-minute return walk on a well-marked track. You can also follow the river upstream on foot from the Gulf Rd picnic area; allow two to three hours return.

🛏 Sleeping & Eating

Longford Riverside
Caravan Park CARAVAN PARK $
(☑03-6391 1470; www.longfordriversidecaravan park.com; 2a Archer St; unpowered/powered sites from $30/36, on-site caravans & studios $85-125; 🛜🐾) Down on the grassy, shady verges of the Macquarie River, this caravan park offers plenty of camp sites, affordable cabins and caravans, decent amenities blocks, camp kitchens, a laundry and the occasional passing trout just begging to be hooked. Extra charges apply for hot showers and use of the BBQs.

Longford Boutique
Accommodation B&B $$
(☑03-6391 2126; www.longfordboutique.com; 6 Marlborough St; d incl breakfast from $165, cottage from $195; ❄🛜) Just off the main street, this National Trust–listed bank (1865) is now a boutique B&B. Luxe benefits include port and chocolates, fluffy bathrobes and a DVD library. There are three rooms in the main building, and a cottage out the back sleeping four (good for families).

JJ's Bakery & Old Mill Café BAKERY $
(☑03-6391 2364; www.facebook.com/jjslaunces ton; 52 Wellington St; items from $4; ⊙6.30am-4.30pm) This bakehouse inside the Old Emerald Flour Mill is always busy, and no wonder. It sells delicious old-fashioned tarts and slices, cakes, pies and bread. Eat in or buy a treat to eat while relaxing in one of the nearby parks.

❶ Getting There & Away

From Monday to Saturday, Tassielink (p306) operates three daily buses to Launceston ($7.30, 50 minutes) via Evandale ($6.10, 25 minutes). The buses stop along Marlborough and Wellington Sts.

Evandale
☑03 / POP 1086

Walk down the main street in Evandale and you'll feel like you've time-warped back a century...precisely why the entire town is National Trust listed. It's a ridiculously photogenic place, and well worth a visit. Allow a few hours so you can admire its historic streetscapes, browse a few boutiques and take a break in the excellent pub and/or bakery. If you visit on a Sunday, the Evandale Market offers light commercial intercourse.

◉ Sights

★Clarendon HISTORIC BUILDING
(☑03-6398 6220; www.nationaltrust.org.au/ places/clarendon; 234 Clarendon Station Rd, Nile, via Evandale; adult/child $15/free; ⊙10am-4pm Thu-Sun Sep-Jun) Located next to the South Esk River, this 1838 mansion was built for wealthy wool grower and merchant James Cox. A Georgian gem, it looks like it's stepped straight out of *Gone with the Wind*. Long the grandest house in the colony, it is now owned by the National Trust. Visitors can take a self-guided tour of the house, which is furnished with antiques, and also

visit its outbuildings – one of these houses the Australian Fly Fishing Museum (www. affm.net.au;; $4; ⊙10am-4pm Fri-Sun).

Evandale Market
MARKET

(☑03-6391 9191; www.facebook.com/evandalesun daymarket; Falls Park, 2-14 Logan Rd; ⊙8am-1.30pm Sun) An exuberant mix of happy locals selling fresh fruit and veg, kids' pony rides (and occasionally a mini-train), food vans, and stalls selling crafts and bric-a-brac.

Water Tower
HISTORIC BUILDING

(cnr High St & Cambock Lane W) As you enter town from the north you'll see this castle-like red-brick water tower (1896), which encloses a convict-dug tunnel designed to supply water to the town. There's still 80,000L inside, maintaining pressure on the walls so they don't collapse.

🎆 Festivals & Events

Evandale Village Fair
FAIR

(www.evandalevillagefair.com; ⊙Feb) During its village fair, Evandale comes out to play. There are breakneck penny-farthing races, musicians and entertainers parading the streets and plenty of other action, including a bustling market. The 'Slow Race' for the penny farthings is hilarious (last bike over the line wins – it's actually really difficult to ride these bad boys slowly).

Glover Art Prize
ART

(www.johnglover.com.au; ⊙Mar) During the March long weekend each year, the historic pavilion in Falls Park hosts an exhibition of finalists' works in the Glover Art Prize competition, Australia's richest. It's a feast of contemporary landscape art.

🛏 Sleeping & Eating

Wesleyan Chapel
COTTAGE $$

(☑0417 641 536; 28 Russell St; cottage from $130; 🐾) Built in 1835, this tiny brick chapel has since been used variously as a druids hall, an RSL hall and a scout hall. Now it's self-contained accommodation. There's a washing machine and fully equipped kitchen in which guests will find homemade breakfast provisions (even the honey is hand-produced).

Grandma's House
RENTAL HOUSE $$

(☑03-6391 8444; www.grandmashouse.com.au; 10 Rodgers Lane; house from $130; 🛜🐾) Sleeping four comfortably, this tempting option occupies the leafy gardens of historic Marlborough House in the centre of town. Relax in the spacious lounge, which has a wood fire, or hang out in the gorgeous garden or on the rear verandah, where there's a BBQ. Facilities include a fully equipped kitchen and a separate laundry.

Ingleside Bakery Cafe
CAFE $

(☑03-6391 8682; www.facebook.com/ingleside bakery; 4 Russell St; mains $8-23; ⊙8.30am-5pm Mon-Fri, to 4pm Sat & Sun; 🚸) Sit in the flowery walled courtyard or under the high ceiling inside this former council chambers (1867), where fresh-baked aromas waft from the wood oven. Expect delicious pies and pasties, a hefty ploughman's lunch and all manner of sweet treats, including Devonshire teas. The providore shelves are packed with Tasmanian products.

🍷 Drinking & Nightlife

⭐Clarendon Arms Hotel
PUB

(☑03-6391 8181; www.clarendonarms.com.au; 11 Russell St; ⊙10am-5pm Thu, 10am-late Fri & Sat, 10am-4pm Sun) Dating from 1847, this venerable pub with its much-loved beer garden was damaged by fire in 2015 and subsequently sold to the owners of the acclaimed Red Feather Inn (p194) in Hadspen. Extensive renovations were almost complete when we visited, with a fab restaurant up-and-running and boutique pub accommodation available from 2018.

ℹ Information

Evandale Visitor Information Centre

(☑03-6391 8128; www.evandaletasmania. com; 18 High St; ⊙10am-4pm) Local info and accommodation bookings. Stocks the *Evandale Heritage Walk* pamphlet ($3), detailing the town's historic riches. The history room here has a display on Victoria Cross–winning WWI soldier Harry Murray, who is commemorated with a statue on Russell St.

ℹ Getting There & Away

From Monday to Saturday, three daily Tassielink (p306) buses travel between Launceston and Evandale ($6.10, 30 minutes), continuing to Longford ($7.30, 55 minutes). The Evandale bus stop is on Scone St.

Ben Lomond National Park

Home to Tassie's best-equipped ski field, this 181-sq-km national park (☑03-6777 2179; www.parks.tas.gov.au; Ben Lomond Rd; parks pass vehicle/person per day $24/12) takes in the whole of the Ben Lomond massif: a craggy alpine plateau whose highest point, Legges Tor (1572m), is the second-highest spot on the island (the highest is the 1617m Mt Ossa). Bushwalkers traipse across the mountain plateau when the snow melts, swooning over alpine wildflowers during spring and summer, marvelling at the views from the precipitous escarpments and spotting native animals, including Bennett's wallabies, wombats, pademelons and Eastern quolls.

Activities

Skiing

Ben Lomond is considered Tasmania's Aspen – well, not quite, but when the snow does fall the lifts grind into action and you can ski here. Coverage can be patchy, but the ski season generally runs from early July to late September. Two 'snow guns' top up the natural snow. Full-day ski-lift passes cost $70/50/30 per adult/teenager/child, while half-day passes cost $45/35/20. Under sevens and over 70s ride free. There are three T-bars and four poma lifts. For snow reports and cams, see www.benlomond.org.au.

Ben Lomond Snow Sports (☎03-6390 6185; www.skibenlomond.com.au; Ben Lomond Rd, Ben Lomond National Park; ⊘9am-4.30pm in ski season) runs a kiosk selling takeaway fare and a shop doing ski, snowboard and toboggan rental, and associated gear. Skis, boots, poles and a lesson cost $90/75 per adult/child; just skis, boots and poles costs $60/45.

National park entry fees apply.

Walking

The park is magnificent in summer, with great bushwalking and a riot of alpine flowers. It's a two-hour walk each way to Legges Tor from Carr Villa, about halfway up the mountain. You can also climb to the top along marked tracks from the alpine village on the plateau, which takes about 30 minutes each way.

If you're happy to go off track, you can walk across the plateau in almost any direction. This is easy enough in fine weather, but not recommended without complete visibility. Unless you're well equipped, walking south of the ski village isn't advised. All walkers and cross-country skiers should sign in at the self-registration booth at the alpine village.

Sleeping & Eating

There's a small Parks & Wildlife Service–maintained camping area at the base of Jacob's Ladder near the park entrance: six unpowered sites with flushing toilets, drinking water, fireplaces and super views. National park entry fees apply (no camping fees or bookings).

When we last visited, there was talk that the Ben Lomond Alpine Hotel, which had been closed for business since 2016, may be reopening. See www.benlomondalpinehotel.com.au for updates.

During the ski season, the cafe at Ben Lomond Snow Sports sells takeaway food, hot snacks and drinks.

Information

National parks passes are available from self-registration boxes at the entry station prior to the Carr Villa Rd turn-off and at the information booth adjacent to the Legges Tor public shelter. Cash only (or buy one online).

Getting There & Away

There's no public transport to the mountain, so driving is your only option.

Note that the road up to the plateau is unsealed and includes Jacob's Ladder, a sensationally steep climb with six white-knuckle hairpin bends and no safety barriers. During the snow season, chains are standard issue – hire them from **Autobarn** (Map p175; ☎03-6334 5601; www.autobarn.com.au/stores/launceston; 6 Innes St; ⊘8am-5.30pm Mon-Fri, 9am-5pm Sat, 9am-4pm Sun) in Launceston ($40 per day, plus $60 deposit). Don't forget antifreeze.

During the ski season, Ben Lomond Snow Sports runs a shuttle bus ($15 per person return) from the bottom car park at the Parks & Wildlife Service registration booth, 7km from the ski field. If you're catching the shuttle, you don't need to hire chains for your car. Call for pick-ups.

Devonport & the Northwest

Best Places to Eat

➡ Mrs Jones (p205)

➡ The Chapel (p218)

➡ Nut Café (p223)

Best Places to Stay

➡ Ikon Hotel (p216)

➡ Beach Retreat Tourist Park (p219)

➡ Grand on Macfie (p204)

Why Go?

Tasmania's northwest is the island in a nutshell – wild and untramelled in parts, quietly sophisticated in others. Home to two national parks – Rocky Cape and Savage River – as well as the spectacular Arthur-Pieman Conservation Area, this part of the island is rich in wilderness and poor in tourists, and you'll have many sites, landscapes and beaches to yourself. Little-visited areas include the ancient rainforests of the Tarkine wilderness – known as takayna to the Tarkininer Aboriginal people – and the remote beaches on Tasmania's northwest tip, blown-over by the powerful Roaring Forties winds, the cleanest gusts on earth. Here, also, are some of the best places in Australia to see platypuses and penguins and to enjoy rustic meals featuring world-class local produce. Your memories of exploring one of the world's last unspoiled corners will linger long after you leave.

When to Go

➡ The northwest blooms in springtime (September to November), with fields of purple poppies, multicoloured tulips and fragrant forest leatherwood.

➡ Over summer (December to February) there's fresh crayfish on offer, plus music and craft festivals, beaches to relax on and rainforests to tramp through. Camp by the dunes and wait for the perfect break.

➡ Batten down the hatches in winter (June to August): the northwest is exhilaratingly wild as the Roaring Forties blow through. You'll still get a warm welcome, but call ahead: some places reduce their hours or close altogether in winter.

Devonport & the Northwest Highlights

① **Stanley** (p220) Scaling the curious ex-volcanic Nut behind this historic town.

② **Boat Harbour Beach** (p220) Lazing on one of Tasmania's prettiest stretches of sand.

③ **Penguin** (p214) Sampling the cafe culture in this laid-back northwest seaside town.

④ **Mole Creek Karst National Park** (p209) Gawping at amazing limestone cave formations lit by glow-worms.

⑤ **Takayna/ Tarkine Wilderness** (p226) Taking a guided walk through ancient, dense rainforest in an untouched part of the island.

⑥ **Table Cape** (p219) Checking out colourful fields of tulips and photo-worthy views on the drive between Wynyard and Boat Harbour.

⑦ **Leven Valley** (p212) Enjoying a scenic drive through this lush agricultural landscape.

⑧ **Deloraine Creative Studios** (p208) Stocking up on handmade crafts, bought directly from their creators.

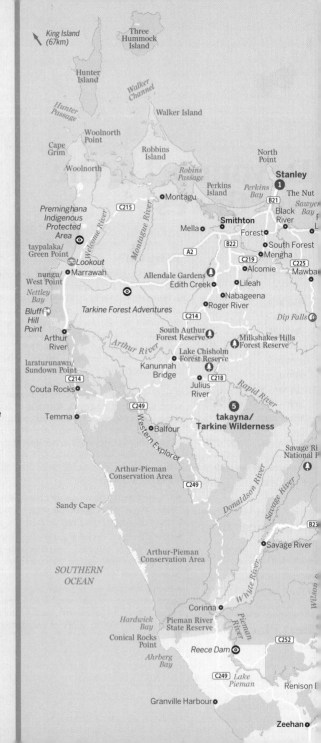

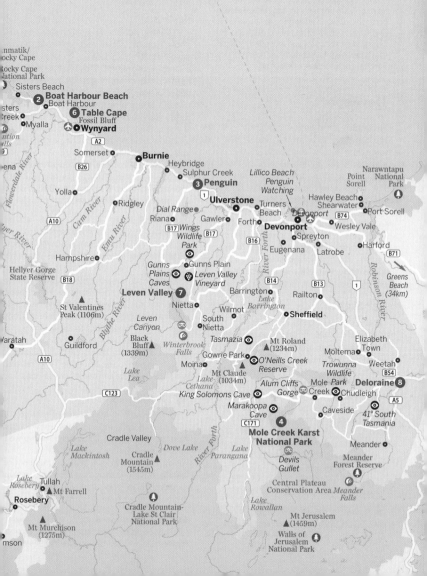

Spirit of Tasmania ferries
to/from Melbourne
(approx. 10 hours
or 360km)

N 0 _____ 20 km
   0 _____ 10 miles

BASS STRAIT

nmatik/
ocky Cape
ational Park

ocky Cape
National Park

Sisters Beach

Boat Harbour Beach ②
Boat Harbour
sters
Creek
Table Cape ⑥
Fossil Bluff
Myalla
Wynyard

ntion
lls
②

Somerset
A2

B26
Burnie
Heybridge
Sulphur Creek
Penguin ③
Yolla
Ulverstone
Lillico Beach
Penguin
Watching
Narawntapu
Point National
Sorell Park
Ridgley
Dial Range
Turners
Beach
Hawley Beach
Shearwater
Port Sorell
Riana
Gawler
Forth
Devonport
B74
Wesley Vale
B17
B17
Devonport
Hampshire
Wings
Wildlife
Park
B16
Spreyton
Eugenana
Latrobe
Harford
B71

Hellyer Gorge
State Reserve
B18
Gunns
Plains
Caves
Gunns Plain
Leven Valley
Vineyard
Barrington
Railton
B14
B13
Greens
Beach
(34km)

Leven Valley ⑦
Nietta
Wilmot
Lake
Barrington
Sheffield

St Valentines
Peak (1106m)
South
Nietta
Leven
Canyon
Elizabeth
Town
Moltema

Guildford
A10
Black
Bluff
(1339m)
Winterbrook
Falls
Tasmazia
Mt Roland
(1234m)
Trowunna
Wildlife
Park
Weetah
B54

Moina
Gowrie Park
O'Neills Creek
Reserve
Mole
Park
Creek
Deloraine ⑧
Chudleigh
A5

Lake
Lea
Mt Claude
(1034m)
Alum Cliffs
Gorge
Caveside
41° South
Tasmania

C123
King Solomons Cave
Marakoopa
Cave ④
C171
**Mole Creek Karst
National Park**
Meander

Cradle Valley
Lake
Mackintosh
Dove Lake
Cradle
Mountain
(1545m)
Lake
Parangana
Devils
Gullet
Meander
Forest Reserve

Lake
Rosebery
Tullah
Mt Farrell
Rosebery
Cradle Mountain–
Lake St Clair
National Park
Central Plateau
Conservation Area
Lake
Rowallan
Meander
Falls

Mt Murchison
(1275m)
mson
Mt Jerusalem
(1459m)
Walls of
Jerusalem
National Park

❶ Getting There & Away

The main road access to this part of the island is via the Bass Hwy, which stretches from Launceston all the way to Marrawah on the west coast. Most roads off this are in good condition and can be tackled in a regular car; the only exceptions are roads deep in the takayna/Tarkine wilderness and Savage River National Park, which can only be accessed by 4WD. Petrol stations are plentiful along the northern coast but in sparse supply on the west coast.

One of Tasmania's major transport hubs – the *Spirit of Tasmania* ferry terminal – is in Devonport, while Devonport and Burnie airports handle flights to and from mainland Australia. Bus services link the cities and most of the major towns hereabouts, but don't extend west beyond Smithton or into takayna/Tarkine.

Devonport

📞 03 / POP 30,500

Tasmania's third-largest city is the port for the *Spirit of Tasmania I* and *II,* the red-and-white ferries that connect the island state with the mainland. It's an evocative sight when, after three deep blasts of the horn, these huge ships cruise past the end of the main street to begin their voyage north. After disembarking, most passengers scatter to other destinations on the island and Devonport slips back into obscurity. Before you do the same, consider popping into town to visit its excellent maritime museum and regional gallery and have a meal at one of the eateries overlooking Mersey Bluff Beach.

◉ Sights

★ Bass Strait Maritime Centre · MUSEUM

(📞 03-6424 7100; www.bassstraitmc.com.au; 6 Gloucester Ave; adult/child/family $10/5/25; ⊙10am-5pm) Housed in the former harbour master's residence (c 1920), this small but impressive museum is home to displays about the geology and maritime history of Bass Strait. Its large collection of ship and ferry models is a crowd-pleaser, but the knockout exhibit is the interactive simulator ($2) that allows museum-goers to steer a steamer along the Mersey River or through Port Phillip Heads. Also of note is a cleverly presented and informative exhibit on the history of container ships.

★ Devonport Regional Gallery · GALLERY

(📞 03-6424 8296; www.devonportgallery.com; 45-47 Stewart St; by donation; ⊙10am-5pm Mon-Fri, noon-5pm Sat, 1-5pm Sun) Currently housed in a decommissioned 1904 Baptist church with a stunning wooden vaulted ceiling, this small but well-curated gallery is slated to move into the new contemporary arts hub within the Devonport Entertainment & Convention Centre in late 2018. A regular exhibition is the excellent biannual (odd-numbered years) City of Devonport National Art Award (aka Tidal), which attracts entries from prominent Australian visual artists. Otherwise, the exhibition program tends to focus on local work.

Home Hill · HISTORIC BUILDING

(📞03-6424 8055; www.nationaltrust.org.au/places/home-hill; 77 Middle Rd; adult/child/concession $15/10/12; ⊙guided tours 2pm Wed-Sun, other times by appointment) This relatively modest house set in a pretty garden was the residence of Joseph Lyons, Australia's only Tasmanian prime minister, and his wife Dame Enid Lyons, the first woman elected to federal parliament. Built in 1916, it was extended in stages to accommodate the power couple and their 12 children. There are plenty of political and family mementos on show on the compulsory guided tour, plus original furnishings. It's located just off the Bass Hwy, a five-minute drive from town.

Don River Railway · MUSEUM

(📞03-6424 6335; www.donriverrailway.com.au; Forth Rd, Don; adult/child/family $19/14/40; ⊙9am-4.30pm Wed-Sun, reduced winter hours) You don't have to be a trainspotter to love this collection of locomotives and brightly painted rolling stock. The entry price includes a half-hour train ride on a diesel locomotive running beside the Don Riverbank (on the hour from 10am to 4pm, Wednesday to Sunday only).

To get here, drive west of Devonport along the Bass Hwy then take the B19 exit towards Don, Devonport and Spreyton. The railway is 4.5km from the centre of Devonport.

🏃 Activities

There's a colony of little (or fairy) penguins at Lillico Beach, on the Bass Hwy 8.5km west of Devonport. These can be viewed on a purpose-built viewing platform. Local volunteers and Parks & Wildlife rangers are usually on-site during the breeding season (September to May) and summer months (mid-December to mid-February).

★ The Julie Burgess · CRUISE

(📞03-6424 7100; www.bassstraitmaritimecentre.com.au/julie-burgess; per person $50; ⊙Wed &

Devonport

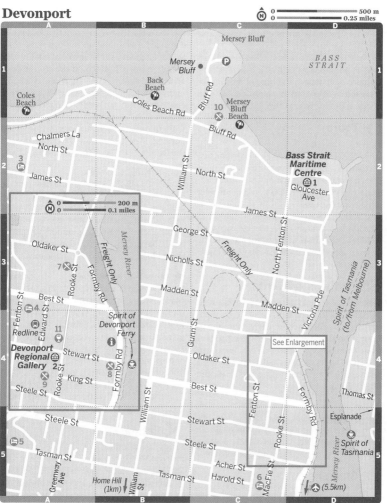

N
0 ————— 500 m
0 ————— 0.25 miles

Devonport

◎ Top Sights
1	Bass Strait Maritime Centre	D2
2	Devonport Regional Gallery	A4

⊜ Sleeping
3	Inspire Boutique Apartment 1	A2
4	Quality Hotel Gateway	A3
5	Tasman Backpackers	A5
6	The Grand on Macfie	C5

⊗ Eating
7	Burger Got Soul	A3
8	Central Restaurant	B4
9	Laneway	A4
10	Mrs Jones	C1

⊝ Drinking & Nightlife
	Formby Hotel	(see 8)
11	Tapas Lounge Bar	A4

Sun) Purpose-built in 1936 to harvest the rich crayfish fields of Bass Strait and Tasmania, this fishing ketch has recently been meticulously restored and now offers two-hour cruises out of the mouth of the Mersey River into Bass Strait towards Don Heads. Tickets should be booked in advance at the Bass Strait Maritime Centre; tours only operate with minimum numbers and in favourable weather conditions.

The cruises depart from Reg Hope Park next to the Mersey Yacht Club in East Devonport. Note that at the time of writing the good ship was undergoing maintenance: call or check the website to check if it's running.

Tours

Murray's Day Out
TOURS

(☑ 0427 252 439, 03-6425 2439; www.murraysday out.com.au; day trips per person from $150) To be shown some of Tasmania by an entirely passionate and charming Tasmanian, consider taking one of these tours. Murray offers 'service with humour' in his comfortable van (seating up to seven). Go all the way west to Marrawah, drop in on Cradle Mountain, or just tootle around the country lanes near Devonport.

Festivals & Events

Taste the Harvest Festival
FOOD & DRINK

(www.tastetheharvestdevonport.com.au; ☉ Feb/ Mar) In late February or early March, this festival on the foreshore celebrates produce from Tasmania's northwest coast. Local eateries and wineries have stalls, and there's a large tent showcasing fruit, vegetables and other produce.

Devonport Jazz
MUSIC

(www.devonportjazz.com; ☉ Jul) Held in late July each year, this four-day festival is staged in different venues around town and features a huge variety of jazz styles and performers.

Sleeping

Tasman Backpackers
HOSTEL $

(☑ 03-6423 2335; www.tasmanbackpackers.com. au; 114 Tasman St; dm $21-23, tw/d/tr with shared bathroom $52/54/72; @ 🛜) This sprawling building once housed nurses from Devonport's hospital, but it's now a well-run hostel that is popular with Asian backpackers doing visa-related farm work. Its six single-sex dorms and variety of twin, double and triple rooms are worn but clean. Facilities include a good kitchen, BBQ courtyard, locker room, pool table, lounge and cinema room. Advance bookings are recommended.

Staff can help with placements for harvesting and fruit-picking jobs. The hostel is situated on a hill above the town centre; a taxi from the ferry will cost $10.

Inspire Boutique Apartment 1
APARTMENT $$

(☑ 0400 012 231; www.stayz.com.au; 134 James St; d from $180) Planning on self-catering? If so, this apartment near Coles Beach is the best option in town. Located on the ground floor of a three-storey property, it offers a large lounge and dining area with TV and DVD, courtyard with barbecue, kitchenette with coffee machine, washing machine, bedroom with queen-size bed and secure off-street parking. Bookings can also be made through the Devonport Visitor Information Centre.

Quality Hotel Gateway
HOTEL $$

(☑ 03-6424 4922; www.gatewayinn.com.au; 16 Fenton St; d/f from $150/180; ❊ 🛜) Clean and modern rooms (some with spa and most with air-conditioning) and good in-house facilities (restaurant, bar, laundry) result in a reliable package at this large place three short blocks back from the waterfront.

★ The Grand on Macfie
B&B $$$

(☑ 03-6424 2000; www.thegrandonmacfie.com.au; 44a Macfie St; r incl breakfast $225-300; 🛜) Built over a century ago, the Grand is just that – a well-located, large and extremely handsome mansion offering five elegant antique-filled rooms, a guest lounge, a balcony with panoramic views and a dining room where a full cooked breakfast is served. On weekend afternoons, a high tea ($39.50) is offered. Guest feedback is extremely positive about hosts Paul and Brendan.

Eating

Burger Got Soul
BURGERS $

(☑ 03-6423 4055; www.burgergotsoul.com; 155 Rooke St; mains $11-18; ☉ 11am-9pm) Like its sister establishments in Hobart and Launceston, this burger bar next to the Entertainment & Convention Centre flips beef, lamb, chicken, fish and veggie burgers to meet orders from a multitude of appreciative repeat clients.

Central Restaurant
PUB FOOD $$

(☑ 03-6424 1601; www.goodstone.com.au/central_ restaurant; Formby Hotel, 82 Formby Rd; mains $22-43; ☉ noon-late) Most Tasmanian pub bistros serve a monotonous and unhealthy menu dominated by fried dishes and grilled steak. Here at the Central, they do things differently. The menu features Asian-influenced shared small plates, pizzas with unorthodox toppings, mains cooked *sous vide* and a battalion of vegetable sides (bravo!). Servings are huge and prices are reasonable.

Laneway CAFE **$$**
(☑03-6424 4333; www.lane-way.com.au; 2/38 Steele St; mains $11-24; ⊙7am-5pm Thu-Tue, to 4pm Wed; 🐾📶) Occupying a former bakery, this cafe on Rooke Lane is as hip as Devonport gets. Large all-day breakfast plates (eggs, beans, waffles, coconut chia pudding) are the order of choice for a loyal local clientele, accompanied by well-made coffee, T2 tea or freshly squeezed fruit juice. Evening events with special dinner menus are sometimes scheduled – check the website for details.

★**Mrs Jones** MODERN AUSTRALIAN **$$$**
(☑03-6423 3881; www.mrsjonesrbl.com.au; 1st fl, 41 Bluff Rd; lunch mains $23-34, dinner $34-41; ⊙noon-late Wed-Sun; 🐾📶) Head to the upstairs level of the surf lifesaving club at Mersey Bluff to discover one of Tasmania's best Mod Oz eateries. The ambitious menu cherrypicks highlights from global cuisines but is particularly strong on Asian dishes – think Thai curries, Japanese-style grills, Vietnamese spring rolls. Decor is casual chic, service is polished and the excellent wine list is predominantly Tasmanian.

🍷 **Drinking & Nightlife**

Formby Hotel PUB
(☑03-6424 1601; www.formbyhoteldevonport. com; 82 Formby Rd; ⊙noon-late) Devonport's most popular pub has a spacious and modern public bar.

Tapas Lounge Bar BAR
(☑03-6424 2727; www.tapasloungebar.com; 97a Rooke St Mall; ⊙5pm-midnight Thu, to 2am Fri, to late Sat) One of the only places to party in town after the pubs close, this lounge bar offers live music and free pool.

ℹ️ **Information**

Devonport Visitor Information Centre (☑03-6424 4466, 1800 649 514; www.tasmaniasnorth west.com.au; 92 Formby Rd; ⊙7.30am-3.30pm Mon-Fri, to 11.30pm Sat & Sun; 🐾) This helpful information office in the town centre can make tour and accommodation bookings, sell national park passes, supply a town map and give advice about travelling in the region. It also offers free baggage storage and wi-fi. Note that weekend hours are extended in summer.

ℹ️ **Getting There & Away**

AIR

QantasLink (☑13 13 13; www.qantas.com.au) has regular flights between Melbourne and **Devonport Airport** (☑13 13 13; www.devonport

airport.com.au; Airport Rd), which is located about 10km east of the town centre.

BOAT

Spirit of Tasmania (☑1800 634 906; www. spiritoftasmania.com.au; ⊙customer info 8am-8.30pm Mon-Sat, 9am-8pm Sun) ferries sail between Station Pier in Melbourne and the ferry terminal on the Esplanade in East Devonport.

BUS

Tassielink (p306) bus services stop at the visitor centre and at the *Spirit of Tasmania* terminal. Services from Devonport include Launceston ($24.50, 1¼ hours), Sheffield ($5.60, 40 minutes), Gowrie Park ($10.20, 55 minutes), Cradle Mountain ($42.40, 1½ hours) and Queenstown ($56.20, 5½ hours). These connect with services to Strahan ($10.60, 45 to 75 minutes).

Redline (☑1300 360 000; www.tasredline. com.au) buses stop at 9 Edward St and the *Spirit of Tasmania* terminal. Buses travel between Launceston and Devonport ($25.40, 1½ hours) via Westbury, Deloraine and (sometimes) Mole Creek. Other services include Ulverstone ($6.50, 25 minutes), Penguin ($8.50, 40 minutes) and Burnie ($11.20, one hour).

Local company **Merseylink** (☑03-6427 7626; www.merseylink.com.au) runs buses between Devonport and Latrobe ($3.30, 25 minutes), operating Monday to Saturday. There is also a service from Devonport to Ulverstone ($6.40, 50 minutes) operating Monday to Saturday. All depart from the Rooke St interchange.

ℹ️ **Getting Around**

Spirit of Devonport Ferry (☑03-6427 7626; www.merseylink.com.au/ferry; one-way adult/ child/family $2.50/2/10; ⊙7am-5.30pm Mon-Fri, 9am-5pm Sat) The small *Spirit of Devonport* ferry crosses the Mersey River on a quick trip between a pontoon near the post office and another at the *Spirit of Tasmania* terminal. It runs on demand – just press the button at either pontoon.

Taxi Combined (☑13 10 08; www.devonport taxis.com.au) Will carry you from the ferry terminal to the centre of town for approximately $16; a fare from the airport will cost approximately $25. The flagfall is higher on weekends.

Latrobe
☑03 / POP 3900

Once a busy shipping port on the Mersey River, this country town 10km southeast of Devonport is attractive but moribund, a victim of the closure of the many mines and wood mills that were once scattered across the surrounding countryside. Still, the House of Anvers chocolate factory is worth a look if you're passing through...and you might spy a platypus!

◉ Sights

Spreyton Cider Co BREWERY
(☑03-6427 3664; www.spreytonciderco.com.au; cnr Sheffield & Melrose Rds, Spreyton; tastings & 1 glass $12; ⊙noon-5pm) Around 6km west of Latrobe along the B19 and C146, this company produces some of Tasmania's best-loved apple and pear ciders. Visit its modern tasting shed to sample its range of six ciders, one ginger beer and one juice and then take a self-guided tour around the apple orchard. Sometimes there's live music to entertain visitors on weekend afternoons.

House of Anvers FOOD
(☑03-6426 2958; www.anvers-chocolate.com.au; 9025 Bass Hwy; ⊙7am-5pm) Fudge and truffle, milk and dark – every taste is catered for at this chocolate factory just out of town. Visitors can watch chocolates being made (weekdays only), enjoy tastings in the salesroom off the car park, and order chocolate and other treats in the well-regarded cafe (breakfast and lunch mains from $8). Be sure to taste the dark ganache truffle (yum!) and the Fortunato No 4, described as the 'rarest chocolate in the world'.

🛏 Sleeping & Eating

Lucinda B&B B&B $$
(☑03-6426 2285; www.sheffieldcradleinfo.com.au/lucinda-b-b-latrobe-tasmania; 17 Forth St; r from $140; 🛜) Built in 1891 as a doctor's residence, this run-down but undeniably handsome mansion on a hill above the town centre now offers old-fashioned B&B accommodation. The three guest rooms have ornate ceiling detailing and are well sized, with TVs and in-room tea and coffee; the best is the recently renovated Reliquaire. Continental breakfasts are served in the ground-floor dining room.

**★Tasmanian Food
& Wine Conservatory** MODERN AUSTRALIAN $$
(☑0499 888 544; www.facebook.com/tasmanianfoodandwineconservatory; 9 Conservatory Rd, Sassafras; mains $20-28; ⊙9am-4pm Tue-Sun) With the laudable aim of showcasing Tasmanian food and wine – especially from boutique and small producers – this stylishly converted conservatory 15km south of Latrobe performs a valuable role and does so to great acclaim. Functioning as a cafe and provedore, it's an excellent breakfast or lunch stop when

travelling on the Bass Hwy. Try the Tasmanian gourmet platter ($40 per person).

🛍 Shopping

★Reliquaire HOMEWARES
(☑03-6426 2599; www.reliquaire.com; 14 Hamilton St; ⊙9am-5pm) After a fire destroyed its Gilbert St outlet, this marvellously eccentric shop and cafe relocated to a 19th-century mansion nearby. Customers travel here from Devonport and beyond to source a huge range of quality imported and Australian toys, homewares and knick-knacks, often staying to enjoy a naturopathic tea or an excellent coffee made with beans roasted by Villino in Hobart.

ℹ Information

Limited tourist information is available at the **Cherry Shed** (☑03-6426 2411, visitor information centre 03-6421 4699; www.thecherryshed.com.au; 243 Gilbert St; ⊙9am-5pm). Also see www.latrobe.tas.gov.au.

ℹ Getting There & Away

Local company **Merseylink** (☑03-6427 7626; www.merseylink.com.au) runs buses between Latrobe and Devonport ($3.30, 25 minutes), operating Monday to Saturday.

Metro (☑13 22 01; www.metrotas.com.au) runs services to/from Ulverstone ($6.40, 30 minutes) and then on to Penguin and Burnie.

Both companies have a number of stops along Gilbert St.

Deloraine

☑03 / POP 2750
Nooked into the base of the Great Western Tiers, Deloraine commands wonderful views at almost every turn. Blessed with the photogene, the town is bisected by the winding Meander River, with Georgian and Victorian buildings scattered around the main street, Emu Bay Rd. There's a vibrant, artsy feel here, with several good eateries and craft studios to visit.

◉ Sights

★41° South Tasmania FARM
(☑03-6362 4130; www.41southtasmania.com; 323 Montana Rd; ⊙9am-5pm Nov-Mar, to 4pm Apr-Oct) FREE Salmon are reared in raised tanks and a wetland is used as a natural biofilter at 41° South Tasmania. This no-waste, no-chemical method of fish farming is the cleanest way of raising fish – and also sup-

plies the base for superb hot-smoked salmon, which you can enjoy in a free tasting or over lunch in the terrace cafe (mains $10 to $12). The farm is 6km out of town towards Mole Creek (signed down Montana Rd).

Truffles of Tasmania FARM
(☑0457 021 571; www.trufflesoftasmania.com. au; 110 Trickets Rd; tours adult/child $50/20) The owners of this *truffière* (truffle plantation) have a 50-hectare stand of evergreen oak and mature deciduous trees that they use to cultivate the prized *Tuber melanosporum* (black truffle). Book in advance to visit their operation, learn about the truffle-growing process and meet their highly trained truffle-hunting dogs. Preserved and frozen truffles are available to purchase.

Deloraine & Districts
Folk Museum MUSEUM
(☑03-6362 5280; www.greatwesterntiers.net.au; 98-100 Emu Bay Rd; adult/child/family $8/2/18; ◉9am-5pm) The centrepiece of this museum is an exquisite four-panel, quilted and appliquéd depiction of the Meander Valley through a year of seasonal change. It's an astoundingly detailed piece of work that was a labour of love for 300 creative local men and women. Each of the four panels entailed 10,000 hours of labour, and the whole project took three years to complete. It's now housed in a purpose-built auditorium, where you can witness a presentation explaining the work every half-hour.

Ashgrove Cheese FOOD
(☑03-6368 1105; www.ashgrovecheese.com.au; 6173 Bass Hwy, Elizabeth Town; ◉7.30am-5pm, cheesemaking 9am-4pm Mon-Fri) This company's cheeses, milk and butter are ubiquitous in Tasmania. Its factory and shop on the highway in Elizabeth Town, 15km north of Deloraine, is a popular stop for locals and tour buses alike. You can watch cheese being made and purchase the result in the large shop. Limited free tastings are also offered.

🏃 Activities

Dominating the southern skyline are the **Great Western Tiers** (their Aboriginal name is Kooparoona Niara, 'Mountain of the Spirits'). The **Meander Forest Reserve** is the most popular starting point for walks here. From the swing bridge over the Meander River – where there are bowers of man ferns and tall trees – you can walk to **Split Rock** (medium-to-hard level of difficulty,

SEEING PLATYPUSES AT LATROBE
Latrobe markets itself – with as much justification as hyperbole, it must be said – as the 'Platypus Capital of the World'. Head to Bells Parade to see a large wooden platypus (dubbed 'The Big Platypus' but not really deserving of the title) and to spot the real things in the river itself, especially at sunset.

three hours return) and **Meander Falls** (medium-to-hard, six hours return).

Other good walking destinations on the Great Western Tiers include **Pine Lake** (easy, 30 minutes return), **Liffey Falls** (medium, one hour return), **Projection Bluff** (medium, one hour return), **Quamby Bluff** (medium-to-hard, five hours return) and **Westmoorland Falls** (medium, two hours return).

For guided walks, contact **Forest Walks Lodge** (☑03-6369 5150; www.forestwalkslodge. com; 669 Jackeys Marsh Rd, Jackeys Marsh; guided walks $65-175).

Note that major floods in 2016 damaged many walking tracks and viewing platforms in this area. They're slowly reopening, but check with Great Western Tiers Visitor Information Centre (p209) in advance to make sure.

The Meander Valley is a popular fly-fishing location. Contact **Driftwater** (☑0408 427 767; www.driftwater.com.au; 4501 Meander Valley Rd; half/full-day fishing per 2 people incl lunch & equipment $500/800) to arrange a guided fishing journey.

🎭 Festivals & Events

Tasmanian Craft Fair FAIR
(www.tascraftfair.com.au; adult/child/family $17/8/40, 4-day pass $28/12/65; ◉Nov) Deloraine's strong artistic community oversees this impressive four-day fair, which is held annually. People from across the country visit hundreds of craft stalls set up around town. Free shuttle buses offer a pick-up, drop-off service between venues.

🛏 Sleeping

There's decent accommodation in both of the pubs on Deloraine's main street; the **Deloraine Hotel** (☑03-6362 2022; www.delo rainehotel.com.au; 1-5 West Barrack St; d/tr & q $120/150, s/d without bathroom $50/100; 🛜) is the best bet. The town's other options are less impressive, other than historic Arcoona Manor B&B on the eastern side of the river, which has reopened since the last time we visited: check www.arcoonamanor.com.au.

Deloraine Apex Caravan Park CAMPGROUND $
(☑03-6362 2345; www.greatwesterntiers.net.au/accommodation/deloraine/deloraine-apex-caravan-park; 51 West Pde; unpowered/powered sites s $15/20, extra person $10) This camping ground is at the bottom of the main street right next to the Meander River, where platypus and ducks are regularly spotted. There's plenty of grass, and facilities are clean but worn. Don't be alarmed if an almighty thundering disturbs your slumber here: the train tracks are adjacent.

Forest Walks Lodge LODGE $$
(☑03-6369 5150; www.forestwalkslodge.com; 669 Jackeys Marsh Rd, Jackeys Marsh; d & tw $140-200, f $225-330, all incl breakfast; ☎) Set on the southern side of Quamby Bluff, this rural retreat offers an abundance of tranquillity and easy access to the attractions of the Great Western Tiers. Rooms are spacious, have comfortable beds and are decorated with locally produced crafts and artwork. Eco-credentials include solar energy and waste recycling, and meals are prepared with organic produce wherever possible.

Blake's Manor APARTMENT $$
(☑03-6362 4724; www.blakesmanor.com; 18 West Goderich St; d $180-220, extra person $30; ☎) American-Australian husband-and-wife Rhett and Dina are enthusiastic and friendly hosts, offering four suites sleeping between two and six in their heritage house. All have kitchenette and TV/DVD and are decorated in an ornate Victorian-era style that won't be to all tastes. Generous breakfast provisions are supplied, along with a welcome treat of port, cheese and nibbles.

 Eating

Van Diemen's Land Creamery ICE CREAM $
(☑03-6362 4200; www.vdlcreamery.com.au; 10 Christmas Hills Rd; ◷10am-5pm) The ice cream, gelato and sorbet on offer here changes every day, rotating between the 40 flavours this artisan company produces. Grab a cone to go or sit down for a light lunch (soup, sandwiches) or a stack of pancakes topped with your choice from the ice-cream display. A glass window allows visitors to watch the icy confections being made.

Christmas Hills
Raspberry Farm Cafe CAFE $$
(☑03-6362 2186; www.raspberryfarmcafe.com; 9 Christmas Hills Rd, Elizabeth Town; mains $10-32; ◷7am-5pm) Come here to indulge in everything raspberry. Set next to a berry farm, this cafe has a lakeside deck and an indoor space with open fire. Menu offerings include raspberry soda and milkshakes, sundaes piled high with ruby-coloured raspberries and scones with raspberry jam and cream. Be sure to sample a chocolate-dipped raspberry in the shop, which sells marvellous jam. The cafe is on the Bass Hwy, 8km north of Deloraine.

Deloraine Deli DELI, CAFE $$
(☑03-6362 2127; www.delorainedeli.com.au; 81 Emu Bay Rd; lunch mains $13-16, dinner $27-37; ◷8.30am-5pm Mon-Thu, to 10pm Fri & Sat, 10am-4pm Sun) Deloraine's best cafe does a bustling coffee trade and serves baguettes, pies, soup and quiche for lunch. Dinner on Friday and Saturday nights is more exotic – think seared lemon-myrtle-spiced wallaby, dukkah-encrusted chicken breast and citrus-glazed pork spare ribs. Dairy- and gluten-free meals are available, as are plenty of vegetarian options. There are also shelves of Tasmanian produce for sale.

 Drinking & Nightlife

Empire Hotel PUB
(☑03-6362 1029; www.theempiredeloraine.com.au; 19 Emu Bay Rd; ◷10am-10pm Tue-Thu & Sun, to 11pm Fri & Sat) Opened in 1902 as an overnight staging post for travellers between Launceston and Devonport, the Empire retains an old-fashioned feel but has been given a modest spruce-up in recent years and now has pleasant public spaces and a welcoming atmosphere. The popular Cycles (lunch mains $7-25, dinner $18-38; ◷11.30am-3pm Tue-Sun, 6-9pm daily) cafe-restaurant is attached.

Shopping

★**Deloraine Creative Studios** ARTS & CRAFTS
(☑03-6362 4455; www.delorainecreativestudios.com; 59-61 Emu Bay Rd; ◷10am-4pm) The arts and crafts being produced in this artist-operated studio space are a cut above many galleries and craft shops on the island. Wander around to see artisans at work in their open studios – if you like the finished products on display, you can usually purchase them. There's woodwork, weaving, fashion, toys, jewellery, glass and furniture to admire.

ℹ Information

Great Western Tiers Visitor Information Centre (☑ 03-6362 5280; www.greatwesterntiers. net.au; 98-100 Emu Bay Rd; ⊙ 9am-5pm) Shares premises with the Deloraine Museum. Staff are helpful and can supply plenty of information about activities in the region as well as book accommodation.

ℹ Getting There & Away

Redline (☑ 1300 360 000; www.tasredline. com.au) buses run to Launceston ($14.30, one hour, three daily), Devonport ($8.50, 45 minutes, two daily) and Mole Creek ($6.50, 30 minutes, one daily).

Tassielink (p306) doesn't drop off passengers in Deloraine but it does pick up passengers en route to Cradle Mountain ($61.50, 2½ hours, at least twice weekly) and Queenstown ($74.80, 5½ hours, twice weekly). From Queenstown, there are connecting services to Strahan ($10.60, 1¼ hours).

Mole Creek

☑ 03 / POP 610

Diminutive Mole Creek, around 23km west of Deloraine, is a quiet rural town with beautiful mountain views. It's also a great base for those wanting to go bushwalking or caving in the nearby national parks. There's a good chance of seeing platypuses (rather than moles) in the town's waterways – keep an eye out just after sunrise and just before sunset.

⊙ Sights

★ Mole Creek Karst National Park   NATIONAL PARK
(☑ 03-6363 5182; www.parks.tas.gov.au; daily national parks pass per person/car $12/24) The major draws in this national park are the Marakoopa (330 Mayberry Rd, Mayberry; adult/child $19/9.50; ⊙ Underground Rivers & Glowworms Tour 10am, noon and 2pm daily, plus 4pm October to May) and the King Solomons Cave (adult/child/family $19/9.50/47.50; ⊙ tours 11.30am, 12.30pm, 2.30pm & 3.30pm daily, plus 10.30am & 4.30pm Dec-Apr). These can be visited on tours operated by the Tasmanian Parks & Wildlife Service. Other caves in the park can be visited by experienced cavers or in a guided tour operated by Wild Cave Tours (☑ 03-6367 8142; www.wildcavetours.com; half-/full-day tours $150/300). Note that visitors who purchase a ticket for a PWS caves tour do not need a national parks pass. Those exploring elsewhere in the park do.

Walls of Jerusalem National Park   NATIONAL PARK
(☑ 03-6701 2104; www.parks.tas.gov.au; via Mersey Forest Rd to Lake Rowallan; daily parks pass per person/vehicle $12/24) This isolated Central Plateau national park features glacial lakes and valleys, alpine flora and the rugged dolerite Mt Jerusalem (1459m). It's a favourite of experienced bushwalkers with a passion for challenging, remote hiking. The most popular day walk here is to the summit of Mt Jerusalem.

The park is reached from Mole Creek by taking Mersey Forest Rd to Lake Rowallan. The last 11km is on well-maintained gravel roads.

Trowunna Wildlife Park   WILDLIFE RESERVE
(☑ 03-6363 6162; www.trowunna.com.au; 1892 Mole Creek Rd; adult/child/family $26/16/75; ⊙ 9am-5pm, guided tours 11am, 1pm & 3pm) Home to Tasmanian devils, wombats, quolls, kangaroos, wallabies and pademelons, this privately owned wildlife park focuses on conservation and education and is a great stop for those headed to/from Cradle Mountain. During the informative tour you'll get to pat a wombat and see devils being fed. While there, don't miss the interactive Devil Education & Research Centre. The park is just off the highway – look for the big Tasmanian devil by the side of the road.

⌖ Tours

Tasmanian Expeditions   WALKING
(☑ 1300 666 856; www.tasmanianexpeditions.com. au) Tasmanian Expeditions conducts a four-day Walls of Jerusalem Experience ($1395), taking in the park's highlights and camping each night at a base camp near a cluster of alpine tarns known as Solomon's Jewels. It also offers a truncated three-day self-guided version ($995).

🛏 Sleeping & Eating

Mole Creek Caravan Park   CAMPGROUND $
(☑ 03-6363 1150; www.molecreek.net.au; cnr Mole Creek & Union Bridge Rds; unpowered/powered sites d $20/25, d cabin $75, extra person camping/cabin $3/10; 🖥) This thin sliver of grassy park is about 4km west of town beside Sassafras Stream, at the turn-off to the caves and Cradle Mountain. There are level sites, a basic camp kitchen and amenities block (hot showers $0.60) and firewood is supplied for the open fireplaces. Platypus are regularly

spotted in the stream and chooks roam free around the camp sites.

Mole Creek Guest House   B&B $$
(☑ 03-6363 1399; www.molecreekguesthouse.com.au; 100 Pioneer Dr; r $145-175, cottage/house d $205/255, extra adult/child $50/20; ☜) The owners here are justifiably proud of their spick-and-span guesthouse, which has six somewhat fussily decorated rooms above the **Pepperberry Cafe** (☑ 03-6363 1399; www.molecreekguesthouse.com.au; 100 Pioneer Dr; mains $16-20; ⊙ 9am-4pm Tue-Thu, to 8pm Fri & Sat, to 4pm Sun; ☜💂), one off the garden and a communal lounge with fireplace and kitchenette. There are also attractively presented houses sleeping five and nine for those wanting to self-cater. Breakfast is $10.

Shopping

R Stephens Apiary   FOOD
(☑ 03-6363 1170; www.leatherwoodhoney.com.au; 25 Pioneer Dr; ⊙ 9am-4pm Mon-Fri) The leatherwood honey produced by this family-owned business has been a permanent fixture in Australian pantries for nearly a century. The company harvests in the catchment area of the Franklin River and produces 35% of Tasmania's commercial honey crop. Head to its Mole Creek factory to taste and buy a jar adorned with the company's distinctive 1930s 'golden bee' labelling.

Melita Honey Farm   FOOD
(☑ 03-6363 6160; www.melitahoneyfarm.com.au; 39 Sorell St, Chudleigh; ⊙ 9am-5pm Sun-Fri Oct-Mar, 9am-5pm Sun-Thu, to 4pm Fri Apr-Sep) Get your fingers sticky while enjoying free tastings of the 50-plus different types of honey on sale at this shop in Chudleigh, 6.6km east of Mole Creek. Be sure to sample a cone of honey ice cream – the blue gum has a mild flavour and the leatherwood is stronger. Also sells honey-based skincare and other bee-related products.

ℹ Information

Mole Creek Caves Office (☑ 03-6363 5182; www.parks.tas.gov.au; Marakoopa Cave, 330 Mayberry Rd, Mayberry; ⊙ 9am-5pm) Tour tickets for Marakoopa Cave and King Solomons Cave, plus information about Tasmania's national parks and reserves, are available at this helpful office close to the Marakoopa Cave entrance.

Mole Creek Community & Information Centre
(☑ 03-6363 2030; www.molecreek.info; 48 Pioneer Dr; ⊙ 10am-4pm Mon & Thu-Sat, to 2pm Tue, 1-4pm Wed; ☜) This small community and information centre offers wi-fi and internet access on fixed computers. Staff can help with information about bushwalking in the area – particularly at the Walls of Jerusalem – and visiting the area's many caves. It also stocks a small range of tourist brochures and maps.

ℹ Getting There & Away

One daily **Redline** (☑ 1300 360 000; www.tasredline.com.au) bus service travels between Mole Creek and Deloraine ($6.50, 30 minutes), Westbury ($8.50, 45 minutes) and Launceston ($22.30, 1½ hours).

There is no public transport to Mole Creek Karst National Park. If driving, take the B12 from Mole Creek, where the turn-off for Marakoopa Cave is 4km west of the town. King Solomons Cave is 15km west of Mole Creek along the B12.

Cradle Mountain Coaches (☑ 03-6427 7626; www.cradlemountaincoaches.com.au) runs shuttles between Launceston or Devonport and Walls of Jerusalem National Park ($260 for a private shuttle or $65 per person for four or more passengers). It can also transport passengers between Walls of Jerusalem and Cradle Mountain for the same cost. The shuttles collect passengers from Launceston or Devonport airport, the *Spirit of Tasmania* terminal or their accommodation.

Gowrie Park

☑ 03 / POP 40

At the foot of Mt Roland, just 14km from Sheffield, the Gowrie Park area makes an excellent base for mountain walks or a rural retreat. There are walks to the summits of Mt Roland (1234m), Mt Vandyke (1084m) and Mt Claude (1034m) and shorter walks in the cool, shady forests of the lower slopes, such as the pleasant meander through the bush at nearby O'Neills Creek Reserve. Bird lovers take note: 94 species have been recorded in the Mt Roland area.

🏃 Activities

The sharp comb of rock that's the dramatic backdrop to the rural views here is **Mt Roland** (1234m). It looks spectacularly difficult but is achievable for confident walkers. There are two tracks – one accessed from O'Neill's Creek (10km, four hours return) and another steeper and more-difficult track from Kings Rd (6.5km, 3½ hours return). Access to both is from the northern side of the mountain. For the easier track, pass through Gowrie Park, turn right into O'Neills Rd near the sportsground and drive approximately 1km to find the car park at the start of the track. To get to the Kings Rd track, drive through the village of Claude Road, turn off at Kings Rd and head south for about 1.5km to the start of the track.

🛏 Sleeping

Gowrie Park
Wilderness Village CABIN, CARAVAN PARK $
(☑03-6491 1385; www.gowriepark.com.au; 1447 Claude Rd; unpowered/powered sites $20/28, dm $40, cabin from $110; 🛜) There are four neat but basic self-contained cabins here sleeping up to six, plus bunk rooms and caravan and camping sites. Facilities include a laundry, games room and camp kitchen with BBQs. Tracks lead right from the grounds to nearby peaks. Wi-fi is available near the reception area only.

Silver Ridge Wilderness Retreat CABIN $$
(☑03-6491 1727; www.silverridgeretreat.com.au; 46 Rysavy Rd; 1-/2-bedroom cottage d from $200/256, extra person $25; 🛜▨) Nestled at the foot of Mt Roland, these self-contained studios and cottages have stunning mountain views. Some have spas, others wood heaters and one is accessible for guests using wheelchairs. You can soak in the heated indoor pool, fish for trout in the property's dams and take evening walks to spot wildlife including wallabies and platypus.

ℹ Getting There & Away

Tassielink (p306) operates buses to/from Launceston ($41.20, 2¼ hours) and Queenstown ($44.70, 3¾ hours), at least twice per week. Change at Queenstown for Strahan services.

Lake Barrington & Around

Created by the Mersey-Forth hydroelectric scheme in 1969, this beautiful lake edged by tall eucalypts and lush rainforest stretches for 20km and is home to the Lake Barrington International Rowing Course. There are a number of vineyards around its shore, and excellent fishing in its waters. The lake is protected as part of the Lake Barrington Nature Recreation Area.

◉ Sights

The lake's mirror-flat surface is home to international-standard water-sports competitions, with a proper rowing course. The recreation area has wood BBQs, picnic shelters and toilets, while the amazing 84m-high

Devil's Gate Dam, which holds the waters back, is engineered to be one of the most devilishly thin concrete dams in the world.

Tasmazia AMUSEMENT PARK
(☑03-6491 1934; www.tasmazia.com.au; 500 Staverton Rd, Promised Land; adult/child/family $25/12.50/70; ⊙9am-5pm Oct-Apr, 10am-4pm May-Sep) Young children love this wacky complex, on the C140 route to Cradle Mountain, which has eight mazes to get lost in (four hedge mazes and four footpath mazes) as well as a whimsical model village called Lower Crackpot and a feature called Embassy Gardens, which includes 60 model buildings representing over 40 countries around the globe.

Wilmot Hills Distillery DISTILLERY
(☑03-6492 1193; www.wilmothills.com; 407 Back Rd, Wilmot; ⊙10am-5pm Thu-Tue) On the western side of Lake Barrington, just north of the village of Wilmot, is this boutique distillery producing apple brandy, grappa, basilico, gin and absinthe. Pop in to purchase a bottle or two from the cellar door.

🛏 Sleeping & Eating

★ Eagle's Nest Retreat LODGE $$$
(☑0429 911 517; www.eaglesnestretreat.com.au; 15 Browns Rd, West Kentish; d $450-650, extra person $100; ▨) Surely the best panoramas around Lake Barrington are to be had at Eagle's Nest Retreat, comprised of three isolated and opulent holiday houses with wall-high glass that frame incredible Mt Roland views. The houses sleep between four and six; two have outdoor spas. You'll find them standing in solitary magnificence off the C141 near West Kentish.

Barringwood Estate CAFE $
(☑03-6287 6933; www.barringwood.com.au; 60 Gillams Rd, Lower Barrington; pickers platter for 2 people $42, sandwiches $12-15, terrine $16.50; ⊙10am-5pm Thu-Mon, breakfast 8-11am Sat & Sun by arrangement) Enjoying a gourmet lunch and glass of wine on the deck or lawn of Tuckshop at Barringwood, the cafe at Barringwood Estate, is a wonderful way to while away an afternoon. There are glorious views over the Don River Valley towards Bass Strait, and tastings of the estate's pinot gris, pinot noir, riesling and schonburger.

ℹ Getting There & Away

Lake Barrington's eastern and southern shores are easily accessible from Sheffield. For the western shore, take the C132 south from the

WORTH A TRIP

THE COAST TO CANYON CIRCUIT

This rewarding driving circuit begins in Ulverstone or Penguin. From Ulverstone, drive to Penguin along the picturesque coast road, then veer south before Sulphur Creek on the B17, continuing south to Riana. From South Riana, a scenic drive brings you to the George Woodhouse Lookout, offering views over the agriculturally rich Leven Valley. More winding road leads to Wings Wildlife Park (☑03-6429 1151; www.wingswildlife.com. au; 137 Winduss Rd, Gunns Plains; adult/child $27/15, family from $80; �---10am-4pm), which is home to an eclectic collection of native and exotic animals.

Close by is Gunns Plains Cave (☑03-6429 1388; www.gunnsplainscaves.com.au; 46 Cave Rd, Gunns Plains; adult/child/family $17/7/45; �---guided tours 10am, 11am, noon, 1.30pm, 2.30pm & 3.30pm), filled with magical limestone formations and glow-worms. Guided tours involve some clambering and ladder work. Back on the B17, you can complete the circuit to Ulverstone or take the C127 and C125 to the Leven Canyon. On the C127 at Gunns Plains is Leven Valley Vineyard (☑03-6429 1140; www.levenvalleyvineyard.com.au; 321 Raymond Rd, Gunns Plains; �---11am-5pm Wed-Sun Sep-May), a boutique vineyard where you can taste its chardonnay and pinot before purchasing a bottle and some cheese and enjoying your lunch in the vineyard's garden. Signposted just off the road near the vineyard are lower and upper Preston Falls: all cascading water and primeval ferns.

Continue via Nietta to Leven Canyon. A 20-minute return walk here leads to the sensational gorge-top Cruickshanks Lookout, a sky platform peering 300m down to the Leven River below. From here, you can head back to Ulverstone on the B15, tasting and purchasing some golden-hued oil at Cradle Coast Olives (☑03-6425 3449; www. cradlecoastolives.com.au; 574 Castra Rd, Abbotsham; �---10am-4pm Sun-Fri) en route.

coast near Forth. There is no public transport to this area.

Sheffield

☑03 / POP 1540

In the 1980s Sheffield was a typical small Tasmanian country town in the doldrums of rural decline. But then some astute townsfolk came up with an idea that had been applied to the small town of Chemainus in Canada, with some surprising and wonderful results. The plan was to paint large murals on walls around town, depicting scenes from the district's pioneer days. Sheffield is now a veritable outdoor art gallery, with more than 50 large-scale murals and an annual mural-painting festival. It's a handy base for people walking around Mt Roland and splashing around in/on Lake Barrington, as well as a pit stop for drivers on Hwy 1.

◉ Sights

★ King George V Park   PARK

Hidden behind Main St's shops (access is via an asphalt path), this park has plenty of trees and lawn, a children's playground, public toilets, picnic tables, BBQs and an utterly charming mosaic walk inspired by local flora and fauna. The mosaics were created by members of the community and are much more attractive than most of the town's murals. The Sheffield Working Art Space (☑0437 795 374; www.sheffieldworking artspace.blogspot.com.au; 2 Albert St; �---10am-4pm) FREE is located at the northern edge of the park.

Seven Sheds   BREWERY

(☑03-6496 1139; www.sevensheds.com; 22 Crockers St, Railton; �---11am-3pm Wed-Sun Jun & Jul, to 5pm Wed-Sun Sep-May, closed Aug) Here brewer and beer connoisseur Willie Simpson has turned a passion for home brewing into one of Tasmania's best boutique breweries. Located in the small town of Railton, 12km northeast of Sheffield, this brewery, meadery and hop gardens offers visitors the opportunity to taste its range of Kentish ale, melomel and a fabulous dry mead. You can also tour its microbrewing operation (noon Wednesday to Sunday; advance bookings essential).

☞ Tours

Mural Audio Tours   WALKING

(☑03-6491 1179; www.sheffieldcradleinfo.com. au/sheffield-murals-audio-tour; Kentish Visitor Information Centre, 5 Pioneer Cres; $5; �---9am-5pm Mon-Fri, 10am-4pm Sat & Sun) Grab a headset from the visitor information centre and take an informative audio tour of Sheffield's outdoor art. The tour takes about 1½ hours (though you can keep the headset all day) and guides you past about 20 of the town's murals. It also leads you through the Sheffield Working Art Space, where you can see local artists at work.

✤ Festivals & Events

Muralfest   ART
(www.muralfest.com.au; ⊙ late Mar–early Apr) This celebration of outdoor art is held each year. It's a massive public paint-off in Mural Park – a theme is set and nine artists compete for a generous cash prize, with the resulting nine murals added to the park for a year. Book accommodation well ahead.

⊨ Sleeping & Eating

Acacia B&B   B&B $$
(⊉ 0413 149 691, 0437 911 502; www.acacia-bandb. com.au; cnr High & Tarleton Sts; tw $130, d & f $140-190; ☞) Ann and Nigel Beeke are justifiably proud of their quiet and meticulously maintained B&B. There are four rooms on offer (the king room with its four-poster bed is the best). The family room has an en-suite bathroom and the others have dedicated bathrooms in other parts of the house. A generous continental breakfast is served.

Kentish Hills Retreat   MOTEL $$
(⊉ 03-6491 2484; www.kentishhills.com.au; 2 West Nook Rd; d/apt from $135/155, extra person $20; ✳@) In a quiet location just west of town, Kentish Hills has a range of accommodation, including double rooms, a spa suite and an apartment sleeping up to six. Rooms are simple but comfortable, and facilities include a BBQ area and a guest laundry. The friendly alpacas that live on-site can be fed by hand.

Apple Tree Cafe   CAFE $
(⊉ 03-6491 1665; www.facebook.com/theapple treesheffield; 43 Main St; scone $3, mains $9-17; ⊙ 8am-5pm Tue-Sat) Aficionados of Devonshire teas will appreciate the Apple Tree Cafe's version, which features delicious homemade berry jam. A friendly and pretty space with stained-glass windows and high ceilings, it serves cakes, soup and toasted sandwiches as well as scones.

❶ Information

Kentish Visitor Information Centre (⊉ 03-6491 1179; www.sheffieldcradleinfo.com.au; 5 Pioneer Cres; ⊙ 9am-5pm Mon-Fri, 10am-4pm Sat & Sun) Sheffield's helpful tourism information centre supplies information on Sheffield,

Latrobe and the greater Kentish region. It also provides maps and can make accommodation and tour bookings.

❶ Getting There & Away

Tassielink (p306) buses stop directly outside the visitor information centre. Services to/from Sheffield include Launceston ($31.20, 2¼ hours), Devonport ($5.60, 50 minutes), Cradle Mountain ($27.60, one hour) and Queenstown ($49.70, 3¾ hours). Change at Queenstown for Strahan.

Ulverstone

📵 03 / POP 14,110

Arranged around the mouth of the Leven River, Ulverstone has a resolutely old-fashioned rural-town feel: you could be forgiven for thinking you've stepped back in time 30 years or so. There are few compelling reasons to spend time in the town itself, but it's a good base for exploring beautiful Leven Valley and the spectacular Leven Canyon.

⊙ Sights

Ulverstone History Museum   MUSEUM
(⊉ 03-6425 3835; www.centralcoasttas.com.au/ ulverstone-history-museum; 48 Main St; adult/child/family $5/2/12; ⊙ 1.30-4.30pm Mon-Sat) Children will love this museum's artefact-rich displays of 19th-century shops and businesses, including a photographer's studio, general store, newspaper office, dairy and blacksmith's forge. There's also a trainmaster's hut and old beach shack in the car park.

☞ Tours

Leven River Cruises   CRUISE
(⊉ 0400 130 258; www.levenrivercruises.com. au; off Tasma Pde; adult/child from $50/25) Spot the endangered azure kingfisher, sea eagles and other local bird species from the deck of one of this company's boats as you cruise up the Leven River. There are four cruises to choose from, with the most popular being the one- and two-hour cruises. All leave from the public pontoon on Tasma Pde; bookings are essential.

⊨ Sleeping & Eating

★ **Boscobel of Tasmania**   B&B $$
(⊉ 0408 474 095; www.boscobeloftasmania.com. au; 27 South Rd, West Ulverstone; r $160-180; ☞) There are four upstairs guest rooms in this handsome, renovated 1885 mansion, all with period-style furniture, comfortable beds and modern bathroom with underfloor heating.

Downstairs, there's a grand dining room where a full breakfast is served, a communal lounge with an open fire and a conservatory overlooking the expansive garden.

Beachway Motel MOTEL $$
(🖉 03-6425 2342; www.beachwayulverstone.com.au; 1 Heathcote St; r $110-130, self-contained apt $230; ❄ 🛜 ⊛) An exemplar of 1960s motel style that has been gently nudged into the 21st century, this place is notable for its keen prices and on-site facilities (laundry, pool, BBQ area). There's also a bar and restaurant (mains $22 to $38). Rooms are set around a large grassed area and have parking at their doors. All are clean and well sized.

★ **Thirty Three Cups** CAFE
(🖉 03-6425 1626; www.facebook.com/thirtythreecups; 27 King Edward St; mains breakfast $17-22, lunch $20-24; ⊙8.30am-4pm Mon-Fri, to 3pm Sat) Towns on Tasmania's northwest coast are known for their cafe culture, and there are plenty of stylish examples where you can enjoy great food and a well-made latte. This is one of the best of that breed, offering excellent coffee made with Ritual beans, huge and super-tasty breakfasts (zucchini fritters, almond-milk porridge, garlic-and-thyme mushrooms) and similarly impressive lunch dishes.

🛍 Shopping

★ **Cradle Coast Farmers' Market** MARKET
(www.cradlecoastfarmersmarket.weebly.com; 3 Wharf Rd; ⊙8.30am-12.30pm Sun) Held every Sunday morning in the Wharf precinct. Stalls include Manu bread, Mount Gnomon pork, Red Cow Dairies cheese, Braefield lamb, Cradle Coast olives and Henry's Ginger Beer.

OFF THE BEATEN TRACK

PENGUIN CRADLE TRAIL

One of Tasmania's most rewarding multiday walks takes you from Penguin down to Cradle Mountain. The 80km **Penguin Cradle Trail** crosses the Dial Range, and takes in Leven Canyon and Black Bluff en route to Cradle Mountain. Note that many of the walking tracks on this trail were significantly damaged during floods in mid-2016 – see the website of the **North West Walking Club** (NWWC; 🖉03-6423 2844; www.nwwc.org.au; membership from $5) for updates. The website also has a route description and map.

❶ Information

Ulverstone Visitor Information Centre (🖉 03-6425 2839; www.coasttocanyon.com.au; 13-15 Alexandra Rd; ⊙9am-5pm Oct-Apr, 9am-5pm Mon-Fri, 10am-4pm Sat & Sun May-Sep; 🛜) This centre has helpful volunteer staff and offers loads of brochures.

❶ Getting There & Away

Redline (🖉1300 360 000; www.tasredline.com.au) buses arrive at and depart from Alexandra Rd, near the War Memorial clock. Daily departures include Burnie ($8.50, 35 minutes) and Devonport ($6.50, 25 minutes).

Metro (🖉13 22 01; www.metrotas.com.au) operates services to/from Latrobe ($6.40, 30 minutes), Penguin ($6.40, 20 minutes) and Burnie ($8.30, 55 minutes). Buses stop at the interchange on King Edward St, near Reibey St.

Penguin

🖉 03 / POP 3850

A large example of Australia's strange obsession with 'big' things stands between the main beach and shopping strip of this pretty town on Tasmania's north coast. The 3m-high penguin signals the fact that this part of the coast is where the world's smallest penguin (*Eudyptula minor*) comes ashore during its breeding season. Many people head here to see these cute critters in the flesh (in the feather?), but the vibrant cafe culture and safe, sandy beach in the town centre are even greater attractions.

◉ Sights

Penguin Market MARKET
(🖉0400 903 031; www.facebook.com/penguinmarket; 11 Arnold St; ⊙9am-3pm Sun) The popular undercover Penguin Market takes place every Sunday. Stalls sell fresh local produce, art and crafts, vintage clothing, gifts and homewares. There is also a licensed food court.

🛏 Sleeping

Happy Backpacker HOSTEL $
(Neptune Grand Hotel; 🖉03-6437 2406; www.thehappybackpacker.com.au; 84 Main Rd; dm/d without bathroom from $28/47; 🛜) This art-deco pub opposite the beach is begging for a boutique makeover, but at the moment backpackers can take advantage of its great location and bargain prices. Dorms have bunk beds (small lockers in the passageway), the cramped and musty doubles have

basins, shared bathrooms are clean and there's an excellent communal kitchen as well as a lounge with TV.

★ Penguin Beachfront Apartments   APARTMENT $$

(☏ 0411 278 473; www.penguinbeachfront.com; 52 Main Rd; d apt $170-190, extra person $30; ❋ 🐾 🐕) Penguin is high on the holiday wish list for families, and these five apartments are perfect choices for those travelling with children as they are located opposite the beach, sleep between four and six, and have excellent kitchens as well as laundry facilities. Couples like them too – especially the two downstairs apartments with their huge lounge areas and beachfront terraces.

★ The Madsen   BOUTIQUE HOTEL $$$

(☏ 03-6437 2588; www.themadsen.com; 64 Main Rd; d $165-220, penthouse d $300, extra adult/child $40/20; 🐕) Housed in a grand former bank building on the beachfront, this friendly and well-managed boutique hotel offers six well-sized rooms with comfortable beds. All are decorated tastefully – the luxurious penthouse and beachfront spa suites are the most impressive. A cooked breakfast is served in the downstairs lounge, which has an honour bar and tea-and-coffee station, or in your room.

Note that at the time of research the Madsen's owners were planning to open a new hotel called the Annexe on King Edward St. This will have a hot tub and wonderful views over the water. Contact the Madsen for details.

✖ Eating

★ Letterbox   CAFE $

(☏ 0498 502 716; www.facebook.com/letterbox cafe; 80a Main Rd; mains $6-20; ⏰ 8am-2pm Sat-Mon, to 3pm Tue-Fri) The sleek and ultra-stylish Victoria Arduino espresso machine at this cute cafe in the post office building is put to good use producing coffees to accompany delicious breakfast dishes (smoked salmon bagels, house-made granola, eggs Benedict) and equally alluring light lunches (frittata, quiche, cheese platters). Sit inside or at one of the streetside tables.

★ Jo & Co Cafe   CAFE $$

(☏ 03-6437 2101; www.facebook.com/joandco cafe; 74 Main Rd; mains $14-20; ⏰ 8am-3.30pm Sat-Wed, 8.30am-8.30pm Thu, 8am-8.30pm Fri; 🐕 🐾) Directly opposite the Big Penguin, this ultra-friendly cafe has a retro decor, quirky vibe and tasty menu that caters to vegetar-

---

WHERE ARE THE PENGUINS?

True to its name, Penguin is a base for the little (or fairy) penguins that nightly come ashore along this stretch of coast from mid-September or October to March or April. There are three places to see them. **Lalico Beach**, 22km east of Penguin, is where the largest breeding colony arrives around sunset. There's a viewing platform and, on most nights in season, there's a park ranger in residence to answer any questions. Contact Penguin's **Visitor Information Centre** for more details. A smaller colony comes ashore at **Sulphur Creek**, 4km west of Penguin, and at **West Beach** in Burnie, behind the Makers' Workshop (19km west of Penguin).

---

ians, vegans and those who are gluten-free. It's a winning combination. Breakfast involves everything from smashed avocado to the full cooked production, lunch focuses on burgers and salad, and the Friday night dinners are themed by cuisine or food style.

ℹ Information

Penguin Visitor Information Centre (☏ 03-6437 1421; www.coasttocanyon.com.au; 78 Main Rd; ⏰ 9am-4pm Oct-May, 9.30am-3.30pm Jun-Sep) Staffed by volunteers, the friendly Penguin visitor centre can supply brochures and advice about visiting nearby attractions. There are public toilets next door.

ℹ Getting There & Away

Regular **Metro** (☏ 13 22 01; www.metrotas.com. au) services travel to/from Ulverstone ($6.40, 20 minutes) and Burnie ($6.40, 30 minutes) on their route between Latrobe and Burnie. **Redline** (☏ 1300 360 000; www.tasredline. au.com) buses go to Burnie ($6.50, 20 minutes) and Devonport ($8.50, 40 minutes) twice daily.

All buses stop at Johnsons Beach, opposite the Penguin Caravan Park.

Burnie

☏ 03 / POP 18,900

Long dismissed as the island's ugly-duckling city, once-industrial Burnie is trying hard to reinvent itself as a 'City of Makers', referring both to its heavy manufacturing past and its present creative flair. The things being made here these days include paper, cheese and whisky – an unusual but interesting mix.

Most visitors are here for business, but its regional museum and penguin centre are well worth a visit if you're on the north coast.

Sights

⭐ Burnie Regional Museum
MUSEUM

(Pioneer Village Museum; ☑03-6430 5746; www.burnieregionalmuseum.net; Little Alexander St; adult/child $8/5; ⊙10am-4.30pm Mon-Fri, 1.30-4pm Sat & Sun) The centrepiece of this absorbing museum is a lovingly crafted recreation of a 1900 Burnie streetscape – including blacksmith's forge and farriers shop, wash house, general store, post and telegraph office, stagecoach depot, inn, dentist's surgery, newspaper office and bootmaker. Each is based on an actual business that once existed in Burnie, incorporates multimedia elements and features excellent interpretative panels. Interesting temporary exhibitions are shown in an adjoining room.

Fern Glade
NATURE RESERVE

(Fern Glade Rd) FREE Fern Glade is renowned as a top spot for platypus spotting at dawn and dusk. It's east of the city centre: turn off the Bass Hwy on to Old Surrey Rd (C112) then take Fern Glade Rd to the left (east).

Makers' Workshop
MUSEUM

(☑03-6430 5831; www.discoverburnie.net/what-to-see/makers-workshop.html; 2 Bass Hwy; ⊙9am-5pm) FREE Part museum, part arts centre, this dramatic structure dominates the western end of Burnie's main beach and is a good place to get acquainted with this city's creative heart. The life-size paper people in odd corners of the workshop's cavernous contemporary interior are the work of Creative Paper (tours adult/child/family $15/8/40; ⊙tours 10am-3.45pm), Burnie's handmade-paper producers. Its tours take you through the production process of making paper from such unusual raw materials as kangaroo poo, apple pulp and rainforest leaves.

Hellyers Road Distillery
DISTILLERY

(☑03-6433 0439; www.hellyersroaddistillery.com.au; 153 Old Surrey Rd; tours per person $19.50; ⊙10am-4.30pm) Henry Hellyer was the first white settler in Emu Bay, and this respected distillery does his memory proud. You can tour the distillery to see how its golden single malt is made. Tours depart at 10.30am, 11.30am, 2pm and 3pm daily.

To get here from the city centre or Bass Hwy, head south up Mount St (B18), following signs for Upper Burnie and Queenstown.

Then turn left onto Old Surrey Rd (C112) towards Wivenhoe and follow signs to the distillery.

Burnie Regional Fine Art Gallery
GALLERY

(☑03-6431 5875; www.burniearts.net; Burnie Arts & Function Centre, 77-79 Wilmot St; ⊙10am-4.30pm Mon-Fri, 1.30-4.30pm Sat & Sun) FREE This art gallery stages exhibitions of contemporary Tasmanian artworks, especially those created by artists based in the region.

Activities

Burnie has some impressive civic and domestic architecture that you can view on two Federation walking trails. The city is also renowned for its art-deco buildings, which you can see on the Burnie Art Deco Trail. The visitor information centre (p218) has trail maps, or check out the art-deco map (and podcasts) on www.artdecotasmania.com.au.

⭐ Little Penguin Observation Centre
BIRDWATCHING

(☑0437 436 803; www.discoverburnie.net/what-to-see/penguins.html; off Bass Hwy, West Beach; ⊙dusk Sep-Mar) FREE A boardwalk on the foreshore leads from Burnie Beach to this centre, skirting the Makers' Workshop along the way. From October to March you can take a free Penguin Interpretation Tour about one hour after dusk when the penguins emerge from the sea and waddle back to their burrows. Volunteer wildlife guides are present to talk about the penguins and their habits. Wear dark clothing.

Festivals & Events

Burnie Shines
CULTURAL

(www.burnieshines.com; ⊙Oct) Local community festival featuring music, visual art, open gardens, food events and children's activities.

Sleeping

⭐ Ikon Hotel
BOUTIQUE HOTEL $$

(☑03-6432 4566; www.ikonhotel.com.au; 22 Mount St; d incl breakfast $185-260; ❋ ⎘) Boutique hotel chic comes to Burnie at this centrally located hotel. Located on the 1st floor of a heritage hotel in the city centre, it offers extremely spacious and stylish suites with compact kitchenettes and sleek bathrooms. Breakfast provisions are modest.

Jones on Wilson
B&B $$

(☑0408 555 360; www.jonesonwilson.com.au; 154 Wilson St; d from $140, extra adult/child $40/20; ⎘) There are three options on offer here: a suite decorated with Marilyn Monroe mem-

Burnie

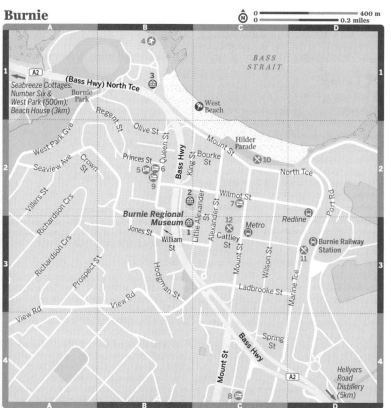

Burnie

orabilia, a self-contained studio featuring attractive landscape photographs and a three-bedroom air-conditioned house. A continental breakfast is included in the price.

Duck House　　　　　　　COTTAGE **$$**
(☎03-6431 1712; www.duckhousecottage.com.au; 26 Queen St; s/d $120/160, extra adult/child $40/20, all incl breakfast; ☎☒) Named after Salvation Army stalwarts Bill and Winifred Duck, who lived here for 30 years, this charming little self-contained two-bedroom cottage sleeps up to five. The decoration, predictably, has an emphasis on ducks. A three-bedroom property next door, **Mrs Philpott's** (28 Queen St; s/d $120/160, extra

adult/child $40/20, all incl breakfast; 🛜 🐾), sleeps up to seven and a third house, **Amelia's** (1 Princes St; s/d $120/160, extra adult/child $40/20, all incl breakfast; 🛜 🐾), has three bedrooms and is located nearby.

✖ Eating

★ The Chapel   CAFE **$**
(📞03-6432 3460; www.chapelcafe.com.au; 50 Cattley St; mains $7-18; ⊗7.30am-3pm Mon-Thu, 7.30am-3pm & 7-10pm Fri, 8am-3pm Sat) This hipsterish cafe is housed in a handsome decommissioned chapel and the quality of the food certainly matches the surrounds. The best cafe in Burnie (and probably the best on the north coast), it serves excellent house-roasted coffee, house-made chai and simply sensational toasted sandwiches made with freshly baked bread.

★ Fish Frenzy   SEAFOOD **$$**
(📞03-6432 1111; www.fishfrenzyburnie.com.au; 2 North Tce; mains $13-27; ⊗8am-9pm; 🚻) This fish and chippery breadcrumbs its super-fresh fish or dowses it in a tempura batter before frying, ensuring that its creations are a cut above the competition. A modern and bustling place right on the water, it also serves oysters and lavish seafood platters ($75 for two persons).

Food + Brew   CAFE **$$**
(📞03-6431 9225; www.foodbrewburnie.com; 1 Cattley St; breakfast mains $8-20, lunch $11-25, dinner $21-38; ⊗7.30am-3pm Mon-Wed, to late Thu & Fri, 8.30am-late Sat & Sun) Worthy of an honourable mention in the list of best cafes on the north coast, this cafe down near the old train station specialises in tasty meals made with fresh local produce and well-made coffee. There's also a good range of spirits and Tasmanian wines.

Bayviews   MODERN AUSTRALIAN **$$$**
(📞03-6431 7999; www.bayviewsrestaurant.com.au; 1st fl, 2 North Tce; lunch mains $20-22, dinner $35-46; ⊗5pm-late Mon-Wed, noon-late Thu & Fri) An upmarket establishment right on the beach, Bayviews serves a limited menu of dishes featuring produce including local free-range pork, the region's amazing grass-fed beef and terrific seafood. You can also order bar snacks or antipasto/seafood/cheese platters in the lounge bar.

🛈 Information

Visitor Information Centre (📞03-6430 5831; www.discoverburnie.net; 2 Bass Hwy; ⊗9am-

5pm) A desk in the foyer of the Makers' Workshop, this volunteer-staffed information centre can provide advice, brochures and a city map.

🛈 Getting There & Away

AIR
Burnie Airport (📞03-6442 1133; www.burnieairport.com.au; 3 Airport St, Wynyard), known as either Burnie or Wynyard airport, is located in Wynyard, 20km northwest of Burnie. Regular flights travel to/from Melbourne (75 minutes) with **Regional Express Airlines** (REX; 📞13 17 13; www.regionalexpress.com.au), and to/from King Island (40 minutes) with **Sharp Airlines** (📞1300 556 694; www.sharpairlines.com).

BOAT
Burnie (somewhat surprisingly) is on the international cruise-ship circuit, with enormous liners regularly docking in the city's deep-water port: see www.burnie.net/burnie/cruise-ship-visits.

BUS
Redline (📞1300 360 000; www.tasredline.com.au) buses stop on Wilmot St, opposite the Metro Cinemas. Useful destinations include Devonport ($11.20, one hour, two daily), Launceston ($39.30, 2½ hours, two daily) and Smithton ($24, 1½ hours, one daily).

Regular suburban **Metro** (📞13 22 01; www.metrotas.com.au) buses travel to/from Penguin ($6.40, 30 minutes), Ulverstone ($8.30, 55 minutes) and Wynyard ($6.40, 30 minutes), departing from the bus interchange on Cattley St, beside the Harris Scarfe department store.

🛈 Getting Around

Burnie/Wynyard Taxi (📞03-6431 2199) meets all flights arriving at **Burnie Airport**. It costs around $45 to get from the airport to Burnie's town centre; the trip usually takes 20 minutes.

Local **Metro** buses stop in Dodgin St, 300m from the airport terminal, on their route between Wynyard and Burnie's town centre. A ticket into Burnie costs $6.40.

Wynyard & Around

📞03 / POP 5990

Clustered around the wooded banks of the sinuous Inglis River, laid-back Wynyard is a smallish town that's a service centre for surrounding agricultural properties. Sheltered from wild westerly weather by prominent Table Cape and Fossil Bluff, it has a friendly vibe and some excellent eating and sleeping options. On its doorstep are unpeopled beaches, wind-blasted lighthouses and an amazing spring display of tulips sprouting from the rich red soils of Table Cape.

◉ Sights

Table Cape   LANDMARK
(via Table Cape Rd) The stunning flat-topped promontory known as Table Cape was named by Matthew Flinders in 1798 during his circumnavigation of the island with George Bass. An extinct volcano, it is now protected as the Table Cape State Reserve. To get here, take the minor road (C234) northwest out of Wynyard and drive to the lookout and lighthouse (☑0499 919 993; www.tasmaniasnorthwest.com.au/attraction/table-cape-lighthouse-tours; Lighthouse Rd; adult/child/family $10/5/25; ⊘11am-3pm Oct-May, by appointment Jun-Sep). Stunning views out to Bass Strait are available from both vantage points.

Fossil Bluff   LANDMARK
(off Golf Links Rd) Created by an ancient tidewater glacier, 275-million-year-old Fossil Bluff is rich in fossils, including the remains of prehistoric whales and the oldest marsupial fossil found in Australia. The species was named *Wynyardia bassiana* in honour of the town. At low tide, it's possible to walk around the base of the bluff and fossick for fossils. You'll find the bluff 3km north of the town centre.

Table Cape Tulip Farm   FARM
(☑03-6442 2012; www.tablecapetulipfarm.com.au; 363 Table Cape Rd; adult/child $12/free; ⊘9am-4.30pm late-Sep–Oct) The volcanic, chocolate-red soils of the cape are extraordinarily fertile, so it's a perfect spot to grow tulips. In October, when the bulbs flower, there's a mesmerising array of colours to marvel at and a canteen serving Devonshire teas. At other times of the year it's possible to buy bulbs in the farm's shop – call ahead.

Ransley Veteran Ford Collection   MUSEUM
(☑03-6443 8330; www.wondersofwynyard.com; 8 Exhibition Link; adult/child $8/free; ⊘9am-5pm Oct-Apr, 10am-4pm May-Jul, 9am-5pm Mon-Fri, 10am-4pm Sat & Sun Aug-Sep) Owned and meticulously restored by a Wynyard local, this extraordinary collection of 17 vintage Ford cars and motorbikes is the pride of the town, and rightfully so. The showpiece is a 1903 Model A Ford, which was the 31st off the factory line and is now the second oldest in existence. Enter through the Wynyard Visitor Information Centre.

✸ Festivals & Events

Bloomin' Tulips Festival   FAIR
(www.bloomintulips.com.au; ⊘Oct) One-day event celebrating the tulip harvest in October.

🛏 Sleeping & Eating

★ **Beach Retreat**
Tourist Park   CARAVAN PARK $
(☑03-6442 1998; www.beachretreattouristpark.com.au; 30b Old Bass Hwy; powered sites d $33, cabins & units from $125) This must be one of the prettiest and friendliest caravan parks in Australia. Located right by the beach, its grounds are meticulously manicured and pleasingly green. There are neat cabins, camp sites, an excellent fully equipped camp kitchen, a laundry and good amenities blocks. It's so good, we'll even forgive the lack of wi-fi.

Waterfront Wynyard   MOTEL $$
(☑03-6442 2351; www.waterfrontwynyard.com; 1 Goldie St; motel r $120-150, pod from $250; ❄🛜🐾) As its name implies, this motel is slap bang on the water. It offers clean and neat motel rooms (some with air-con and recently renovated bathrooms) and two absolutely sensational 'Coastal Pod' suites constructed from shipping containers. Each of these has a deck overlooking the river, large kitchen, lounge and dining area, two bedrooms, laundry facilities and air-con.

Wynyard Seafoods   FISH & CHIPS $
(☑03-6442 1596; www.facebook.com/wynyardseafoodsonthewharf; Wynyard Wharf, 3 Goldie St; fish & chips $10-18; ⊘10.30am-7pm Mon-Fri, to 7.30pm Sat & Sun) There's only one place to truly enjoy fish and chips, and that's outside. Head to this takeaway shop on the Wynyard Wharf, order your fried morsels of choice and eat them at one of the river-facing picnic tables.

★ **Splash Café**   CAFE $$
(☑03-6442 5333; www.splashcafetasmania.com; 30a Old Bass Hwy; mains $8-18; ⊘9am-4pm; 🛜) Well, here's an unexpected treat. Located at the entrance to the tourist park on the eastern edge of town, Splash serves delicious food and excellent coffee. How do housemade bagels or eggs Benedict sound for breakfast? Sit indoors or outdoors but don't expect swift service.

ℹ Information

Wynyard Visitor Information Centre (☑03-6443 8330; www.wondersofwynyard.com/visitor-information; 8 Exhibition Link; ⊘9am-5pm

Oct-Apr, 10am-4pm May-Jul, 9am-5pm Mon-Fri, 10am-4pm Sat & Sun Aug-Sep; 🛜) An extremely helpful information office offering maps, brochures, advice, clean toilets and free wi-fi. Ask here for the brochures *Wynyard Heritage Walk* and *Scenic Walks of Wynyard and the Surrounding Districts* if you're keen to explore on foot.

ℹ️ Getting There & Away

AIR

The Burnie Airport (p218), oddly, is just one block from Wynyard's main street. Regional Express (p218) connects Wynyard to Melbourne (75 minutes), while Sharp Airlines (p218) has regular flights to/from King Island (40 minutes).

BUS

Metro (☑ 13 22 01; www.metrotas.com.au) buses to/from Burnie to Wynyard ($6.40, 30 minutes) stop on Jackson St.

Boat Harbour Beach & Around

☑ 03 / POP 430

This may well be paradise. Picture-perfect Boat Harbour Beach has the kind of pristine white sand and sapphire-blue waters that make you feel like you've taken a wrong turn off the Bass Hwy and ended up somewhere in the Caribbean. The usually calm seas are patrolled in summer and perfect for kids, and one of the north coast's best casual eateries is located in the surf lifesaving club. The beach is 4.5km west of the small settlement of Boat Harbour, off the Bass Hwy.

🛏️ Sleeping & Eating

Tidal Whispers   RENTAL HOUSE **$$$**

(☑ 0458 591 777; www.tidalwhispers.com; 268 Port Rd; d/tr/q $230/260/290; 🛜) Right on the water, this beach house can sleep up to four in two bedrooms (one queen and single bunks). It includes two decks with panoramic sea views, a fully equipped kitchen and a laundry with washer and drier.

Paradise House   RENTAL HOUSE **$$$**

(☑ 03-6445 1390, 0408 451 710; www.paradise-house.com.au; 263 Port Rd; 1-6 people from $290; ❄️🛜) This beach house offers top-notch accommodation for up to six guests in three bedrooms (one with en suite), and has a large open-plan living area with internet-enabled TV. Use of bikes, fishing gear, surfboards, boogie boards and all manner of beach gear comes free.

Illume Restaurant   CAFE **$$**

(☑ 0458 775 889, 03-6445 1400; Surf Lifesaving Club, 17254 Bass Hwy; lunch mains $19-34, dinner $25-48; ⏱️ 11am-10pm Wed & Thu, to 11pm Fri & Sat, to 8pm Sun) Head to this licensed beachfront cafe to enjoy blissfully balmy breezes on the beachside deck or shelter from less-benign winds at a table inside the surf lifesaving club building. The menu is simple (fish and chips, oysters, pizzas, steaks) but is exceptionally well cooked and very tasty. There's a children's playground nearby.

ℹ️ Getting There & Away

Daily Redline (p218) buses from Burnie ($10.50, 30 minutes) and Wynyard ($6.10, 10 minutes) drop passengers at Boat Harbour Store, which is an unfortunate 4km trudge from the beach.

If driving from Wynyard, the best route is to follow the C234 northwest – there are some wonderful views of the cliffs and rocky coast.

Stanley

☑ 03 / POP 490

Stanley is little more than a scatter of brightly painted heritage cottages sheltering in the lee of an ancient volcano, the Nut (also known as Circular Head). But it sure is atmospheric: fishing boats piled high with cray pots and orange buoys bob in the harbour, locals chat on door stoops and the blast of the Roaring Forties ensures that the air is exhilaratingly clear. With a couple of top-drawer tourist attractions (Highfield and the Nut), an array of excellent accommodation options and a few good eateries, it's an understandably popular place to while away a day or two.

👁️ Sights

⭐**Highfield Historic Site**   HISTORIC BUILDING

(☑ 03-6458 1100; www.parks.tas.gov.au; 143 Green Hills Rd; adult/child/family $12/6/30; ⏱️ 9.30am-4.30pm daily Sep-May, Mon-Fri Jun-Aug) Built in 1835 for the chief agent of the Van Diemen's Land Company, this homestead 2km north of town is an exceptional example of domestic architecture of the Regency period in Tasmania. Managed by the Parks & Wildlife Service, it can be visited on a self-guided tour that covers the house, pretty garden and outbuildings including stables, grain stores, workers' cottages and the chapel.

The Nut   LANDMARK

(off Browns Rd) FREE Known to the area's Indigenous people as Monatteh and labelled

'Circular Head' by Matthew Flinders, this striking 143m-high, 12-million-year-old core of an extinct volcano can be seen for many kilometres around Stanley. To get to the summit it's a steep 20-minute climb or a ride on the chairlift (☑03-6458 1482; www.thenutchairlift.com.au; Browns Rd; adult one-way/return $10/16, child $5/10, family $30/45; ⊙9.30am-5.30pm Sep-May). The best lookout is a five-minute walk to the south of the chairlift. When at the top you can take a 2km walk (about 35 minutes) on a dedicated path.

Rocky Cape National Park
NATIONAL PARK

(www.parks.tas.gov.au; day pass per vehicle/person $24/12) Tasmania's smallest national park stretches 12km along Bass Strait's shoreline. Known in local Aboriginal dialect as pin-matik, it has great significance to the local Indigenous people, who made their homes in the sea caves here 8000 years before European occupation. Inland the park is made up of coastal heathland and rare *Banksia serrata* forests. On Rocky Cape itself, you can drive out to a squat lighthouse and enjoy fine Bass Strait views. Parks passes are available at the Sisters Beach General Store.

Information about the park can be supplied over the phone by the Stanley Field Centre Office (☑03-6458 1480).

Stanley Discovery Museum
MUSEUM

(☑03-6458 2091; www.facebook.com/stanleydiscoverymuseum; 37 Church St; adult/child $3/0.50; ⊙11am-3pm Sep-May) Housed in a small hall next to the 1880s St Paul's Anglican Church, Stanley's local history museum has a collection of historic photographs as well as exhibits on marine history. Its main focus is family history (research assistance $10).

Lyons Cottage Historic Site
HISTORIC SITE

(☑0408 063 571; www.parks.tas.gov.au; 14 Alexander Tce; admission by donation; ⊙11am-3pm) This modest cottage was the birthplace of Prime Minister Joseph Lyons (1879–1939).

🏃 Activities

Under the Nut – Stanley Heritage Walk, available from the visitor information centre (p223), takes in 15 of Stanley's more beautiful and/or interesting historic buildings; the booklet contains detailed notes on each. The map is also available at www.stanleyheritagewalk.com.au.

Stanley Seal Cruises
BOATING

(☑03-6458 1294; www.stanleysealcruises.com.au; Fisherman's Dock, Wharf Rd; adult/child $55/18; ⊙Sep–mid-Jul) These excellent 75-minute cruises on the MC *Sylvia C* take passengers to see up to 500 Australian fur seals sunning themselves on Bull Rock on the Bass Strait coast. Departures are at 10am and 3pm from September to April, and at 1pm from May to mid-July, sea conditions permitting – book ahead to make sure they're running.

🛏 Sleeping

Stanley Cabin & Tourist Park
CARAVAN PARK $

(☑03-6458 1266, 1800 444 818; www.stanleycabinpark.com.au; 23a Wharf Rd; powered/unpowered sites per 2 people $33/25, dm $26, cabins d $90-180; 🐾) Commanding expansive views of Sawyer Bay in one direction and the Nut in the other, this park offers waterfront camp sites, a camp kitchen and laundry, a games room with ping-pong, neat but basic self-contained cabins, a backpackers lodge and a lounge with TV and communal kitchen. Linen is supplied, but it's BYO towels.

★ Cable Station Accommodation
B&B $$

(☑03-6458 1312, 0405 819 728; www.cablestationstanley.com.au; 435 Green Hills Rd; d $165, tr $185; 🐾🍽) Perched on a windswept plateau close to Perkin's Bay, this 1930s building was constructed as a telecommunications centre that would carry Tasmania's first telephone link to the mainland. It now houses two delightful guest units sleeping two or three; each has a TV and large modern bathroom. The helpful managers supply breakfast provisions including freshly baked bread and homemade jams.

The Ark
BOUTIQUE HOTEL $$

(☑0421 695 224; www.thearkstanley.com.au; 18 Wharf Rd; d/ste from $180/240; ❄🍽) Polished wooden floors, wrought-iron furnishings, luxury linens, espresso machines, goose-down duvets...the five individually styled rooms here take the concept of attention to detail to a whole new level. Water views are to be had from four of the rooms and the service is discreet but attentive. The owners have recently opened a second B&B, Noah's (3 Victoria St; d from $160; ❄🍽), near the Stanley Pub.

Stanley Seaview Inn
MOTEL $$

(☑03-6458 1300; www.stanleyseaviewinn.com.au; 58 Dovecote Rd; d $125-180, f $180, 2-bed apt $195, ste $220, extra person $30; 🐾) This welcoming option has a selection of motel rooms and self-contained accommodation with million-dollar views of the Nut, harbour and township. Rooms are modern, clean

Stanley

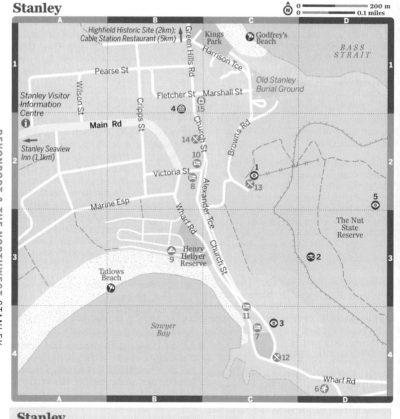

Stanley

⊚ Sights
1 Chairlift	C2
2 Lookout	D3
3 Lyons Cottage I listoric Site	C4
4 Stanley Discovery Museum	B1
5 The Nut	D2

⊕ Activities, Courses & Tours
6 Stanley Seal Cruises	D4

🛏 Sleeping
7 @VDL	C4
8 Noah's Luxury B&B	B2

9 Stanley Cabin & Tourist Park	B3
10 Stanley Hotel	B2
11 The Ark	C4

⊗ Eating
12 Hursey Seafoods	C4
13 Nut Café	C2
Stanley Hotel	(see 10)
14 Xanders	B2

🛍 Shopping
15 Providore 24	B1

and comfortable; many of them have kitchenettes. The apartments are best. Facilities include two children's playgrounds, a guest laundry, bar and BBQ area.

Stanley Hotel   HOTEL $$
(☏ 03-6458 1161, 1800 222 397; www.stanley tasmania.com.au; 19-21 Church St; d with/without bathroom $125/85; 🛜) This historic pub has a

rabbit warren of rooms. They're clean, neat and comfortable – truly excellent pub accommodation. It also runs the six self-catering **Abbey's Cottages** (www.abbeyscottages.com. au; d incl breakfast $155-235, extra person $30; 🛜).

★ **@VDL**   BOUTIQUE HOTEL $$$
(☏ 03-6458 2032; www.atvdlstanley.com.au; 16 Wharf Rd; ste $185-250, loft $285-350; 🛜) What's

been done within the bluestone walls of this 1840s warehouse on the seafront is quite incredible. This ultra-hip boutique offering has two suites and a self-contained loft apartment. The decor and amenities are top class, featuring designer furniture, contemporary art, sleek bathrooms and coffee machines.

✗ Eating

★ Nut Café   CAFE $
(☑03-6458 1186; www.stanley.com.au/restaurants; Browns Rd; breakfast mains $9-20, lunch $10-23, 1/2 scones $6.50/8.50; ☺9.30am-3pm) Cafes at popular tourist attractions are often substandard, but that's decidedly not the case here. Stanley's best eatery by a long shot, the Nut Café serves gourmet breakfasts, delicious lunches and the best Devonshire tea on the island (and that's really saying something). Be sure to purchase some of the homemade jam to take home.

Hursey Seafoods   FISH & CHIPS $
(☑03-6458 1103; www.hurseyseafoods.com.au; 2 Alexander Tce; fish & chips $11-23; ☺restaurant noon-2.45pm & 5.45-7.45pm, takeaways 11.30am-7.30pm) Hursey's operates a fleet of nine fishing boats and is known for its catches of fish, crabs and southern rock lobster. There's a cavernous restaurant upstairs, but most locals recommend ordering takeaway from the ground-floor shop instead.

Stanley Hotel   PUB FOOD $$
(☑1800 222 397; www.stanleytasmania.com.au; 19 Church St; mains $19-49; ☺noon-2pm & 6-8pm) This pub serves good bistro fare, including year-round fresh seafood – crayfish in season – and servings the size of the Nut itself. There's a scattering of vegetarian and vegan options on the menu.

Xanders   MODERN AUSTRALIAN $$$
(☑03-6458 1222; www.xanders.com.au; 25 Church St; mains $34-48; ☺6-8pm Wed-Sun) The views from the rear windows of this fine diner on the main street are impressive, and the dining room's interior is very attractive, making it a lovely setting for a meal. The menu takes advantage of top-quality local produce (the lamb we enjoyed on our most recent visit was sublime), but the execution can be needlessly fussy. Service is polished and attentive.

🛍 Shopping

Providore 24   FOOD & DRINKS
(☑03-6458 1323; www.providore24.com.au; 24 Church St; ☺10am-5pm) Cheeses, oils, wines

and other edible goodies that Tasmania has to offer fill this classy gourmet food and homewares store at the top of the main street.

ℹ Information

Stanley Visitor Information Centre (☑03-6458 1330, 1300 138 229; www.stanley.com.au; 45 Main Rd; ☺10am-5pm; 🛜) A mine of information on Stanley and surrounding areas. Offers bicycle hire (adult/child $22/15 for three hours) and free wi-fi.

ℹ Getting There & Away

Redline (☑1300 360 000; www.tasredline.com.au) buses stop at the visitor centre en route to/from Burnie ($21.10, 75 minutes, daily) and Smithton ($6.10, 25 minutes, daily).

Smithton & Around
☑03 / POP 3940

When in Smithton, take deep lungfuls of the air: the Baseline Air Pollution Station off nearby Cape Grim declares the air here to be the cleanest in the world. On 22km of rugged coast west of Stanley, the town stretches along the banks of the Duck River and is a service centre for local beef and dairy farming and vegetable cropping. It's a gritty town, with a few worthy distractions.

🅞 Sights

Allendale Gardens   GARDENS
(☑03-6456 4216; www.stanley.com.au/activities/allendale-gardens; Blanch Rd, Edith Creek; adult/child $10/3.50; ☺10am-4pm Tue-Sat Oct-Apr) Allendale Gardens is the life's work and passion of green-fingered Max and Lorraine Cross, who created and nurture it. Here you can wander through an incredible variety of trees and flowering plants – there's the glorious birch walk, a spectacular dahlia-and-rose garden, a wisteria pergola, spring blossoms, autumn colours and a panoply of trees, from Himalayan spruces to redwoods, tulip trees and the exquisite Chinese dove tree.

🖝 Tours

Woolnorth Tours   OUTDOORS
(☑03-6452 1493; www.woolnorthtours.com.au; Bluff Point Wind Farm Gate, 1907 Woolnorth Rd; tours adult/child $66/44; ☺tours 9.30am & 11.30am) Woolnorth, a historic 220-sq-km

cattle and sheep property, sprawls across the northwestern tip of Tasmania, 25km from Smithton. Today it's also home to enormous wind turbines that harness the power of the Roaring Forties. Woolnorth Tours offers two-hour tours visiting the wind farm, Cape Grim and the Woolnorth property.

Tall Timbers Adventure Tours   ADVENTURE
(☑1800 628 476; www.talltimbershotel.com.au; 5/15 Scotchtown Rd; day tours per person $145-270) From September to June, Tall Timbers offers full-day 4WD adventure tours to the takayna/Tarkine wilderness. It also runs mine tours, Aboriginal heritage tours and helicopter sightseeing in several variations. Flights start at $495 for 45 minutes.

🛏 Sleeping & Eating

★ **Tall Timbers**   HOTEL $$
(☑1800 628 476, 03-6452 2755; www.talltimbers hotel.com.au; 5/15 Scotchtown Rd; d $150-200, 1- & 2-bedroom apt from $235; 🛜🐕) Set in 8 hectares of landscaped bushland on the edge of Smithton, this impressive resort offers facilities including a sports bar with pool tables, **bistro** (pizzas $9-20, mains $18-42; ⊙7-9am, noon-2pm & 6-8pm Mon-Sat, from 8am Sun; 🖐), kids' games room, heated indoor pool, gym and tennis courts. The modern lakeside apartments are outstanding, featuring air-con, fully equipped kitchen and laundry, lounge and deck over the water. No air-con, but rooms are well sized.

Tassie Cottages   RENTAL HOUSE $$
(☑0418 595 314; www.tassiecottages.com.au; d from $130, extra adult/child $40/15) Owner Michael Whish-Wilson offers two self-contained cottages in Smithton, plus one at Cowrie Point off the road to Stanley and another at Arthur River. Cowrie Point, Arthur River and Island View have wonderful views.

Time Out on Emmett   CAFE $
(☑03-6452 3420; www.facebook.com/onemmett; 61 Emmett St; items $2-8; ⊙5am-5.30pm Mon-Sat) A local institution, this cafe and bakery is owned by Bunny and Cheryl, who make the delicious sausage rolls and pies – try the curried scallop, seafood mornay or steak-and-kidney versions. There's also a range of slices and pastries, freshly squeezed juice and tea and coffee.

ℹ Getting There & Away

Redline (☑1300 360 000; www.tasredline. com) has bus services to/from Burnie ($24,

1½ hours, daily) via Stanley ($6.10, 15 minutes) and Wynyard ($13.50, 75 minutes). The bus stop is on Smith St, opposite the police station.

Marrawah
☑03 / POP 410

Untamed and unspoilt, Marrawah is a domain of vast ocean beaches, mind-blowing sunsets and green, rural hills. The power of the ocean here is astounding, and the wild beaches, rocky coves and headlands have changed little since they were the homeland of Tasmania's first people. This coast is abundant with signs of Aboriginal Tasmania – especially in the fascinating Preminghana Indigenous Protected Area just north of town. Sometimes the Southern Ocean throws up the remains of long-forgotten shipwrecks here – things tumble in on waves that can reach more than 10m in length. Experienced surfers and windsurfers also come here for the challenging breaks.

🏃 Activities

There's a lengthy beach walk from **Bluff Hill Point** to **West Point** (four hours one way) and a coastal walk from **Bluff Hill Point** to the mouth of the **Arthur River** (two hours one way). There's also a highly scenic walk north along the beach from **Green Point** to **Preminghana** (around three hours return).

🛏 Sleeping

Marrawah Beach House   RENTAL HOUSE $$
(☑0428 571 285, 03-6457 1285; www.marrawah beachhouse.com.au; 19 Beach Rd; d from $165, extra person $25) Perched on the slopes of a working farm overlooking the wild Southern Ocean, these two self-contained cabins are extremely well maintained and are great options for those wanting a beach break. One sleeps four in two bedrooms, the second is a studio sleeping two. Both command magnificent views. You'll find them just up the hill from Green Point Beach. No wi-fi or TV reception.

Ann Bay Cabins   CABIN $$
(☑0428 548 760, 03-6457 1361; www.annbaycab-ins.com; 99 Green Point Rd; d from $160) These two cosy wooden cabins are just the place to hang out and get away from it all. You can sit on the deck and admire the views, or luxuriate in the deep spa bath, with bathing essentials supplied.

NORTHWEST ABORIGINAL SITES

The far northwest of Tasmania has been home to the Tasmanian Aboriginal Tarkininer people for more than 35,000 years. Evidence of their habitation is clearly visible along much of the takayna/Tarkine coast, and experts call this one of the most important archaeological regions in the world.

There's a significant Aboriginal site along the road to Arthur River called the **West Point State Reserve** (nungu in Aboriginal dialect). This has hut sites and middens (these days called 'living sites'). Beyond the small seasonal settlement at Sundown Point is the **Sundown Point State Reserve**, a site containing several dozen mudstone slabs engraved with petroglyphs (rock carvings). Sundown Point is known as laraturunawn in Aboriginal dialect. The Arthur-Pieman Conservation Area, further south, has a particularly dense concentration of living sites and, slightly further afield, there are also several important cave sites at Rocky Cape National Park (known as pinmatik in the local Aboriginal dialect).

Arguably the most significant Indigenous site on the west coast is 7km north of Marrawah at **Preminghana** (formerly known as Mt Cameron West). Now called the **Preminghana Indigenous Protected Area** (☑ 03-6234 0700, 1800 132 260; http://tacinc. com.au), it is 5km long and 1km wide and is home to low-lying slabs of rock with petroglyphs dating back two millennia, tool quarries and living sites. Flora includes manuka thicket, tea-tree swamps, eucalyptus woodlands, coast wattle and honeysuckle.

Preminghana was returned to the Aboriginal people in 1995 and is currently maintained and protected by Aboriginal supervisors. You can drive to their work camp and ask for permission to explore the site; there is someone there most days. If you'd like to be authoritatively guided around this and other significant Aboriginal sites on the island, contact the **Tasmanian Aboriginal Centre** (☑ 03-6234 0700, 1800 132 260; http://tacinc.com.au).

🛈 Getting There & Away

Marrawah lies 50km southwest of Smithton along a sealed road. There is no public transport to this corner of the island. If you are heading down the Western Explorer from Marrawah, fill up your fuel tank at the **Marrawah General Store** (☑ 03-6457 1122; www.facebook.com/marrawahgeneralstore; 800 Comeback Rd; ⊗7am-6.30pm Mon-Fri, 7.30am-6.30pm Sat & Sun) as there's no other petrol outlet until Zeehan or Waratah, some 200km away.

Arthur River

☑ 03 / POP 380

There are only a few hardy souls who call Arthur River their full-time home – the rest of the population is made up of 'shackies' and fisherfolk who love the wild remoteness of the country around here. Seemingly teetering on the very edge of the world, Arthur River is the starting point for many a fine adventure into the Arthur-Pieman Conservation Area and down the Western Explorer road to Strahan.

👁 Sights & Activities

Gardiner Point   VIEWPOINT
(Edge of the World; off Airey St) Gardiner Point, signposted off the main road on the southern side of Arthur River, is Tasmania's official

Edge of the World: the sea here stretches uninterrupted all the way to Argentina. There's a plaque at the point – a great place to take those leaning-into-the-wind, world's-end photos.

Arthur River Canoe & Boat Hire   BOATING
(☑ 03-6457 1312; www.arthurrivercanoe.wordpress. com; 1429 Arthur River Rd; canoe hire per hr/day from $14/60, dinghy $30/180; ⊗9am-5pm mid-Sep–late Apr) You can explore the amazing Arthur River on watercraft hired through Jaynee and Barry, the friendly owners of this local company. They offer information on river conditions and will store your gear while you're on the water. Single and double Canadian canoes and a motorised aluminium dinghy can be hired by the hour or day.

👉 Tours

⭐ **AR Reflections River Cruises**   BOATING
(☑ 03-6457 1288; www.arthurriver.com.au; off Arthur River Rd; adult/child $95/48; ⊗10.15am Sep-May) The most modern and best of the cruise boats on the Arthur River, offering upper-level viewing. The MV *Reflections* departs daily for a 5½-hour return trip to Warra Landing, where passengers can enjoy a guided rainforest walk and gourmet lunch.

OFF THE BEATEN TRACK

THE WESTERN EXPLORER

The Western Explorer (C249) is probably Tasmania's most excitingly remote road journey. It delves deep into the buttongrass wilderness of the Arthur-Pieman Conservation Area of the western takayna/Tarkine. Dubbed the 'Road to Nowhere', it was controversially upgraded from a barely there 4WD track into a wide gravel road in 1995 to the dismay of conservationists, who saw the upgrade as opening this vulnerable wilderness to damage and exploitation. Despite these troubled beginnings, the road is now a well-established means of traversing this rugged part of Tasmania, and it's an unmissable journey if you're in the region.

Road conditions vary from season to season, but it is usually easily navigable by 2WD. For an up-to-date assessment of road conditions, contact the Parks & Wildlife Service's Arthur River Field Office.

Arthur River Cruises BOATING
(📞 0427 885 792; www.arthurrivercruises.com.au; adult $95, child $20-35; ⏰ 10am Sep-May) The reflections on the Arthur River have to be seen to be believed, and you can get out among them on board this company's jaunty red boat, the MV *George Robinson*. On the five-hour, 28km round trip into the rainforest, you'll see sea eagles and kingfishers, stroll in the rainforest and enjoy a morning tea and BBQ lunch.

🛏 Sleeping

Arthur River's Parks & Wildlife Service manages two serviced camp sites: Manuka Campground just north of Arthur River and Peppermint Campground (📞 03-6457 1225; www.parks.tas.gov.au; off Arthur River Rd; unpowered sites per 2 people $13, extra adult/child $5/ free) in Arthur River. Both have unpowered sites with basic facilities (no bins). There are also unserviced camp sites nearby at Prickly Wattle, Nelson Beach, Green Creek, Camp Elsewhere and Stinking Beach ($6 for two people, extra adult/child $3/free).

Arthur River Cabin Park CAMPGROUND $
(📞 03-6457 1212; www.arthurrivercabinpark.com; 1239 Arthur River Rd; unpowered/powered sites per 2 people $32/35, s/d cabin from $80/95, extra adult $30) There are hot showers, a laundry and a camp kitchen with BBQ at this neat but atmosphere-free camp site, which is a 25-minute walk from the beach. The spick-and-span cabins have basic cooking facilities and are excellent value. Various wildlife – including devils – visits in the evening.

Arthur River Beach House RENTAL HOUSE $$
(📞 0438 454 311; www.arthurriverbeachhouse. com.au; 24 Gardiner St; d $160, extra person $20) You can't get much closer to the water when staying in Arthur River, so it's not surprising that this rental accommodation is so popular. There are three bedrooms, a fully equipped kitchen and laundry. The property even has its own private boat landing.

Arthur Riverfront & Sea Lodge APARTMENT $$
(📞 0429 901 644; www.arthurriveraccommodation. com.au/arthurriverfrontandsealodgeupstream; 22 Gardiner St; d $135-205, extra adult/child $35/17; ❇) This house can be rented as two separate apartments (one two-bedroom, one three-bedroom) or opened up into one big house, sleeping up to 12. It's absolutely on the waterfront and well equipped with spacious living areas, wood stoves, expansive decks and wonderful views. One of the apartments is fully wheelchair-accessible.

ℹ Information

Arthur River Field Office (📞 03-6457 1225; www.parks.tas.gov.au; Arthur River Rd; ⏰ 8am-4pm) Operated by the Parks & Wildlife Service, this visitor centre on the northern side of the river supplies camping information, gas, national parks passes and permits for off-road vehicles ($30 for one month).

ℹ Getting There & Away

Fuel is not available here – the closest petrol pumps are in Marrawah and Redpa.

Takayna/Tarkine Wilderness

Known as takayna in local Aboriginal dialect, the Tarkine is a 4470-sq-km stretch of temperate rainforest between the Arthur River in the north, the Pieman River in the south, the Murchison Hwy to the east and the Southern Ocean to the west. It's a globally significant ecosystem that encompasses vast forests of myrtle, leatherwood and pine trees, endless horizons of button-grass plains, savage ocean beaches, sand dunes and extensive coastal heathland. It's also believed to be one of the oldest rainforests in Australia, and is home to several endangered species and extensive, ancient archaeological sites. Because of its remoteness, ferocious weather and isolation, the takayna/Tarkine survived almost untouched by modernity well into the 20th century and the region still offers a frontier-style experience for those keen to explore it.

◉ Sights & Activities

To download a handy activity guide to the takayna/Tarkine, go to www.stanley.com.au (click on 'Things to do' then 'Tarkine').

Arthur-Pieman
Conservation Area NATURE RESERVE
(☑ 03-6457 1225; www.parks.tas.gov.au; via Arthur River or Corinna; 4WD off-road-only recreational driver pass $50) This 1000-sq-km coastal section of the takayna/Tarkine wilderness takes in the remote fishing settlement of Temma, the mining ghost town of Balfour, magnificent beaches such as Sandy Cape Beach, the rugged Norfolk Range, the Thornton and Interview Rivers and wild Pieman Heads. The conservation area's northern boundary begins just to the north of the Arthur River, while its southern boundary follows the Pieman River. From its west-coast border, the reserve extends east to the Frankland and Donaldson Rivers.

★ Tarkine Forest
Adventures ADVENTURE SPORTS
(☑ 03-6456 7138; www.dismalswamptasmania.com.au; 26059 Bass Hwy, Togari; adult/child $20/10, plus per slide $2; ☉ 9am-5pm Dec & Jan, 10am-4pm Feb-May & Sep-Nov; ⊞) Formerly known as Dismal Swamp (yes, really), this forest adventure centre 32km southwest of Smithton (just off the A2) is home to a 110m-long 'serpent slide' that provides a thrilling descent through the dense blackwood canopy to boardwalks down on the forest floor – sliders must be over eight years of age and at least 90cm tall.

☞ Tours

★ Tarkine Trails WALKING
(☑ 0405 255 537; www.tarkinetrail.com.au; per person $1799) Tarkine Trails takes bushwalkers on a four-day Tarkine Rainforest Walk including all meals, gear and accommodation in fab rainforest safari tents. Hikers venture out on day walks from the exclusive and deliciously remote Tiger Ridge Base Camp, where you can ogle the surrounding giant tree ferns from the lodge's cantilevered verandah.

Tarkine Wilderness Walks WALKING
(☑ 03-6445 9184; www.tarkinelodge.com.au; Tarkine Wilderness Lodge, Newhaven Track, Meunna; walk only $35, walk & lunch $55; ☉ 10.30am) Take a guided 2½-hour stroll through the rainforest surrounding the Tarkine Wilderness Lodge, spotting flora and fauna unique to the region. Walks are weather permitting; advance bookings essential.

Tasmanian Expeditions ADVENTURE
(☑ 1300 666 856; www.tasmanianexpeditions.com.au; 4-day guided walk $1799) Tasmanian Expeditions offers a number of four-day takayna/Tarkine experiences, with hiking, canoeing and rafting all part of the possible mix.

☲ Sleeping

Tarkine Wilderness Lodge LODGE $$$
(☑ 03-6445 9184; www.tarkinelodge.com.au; 1 Newhaven Track, Meunna; r from $410) 🗲 Hidden in the forests behind Rocky Cape National Park, this lodge offers luxury accommodation and a host of activities for getting out into the forest. Breakfast (from $12), lunch ($20) and dinner ($50) are offered.

❶ Getting There & Away

Tassielink (p306) runs a twice-weekly bus service between Strahan and Burnie via Waratah along the eastern fringe of takayna/Tarkine: Burnie to Waratah ($13.10, 50 minutes); Waratah to Strahan ($37.20, 2¾ hours).

The **Waratah Roadhouse** (☑ 03-6439 1110; 11 Smith St; items from $3; ☉ 7.30am-7pm) sells petrol. Major highways and roads are navigable by 2WD but you'll need a 4WD for tracks and minor roads. Drive with great care here: there's potential to skid on treacherous road surfaces. Also, don't drive at night or in bad weather. Fill up your petrol tank at Marrawah if you're travelling south, or at Zeehan, Tullah or Waratah if heading north: there's no petrol in between.

Corinna &
the Pieman River

In the rip-roaring gold-rush days Corinna was a humming mining settlement with two hotels, a post office, plenty of shops and a population that numbered 2500 souls. These days, it's a tranquil place with only one business: Corinna Wilderness Experience. An outfit providing visitors the chance to experience a sense of adventure and immersion in the rainforest without forsaking too many comforts, it offers accommodation in camp sites and cabins, a restaurant and cafe-bar, cruises down the Pieman River and kayak hire.

🏃 Activities

Corinna is the trailhead for some fabulous bushwalking from short strolls to more serious rainforest undertakings. Possibilities include Mt Donaldson (four hours return), Philosopher's Falls (two hours return) and Whyte River (one hour return). The latter can offer good platypus spotting around dusk. There's also a short (20-minute) Huon Pine Walk, where you can see some of these famous trees.

Also on offer are kayaks on the Pieman (per four/eight hours $30/50) and boat trips (per person $30) to Lovers' Falls, where you can be dropped with a picnic hamper to sigh at the beauty of it all. Longer cruises on the Pieman River are also available. For details, ask at the reception of Corinna Wilderness Experience.

OFF THE BEATEN TRACK

SAVAGE RIVER NATIONAL PARK

Now this *really* is the wilderness. The remote 180-sq-km Savage River National Park (☑ 1300 135 531; www.parks. tas.gov.au; parks day pass per vehicle/ person $24/12) is inaccessible to all but 4WD vehicles, and even then access is limited. The park protects part of the largest contiguous region of cool temperate rainforest surviving in Australia, as well as pristine blanket bogs, undisturbed river catchments and rare wildlife. There are no roads and no facilities for visitors. Only the very hardiest of bushwalkers make it in here.

Limited access into the adjacent Savage River Regional Reserve is possible by 4WD from the east via the Murchison Hwy and from the south via the Waratah–Corinna Rd.

Pieman River Cruises BOATING
(☑ 03-6446 1170; www.corinna.com.au/river-cruises; ⊙ Pieman River Cruise adult/child $90/50, Sweetwater Cruise per person $30) When in Corinna, be sure to take one of these cruises. The 4½-hour Pieman River Cruise departs at 10am daily and sails downstream to where the Pieman River meets the Southern Ocean. Morning tea and a packed lunch is included. Also on offer is a one-hour Sweetwater Cruise to Lovers' Falls and the SS *Croydon* shipwreck, which departs at 3pm. Book well ahead.

🛏 Sleeping & Eating

Corinna Wilderness Experience COTTAGE $$
(☑ 03-6446 1170; www.corinna.com.au; Corinna Rd; unpowered sites $40, cottage d $165-220, f $270-370) Corinna's tranquil wilderness village offers accommodation in one- and two-bedroom timber cottages scattered in the attractive rainforest above the riverside lodge. These sleep up to five and are solar powered; all have a kitchen or kitchenette, a wood stove or fire, a simple bathroom and a deck. There are also camp sites and a camp kitchen with BBQ.

The lodge has a cafe-bar and the Tannin Restaurant (mains lunch $10-18, dinner $22-37; ⊙ noon-2pm & 6-8pm) offers hearty meals.

ⓘ Getting There & Away

Heading south, you can approach Corinna from Somerset, just west of Burnie, via the Murchison Hwy through magnificent Hellyer Gorge (perfect for picnic stops). After Waratah, the C247 is sealed as far as Savage River, after which it's 26km of unsealed but well-maintained gravel that's almost always passable in a 2WD. If you're taking the C249 Western Explorer Rd from Arthur River, it's 109km of unsealed road to Corinna. On the southern side of the Pieman River, the road is unsealed for 5km and then sealed for the remaining 50km to Zeehan. The **Fatman Vehicle Barge** (☑ 03-6446 1170; www.corinna.com.au/barge-access-and-times; motorbike/car/caravan/pedestrian $12.50/25/30/10; ⊙ 9am-5pm Apr-Sep, to 7pm Oct-Mar) ferries passengers and their vehicles across the river.

King Island

☑ 03 / POP 1600

King Island (or 'KI', as the locals call it) is a skinny sliver of land 64km long and 27km wide – a fabulously laid-back place where everyone knows everyone. The island's green pastures famously produce a rich dairy bounty (you'll be testing how much cheese it's actually possible to ingest over the space of a few days) and its surrounding seas supply fabulously fresh seafood. The island's main settlement is the town of **Currie** (population 700) on the west coast, and there are east-coast settlements at **Grassy** (population 280) and **Naracoopa** (population 200).

Interestingly, recent talk on the island has been of seceding from Tasmania and becoming part of Victoria. Poor shipping service from mainland Tasmania has raised the ire of residents, who believe a shift of state allegiance to Victoria would improve the situation. Watch this space!

Sights

King Island Dairy DAIRY
(📞03-6462 0947; www.kingislanddairy.com.au; 869 North Rd, Loorana; ⊙10am-5pm) **FREE** Low-key but top quality, King Island Dairy's fromagerie is 8km north of Currie (just beyond the airport). Taste its award-winning bries, cheddars and feisty blues, watch a 15-minute video about the cheesemaking process and then stock up in its shop on cheeses that are budget priced – only here – to fuel your King Island exploring.

Cape Wickham Lighthouse LIGHTHOUSE
(Cape Wickham Rd) You can drive right up to the tallest lighthouse in the southern hemisphere at Cape Wickham, on KI's northern tip. This 48m-high tower was built in 1861 after several ships had been wrecked on the island's treacherous coastline. Most famous of all King Island shipwrecks is the *Cataraqui* (1845), Australia's worst civil maritime disaster, which resulted in the loss of 400 lives.

Kelp Industries' Visitor Centre MUSEUM
(📞03-6462 1340; www.kelpind.com.au; 89 Netherby Rd, Currie; ⊙8am-5pm Mon-Fri) **FREE** Come here to find out why you see tractors gathering kelp on the island's beaches. The huge straps of bull kelp being air-dried here are exported to factories in Scotland and Norway, which extract alginates for use in products such as sauces, lotions and detergents.

King Island Historical Museum MUSEUM
(📞03-6462 1512; www.kingisland.org.au/excursions; 36 Lighthouse St, Currie; adult/child $7/2; ⊙2-4pm Tue, Thu & Sat) Exhibits on lightkeeping, shipwrecks, local monuments and the island's soldier settlement history.

OFF THE BEATEN TRACK

THE TAKAYNA/TARKINE DRIVE

Tasmania offers the motorist many memorable scenic drives, but it is hard to upstage this loop from Stanley or Smithton to Marrawah, down to Arthur River and then through temperate rainforest to Trowutta and back to your starting point. You'll drive sealed roads and see towering eucalypt forests, open plains of buttongrass and heathland, magnificent rainforests, wild rivers and mysterious blackwood swamps. Watch out for the wildlife, remember that petrol stations are few and far between, and be aware of logging traffic. For a brochure outlining the route, go to www.stanley.com.au.

Activities

Being an island, the wind is offshore somewhere every day, ensuring excellent **surfing**. Indeed, the break at Martha Lavinia is often described as one of the best in Australia. Named after an 1852 shipwreck, it is located just outside Currie. Other stellar breaks can be found at Phoques Bay on the northwest coast; Red Hut Point, south of the island; Porky Beach, behind the King Island Dairy; and British Admiral Beach near the Kelp Industries in Currie.

Surf and freshwater **fishing** almost guarantee a good catch, and you can **swim** at many of the island's unpopulated beaches (beware rips and currents) and freshwater lagoons. Bring your own gear for the legendary snorkelling and diving here.

For **hiking**, pick up a map from King Island Tourism (p230) and go independently, or take a guided walk. Tour companies are listed on the King Island Tourism website.

You don't even need to get out on foot for **wildlife spotting** on KI: it's just about everywhere you look. There are rufus and Bennett's wallabies, pademelons, snakes, echidnas and platypuses, and you may even glimpse seals. The island has 78 bird species and, on summer evenings, little penguins come ashore around the Grassy breakwater.

Festivals & Events

Festival of King Island CULTURAL
(FOKI; www.foki.com.au; multiday ticket adult/child $50/free, camping per person per night $10; ⊙late

Jan) Live music, horse racing, pie-eating competitions and a raft race.

🛌 Sleeping

The King Island Tourism (p230) website lists accommodation options around the island; the majority are self-catering and are in or around Currie. There are limited choices in Grassy and Naracoopa.

Island Breeze Motel MOTEL **$$**
(✉03-6462 1260; www.islandbreezemotel.com. au; 95 Main St, Currie; d $170, 2-/3-bedroom cabin $190/200, all incl breakfast; 🖥) Popular with those playing at the nearby Cape Wickham Golf Course, this motel offers attractive, well-heated rooms with comfortable beds and tea- and coffee-making facilities. There are also two self-catering cabins with three bedrooms. The friendly and efficient manager can supply plenty of advice about touring the island. A continental breakfast is included in the price.

King Island Accommodation Cottages RENTAL HOUSE **$$**
(✉03-6461 1326; www.kingislandaccommodation cottages.com.au; 125 Esplanade, Naracoopa; 1-/2-bedroom cottages from $130/140, extra adult/ child $25/15; 🖥) Right on the coast and beautifully maintained, these quiet self-catering cottages are an excellent choice. If they were on the mainland, they'd cost double this price. Wi-fi in public areas only.

Portside Links APARTMENT **$$**
(✉03-6461 1134; www.portsidelinks.com.au; 255 Grassy Harbour Rd, Grassy; apt $190) Located on the slopes of a disused golf course (hence the name), these two stylish and well-equipped self-catering apartments are a great base when exploring the island. It's a short stroll to pretty Grassy Harbour and Sand Blow Beach, where fairy penguins return to their colony at dusk. The owners also operate a gallery and cafe here. Minimum two-night stay.

🍴 Eating

King Island Bakehouse BAKERY **$**
(✉03-6462 1337; www.facebook.com/kingisland bakehouse; 5 Main St, Currie; snacks $5-18; ⊘6am-5pm Mon-Fri, 7am-3pm Sat & Sun) Best pies for miles, with unusual fillings including wallaby and crayfish. Also makes cakes, bread and coffee.

Wild Harvest MODERN AUSTRALIAN **$$$**
(✉03-6461 1176; www.wildharvestkingisland.com. au; 4 Bluegum Dr, Grassy; mains $28-55; ⊘6pm-late) Sea to table, paddock to plate – most of the produce used by the chefs at this eatery overlooking Grassy Harbour is local, seasonal and fresh. The result is a menu of tasty dishes with global accents accompanied by Tasmanian wines. Winter meals here are enjoyed in front of a roaring log fire; in summer guests can dine outside.

ℹ️ Information

King Island Tourism (✉03-6462 1355, 1800 645 014; www.kingisland.org.au; 5 George St, Currie; ⊘10.30am-5pm Mon-Fri, 10am-noon Sat) Supplies brochures outlining the King Island Grazing Trail and Maritime Trail at both the airport and its office in town. Its website is an excellent pretrip planning resource, with suggested itineraries and loads of information about activities, tours and accommodation.

ℹ️ Getting There & Away

Three airlines fly into King Island's small airport at Loorana, 8km northeast of Currie. **King Island Airlines** (✉03-9580 3777; www.kingisland air.com.au) flies to/from Melbourne's Moorabbin airport (one-way $210, one hour) once or twice daily; **Regional Express** (REX; ✉13 17 13; www. regionalexpress.com.au) flies daily to/from Melbourne's Tullamarine airport (one-way from $130, 55 minutes); and **Sharp Airlines** (✉1300 556 694; www.sharpairlines.com) flies to/from Melbourne's Essendon airport (one-way from $125, 45 minutes, twice daily) and daily from Burnie (one-way from $220, 40 minutes).

ℹ️ Getting Around

King Island Car Rental (✉1800 777 282; www.kingisland.org.au/transport/car-hire; 2 Meech St, Currie; per day from $73; ⊘office 8am-5pm Mon-Fri) and **P&A Car Rental** (✉03-6462 1603; www.kingisland.org.au/transport/ car-hire; 2a Meech St, Currie; per day from $73; ⊘office 8am-5pm Mon-Fri) offer car hire.

Cradle Country & the West

Best Places to Eat

➜ Bushman's Bar & Cafe (p242)

➜ Hellyers Restaurant (p254)

➜ Union Takeaway (p242)

➜ Tracks Cafe (p246)

Best Places to Stay

➜ Pumphouse Point (p255)

➜ Cradle Mountain Wilderness Village (p253)

➜ Mt Lyell Anchorage (p246)

➜ Ormiston House (p242)

Why Go?

Welcome to the island's wild west, a land of endless ocean beaches, ancient mossy rainforests, tannin-tinted rivers, glacier-sculpted mountains, wildflower-strewn high plains and boundless horizons – a place where you'll often feel like you are the only soul on earth. This is Tasmania's vast outdoor playground, replete with national parks, conservation reserves and World Heritage–protected wilderness, where your options for adventure are varied and plentiful.

Come here for the toughest multiday hikes (or gentle rainforest wanders); come to shoot rapids on untamed rivers (or cruise mirror-calm waters); and come to kayak into some of the last untouched temperate wilderness on earth (or fly over it all in a light plane). You can visit independently or with a guided group – however you choose to arrive, one thing is sure: you won't want to leave.

When to Go

➜ Western Tasmania comes to life in the warmest months (December to March). Things get busy, but long summer days afford more time in the great outdoors, and visitor services are at the top of their game.

➜ Tasmania's alpine heart can be gorgeously ice-encrusted over winter (June to August). Just a few hardy souls hike along the trails: if you're equipped for a chilly – even snowy – wilderness adventure, it's an atmospheric time to visit.

➜ In spring (September to November) the southwest glories in splendid isolation: intrepid hikers have the place to themselves. The odd western gale still blows through – come prepared!

Cradle Country & the West Highlights

① Overland Track (p234) Walking through World Heritage–listed landscape from Cradle Mountain to Lake St Clair.

② West Coast Wilderness Railway (p243) Travelling through the wilderness in style on this scenic rail journey.

③ Gordon River Cruise (p240) Sailing up this rainforest-edged waterway, stopping at historic Sarah Island en route.

④ Franklin River (p248) Shooting the rapids on a rafting journey down Tasmania's wildest river.

⑤ Lake St Clair (p251) Gliding over

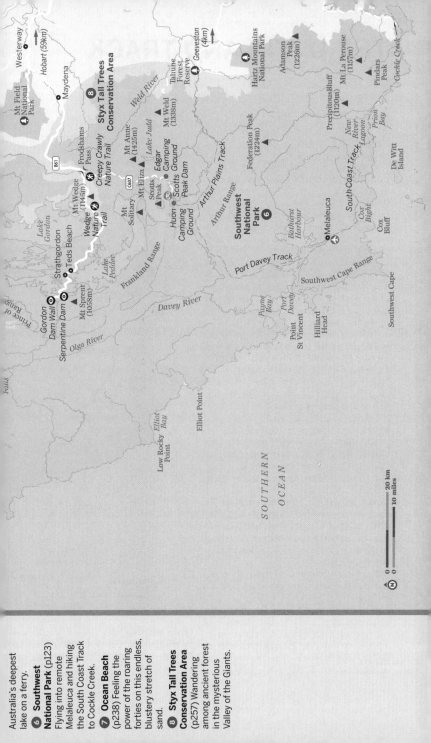

Australia's deepest lake on a ferry.

⑥ Southwest National Park (p123) Flying into remote Melaleuca and hiking the South Coast Track to Cockle Creek.

⑦ Ocean Beach (p238) Feeling the power of the roaring forties on this endless, blustery stretch of sand.

⑧ Styx Tall Trees Conservation Area (p257) Wandering among ancient forest in the mysterious Valley of the Giants.

THE OVERLAND TRACK

THE HIKE

START CRADLE MOUNTAIN
END CYNTHIA BAY, LAKE ST CLAIR
DURATION/DISTANCE 65KM/FIVE TO SEVEN DAYS
DIFFICULTY MODERATE

Most hikers walk the Overland Track during summer when alpine plants are fragrantly in flower, daylight hours are long and you can work up enough heat to swim in one of the frigid alpine tarns. The track is very busy at this time and is subject to a crowd-limiting permit system. Outside of the booking season, the track is usually quiet and icily beautiful, and can be hiked in either direction.

The trail is well marked for its entire length. Side trips lead to features such as Mt Ossa (Tasmania's loftiest peak at 1617m), and some fantastic waterfalls – so it's worth budgeting time for some of these. You can expect to meet many walkers each day except in the dead of winter. The walk itself is extremely varied, negotiating high alpine moors, rocky scree, gorges and tall forest.

There are unattended huts with bare wooden bunks and heaters spaced handily along the track – at Waterfall Valley, Lake Windermere, Pelion, Kia Ora, Windy Ridge and Narcissus – anywhere from 7.8km to 16.8km apart. It pays to bring a tent too, in case the huts are full (there are tent platforms adjacent to huts). From Narcissus you can walk around Lake St Clair (17.5km) back to Derwent Bridge, or book the ferry (p255) across the lake.

Note that campfires are banned on the track, so you'll need to carry a fuel stove for cooking.

If you don't want to hike the track independently, there are a couple of couple of commercial guided-walk companies operating here, including **Tasmanian Expeditions** (☑ 1300 666 856; www.tasmanianexpeditions.com.au; 6-day hike from $2095; ☉ Oct-early May) and

Cradle Mountain Huts (☑ 03-6392 2211; www.cradlehuts.com.au; Quamby Estate, 1145 Westwood Rd, Hagley; walks from $2350; ☉ Oct-May), with accommodation in very decent huts.

Tasmania's iconic alpine Overland Track is a 65km, five- to seven-day odyssey (with backpack) through incredible World Heritage–listed mountainscapes, from Cradle Mountain to the southern shores of Lake St Clair.

THE FACTS

For all the latest info on the track and walk planning, and to check availability and make bookings, visit www.parks.tas.gov.au.

To help keep walker numbers manageable and the walking experience one of wilderness, not crowd dodging, the following rules apply.

There's a booking system in place from 1 October to 31 May, when a maximum of 34 independent walkers can depart each day. There are fees of $200/160 per adult/child aged five to 17 and concession, to cover the costs of sustainable track management (these apply from October to May only). The compulsory walking direction from October to May is north to south.

The best reference map for the track and surrounds is the 1:100,000 *Cradle Mountain–Lake St Clair* map published by Tasmap (www.tasmap.tas.gov.au). For further notes on the tracks in the park, read *Cradle Mountain–Lake St Clair and Walls of Jerusalem National Parks* by John Chapman, Monica Chapman and John Siseman. A handy pocket-sized reference for the walk is the Parks & Wildlife Service's *The Overland Track: One Walk, Many Journeys*, which has notes on ecology and history plus illustrations of flora and fauna you may see along the way.

TRACK ACCESS

For Overland Track walkers, Tassielink (p306) offers a Launceston–Cradle Mountain and Lake St Clair–Hobart package fare costing $104. Package fares cost $135 from Launceston to Cradle Mountain and Lake St Clair to Launceston via Hobart and $137 from Devonport to Cradle Mountain and Lake St Clair to Devonport via Hobart.

Cradle Mountain Coaches (☏03-6427 7626; www.cradlemountaincoaches.com.au) operates bushwalker shuttle services between Launceston and Cradle Mountain or Lake St Clair ($320 or $80 per person for four or more passengers) and between Devonport and Cradle Mountain ($260/$65). Shuttles also run from Lake St Clair to Hobart ($360 for private shuttle or $90 per person for four or more passengers).

Cradle Mountain Coaches also offers bushwalker shuttles each way between Lake St Clair and Cradle Mountain ($100 per person for four or more passengers, $400 for private shuttle). These are popular with walkers who leave their vehicles at Cradle Mountain and so need to return there from Lake St Clair.

Tassie Road Trips (p310) also shuttles bedraggled hikers back to Hobart from the Lake St Clair end of the track. Minimum two people ($135 per person); prices come down for larger groups (three people $95 per person, four people $90, five people $85 etc).

If you're planning to use the Lake St Clair Ferry (p255) at the end of your Overland Track hike, for which bookings are essential, you must radio the ferry operator when you arrive at Narcissus Bay to reconfirm your booking.

ℹ️ Getting There & Away

Tassielink (p306) buses travel from Launceston to Queenstown via Cradle Mountain, Tullah, Rosebery and Zeehan. There are also services from Hobart to Queenstown via Derwent Bridge and Lake St Clair. From Queenstown, the company operates separate services to Strahan.

To reach the remote Southwest National Park, you'll need to drive and walk in, or fly in on a Par Avion (p257) service.

Tullah

 03 / POP 200

A quiet place offering excellent trout fishing and some challenging mountain walks, the little town of Tullah has long been isolated in the rainforests of the West Coast Range. The name Tullah comes from an Aboriginal word meaning 'meeting of two rivers'; the town is, in fact, almost an island, surrounded by deep, tannin-brown waterways. It's nooked into the nape of majestic Mts Farrell and Murchison, and the waters of Lake Rosebery lap close.

🏃 Activities

The area's best walks include 712m **Mt Farrell** (three to four hours return) and the tallest mountain in the West Coast Range, 1275m **Mt Murchison** (six hours return). There are also beautiful, short lakeside walks starting near the jetty and boat ramp. You might see platypuses at play.

Lake Rosbery is well stocked with atlantic salmon, rainbow trout and brown trout. Tullah Lakeside Lodge can organise fishing charters.

Wee Georgie Wood Steam Railway   RAIL

(📋 03-6473 2228; www.weegeorgiewood. au; Murchison Hwy; adult/child/family $10/5/25; ⏱ 10am-3pm 1st Sun & last weekend of the month Oct-May) To commemorate the days of steam – when Tullah's only link to the outside world was by train – local residents have restored *Wee Georgie*, one of the narrow-gauge steam locomotives that operated on the town's original railway. Now it takes

---

ℹ️ **WATCH YOUR STEP**

If walking off marked tracks in the bush close to Zeehan or at Trial Harbour, beware of abandoned mine shafts hidden by vegetation.

---

passengers on a 20-minute ride through the surrounding rainforest.

🍴 Sleeping & Eating

Tullah Lakeside Lodge   HOTEL, CABIN $$

(📋 03-6473 4121; www.tullahlakesidelodge.com. au; 1 Meredith St; r $100-150; 🌐🍽️) Here, it's all about the location. A cluster of barracks-like cabins is set on the edge of Lake Rosbery, commanding lovely views over the water and surrounding rainforest. Rooms are basic but clean; there is little discernible difference between room types. The on-site Lakeside Bar & Grill is the best eatery in town. Breakfast is included.

Lakeside Bar & Grill   PUB FOOD $$

(📋 03-6473 4121; www.tullahlakesidelodge.com. au; Tullah Lakeside Lodge, 1 Meredith St; mains $18-30; ⏱ noon-2pm & 6-8pm) Enjoy your meal or drink on the grassed terrace or around the wood stove in the tentlike dining room at Tullah's best eating option. Lunch is a simple affair, with soup, pies and toasted sandwiches on offer. Dinner choices include steaks, ribs and grilled salmon. The oversized outdoor chess set is a draw, as is the magnificent view of the lake and forest.

ℹ️ Getting There & Away

Twice-weekly Tassielink (p306) bus services to/from Burnie ($21.10, 1½ hours), Launceston ($53.30, 4¾ hours) and Queenstown ($22.60, 85 minutes) stop at the service station on the corner of Arthur St and Primrose Rd. Change at Queenstown to reach Strahan.

Rosebery

 03 / POP 930

Rosebery's best asset is its beautiful setting in a valley of temperate rainforest with Mt Murchison to the east, imposing Mt Black (950m) to the north and Mt Read to the south. Located on the Murchison Hwy between Tullah and Zeehan, the town is home to the MMG polymetallic base-metal mine and little else. Impressive Montezuma Falls, one of the highest waterfalls in Tasmania, is located approximately 8km south of town.

🏃 Activities

The picnic area at the southern entrance to town is the start of a short (10-minute) walk along the Stitt River and over Park Rd to pretty **Stitt Falls**.

HARBOURS & WEST COAST BACKBLOCKS

To experience the west coast in the raw, visit the tiny wave-lashed settlements of **Trial Harbour** and **Granville Harbour**. Directly west of Zeehan, the gravel C248 leads to the former. Once Zeehan's port, it is now a ragged collection of holiday shacks and the odd permanent home. There are coastal walks here, good fishing and great free camping in the vicinity – but no shops or facilities.

Further north, tiny Granville Harbour (reached via the gravel Granville Harbour Rd off the paved C249) is one of the best spots in Tasmania for crayfish (you'll need a licence). The C249 (which becomes gravel as you head north) also leads to peaceful **Corinna**, which is the jumping-off point for the Pieman River Cruise (p228) and the Western Explorer road (p226).

A more accessible beach alternative lies 14km along the road from Strahan to Zeehan: the spectacular **Henty Dunes**, a series of 30m-high sugar-fine sand dunes backing **Ocean Beach**. From the picnic area take the 1½-hour return walk through the dunes and out to Ocean Beach; remember to carry drinking water.

South of town the spectacular 104m-tall **Montezuma Falls** plume down a rainforest cliff. To head there, drive out of Rosebery towards Strahan and take the signed turnoff to reach Williamsford, the site of an abandoned mining town. From here an easy three-hour return walk leads to the falls, where you can venture out onto the narrow swing bridge suspended over the yawning chasm for a great view.

✾ Festivals & Events

Rosebery Festival   CULTURAL
(www.roseberyfestival.org; ⊙ Feb) At the beginning of every year (usually in February), Rosebery hosts a four-day festival where locals enjoy trail runs, pet parades, cake-decorating competitions, live-music performances, a craft market and other activities.

❶ Getting There & Away

Twice-weekly Tassielink (p306) bus services to/from Launceston ($55.60, five hours) and Queenstown ($20, one hour) stop on Agnes St. Change at Queenstown to reach Strahan.

Zeehan

📞 03 / POP 720

Zeehan owes its existence to mining. In 1882 Frank Long discovered silver and lead on the banks of Pea Soup Creek, and in no time what had been a small mining field became known as 'Silver City', with a population of 10,000 people. Service industries included 27 pubs, the famous Gaiety Theatre and even a stock exchange. However, times have changed: Zeehan now has a one-horse, tumbleweed-town vibe. But it is worth pausing to visit the West Coast Heritage Centre and amazing old Gaiety Theatre.

◉ Sights

West Coast Heritage Centre   MUSEUM
(📞 03-6471 6225; www.wchczeehan.com.au; 114 Main St; adult/child/family combined ticket with Gaiety Theatre $25/5/55; ⊙ 9.30am-4.30pm) Housed in the 1894 School of Mines & Metallurgy, this museum is the pride of the local community and the town's major tourism drawcard. There's plenty to see, including a huge mineral display, photographs and documents tracing the history of the west coast, an underground-mine simulation and steam locomotives and carriages from the early west-coast railways. The centre also incorporates the Gaiety Theatre, a blacksmith shop and wheelwright workshop and the town's historic Freemasons lodge and police station/courthouse.

Gaiety Theatre   HISTORIC BUILDING
(www.wchczeehan.com; Main St; entry via West Coast Heritage Centre adult/child/family $25/5/55; ⊙ 9.30am-4.30pm) When the Gaiety opened in February 1898, a troupe of 60 performers was brought to town from Melbourne and played to 1000 spectators every night for a week. Soon, this grand theatre building was hosting films, plays, vaudeville reviews and concerts. Now restored to its former glory, it screens two hour-long silent-film sessions per day, one of which features parts of the world's first feature film, *The Story of the Kelly Gang* (first shown here in May 1907).

Spray Tunnel
HISTORIC SITE

(www.discovertasmania.com.au/home/local-tips/spray-tunnel-in-zeehan; off Fowler St; ⊙24hr) **FREE** This 100m-long glowworm-filled railway tunnel was constructed as part of silver-mining operations in 1904. You can now take a short walk through it along a boardwalk to spy the remains of the **Spray Silver Mine** on the other side before looping back to your start point. To access the boardwalk, turn southwest into Fowler St from Main St and drive through the golf course and down the narrow and winding dirt road.

✦ Festivals & Events

Zeehan Gem & Mineral Fair
FAIR

(www.zeehangemandmineralfair.com; ⊙Nov) Held over two days in early November, this festival hosts up to 100 stalls selling gems, jewellery, minerals, crystals and fossils. It also stages specimen competitions and fossicking-related activities such as gem sieving and gold panning.

🛏 Sleeping & Eating

Heemskirk Motor Hotel
MOTEL $$

(☑03-6471 6107; www.heemskirkmotorhotel.com.au; 1/25 Main St; r $130-140, 2-bed apt $180-190; ❄️🐾) This efficiently operated motel on the eastern edge of town is hands down the best place to sleep and eat while in Zeehan. It offers a popular **bistro** (mains $15-30; ⊙6-9am, noon-2pm & 6-8pm) and comfortable if characterless rooms with tea- and coffee-making facilities. Self-caterers can opt for a two-bedroom apartment with fully equipped kitchen (a supermarket is next door). Wi-fi access is restricted to the reception area.

Carol's on Main
CAFE $

(☑03-6471 6505; 110 Main St; mains $5-17; ⊙7.30am-5pm Mon-Sat) One of a couple of decent cafes on Zeehan's main street, this place serves fish and chips, homemade sausage rolls, sandwiches and ice cream. It often closes for a period over winter.

ℹ Information

West Coast Heritage Centre (p237) has limited visitor information.

ℹ Getting There & Away

Twice-weekly Tassielink (p306) bus services to/from Burnie ($34.90, 2¼ hours), Launceston ($64.50, 5¼ hours) and Queenstown ($10.20, 40 minutes) stop at the supermarket on Main St. Change at Queenstown for Strahan services.

Strahan
☑03 / POP 710

The *Chicago Tribune* newspaper once dubbed Strahan 'the best little town in the world' and it's easy to imagine why it did so. The town's pure air, affable locals and picturesque location tucked between Macquarie Harbour and the rainforest combines with top-drawer tourist attractions – Gordon River cruises and the West Coast Wilderness Railway (p243) – to make it one of Tasmania's most popular and family-friendly tourist destinations.

◉ Sights

Ocean Beach
BEACH

(via Ocean Beach Rd) Head 6km west of Strahan's town centre to find Ocean Beach, awesome as much for its 40km length as for the strength of the surf that pounds it. This stretch of sand and sea runs uninterrupted from Trial Harbour in the north to Macquarie Heads in the south and is an evocative place to watch the orange orb of the sun melt into the sea. The water is treacherous: don't swim here.

West Coast Reflections
MUSEUM

(☑1800 352 200; www.westernwilderness.com.au; West Coast Visitor Information Centre, Esplanade; adult/child/family $2/1/5; ⊙10am-5pm) The West Coast Visitor Information Centre is home to this creative and thought-provoking display on the history of the west coast. It includes a refreshingly blunt appraisal of the region's environmental disappointments and achievements, including the Franklin Blockade, the 1982 protest against the damming of the Franklin River.

West Strahan Beach
BEACH

(off Beach St) The beach next to the caravan park has a gently shelving sandy bottom that provides safe swimming. Don't be discouraged by the water colour – it's tinted with natural tannin.

Cape Sorell Lighthouse
LIGHTHOUSE

(Macquarie Heads) Located 12km southwest of Strahan at the harbour's southern head, this 40m-high lighthouse dates from 1899 and is purportedly the second highest in Australia. You'll need a boat to cross the heads, unless you can find an accommodating fishing boat to take you over. A return walk of two to three hours along a vehicle track from

Strahan

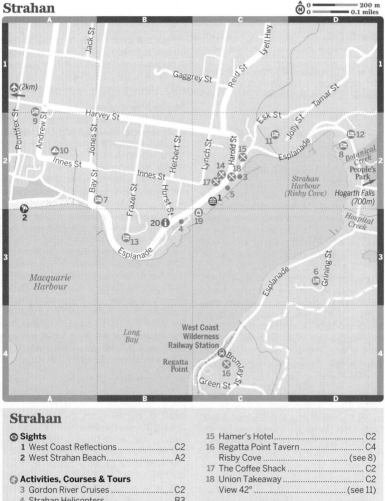

CRADLE COUNTRY & THE WEST STRAHAN

the jetty at Macquarie Heads leads to the lighthouse.

Hogarth Falls   WATERFALL

(off Esplanade) A pleasant 50-minute return walk through the rainforest to these falls follows platypus-inhabited Botanical Creek. The track starts at People's Park, off the Esplanade opposite Risby Cove.

☞ Tours

Most visitors to Strahan take a **Gordon River cruise**. The dense rainforest that lines the riverbank and the sense of peace in these trackless wilds makes this experience quite unforgettable.

You can cruise the Gordon on a large, fancy catamaran in the company of a crowd of fellow river admirers (with plenty of comforts laid on), or be a bit more adventurous and visit with a small group by sailing boat. All cruises cross vast Macquarie Harbour before entering the mouth of the Gordon and proceeding to Heritage Landing for a rainforest walk. Most cruises visit Sarah Island, site of Van Diemen's Land's most infamously cruel penal colony, as well as Macquarie Heads and Hells Gates (the narrow harbour entrance). If you visit under sail, you can sneak a little further up the river than other cruise vessels are allowed to go, to beautiful Sir John Falls.

World Heritage Cruises   CRUISE

(☑03-6471 7174; www.worldheritagecruises.com. au; 19 Esplanade; adult $115-160, child $60-90, family $290-370; ☉9am mid-Aug–mid-Jul) The Grining family have been taking visitors to the Gordon since 1896 and they are true river experts. Join them aboard their low-wash, environmentally sensitive catamaran, the *Harbourmaster,* for a six-hour cruise through Macquarie Harbour out through Hells Gates, to Sarah Island and up the Gordon River. Prices vary depending on whether you take a window seat (premium, or, if

on the upper deck, gold) or one in the centre of the boat (standard). All prices include a buffet meal.

Note that there may be an additional departure at 3.15pm and returning at 8.30pm in the height of summer, and there is no service at all in the depths of winter. Students and seniors are eligible for a 10% discount.

Gordon River Cruises   CRUISE

(☑03-6471 4300; www.gordonrivercruises.com. au; 24 Esplanade; cruise adult $115-230, child $62-230, family from $280) Operated by the Royal Automobile Club of Tasmania, the 5½-hour Gordon River Cruise departs at 8.30am and sails up the Gordon as far as Heritage Landing, stopping at Sarah Island en route. Prices depend on whether you opt for the standard package, premium window seating or the lavishly catered 'upper deck' experience. Advance bookings are recommended.

The outfit's other cruise offerings include a 2½-hour Bonnet Island Experience (adult/child/family $105/45/255) that visits the island's penguin colony at sunset and includes wine and cheese; a 3½-hour afternoon highlights cruise (adult/child from $75/50) departing at 3.30pm in late December and January only; and a Convict Explorer cruise (adult/child $85/45) across Macquarie Harbour to Sarah Island departing at 10am.

West Coast Yacht Charters   BOATING

(☑03-6471 7422; www.westcoastyachtcharters. com.au; 59 Esplanade; Upper Gordon cruise adult/child $320/160; ☉Oct-Apr) If you'd like your Gordon River experience with a little adventure (and fewer people), sailing on the *Stormbreaker* may be the way to go. This 20m ketch has the only licence to cruise the Upper Gordon; it departs at 1pm and returns at noon the next day (minimum numbers apply, meals and accommodation included).

Other offerings include an overnight trip up the Gordon (adult/child $380/190, meals and accommodation included) and a 2½-hour kayaking and fishing cruise (full charter $720 for two to eight people). Minimum numbers apply for both.

Strahan ATV
Adventures   ADVENTURE SPORTS

(☑0407 343 797; www.strahanatvadventures.com. au; adult/child/family $75/40/230; ☉10am, noon, 2pm & 4pm) Take to the Henty Dunes on a one-hour ATV (quad bike) tour departing from Strahan. There's also a 1½-hour Macquarie Heads sunset tour ($140 per person).

---

❶ PARKING IN STRAHAN

Parking here can get tight. The public car park next to the visitor centre charges $5 per day between 6am and 6pm; the private parking next to the Strahan Village reception charges $6 per day. A few free spaces in front of the main shopping strip have 30- to 60-minute time limits.

Call or book online. All drivers must have a valid Australian driver's licence; L-plate drivers must be accompanied by a licensed driver.

Strahan Helicopters
SCENIC FLIGHTS

(☑0419 656 974; www.strahanhelicopters.com.au; Esplanade; ⊙ Nov-May) The west coast is a rugged and remote region, so one of the easiest ways to see its scenery is on a helicopter ride. Possibilities include a 20-minute fight over Hells Gate and Ocean Beach (per person $250) and a 30-minute flight following the West Coast Wilderness Railway line between Regatta Point, Teepookana and Dubbil Barril stations ($750 per flight).

Other packages include a one-hour 'West Coast and Mountain Adventure' flight over the West Coast Range ($1560 per flight). Flights can be booked online or through the West Coast Visitor Information Centre (p243).

🛏 Sleeping

Strahan Holiday Retreat
CARAVAN PARK $

(☑03-6471 7442; www.strahanretreat.com.au; 10 Innes St; unpowered/powered sites $20/45, cabins & cottages from $159; ☜) Close to Strahan's West Beach, this well-maintained park offers camp and caravan sites, self-contained cabins and multiroom cottages. There's not much grass and accommodation is cheek-by-jowl, but the facilities, including a camp kitchen, BBQs, laundries and a games room, compensate. The retreat also offers kayak/ sand board/bicycle hire ($40/10/30 per day). Platypuses are regularly spotted in the on-site creek.

Macquarie Heads
CAMPGROUND $

(☑03-6471 4700; www.westcoast.tas.gov.au/ camping; off Ocean Beach Rd; unpowered sites $7) Camping is possible at a basic site at Macquarie Heads, 15km southwest of Strahan; follow the signs to Ocean Beach and see the caretaker. There are pit toilets on-site and limited water is available, but there are no showers or kitchen facilities.

Gordon Gateway
MOTEL $$

(☑1300 134 425; www.gordongateway.com.au; 4 Grining St; studios/2-bedroom ste from $125/210; ❄) On the hillside on the way to Regatta Point, this place offers 10 well-priced studio units sleeping four persons. All have equipped kitchenettes, cramped bathrooms and sweeping water and township views. There's a guest laundry on-site.

Strahan Bungalows
APARTMENT $$

(☑03-6471 7268, 0412 870 684; www.strahanbungalows.com.au; cnr Andrew & Harvey Sts; d $160-210; ☜) Decorated with a nautical theme, these two-bedroom bungalows are clean, well maintained and equipped with everything you need for a self-contained stay. They sleep up to five persons but are compact, so things would be cramped for larger groups. The location is reasonably close to the beach and the golf course, and less than a 15-minute walk from the town centre.

Strahan Village
HOTEL $$

(☑03-6471 4200, 1800 628 286; www.strahanvillage.com.au; Esplanade; d in hotel/cottage from $180/240; ☜) Managed by the Royal Automobile Club of Tasmania, this outfit has a reception area on the Esplanade in the town centre. Its major property is a 140-room hotel on a hilltop overlooking town. A few have wonderful harbour views, as does the on-site View 42° (p242) restaurant, bar and lounge.

Down near the waterfront, the company offers cottages with motel-style rooms. These are on the main street so can be noisy. Wi-fi is only available in the reception centre and the restaurant. You'll need a car if staying at the hotel, as it's a very steep climb from the town centre.

The Crays
COTTAGE $$

(☑03-6471 7422, 0419 300 994; www.thecrays accommodation.com; 59 Esplanade; d studios from $180, 2-/3-bedroom cottages from $190/220; ☜) The Crays has six simple studios and cottages with basic kitchenette and bathroom on the Esplanade, opposite Risby Cove, as well as two self-contained units on Innes St. Wi-fi is available at some of the Esplanade cottages, but not all; there is no wi-fi at Innes St. The business was for sale when we last visited, so details may change – check ahead.

★ Wheelhouse Apartments
RENTAL HOUSE $$$

(☑0429 356 117; www.wheelhouseapartments.com.au; 4 Frazer St; d $320; ❄) Talk about a room with a view! Perched high above the town centre, this pair of swish two-bedroom town houses have seamless walls of glass framing a jaw-dropping view over Macquarie Harbour. They feature a well-equipped kitchen with oven and espresso machine, lounge with huge TV, downstairs bedroom and bathroom, and a spiral staircase leading to a master bedroom with spa.

CRADLE COUNTRY & THE WEST STRAHAN

★ **Ormiston House**   B&B $$$
(☑ 03-6471 7077; www.ormistonhouse.com.au; 1 Esplanade; d $200-240; 🐾) Built by Frederick Ormiston (Strahan's founder), this handsome red-brick mansion dating from 1899 now offers B&B accommodation in five well-sized, antique-filled rooms. A recent change of management isn't expected to lead to many changes – expect comfortable beds, a generous continental breakfast and a relaxing ambience. Ask to visit the small museum about Strahan's history housed in the mansion's tower.

Risby Cove   HOTEL $$$
(☑ 03-6471 7572; www.risbycove.com.au; Esplanade; d studio from $210, 1-/2-bedroom ste from $250/260; 🐾) Though overpriced, these studios and suites have kitchenettes and comfortable beds with nice linen. Some of the suites have spa baths and others have desks overlooking the water. There's an onsite **restaurant** (mains $28-38; ☺6-8pm; 🔧) and **craft shop** (☺8am-5pm Dec-Feb, 9am-4pm Mar-Nov).

🍴 Eating

★ **Union Takeaway**   FISH & CHIPS $
(☑ 03-6471 7500; 23-25 Esplanade; $2 per oyster, fish & chips $13-22; ☺noon-8pm daily Oct-Mar, 5-8pm Tue-Sat Apr-Sep) You're at the beach, so eating fish and chips at least once is obligatory. And in Strahan, the best place for a fishy fry-up is this takeaway joint on the main street. As well as whiting, flake or scallops with chips, it offers fresh oysters.

The Coffee Shack   CAFE $
(☑ 03-6471 7095; www.facebook.com/thecoffee shackstrahan; 19 Esplanade; items from $2.50; ☺6am-5pm Sun-Thu, daily Christmas-Mar) If we were to quibble, we would describe this cute-as-a-button cafe as a shed rather than a shack. Why bother, though? The important thing to say is that owner Tracy had an inspired idea when she decided to set up this makeshift operation on the Esplanade and serve coffee accompanied by homemade muffins, cakes and slices.

★ **Bushman's Bar
& Cafe**   MODERN AUSTRALIAN $$
(☑ 03-6471 7612; www.bushmanscafe.com.au; 1 Harold St; mains $17-39; ☺7.30am-8pm daily Dec-Feb, 11am-8pm Mon-Sat Mar-Nov) A focus on local produce, including Petuna salmon, Spring Bay scallops and Sassafras lamb, is the defining feature of the menu at Strahan's best restaurant. Lunch is a laid-back affair featuring homemade pies, salads, pasta dishes and burgers. Dinner is a more sophisticated proposition, featuring dishes such as slow-cooked pork belly, *paillard* of salmon and rack of lamb. Book ahead for dinner.

Regatta Point Tavern   PUB FOOD $$
(☑ 03-6471 7103; www.regattapointtavern.com.au; Esplanade; mains $18-35; ☺noon-2pm & 6-8pm) To eat with the locals, make your way to this friendly and down-to-earth pub near the railway terminus 2km around the bay from Strahan's centre. The dining room overlooks the water and the menu offers steaks, burgers and plenty of fresh seafood. Kids meals are also available ($11 to $15).

View 42°   MODERN AUSTRALIAN $$$
(☑ 03-6471 4200; www.strahanvillage.com.au; Strahan Village, Esplanade; buffet adult/child breakfast $27/13.50, dinner $57/28.50; ☺6.30-10am & 6-8.30pm) Though our natural inclination is to avoid buffets, the spread in Strahan Village's hilltop hotel was a pleasant surprise, featuring well-prepared Tasmanian produce including plenty of fresh seafood. On top of that, the deck and window tables offer wonderful harbour views. There's also a limited à la carte menu in the lounge bar (antipasto, cheese, seafood or meat platters cost $40 to $55).

🍷 Drinking & Nightlife

Hamer's Hotel   PUB
(☑ 03-6471 4335; www.strahanvillage.com.au; 31 Esplanade; ☺11.30am-9pm Sun-Wed, to 10pm Thu-Sat) The most centrally located drinking den in town, with decent **pub grub** (mains $25-40; ☺5.30-8.30pm).

☆ Entertainment

★ **The Ship That Never Was**   THEATRE
(☑ 03-6471 7700; www.roundearth.com.au; West Coast Visitor Information Centre, Esplanade; adult/child/concession $25/2.50/12.50; ☺performance 5.30pm Sep-May, movie 5.30pm Jun-Aug) Presented in a small amphitheatre attached to the West Coast Visitor Information Centre, this 1½-hour, two-performer play tells the picaresque tale of a group of convicts who escaped from Sarah Island in 1834 by hijacking a ship they were building. A Strahan institution (it's been staged for over two decades), the hugely entertaining performance involves audience participation and is suitable for all age groups.

THE WEST COAST WILDERNESS RAILWAY

Love the romance of the days of steam? The old wood-lined carriages with shiny brass trimmings, the breathy puffing of steam engines and the evocative, echoing train whistle? Then hop on board the **West Coast Wilderness Railway** (☑03-6471 0100; www.wcwr. com.au; Queenstown Station, 1 Driffield St; ⊙ticket office 8am-4.30pm Mon-Sat, 9am-4pm Sun), which runs through breathtaking rainforest between Strahan and Queenstown.

When it was first built in 1896, this train and its tortuous route through remote country was a marvel of engineering. It clings to the steep-sided gorge of the (once-polluted, now-recovering) King River, passing through dense myrtle rainforest over 40 bridges and on gradients that few other rolling stock could handle. The railway was the lifeblood of the Mt Lyell Mining & Railway Co in Queenstown, connecting it for ore and people haulage to the port of Teepookana on the King River, and later with Strahan. The original railway closed in 1963.

Ride options on offer include standard carriages where you pay for a seat only, and wilderness carriages where you are allocated a seat but can also take advantage of an outdoor viewing platform and enjoy a glass of sparkling wine and either morning tea and lunch or a high tea. Expect reduced services outside the high season (especially June and July) and always check the website for schedule and price updates.

Rack & Gorge (standard carriage adult/child/family $110/55/245, wilderness carriage adult/child $175/100) Departs Queenstown at 9am (and 2.15pm during summer), looping through the King River Gorge to Dubbil Barril and then returning to Queenstown.

River & Rainforest (standard carriage adult/child/family $110/55/245, wilderness carriage adult/child $175/100) Departs Strahan at 9am (and 2.15pm during summer). The route skirts the harbour, enters the rainforest and then returns to Strahan after crossing many of the route's spectacular bridges.

Queenstown Explorer (standard carriage adult/child/family $185/80/390, wilderness carriage adult/child $239/130) Departs Strahan at 8.30am and runs the railway's full length through gorge and rainforest to Queenstown (where there's a one-hour stop), before returning to Strahan at 5.30pm.

CRADLE COUNTRY & THE WEST STRAHAN

🛍 Shopping

Wilderness Woodworks ARTS & CRAFTS
(☑03-6471 7244; www.wildernesswoodworks.com. au; 12 Esplanade; ⊙8am-5pm) Here you can see Huon pine being turned, and then buy the end results: kitchen utensils, platters, bowls, ornamental objects and furniture.

ℹ Information

Parks & Wildlife Service (☑03-6472 6020; www.parks.tas.gov.au; Customs House Building, 13 Esplanade; ⊙9am-5pm Mon-Fri) The Strahan office of the Parks & Wildlife Service is located in the handsome Customs House building, adjacent to the library and post office. Though officially meant to be open during business hours, its actual opening hours are extremely limited.

West Coast Visitor Information Centre (☑1800 352 200, 03-6472 6800; www.west ernwilderness.com.au; Esplanade; ⊙10am-5pm; 🐾) This extremely friendly and helpful visitor centre supplies information about Strahan and other destinations on the west coast.

Staff can also make tour and accommodation bookings. It is the location of the West Coast Reflections (p238) museum and The Ship That Never Was performance.

ℹ Getting There & Away

Tassielink (p306) operates a once-daily bus service to Queenstown ($10.60, 45 to 75 minutes) during the school term, Monday to Friday; outside these periods services depart Monday to Thursday. From Queenstown, buses continue to Launceston ($74.80, six hours) and Hobart ($67.60, 5¼ hours) two to four times weekly. Services arrive at/depart from the Esplanade in the town centre.

See also West Coast Wilderness Railway.

ℹ Getting Around

Bicycle hire is available for $10/30 per hour/day $10/30 at the Strahan Village (p241) and at for $25/35 per half-/full day at Strahan Holiday Retreat (p241).

Queenstown

🛪 03 / POP 1980

Most of western Tasmania is green. Queenstown is orange or red. The winding descent into Queenstown from the Lyell Hwy is unforgettable for its moonscape of bare, dusty hills and eroded gullies where rainforest once proliferated. Copper was discovered here in the 1890s and mining has continued ever since, but today – thankfully – pollution is closely monitored and sulphur emissions are controlled. The town itself retains a rough-and-ready pioneer feel and though clearly suffering the economic aftershocks of mine closures, it is trying hard to reinvent itself as a tourism destination.

⊙ Sights

Iron Blow Lookout   VIEWPOINT

(off Lyell Hwy) On top of Gormanston Hill on the Lyell Hwy, just before the final descent along hairpin bends into Queenstown, is a sealed side road leading to an utterly spectacular lookout over the geological wound of Iron Blow. This decommissioned open-cut mine, where Queenstown's illustrious mining career began, is awesomely deep and is now filled with emerald water. You can get an eagle's-eye view from the 'springboard' walkway projecting out into thin air above the mine pit.

Q Bank Gallery   GALLERY

(www.qbankgallery.com.au; 37 Orr St; ⊙ hours vary) Run by a group of friends who fell in love with the town and its handsome but faded bank building, this gallery is home to the Queenstown Artists In Residence Initiative (QuARI), which hosts visiting visual artists keen to engage with the local community and landscape. Most are happy to show their works-in-progress to visitors, and all stage exhibitions at the end of their residencies.

Upstairs there's a three-bedroom flat with kitchen and laundry available for rent (from $135).

Paragon Theatre   THEATRE

(🛪 0428 429 962; www.theparagon.com.au; 11 McNamara St; self-guided tour adult/child $5/2; ⊙ tours 9am & 2pm) This 1930s behemoth is the town's major landmark and in its heyday it was the epicentre of a thriving social scene. Lovingly restored to a semblance of its original grandeur by a local doctor and cinephile, it is now open for self-guided

tours. There are plans underway to turn it into an events venue and pop-up restaurant.

Pioneer Cemetery   CEMETERY

(🛪 03-6471 4700; www.westcoast.tas.gov.au/cemeteries; Conlan St) Queenstown's story is told in this intriguing cemetery with more than 500 graves and some fascinating inscriptions on the crumbling headstones.

LARQ Studio   GALLERY

(🛪 03-6471 2805; www.landscapeartresearchqueenstown.wordpress.com; 8 Hunter St; ⊙ by appointment) FREE Well-known printmaker and painter Raymond Arnold and his artist partner Helena Demczuk are two of a small community of visual artists living and working in the Queenstown area. Their studio, known as Landscape Art Research Queenstown (LARQ), can be visited by appointment.

Spion Kop Lookout   VIEWPOINT

(off Latrobe St) The panoramic views of town from this lookout, which was named by soldiers after a battle in the Boer War, are excellent. Try to arrive at sunset, when the bare hills are flaming orange. To get here, follow Hunter St uphill, turn left onto Bowes St, then do a sharp left onto Latrobe St to a small car park. From here a short, steep track leads to the summit.

Eric Thomas Galley Museum   MUSEUM

(🛪 03-6471 1483; www.discovertasmania.com.au/attraction/ericthomasgalleymuseum; 1-7 Driffield St; adult/student & child/family $6/4/13; ⊙ 9am-5pm Oct-Apr, 9.30am-4.30pm May-Sep) This museum started life as the Imperial Hotel in 1897 and now houses an extensive and idiosyncratically captioned photographic collection documenting the people and places of Tasmania's west coast. These include an exposé of the 1912 Mt Lyell mining disaster, which claimed 42 lives. There's also a clutter of old memorabilia, household items and clothing.

☞ Tours

See also West Coast Wilderness Railway (p243).

Queenstown Heritage Tours   HISTORY

(🛪 0407 049 612; www.queenstownheritagetours.com; power-plant tour adult/child $65/35; ⊙ by appointment) Operated by the knowledgable Anthony Coulson, this company offers industrial-heritage buffs the opportunity to visit an early 20th-century hydroelectric

Queenstown

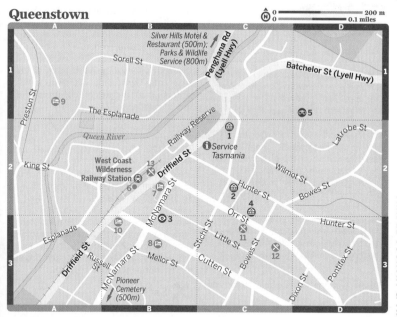

Queenstown

⊙ Sights
1 Eric Thomas Galley Museum C2
2 LARQ Studio C2
3 Paragon Theatre B3
4 Q Bank Gallery C2
5 Spion Kop Lookout D1

⊕ Activities, Courses & Tours
6 Town Centre Walking Tour B2
 West Coast Wilderness
  Railway .... (see 6)

⊜ Sleeping
7 Empire Hotel B2
8 Mt Lyell Anchorage B3
9 Penghana A1
10 Railway Hotel B3

⊗ Eating
11 Cafe Serenade C3
 Empire Hotel .... (see 7)
12 Maloney's Restaurant C3
13 Tracks Cafe B2

power plant on Lake Margaret, but its most popular offering is a 'Lost Mines, Ancient Pines' tour (adult/child $75/45), which goes underground at old copper and gold mines and visits a commercial sawmill and stand of Huon-pine rainforest.

Town Centre Walking Tour WALKING
(☏ 03-6471 0100; www.wcwr.com.au; Queenstown Station, 1 Driffield St; ⊘ every Queenstown Explorer train arrival) FREE Local amateur historian Charlie meets the *Queenstown Explorer* when it arrives in town and takes passengers on a 15-minute guided walking tour from the train station up Queenstown's main street.

🎎 Festivals & Events

The Unconformity CULTURAL
(www.theunconformity.com.au; ⊘ Oct) Biannual arts festival held in October on even years (2018, 2020 etc). The edgy programming features theatre, music and visual arts, with an overriding theme of cultural paradox.

🛏 Sleeping

Railway Hotel PUB $
(☏ 03-6471 1511; www.therailwayhotel.com.au; 27-33 Driffield St; s/tw/d $30/45/50) The rooms in a breeze-block-style structure at the rear of this pub are spartan and have little natural light, but they are clean, centrally located and the cheapest accommodation option in town. The shared bathrooms have copious hot water. New licensees Karen and Darren Stewart are helpful and enthusiastic hosts

WORTH A TRIP

LAKE BURBURY

Approximately 20km east of Queens-town along the Lyell Hwy is the southern shore of Lake Burbury, a water reservoir created when the Crotty Dam inundated the upper King River valley. The lake is surrounded by the Princess River Conservation Area, and the scenery around it is magnificent – especially when there's snow on the nearby peaks. There are impressive vistas from the attractive shoreline campground (www.westcoast.tas. gov.au/camping; Lyell Hwy; unpowered sites $7) just east of Bradshaw Bridge, which offers unpowered sites, toilets, a public picnic area with sheltered electric barbecues and a children's playground. Fishers say the trout in Lake Burbury make for some of the best fishing in Tasmania.

who are working hard to reinvigorate this business.

Empire Hotel
PUB $

(☑03-6471 1699; www.empirehotel.net.au; 2 Orr St; tw/d/f $115/120/143, s/d/tr without bathroom $55/80/100; P☺☜) The rooms here aren't as magnificent as the building's imposing blackwood staircase, which is a National Trust–listed treasure, but they have a certain jaded pub charm and are generally kept clean. A simple continental breakfast is included.

★ Mt Lyell Anchorage
B&B $$

(☑03-6471 1900; www.mtlyellanchorage.com; 17 Cutten St; r $170-180; ☜) Though you wouldn't guess it from the outside, this 1890s weatherboard home has been transformed into a welcoming guesthouse with comfortable rooms featuring excellent beds. Three of the rooms have stylish bathrooms (a fourth has private facilities across the hall) and there's a shared fully equipped kitchen next to a comfortable communal lounge. Owner Joy is a mine of local information.

On the other side of the guesthouse's herb and vegetable garden are three self-contained apartments sleeping up to four (double $170, extra person $30). Basic breakfast provisions are provided for both rooms and units.

★ Penghana
GUESTHOUSE $$

(☑03-6471 2560; www.penghana.com.au; 32 Esplanade; d $180-195, d without bathroom $160, 2-bedroom apt from $200; ☜) Built in 1898 for the general manager of the Mt Lyell Mining & Railway Co, this National Trust–owned mansion is located on a hill above town amid a beautiful garden. The views from here are magnificent. The managers are gradually refurbishing all six rooms in great style – the Owen and Lyell rooms have en suites and are the pick of the bunch. Breakfast is included.

Silver Hills Motel & Restaurant
MOTEL $$

(☑03-6471 1755; www.silverhillsmotel.com.au; Penghana Rd; d/f from $113/139; ☜) It may lack atmosphere, but this efficiently run motel at the northern entrance to town offers 57 simple and well-maintained rooms that are clean, well priced and worth considering. Family rooms sleep four; some have kitchenettes. The popular on-site restaurant (dinner from 5.30pm Monday to Saturday, mains $28 to $49) and bar has an open fire and serves continental breakfasts ($13).

 Eating

Cafe Serenade
CAFE $

(☑0458 712 199; 40-42 Orr St; mains from $6; ☺7.30am-4pm Mon-Fri, 9am-2pm Sat, 10am-1pm Sun) A popular place near the post office on the main street, the Serenade won't win any awards for its decor or its food, but it is a reliable choice for coffee, pies and toasted sandwiches.

Tracks Cafe
CAFE $$

(☑03-6471 0100; www.wcwr.com.au; Queenstown Station, Driffield St; mains $6-19; ☺8am-4.30pm Mon-Sat, 9am-4pm Sun; ☜) Though located in the historic Queenstown railway station, Tracks has been given a resolutely modern fit-out. The light and airy interior is warmed by a wood stove in winter and it's the best spot in town to pause for a simple breakfast or lunch (soups, wraps, toasted sandwiches).

Empire Hotel
PUB FOOD $$

(☑03-6471 1699; www.empirehotel.net.au; 2 Orr St; mains lunch $12-16, dinner $18-35; ☺noon-2pm & 5.30-8pm) This old miners' pub has survived the ages and includes an atmospheric heritage dining room serving a changing menu of hearty pub standards, including well-cooked parmas, pastas and steaks. The menu focuses on meat dishes, but vegetarians are catered for with a massive veggie stack. The friendly bar is the town's major meeting place.

Maloney's Restaurant BISTRO **$$**
(☑03-6471 1866, 1800 684 997; www.queens townmotorlodge.com.au; Queenstown Motor Inn, 54-58 Orr St; mains $24-35; ☺6-8pm Mon-Sat; 🖼) Who would expect such good food in an otherwise-unremarkable small-town motel? It's quite sophisticated fare here, all cooked fresh to order. Try the house speciality (chicken breast stuffed with camembert and sun-dried tomatoes) or opt for alternatives including dukkah-crusted salmon, vegetable lasagne or fillet mignon. There's also a well-priced kids menu ($12).

ℹ Information

Parks & Wildlife Service (Queenstown Field Centre; ☑03-6471 5920; www.parks.tas. gov.au; Penghana Rd; ☺hours vary) If you're planning a visit to Franklin-Gordon Wild Rivers National Park, the park rangers at this office can supply current information on permits, weather, regulations and environmental considerations. Try to catch them between 8am and 9.30am before they set off for the day. The office is located on the northern edge of town.

West Coast Community Services Hub (☑03-6495 1530; www.linc.tas.gov.au; 9-13 Driffield St; ☺9.30am-5pm Mon-Fri; 🛜) There's no tourist information centre in Queenstown, but this excellent community-services hub offers a library with free wi-fi and internet access. You can also access information, charge your phone and read Tasmanian and mainland newspapers here. An on-site **Service Tasmania** (☑1300 135 513; www.service.tas.gov.au; ☺9.30am-4.30pm Mon-Fri) office sells good maps of the nearby national park.

ℹ Getting There & Away

Tassielink (p306) buses arrive at and depart from the West Coast Wilderness Railway Station on Driffield St. Services travel to/from Hobart ($67.60, 5½ hours) via Derwent Bridge and Lake St Clair three times weekly, and to/from Launceston ($74.80, six hours) via Cradle Mountain and Devonport at least twice weekly; all services connect with buses to Strahan ($10.60, 45 minutes).

Franklin-Gordon Wild Rivers National Park

Named after the wild rivers that twist and cascade their way through its infinitely rugged landscapes, this magnificent national park (www.parks.tas.gov.au; vehicle/person per day $24/12) is part of the Tasmanian Wilderness World Heritage Area and encompasses the catchments of the Franklin, Olga and Gordon Rivers. It was proclaimed a national

---

SAVING THE FRANKLIN

The Franklin-Gordon Wild Rivers National Park is probably best known as the site of Australia's biggest-ever environmental battle, the Franklin River Blockade, which drew national and international attention and was ultimately successful in saving the wilderness from further dams.

The battle to save the lower Gordon and Franklin Rivers was played out in Tasmania in the early 1980s. Despite national-park status and then World Heritage nomination, dam-building plans by the then Hydro Electric Commission (HEC) continued. In the aftermath of the controversial damming and subsequent flooding of nearby Lake Pedder, public opinion on the matter was clear – when a 1981 referendum asked Tasmanians to decide between two different dam schemes, 46% of voters scribbled 'No Dams' across their ballot papers. When the World Heritage Committee eventually announced the area's World Heritage listing and expressed concern over the proposed dam, the new state premier attempted to have the listing withdrawn.

Dam construction began in 1982 and protesters from all over Tasmania set off from Strahan to stage what became known as the 'Franklin River Blockade'. Press pictures from the time show flotillas of blow-up dinghies stretched across the river, blocking the HEC boats' access to the dam work site. Despite the peaceful protests, the Tasmanian government passed special laws allowing protesters to be arrested, fined and jailed. In the summer of 1982–83, 1400 people were arrested in a confrontation so intense it received international news coverage.

The Franklin River became a major issue in the 1983 federal election, which was won partly on a 'No Dams' promise by the incoming Australian Labor Party, which then fully implemented the Franklin and Gordon Rivers' World Heritage assignation, wholly protecting the rivers and forests.

OFF THE BEATEN TRACK

MT JUKES

To begin one of the region's more scenic drives, head south out of Queenstown along Driffield and Conlan Sts to Mt Jukes Rd (22km one way), which will take you to side roads leading to sections of the **West Coast Wilderness Railway** (p243). Further along this scenic road (9km south of Queenstown) is **Newall Creek**, where a platform provides access to a patch of superb King Billy and Huon-pine rainforest. The bitumen section of the road ends at Lake Burbury (p246), a hydroelectric dam that can be seen to stunning effect from a lookout on the descent to its shores.

park in 1981 after the failed campaign to stop the flooding of precious Lake Pedder (p247) under the Pedder-Gordon hydroelectric dam scheme and is now a popular destination for bushwalkers, rafters and 4WD enthusiasts. The park's most significant peak is Frenchmans Cap (1443m), with a white-quartzite top formed by glacial action.

The park contains a number of unique plant species and major Aboriginal sites, the most significant of which is **Kutikina Cave**, where over 50,000 artefacts have been found. These date from the cave's 5000-year-long occupation between 14,000 and 20,000 years ago. The cave is located on Aboriginal land in remote forest and can only be reached by rafting down the Franklin River. Note, however, that this cave is protected by the local Indigenous community and it is usually off limits to visitors.

🏃 Activities

Rafting the Franklin River is the most popular activity in the park. The **Collingwood River**, a tributary of the Franklin, is the usual put-in point. Much of the park consists of deep river gorges and impenetrable rainforest, but the Lyell Hwy traverses its northern end. Most walking tracks are found off the Lyell Hwy. Frenchmans Cap is a popular hiking and climbing destination.

Walking

Along the Lyell Hwy are a number of signposted features of note, including a few short walks that you can take to see just what this park is all about.

Donaghy's Hill Wilderness Lookout Walk Located 4km east of the bridge over the Collingwood River, the lookout on Donaghy's Hill is accessed on a 30- to 40-minute return walk on a well-graded track. Rising above the junction of the Collingwood and Franklin Rivers, it has spectacular views of the Franklin River valley and Frenchmans Cap.

Nelson Falls Nature Trail An easy 20-minute return walk on a well-graded track through cool temperate rainforest to 35m-high Nelson Falls just east of Lake Burbury, at the bottom of Victoria Pass. Signs beside the track highlight common plants of the area.

Franklin River Nature Trail This 1km nature trail, taking 20 to 30 minutes return, has been marked through the forest from the picnic ground where the highway crosses the Franklin River.

Frenchmans Cap Walking Track Starting 3km west of the Franklin River Nature Trail, this hike along a good hardened track takes experienced bushwalkers four to five days. Though there are two shelter huts along the way, you should carry a tent. The Tassielink (p306) Hobart–Strahan service stops on request at the beginning of the Frenchmans Cap track. You can also do the walk as a guided six-day trip with Tasmanian Expeditions.

Rafting the Franklin River

Rafting the Franklin River is about as wild and thrilling a journey as it's possible to make in Tasmania. This is really extreme adventure and a world-class rafting experience. Experienced rafters can tackle it independently if they're fully equipped and prepared, but for anyone who's less than completely river savvy (and that's about 90% of all Franklin rafters), there are tour companies offering complete rafting packages.

If you go with an independent group you must contact the park rangers at Queenstown's Parks & Wildlife Service (p247) field office for current information on permits, regulations and environmental considerations. You should also check out the Franklin rafting notes on the Parks & Wildlife Service website. All expeditions should register at the booth at the point where the Lyell Hwy crosses the Collingwood River, 49km west of Derwent Bridge.

The trip down the Franklin, starting at Collingwood River and ending at Sir John Falls, takes between eight and 14 days, depending on river conditions. Shorter trips on certain sections of the river are also possible. From the exit point at Sir John Falls, you can be picked up by Strahan Helicopters (p241), or by the West Coast Yacht Charters' (p240) yacht *Stormbreaker* for the trip back to Strahan.

The upper Franklin, from Collingwood River to the Fincham Track, passes through the bewitchingly beautiful Irenabyss Gorge and you can scale Frenchmans Cap as a side trip. The lower Franklin, from the Fincham Track to Sir John Falls, passes through the wild Great Ravine.

☞ Tours

Franklin River Rafting RAFTING
(☑0422 642 190; www.franklinriverrafting.com; 8-/10-day trip $2860/3190; ☉Oct-Apr) Excellent eight- and 10-day guided and fully catered trips from Collingwood Bridge, with the final leg to Strahan on the *Stormbreaker*. The longer trip includes the chance to climb Frenchmans Cap. Both trips include pick-up in Hobart.

Tasmanian Expeditions RAFTING, HIKING
(☑1300 666 856; www.tasmanianexpeditions.com. au; ☉Frenchmans Cap trek $1795, 9-/11-day rafting trips $2895/2995) Tasmanian Expeditions offers treks and rafting trips. Starting and ending in Launceston, the classic Franklin River trips are guided and fully catered, with the final leg on the *Stormbreaker*. The longer option includes the Frenchmans Cap climb. On the six-day, 46km guided Frenchmans Cap trek you will stay in cabins at Derwent Bridge and camp at Lake Vera.

Water By Nature RAFTING
(☑1800 111 142, 0408 242 941; www.franklin rivertasmania.com; 5-/7-/10-day trips $2290/2690/3180) This outfit provides five-, seven- and 10-day guided and fully catered trips down the Franklin. The 10-day trip includes an optional climb of Frenchmans Cap. Trips start and end in Hobart and include a final leg aboard the *Stormbreaker*.

ⓘ Information

Information on permits, weather, regulations and environmental considerations is available at the Parks & Wildlife Service (p247) in Queenstown. Get there early before the park rangers head to the park for the day.

If there's a ranger at Strahan's Parks & Wildlife Service (p243) when you drop by, they should be able to offer advice on visiting the park.

ⓘ Getting There & Away

Tassielink (p306) buses travel between Launceston and Queenstown ($74.80, six hours) via Devonport and Cradle Mountain at least twice weekly. There are connecting services to Strahan ($10.60, 45 minutes to 75 minutes).

Buses run between Strahan and Hobart ($78.20, six hours, three weekly) via Queenstown and Lake St Clair; these stop at Frenchmans Cap en route ($29.90 and 2¾ hours from Strahan; $55.70 and 4½ hours from Hobart).

Cradle Mountain-Lake St Clair National Park

Part of the Unesco World Heritage–listed Tasmanian Wilderness, this 1262-sq-km national park (☑03-6492 1110; www.parks. tas.gov.au; day pass per person/vehicle $12/24) incorporates glacier-sculpted mountain peaks, river gorges, lakes, tarns and tracts of wild alpine moorland. Though it extends all the way from the Great Western Tiers in the north to Derwent Bridge in the south, its most beloved landscapes and walks – including parts of the world-renowned 65km Overland Track – are around Cradle Mountain. The park encompasses Mt Ossa (1617m), Tasmania's highest peak, and Lake St Clair, the deepest (200m) lake in Australia. Within the park's boundaries are plenty of wildlife-watching opportunities – sightings of wombats, Bennett's wallabies and pademelons are almost guaranteed, and Tasmanian devils and platypuses are often spotted. The main tourist hubs are Cradle Mountain Village, a tourist settlement scattered along Cradle Mountain Rd, and the smaller Derwent Bridge near Cynthia Bay on Lake St Clair.

◉ Sights

Devils@Cradle WILDLIFE RESERVE
(☑03-6492 1491; www.devilsatcradle.com; 3950 Cradle Mountain Rd; adult/child $18/10, family from $50, night feeding tours adult/child $30/15, family from $80; ☉10am-4pm Apr-Sep, to 5pm Oct-Mar) A refuge for Tasmanian devils, this excellent wildlife sanctuary also plays host to occasional eastern and spotted-tail quolls. Though open all day for self-guided visits, try to sign up for a tour (preferably at night, as this is when the mainly nocturnal animals are best observed). Tours run at 10.30am, 1pm and 3pm, with night tours at 5.30pm year-round and 8.30pm October to

Cradle Mountain–Lake St Clair National Park

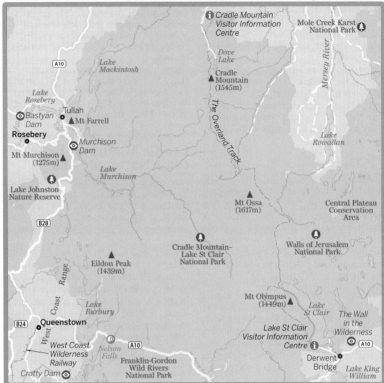

March. Day tours take 45 minutes and night tours 75 minutes. Extra information about the animals is given in an interesting DVD presentation.

As well as the standard tours, the sanctuary offers a 'Dine with the Devil' experience ($99) between 7pm and 8pm daily from November to the end of Easter. This includes drinks and snacks and gives participants an opportunity to interact with the animals.

Wilderness Gallery   GALLERY
(✆03-6492 1404; www.wildernessgallery.com.au; Cradle Mountain Hotel, 3718 Cradle Mountain Rd; ⊙9am-5pm) FREE Located in the Cradle Mountain Hotel, this 10-room commercial gallery showcases the work of local photographers and artists whose work is inspired by the wilderness. It incorporates two small theatres, one of which screens a tribute to the late Peter Dombrovskis, an acclaimed nature photographer whose photograph *Morning Mist, Rock Island Bend, Franklin River* was the signature image of the 1980s 'No Dams' movement. Prints of the photographs on display are offered for sale, as are local handicrafts and produce.

Wall in the Wilderness   LANDMARK
(✆03-6289 1134; www.thewalltasmania.com; Lyell Hwy, Derwent Bridge; adult/child $13/5; ⊙9am-5pm Oct-Apr, to 4pm May-Sep) Wood sculptor Greg Duncan is the genius behind this 100m-wide panorama depicting the history of the Tasmanian highlands, which is presented in a purpose-built structure 2km outside Derwent Bridge. The skill and detail of Duncan's carving is quite extraordinary – he manages to portray everything from the veins in the workers' hands to the creases in their shirts and even the hair of their beards. It's closed for two weeks mid-August.

✖ Activities

Cradle Valley Walks

The starting point of the epic Overland Track (p234) is here, but Cradle Valley has plenty of other accessible trailheads. The following is by no means an exhaustive list.

Knyvet Falls (45 minutes return) Begins opposite Cradle Mountain Lodge (p253) and follows Pencil Pine Creek to a lookout over the falls.

Crater Lake (two to three hours return) Climb up to this lake-filled crater from the Ronny Creek car park.

Cradle Valley Walk (two hours one way) An easy 8.5km walk from the interpretation centre to Dove Lake. It's boardwalked as far as Ronny Creek (5.5km); the rest of the track to Dove Lake can get quite muddy and is sometimes closed after heavy rain.

Main Dove Lake Circuit (two- to three-hour loop) Go all the way around the lake from Dove Lake car park, with near-constant Cradle Mountain views.

Cradle Mountain Summit (six to eight hours return) A tough but spectacular climb with incredible views in fine weather; not recommended in bad visibility or when it's snowy and icy in winter. Begin at either Dove Lake car park or Ronny Creek.

Cynthia Bay Walks

If you're at the southern, Lake St Clair end of the national park, these are our top picks of the day hikes on offer. Always check weather and other conditions with the Lake St Clair Visitor Information Centre (p255) at Cynthia Bay before setting out.

Larmairremener tabelti (one hour return) Aboriginal cultural-interpretative walk that winds through the traditional lands of the Larmairremener, the Indigenous people of the region who know Lake St Clair as Leeawuleena (Sleeping Water). The walk starts at the visitor information centre and loops through the lakeside forest before heading along the shoreline back to the centre.

Platypus Bay Circuit (one hour return) From Watersmeet, near the visitor information centre, to the lake shore, from where uninterrupted views across the lake to the Traveller Range can be enjoyed.

Shadow Lake Circuit (four to five hours return) Mixture of bush tracks and board-walks through rainforest, stringybark trees and subalpine forests.

Mt Rufus Circuit (seven to eight hours return) Climbs Mt Rufus through alpine meadows and past lakes and sandstone outcrops with fine views over Lake St Clair.

Lake St Clair Lakeside Walk Catch the ferry to Echo Point (three to four hours back to Cynthia Bay) or Narcissus Hut (five to seven hours back to Cynthia Bay) and walk back along the lakeshore.

☞ Tours

Lake St Clair Scenic Cruise   CRUISE
(☑ 03-6289 1137; www.lakestclairlodge.com.au/about-lake-st-clair/lake-st-clair-ferry; adult/child $80/40; ⊘ 9am, 12.30pm & 3pm Oct-Apr, on demand May-Sep) Hop aboard the *Ida Clair* for a 1½-hour ferry trip from Cynthia Bay to Echo Point and Narcissus Bay and back, admiring pristine Lake St Clair and the peaks of Mt Hugel, Mt Olympus, Mt Orthys, Mt Byron and Mt Ida along the way. Advance bookings are advised.

Cradle Country Adventures   HORSE RIDING
(☑ 1300 656 069; www.cradleadventures.com.au; 1½hr ride adult/child $129/99, 4hr ride per person $360; ⊘ rides 9.30am & 12.30pm Nov-Apr)

FAMILY WALKS

Many of the walks in Cradle Valley are suitable for children of reasonable fitness. If your kids are *really* young, the following might appeal.

Rainforest Walk & Pencil Pine Falls (10 minutes return) Begins at the interpretation centre (p255). It's easy, boardwalked and quite spectacular.

Enchanted Nature Walk (20 minutes return) Begins near Cradle Mountain Lodge (p253) and runs alongside Pencil Pine Creek; accessible for prams and wheelchairs for most of the way.

Weindorfers Forest Walk (20 minutes return) Begins next to Waldheim Cabins (p253) and climbs up through the forest; not pram or wheelchair accessible.

Ronny Creek (20 to 25 minutes return) The boardwalks that mark the start of the Overland Track are ideal for families, with plenty of wombats in the vicinity.

THE WEINDORFERS' LEGACY

If not for the forward-looking vision of one Gustav Weindorfer, Cradle Mountain might never have been incorporated into a national park. Weindorfer, an Austrian immigrant, first came to Cradle in 1910 and built a wooden cabin, Waldheim (German for 'Forest Home'), in 1912. Weindorfer and his Australian wife, Kate, took their honeymoon at Waldheim and fell in love with the area. Recognising its uniqueness, they lobbied successive governments for its preservation.

Kate Weindorfer had a passion for botany and became an expert in the area's bushland and flora, encouraging Gustav's appreciation of the landscape. Their spirit was tenacious – in those days a horse and cart could only get within 15km of Cradle Mountain, and from there they walked to Waldheim while packhorses carried supplies. The Weindorfers encouraged visitors to come to this remote place and share in its marvels.

Kate died in 1916 from a long illness, and Gustav moved to Waldheim permanently, devoting his life to preserving the mountain area he loved. Cradle Mountain was declared a scenic reserve in 1922 and a national park in 1971, nearly 40 years after Gustav's death in 1932.

The original Waldheim chalet was deemed structurally unsound and demolished in 1976 but was rebuilt using traditional carpentry techniques and stands as a monument to the Weindorfers. Just inside the doorway is Gustav's original inscription: 'This is Waldheim/Where there is no time/And nothing matters'.

Horseback is a great way to explore the Cradle Mountain area, and this company offers guided trail rides through and along native eucalypt and plantation forests, historic farmland and rivers. Tours can be tailored for novice or experienced riders. Maximum two riders per group.

Cradle Mountain Canyons ADVENTURE
(☑1300 032 384; www.cradlemountaincanyons.com.au; 4057 Cradle Mountain Rd, Cradle Mountain; adult $110-220, child $100-195; ☉departures 8.30am, 9.30am & 1.30pm Nov-Apr, subject to bookings) Located in the Cradle Mountain Visitor Information Centre (p255) complex, this company takes small groups of wetsuit-clad thrill-seekers scrambling, abseiling and climbing down a procession of pools and waterfalls. Choose between the Lost World Canyon (for beginners) or Dove Canyon or Machinery Creek (both for more advanced canyoning) and see the region's extreme beauty up close and personal.

McDermott's Coaches BUS
(☑03-6492 1070; www.mcdermotts.com.au; 4057 Cradle Mountain Rd, Cradle Mountain; tours adult/child $49/29) McDermott's two-hour sunrise tour includes a visit to Dove Lake and the King Billy Pine Forest; the tour price does not include the national-parks pass. The company also offers a two-hour wildlife-spotting tour at dusk that combines seeing the devil feeding at Devils@Cradle (p250) and night-time wildlife-spotting in a 4WD. Buses will collect and drop off passengers at their accommodation.

A day tour from Launceston is also available; see the website for details.

Grayline BUS
(☑1300 858 687; www.grayline.com; adult/child $168/84) Offers a day coach tour from Launceston to Cradle Mountain, including a short hike around Dove Lake and along the Enchanted Forest Walk. The fare includes your national-park entrance fee.

Cradle Mountain Helicopters SCENIC FLIGHTS
(☑03-6492 1132; www.cradlemountainhelicopters.com.au; 4057 Cradle Mountain Rd, Cradle Mountain; 20min flights adult/child from $250/150) Snaffle a spectacular bird's-eye view over Tasmania's alpine heart by taking a helicopter joy ride from the helipad next to the Cradle Mountain Visitor Information Centre. While in the air you'll enjoy postcard-perfect shots of sights such as Cradle Mountain, Dove and Crater Lakes, Waterfall Valley and little-seen Fury Gorge.

☆ Festivals & Events

Tastings at the Top FOOD & DRINK
(www.cradlemountainlodge.com.au/food-wine/tastings-at-the-top) Cradle Mountain Lodge organises and hosts this three-day event showcasing Tasmanian food and wine. It's usually held in winter or spring, in even-numbered years.

🛏 Sleeping & Eating

🛏 Cradle Mountain

Discovery Holiday Parks Cradle Mountain
CAMPGROUND $

(📞03-6492 1395; www.discoveryholidayparks.com.au; 3832 Cradle Mountain Rd; unpowered sites for 2 people $36-52, powered sites $50-62, dm $36, cabin d $150-$290) There are options aplenty at this well-run holiday park. Camp sites are well spaced; single-sex dorms are set in bushland and sleep four; basic cabins include kitchens and small bathrooms; and larger versions have gas fires and TVs with DVD player and Playstation. Communal facilities include a laundry, squeaky-clean ablutions blocks and camp kitchens with stoves, BBQs and pizza ovens.

Cradle Mountain Highlanders
CABIN $$

(📞03-6492 1116; www.cradlehighlander.com.au; 3876 Cradle Mountain Rd; d $135-240, extra adult/child $35/25; 📶) The friendly hosts at this rustic retreat opposite the Cradle Mountain Visitor Information Centre offer 16 immaculately kept timber cottages sleeping between two and seven people. All have wood or gas fires, electric blankets, TV and DVD and equipped kitchens. Four cabins include a spa, and all are serviced daily. There's a communal BBQ area and laundry. On-site wi-fi is intermittent.

Waldheim Cabins
CABIN $$

(📞03-6491 2158; www.parks.tas.gov.au; d $95-185; P♨) Set in forest near the Weindorfers' chalet inside the park are eight rustic wood-lined cabins managed by the Tasmanian Parks and Wildlife Service. Each has heating, basic kitchen facilities and between four and eight single bunk beds. Despite their simplicity (no power points and a shared shower and toilet block), the gorgeous set-ting means that these cabins are deservedly popular.

⭐Cradle Mountain Wilderness Village
CABIN $$$

(📞03-6492 1500; www.cradlevillage.com.au; 3816 Cradle Mountain Rd; d cabins $220-370; 📶) Cleverly camouflaged in the bushland, the 44 cabins here are clean, comfortable, well equipped and extremely family friendly – all have TV with DVD player and there's a purpose-built children's playground next to the BBQ shelter. The elevated premium chalets are the best of the bunch, with the romantic spa cottage a strong runner-up. Wi-fi is available in the main building only. Hellyers Restaurant (p254) serves the area's best food.

Cradle Mountain Hotel
HOTEL $$$

(📞03-6492 1404; www.cradlemountainhotel.com.au; 3718 Cradle Mountain Rd; r $279-359; 📶) Operated by the Royal Automobile Club of Tasmania, this sleek hotel offers 60 spacious, well-presented and comfortable rooms. All have tea- and coffee-making facilities and TVs and the split-level and deluxe rooms have spa baths. On-site facilities include a small sauna and spa (massages $95 to $150), guest laundry and large lounge bar with pool table.

The on-site Altitude restaurant serves lacklustre food (buffet adult/child $45/21, à la carte mains $29 to $35) with *Fawlty Towers*–style levels of service. Breakfast costs $14 to $27 per person.

Cradle Mountain Lodge
LODGE $$$

(📞03-6492 2100, 1300 806 192; www.cradlemountainlodge.com.au; 4038 Cradle Mountain Rd; d $299-930; ❄📶) Though often described as Cradle Mountain's best accommodation option, we don't think this claim bears scrutiny. The cabins are comfortable but their decor is tired, and the on-site restaurant (p254)

WATCHING WILDLIFE

Cradle Mountain is known for its abundant native wildlife. In addition to the following, it's possible to see Tasmanian devils, echidnas, spotted-tailed quolls and eastern quolls.

Common wombat Seen regularly throughout the park, but best found along the Ronny Creek valley before dusk.

Tasmanian pademelon This small, plump, wallaby-like creature is commonly seen throughout the park, especially around accommodation such as Cradle Mountain Hotel.

Bennett's wallaby Not as common as the pademelon, but still seen regularly, including around Ronny Creek.

Platypus Present in most of the park's rivers, but try Ronny Creek close to dawn or dusk.

is extremely disappointing. Service levels are low too. On the bright side, the lodge puts on plenty of activities and guided walks (most charged), and operates the Waldheim Alpine Spa (massages $140 to $200).

Lemonthyme Wilderness Retreat   LODGE **$$$**
([✓]03-6492 1112; www.lemonthyme.com.au; 770 Dolcoath Rd, Moina; 1- & 2-bedroom cabins $210-365; [@]) A secluded mountain retreat offering cabins with somewhat-tired decor, Lemonthyme has recently acquired new owners so changes may be in the pipeline. It's set in dense forest 22km from the Cradle Mountain Visitor Information Centre and its isolation means that internet access is limited and TV reception nonexistent. The timber-panelled in-house restaurant offers simple meals (mains $23 to $38).

Driving to Cradle Mountain from Devonport, turn onto the gravel Dolcoath Rd, 3km south of Moina, and follow it for a scenic 8km to get here.

Cradle Mountain Cafe   CAFE **$**
([✓]03-6492 1110; www.parks.tas.gov.au; Cradle Mountain Visitor Information Centre, 4057 Cradle Mountain Rd; mains $10-13; [◷]9am-4.30pm) Staff at the hybrid gas station and cafe inside the Cradle Mountain Visitor Information Centre (p255) flit from pumping petrol to manning the coffee machine, so it's perhaps not surprising that the quality of the espresso leaves something to be desired. It's a convenient stop if you wish to pick up a simple sandwich or pie to eat in or take away.

Tavern Bar & Bistro   BISTRO **$$**
([✓]03-6492 2100; www.cradlemountainlodge.com.au; Cradle Mountain Lodge, 4038 Cradle Mountain Rd; mains $23-37; [◷]11.30am-9pm) Hearty fare, a pool table, TVs and a roaring open fire make this barnlike dining space at Cradle Mountain Lodge (p253) popular with families. The menu features pasta, burgers and steaks.

★**Hellyers Restaurant**   MODERN AUSTRALIAN **$$$**
([✓]03-6492 1320; www.cradlevillage.com.au; Cradle Mountain Wilderness Village, 3816 Cradle Mountain Rd; mains $30-42; [◷]7.30-11am, 2-5pm & 5.30-9pm Tue-Sat; [♿]) Head to this restaurant in the Cradle Mountain Wilderness Village (p253) to enjoy the mountain's best food and friendliest service. Serves are enormous and extremely tasty, with steaks and Mediterranean dishes featuring. Large windows look out onto bush and there's a big open fire to keep quests warm in winter. Advance bookings essential.

Highland Restaurant   MODERN AUSTRALIAN **$$$**
([✓]03-6492 2100; www.cradlemountainlodge.com.au; Cradle Mountain Lodge, 4038 Cradle Mountain Rd; mains $32-46; [◷]6-9pm) The quality of food and service doesn't live up to the relatively high prices at the self-professed fine-dining restaurant at Cradle Mountain Lodge (p253). The interior with its large open fire and lake view is pleasant, but the grills and other meat-dominated dishes on offer are unre-

---

ⓘ PARK ACCESS & WEATHER CONDITIONS

Traffic at the Cradle Valley entrance to the park is strictly controlled and once the vehicle quota (or parking capacity) is reached, the boom gates near the Cradle Mountain Lodge won't open to let vehicles in until enough vehicles have left; this can be a particular problem in the morning.

To keep traffic out of the park itself, most access is now by shuttle bus. Buses run every 10 to 20 minutes between 8.30am and 5pm (extended hours during daylight savings) from the Cradle Mountain Transit Centre (next to the visitor information centre). There is plenty of parking behind the visitor centre. The fare is included in a valid parks pass. Buses stop at the unmanned Rangers Station & Interpretation Centre, Snake Hill, Ronny Creek and Dove Lake. Because of the way the shuttle bus operates, we recommend that you visit the interpretation centre on your way out of the park, rather than on the way in. There is limited parking for cars (no campervans) at Dove Lake on a first-come, first-served basis. You'll need a valid parks pass.

Whatever time of the year you visit, be prepared for cold, wet weather in Cradle Valley and on the Overland Track; it rains on seven out of 10 days, is cloudy on eight out of 10 days, the sun shines all day only one day in 10, and it snows in Cradle Valley on average 54 days each year. You could find yourself camping in the snow at any time of year, but you also need to be aware of sunburn, not just in summer. Winds can be extreme.

fined and weren't well cooked on our recent visit. Service is friendly but unpolished.

Lake St Clair

★ Pumphouse Point   BOUTIQUE HOTEL $$$

(☑ 0428 090 436; www.pumphousepoint.com.au; 1 Lake St Clair Rd; shorehouse r $280-420, pumphouse r $460-570; P ⊜) One of Australia's most unique and impressive hotels occupies a five-storey hydroelectric pumphouse built in 1940 on Lake St Clair, accessed via a narrow walkway, as well as a smaller art deco substation on the shoreline. Pumphouse rooms are best. The location, interior fit-out and level of service are world-class, offering guests the experience of a lifetime.

Delicious buffet breakfasts and set-menu dinners ($50 per head) are served on communal tables in the Shorehouse dining room, and every room has a larder stocked with a generous array of Tasmanian food and wine that guests can purchase. Children are not allowed, and there is no wi-fi. Book well in advance, especially if you wish to visit over summer.

Derwent Bridge

Derwent Bridge Chalets & Studios   COTTAGE $$

(☑ 03-6289 1000; www.derwent-bridge.com; 15,478 Lyell Hwy; studio d $155-175, chalet d $195-235, extra adult/child $40/25; ☎) There's a wide range of closely located studios and small chalets on offer here. All are well maintained and equipped, five have wood fires, two have spas and one is set up for guests with disabilities. Some have a kitchenette, others have a full kitchen. The on-site guest laundry and free wi-fi are welcome added extras.

Derwent Bridge Wilderness Hotel   HOTEL $$

(☑ 03-6289 1144; www.derwentbridgewilderness hotel.com.au; Lyell Hwy; dm $35, d with/without bathroom from $165/145, extra adult/child $25/15) A warm and welcoming vibe await at this chalet-style pub. Hotel rooms (breakfast included) are plain but comfortable, while the single backpackers cabins are cold, resemble army barracks and use poorly maintained amenities blocks. There's a massive log fire in the bar and the restaurant serves commendable pub fare (mains $27 to $60) including steaks, parmas and the occasional curry.

Hungry Wombat Café   CAFE $

(☑ 03-6289 1125; 15488 Lyell Hwy; mains $5-16; ☉ 8.30am-5.30pm) The food is homemade and served with pride at this ultrafriendly cafe inside the service station on the highway. The hearty breakfasts are sure to keep bushwalkers going all day, and sandwiches, pies, burgers and sweet slices are available at other times. There's a small grocery section too.

ⓘ Information

There are no ATMs at Cradle Mountain or Derwent Bridge. You'll need to access cash at Sheffield or Queenstown. Note that there is little to no mobile reception at Cradle Mountain. The only provider that has coverage is Telstra, and its coverage is spotty.

Cradle Mountain Visitor Information Centre
(☑ 03-6492 1110; www.parks.tas.gov.au; 4057 Cradle Mountain Rd; ☉ 8.30am-4.30pm; ☎) Located just outside the park boundary, this visitor information centre sells parks passes, rents personal locator beacons and provides all-terrain wheelchairs. The helpful staff can provide detailed bushwalking information and maps, weather condition updates, and advice on bushwalking gear, bush safety and bush etiquette. There is some bushwalking clothing and equipment for sale too. The centre has wheelchair-accessible toilets and an on-site cafe and petrol station. There's no ATM or drinking water to fill up with here, only bottled water to buy in the shop.

Lake St Clair Visitor Information Centre
(☑ 03-6289 1172; www.parks.tas.gov.au; Cynthia Bay; ☉ 9am-4pm Apr-Sep, 8am-5pm Oct-Mar) Located at Cynthia Bay, on the southern boundary of the park. Helpful rangers provide park and walking information and a small shop sells a limited range of bushwalking equipment and clothing. There are also displays on the area's geology, flora and fauna and Aboriginal heritage. An attached privately operated cafe offers coffee and meals of average quality at relatively hefty prices.

Rangers Station & Interpretation Centre
(☑ 03-6492 1110; www.parks.tas.gov.au; Cradle Mountain; ☉ 9.30am-4pm) Just inside the park boundary, this unmanned interpretation centre houses displays about local geology, flora, fauna and Aboriginal heritage. There are wheelchair-accessible toilets here, as well as picnic shelters with electric BBQs.

ⓘ Getting There & Away

BOAT

The Lake St Clair Lodge operates the **Lake St Clair Ferry** (☑ 03-6289 1137; www.lakestclair lodge.com.au) between Cynthia Bay and

Narcissus Bay (one-way adult/child $40/20) at Lake St Clair's northern end. The ferry departs Cynthia Bay three times daily (9am, 12.30pm and 3pm) year-round (or on demand), reaching Narcissus Bay about 30 minutes later and returning at 9.45am, 1pm and 3.45pm. Winter departures are by demand and advance bookings are essential. Rates are for a minimum of six people; the six-person rate applies to bookings of less than six people.

For those wishing to use the ferry service at the end of Overland Track hikes, bookings are essential; you'll need to radio the ferry operator when you arrive at Narcissus Bay to reconfirm your booking.

You can also ride the ferry from Cynthia Bay to Echo Point (adult/child $35/17), and then walk back to Cynthia Bay (two to three hours).

BUS

Cradle Mountain

Tassielink (p306) buses travel between Launceston ($61.50, 3¼ hours) and the Cradle Mountain Visitor Information Centre four times per week, stopping at the *Spirit of Tasmania* dock in East Devonport, at the Devonport town centre and in Sheffield en route. They continue to Queenstown ($74.80, six hours) twice weekly, where there are connections to Strahan.

To get from Hobart to Cradle Mountain, you'll need to travel via Launceston or Queenstown. Tassielink services travel from Hobart to Queenstown via the visitor centre at Lake St Clair ($53.60, 2¾ hours) four times per week, stopping at destinations including New Norfolk, Bronte Junction and Derwent Bridge en route. The Hobart to Launceston route is a daily service ($35, 2½ hours).

Lake St Clair

Tassielink services travel from Hobart to Queenstown via the visitor centre at Lake St Clair ($53.60, 2¾ hours) four times per week, stopping at destinations including New Norfolk, Bronte Junction and Derwent Bridge en route.

To get from Launceston to Lake St Clair, head to Hobart and take the bus to Queenstown via Lake St Clair, or take the service to Queenstown ($74.80, six hours, twice weekly), overnight there, then take the Queenstown–Hobart bus to Lake St Clair ($32.10, 1¾ hours) the following day.

CAR & MOTORCYCLE

If driving, fill up with petrol before heading to Cradle Mountain – although petrol is sold at the visitor centre (p255), prices are higher there than in the towns. There's a petrol station at Derwent Bridge where the same caveat applies. If you park at the visitor centre, shuttle buses run into the park every 10 to 20 minutes throughout the day.

The Southwest

The wild southwest corner of this island state is an edge-of-the-world domain made up of primordial forests, rugged mountains and endless heathland, all fringed by untamed beaches and turbulent seas. This is among the last great wilderness areas on earth: an isolated, magisterial place that's ripe for adventure.

Just one road enters the 6000-plus-sq-km Southwest National Park, the largest national park in Tasmania and part of the Unesco-listed Tasmanian Wilderness World Heritage Area, and this only goes as far as the hydro-electric station on the Gordon Dam. Otherwise, all access is by light plane to the gravel airstrip at Melaleuca, by sailing boat around the tempestuous coastline, or on foot.

History

When the first humans came to this part of the world, they inhabited a planet in the grip of an ice age. The southwest was then covered in frigid open grasslands – ideal for hunting game and covering large distances on foot. Between 18,000 and 12,000 years ago, as the ice retreated, the landscape changed dramatically. Rising sea levels drowned river valleys and formed land-locked waterways like Bathurst Harbour. Warmer temperatures also brought more extensive forest cover, which Indigenous Tasmanians burnt periodically to keep it open for hunting.

European explorers were at first appalled by the landscape. Matthew Flinders, the first to circumnavigate Tasmania, described the southwest, and in particular its ragged mountains, as 'the most dismal that can be imagined. The eye ranges over these peaks… with astonishment and horror.' Most of the early explorers were surveyors who cut tracks here and endured great hardships in the name of opening the region for development. But the acidic soils of the southwest, its remoteness and harsh weather conditions meant little farming ever got off the ground. Mineral deposits also proved less than anticipated, so although a road was cut as far as Gordon Bend in the 1880s, no permanent access to the southwest was established. Apart from the hardy few who came to Bathurst Harbour to hunt for Huon pine, and a few stalwart miners at Adamsfield and Melaleuca, early European Tasmanians left the southwest well alone. They simply re-

THE GIANTS OF THE STYX

The Styx: even the name is evocative, speaking of the ancients and underworlds. If you come to this valley in Tasmania – a spot formally called the **Styx Tall Trees Conservation Area** but usually referred to as the Valley of the Giants – you'll be absorbed in a domain of ancient tall trees and forests so mysteriously beautiful you'd be forgiven for thinking you have indeed crossed to another world. The subject of heated battles between conservationists and loggers over many decades, the valley was added to the Tasmanian Wilderness World Heritage Area in 2013 and the entire Styx River area was designated a regional reserve.

In the rich and heavily watered soils of the valley, trees grow exceptionally tall. The *Eucalyptus regnans* (swamp gums) here are the loftiest trees in the southern hemisphere, and the highest hardwood trees on earth. Trees of up to 95m in height have been recorded in the valley, and many of the trees here reach more than 80m above the ground.

For a self-drive and walking guide to the Styx, check out the Wilderness Society website (www.wilderness.org.au/styx-self-drive-and-walking-guide).

Note that the roads here are unsealed and, though manageable by 2WD vehicles, are slippery after rain. To get here from Maydena, travel 2.5km west along the B61 and turn right into Florentine Rd and then right again into Styx Rd, looping through the overpass and continuing around 20km along Styx Rd to Big Tree Forest Reserve and Styx Tall Trees Forest Reserve.

---

garded it as uninhabitable. The first tranche of the national park was declared in 1955. In 1972 parts of the southwest were flooded to establish hydroelectric dams.

🏃 Activities

For the well-prepared wanderer, there's plenty on offer: challenging multiday walks (as well as shorter wanders), trout fishing and kayaking on Lakes Gordon and Pedder, and remote sea kayaking on the waterways of Bathurst Harbour and Port Davey. Those who prefer aerial pleasures can take a mind-blowing abseil down the curvaceous wall of the Gordon Dam, or swoop over the valleys and mountains on a scenic southwest joy flight.

There are two main walking tracks in the park: the 70km four- to five-day **Port Davey Track**, between Melaleuca and Scott's Peak road near Lake Pedder; and the 85km, six- to eight-day **South Coast Track**, between Melaleuca and Cockle Creek, near Southport close to the park's southeast edge.

👉 Tours

Par Avion SCENIC FLIGHTS
(☑ 03-6248 5390; www.paravion.com.au; adult/child half-day $395/345, full day $495/445) You can swoop over the southwest on a scenic small-plane flight with this Cambridge-based operator. On a clear day you can see the whole of this corner of Tasma-

nia as you buzz over wild beaches and jagged peaks before landing at Melaleuca and heading out onto Bathurst Harbour on a boat. Half- and full-day tours are available.

Bushwalker transfers to Melaleuca (for the South Coast Track) are $300 one way.

Tasmanian Expeditions WALKING
(☑ 1300 666 856; www.tasmanianexpeditions. au) Tasmanian Expeditions offers numerous walking-tour options in the southwest, including the five-day Mt Anne Circuit ($1795 per person), the seven-day Port Davey Track ($2495), the nine-day South Coast Track ($2295) and 16-day Port Davey and South Coast Track ($4890). It also offers a seven-day kayaking trip on Bathurst Harbour and Port Davey ($3250).

Roaring 40s Kayaking KAYAKING
(☑ 0455 949 777; www.roaring40skayaking.com. au; 3-/7-day trip $2250/3250) To experience this wilderness area from the water, consider a sea-kayaking adventure. From November to early April, Hobart-based Roaring 40s Kayaking offers camp-based kayaking trips exploring Port Davey and Bathurst Harbour with access by light plane to/from Hobart.

ℹ️ Getting There & Away

The two major access points for the Southwest National Park are the tiny town of Southport, 1½ hours and 97km south of Hobart on the A6 (the most southerly township in Australia); and the tiny settlement of Strathgordon on Lake Pedder, accessed via the B61 highway. Strathgordon is a 2½-hour, 155km drive west of Hobart; there's no fuel available past Maydena on this drive, and even there you may not have any luck – it's best to fill the tank at Westerway. Neither Strathgordon nor Southport are serviced by public transport.

Par Avion (p257) flies bushwalkers into remote Melaleuca from Hobart.

Maydena

03 / POP 230

This little town in the Tyenna Valley is surrounded by hills and eucalypt forests and is the northern access point for the Southwest National Park. Previously semisomnolent, Maydena's mood is expected to lift now that the multi-million-dollar cross-country Maydena Bike Park (www.maydena bikepark.com) is open. Previously, most visitors stopped only momentarily en route to Strathgordon and Lake Gordon, or to the Styx Tall Trees Conservation Area (aka Valley of the Giants), 25km southeast.

🏃 Activities

Junee Cave   WALKING

(☑ 03-6288 1149; www.parks.tas.gov.au; off Junee Rd) A waterfall cascades out of the mouth of this cave located approximately 3.7km northwest of Maydena. Part of a 30km-long series of caverns known as the Junee River karst system, it's easy to access. To get here from Gordon River Rd (B61), take Junee Rd north out of town for about 10 minutes to reach the start of the walking track.

From the start of the track it's about a 10-minute walk to the mouth of the cave. The Junee River system includes Niggly Cave, reputedly the deepest cave in Australia, at 375m. Cave divers make hair-raising journeys through the flooded underground passageways, but other visitors can't enter.

🛏️ Sleeping & Eating

Giants' Table & Cottages   COTTAGE $$

(☑ 0407 139 497; www.giantstable.com.au; 13 Junee Rd; d $135-185, extra person $25; 🐾) Named for the giant trees in the Styx, these were once simple workers' cottages. Now restored, they're clean, comfortable and warm self-catering choices. Some sleep two, others can accommodate large families and groups. Platypuses are a frequent sight in the property's ponds, and guests can participate in daily feedings of the alpacas, geese, miniature goats and sheep that live on-site.

Maydena Country Cabins   CABIN $$

(☑ 03-6288 2212; www.maydenacabins.com.au; 46 Junee Rd; d $175; 🐾) On offer here are two cosy timber-lined cabins, one sleeping two and the other up to four. Both have glorious mountain views. There's also an in-house B&B option, and the friendly owners are a mine of information on the area. Breakfast costs $7.50 per person. There's a small herd of resident alpacas

Mountain Cafe   CAFE $

(☑ 03-6288 3048; www.facebook.com/mountain cafemaydena; 38 Kallista Rd; mains $6-16; ⊙ 10am-8pm Fri, to 3pm Sat & Sun Apr-Dec, to 4pm daily Jan-Mar; 🐾) The last coffee stop for those making their way into the Southwest National Park, this cafe offers simple food, hot drinks and a wood fire to keep customers warm in the cooler months. It sometimes closes when business is slow (particularly in winter). You'll find it at the eastern entrance to town.

ℹ️ Getting There & Away

Maydena is about 90km west of Hobart, on the B61. There are no public-transport options here. Fuel is sold at the Mountain Cafe, but opening hours are shaky – it's safer to fill up in Westerway on the way in.

Lake Pedder Impoundment

This vast flooded valley system at the northern edge of the southwest wilderness covers the area that once cradled the original Lake Pedder, a spectacularly beautiful natural lake that was the region's ecological jewel. The largest glacial outwash lake in the world, its shallow, whisky-coloured waters covered 3 sq km. The lake was home to several endangered species and considered so important that it was the first part of the southwest to be protected within its own national park. But even this status failed to preserve it and Lake Pedder disappeared beneath hydroelectric dam waters in 1972.

These days, the artificial replacement is 242 sq km and is the largest freshwater lake in Australia. At its northern tip is the tiny settlement of Strathgordon.

🏃 Activities

Trout fishing is popular here. The lake is well stocked, and fish caught range from 1kg to the occasional 20kg monster. Only artificial lures can be used. Small boats or dinghies are discouraged because the lake is

55km long and prone to dangerously large waves.

Ted's Beach, about 4km before Strathgordon, is a popular fishing spot with a boat launching area. Another popular site is the Edgar Dam area, 30km along the Scotts Peak Rd, just before Scotts Peak. **Kayaking** is also popular.

Always check the weather before you go out onto the water. Conditions here can change rapidly and there can be swells of up to 1.5m in certain wind conditions.

🛏 Sleeping

There are two camping grounds near the lake's southern shore, the **Edgar Camping Ground** (☑03-6288 1149; www.parks.tas.gov.au; off Scotts Peak Rd) and the **Huon Campground** (off Scotts Peak Rd), as well as **Ted's Beach Campground** (Gordon River Rd), near Strathgordon. All three camping grounds are free; no advance bookings can be made.

Pedder Wilderness Lodge in Strathgordon offers rooms and self-contained apartments.

❶ Getting There & Away

The only road into the park (the B61) goes to Strathgordon and the Gordon Dam. No public transport braves these locales. Note that no fuel is available past Maydena on the road in, and even there you may not have any luck – fill up at Westerway.

Strathgordon

☑03 / POP 10

Built in 1969 to house 2000 Hydro Electric Commission (HEC) employees during the construction of the Gordon Dam, Strathgordon remains the base for those who operate the power station today. About 2km past the ex-Hydro settlement is Lake Pedder Lookout, with good views over the lake. A further 10km west is the **Gordon Dam** itself, built in the 1970s with a concrete wall 198m long and 140m high. From the car park, visitors can walk down a flight of steps and walk out along the perfect curve of the dam wall – a spectacular and slightly scary experience.

🏃 Activities

Aardvark Adventures   ADVENTURE SPORTS
(☑03-6273 7722; www.aardvarkadventures.com.au; per person $210) You can abseil over the edge of the Gordon Dam wall with Hobart-based Aardvark Adventures, which organises abseiling trips here (suitable for beginners, minimum two people). It's

claimed to be the highest commercial abseil in the world.

🎊 Festivals & Events

End of the Earth Festival   MUSIC
(www.endoftheearth.com.au; ⊙Feb) The Pedder Wilderness Lodge hosts this two-day outdoor music festival at the start of February each year.

🛏 Sleeping

Pedder Wilderness Lodge   LODGE $$
(Lake Pedder Chalet; ☑03-6280 1166; www.pedderwildernesslodge.com.au; Gordon River Rd; d/tr from $140/170, units $210-240, ste $390; 🛜🐾) There's a wide range of comfortable accommodation at this former hydro-workers lodge, including budget rooms, self-contained apartments sleeping four, family rooms, spa suites and lodge rooms with or without lake views. The **Twelvetrees Restaurant** (set breakfast $10 to $18, lunch mains $18 to $24, dinner $20 to $36) has a bar and an open fire. Leisure facilities include an indoor pool, gym and tennis courts.

❶ Getting There & Away

Strathgordon is accessed via the B61 highway, a 2½-hour, 155km drive west of Hobart. The town isn't serviced by public transport and no fuel is available past Maydena, and even there you may not have any luck – fill up at Westerway.

Southwest National Park

The state's largest national park is made up of remote, wild country: forests, mountains, grassy plains and seascapes. Home to both the Huon pine, which lives for 3000 years, and the swamp gum, the world's tallest flowering plant, it also hosts about 300 species of lichen, moss and fern – some very rare. These festoon the rainforests, and the alpine meadows are replete with wildflowers and flowering shrubs. Through it all run wild rivers, their rapids tearing through deep gorges and their waterfalls plunging over cliffs. All of this, combined with majestic Mt Anne, the Frankland Range and the jagged crest of the Western Arthur Range, renders the park irresistible to photographers, bushwalkers and nature enthusiasts.

🏃 Activities

Day Walks

The **Creepy Crawly Nature Trail**, a 10-minute duck-in, duck-out stroll through

ℹ ACCESSING THE SOUTH COAST TRACK

The start or finish point of the South Coast Track, **Melaleuca** is little more than a quartzite gravel airstrip with a wooden shed for an airport. If you're flying in, you'll see the workings of the earth from the tin mining carried out by hardy bushmen over the years. All around are button-grass plains, mountains, water and wilderness. You can also visit the excellent bird hide, where you might see the extremely rare orange-bellied parrot.

There are two extremely basic walkers huts at Melaleuca, and there's camping nearby. A toilet, water and mattresses are available, but there are no cooking facilities. You'll need to bring your own fuel stove. No supplies are available here, so you'll need to carry everything with you.

rainforest, starts about 2km after the Scotts Peak turn off from the Gordon River Rd.

From Scotts Peak Rd you can climb to **Mt Eliza**, a steep, five-hour return walk giving panoramic views over the Lake Pedder Impoundment and **Mt Solitary**. Another challenging eight-hour walk for experienced hikers is from Red Tape Creek (29km south of the main road, along Scotts Peak Rd) to **Lake Judd**.

From the Huon Campground at the Lake Pedder Impoundment, the best short walk follows the start of the **Port Davey Track** through forest and button-grass plains. **Mt Wedge** is a popular five-hour return walk (signposted off the main road) that offers great views of the Lake Pedder Impoundment and Lake Gordon.

Multiday Walks

There are two well-known walks in the southwest. One is the 70km **Port Davey Track**, between Scotts Peak Rd near Lake Pedder and Melaleuca, which takes four to five days. The other is the considerably more popular, 85km **South Coast Track**, between Melaleuca and Cockle Creek, near Southport close to the park's southeastern edge, which takes six to eight days.

When walking here, hikers should be prepared for weather that could bring anything from sunburn to snow flurries. Par Avion flies bushwalkers into or out of the southwest, landing at Melaleuca, and there's vehicle access to Cockle Creek. Comprehensive South Coast Track information is available at www.parks.tas.gov.au.

Of the more difficult walks that require a high degree of bushwalking skill, the shortest is the three-day circuit of the **Mt Anne Range**, a challenging walk with some difficult scrambling. The walk to **Federation Peak**, which has earned a reputation as the most difficult bushwalking peak in Australia, will take a highly experienced walker seven to eight days. The spectacular **Western Arthur Range** is an extremely difficult traverse, for which seven to 11 days are recommended.

ℹ Information

Get your national-parks pass and information about the southwest at the Mt Field National Park Visitor Centre (p93), near Maydena.

ℹ Getting There & Away

Only one road (the B61) enters the park, and this only goes as far as the hydroelectric station on the Gordon Dam at Strathgordon. Otherwise, all access is by by sailing boat around the tempestuous coastline, on foot, or by a **Par Avion** (☑ 03-6248 5390; www.paravion.com.au) flight to the gravel airstrip at Melaleuca. Par Avion operates on-demand 45-minute flights in a twin-engine aircraft between Cambridge near Hobart and Melaleuca (one way $300). No public transport services the park.

Understand
Tasmania

Tasmania Today

There's an expression from the 1980s: 'Wake up, Australia, Tasmania is floating away!' Mainlanders might not have been too interested in Tasmania back then, but today Australia is wide awake to Tasmania's loveliness. Tree-change migrants are escaping to the island – with its natural beauty, fab food, compact cities and relatively affordable real estate – reversing the historical drift of young Tasmanians heading north for careers or study. Meanwhile, Tasmania's never-ending conservation battle continues: will tourism be the healer?

Best on Film
The Hunter (2011) Grumpy Willem Dafoe hunts the last Tasmanian tiger.
The Light Between Oceans (2016) Michael Fassbender and lighthouses; partly filmed in Stanley.
The Sound of One Hand Clapping (1998) A father and daughter at odds in Tasmania's Central Highlands.
Lion (2016) An adopted son finds his parents using Google Earth; partly filmed in Hobart.
The Tale of Ruby Rose (1988) Ruby gets spooked in the Tasmanian wilds.

Best in Print
The Narrow Road to the Deep North (Richard Flanagan; 2014) From Hobart to the infamous Thai–Burma railway. The 2014 Man Booker Prize winner.
In Tasmania (Nicholas Shakespeare; 2004) A British spin on the island's history, heritage and culture.
Wood Green (Sean Rabin; 2016) An ode to Hobart disguised as a novel.
Shadow of the Thylacine (Col Bailey; 2013) An optimistic assertion of the Tasmanian tiger's continued existence. *Lure of the Thylacine* is Bailey's follow-up (2016).
For the Term of His Natural Life (Marcus Clarke; 1874) Classic account of convict life at Port Arthur.

An Outdoor State of Mind

The modern Tasmanian identity is mirrored in the island's ancient and remarkable landscape. Dark foliage and craggy peaks are whipped by notorious winds, and stunted winter days are infused with the stark clarity of southern light. This gothic environment fosters a keen sense of adventure and an understated resilience. Rather than hiding indoors behind sandstone walls, Tasmanians embrace their wilderness: getting into it, over it, or on top of it is something the Tasmanian work–life balance absolutely mandates. Beneath woollen beanies and layers of thermals, locals need little provocation to go camping, bushwalking, caving, kayaking...

New Urban Vibes

Hobart and Launceston's growing urban fizz is proving irresistible to ex-Tasmanians, who are heading back home, confident they're not missing out on anything that Melbourne, Sydney or London can offer. Well, maybe not London...but Hobart does have water views to rival Sydney's, and it continues to evolve into a cosmopolitan hub with craft-beer bars, hip coffee hang-outs, art-house cinema, gourmet providores and farmers markets. Meanwhile, Launceston has been busily transforming itself from 'bogan' backwater into a boutique river city full of students on the run from the books. If you're after a live band or a beer, you're in the right town. Tourism is doing well here, too, with two big new hotels being built.

On Your Plate & in Your Glass

A highlight of any Tasmanian trip is getting stuck into the island's food and drink, especially fresh seafood, luscious fruit, craft beer and stellar wines. This cool-climate combo is a hit with both Australian and international chefs: local salmon is served in the restaurants of Tokyo, while whiffy Tassie cheeses provide the perfect finish to meals in Melbourne and Sydney bistros. And how about the whisky! Hobart's Sullivans Cove whisky won the coveted gold medal at the 2014 World Whisky Masters in London. This success spawned a whisky explosion: there are now a dozen distillers across the state producing superb single malts. And, of course, the classic Tasmanian snack on-the-run remains the curried-scallop pie – a peppery, lurid-yellow concoction sheathed in pie pastry that will fuel your wilderness adventure, solve your morning hang-over or prepare you for tomorrow's.

Small Island, Big Issues

The passionate environmental debates that regularly erupt in Tasmania often overflow to become federal issues, with conflict developing over what the big island thinks the little island should be protecting. Should it fight for a close-knit community, jobs for locals and a sequestered way of life? Or should it safeguard the wilderness, justly famous beyond these island shores? Meanwhile, tourism and hospitality have been bubbling away nicely here. It seems that, regardless of the bitter pro- and anti-conservation divide, Tasmania is perceived elsewhere as an increasingly desirable place to visit – perhaps tourism is the pathway to future prosperity.

Wanna Buy a House?

As the mainland Australian real-estate sector continues its dizzying ascent into uncharted price terrain – especially in Sydney and Melbourne, where first-home aspirants have next to no chance of breaking into the market – it's little wonder that buyers are now looking to Tasmania for a decent deal. Despite a mini-boom in 2016–17, median house prices here are still reasonable compared with the mainland, and the housing stock itself is a superb collation of well-preserved architectural styles. This is particularly evident in Launceston, where the city's historically lethargic economy has meant there's been little cash around to knock stuff down and rebuild. Now all you need to fast-track your move to Tassie is a job!

POPULATION: **519,200**

AREA: **68,401 SQ KM**

GDP: **$26 BILLION**

INFLATION: **1.8%**

UNEMPLOYMENT: **6.1%**

if Tasmania were 100 people

42 would live in Hobart
22 would live in Launceston
6 would live in Devonport
4 would live in Burnie
3 would live in Kingston
23 would live in other places

Belief Systems

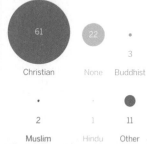

61 Christian
22 None
3 Buddhist
2 Muslim
1 Hindu
11 Other

population per sq km

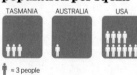

TASMANIA   AUSTRALIA   USA

👤 ≈ 3 people

History

Tasmania's short written history is bleak and powerful. But, like the rest of Australia, it has a much longer story – that of its *palawa* (first man), the term some Tasmanian Aboriginal people use to describe themselves. Though they can be seen as a people all but wiped out in an attempted genocide, their culture survives today despite the fact that their home became Britain's prison island in the first half of the 19th century.

Tasmania's Aboriginal Peoples

Tasmania was part of the super-continent Gondwana until it broke away and drifted south some 160 million years ago. Aboriginal people probably migrated across a land bridge that joined Tasmania to the rest of Australia at least 35,000 years ago. Sea levels were much lower then and the Tasmanian climate much drier and colder. Aboriginal peoples settled in the extensive grasslands on the western side of Tasmania, where they hunted wallabies. When the last ice age ended between 18,000 and 12,000 years ago, glaciers retreated, sea levels rose and tall forests became established on Tasmania's western half. In the east, rainfall increased and new grasslands developed. Cut off by the rising sea, Tasmania 'floated away' from mainland Australia, and a distinctive existence began for the people, animals and plants of the island.

Life on the Smaller Island

The culture of the Tasmanian Aboriginal people diverged from the way people were living on the mainland, as they developed a sustainable, seasonal culture of hunting, fishing and gathering. The islanders produced sophisticated boats and used them to hunt seals and mutton birds on and around the offshore islands.

Those who remained in the west lived mainly on the coast. Aboriginal women collected shellfish (mussels, abalone and oysters), the remains of which comprise the enormous middens still found around Tasmania's coastline. Both men and women wore necklaces of shell. They sheltered in bark lean-tos and protected themselves from the

TIMELINE	12,000–8000 BC	1642	1700s
	Tasmania's Aboriginal peoples arrive on the Australian continent from 60,000 to 35,000 BC. They become separated from the mainland when sea levels rise following the last ice age.	Dutch explorer Abel Tasman eyeballs Tasmania and lands at Blackmans Bay south of Hobart. He names the island Van Diemen's Land after a Dutch governor.	Visiting Captain Bligh cleverly plants the isle's first apple tree. Three centuries later the growers of the Huon Valley still toast their good fortune with zingy cider.

island's cold weather with furs and by applying a thick mix of ochre, charcoal and fat to their skin.

European Impact

The first European to spy Tasmania was Dutch navigator Abel Tasman, who bumped into it in 1642. He named this new place Van Diemen's Land after the Dutch East Indies' governor. It's estimated that there were between 5000 and 10,000 Indigenous people in Tasmania when Europeans arrived, living in 'bands' of around 50 people, each claiming rights over a specific area of land and being part of one of nine main language groups.

European sealers began to work Bass Strait in 1798, raiding tribal communities along the coast and kidnapping Aboriginal women to act as forced labour and sex slaves. The sealers were uninterested in Aboriginal land and eventually formed commercial relationships with the Aboriginal people, trading dogs and other items so that they could take Aboriginal women back to their islands.

Stone engravings have been found along Tasmania's west coast; these are thought to be important symbols of Tasmanian Aboriginal beliefs. The island's Indigenous population also had a knowledge of astronomy.

HISTORY EUROPEAN IMPACT

Australia's Second European Settlement

In the late 1790s Governor King of New South Wales decided to establish a second settlement in Australia, south of Sydney Cove. Port Phillip Bay in Victoria was initially considered, but the site was rejected due to a lack

---

MAPPING VAN DIEMEN'S LAND

Nearly 130 years after Abel Tasman's efforts, Tasmania was visited by a series of other European sailors, including captains Tobias Furneaux, James Cook and William Bligh. Between 1770 and 1790 they all visited Adventure Bay on Bruny Island and believed it to be part of the Australian mainland, rather than an island off an island (off an island).

In 1792 Admiral Bruni D'Entrecasteaux explored the southeastern coastline more thoroughly, mapping and naming many of its features. Many major landmarks in this area still bear the French names he gave them.

In 1798 Lieutenant Matthew Flinders circumnavigated Van Diemen's Land and proved that it was indeed an island.

In 1828 George Frankland was appointed Tasmania's surveyor-general. Determined to map the entire state, he sent many surveyors on long, arduous journeys during the 1830s, often accompanying them. By 1845, when Frankland died, most of the state was roughly mapped and catalogued.

Building roads across the mountainous west was difficult and many were surveyed across all sorts of landscapes before being abandoned. It wasn't until 1932 that the Lyell Hwy from Hobart to Queenstown finally opened for business, linking the west coast and Hobart.

1788	1798	1803	1804
The First Fleet arrives at Sydney with its cargo of convicts. More than 200 years later, family connections to these colonists are still a badge of honour for contemporary Australians.	'Straitsmen', a rough bunch of sealers, make their home and their living in Bass Strait. It's a tough life, characterised by long periods working this unforgiving stretch of water.	The *Lady Nelson* floats into Risdon Cove north of Hobart, Australia's second British penal site. A massacre ensues; the site is eventually returned to the Tasmanian Aboriginal community in 1995.	The Risdon Cove settlement relocates to Sullivans Cove (the present-day Hobart waterfront). Another settlement at George Town on the island's north coast is also established.

of water on the Mornington Peninsula and, in 1803, Tasmania's Risdon Cove was chosen. A year later, the settlement was moved 10km south to the present site of Hobart on the other side of the Derwent River. The threat of French interest in the island suggested the need for a settlement up north; a site called George Town was proclaimed on the Tamar River in 1804.

That same year 74 convicts were shipped out to Van Diemen's Land, with 71 soldiers, plus their 21 wives and 14 children. Penal settlements were built in the island's most inhospitable places. Macquarie Harbour, on the harsh west coast, became Tasmania's first penal site in 1822, and by 1833 roughly 2000 convicts a year were sent to this end-of-the-earth colony as punishment for often-trivial crimes.

The community quickly developed a very particular character: law-lessness and debauchery were rife. Nascent Van Diemen's Land was dominated by a mentality of 'If it grows, chop it down; if it runs, shoot it'. Yet it was also defined by great pioneering innovation and courage.

Settlers initially spread along the island's southeast coast towards Port Arthur, along the east coast and around the Launceston area. By 1807 an overland route from Hobart to Launceston had been forged. Stone was readily available for construction work and many early stone buildings still survive. Some of the best examples can be found in Richmond and in Ross and Oatlands along the Midland Hwy.

To the settlers, Tasmania's big unknowns were its rugged western and central hinterlands, where difficult, mountainous country barred the way. The first Europeans to cross the island were escapees from Macquarie Harbour – many escaped, but only a few survived the journey to Hobart Town.

The reference to 'Truganini in chains' in the Midnight Oil song 'Truganini' is not factually correct. It's more likely to be a metaphor for the appalling treatment of Tasmania's Aboriginal people.

The Black Wars

While Van Diemen's Land's new settlements were finding their feet, initial exchanges with Indigenous islanders were friendly enough. But things soon turned hostile as European fences and farming encroached on Aboriginal hunting grounds and significant places. In return, Aboriginal people began to carry out their own raids. In 1816 Governor Thomas Davey produced his 'Proclamation to the Aborigines', which represented settlers and Indigenous Tasmanians living together amicably – in direct contrast to the realities of a brutal conflict.

By the 1820s these territorial disputes had developed into the so-called Black Wars, as Aboriginal people increasingly refused to surrender their lands, women and children without a fight. In 1828 martial law was declared by Lieutenant-Governor Arthur. Aboriginal groups were systematically murdered, arrested or forced at gunpoint from districts settled by whites – arsenic on bread and steel traps designed to catch humans

1811	1822–53	1824	1830
Governor Lachlan Macquarie arrives from Sydney and draws up initial plans for Hobart's streets. Public buildings erected at this time include the Mt Nelson Signal Station.	Convicts are imprisoned at various penal settlements around the state, including Sarah Island and Port Arthur. For some it (eventually) presents the opportunity of a new start.	The Cascade Brewery opens in Hobart under the shadow of Mt Wellington, making it Australia's oldest continuously operating brewery.	The Black Line, a slow-moving human chain of 2200 men, fails to flush out Tasmania's Aboriginal inhabitants. The intention was to corral all Aboriginal people on the Tasman Peninsula south of Eaglehawk Neck.

were used. Many more people succumbed to European diseases, against which they had no immunity.

Meanwhile, around Bass Strait, a disapproving Van Diemen's Land establishment contemptuously termed the descendants of sealers and Aboriginal women 'half-castes', applying continual pressure on Bass Strait islanders to adopt European farming ways and assimilate with mainlanders.

The Black Line

As the Black Wars continued, the British were growing concerned about how it might look to the world if their actions led to the extinction of an entire race of people. In 1830, in an attempt to contain all Aboriginal people on the Tasman Peninsula for their security and to preserve

TRUGANINI'S LEGACY

One of the last surviving 'full-blooded' Tasmanian Aboriginal people, Truganini lived through the white invasion of her land, and her death has become a symbol of the attempted genocide of her people.

Truganini was born on Bruny Island in 1812, the daughter of Mangana, the chief of the Nuenonne people. Along with her husband, Woureddy, she left her island home to travel with George Robinson – accounts also suggest she lived with sealers as a young woman, an experience that left her unable to bear children. When she was older, Truganini lived with fellow Tasmanian Aboriginals in the derelict environment of Wybalenna on Flinders Island and afterwards at the disastrous Oyster Cove settlement.

It is remarkable, given the times, that Truganini lived into her 60s. When she died in Hobart in 1876, the Tasmanian government declared that she was the last of the island's Indigenous peoples and that her race was extinct (in fact, she was outlived by Suke and Fanny Cochrane, two women of tribal parentage – and of course the many other mixed-race Tasmanian Aboriginal people who survive today). The announcement of her death, and the resulting funeral procession through Hobart, aimed to 'end the native problem'. The demise of the Tasmanian Aboriginal race was taken as fact – and still endures in some encyclopedias and school history lessons.

Against her wishes to be buried in the mountains behind Oyster Cove, or dropped deep into D'Entrecasteaux Channel, Truganini's 4ft-tall skeleton was instead displayed for many years as a public curio in the Tasmanian Museum. Much to the chagrin of the Royal Society in Tasmania, other parts of her contested remains were shipped to Britain by the Royal College of Surgeons in London and were only repatriated in 2002. It took more than a lifetime for Truganini's wishes to be granted and her ashes finally scattered in the channel beside her beloved Bruny Island. You can visit a memorial to Truganini at the Neck on Bruny Island, and there's a memorial on Mt Nelson behind Hobart, at the top of the Truganini Track.

their culture, a human chain of 2200 men known as the Black Line was formed by settlers and soldiers, moving through the settled areas of the state from Moulting Lagoon, through Campbell Town to Quamby Bluff. Three weeks later this farcical manoeuvre had succeeded in capturing only an old man and a boy, and this confirmed settlers' fears that they could not defeat the Aboriginal people by force of arms. The *Hobart Courier* mocked the exercise: it had cost half the colony's annual budget. In turn, it must have given the Aboriginal people an awful sense that their time was running out.

Misguided Conciliation

Following the failure of the Black Line, Lieutenant-Governor Arthur consented to George Augustus Robinson's plan to 'conciliate' the Aboriginal people. In effect, Robinson enticed and cajoled virtually all of the Aboriginal people in mainland Tasmania to lay down their arms, leave their traditional lands and accompany him to new settlements. In doing so he became the first European to walk across much of the state, adding the title of explorer to that of missionary. There is strong historical evidence that the people of Oyster Bay, including their prominent chief Tongerlongetter, whom Robinson regarded as 'a man of great tact and judgement', followed him to a succession of settlements in the Furneaux Islands based on the promise of sanctuary and land. Instead, they were subjected to attempts to 'civilise' and Christianise them, and made to work for the government.

After enduring a number of moves, including to Sarah Island on the west coast, Tasmania's Indigenous inhabitants were finally settled at Wybalenna (Black Man's Houses) on Flinders Island. One by one the people began to die from a potent mixture of despair, homesickness, poor food and respiratory disease. In 1847 those who had managed to survive petitioned Queen Victoria, complaining of their treatment and referring to the 'agreement' they thought Robinson had made with Lieutenant-Governor Arthur on their behalf. Wybalenna was eventually abandoned and the survivors transferred to mainland Tasmania. Of the 135 who had been sent to Flinders Island, only 47 lived to make the journey to Oyster Cove, south of Hobart. The new accommodation here proved to be substandard and the Aboriginal people once again experienced the criminal neglect of the authorities, and growing demoralisation. Within a decade, half of the 47 were dead.

Convict Life

The actual site of the first penal settlement in Tasmania was on small Sarah Island, in Macquarie Harbour on the west coast. The prisoners sent there were those who had committed further crimes after arriving

Bridges to the Past
....
Richmond Bridge (p88), Richmond
....
Ross Bridge (p129), Ros
....
Red Bridge (p131), Campbell Town
....
Spiky Bridge (p144), near Swansea

1932	1934	1935	1936
Born in Stanley in 1879, Joseph Lyons becomes Australia's first (and only) Tasmanian prime minister. The suburb of Lyons in Canberra is named after him in 1965.	Construction of the 7km Pinnacle Rd up Mt Wellington begins, creating employment for thousands of men during the Depression.	Debonair Tasmanian Errol Flynn stars in *Captain Blood*, a rollicking tale in which his character is sold as a slave to Olivia de Havilland, escapes and becomes a pirate.	The last known thylacine (aka Tasmanian tiger) dies in Hobart's Beaumaris Zoo. Wild sightings continue into the 21st century, but no evidence of the species' continued survival is ever produced.

in Australia. Their severe punishment was hard manual labour, cutting down Huon pine in the rainforest. It's believed conditions were so dreadful that some prisoners committed murder in order to be sent for trial and execution in Hobart.

The number of prisoners sent to Van Diemen's Land increased in 1825. In the same year the island was recognised as a colony independent of NSW, and another penal settlement was established, this one off the east coast on Maria Island, where prisoners were treated more humanely.

In 1830 a third penal settlement was established at Port Arthur on the Tasman Peninsula. Shortly after its construction, the other two penal settlements closed – Maria Island in 1832 and Sarah Island in 1833.

Punishments meted out to convicts at Port Arthur included weeks of solitary confinement. The worst prisoners were sent to work in the coal mines of the nearby Saltwater River, where they were housed in miserably damp underground cells. A visit to Port Arthur evokes the terrible conditions suffered by prisoners during this era.

A Name Change & A New Image

In 1840 convict transportation to NSW ceased, resulting in an increase in the number of convicts being sent to Van Diemen's Land; there was a peak of 5329 new arrivals in 1842. In 1844 control of the Norfolk Island penal settlement (in the Pacific Ocean, 1610km northeast of Sydney) was transferred from NSW to Van Diemen's Land and by 1848 'VDL' was the only place in the British Empire to which convicts were still being transported.

Vociferous opposition to the continued transportation of convicts came from free settlers, who in 1850 formed the Anti-Transportation League to successfully lobby for change. The last convicts transported to the colony arrived in 1853.

Van Diemen's Land had been the most feared destination for British prisoners for more than three decades. During those years a total of 74,000 convicts had been transported to the island. The majority of these people had served out their sentences and settled in the colony, yet so terrible was its reputation that in 1856 – the year it achieved responsible self-government – it changed its name to Tasmania in an attempt to free its image once and for all from the shackles of its past.

Tasmanian culture has since undergone a transition from shame, and an increasing number of Tasmanians of European descent now identify with their convict past. There has also been an increase in pride in being Tasmanian and, driven by compelling tourism marketing and a burgeoning food-and-wine scene, the state's positive and cosmopolitan profile is far removed from the negative preconceptions of just a few decades ago.

Looking for a convict in your family tree? To help with genealogy searches, check the website of the Tasmanian Family History Society (www.tasfhs.org).

Experience Convict Life

Port Arthur Historic Site (p103)

Coal Mines Historic Site (p99), Saltwater River

Hobart (p60) and Ross (p130) Female Factories

Darlington (p143), Maria Island

1945	1967	1972	1975
The epic 1170km Sydney to Hobart Yacht Race is run for the first time. The winning time of 43 hours, 23 minutes and 12 seconds, set by *Wild Oats IV* in 2012, is the current race record.	Tasmania's deadliest bushfires kill 62 people, injure over 900 and leave more than 7000 homeless. The 'Black Tuesday' fires affected 2640 sq km, from the Midlands to the D'Entrecasteaux Channel.	Lake Pedder is flooded as part of a hydroelectric scheme. The Lake Pedder Restoration Committee (www.lakepedder.org) is now dedicated to restoring the lake to a natural wilderness state.	Hobart's Tasman Bridge collapses, killing 12, when the ore carrier *Lake Illawarra* crashes into it and sinks. Seven of the dead are crew members.

Gold, But No Great Rush

In the 1870s gold was discovered near the Tamar River, as was tin in the northeast. These discoveries prompted a deluge of international prospectors. In the northeast hundreds of Chinese miners arrived, bringing their culture with them. The themed Trail of the Tin Dragon tourist path (www.trailofthetindragon.com.au) through the northeast highlights this aspect of the state's history.

Mining was a tough way of life and most people didn't make their fortunes. Individual prospectors grabbed the rich, easily found surface deposits, but once these were gone the miners had to form larger groups and companies to reach deeper deposits, until eventually these either ran out or became unprofitable to work. The Beaconsfield Mine & Heritage Centre north of Launceston is still operational and can be visited today.

Once it was realised that there was mineral wealth to be found, prospectors randomly explored most of the state. On the west coast, discoveries of large deposits of silver and lead resulted in a boom in the 1880s and an associated rush at Zeehan. In fact, so rich in minerals was the area that it ultimately supported mines significant enough to create the towns of Rosebery, Tullah and Queenstown. Geological exploitation went unchecked, however, and by the 1920s copper mining at Queenstown had gashed holes in the surrounding hills, while logging, pollution, fires and heavy rain stripped the terrain of its vegetation and topsoil. The environment has only begun repairing itself over the past few decades.

The rich belt of land from Queenstown to the north coast is still being mined in several places, but this is now being done with a little more environmental consideration and fewer visible effects than in the past.

Walking Through History

....

Hobart Historic Tours (p66)

....

Her Story (p60)

....

Port Arthur Historic Site (p104) guided walks

....

Launceston Historic Walks (p179)

Tasmania in the 20th Century

Although it was ignored in the initial federal ministry, Tasmania officially became a state when Australia's Federation took place in 1901. For Tasmanians, as for mainlanders in the new Commonwealth of Australia, the first half of the 20th century was dominated by war, beginning with the dispatch of a contingent of 80 Tasmanian soldiers to South Africa to fight in the Boer War, through WWI and WWII, with the Depression of the 1930s thrown in for bad measure.

The state's post-WWII economy was reassuringly buoyant, with industrial success embodied by Bell Bay's aluminium refinery and the ongoing developments of the powerful Hydro-Electric Commission. However, by the 1980s it had suffered a worrisome decline. Subsequent years saw economic unease reflected in climbing 'brain drain' levels to the mainland (especially among the under-30s) and falling birth rates.

1982	1982–83	1996	1997
Taking in the southwest, Franklin-Gordon Wild Rivers and Cradle Mountain-Lake St Clair National Parks, the expansive Tasman Wilderness World Heritage Area is established.	The Franklin River Blockade is staged to oppose construction of a dam in the area, and is ultimately successful. The action is a substantial boost to Tasmania's conservation lobby.	The massacre of 35 people at the Port Arthur Historic Site stuns the world and eventually results in stricter gun-control laws in Australia.	Homosexuality is finally decriminalised in Tasmania. In 2010 Tasmania becomes the first state to recognise same-sex marriages performed in other jurisdictions as registered partnerships.

A Disputed Wilderness

Since the early 1970s the key influence on Tasmanian history has been the ongoing battle between pro-logging companies and environmental groups. Tasmania is poorer and has fewer employment opportunities than mainland states, but it's also an island with world-class wilderness and scenic beauty. With these two contemporary markers of Tasmanian society, the ideological fault lines often evident in Tasmanian history are not difficult to trace back and understand.

In 1910 Austrian Gustav Weindorfer reached the summit of Cradle Mountain. Throwing his arms out, he declared that the magnificence of the place, 'where there is no time and nothing matters', was something the people of the world should share. It later became a national park. In the 20th century the extinction of the thylacine and the flooding of Lake Pedder led to the birth of Australia's environmental movement in 1972, when concerned people formed the United Tasmania Group. Ten years later, thousands of people acted to stop the damming of the Franklin River. Leaders in these movements became a force in Australian federal politics: the Greens Party, under the leadership of Tasmanian Bob Brown, who was a senator from 1996 until 2012.

> **History Museums**
> ....
> *Queen Victoria Museum (p174), Launceston*
> ....
> *Tasmanian Museum & Art Gallery (p59), Hobart*
> ....
> *Narryna Heritage Museum (p60), Hobart*
> ....
> *Low Head Maritime Museum (p191)*

Tasmania in the 21st Century

Backed by strong tourism campaigns, vocal supporters in mainstream media, a respected arts scene and the emergence of some excellent local brands that wind up in shopping trolleys across the country, Tasmania's image change is crystallising as it fosters its reputation as a 'pure' holiday isle, artisan food producer and lifestyle haven.

The long-running debate between pro-logging groups, pro-pulp-mill corporations and conservationists keen to protect Tasmania's old-growth forests and wild heritage continues. In 2010 a breakthrough was achieved with the signing of the Statement of Principles agreement – a 'peace deal' between pro-forestry and pro-environmental groups. Following this, in 2011 the Tasmanian Forests Intergovernmental Agreement was signed

THE NATIONAL TRUST

As you explore Tasmania you'll often come across gracious old heritage estates and properties managed by the National Trust (www.nationaltrust.org.au/tas). Many are staffed by volunteers and have rather specific opening hours, but if you do fancy a spot of time travel, be sure to talk with the attendants: they are often passionately knowledgeable about local stories and heritage. Step onto the well-worn flagstones of the Georgian Regency mansion Clarendon near Evandale, the convict-built Franklin House in Launceston and the colony's first lawyer's digs, Runnymede in Hobart. All are well worth a visit.

1998	2008	2010	2011
The Sydney to Hobart Yacht Race is marred by tragedy when hurricane-force conditions cause five boats to sink with the loss of six lives.	Prime Minister Kevin Rudd apologises to Australia's Aboriginal stolen generations. Tasmanian Aboriginal activist Michael Mansell questions whether financial compensation will follow.	Signed in December 2010, the Statement of Principles agreement is promoted as a peace deal between pro-forestry and pro-environmental groups in Tasmania.	Tasmania's first female premier – Lara Giddings, from the left-wing Labor Party – is elected, keeping the top job until 2014.

by Australian prime minister Julia Gillard, Tasmanian premier Lara Giddings and conservation and forestry groups, creating new areas of forest reserves while guaranteeing ongoing native- and plantation-timber access for the forestry industry. In 2012 the key actor on the pro-logging side of the debate – forestry company Gunns Ltd – was placed in voluntary administration.

The Tasmanian Forests Intergovernmental Agreement was passed into law by the Tasmanian parliament in 2013 but was repealed by a new conservative state government in 2014. A six-year moratorium period then came into effect, after which the impact of resuming logging in Tasmania's old-growth forests is to be re-examined.

Indigenous Rights

Of course, Truganini and Suke and Fanny Cochrane were not the last Tasmanian Aboriginal people. They may have been the last 'full-blooded' representatives of their race, but countless Tasmanians of mixed heritage survived.

Over recent decades the state's Indigenous population has found a new voice, sense of community and identity. Tasmanian Aboriginal people continue to claim rights to land and compensation for past injustices. Acknowledgement of the treatment meted out to Indigenous peoples by Europeans has resulted in the recognition of native titles to land. In 1995 the state government returned 12 sites to the Tasmanian Aboriginal community, including Oyster Cove, Risdon Cove, Kutikina Cave and Steep Island. Wybalenna was added to this list in 1999, and areas of Cape Barren and Clarke Islands in 2005. The Tasmanian government has also launched an Aboriginal Dual Naming Policy, with 13 places now officially known by both Aboriginal and European names. These include kunanyi (Hobart's Mt Wellington), kanamaluka (Launceston's Tamar River), yingina (Great Lake in the Central Highlands) and takayna (the Tarkine).

Historic Pubs

The Whaler (p80), Hobart

Ross Hotel (p130), Ross

Stanley Hotel (p223), Stanley

Deloraine Hotel (p207), Deloraine

Royal Oak Hotel (p184), Launceston

2013	2014	2015	2017
Southeastern Australia's 'Angry Summer' delivers Hobart's hottest-ever day (41.8°C on 4 January), along with bushfires that burn more than 24,000 hectares and 100-plus properties.	Tasmania author Richard Flanagan reaches the pinnacle of global literary success, winning the Man Booker Prize for his novel *The Narrow Road to the Deep North*.	State Growth Minister Matthew Groom warns that Tasmania faces a population 'death spiral' unless a target of 650,000 residents isn't achieved by 2050.	MONA and the Macquarie Point Development Corporation submit plans to Hobart City Council for the reimagining of this prime waterfront terrain.

Gourmet Tasmania

Tasmania has been dubbed the 'provedore island' – an astute moniker given the state's booming foodie scene. Super seafood, juicy berries and stone fruits, splendidly calorific dairy products, craft beers, excellent cool-climate wines and winning whisky compete for your attention on the Tasmanian menu. Around the state, organic farms, orchards, vineyards and small enterprises are busy supplying fresh local produce, and buyers (restaurants, markets, provedores and individuals) are snapping it up.

Local Produce

Visitors may find themselves underwhelmed by menus in some country towns, especially if the local pub is the only eatery. However, excellent provedores are popping up around the island selling local produce, so a DIY Tasmanian picnic is usually an option.

Seafood

Like the rest of Australia, Tasmania is 'girt by sea' (to steal a phrase from the national anthem). It's a no-brainer that the seafood here is magnificent, harvested from some of the cleanest ocean water on the planet.

Essential specialities include oysters on Bruny Island, at Coles Bay, in Swansea and at Barilla Bay near Hobart; and ocean trout from the waters of Macquarie Harbour. Deep-sea fish such as trevalla (blue eye) and striped trumpeter are delicious, as is the local Atlantic salmon, extensively farmed in the Huon estuary and D'Entrecasteaux Channel south of Hobart. Squid (calamari), rock lobster (known as crayfish in these latitudes), abalone, scallops and mussels are also menu regulars.

From a humble curried-scallop pie or fish and chips at Hobart's Constitution Dock to an innovative meal at one of Hobart's gourmet restaurants or a menu-topping abalone meal at a Chinese eatery, Tasmania is a spectacular seafood destination.

Meat

Tasmania is known for its high-quality beef, based on a natural, grass-fed (as opposed to grain-fed) production system and free from growth hormones, antibiotics and chemical contaminants. Beef from King Island and Flinders Island is sublime, and if you see it on a menu and the wallet allows, tuck into premium Wagyu beef from Robbins Island, also in Bass Strait. Flinders Island also farms prime lamb. Cape Grim, on the northwestern tip of mainland Tasmania, has similarly gained market traction for its beef. These meats have made the grade in upmarket restaurants throughout Australia, and command a ransom in overseas markets such as Tokyo.

Game meats feature on menus too, with quail, wallaby, kangaroo and farmed venison often available. Wallaby and kangaroo meat is tender, lean, flavoursome and packed with protein – if you can banish the imagery of these doe-eyed animals cavorting in the wild from your mind, you're in for a treat.

Travellers who want to eat their way around the Apple Isle should go to www.discovertasmania.com.au – click on 'What to Do', then 'Food and Drink', and start planning your next meal.

Fruit

Tasmania's cool climate equates to fabulous berries and stone fruit; picking your own (in season) is a great way to enjoy them. Sorell Fruit Farm (p98) near Hobart is a favourite: raspberries, cherries, apples, pears... Impromptu stops at roadside stalls in the Huon and Tamar Valleys offer the chance to buy freshly picked fruits. Other places worth a visit include Kate's Berry Farm (p147) outside Swansea, Eureka Farm (p158) in Scamander and Hillwood Berry Farm (p190) near George Town.

Jams, sauces, fruit wines, ciders and juices made from Tasmanian fruits are also excellent. Many varieties are available at gourmet food stores and provedores statewide, and from stalls at Hobart's Salamanca Market (p61) and Farm Gate Market (p83), and Launceston's Harvest (p184) market.

Cheese

Tasmania has an impressive cheese industry, somewhat hampered by the fact that all milk here must be pasteurised, unlike in Italy and France. Despite this legal inconvenience, the results are fabulous – just slap some local leatherwood honey over a slice of blue cheese for tasty confirmation.

Visit the Pyengana Dairy Company (p160), not far from St Helens, for sensational cheddar. Grandvewe Cheeses (p115), just south of Woodbridge, produces organic cheese from sheep's and cow's milk. Ashgrove Cheese (p207) near Deloraine conjures up traditional cheeses such as Rubicon red, smoked cheddar and creamy Lancashire, while the Bruny Island Cheese Co (p114) produces Italian and French styles. In provedores and restaurants, keep an eye out for the superb brie from King Island Dairy (p228). If you do find yourself on King Island, a visit to the walk-in refrigerated tasting room here is one of the more generous foodie experiences you'll ever have (don't eat beforehand).

Wasabi, Truffles & Other New Directions

Not content with seafood successes and champion cheese, Tasmanian producers are getting creative and showing off their agricultural skill, growing or harvesting some wonderfully diverse products, including buckwheat, walnuts, wasabi, wakame (a type of seaweed) and saffron. Black truffles are being harvested in the north of Tasmania, with an idea to capture the European market during the French off season.

Tasmania also produces fantastic honey, chocolate and fudge, mushrooms, asparagus, olive oil, mustards and relishes. To stock up, check out Hobart's Farm Gate Market and Salamanca Market or Launceston's Harvest market, or hit provedores statewide.

Where to Eat

Cafes

Like the rest of Australia, Tasmania has fallen hard for coffee, and the humble bean is taken super-seriously at city cafes such as Pilgrim Coffee (p74), Yellow Bernard (p72) and Mulberry Street Espresso (p72) in Hobart; the Chapel (p218) in Burnie; Milkbar (p181) and Sweetbrew (p182) in Launceston; and Laneway (p205) in Devonport.

Cafes are the traveller's best option for breakfast and brunch; expect to pay $12 to $20 for main-course menu items. You will find good cafes outside the big cities too: towns like Bridport, Cygnet, Dunalley, Longford, Penguin, Wynyard and Ranelagh have some of the best cafes in the state.

Listing foodie haunts, wineries, breweries, distilleries and other purveyors of gastronomic bounty, the *Tasmania Wine & Gastronomy Map with Breweries and Distilleries* is an essential for galloping gourmets. Pick one up online at www.vwmaps.com/australian-wine-maps/tasmania or in Hobart's main bookshops.

When We Eat: A Seasonal Celebration of Fine Tasmanian Food and Drink, by Liz McLeod, Bernard Lloyd and Paul County, is the companion guide to *Before We Eat*. It covers the availability of seasonal foods in the state, accompanied by great recipes and photographs.

Pubs

The quality of Tasmanian pub food swings between gourmet and grossly outmoded. Upmarket city pubs brim with international flavours and innovation, while utilitarian country pubs proffer a more predictable slew of schnitzels, roasts and stodgy frozen-then-deep-fried seafood. Still, a quick pub meal is a good option if you're travelling with kids or don't want to break the bank (main courses are generally $15 to $30). At most pubs you can eat in the bistro/dining room out the back, or in the front bar (often accompanied by horse racing on the TV and blokey airs/aromas).

In Hobart, the Shipwright's Arms Hotel (p81), the New Sydney Hotel (p79) and the Republic Bar & Café (p81) plate up the state's best pub grub. The Ross Hotel (p130) in Ross is also a solid option.

Fine Dining

Tasmania's best fine-dining restaurants rival anything on the Australian mainland, and local chefs are renowned for making the most of the island's excellent produce. Menu items can be expensive (mains sometimes exceed $35), but diners are guaranteed innovative and thoughtful interpretations of local seafood, beef and lamb, partnered with the best Tasmanian wines.

In Hobart, Franklin (p75) and Aløft (p76) are outstanding. Meanwhile, Geronimo (p183) delivers Launceston's most interesting high-end tastes. Elsewhere on the island, Edge (p152) at Coles Bay, Mrs Jones (p205) in Devonport, Piermont (p146) in Swansea and the Home Hill Wines (p118) restaurant in Huonville are all excellent.

Vegetarian Dining

Vegetarian menu selections are common in large Tasmanian towns and tourist areas, but dedicated vegetarian/vegan restaurants are thin on the ground here. Indian and Asian eateries are usually your best bet for dinner. During the day, Tasmanian cafes usually have a few vegetarian options, but vegans will find the going much tougher. In Hobart, try the **Heartfood Cafe** (Map p62; ☑0402 351 689; 66 Liverpool St, Hobart; 1/2/3 dishes $8/10/12; ☺10am-4pm Mon-Fri, 11am-3pm Sat; ☑); in Launceston head for **Earthy Eats** (Map p178; ☑03-6380 9426; www.earthyeats.com.au; 19 Kingsway; mains $6-12; ☺8.30am-4pm Mon-Fri, 9am-3pm Sat; ☜☑). Also see www.happycow.net for vegetarian-eatery locations.

Foodie Tours

....

Gourmania (p66), departing Hobart

Tasmanian Seafood Seduction (p65), boat tours departing Hobart

Tamar Valley Winery Tours (p186), departing Launceston

....

Drink Tasmania (p66), whisky and wine; departing Hobart

TOP FARM GATES & ARTISAN FOOD PRODUCERS

Chat with the farmer, fisher, fruiterer or orchard owner at these top spots to pick up the freshest of local Tasmanian produce.

Get Shucked Oyster Farm (p114), Bruny Island

King Island Dairy (p228), King Island

Sorell Fruit Farm (p98), Sorell

Freycinet Marine Farm (p152), Coles Bay

Grandvewe Cheeses (p115), Woodbridge

Cradle Coast Olives (p212), Ulverstone

Pyengana Dairy Company (p160), Pyengana

41° South Tasmania (p206), Deloraine

Melshell Oysters (p147), Swansea

Eureka Farm (p158), Scamander

Tasting Tasmania

Welcome to Australia's finest food destination. Fire your creativity with a cooking class, fill your basket at a farmers market or tour the state's artisan producers. Rather eat without the effort? Time your trip to coincide with one of Tassie's fab food festivals.

To Market, To Market

Hobart's Salamanca Market is prime local-produce territory, while the Farm Gate Market in the CBD offers a 100% foodie focus, with baked goods, wine, smoked meats, eggs, fruit, veg, honey, beer, coffee, nuts, oils and condiments. Harvest in Launceston is a similar scene.

Cooking Schools

Get crafty in the kitchen at one of Tasmania's cool cooking schools. The Agrarian Kitchen (p44) in the Derwent Valley has its own organic farm; the Red Feather Inn in Hadspen combines plush accommodation with a slow-food emphasis. Fat Pig Farm in Cygnet also runs cooking classes.

Briny Bounty

Tasmania is an island: the seafood here is awesome! Highlights include fresh-off-the-boat fish in St Helens, oysters from Bruny Island and the east coast, and curls of calamari from the floating fish punts at Hobart's Constitution Dock.

Food Festivals

Locals love to to blow their culinary trumpet. Fill your insides at Hobart's long-running Taste of Tasmania festival around Christmas/New Year, Launceston's Festivale or Huonville's Taste of the Huon festival.

Gourmet Farmer

For onscreen inspiration, source the excellent SBS television series *Gourmet Farmer* (four seasons from 2010) following ex–food critic Matthew Evans as he retreats from Sydney to Cygnet to try his hand at organic farming. Evans' new restaurant at Fat Pig Farm is now open.

CONFERENCE Pears

GOOD SWEET EATING

KEEP AT ROOM TEMPERATURE OUT OF DIRECT SUNLIGHT.

$5.50 kg.

1. Salamanca Market (p61), Hobart 2. Fresh seafood platter 3. Taste of Tasmania festival (p67), Hobart

Tasmanian Wine

Since the mid-1950s, Tasmania has been building a rep for quality cool-climate wines, characterised by full, fruity flavours and high acidity. Today vineyards across the state are producing sublime pinot noir, riesling and chardonnay, with many producers focusing on sparkling wine as their future.

Tasmania can be split into three key wine regions: the north around Launceston, the east around Swansea and the south around Hobart. There are plenty of large, professional outfits with sophisticated cellar doors, but you'll also find smaller, family-owned vineyards with buckets of charm.

Some wineries' tastings are free, while most charge a small fee that's refundable if you buy a bottle.

Download the *Tasmanian Fruits Farm Gate Guide* from the Fruit Growers of Tasmania website (www.fruitgrowerstas.com.au). This annual publication lists the best places to secure a drive-in, pick-your-own summertime vitamin hit of stone fruit, cherries and berries.

The North & East

The Tamar Valley and Pipers River areas north of Launceston are Tasmania's best-known wine regions, and are home to a number of big-name wineries, including Pipers Brook (p192) and Jansz Wine Room (p192), home to the best sparkling white this side of Champagne. Holm Oak (p188) in Rowella, Bay of Fires Wines (p192) at Pipers River and Tamar Ridge (p186) in Rosevears are some regional faves.

Six excellent wineries are dotted down the east coast from Bicheno to Orford, including the well-respected Freycinet Vineyard (p146) and progressive Devil's Corner (p146) near Swansea.

Around Hobart & the South

A major producer in Hobart's northern suburbs (next to MONA!) is Moorilla (p61). Established in 1958, it's the oldest vineyard in southern Tasmania. A little further up the Derwent River is the very 'Med' Stefano Lubiana Wines (p90), with a fabulous view and *osteria* (tavern). Just east of Hobart, the Coal River Valley is home to an increasing number of wineries, most notably Frogmore Creek (p85) and Puddleduck Vineyard (p85).

CRAFT-BEER CRAZY

The Cascade-Boag's beer duopoly is under siege: Tasmanian craft beers are the flavour of the decade, and you don't have to travel far to find a brewery bar in which to sit, sip and savour. There are 20-odd craft breweries in the state now, with new ones opening up all the time: the Tasmanian Beer Trail website (www.tasbeertrail.com) has a catch-all list.

Craft-beer boffins may want to time their Tasmanian sojourn around the Hobart Beerfest (p67) and Esk BeerFest (p180) in Launceston, both in January. Otherwise, here are our five favourite craft breweries around the state:

T-Bone Brewing Co (p81) Savvy shopfront brewhouse on the fringes of the North Hobart strip. Try the pale ale.

Seven Sheds (p212) Specialises in a malty Kentish ale, plus seasonal brews and honey-infused mead. In Railton near Devonport.

Iron House Brewery (p157) Makes a crisp lager, a hoppy pale ale and a Czech-style pilsner. On the east coast near Scamander.

Two Metre Tall (p90) Real ale and ciders, with ingredients sourced on-site in the Derwent Valley, 45 minutes northwest of Hobart. Friday-night and Sunday-afternoon 'Farm Bar' sessions are a hoot.

Hobart Brewing Company (p80) This big, raffish red shed is delightfully anomalous on the polished Hobart waterfront. Try the Harbour Master Ale.

> **BILLS & TIPPING**
> ●
> In Tasmania the total at the bottom of a restaurant bill is all you really need to pay. It will include GST and there is no 'optional' service charge added. Waiters are paid a reasonable salary – they don't rely on tips to survive. Often, though, especially in the cities, people tip a few coins in a cafe, while the tip for excellent service in a whiz-bang restaurant can go as high as 15%, depending on your level of satisfaction.

Further south, in the Huon Valley area, you'll find Hartzview Vineyard (p115), Panorama Vineyard (p116) and Home Hill Wines (p118). Cross on the ferry to Bruny Island Premium Wines (p110) – Australia's southernmost vineyard – or continue south to Dover and St Imre Vineyard (p121) for Hungarian-style wines.

Tasmanian Beer & Cider

The definitive example of Tasmanian parochialism is the traditional local loyalty to regionally brewed beer. In the south it's Cascade, brewed in South Hobart; in the north Launceston's James Boag flies the flag. Until quite recently you could draw an invisible line from Strahan through Ross to Bicheno, north of which no sane publican would serve Cascade. South of this hoppy division, any mention of Boag's would provoke confusion and ridicule. These days things are much less definitive and you'll find Cascade and Boag's both freely available in 'enemy territory'.

Cascade highlights include the very drinkable premium lager, a pale ale, the ever-present draught and saucy winter stouts. Boag's produces similar beers to the Cascade brews, such as its premium lager and draught.

Tasmanian cider has had a real resurgence of late, filling the bar taps in pubs around the state and across Australia. Don't miss the Apple Shed (p118) and Pagan Cider (p116) in the Huon Valley, and Spreyton Cider Co (p206) near Latrobe in the northwest. How do you like them apples!

Tasmanian Whisky

In recent years Tasmania, with its chilly Scotland-like highlands and clean water, has become a whisky-producing hot spot. There are about a dozen distillers around the state now, bottling superb single malts for a growing international market (and a few good gins to boot). Sullivans Cove Whisky (p87), based at Cambridge near Hobart, has been racking up world whisky awards and now runs tours and tastings. If you're keen for a wee dram, worthy distillers to visit include **Lark Distillery** (Map p62; ☑03-6231 9088; www.larkdistillery.com; 14 Davey St, Hobart; ◷10.30am-7pm Thu-Sun, to 11pm Fri & Sat) in Hobart, Shene Estate (p128) in Pontville, **Nonesuch Distillery** (☑0408 616 442; www.nonesuchdistillery.com.au; 491 Arthur Hwy, Forcett; ◷by appointment only) near Sorell, Old Kempton Distillery (p128) in Kempton, Nant Distillery (p133) in Bothwell and Hellyers Road Distillery (p216) in Burnie. Or try them all at the Bruny Island House of Whisky (p114) – who's driving?

For the comprehensive low-down on Tassie's burgeoning beer and whisky scenes, check out the Tasmanian Beer Trail (www. tasbeertrail.com) and Tasmanian Whisky Trail (www.taswhisky trail.com) websites.

Drinking Down South

There simply are no reasons not to have a drink in Tasmania. Local cool-climate wines grace the state's menus, and Tasmanian single malt whisky has become a global smash. Meanwhile, the local craft-beer scene is bubbling along nicely.

Top Tassie Drops

The cool-climate Tamar Valley and Pipers River regions north of Launceston are Tasmania's key wine-producing areas. Spend a day vineyard-hopping, filling the car boot with pinot noir, riesling and bottles of bubbles.

The Beer Down Here

Tasmanian craft-beer breweries are taking off! Visit T-Bone Brewing Co, Hobart Brewing Co and Shambles Brewery in Hobart; Iron House Brewery near Scamander on the east coast; Two Metre Tall near New Norfolk; and Little Rivers Brewing Company in Scottsdale (among many others!). Try them all at the Weldborough Hotel in the northeast.

1. Lark Distillery (p279), Hobart **2.** Cascade Brewery (p60), H
3. Frogmore Creek (p85), Cambridge

A Cascade of History

South Hobart's Gothic-looking Cascade Brewery has been bottling the good stuff since 1824 – it's Australia's oldest brewery. Take a tour of the workings, then sample its globally acclaimed stouts, ales and lagers.

Southern Wine Touring

Just east of Hobart is the fast-emerging Coal River Valley wine region; just north is the excellent Stefano Lubiana Wines near New Norfolk. Further south, Bruny Island Premium Wines is Australia's most southerly vineyard.

Make Mine a Double

Wait a minute...this place looks just like the Scottish highlands! Must-visit Tasmanian single-malt distilleries include Sullivans Cove at Cambridge near Richmond, Nant Distillery in Bothwell, Old Kempton Distillery in Kempton and Hellyers Road Distillery in Burnie.

Wilderness & Wildlife

Tasmania is the size of a small European country – there's plenty of room for the island's unique flora and fauna to live, thrive and survive. A roll call of quirky species reinforces Tasmania's unique appeal, and travellers have plenty of opportunities, both structured and spontaneous, to see a Tasmanian devil, a platypus, a Cape Barren goose... The backdrop to this animal hubbub is the state's amazing wilderness, comprising some of the planet's most important natural-heritage areas.

The Tasmanian Wilderness

Welcome to Australia's most compact yet diverse state. Unlike in much of mainland Australia, flat land is a rarity here. Tasmania's highest mountain, Mt Ossa, peaks at just 1617m, but much of the island's interior is extremely vertiginous. One indication of the lack of level ground is the proximity of central Hobart and Launceston to some rather impressive hills – life in the suburbs here often involves having steep driveways and strong leg muscles!

Tasmania's intricate coastline is laced with coves and beaches, shallow bays and broad estuaries – the result of river valleys flooding as sea levels rose after the last ice age. By contrast, the island's Central Highlands were covered by a single ice sheet during that ice age. This bleak (but amazingly beautiful) landscape remains a harsh environment, dotted with lakes, dappled with winter snow and completely unsuitable for farming.

Showing the scars of recent glaciation, most of Tasmania's west coast is a twisted nest of mountain ranges, ridges and formidable ocean beaches. The climate here is inhospitable: the coastline is pummelled by uncompromising seas and annual rainfall clocks in somewhere upwards of 3m. But on an overpopulated planet, this kind of wilderness is increasingly rare; the west's cliffs, lakes, rainforests and wild rivers are among Tasmania's greatest attractions and are irresistible temptations for walkers, adventurers and photographers.

By the time the rain clouds make it over to the east coast, they've usually dumped their contents out west and have become fluffy and benign rather than grey and menacing. The east coast is sunny and beachy, with a sequence of laid-back holiday towns and photogenic white-sand beaches.

The fertile plains of the Midlands area make up Tasmania's agricultural heartland – east of the harsh Central Highlands but not so far east that rainfall becomes an anomaly.

National Parks

A greater percentage of land – around 40% – is allocated to Tasmania's national parks and reserves than any other Australian state. Walk along a trail and scale a peak, or visit a few parks and come to grips with the island's environmental diversity, which includes highland lakes, surging rivers, ocean-swept beaches, craggy coves, wildlife-rich islands, jagged ranges and lush temperate rainforest.

Public access to the national parks is encouraged as long as safety and conservation regulations are observed. The golden rules: don't damage or alter the natural environment, and don't feed wild animals. Most of the parks are easily accessed by vehicle, but two – Savage River in the heart of the Tarkine wilderness, and the Kent Group of islets in Bass Strait – are virtually inaccessible. Walls of Jerusalem National Park has no direct road access, but there's a car park a steep 30-minute walk down from the park boundary.

When to Visit

Most people visit Tasmania's national parks during summer (December to February) to enjoy long days and warm weather (although Tasmania can receive snow in December!). Visiting outside these months sees smaller crowds and seasonal diversity: autumn features mild weather and the changing colours of deciduous beech forests; winter sees snow on the peaks; spring brings on a surge of wild flowers.

Park Fees

Visitor fees apply to all national parks, even when there's no rangers' office or roaming ranger on duty. Funds from entry fees remain with the Parks & Wildlife Service and go towards constructing and improving walking tracks, camping grounds, toilets, lookouts and picnic facilities, as well as funding a program to train new rangers and the popular summer 'Discovery Ranger' activities for younger visitors.

There are two main types of passes available for short-term visitors: 24-hour and holiday passes. A 24-hour pass costs $12/24 per person/vehicle; a holiday pass lasts for eight weeks and costs $30/60 per person/vehicle. Vehicle passes cover up to eight people. Annual passes ($96 per vehicle) and two-year passes ($123 per vehicle) are also available if you're a frequent visitor.

For most travellers the eight-week holiday pass is the best bet. Passes are available at most park entrances, at many visitor centres, aboard the *Spirit of Tasmania* ferries, from Service Tasmania (p299) and online at www.parks.tas.gov.au.

Access & Facilities

Information centres with walking information and history and ecology displays are at both ends of Cradle Mountain-Lake St Clair National Park, as well as at Freycinet, Mt Field and Narawntapu National Parks.

The 16 most accessible parks (that is, not the Savage River, Kent Group and Walls of Jerusalem National Parks) all have short walking tracks, toilets, shelters and picnic areas for day visitors to use; many also have barbecues. The entire Tasmanian Wilderness World Heritage Area and most national-park areas have been declared 'fuel stove only' to protect the natural environment – this means no campfires. Dogs are definitely not allowed in any of the national parks.

The website of the Parks & Wildlife Service (www.parks.tas.gov.au) is an absolute goldmine of information on the Tasmanian wilderness and how best to access it. Download fact sheets on national parks, bushwalks, plants and wildlife, camping grounds within parks and loads more.

WILDERNESS & WILDLIFE THE TASMANIAN WILDERNESS

MARINE RESERVES

The PWS also manages seven offshore marine reserves and 14 marine conservation areas, together covering 1351 sq km, or around 7.9% of Tasmania's state coastal waters. Fishing or collecting living or dead material within Tasmanian marine reserves is illegal. Reserves include Tinderbox near Hobart, around the northern part of Maria Island, around Governor Island off the coast at Bicheno, at Port Davey and Bathurst Harbour in the southwest, and Macquarie Island. See www.parks.tas.gov.au for detailed information.

Established camp sites are available in all accessible parks, except for the Hartz Mountains, Mole Creek Karst and Rocky Cape National Parks. Some sites are free, while others have a small charge per person (generally $6 to $13 for an unpowered site) in addition to park entry fees. Ben Lomond, Cradle Mountain-Lake St Clair, Freycinet, Maria Island and Mt Field National Parks also have accommodation options inside their boundaries, ranging from rustic huts to five-star resorts. Click on 'Recreation', then 'Camping' on www.parks.tas.gov.au for detailed information for each park.

There are short walks suitable for wheelchair users and some prams at the Cradle Mountain-Lake St Clair, Freycinet, Mt Field, Tasman and Franklin-Gordon Wild Rivers National Parks (though wheelchair users may require assistance on these walks).

World Heritage Areas

The internationally significant **Tasmanian Wilderness World Heritage Area** (☑03-6288 1283; www.parks.tas.gov.au/wha; ☉24hr) contains the state's four largest national parks – Southwest, Franklin-Gordon Wild Rivers, Cradle Mountain-Lake St Clair and Walls of Jerusalem – plus the Hartz Mountains National Park, the Central Plateau Conservation Area, the Adamsfield Conservation Area, a section of Mole Creek Karst National Park, the Devils Gullet State Reserve and part of the Liffey Falls State Reserve.

Unesco granted the region World Heritage status in 1982, acknowledging that these parks make up one of the planet's last great temperate-wilderness areas. An area nominated for World Heritage status must satisfy at least one of 10 criteria – the Tasmanian Wilderness World Heritage Area fulfilled a record seven categories! The area comprises a grand 15,840 sq km – around 20% of Tasmania.

In 1997 the Macquarie Island World Heritage Area – a remote sub-Antarctic island 1500km southeast of mainland Tasmania – was proclaimed for its outstanding geological and faunal significance.

Access & Tours

Most of the World Heritage area is managed by the Parks & Wildlife Service as a publicly accessible wilderness. Getting into the true heart of the area usually means trudging off on a long-range bushwalk with a tent and a week's supply of food – either independently or on a guided hike. For a considerably less demanding experience, scenic flights depart from Hobart, Strahan and Cradle Valley near Cradle Mountain.

Unless you have your own ocean-going vessel, the only realistic way to visit the Macquarie Island World Heritage Area is on a cruise (p305).

Tasmanian Wildlife

Many of the distinctive mammals of mainland Australia – the marsupials and monotremes isolated here for at least 45 million years – are also found in Tasmania. But the island's fauna is not as varied as that of the rest of Australia, and there are relatively few large mammals here – no koalas and few big kangaroos, for example. Smaller mammals proliferate but can be difficult to spot in the bush. Fortunately, there are plenty of wildlife parks around the state where you can get a good look at them. Also on view here are a dozen endemic bird species, some impressive snakes and creepy-crawlies, and whales cruising the coastline.

Marsupials

Marsupial mammals give birth to partially developed young that they then protect and suckle in a pouch. The island's best-known marsupials are of course the Tasmanian tiger and Tasmanian devil.

The Tasmanian Wilderness World Heritage Area is one of only 206 natural World Heritage areas in the world. To find out what gives these places 'outstanding universal value', check out whc.unesco.org/en/criteria.

TASMANIA'S NATIONAL PARKS

PARK	FEATURES	ACTIVITIES	BEST TIME TO VISIT
Ben Lomond National Park	alpine flora, the state's main ski field	walking, skiing, rock climbing	year-round
Cradle Mountain-Lake St Clair National Park	moorlands, mountain peaks, the famed Overland Track, Australia's deepest freshwater lake	walking, scenic flights, wildlife spotting	year-round
Douglas-Apsley National Park	dry eucalypt forest, river gorges, waterfalls, wildlife, waterhole swimming	walking, swimming	summer
Franklin-Gordon Wild Rivers National Park	two grand wilderness watercourses, deep river gorges, rainforest, Frenchmans Cap, Aboriginal sites	rafting, river cruises (from Strahan)	summer
Freycinet National Park	picturesque coastal scenery, Wineglass Bay, granite peaks, great beaches, walks	walking, abseiling, sea kayaking, scenic flights, fishing	year-round
Hartz Mountains National Park	alpine heath, rainforest, glacial lakes, views of the southwest wilderness	walking, wild flowers	spring, summer
Kent Group National Park	Bass Strait islets (mostly inaccessible), fur seals, seabirds, historical significance	wildlife watching	year-round
Maria Island National Park	traffic-free island with convict history, peaceful bays, fossil-filled cliffs	walking, mountain biking, swimming	spring, summer
Mole Creek Karst National Park	more than 200 limestone caves & sinkholes, some open to the public	caving, walking	year-round
Mt Field National Park	abundant flora & fauna, alpine scenery, high-country walks, Russell Falls, Mt Mawson ski field	walking, skiing, wildlife watching	year-round
Mt William National Park	long sandy beaches, protected Forester kangaroos	walking, fishing, swimming	spring, summer
Narawntapu National Park	north-coast lagoons, wetlands, tea-tree mazes, native wildlife	swimming, walking, wildlife watching	summer, autumn
Rocky Cape National Park	bushland, rocky headlands, Aboriginal caves, exceptional marine environment	swimming, fishing, walking	summer, autumn
Savage River National Park	cool temperate rainforest inside the Tarkine wilderness – utterly secluded, no road access	walking	summer
South Bruny National Park	wild cliffs, surf & swimming beaches, heathlands, wildlife	walking, swimming, surfing, wildlife watching, eco-cruises	spring, summer
Southwest National Park	vast multi-peaked wilderness, one of the world's most pristine natural wonders	walking, swimming, scenic flights, mountaineering, sea kayaking	summer
Strzelecki National Park	mountainous slice of Flinders island, rare flora & fauna	walking, rock climbing, wildlife watching, swimming	summer
Tasman National Park	spectacular sea cliffs & rock formations, offshore islands, forests, bays & beaches, the new Three Capes Track	walking, diving, surfing, eco-cruises, fishing, sea kayaking	year-round
Walls of Jerusalem National Park	spectacular, remote alpine & mountain wilderness, no road access	walking	summer

1. Brushtail possum (p288) 2. South Cape Bay (p123)
3. The Overland Track (p234) and Cradle Mountain (p250)
4. Takayna/Tarkine wilderness (p226)

TOM JASTRAM / SHUTTERSTOCK ©

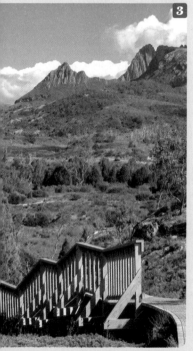

Wilderness & Wildlife

Sign out of civilisation for a few days and head for Tasmania's wild forests, alpine plateaus and empty beaches. Trudge off with a tent and a backpack, or take it easy on a guided hike with upmarket accommodation. Once you exit the cities, Tasmania's unique native wildlife is everywhere.

Tasmanian Wilderness World Heritage Area

Yes, it's big, cold and wet. But the Tasmanian Wilderness World Heritage Area – around one-fifth of the state – is also unique, timeless and inspiring. It's one of the last true wilderness areas on this lonely planet. For a good look at it, tackle the epic five-day Overland Track.

East-Coast Critters

Tassie's sunny east coast is a top spot to see fairy penguins, dolphins, migrating whales, possums, Tasmanian devils, wallabies and snakes – some of them neatly presented for tourist appreciation, some of them incidental encounters.

Takayna/Tarkine Wilderness

In Tasmania's little-visited northwest, the takayna/Tarkine wilderness is an ancient collusion of rainforests, rugged button-grass plains and wild, windy beaches – the most diverse wilderness area in Tasmania. Come prepared for glorious isolation and capricious weather.

Maria Island National Park

A short boat ride off Tassie's east coast, Maria Island is a hit with peak baggers, guided gourmet hikers and wildlife-spotters. It's a veritable zoo: wombats, Tasmanian devils and Cape Barren geese far outnumber humans.

South Coast Track

This is it: the end of the earth. For a true taste of oblivion, this 85km wilderness hike along the bottom fringes of Southwest National Park delivers the goods.

Kangaroos & Wallabies

Tasmania's kangaroos and wallaby species are related to those found on the mainland, but they're generally smaller than their northern kin.

Tasmania's largest marsupial is the Forester kangaroo *(Macropus giganteus)*. Following increasing pressure from the growth of farming, Narawntapu National Park in the state's north and Mt William National Park in the northeast have been set aside to preserve these impressive animals.

The Bennett's wallaby *(Macropus rufogriseus)* thrives in colder climates (Tasmania certainly fits the bill) and is often seen angling for food at Cradle Mountain-Lake St Clair and Freycinet National Parks. They may seem cute, but please don't feed them. Animals in the wild should be feeding themselves: giving them processed foods such as bread crusts or biscuits not only teaches them to rely on visitors as their main food source but also can cause a fatal disease called 'lumpy jaw'. Bennett's wallabies are smaller than Forester kangaroos – just over 1m tall at the most – but like all native animals they can sometimes be aggressive. It is best to approach with caution.

The Mammals of Australia, edited by Ron Strahan, is a complete survey of Australia's somewhat offbeat mammal species. Every species is illustrated and much of what's known about them is covered in individual species accounts, written by the nation's experts.

Tasmanian Devils

If the thylacine (p290) is indeed no more, the Tasmanian devil *(Sarcophilus harrisii)* is the largest carnivorous marsupial in the world. Devils mostly eat insects, small birds, rodents and carrion and can often be seen at night feasting on roadkill – a habit that unfortunately often leads to their becoming roadkill themselves. Mature devils grow up to about 75cm long, with short, stocky bodies covered in black fur with a white blaze across their chests.

Sadly, devil facial tumour disease (DFTD; a fatal, communicable cancer) infects up to 75% of the wild population. Quarantined populations have been established in places such as Maria Island off the east coast, but efforts to find a cure have thus far proved fruitless. Check out www.tassiedevil.com.au for more on DFTD and the efforts to eradicate it.

Possums

There are several varieties of possum in Tasmania. The sugar glider *(Petaurus breviceps)* has developed impressive webs between its legs, enabling it to glide from tree to tree. The most common and boldest of the species is the brushtail possum *(Trichosurus vulpecula),* which lives and sleeps in trees but descends to the ground in search of food. Brushtails show little fear of humans and regularly conduct late-night food heists at camping grounds (you've been warned!). Don't forget to zip up your tent and carefully store leftover food, and don't panic if you hear something akin to an asthmatic Darth Vader roaming around outside your hut: possums hiss and growl at each another, particularly during mating season. A shyer (and much quieter) relative is the smaller ringtail possum *(Pseudocheirus peregrinus).*

Pademelons, Bettongs & Quolls

Like the Tasmanian devil, the Tasmanian pademelon *(Thylogale billardierii,* aka the rufous wallaby) is unique to the island – a small, rounded species sometimes seen hiding in forests. It's a notoriously shy creature that you'll be lucky to see in the wild – tread quietly if you do spot one.

Other endemic marsupials include the Tasmanian bettong *(Bettongia gaimardi),* found exclusively in the east of the state and growing only to a compact 2kg, and the carnivorous eastern quoll *(Dasyurus viverrinus),* approximately the size of a domestic cat. The eastern quoll was declared extinct on the Australian mainland in 1964 (the last known sighting was believed to be in Sydney's exclusive eastern suburb of Vaucluse), but it's common and fully protected in Tasmania.

Wombats

Weighing up to 35kg, Tasmania's subspecies of the common wombat *(Vombatus ursinus tasmaniensis)* is a very solid, powerfully built marsupial with a broad head and short, stumpy legs. Wombats live in underground burrows that they excavate, and are usually very casual, slow-moving characters, partly because they don't have any natural predators to worry about. Maria Island and Cradle Mountain are good places to see them. Another subspecies, *Vombatus ursinus ursinus,* once lived on all the Bass Strait islands but is now only found on Flinders Island.

Monotremes

The platypus and echidna are the world's only two living monotremes (mammals that lay eggs).

Platypus

Up to 50cm long, the platypus *(Ornithorhynchus anatinus)* lives in fresh water and burrows into riverbanks. It has a leathery, duck-like bill, webbed feet and a beaverish body. You're most likely to see one in a stream or lake, searching out food in the form of crustaceans, worms and tadpoles with its electro-sensitive bill. They're notoriously shy: if you want to spot one in the wild, look for telltale lines of small bubbles tracking across the surface of a waterway and sit very still! Latrobe in the northwest bills itself as the 'Platypus Capital of the World'. Geeveston in the southeast is another likely spot to spy one.

Echidnas

The land-based echidna *(Tachyglossus aculeatus)* is totally different to the platypus. It looks similar to a porcupine, and is covered in impressively sharp spikes. Echidnas primarily eat ants and have powerful claws for unearthing their food and digging into the dirt to protect themselves when threatened. They're common in Tasmania, but if you approach one all you're likely to see up close is a brown, spiky ball. However, if you keep quiet and don't move, you might be lucky – they have poor eyesight and will sometimes walk right past your feet.

Birds

Tasmania has a wide variety of seabirds, parrots, cockatoos, honeyeaters, hawks, owls, falcons, eagles and wrens, flitting through the undergrowth, on the prowl at night and soaring around sea cliffs. There are 12 bird species endemic to Tasmania, including the forty-spotted pardalote, black currawong, Tasmanian thornbill, green rosella and Tasmanian native hen. If you're a mad-keen twitcher, sign up for a comprehensive tour with Bruny Island's Inala Nature Tours (p111). Inala is also a driving force behind October's annual Bruny Island Bird Festival (p113).

Black Currawongs

The black currawong *(Stepera fuliginosa),* found only in Tasmania, lives primarily on plant matter and insects but will sometimes kill small mammals or bird hatchlings. You'll often see this large, black, fearless bird goose-stepping around picnic areas.

Muttonbirds

The mutton bird is more correctly called the short-tailed shearwater *(Puffinus tenuirostris).* It lives in burrows in sand dunes and migrates annually to the northern hemisphere. These small birds fly in spectacular flocks on their way back to their burrows (the same ones every year) at dusk. They are still hunted by some Tasmanians, notably around

WILDERNESS & WILDLIFE TASMANIAN WILDLIFE

In 1964 the original cartoon series featuring 'Taz', the tempestuous Warner Bros Tasmanian devil character, lasted just five short episodes. Such was the cult status Taz achieved, however, that he was resurrected for three seasons of his own show in 1991.

If threatened, a wombat will often dive head first into one of its tunnels, blocking the entrance with its extremely tough rear end, which is clad in extra-thick skin.

Flinders Island, and there are certain places where you will occasionally see cooked mutton bird advertised for sale.

Penguins

The little penguin *(Eudyptula minor)* is the smallest penguin in the world, and lives in burrows in Tasmania's sand dunes. Penguin spotting is a drawcard activity for tourists and is particularly fun for kids. Visitors can see Tassie's penguins waddle from the ocean to their nests just after sunset at Bruny Island, Burnie, Bicheno, Low Head and Penguin (naturally). Bring a picnic, settle in to watch the sun go down and (quietly and unobtrusively) enjoy the show.

Snakes & Spiders

As in the rest of Australia, there are plenty of creatures in Tasmania that can do you a disservice.

There are three types of snake here, and they're all poisonous. The largest and most venomous is the tiger snake *(Notechis scutatus)*. There's also the copperhead *(Austrelaps superbus)* and the smaller white-lipped whip snake *(Drysdalia coronoides)*. Bites are rare, as most snakes are shy and try to avoid humans. Tiger snakes can sometimes get a bit feisty, particularly in late summer and especially if you tread on one (watch your step when stepping over logs into sunny patches where they may be basking). If you are bitten, don't try to catch the snake for identification, as there's a common antivenin for all three species. Instead remain as still as possible, bandage the bite site firmly and get someone else to ship you to hospital for treatment.

TIGER, TIGER BURNING BRIGHT

The story of the Tasmanian tiger (thylacine), a striped, nocturnal, dog-like predator once widespread in Tasmania and in parts of mainland Australia, has two different endings.

Version one says that thylacines were hunted to extinction in the 19th and early 20th centuries, with the last captive tiger dying in Hobart Zoo in 1936. Harangued, diseased and deeply misunderstood, the thylacine didn't stand much of a chance once European interests started to encroach on its terrain. It was officially declared extinct in 1986, the requisite 50 years after that last, lonely thylacine died. No specimen, living or dead, has been conclusively discovered since then, despite hundreds of alleged sightings.

Version two maintains that thylacines continue a furtive existence deep in the Tasmanian wilderness. Scientists dismiss such ideas, suggesting that inbreeding among limited numbers of survivors would have put an end to the species just as readily as the hunters' rifles.

But such is the ongoing fascination with the thylacine that sightings still occasionally make the nightly news, however frustratingly unconfirmed they may be (no one ever seems to have their camera/phone handy...and if they do, digital images these days are all too easily doctored and debunked). The tantalising possibility of surviving tigers also makes them prime corporate fodder: Tasmanian companies plaster tiger imagery on everything from beer bottles to licence plates and record labels.

In recent years scientists at Sydney's Australia Museum began scripting another possible ending to the tiger saga. Kicking off version three of the story, biologists managed to extract DNA from a thylacine pup preserved in alcohol since 1866. Their aim was to successfully replicate the DNA, with the long-term goal of cloning the species. Needless to say, there were many obstacles and the project drew criticism from those who would rather have seen the money spent on helping current endangered species. In 2005 the project was shelved due to the poor quality of the extracted DNA, but work done since by the University of Melbourne has raised the possibility of future success.

THE IMPACT OF HUMANS

Since Europeans arrived, Tasmania has lost more than 30 species of plants and animals – most famously, the thylacine (Tasmanian tiger). Currently over 600 types of flora and fauna are listed under the state's Threatened Species Protection Act.

Among Tasmania's threatened birds are the forty-spotted pardalote, orange-bellied parrot (which breeds in Tasmania then wings it back to mainland Australia) and wedge-tailed eagle. Tasmania is also home to the largest invertebrate in the world: the giant freshwater crayfish, whose numbers have been so depleted by recreational fishing and habitat destruction that it's now illegal to take any specimens from their natural habitat.

Introduced species are also having an impact. In 2001 it was reported that a fox had been spotted near Longford in the state's north. Fox predation puts nearly 80 of the island's indigenous land species at enormous risk because of their vulnerability to attack from an animal against which they have no defence. Subsequent reported sightings of the European red fox in other parts of the state confirmed that the animal had been deliberately introduced to Tasmania, probably for the purposes of hunting. The Fox Eradication Program was set up by the state government in 2006, and ran until 2014, when it was shut down after no credible fox evidence had been found for three years. But if you do see a fox, phone the Fox Hotline: 1300 369 688.

WILDERNESS & WILDLIFE TASMANIAN FLORA

An eight-legged local with a long reach (up to 18cm) is the Tasmanian cave spider *(Hickmania troglodytes)*, which spins horizontal mesh-webs on the ceiling of a cave to catch insects such as cave crickets (it's harmless to humans). On the toxic side of the fence are the Tasmanian funnel-web, redback and white-tailed spiders. If you're bitten by a funnel web or redback, seek immediate medical attention. White-tailed spider bites aren't life-threatening but can be painful and sometimes cause ulceration.

Whales

Southern right whales *(Eubalaena australis)* migrate annually from Antarctica to southern Australia to give birth to their calves in shallow waters. So named because they were the 'right' whales to kill, they were hunted to the point of extinction around Tasmania while sustaining a lucrative industry. Numbers have recovered: they're now regularly seen migrating along the east coast (in November and December especially). Whales have also made a return to Hobart's Derwent River estuary, where they were once so plentiful that locals joked that they could walk across the river on the whales' backs.

Long-finned pilot whales *(Globicephala melas)* are also common, and sadly are often involved in beach strandings around the Tasmanian coast.

Tasmanian Flora

Tasmania's myriad flora ranges from the dry forests of the east, through the alpine moorlands and buttongrass plains of the centre, to the temperate rainforests of the west. Many of the state's plants are unlike those found in the rest of Australia, with ties to species that grew millions of years ago when the southern continents were joined at the hip as Gondwana. Similar plants are found in South America and fossilised in Antarctica.

The Parks & Wildlife Service website (www.parks.tas.gov.au) has comprehensive information on Tasmanian flora: click on 'Nature & Conservation' then 'Plants'.

Huon Pine

Prized by shipwrights and furniture makers for its rich, golden hue, rot-resistant oils, fine grain and fragrance, Tasmania's Huon pine

See B&W footage of a Tasmanian tiger at Hobart's Tasmanian Museum & Art Gallery. For an insightful read, pick up David Owen's *Thylacine* (2011) or Col Bailey's *Shadow of the Thylacine* (2013) or *Lure of the Thylacine* (2016). For a Hollywood spin, check out surly Willem Dafoe in *The Hunter* (2011).

(*Lagarostrobos franklinii*) is one of the slowest-growing and longest-living trees on the planet. Individual trees can take 2000 years to reach 30m in height and can live to 3000 years, a situation overlooked by 19th-century loggers and shipbuilders, who plundered the southwest forests in search of this 'yellow gold'. Fortunately, it's now a protected species. Most of the Huon pine furniture and timber work you'll see around the state is recycled, or comes from dead trees salvaged from riverbeds and hydroelectric dams. Some older trees remain: one 2500-year-old beauty can be viewed during cruises on the Gordon River.

Beech & Eucalyptus

The dominant tree of the wetter forests is myrtle beech, similar to European beeches. Tasmania's many flowering trees include the leatherwood, which is nondescript most of the year but erupts into bright flowers during summer. Its white and pale-pink blooms yield a uniquely fragrant honey.

Many of Tasmania's eucalyptus trees also grow on the mainland, but down on the island they often grow ludicrously tall. The swamp gum (*Eucalyptus regnans;* known as mountain ash on the mainland) can grow to 100m in height and is the tallest flowering plant in the world. Look for it in the forests of the southwest, where you'll also find the state's floral emblem, the Tasmanian blue gum (*Eucalyptus globulus*).

In autumn you might catch an eyeful of the deciduous beech, the only truly deciduous native plant in Australia. It usually grows as a fairly straggly bush with bright green leaves. In autumn, however, the leaves become golden and sometimes red, adding a splash of colour to the forests. The easiest places to see this lovely autumnal display are the Cradle Mountain-Lake St Clair and Mt Field National Parks.

Horizontal Scrub

The skinny horizontal scrub (*Anodopetalum biglandulosum*) is a feature of the undergrowth in many parts of Tasmania's southwest. It grows by sending up thin, vigorous stems whenever an opening appears in the forest canopy. The old branches soon become heavy and fall over, then put up shoots of their own. This continuous process of growth and collapse creates dense, tangled thickets – bushwalkers have been rumoured to completely disappear into it when venturing off the beaten track. You can see twisted examples of horizontal scrub in the southwest's forests and in the Hartz Mountains.

King's Lomatia

This member of the Proteaceae family has flowers similar to those of the grevillea, and grows in the wild in only one small part of the Tasmanian Wilderness World Heritage Area. Studies of the plant's chromosomes have revealed that it's incapable of reproducing sexually, which is why it must rely on sending up shoots to create new plants. Further research has shown that there's absolutely no genetic diversity within the population, which means that every king's lomatia in existence is a clone. It's the oldest known clone in the world, thought to have been around for at least 43,600 years.

WATCH YOUR STEP

The cushion plant, found in alpine areas, at first sight resembles a green rock. In fact, it's an extremely tough, short plant that grows into thick mats ideally suited to helping it cope with its severe living conditions. It's not so tough, however, that it can tolerate footprints – stepping on one can destroy thousands of tiny leaves, which take decades to regenerate.

Survival Guide

Directory A–Z

Accommodation

Tourist centres are heavily booked in summer, over Easter and on public holidays – get in early. Weekend trips are popular with mainlanders (the 'MONA effect') – so look for cheaper midweek fares.

Self-contained accommodation Beach houses, city apartments and historic cottages.

Camping and caravan parks Tasmanian camping grounds and caravan parks don't skimp on the wilderness.

B&Bs and boutique stays Many B&Bs are historic homes with tales to tell. Boutique hotels up the ante.

Hotels and motels Heritage hotels (plus a few contemporary ones) and myriad drive-up motels.

Hostels Backpacker joints in Tasmania can be hit-and-miss... but there are some good ones.

Booking Services

Discover Tasmania (www.discovertasmania.com) Tasmania's official tourism website offers online accommodation booking.

Green Getaways Australia (www.greengetawaysaustralia.com.au) Concise listings of environmentally aware accommodation.

Lonely Planet (www.lonelyplanet.com/australia/hotels) Recommendations and bookings.

B&Bs & Boutique Stays

Tasmania's B&Bs occupy everything from restored convict-built cottages to up-market country manors and beachside bungalows. Some places advertised as B&Bs are actually self-contained cottages with breakfast provisions supplied. Only in the cheaper B&Bs will bathroom facilities be shared. Some B&B hosts may cook dinner for guests (usually 24 hours' notice is required). Rates usually range from $150 to $300 per double.

There's an increasing number of top-flight boutique hotels in Tasmania, in places as urban as Hobart and Burnie, and as far-flung as Lake St Clair and Stanley. Rates are certainly lofty – at least $300 a night and sometimes a *lot* more – but you definitely get what you pay for.

Beautiful Accommodation (www.beautifulaccommodation.com) A select crop of luxury B&Bs and self-contained houses.

Hosted Accommodation Australia (www.tasmanianbedandbreakfast.com) B&Bs, homestays and farmstays.

Oz Bed & Breakfast (www.ozbedandbreakfast.com) Nationwide website with good Tasmanian listings.

Tasmania Luxury Accommodation (www.tasmanialuxuryaccommodation.com.au) Resorts, boutique hotels and luxury B&B accommodation – high-end stuff.

Camping

Camping in most national parks requires you to purchase a parks pass and then pay a small (unpowered) site fee (usually couple/child $13/free, additional adult $5). Facilities are generally pretty basic but often include toilets, picnic benches and fireplaces (BYO wood). There are also plenty of free camp sites in national parks, with minimal facilities.

Other than at a few particularly popular places (eg Freycinet National Park on the east coast) it's not possible to book national-park camp sites...so arrive early! Organise parks passes in advance (unless there's a visitor centre where you can purchase one on-site). Camping fees are payable either on-site in deposit boxes or at visitor centres.

Parks & Wildlife Service (www.parks.tas.gov.au) Click on 'Recreation', then 'Camping'. Also the hub for info on parks passes.

Camping Tasmania (www.campingtasmania.com) A deep reservoir of Tasmanian camping info.

Caravan Parks

Tasmania also has plenty of commercial caravan parks, with hot showers, kitchens and laundry facilities. Unpowered sites for two people generally fall into the $25 to $30 price bracket; powered sites usually range from $30 to $40. Some parks offer cheap dorm-style accommodation and cabins. Cabin configurations vary, but expect to pay $100 to $170 for two people in a cabin with a small bathroom and kitchenette.

Caravan Parks Tasmania (www.caravanparkstasmania.com) Comprehensive website, detailing all of Tasmania's caravan parks.

Tasmanian Tourist Parks (www.tasmaniantouristparks.com.au) Selected caravan-park listings around the state.

Hotels & Motels

In Tasmania's cities, hotel accommodation is typically comfortable and anonymous, often with a kitsch heritage bent (though some newer contemporary options are appearing). Aimed at business travellers and midrange tourists (doubles generally upwards of $160), they tend to have a restaurant/cafe, room service, a gym and various other facilities.

Midrange drive-up motels have similar facilities to hotels (tea- and coffee-making facilities, fridge, TV, bathroom). There's rarely a cheaper rate for singles, so they're a better option if you're travelling as a couple or a group of three. Prices reflect standards, but you'll generally pay between $120 and $160 for a room.

Inkeepers Tasmania (www.innkeeper.com.au) Midrange hotels, motels, lodges and apartments.

Hostels

The established YHA network in Tasmania comprises just three hostels, but backpacker accommodation can be found in most major towns. Often you'll need to supply your own bed linen, or sheets can be rented for around $5. Sleeping bags are usually a no-no.

INDEPENDENT HOSTELS

Tasmania has plenty of independent hostels, but standards vary enormously. Many are old rabbit-warren pubs that have been transformed into backpackers, with rowdy bar areas and makeshift

bathroom facilities, while others are converted motels where all rooms have private bathrooms. Newer purpose-built hostels generally have tidier facilities, with good communal areas and plenty of bathroom space. Other good places are small, intimate hostels where the owner is also the manager.

Independent backpacker establishments typically charge $27 to $37 for a dorm bed and $80 to $100 for a twin or double room with shared bathroom (upwards of $100 if there's a private bathroom).

YHA HOSTELS

Tasmania has three hostels as part of the Youth Hostels Association (www.yha.com.au): in Hobart, Bridport in the northeast and Coles Bay on the east coast. YHA hostels offer dorms, twin and double rooms, and cooking and laundry facilities. The vibe is generally less 'party' than in independent hostels...but there's always plenty of cutlery.

Nightly charges start at $27 for members; hostels also take non-YHA members for an extra $3. Australian residents can become YHA members for $15 for one year; join online or at any YHA hostel (sometimes it's thrown in for free as part of your first booking). Families can also join: just pay the adult price, then kids under 18 can join for free.

The YHA is part of Hostelling International (www.hihostels.com). If you already have HI membership in your own country, you're entitled to YHA rates in Tasmanian hostels.

Pubs

Some Tasmanian pubs have been restored – the new **Alabama Hotel** (p69) in Hobart is a prime specimen – but generally, pub rooms remain small and weathered, with a long amble down the hall to the bathroom. They're usually central and cheap – singles/doubles with shared facilities start at $70/90 – but if you're a light sleeper, avoid booking a room above the bar and check whether a band is playing downstairs that night.

Self-Contained Accommodation

Self-contained holiday houses and apartments in Tasmania are largely midrange affairs rented on a nightly or weekly basis – a great option if you're travelling with kids or a group of mates, or just want to cook dinner once in a while. Historic cottages are pricier, starting at around $200 per night, but often include breakfast provisions.

Cottages of the Colony (www.cottagesofthecolony.com.au) Self-contained historic cottages around the state.

> **EATING PRICE RANGES**
>
> ·········
>
> The following price ranges refer to a main course.
>
> **$** less than $15
>
> **$$** $15–$30
>
> **$$$** more than $30

Home Away (www.homeaway.com.au) Self-contained historic cottages and rental properties.

Tas Villas (www.tasvillas.com) Self-catering accommodation.

Other Accommodation

Long-term accommodation
If you want to stay longer in Tasmania, noticeboards in universities, hostels, bookshops and cafes are good places to start looking for digs. Shared-flat vacancies are also listed in the classified sections of the daily newspapers (and on their websites). Online, check out Gumtree (www.gumtree.com.au).

WWOOFing See Willing Workers on Organic Farms (www.wwoof.com.au) for info on working on farms in return for bed and board.

Activities

Are you the outdoors type? If you're looking to do some bushwalking, fishing, rafting, sea kayaking, sailing, scuba diving or surfing, Tasmania could be your personal promised land!

Resources

Bureau of Meteorology (www.bom.gov.au/tas) Tasmanian weather can be fickle: check the forecast before you head into the wilds.

Canoe Tasmania (www.tas.canoe.org.au) Canoe- and kayak-club info around the state.

Inland Fisheries Service (www.ifs.tas.gov.au) Info on fishing regulations around the state.

Parks & Wildlife Service (www.parks.tas.gov.au) Click on 'Recreation' for oodles of bushwalking and camping info.

Royal Yacht Club of Tasmania (www.ryct.org.au) Sailing advice for around the island.

Service Tasmania (www.service.tas.gov.au) For detailed bushwalking maps; outlets around the state.

Tasmanian Scuba Diving Club (www.tsdc.org.au) Scuba advice and events.

Tassie Surf (www.tassiesurf.com) Daily surf photos and weather updates.

Tourism Tasmania (www.discovertasmania.com.au) Extensive outdoor-activity info and operator listings; click on 'What to Do', then 'Outdoors & Adventure'.

Trout Guides & Lodges Tasmania (www.troutguidestasmania.com.au) Trout-fishing guides and Central Highlands accommodation options.

Customs Regulations

There are stringent rules in place to protect the 'disease-free' agricultural status of this island state: fresh fruit, vegetables and plants cannot be brought into Tasmania. Tourists must discard all such items prior to their arrival (even if they're only travelling from mainland Australia). There are sniffer dogs at Tasmanian airports, and quarantine inspection posts at the Devonport ferry terminal. Quarantine officers are entitled to search your car and luggage for undeclared items. See www.dpipwe.tas.gov.au/biosecurity-tasmania for a detailed traveller's guide.

Discount Cards

iVenture Card (☑02-8594 7200; www.iventurecard.com/au/tasmania; 3-ticket pass adult/child $109/69) Flexible combo passes to a selection of tourist lures around the state.

Senior cards Travellers over 60 with some form of identification (eg a Seniors Card – www.australia.gov.au/content/seniors-card) are often eligible for concession prices. Most Australian states and territories issue their own versions of these, which can be used Australia-wide.

Student and youth cards The internationally recognised International Student Identity Card (ISIC; www.isic.org) is available to full-time students aged 12 and over. The card gives the bearer discounts on accommodation, transport and admission to various attractions. The same organisation also produces the International Youth Travel Card (IYTC), issued to people aged under 26 years who are not full-time students, and has benefits equivalent to those of the ISIC. Also similar is the International Teacher Identity Card (ITIC), available to teaching professionals. All three cards ($30 each) are available online or from student-travel companies.

Electricity

Type I
230V/50Hz

Climate

Hobart

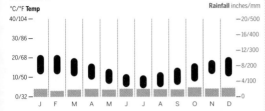

Launceston

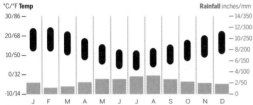

Strahan

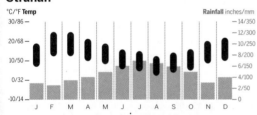

Food

Eating (p273) in Tasmania these days is a pleasure: booking on the day of your meal is usually fine. Top-end restaurants should be booked a couple of weeks ahead.

Cafes Tasmanian cafes are the hubs of local life – meeting places, conversation backdrops and breakfast/lunch stalwarts. And the coffee here is usually pretty great!

Restaurants Restaurant dining ranges from reliable bistro encounters to amazing high-end gourmet experiences using organic local fare. Seafood and beef are standout ingredients.

Pubs Head to the pub for a quick-fire steak/schnitzel/seafood lunch or dinner, plus a couple of beers and maybe some ice cream for the kids.

Health

Before You Go
HEALTH INSURANCE

Health insurance is essential for all travellers. You may prefer a policy that pays doctors or hospitals directly rather than requiring you to pay on the spot and claim later. If you have to claim later make sure you keep all documentation. Check that the policy covers ambulances and emergency medical evacuations by air.

RECOMMENDED VACCINATIONS

If you're travelling to Australia from overseas, visit a physician four to eight weeks before departure. Ask your doctor for an International Certificate of Vaccination (aka the 'yellow booklet'), which will list the vaccinations you've received.

If you're entering Australia within six days of having stayed overnight or longer in a yellow-fever-infected country, you'll need proof of yellow-fever vaccination. For a full list of these countries visit Centers for Disease Control & Prevention (www.cdc.gov/travel).

The World Health Organization (www.who.int) recommends that all travellers should be vaccinated against diphtheria, tetanus, measles, mumps, rubella, chicken pox and polio, as well as hepatitis B, regardless of their destination. While Australia has high levels of childhood vaccination coverage, outbreaks of these diseases do occur.

MEDICAL CHECKLIST

➡ acetaminophen (paracetamol) or aspirin
➡ adhesive or paper tape
➡ antibiotics (also bring any prescriptions)
➡ antidiarrhoeal drugs (eg loperamide)
➡ antihistamines (for hayfever and allergic reactions)
➡ anti-inflammatory drugs (eg ibuprofen)
➡ antibacterial ointment in case of cuts or abrasions
➡ bandages, gauze, gauze rolls
➡ DEET-containing insect repellent for the skin
➡ iodine tablets or water filter (for water purification)
➡ oral rehydration salts
➡ permethrin-containing insect spray for clothing, tents and bed nets
➡ pocket knife
➡ scissors, safety pins, tweezers
➡ steroid cream or cortisone (for allergic rashes)
➡ sunscreen
➡ thermometer

MEDICATIONS

Painkillers, antihistamines for allergies and skincare products are widely available at chemists throughout Tasmania. You may find that medications available over the counter in some countries are only available in Australia by prescription. These include the oral contraceptive pill, some medications for asthma and all antibiotics.

REMOTE LOCATIONS

In Tasmania's remote locations, there could be a significant delay in emergency services reaching you in the event of serious accident or illness. An increased level of self-reliance and preparation is essential. Also take a comprehensive first-aid kit that is appropriate for the activities planned, and ensure that you have adequate means of communication. Tasmania's sometimes-limited mobile-phone coverage can mean that additional radio communication is important for remote areas.

TAP WATER

Tap water in Tasmania is safe to drink, right across the state (and is the best tasting in Australia!).

Insurance

A good travel-insurance policy covering theft, loss and medical problems is essential. Some policies specifically exclude designated 'dangerous activities' such as scuba diving, skiing and even bushwalking. Make sure your policy fully covers you for your activity of choice, and covers ambulances and emergency medical evacuations by air.

Worldwide travel insurance is available at www.lonelyplanet.com/travel-insurance. You can buy, extend and claim online anytime – even if you're already on the road.

WEBSITES

There's a wealth of travel health advice on the internet: Lonely Planet (www.lonelyplanet.com) is a good place to start.

World Health Organization (www.who.int/ith) Publishes *International Travel and Health*, revised annually and available free online.

MD Travel Health (www.redplanet.travel/mdtravelhealth) Provides complete travel-health recommendations for every country, updated daily.

Government travel-health websites include the following:

Australia (www.smartraveller.gov.au)

Canada (www.hc-sc.gc.ca)

UK (www.nhs.uk/livewell/travelhealth)

USA (www.cdc.gov/travel)

In Tasmania
MEDICAL SERVICES

Like the rest of Australia, Tasmania has an excellent health-care system: a mixture of privately run medical clinics and hospitals alongside public hospitals funded by the Australian government. There are also excellent specialised public health facilities for women and children in major centres.

You'll find general practitioners (GPs) working in most Tasmanian towns and available for prebooked appointments, and hospitals with emergency departments in the cities.

The Medicare system covers Australian residents for some health-care costs. Visitors from countries with which Australia has a reciprocal health-care agreement – New Zealand, the Republic of Ireland, Sweden, the Netherlands, Finland, Italy, Belgium, Malta, Slovenia, Norway and the UK – are eligible for benefits specified under the Medicare program. Online, see www.humanservices.gov.au/customer/dhs/medicare. But even if you're not covered by Medicare, a short consultation with a local GP will usually only set you back around $70.

Internet Access

Access No one goes to internet cafes any more, do they? They're very hard to find these days. At a pinch, try the free terminals at libraries or government-funded Online Access Centres, which operate in dozens of small Tasmanian towns. For a complete listing of these centres, see www.linc.tas.gov.au/locations.

Wi-fi Wireless access is fast becoming a given in most Tasmanian accommodation (even across some entire town centres), but access is still limited in more isolated areas such as Bruny Island and the southwest. See www.freewifi.tas.gov.au for free government-sponsored wi-fi locations around the state. If you're travelling here from overseas with your smartphone, you might be better off buying a local SIM card with a data allowance you can top up.

Tasmanian cafes and pubs have been slow to adopt free wi-fi for customers, though you can find it (you might have to ask). At your accommodation, if access is not totally free, you might still get a certain amount of data gratis, then pay-per-use after that.

Legal Matters

Most travellers will have no contact with Tasmania's police or legal system. If you do, it's most likely to be while driving.

Driving There's a significant police presence on Tasmanian roads – police have the power to stop your car, see your licence (you're required to carry it), check your vehicle for roadworthiness and insist that you take a breath test for alcohol (and sometimes illicit drugs).

Drugs First-time offenders caught with small amounts of illegal drugs are likely to receive a fine rather than go to jail, but the recording of a conviction against you may affect your visa status.

Visas If you remain in Australia beyond the life of your visa, you'll officially be an 'overstayer' and could face detention and then be prevented from returning to Australia for up to three years.

Arrested? It's your right to telephone a friend, lawyer or relative before questioning begins. Legal aid is available only in serious cases; for Legal Aid office info, see www.legalaid.tas.gov.au. However, many solicitors do not charge for an initial consultation.

LGBTIQ+ Travellers

It wasn't always the case, but LGBTIQ-rights groups now consider homosexual and heterosexual people to have greater equality under the law in Tasmania than they do in most other Australian states. But beyond the law, a lack of discrimination outside urban centres should never be assumed.

Hobart has one gay bar – **Flamingos Dance Bar** (p79) – but most urban venues are open-minded.

Gay Tasmania (www.gaytasmania.com.au) Accommodation and travel info.

TasPride (www.taspride.com) Based in Hobart, but a Tasmania-wide support group. A good source of info on upcoming events, including November's annual TasPride Festival.

Maps

One of the best road maps of the state (1:500,000) is produced by the Royal Automobile Club of Tasmania (www.ract.com.au) and is on sale in the organisation's offices around the island. This sheet map includes detail of main city centres.

For more detail, including contours, try the maps (1:250,000) published by Tasmap (www.tasmap.tas.gov.au). Tasmap also produces more detailed 1:25,000 topographic sheets appropriate for bushwalking, ski touring and other activities requiring large-scale maps.

Many of the more popular sheets, including day walks and bushwalks in national parks, are usually available over the counter at shops specialising in bushwalking gear and outdoor equipment, and also at urban and national-park visitor centres. **Service Tasmania** (☑1300 135 513; www.service.tas.au; 134 Macquarie St, Hobart; ⏰9am-5pm Mon-Fri) and the **Tasmanian Map Centre** (Map p62; ☑03-6231 9043; www.map-centre.com.au; 110 Elizabeth St, Hobart; ⏰9.30am-5pm Mon-Fri, to 1.30pm Sat).

The best atlas is *Tasmania Hobart & Launceston* ($35), published by UBD. It contains clear, detailed maps of 40 significant towns in the state.

Money

The Australian dollar comprises 100 cents. There are 5c, 10c, 20c, 50c, $1 and $2 coins, and $5, $10, $20, $50 and $100 notes.

ATMs & Debit Cards

ATMs Tasmanian cities are flush with ATMs, but they're often absent in smaller towns. In towns without banks, the local post office sometimes acts as a bank agent. You'll also sometimes find a multicard ATM in the local grocery store, pub or petrol station.

Debit cards For international travellers, debit cards connected to the international banking networks – Cirrus, Maestro, Plus and Eurocard – will work fine in Tasmanian ATMs. Expect substantial fees. A better option may be prepaid debit cards (such as MasterCard and Travelex 'Cash Passport' cards) with set withdrawal fees and a balance you can top up from your bank account while on the road.

Credit Cards

Credit cards such as MasterCard and Visa are widely accepted for most accommodation and services, and a credit card is essential (in lieu of a fat wad of cash) to hire a car. They can also be used to get cash advances over the counter at banks and from many ATMs, depending on the card – but be aware that these withdrawals incur immediate interest. Diners Club and American Express cards are not as widely accepted.

Taxes & Refunds

Australia has a flat 10% tax on all goods and services (the GST); this is included in quoted/shelf prices. A refund is sometimes possible under the Tourist Refund Scheme (TRS): see www.border.gov. au/trav/ente/tour/are-you-a-traveller.

Opening Hours

Opening hours are fairly consistent: you'll more likely find venues closing for certain days during winter rather then shortening hours on the days they remain open.

Banks 9.30am to 4pm Monday to Thursday, to 5pm Friday

Cafes 7.30am to 4pm

Post offices 9am to 5pm Monday to Friday; some open Saturday morning in cities

Pubs and bars 11am to 10pm (closing later in cities)

Restaurants Lunch noon to 2pm, dinner 6pm to 8.30pm

Shops 9am to 5pm Monday to Friday, to noon or 5pm Saturday, 'late-night' Hobart shopping to 8pm Friday

Post

Australia Post (www.auspost. com.au) is the nationwide provider. Most substantial Tasmanian towns have a post office, or an Australia Post desk within a local shop. Services are reliable, but slower than they used to be (recent cost-saving cutbacks are to blame). Express Post delivers a parcel or envelope interstate within Australia by the next business day; otherwise allow four days for urban deliveries, longer for country areas.

Public Holidays

The holidays listed are statewide unless otherwise indicated.

New Year's Day 1 January

Australia Day 26 January

Hobart Regatta Day 2nd Monday in February (southern Tasmania)

Launceston Cup Last Wednesday in February (Launceston only)

King Island Show 1st Tuesday in March (King Island only)

Eight Hour Day 2nd Monday in March

Easter March/April (Good Friday to Easter Tuesday inclusive)

Anzac Day 25 April

Queen's Birthday 2nd Monday in June

Burnie Show 1st Friday in October (Burnie only)

Launceston Show 2nd Thursday in October (Launceston only)

Hobart Show 3rd Thursday in October (southern Tasmania)

Flinders Island Show 3rd Friday in October (Flinders Island only)

Recreation Day 1st Monday in November (northern Tasmania)

Devonport Show Last Friday in November (Devonport only)

Christmas Day 25 December

Boxing Day 26 December

School Holidays

The Christmas/summer school-holiday season runs from mid-December to late January. Accommodation often books out. Book early for *Spirit of Tasmania* ferry services. Three shorter school-holiday periods occur during the year: roughly from early to mid-April, late June to mid-July, and late September to early October.

Safe Travel

Tasmania is a relatively safe place, but you should still take reasonable precautions.

At the Beach

Surf beaches can be dangerous places if you aren't used to the conditions. Undertows (or 'rips') are the main problem. If you find yourself being carried out by a rip, the important thing to do is just keep afloat – don't panic or try to swim against the current, which will exhaust you. In most cases the current stops within a couple of hundred metres of the shore: you can then swim parallel to the shore for a short way to get out of the rip and make your way back to land.

Insects

In the warmer months of the year, expect mosquitoes, especially around sunset. Insect repellents will deter them, but it's best to cover up. Ticks are found in moist bushy areas and can be avoided by covering up in light clothing. Most people experience little or no symptoms of bites, but occasionally paralysis or allergic reaction to their toxins can occur. If you find a tick lodged somewhere on your body, gently remove it with a pair of fine-pointed tweezers by grasping as close to the skin as possible.

Jack jumper ants have a black body and orange pincers. They are aggressive and can sometimes 'jump' from the vegetation. Bull ants (aka inchmen) are larger, with dark browny-red bodies. Bites from both cause an allergic reaction, followed by devilish itching. Signs of an ant nest can include small pebbles at the entrance to the hole.

Leeches

Leeches may be present in damp rainforest conditions: bushwalkers often find them on their legs or in their boots. Salt or a lit cigarette end will make them fall off. Do not pull them off, as the bite is then more likely to become infected. Clean and apply pressure if the point of attachment is bleeding. An insect repellent may keep them away and gaiters are a good idea when you're walking.

Sharks

Despite the bad rep, shark attacks are rare in Tasmania, with only six deaths in the last 50 years in state waters. That said, the sea is their house: if you walk through the front door, someone might be home.

Snakes

Tasmania is home to three snake species: tiger, white-lipped and lowland copper-head snakes; see www.parks. tas.gov.au/wildlife. All three are venomous, but they are not aggressive and, unless you have the ill fortune to stand on one, it's unlikely you'll be bitten. Snakes are most active in summer and are often spotted on bushwalking trails around the state.

To minimise your chances of being bitten, always wear boots, socks and long trousers (ideally gaiters) when walking through undergrowth. Don't put your hands into holes and crevices and be careful if collecting firewood.

Spiders

There are a few spiders to watch out for in Tasmania. The white-tailed spider is a long, thin, black spider with a white tip on its tail. It has a fierce bite that can lead to local inflammation. It is a ground scavenger and can sometimes crawl into piles of stuff left on the floor. Tasmanian funnel-web and redback spiders are venomous; if you're bitten, seek medical help ASAP. The disturbingly large huntsman spider has a nonvenomous bite.

Telephone

Australia's main telecom-munication companies all operate in Tasmania:

Telstra (www.telstra.com.au) The main player, with the best mobile coverage. Offers landline and mobile-phone services.

Optus (www.optus.com.au) Telstra's main rival. Landline and mobile-phone services.

Vodafone (www.vodafone.com. au) Mobile-phone services.

Information & Toll-Free Calls

➡ Numbers starting with ✆190 are usually recorded-information services, charged at anywhere from 35c to $5 or more per minute (more from mobiles).

➡ Toll-free numbers beginning with ✆1800 can be called free of charge from anywhere in Australia, though they may not be accessible from certain areas or from mobile phones.

➡ Calls to numbers beginning with ✆13 or ✆1300 are charged at the rate of a local call; the numbers can usually be dialled Australia-wide but may be applicable only to a specific state or Subscriber Trunk Dialling (STD) district.

➡ Telephone numbers beginning with ✆1800, ✆13 or ✆1300 cannot be dialled from outside Australia.

International Calls

➡ When calling overseas you need to dial the international access code from Australia (✆0011), the country code and the area code (without the initial 0).

➡ If calling Australia from overseas the country code is ✆61 and you need to drop the 0 in the state/territory area codes.

Local Calls

➡ Local calls from private phones cost 30c and are untimed.

➡ Local calls from public phones cost 50c and are untimed.

➡ Calls to mobile phones cost more and are timed.

Long-Distance Calls & Area Codes

Australia uses four long-distance STD area codes:

State/territory	Area code
ACT	✆02
NSW	✆02
NT	✆08
Qld	✆07
SA	✆08
Tas	✆03
Vic	✆03
WA	✆08

➡ STD calls can be made from virtually any public phone and are cheaper during off-peak hours (7pm to 7am).

➡ Long-distance calls (more than 50km away) within these areas are charged at long-distance rates, even though they have the same area code.

➡ When calling from one area of Tasmania to another, there's no need to dial 03 before the local number.

➡ Local numbers start with 62 in Hobart and southern Tasmania, 63 in Launceston and the northeast, and 64 in the west and northwest.

Mobile Phones

Australia's main service providers (Telstra, Optus and Vodafone) all have prepaid mobile systems. Buy a starter kit, which may include a phone or, if you have your own phone, a SIM card and a prepaid charge card.

Numbers Local numbers with the prefix ✆04 belong to mobile phones.

Reception If you're not on the Telstra network, coverage can be patchy in remote areas (and sometimes even if you are with Telstra).

Networks Australia's digital network is compatible with GSM 900 and 1800 (used in Europe) but generally not with the systems used in the USA or Japan. For overseas visitors GSM 900 and 1800 mobiles can be used in Australia if set up at home first; contact your service provider before you travel.

Phonecards & Public Phones

A variety of phonecards can be bought at newsagents, hostels and post offices for a fixed dollar value (usually $10, $20 etc) and can be used with any public or private phone. Shop around.

Most public phones use phonecards; some also accept credit cards. Old-fashioned coin-operated public phones are becoming increasingly rare.

Time

Australia is divided into three time zones:

Western Standard Time (GMT/UTC plus eight hours) Applies in Western Australia (WA).

Central Standard Time (GMT/UTC plus 9½ hours) Covers the Northern Territory (NT) and South Australia (SA).

Eastern Standard Time (GMT/UTC plus 10 hours) Covers Tasmania, Victoria, New South Wales (NSW), the Australian Capital Territory (ACT) and Queensland.

Daylight Saving

Daylight saving in Tasmania begins on the first Sunday in October and ends on the first Sunday in April. These arrangements are in line with Victoria, NSW, SA and the ACT. Daylight saving does not operate in Queensland, WA or the NT.

Toilets

➜ Toilets in Tasmania are sit-down Western-style (though you mightn't find this prospect too appealing in some remote spots).

➜ See www.toiletmap.gov.au for public-toilet locations.

Tourist Information

Tourism Tasmania (www.discovertasmania.com) Tasmania's official tourism promoter. The main Tasmanian Travel &

Information Centre in Hobart is a helpful spot for planning statewide travel and can handle bookings of all sorts.

Tasmanian Travelways (www.travelways.com.au) Online version of the tourist newspaper of the same name.

National Trust (☑03-6344 6233; www.nationaltrust.org.au/tas) Keepers and protectors of many of Tasmania's gorgeous old heritage buildings.

Local Tourist Offices

Tasmania's main visitor centres supply brochures, maps and local info and can often book transport, tours and accommodation. They generally open from around 8.30am or 9am to 5pm or 5.30pm weekdays, with slightly shorter hours at weekends. Info centres in smaller towns are usually staffed by volunteers (chatty, benign retirees), resulting in less regular opening hours.

Travellers with Disabilities

An increasing number of accommodation providers and key attractions have access for those with limited mobility, and tour operators often have the appropriate facilities; call ahead to confirm.

Download Lonely Planet's free Accessible Travel guide from http://lptravel.to/AccessibleTravel. Also check out the *Hobart CBD Mobility Map* from Hobart's visitor centre.

National Information Communication & Awareness Network (www.nican.com.au) Australia-wide directory providing information on access, accommodation, sports and recreational activities, transport and specialist tour operators.

ParaQuad Association of Tasmania (☑03-6272 8816; www.paraquadtas.org.au) Information for travellers with disabilities. Download *The Wheelie Good Guide*.

Parks & Wildlife Service (☑1300 135 513; www.parks.tas.gov.au) *Parks for all People* (PDF download) outlines access for mobility-impaired visitors to Tasmania's national parks and reserves. Click on 'Recreation', then 'Disabled Access'.

Visas

All visitors to Australia, and thus Tasmania, need a visa. Apply online through the Department of Immigration & Border Protection (www.border.gov.au), unless you are a New Zealander (Kiwis are granted a special visa upon entering Australia).

eVisitor (651)

➜ Many European passport-holders are eligible for a free eVisitor visa, allowing visits to Australia for up to three months at a time within a 12-month period.

➜ eVisitor visas must be applied for online. They are electronically stored and linked to individual passport numbers, so no stamp in your passport is required.

➜ It's advisable to apply at least 14 days prior to the proposed date of travel to Australia.

Electronic Travel Authority (ETA; 601)

➜ Passport-holders from many of the European countries eligible for eVisitor visas, plus passport-holders from Brunei, Canada, Hong Kong, Japan, Malaysia, Singapore, South Korea and the USA, can apply for either a visitor ETA or business ETA.

➜ ETAs are valid for 12 months, with multiple stays of up to three months permitted.

➜ ETA visas cost $20; apply via travel agents worldwide, or online.

Visitor (600)

➜ Short-term Visitor visas have largely been replaced by the eVisitor and ETA.

However, if you're from a country not covered by either, or you want to stay longer than three months, you'll need to apply for a Visitor visa.

➡ Standard Visitor visas allow one entry for a stay of up to three, six or 12 months, and are valid for use within 12 months of issue.

➡ Visitor visas cost from $140 to $1020.

Work & Holiday (462)

➡ Nationals from Argentina, Bangladesh, Chile, China, Indonesia, Israel, Luxembourg, Malaysia, Peru, Poland, Portugal, San Marino, Singapore, the Slovak Republic, Slovenia, Spain, Thailand, Turkey, the USA, Uruguay and Vietnam who are aged between 18 and 30 can apply for a Work and Holiday visa prior to entry to Australia.

➡ Once granted, this visa allows the holder to enter Australia within three months of issue, stay for up to 12 months, leave and reenter Australia any number of times within those 12 months, undertake temporary employment to supplement a trip, and study for up to four months.

➡ The application fee is $440.

Working Holiday (417)

➡ Young (aged 18 to 30) visitors from Belgium, Canada, Cyprus, Denmark, Estonia, Finland, France, Germany, Hong Kong, Ireland, Italy, Japan, the Republic of Korea, Malta, the Netherlands, Norway, Sweden, Taiwan and the UK are eligible for a Working Holiday visa, which allows you to visit for up to 12 months and gain casual employment.

➡ Holders can leave and reenter Australia any number of times within those 12 months.

➡ Holders can only work for any one employer for a maximum of six months.

➡ Apply prior to entry to Australia (up to a year in advance) – you can't change from another tourist visa to a Working Holiday visa once you're in Australia.

➡ Conditions include having a return air ticket or sufficient funds ($5000) for a return or onward fare.

➡ The application fee is $440.

➡ Second Working Holiday visas can be applied for once you're in Australia, subject to certain conditions.

Visa Extensions

If you want to stay in Australia for longer than your visa allows, you'll need to apply for a new visa (usually a Visitor visa 600). Apply online at least two or three weeks before your visa expires.

Volunteering

Volunteering is an excellent way to meet people and visit some interesting places, with a number of worthy projects active in Tasmania.

Conservation Volunteers Australia (☏1800 032 501; www.conservationvolunteers.com.au) Helps volunteers get their hands dirty with tree planting, walking-track construction and flora and fauna surveys.

Greening Australia (☏03-6235 8000; www.greeningaustralia.org.au) Helps volunteers get involved with environmental projects in the bush or in plant nurseries.

Volunteering Tasmania (☏1800 677 895; www.volunteeringtas.org.au) Useful resource bringing volunteers and volunteer projects together.

Willing Workers on Organic Farms (WWOOF;☏03-5155 0218; www.wwoof.com.au) WWOOFing is where you do four to six hours' work each day on a farm in return for bed and board. Most hosts are concerned to some extent with alternative lifestyles, and require a minimum stay of two nights. Join online (one year/six months $70/50), then get started (farm listings, maps etc also online). An app is available.

Women Travellers

Tasmania is generally a safe place for women travellers, although the usual sensible precautions apply. Sexual harassment is rare, though some macho Aussie males still slip – particularly in rural areas when they've been drinking. Hitchhiking isn't such a great idea anywhere in Australia these days, even when travelling in pairs.

Work

Casual work can usually be found during summer in the major tourist centres, mainly working in tourism, hospitality, labouring, gardening or farming.

Seasonal fruit picking is hard work and pay is proportional to the quantity and quality of fruits picked. Harvest is from December to April in the Huon and Tamar Valleys. Grape-picking jobs are sometimes available in late autumn and early winter, as some wineries still hand-pick their crops.

Australian JobSearch (www.jobsearch.gov.au) Myriad jobs across the country.

Harvest Trail (www.harvesttrail.gov.au) Harvest job specialist.

National Harvest Telephone Information Service (☏1800 062 332; www.employment.gov.au/harvest-labour-services) Advice on when and where you're likely to pick up harvest work.

Seek (www.seek.com.au) General employment site; good for metropolitan areas.

Travellers at Work (www.taw.com.au) Excellent site for working travellers in Australia.

Transport

GETTING THERE & AWAY

There are no direct international flights to Tasmania. Visitors need to get to one of Australia's mainland cities and connect to a Tasmania-bound domestic flight to Hobart, Launceston or Devonport. Melbourne and Sydney (and, to a lesser extent, Brisbane) airports have the most frequent direct air links. Also popular is the *Spirit of Tasmania* passenger and car ferry, sailing between Melbourne and Devonport in Tasmania's north.

Flights, cars and tours can be booked online at lonelyplanet.com/bookings.

Entering Tasmania

Security at mainland Australian airports has increased in recent years, at both domestic and international termi-

nals, but Tasmania's arrivals procedures are generally less time-consuming.

Passport

There are no restrictions for citizens of any particular countries entering Australia, and thus Tasmania. If you have a current passport and visa, you should be fine.

Air

There are major airports in Hobart and Launceston, as well as smaller operations at Burnie and Devonport. One-way flights to Hobart or Launceston start at around $100 from Melbourne and $150 from Sydney.

Airports & Airlines

Burnie Airport (☎03-6442 1133; www.burnieairport.com. au; 3 Airport St, Wynyard) On the southern edge of Wynyard, 19km west of Burnie. Some Tasmanians call the airport 'Burnie',

others call it 'Wynyard'...maybe it should be 'Burnie/Wynyard'.

Devonport Airport (☎13 13 13; www.devonportairport.com.au; Airport Rd) About 10km east of central Devonport.

Hobart Airport (☎03-6216 1600; www.hobartairport.com. au; 6 Hinkler Rd, Cambridge) At Cambridge, 19km east of Hobart.

Launceston Airport (☎03-6391 6222; www.launcestonairport. com.au; 201 Evandale Rd, Western Junction) About 15km south of Launceston, on the road to Evandale.

Airlines flying into Tasmania from mainland Australia include the following:

Jetstar (www.jetstar.com.au) Direct flights from Melbourne, Sydney and Brisbane to Hobart and Launceston. Also flies Adelaide to Hobart.

Qantas (www.qantas.com. au) Direct flights from Sydney, Brisbane and Melbourne to Launceston, and from Sydney and Melbourne to Hobart. Also

---

CLIMATE CHANGE & TRAVEL

Every form of transport that relies on carbon-based fuel generates CO_2, the main cause of human-induced climate change. Modern travel is dependent on aeroplanes, which might use less fuel per kilometre per person than most cars but travel much greater distances. The altitude at which aircraft emit gases (including CO_2) and particles also contributes to their climate change impact. Many websites offer 'carbon calculators' that allow people to estimate the carbon emissions generated by their journey and, for those who wish to do so, to offset the impact of the greenhouse gases emitted with contributions to portfolios of climate-friendly initiatives throughout the world. Lonely Planet offsets the carbon footprint of all staff and author travel.

flies between Melbourne and Devonport.

Regional Express (Rex; www.regionalexpress.com.au) Flies from Melbourne to Burnie and King Island.

Tiger Air (www.tigerair.com.au) Flies from the Gold Coast to Hobart.

Virgin Australia (www.virginaustralia.com) Direct flights from Melbourne, Sydney, Brisbane and Canberra to Hobart, and from Melbourne, Brisbane and Sydney to Launceston.

Land

It is not possible to travel here by land (the land bridge that once linked Tasmania and Victoria disappeared under Bass Strait after the last ice age).

Sea
Ferry

Two big, red **Spirit of Tasmania** (☑1800 634 906, 03-6419 9320; www.spiritoftasmania.com.au) ferries ply Bass Strait nightly in each direction between Melbourne and Devonport on Tasmania's northwest coast. The crossing takes around 11 hours, departing either mainland Australia or Tasmania at 7.30pm and arriving at 6.30am. During peak periods, including Christmas, Easter and key holiday weekends, the schedule is ramped up to two sailings per day, departing at 9am and 9pm. Check the website for details.

Each ferry can accommodate 1400 passengers and around 650 vehicles and has restaurants, bars and games facilities. The whole experience is a bit of an adventure for Australians, who are used

to flying or driving everywhere; kids especially get a kick out of it.

The ships' public areas have been designed to cater for wheelchair access, as have a handful of cabins.

DEPARTURE POINTS
The Devonport terminal is on the Esplanade in East Devonport; the Melbourne terminal is at Station Pier in Port Melbourne.

CABIN & SEATING OPTIONS
There's a range of seating and cabin options on 'the *Spirit*'. Recliner seats are the cheapest – a bit like airline seats (BYO earplugs and eye mask if you actually want to get some sleep). Cabins are available in twin or three- or four-berth configurations, with or without porthole windows. Or you can up the ante to a 'deluxe' cabin with a queen-size bed, a TV and two windows. All cabins have a private bathroom. Child, student and pensioner discounts apply to all accommodation, except for deluxe cabins. Prices do not include meals, which can be purchased on board from the restaurant or cafeteria.

FARE OPTIONS
Fares depend on whether you're travelling in the peak period (mid-December to late January, and Easter), or in the off-peak period (all other times). For the peak season and during holiday weekends, booking ahead as early as possible is recommended.

One-way online prices (per adult) are as follows. Fares per person come down if there's more than one person per cabin. It's cheaper again if you're prepared to share a cabin with

same-gender passengers who aren't travelling with you (mini dormitories!). Fares listed here are the less-flexible, nonrefundable 'Spirit Fare' prices (conditions are similar to discount airlines). Check online for specials.

Fare	Peak	Off-Peak
Recliner seat	$130	$99
Inside three- or four-berth cabin	$262	$231
Inside twin cabin	$310	$279
Deluxe cabin	$590	$559
Daytime sailings (seats only)	$110	n/a
Standard vehicles	$99	$89
Campervans up to 7m long	$109	$99
Motorcycles	$69	$59
Bicycles	$5	$5

Cruise Ship

During the summer season, passengers from gargantuan international cruise ships regularly disembark onto the Hobart and Burnie waterfronts and wander around looking disoriented and splashing their cash. **P&O Cruises** (☑1300 159 454; www.pocruises.com.au) is one of the main players. The TasPorts (www.tasports.com.au) website lists all the expected cruise-ship arrivals.

Just about the only way to see the remote Macquarie Island, proclaimed Tasmania's second World Heritage area in 1997, is to take one of the sub-Antarctic-islands cruises scheduled by New

Zealand-based Heritage Expeditions (www.heritage-expeditions.com).

GETTING AROUND

Air

Distances within Tasmania are far from huge, so air travel within the state is not very common. Of more use to travellers are the air services for bushwalkers in the southwest, and flights to King and Flinders Islands.

Par Avion (☑1800 017 557; www.paravion.com.au) Flies regularly from Launceston to Cape Barren Island (one way from $124), just south of Flinders Island. Also runs scenic flights over the east coast and southwest, plus bushwalker transport between Hobart and Melaleuca (one way from $290) for the South Coast Track or Port Davey Track.

Sharp Airlines (☑1300 556 694; www.sharpairlines.com) Flies between Melbourne (Essendon Airport) and Flinders Island (one way $252), and Launceston and Flinders Island ($185). Also services King Island from Launceston ($286), Melbourne ($215) and Burnie/Wynyard ($219).

Bicycle

Cycling Tasmania is one of the best ways to get close to nature (and, it has to be said, to logging trucks, rain, hills, roadkill...). Roads are generally in good shape, and traffic outside the cities is light. If you're prepared for occasional steep climbs and strong headwinds, you could enjoy the experience immensely.

Transport It's worth bringing your own bike, especially if you're coming via ferry: bike transport on the *Spirit of Tasmania* costs just $5 each way year-round. Another option is buying a bike in Hobart or

Launceston and reselling it at the end of your trip – hit the bike shops or the noticeboards at backpacker hostels.

Rental Bike rental is available in the larger towns, and a number of operators offer multiday cycling tours or experiences such as mountain biking down kunanyi/Mt Wellington in Hobart.

Road rules Bicycle helmets are compulsory in Tasmania, as are white front lights and red rear lights if you're riding in the dark. See www.biketas.org.au for more information.

Boat

There are a few handy regional ferries around Tasmania, accessing the islands off the island.

Bruny Island Ferry (☑03-6273 6725; www.brunyislandferry. com.au; Ferry Rd, Kettering; car return $33-38, motorcycle/ bike/foot passenger return $6/6/free) Vehicle/passenger ferry running at least 10 times a day from Kettering to Bruny Island in Tasmania's southeast.

Furneaux Freight (☑03-6356 1753; www.furneauxfreight.com. au; Main St, Bridport; adult/ child/car return $115/60/505) Small weekly passenger and car ferry from Bridport in Tasmania's northeast to Lady Barron on Flinders Island.

Encounter Maria Island (☑03-6256 4772; www.encounter maria.com.au; Charles St, Triabunna; return incl national-park entry adult/child $50/33, per bicycle/kayak $10/20; ☺9am, 10.30am, noon, 2.45pm & 4.15pm Sep-Apr, 10.30am, noon & 2.45pm May-Aug) Runs at least three ferries daily from Triabunna on the east coast to Maria Island National Park; carries passengers and bicycles.

Bus

Tasmania has a reasonable weekday bus network connecting the major towns and centres, with reduced week-

end services. There are more buses in summer than during winter. Small operators run useful services along key tourist routes and to smaller regional towns. The two main players – Tassielink and Redline – don't currently offer multitrip bus passes.

Operators include the following:

Calow's Coaches (Map p178; ☑0400 570 036, 03-6376 2161; www.calowscoaches. com) Services the east coast (St Marys, St Helens, Bicheno) from Launceston. Also runs into Coles Bay and Freycinet National Park, connecting with Tassielink buses to/from Hobart at the Coles Bay turn-off.

Lee's Coaches (Map p178; ☑0400 937 440; www.lees coaches.com) Services the East Tamar Valley region from Launceston. Buses stop on Brisbane St.

Manions' Coaches (Map p178; ☑03-6383 1221; www.manions coaches.com.au) Services the West Tamar Valley region from Launceston. Buses stop on Brisbane St.

Redline Coaches (☑1300 360 000; www.tasredline.com.au) The state's second-biggest operator. Services the Midland Hwy between Hobart and Launceston, and the north-coast towns between Launceston and Smithton. Also available are shuttles to Hobart and Launceston airports, called the **Hobart Airporter** (☑1300 385 511; www.airporter hobart.com.au; adult/child $20/18 one way, return $35/31) and the **Launceston Airporter** (☑1300 360 000; www.airporterlaunceston. com.au; adult/child one way $15/14).

Sainty's North East Bus Service (Map p178;☑0437 469 186, 0400 791 076; www. saintysnortheastbusservice. com.au) Buses between Launceston and Lilydale, Scottsdale, Derby and Bridport.

Tassielink (☑03-6235 7300, 1300 300 520; www.tassielink. com.au) The main player, with extensive statewide services. From Hobart buses run south to Dover via the Huon Valley, southeast to Port Arthur, north to Richmond, to Launceston via the Midlands Hwy, to the east coast as far as Bicheno, and to Strahan on the west coast via Lake St Clair. From Launceston buses run south to Cressy, to Hobart via the Midlands Hwy, and west to Devonport, continuing to Strahan on the west coast via Cradle Mountain and Queenstown. Express services from the *Spirit of Tasmania* ferry terminal in Devonport to Launceston and Hobart are also available. Buses also link Burnie in the northwest with Strahan on the west coast, via a (relatively) wild northwest route.

Car & Motorcycle

For maximum freedom and flexibility, travelling around Tassie with your own wheels is definitely the way to go. You can also BYO vehicle from the mainland to Tasmania on the *Spirit of Tasmania* ferries, which might save you some dollars in car rental.

Motorcycles are a hip way to get around the island, but be prepared for all kinds of weather in any season.

Automobile Associations

The **Royal Automobile Club of Tasmania** (RACT; ☎03-6232 6300, roadside assistance 13 11 11; www.ract. com.au; cnr Murray & Patrick Sts, Hobart; ⊗8.45am-5pm Mon-Fri) is the local body, providing emergency breakdown service to members (and affiliate members).

Fuel

In small towns there's often just a pump outside the general store, but all the larger towns and cities have conventional service stations. Most are open from 7am to around 10pm daily, plus you'll find a few 24-hour petrol stations in Hobart and Launceston.

Unleaded petrol, diesel and gas are all widely avail-

able. In small rural towns, prices often jump about 10c per litre from urban rates, so fill up before leaving a bigger centre.

Insurance

THIRD-PARTY INSURANCE

Third-party personal-injury insurance is included in vehicle-registration costs, ensuring that every registered vehicle carries at least minimum insurance. Extending that minimum to at least third-party property insurance is highly recommended: minor collisions can be amazingly expensive.

RENTAL VEHICLES

When it comes to hire cars, understand your liability in the event of an accident. Rather than risk paying out thousands of dollars, consider taking out comprehensive car insurance or paying an additional daily amount to the rental company for excess reduction – this reduces the excess payable in the event of an accident from between $2000 and $5000 to a few hundred dollars.

EXCLUSIONS

Be aware that if travelling on dirt roads you usually won't be covered by insurance unless you have a 4WD (read the fine print). Also, many insurance companies won't cover the cost of damage to glass (including the windscreen) or tyres. Note that many rental companies won't let you take their vehicles onto Bruny Island in the southeast.

Purchase

If you're touring Tassie for several months, buying a secondhand car may be cheaper than renting. You'll probably pick up a car more cheaply by buying privately online rather than through a car dealer, but buying through a dealer does have the advantage of some sort of guarantee.

Online, check out Car Sales (www.carsales.com.au) or Gumtree (www.gumtree. com.au).

LEGALITIES

When you buy a car in Tasmania, you and the seller need to complete and sign a Transfer of Registration form. Inspections or warrants of fitness aren't required, but ensuring the vehicle registration is paid becomes your responsibility. See http:// www.transport.tas.gov.au/ registration/buying-selling for details.

It's also your responsibility to ensure that the car isn't stolen and that there's no money owing on it: check the car's details with the Australian government's Personal Property Securities Register (www.ppsr.gov.au).

Rental

CARS

Practicalities Before hiring a car, ask about any kilometre limitations and find out exactly what the insurance covers. Note that some companies don't cover accidents on unsealed roads, and hike up the excess in the case of any damage on the dirt – a considerable disadvantage, as many of the top Tasmanian destinations are definitely off-piste! Some companies also don't allow their vehicles to be taken across to Bruny Island.

Costs Expect to pay anywhere from $30 to $90 per day for a week's hire of a small car in any season; local operators are cheaper. Book in advance for the best prices.

Autorent-Hertz (☎1800 030 500; www.autorent.com.au) Also has campervans for hire and sale.

Avis (☎13 63 33; www.avis. com.au) Also has 4WDs.

Bargain Select (☎1800 300 102; www.selectivecarrentals. com.au) Branches in Hobart and Devonport, plus at Hobart and Launceston Airports.

Budget (☎1300 362 848; www. budget.com.au) Car rental.

Europcar (☑1300 131 390; www.europcar.com.au) Car rental.

Lo-Cost Auto Rent (☑03-6231 0550; www.locostautorent. com) Has a branch in Hobart, plus at Hobart and Launceston Airports.

Rent For Less (☑1300 883 728; www.rentforless.com. au) Hobart, Hobart Airport and Launceston Airport locations.

Thrifty (☑1300 367 227; www. thrifty.com.au) Car rental.

CAMPERVANS
Campervan hire in Tasmania starts at around $90 per day for a two-berth van, or $150 for a four-berth van, usually with unlimited kilometres and a minimum five-day hire. For rate comparisons, see www.fetchcampervanhire. com.au. Operators include the following:

Apollo (☑1800 777 779; www. apollocamper.com) Also has a backpacker-focused brand called Hippie Camper.

Britz (☑1300 738 087; www. britz.com.au) Campervan hire; also has 4WDs.

Cruisin' Tasmania (☑1300 664 485; www.cruisintasmania.com. au) Campervan rental.

Leisure Rent (☑0429 727 277; www.leisurerent.com.au) Campervan hire.

Maui (☑1800 827 821; www. maui.com.au) Campervan rental.

Tasmanian Campervan Hire (☑0438 807 118; www.tas camper.com) Specialises in two-berth vans.

Tasmanian Campervan Rentals (☑03-6248 4418; www.tas maniacampervanrentals.com. au) Campervan rental. Based in Hobart.

Tasmanian Motor Shacks (☑03-6248 4418; www. tassiemotorshacks.com.au) Hobart-based campervan rental.

MOTORCYCLES
Tasmanian Motorcycle Hire (☑0418 365 210; www.tas motorcyclehire.com.au) has a range of touring motorbikes for rent from around $120 per day (cheaper rates for longer rentals); see the website for full pricing details. Based in Launceston.

Road Conditions & Hazards
Road conditions in Tasmania are generally pretty good, but there are a few hazards to watch out for.

FOUR-WHEEL DRIVE TRACKS
Anyone considering travelling on 4WD tracks should read the free publication *Cruisin' Without Bruisin'*, available online from the Parks & Wildlife Service (www.parks.tas.gov.au): click on 'Recreation', then 'Other Activities'. It sets out a code of practice to minimise your impact on the regions you drive through.

BLACK ICE
In cold weather be wary of 'black ice', an invisible layer of ice over the tarmac, especially on the shady side of mountain passes. Slippery stuff.

CYCLISTS & LOG TRUCKS
Cycle touring is popular on some roads, particularly on the east coast in summer. When encountering bicycles, wait until you can pass safely to avoid clipping, scaring or generally freaking out cyclists. Log trucks piled high and coming around sharp corners also demand caution.

DISTANCES
Distances may appear short when you peruse a map of Tasmania, especially compared with the vast distances on mainland Australia. But many roads here are narrow and winding, with sharp bends and occasional one-lane bridges. Getting to where you want to be usually takes longer than expected.

UNSEALED ROADS
Most of the main roads around Tasmania are sealed and in good nick, but there are also many unsealed roads leading to off-the-beaten-track spots. Ask your car-rental company if it's cool with your going off-tarmac.

WILDLIFE
Watch out for wildlife while you're driving around the island, especially at night – the huge number of car-casses lining highways tells a sorry tale. Many local animals are nocturnal – try to avoid driving in rural areas at dusk and after dark. If it's unavoidable, slow down. If you do hit and injure an animal, contact the **Parks & Wildlife Service** (☑03-6165 4305; www.parks.tas.gov.au) for advice.

Road Rules
Cars are driven on the left-hand side of the road in Tasmania (as per the rest of Australia). An important road rule is to 'give way to the right' – if an intersection is unmarked (unusual), you must give way to vehicles entering the intersection from your right.

The speed limit in built-up areas is 50km/h. Near schools, the limit is 40km/h in the morning and afternoon. On the highway it's 100km/h or 110km/h.

Random breath tests (for alcohol and illegal drugs) are common. If you're caught with a blood-alcohol level of more than 0.05% expect a fine and the loss of your licence. Talking on a mobile phone while driving is also illegal (excluding hands-free technology).

Hitching & Ride-Sharing
Hitching is never entirely safe in any country in the world, and we don't recommend it. Travellers who decide to hitch should understand that they are taking a small but potentially serious risk. People who do choose to hitch will be safer if they travel in

pairs and let someone know where they are planning to go.

People looking for travelling companions for car journeys around the state often leave notices on boards in hostels and backpacker accommodation.

Taxi-but-not-a-taxi operator Uber (www.uber. com) is now operating in Tasmania. You might also try ride-share hub www.cool-pooltas.com.au.

Local Transport

Metro Tasmania (📞13 22 01; www.metrotas.com.au) operates local bus networks in Hobart, Launceston and Burnie, offering visitors inexpensive services around the city suburbs and to a few out-of-the-way areas, including the Channel Hwy towns south of Hobart, and

Hadspen south of Launceston. Check online for schedules and fares.

Tours

Backpacker-style, outdoorsy or more formal bus tours offer a convenient way to see some of Tasmania's more remote corners, or just to get from A to B and check out the sights on the way. Operators include the following:

Adventure Tours (📞1300 654 604; www.adventuretours. au) An Australia-wide company offering six-day tours around Tasmania, including hostel accommodation.

Jump Tours (📞03-6288 7030; http://jumptours.com.au) Youth/backpacker-oriented one-to seven-day Tassie tours.

Tarkine Trails (📞0405 255 537; www.tarkinetrails.com.

au) 🍃 Green-focused group offering guided walks in the takayna/Tarkine wilderness.

Tasmania Tours (📞1800 994 620; www.tasmaniatours. com.au) Multi-day coach tours around the island, from four to 13 days. Prices include accommodation.

Tasmanian Expeditions (📞1300 666 856; www.tasmanianexpeditions.com.au) Offers an excellent range of activity-based tours – bushwalking, cabin-based walks, rafting, rock climbing, cycling, sea kayaking – in remote parts of the state.

Tasmanian Safaris (📞1300 882 415; www.tasmaniansafaris.com) 🍃 Multiday all-inclusive, eco-certified 4WD tours out of Launceston heading to Hobart via the east coast, or from Hobart to Launceston via the west coast. There's bushwalking, bush camping and lots

ROAD DISTANCES (KM)

	Burnie	Deloraine	Devonport	Geeveston	Hobart	Launceston	New Norfolk	Oatlands	Port Arthur	Queenstown	St Helens	Scottsdale	Smithton	Sorell	Strahan	Swansea
Deloraine	100															
Devonport	50	50														
Geeveston	381	281	331													
Hobart	328	228	278	53												
Launceston	137	51	87	254	201											
New Norfolk	290	190	240	91	38	197										
Oatlands	246	146	196	136	83	118	79									
Port Arthur	386	286	336	148	95	258	133	140								
Queenstown	148	204	198	312	259	251	221	261	354							
St Helens	293	207	243	304	251	156	247	168	299	407						
Scottsdale	197	111	147	314	261	60	257	178	318	311	96					
Smithton	88	188	138	469	416	225	378	334	474	236	381	285				
Sorell	316	216	266	78	25	188	63	70	70	284	229	248	404			
Strahan	183	222	209	353	289	271	253	370	388	41	405	330	224	325		
Swansea	264	164	214	189	136	136	174	114	181	395	118	214	352	111	352	
Triabunna	314	214	264	139	86	186	124	131	131	345	168	264	402	61	249	50

These are the shortest distances by road; other routes may be considerably longer.
For distances by coach, check the companies' leaflets.

of wilderness. Canoe trips also available.

Under Down Under (Tassie Day Tours; ☎1800 444 442; www.underdownunder.com.au) Offers pro-green, nature-based, backpacker-friendly trips. Tours from one to nine days heading all over the state.

Tassie Road Trips (☎0455 227 536; www.tassieroadtrips.com) Day tours around Hobart (Bruny Island, Port Arthur, Huon Valley, Richmond etc), plus bushwalker transport back to civilisation from the ends of the Overland Track and the South Coast Track.

Eco Tours Tasmania (☎0407 636 014; www.ecotours tasmania.com.au; half-/full-day tours from $80/135) Day tours out of Hobart with a distinctly eco bent: Styx Valley, Huon Valley and dedicated native-orchid-spotting trips in spring.

Train

For economic reasons, passenger rail services in Tasmania sadly ceased in the late 1970s. There are a couple of small, scenic tourist routes still running, however, including the **West Coast Wilderness Railway** (Map p245; ☎03-6471 0100; www.wcwr.com.au; Queenstown Station, 1 Driffield St; standard carriage adult/child/family $110/55/245, wilderness carriage adult/child $175/100; ⏰ticket office 8am-4.30pm Mon-Sat, 9am-4pm Sun) between Queenstown and Strahan (34km) and the **Ida Bay Railway** (☎03-6298 3110, 0428 383 262; www.idabayrailway.com.au; 328 Lune River Rd, Lune River; adult/child/family $32/17/75; ⏰10am, noon, 2pm & 4pm Jan, 10am, noon & 2pm Feb-Apr, 10am & 12.30pm Thu-Sun May-Dec) in the southeast.

Behind the Scenes

SEND US YOUR FEEDBACK

We love to hear from travellers – your comments keep us on our toes and help make our books better. Our well-travelled team reads every word on what you loved or loathed about this book. Although we cannot reply individually to your submissions, we always guarantee that your feedback goes straight to the appropriate authors, in time for the next edition. Each person who sends us information is thanked in the next edition – the most useful submissions are rewarded with a selection of digital PDF chapters.

Visit **lonelyplanet.com/contact** to submit your updates and suggestions or to ask for help. Our award-winning website also features inspirational travel stories, news and discussions.

Note: We may edit, reproduce and incorporate your comments in Lonely Planet products such as guidebooks, websites and digital products, so let us know if you don't want your comments reproduced or your name acknowledged. For a copy of our privacy policy visit lonelyplanet.com/privacy.

OUR READERS

Many thanks to the travellers who used the last edition and wrote to us with helpful hints, useful advice and interesting anecdotes: Justin Davies, Michelle Gralike, Mike Hawkins, Janine Matheson, Allen Nelson, Rochelle Robinson, WY Yau

WRITER THANKS
Charles Rawlings-Way

Huge thanks to Tasmin Waby for the gig, Niamh O'Brien for the ongoing support, and to all the helpful souls I talked to and friends I reconnected with on the road in Tasmania. 'Coming home' means something different for everyone: for me, Tasmania is always where the heart is. Biggest thanks of all to Meg, who held the increasingly chaotic fort at home while I was scooting around my beloved island state ('Where's Daddy?') – and made sure that Ione, Remy, Liv and Reuben were fed, watered, schooled, tucked-in and read-to.

ACKNOWLEDGEMENTS

Climate map data adapted from Peel MC, Finlayson BL & McMahon TA (2007) 'Updated World Map of the Köppen-Geiger Climate Classification', Hydrology and Earth System Sciences, 11, 16-3344.

Cover photograph: The Neck, Bruny Island, Artie Photography (Artie Ng)/Getty Images ©

THIS BOOK

This 8th edition of Lonely Planet's *Tasmania* guidebook was curated by Charles Rawlings-Way, and written and researched by Charles and Virginia Maxwell. The previous edition was written by Anthony Ham, Charles Rawlings-Way and Meg Worby. This guidebook was produced by the following:

Destination Editors
Tasmin Waby, Niamh O'Brien

Senior Product Editor
Kate Chapman

Product Editor Ross Taylor

Senior Cartographer
Julie Sheridan

Book Designer
Virginia Moreno

Assisting Editors
Sarah Bailey, Judith Bamber, Katie Connolly, Gabby Innes, Kate James, Anne Mulvaney, Rosie Nicholson, Charlotte Orr

Assisting Cartographer
James Leversha

Assisting Book Designer
Mazzy Du Plessis

Thanks to
Amanda Williamson

Index

Map Legend

Sights
- Beach
- Bird Sanctuary
- Buddhist
- Castle/Palace
- Christian
- Confucian
- Hindu
- Islamic
- Jain
- Jewish
- Monument
- Museum/Gallery/Historic Building
- Ruin
- Shinto
- Sikh
- Taoist
- Winery/Vineyard
- Zoo/Wildlife Sanctuary
- Other Sight

Activities, Courses & Tours
- Bodysurfing
- Diving
- Canoeing/Kayaking
- Course/Tour
- Sento Hot Baths/Onsen
- Skiing
- Snorkelling
- Surfing
- Swimming/Pool
- Walking
- Windsurfing
- Other Activity

Sleeping
- Sleeping
- Camping
- Hut/Shelter

Eating
- Eating

Drinking & Nightlife
- Drinking & Nightlife
- Cafe

Entertainment
- Entertainment

Shopping
- Shopping

Information
- Bank
- Embassy/Consulate
- Hospital/Medical
- Internet
- Police
- Post Office
- Telephone
- Toilet
- Tourist Information
- Other Information

Geographic
- Beach
- Gate
- Hut/Shelter
- Lighthouse
- Lookout
- Mountain/Volcano
- Oasis
- Park
- Pass
- Picnic Area
- Waterfall

Population
- Capital (National)
- Capital (State/Province)
- City/Large Town
- Town/Village

Transport
- Airport
- Border crossing
- Bus
- Cable car/Funicular
- Cycling
- Ferry
- Metro station
- Monorail
- Parking
- Petrol station
- Subway station
- Taxi
- Train station/Railway
- Tram
- Underground station
- Other Transport

Routes
- Tollway
- Freeway
- Primary
- Secondary
- Tertiary
- Lane
- Unsealed road
- Road under construction
- Plaza/Mall
- Steps
- Tunnel
- Pedestrian overpass
- Walking Tour
- Walking Tour detour
- Path/Walking Trail

Boundaries
- International
- State/Province
- Disputed
- Regional/Suburb
- Marine Park
- Cliff
- Wall

Hydrography
- River, Creek
- Intermittent River
- Canal
- Water
- Dry/Salt/Intermittent Lake
- Reef

Areas
- Airport/Runway
- Beach/Desert
- Cemetery (Christian)
- Cemetery (Other)
- Glacier
- Mudflat
- Park/Forest
- Sight (Building)
- Sportsground
- Swamp/Mangrove

Note: Not all symbols displayed above appear on the maps in this book

OUR STORY

A beat-up old car, a few dollars in the pocket and a sense of adventure. In 1972 that's all Tony and Maureen Wheeler needed for the trip of a lifetime – across Europe and Asia overland to Australia. It took several months, and at the end – broke but inspired – they sat at their kitchen table writing and stapling together their first travel guide, *Across Asia on the Cheap*. Within a week they'd sold 1500 copies. Lonely Planet was born.

Today, Lonely Planet has offices in Franklin, London, Melbourne, Oakland, Dublin, Beijing and Delhi, with more than 600 staff and writers. We share Tony's belief that 'a great guidebook should do three things: inform, educate and amuse'.

OUR WRITERS

Charles Rawlings-Way

Charles is a veteran travel writer who has penned 30-something titles for Lonely Planet – including guides to Singapore, Toronto, Sydney, New Zealand, the South Pacific and Australia – and numerous articles. After dabbling in the dark arts of architecture, cartography, project management and busking for some years, Charles hit the road for LP in 2005 and hasn't stopped travelling since.

Virginia Maxwell

Although based in Australia, Virginia spends at least half of her year updating Lonely Planet destination coverage in Europe and the Middle East. The Mediterranean is her favourite place to travel, and she has covered Spain, Italy, Turkey, Syria, Lebanon, Israel, Egypt and Morocco for Lonely Planet guidebooks – there are only eight more countries to go! Virginia also writes about Armenia, Iran and Australia. Follow her @maxwellvirginia on Instagram and Twitter.

Published by Lonely Planet Global Limited
CRN 554153
8th edition – November 2018
ISBN 978 1 78657 177 9
© Lonely Planet 2018   Photographs © as indicated 2018
10 9 8 7 6 5 4 3 2 1
Printed in Singapore